D1708094

THE EARLIEST ADVOCATES OF THE ENGLISH BIBLE

The Texts of the Medieval Debate

One of the major debates in English cultural, literary and religious history concerned whether or not the Bible should be translated into English. The Middle English texts edited in this book all argue on the same side of the debate: that is, that there should be a Bible in English. But they also include many of the arguments put forward on the other side, in order to refute them.

Mary Dove's edition

- brings together for the first time the English texts of the debate concerning whether or not the Bible should be translated into English
- furnishes the reader with an appreciation of the crucial place the Bible in English occupied in late-medieval England
- provides an invaluable context for the decision of Archbishop Arundel and the English Church to seek to control lay access to vernacular texts in the years following 1409.

The late **Mary Dove** was Professor in the School of English at the University of Sussex. This edition builds on her well-received monograph of 2007: *The First English Bible: The Text and Context of the Wycliffite Versions* (CUP).

EXETER MEDIEVAL TEXTS AND STUDIES

Series Editors: Vincent Gillespie and Richard Dance

Founded by M.J. Swanton
and later co-edited by Marion Glasscoe

The Earliest Advocates of the English Bible

The Texts of the Medieval Debate

edited by

MARY DOVE

UNIVERSITY
of
EXETER
PRESS

First published in 2010 by
University of Exeter Press
Reed Hall, Streatham Drive
Exeter EX4 4QR
UK

www.exeterpress.co.uk

© Mary Dove 2010

The right of Mary Dove to be identified as author of this
work has been asserted by her in accordance with
the Copyright, Designs and Patents Acts 1988.

British Library Cataloguing in Publication Data
A catalogue record for this book is available
from the British Library.

ISBN 978 0 85989 852 2

Typeset in Adobe Garamond 11/13
by Carnegie Book Production, Lancaster
Printed in Great Britain
by CPI Antony Rowe

Contents

Publisher's Note

When Mary Dove was in Oxford about a month before her tragically early and sudden death, she indicated that she expected to complete the present book within the following three months; there remained, she said, a little checking and revision to be done. Sadly she did not live to carry this through. The material she left was for the most part in admirably good order, and proofs were set up from her electronic files and hard copy without changes.

A decision was taken early on to fix the lineation of the texts in accordance with Mary's files since all her editorial apparatus refers to the original lineation. This seemed the most practical solution to a problem recurrent with prose works, and explains the left-aligned presentation of the texts.

No attempt has been made to revisit wholesale the accuracy of the material. However, Anne Hudson kindly agreed to oversee the painstaking process of preparing the book for publication and, following consultation on various issues that arose, minor editorial interventions have been made.

- Editorial notes have been added on pp. xii, 2, 225 and 230 to help the reader.

- In a few instances inconsistency within the material was noticed, and where this inconsistency involved citation of the edited texts, the reading of those texts (rather than the cross references etc) has been taken as correct.

- The conventions which were followed in the variants were also not entirely consistent, and some effort has been made to make this material easier to use (although the need to keep to line and page numbering already established means that this was not always possible).

Acknowledgments

I am grateful to the following for their advice, expertise and generosity: Mishtooni Bose, Vincent Gillespie, Anna Henderson, Patrick Hornbeck, Anne Hudson, Ian Christopher Levy, Richard Marsden, Paul Needham, Fiona Somerset, Toshiyuki Takamiya and Norman Vance. I am especially grateful to Simon Hunt for allowing me to cite his unpublished dissertation.

One of the pleasures of working with manuscripts is the opportunity to meet knowledgeable and patient librarians: in the case of this edition, librarians at Corpus Christi College Cambridge; Emmanuel College Cambridge; Trinity College Cambridge; Cambridge University Library; Sächsische Landesbibliothek Dresden; Trinity College Dublin; Glasgow University Library; Hereford Cathedral Library; the Huntington Library; the British Library; Lambeth Palace Library; the John Rylands Library; Norwich Castle Museum; the Bodleian Library; Christ Church Oxford; Corpus Christi College Oxford; The Queen's College Oxford; St John's College Oxford and Princeton University Library.

I owe a great debt to the Leverhulme Trust and to the President and Fellows of Clare Hall Cambridge.

This edition is dedicated to the memory of the writers of the texts it contains, who chose to be nameless.

Abbreviations

Arnold, *SEW*	Thomas Arnold, *Select English Works of John Wyclif*, 3 vols (Oxford: Clarendon Press, 1869–71)
AV	Authorised Version
Biblia Sacra	see Latin Bible
BL	British Library
CCCM	*Corpus Christianorum Continuatio Medievalis* (Turnhout: Brepols, 1971–)
CCSL	*Corpus Christianorum Series Latina* (Turnhout: Brepols, 1952–)
CUL	Cambridge University Library
Deanesly, *LB*	Margaret Deanesly, *The Lollard Bible and Other Medieval Biblical Versions* (Cambridge: Cambridge University Press, 1920)
Dove, *FEB*	Mary Dove, *The First English Bible: The Text and Context of the Wycliffite Versions* (Cambridge: Cambridge University Press, 2007)
EETS	Early English Text Society
EV	Earlier Version of the Wycliffite Bible
EWS, I	Anne Hudson, ed., *English Wycliffite Sermons*, vol. I (Oxford: Clarendon Press, 1983)
Hudson, *LB*	Anne Hudson, *Lollards and their Books* (London: Hambledon Press, 1985)
Hudson, *PR*	Anne Hudson, *The Premature Reformation: Wycliffite Texts and Lollard History* (Oxford: Clarendon Press, 1988)
Hudson, *SEWW*	Anne Hudson, *Selections from English Wycliffite Writings* (Cambridge: Cambridge University Press, 1978)
Hudson, *WLP*	Anne Hudson, *The Works of a Lollard Preacher* (Oxford: Oxford University Press, 2001; EETS 317)
Hunt, *TFST*	Simon Hunt, 'An Edition of Tracts in Favour of Scriptural Translation and of Some Texts Connected with Lollard Vernacular Biblical Scholarship', DPhil thesis, 2 vols, University of Oxford (1994)

IMEP	R.E. Lewis, N.F. Blake and A.S.G. Edwards, eds, *Index of Middle English Prose* (Cambridge: D.S. Brewer, 1984–)
IPMEP	R.E. Lewis, N.F. Blake and A.S.G. Edwards, eds, *Index of Printed Middle English Prose* (New York: Garland, 1985)
Jolliffe	P.S. Jolliffe, *A Check-list of Middle English Prose Writings of Spiritual Guidance* (Toronto: PIMS, 1974)
LALME	Angus McIntosh, M.L. Samuels and Michael Benskin, *A Linguistic Atlas of Late Mediaeval English*, 4 vols (Aberdeen: Aberdeen University Press, 1986)
Latin Bible	Robert Weber, ed., rev. Roger Gryson, *Biblia Sacra iuxta vulgatam versionem* (Stuttgart: Deutsche Bibelgesellschaft, 2007)
Lindberg, no.	the number given in Conrad Lindberg, 'The Manuscripts and Versions of the Wycliffite Bible: a preliminary survey', *Studia Neophilologica* 42 (1970), 333–47
LV	Later Version of the Wycliffite Bible
Manual	J. Burke Severs, Albert E. Hartung and Peter G. Beidler, eds, revision of J.E. Wells, *A Manual of the Writings in Middle English 1050–1500*, 11 vols so far published (New Haven, Connecticut: Connecticut Academy of Arts and Sciences, 1967–)
Matthew	F.D. Matthew, *The English Works of Wyclif hitherto unprinted* (EETS 74, 1880, 2nd edition 1902)
MED	H. Kurath, S.M. Kuhn et al., eds, *Middle English Dictionary* (Ann Arbor: University of Michigan Press, 1952–2001)
NT	New Testament
ODNB	*Oxford Dictionary of National Biography* 2001–4
OT	Old Testament
PG	*Patrologia Graeca*, ed. J.P. Migne, 161 vols (Paris, 1857–66)
PL	*Patrologia Latina*, ed. J.P. Migne, 221 vols (Paris, 1844–64)
Richter and Friedberg	E. Richter and E.L. Friedberg, eds, *Corpus Iuris Canonici*, 2 vols (Leipzig: Tauchnitz, 1879–81)
WB	Wycliffite Bible
WB	Josiah Forshall and Frederic Madden, eds, *The Holy Bible, Containing the Old and New Testaments, with the Apocryphal Books, in the Earliest English Versions Made from the Latin Vulgate by John Wycliffe and his Followers*, 4 vols (Oxford: Clarendon Press, 1850)

Abbreviations for the texts in this volume:

CT	The Twelve Cambridge Tracts – numbered I to XII
FSB	*First seiþ Bois*
GG	Glossed Gospel Prologues and Epilogue – numbered I to V
HPD	*The Holi Prophete Dauid*
IB	*In þe biginnyng*
PIP	The Prologue to Isaiah and the Prophets
PNII	*Pater Noster II*
PWB	The Prologue to the Wycliffite Bible

Manuscript sigla

Listed below are the manuscripts used in the present volume, with their sigla and a page reference to the main place in the Introduction where they are mentioned; in most cases the major content of each is provided at the specified page. The accounts given follow the normal conventions, including those of dating, as set out by N.R. Ker, *Medieval Manuscripts in British Libraries i. London* (Oxford: Clarendon Press, 1969), pp. vii–xiii. Full collation is not always provided: for manuscripts less important to the texts a reference is given to a source of information, rather than a full description.

sigla	Manuscript	page
A	British Library Royal I C.viii (PIP, PWB)	xxviii
α	British Library Harley 1666 (PWB)	xxviii
β	University College Oxford 96 (PWB)	xxvii
C	Cambridge University Library Ii.6.26 (CT)	xxxiv
C1	Corpus Christi College Cambridge 298 (*FSB*)	lii
C2	Trinity College Cambridge B.1.26 (*FSB*)	liii
C3	Trinity College Cambridge B.1.38 (GGI)	lxii
C4	Trinity College Cambridge B.14.38 (*PNII*)	lviii
C5	Trinity College Cambridge B.14.50 (*FSB*)	lii
C6	Cambridge University Library Additional 6680 (PIP)	xxxi
C7	Cambridge University Library Ff.6.31 (*HPD*)	lvi
C8	Cambridge University Library Nn.4.12 (*PNII*)	lviii
C9	Emmanuel College Cambridge 21 (PIP)	xxxi
D	Sächsische Landesbibliothek Dresden Od. 83 (CTII, GGII)	xxxix
D76	Trinity College Dublin 76 (CTII, GGII, *IB*)	xxxix
E	British Library Arundel 104 (PIP)	xxxi
F	Sion College Arc.L.40.2 / E.1 (PIP)	xxxii
G	Lincoln College Oxford lat. 119 (PIP, PWB)	xxviii

Manuscripts by location

Cambridge

S   Corpus Christi College Cambridge Parker 147 (PIP, PWB)

C1   Corpus Christi College Cambridge 298 (*FSB*)

C9   Emmanuel College Cambridge 21 (PIP)

C2   Trinity College Cambridge B.1.26 (*FSB*)

C3   Trinity College Cambridge B.1.38 (GGI)

C4   Trinity College Cambridge B.14.38 (*PNII*)

C5   Trinity College Cambridge B.14.50 (*FSB*)

C6   Cambridge University Library Additional 6680 (PIP)

R   Cambridge University Library Dd.1.27 (PIP)

C7   Cambridge University Library Ff.6.31 (*HPD*)

C   Cambridge University Library Ii.6.26 (CT)

ι   Cambridge University Library Kk.1.8 (PWB)

Q   Cambridge University Library Mm.2.15 (PIP, PWB)

C8   Cambridge University Library Nn.4.12 (*PNII*)

P1   Peterborough Cathedral 8 (conserved in CUL) (CTII, GGII, *IB*)

Dresden

D   Sächsische Landesbibliothek Dresden Od. 83 (CTII, GGII)

Dublin

Y   Trinity College Dublin 67 (PIP)

T   Trinity College Dublin 75 (PWB)

D76 Trinity College Dublin 76 (CTII, GGII, *IB*)

Glasgow

G1   Glasgow University Gen. 223 (CTII, GGII, *IB*)

Hereford

X   Hereford Cathedral Library O.vii.I (PIP)

London

L   British Library Additional 28026 (GGIII)

E   British Library Arundel 104 (PIP)

L1   British Library Arundel 254 (CTII, GGII, *IB*)

L2   British Library Cotton Claudius E.ii (PIP)

L3   British Library Cotton Vitellius D.vii (*FSB*)

L4   British Library Harley 425 (*FSB*)

α   British Library Harley 1666 (PWB)

L5   British Library Harley 2322 (CTVI)

L6   British Library Harley 2398 (*PNII*)

o   British Library Harley 6333 (CTII, GGII)

L7   British Library Additional 41175 (GGI)

A   British Library Royal I C.viii (PIP, PWB)

U   Lambeth Palace Library 25 (PIP)

L8   Lambeth Palace Library 594 (*FSB*)

V   Lambeth Palace Library 1033 (PIP)

F   Sion College Arc.L.40.2 / E.1 (conserved in Lambeth Palace Library) (PIP)

Manchester

R77   John Rylands Manchester Eng. 77 (CTII, GGII)

R85   John Rylands Manchester Eng. 85 (*PNII*)

R90   John Rylands Manchester Eng. 90 (*PNII*)

R91   John Rylands Manchester Eng. 91 (PIP)

New York

N1 Pierpont Morgan New York 648 (*FSB*)

Norwich

N2 Norwich Castle Museum 158.926.4g(3) (*PNII*)

Oxford

O   Bodleian Library Bodley 143 (GGIV)

O1 Bodleian Library Bodley 243 (GGV)

I   Bodleian Library Bodley 277 (PIP, PWB)

O2 Bodleian Library Bodley 938 (*PNII*)

O3 Bodleian Library Additional B.66 (CTVI)

K   Bodleian Library Fairfax 2 (PIP)

O4 Bodleian Library Laud misc. 235 (CX, GGII, GGIII)

O5 Bodleian Library Laud misc. 524 (CTIX)

O6 Christ Church Oxford Allestree L.4.1 (GGII)

H   Corpus Christi College Oxford 20 (PIP)

G   Lincoln College Oxford lat. 119 (PIP, PWB)

M   Queen's College Oxford 388 (PIP)

N   St John's College Oxford 7 (PIP)

β   University College Oxford 96 (PWB)

Princeton

P   Princeton University William H. Scheide 12 (PIP, PWB)

P2 Princeton University Robert Taylor 16 (*PNII*)

San Marino, California

S1 Huntington Library HM 502 (*PNII*)

Introduction

An English Bible translated by men sympathetic to Wyclif was completed *c*.1390.[1] In 1407, the constitutions against heresy issued at the Council of Oxford by the archbishop of Canterbury, Thomas Arundel, inhibited any public or private use or dissemination of the translation of the Bible made in Wyclif's time, or of any translation made later than that, unless licensed by the diocesan bishop or by a provincial council.[2] Legislation against the Wycliffite Bible was by no means a snap decision on the English church's part: it was made in the context of a debate about translation of the Bible into English which had begun in the Prologue to the Wycliffite Bible (see the introduction, pp. xx–xxx). From the beginning, advocacy of an English Bible was adversarial, directed implicitly or explicitly 'against those who say holy writ should not or may not be translated into English' (see the heading to *First seiþ Bois*, included in this edition, p. 143).

Because the first English Bible was produced by Wycliffite translators and because archbishop Arundel explained his prohibition of the Wycliffite Bible to Pope John XXIII by saying that it was part of the arch-heretic's project to attack the faith and doctrine of holy church[3] it has sometimes been assumed that advocacy of the English Bible was predominantly a Wycliffite phenomenon, and that anyone who wrote in favour of scripture in English was sympathetic to Wyclif. But while some of the writings advocating God's law in the people's language can be identified as Wycliffite because of their context—notably the Prologue to the Wycliffite Bible (PWB in this edition, pp. 3–85) and the Prologues and Epilogue to the Wycliffite Glossed Gospels (GGI–GGV, pp. 172–86)—and some because they include ideas or terms characteristic of Wycliffite texts—for example, *Pater Noster II* and the related Cambridge Tract VII—others are certainly not Wycliffite (for example, Richard Ullerston's Latin *determinacio*, on which see the introduction to *First seiþ Bois*, pp. xlix–liv). Some of the twelve Cambridge Tracts may reasonably be identified as Wycliffite, while others are as far from Lollardy as could be imagined (see the introduction to these tracts, pp. xxxiii–xlix). Neither arguing in favour of an English Bible nor assembling

---

[1] The so-called 'Later Version' was completed *c*. 1390; Dove, *FEB*, 79, 150.

[2] C.R. Cheney, *Medieval Texts and Studies* (Oxford: Clarendon Press, 1973), pp. 123, 172; David Wilkins, ed., *Concilia Magnae Britanniae et Hiberniae*, vol. III (London, 1737), p. 317. The legislation remained in place until 1529.

[3] Wilkins, *Concilia*, vol. III, p. 350.

a collection of writings in favour of an English Bible were intrinsically Wycliffite activities, although it was natural that Wycliffites would wish to argue for the Bible that associates of theirs had produced.

The Cambridge Tracts were probably assembled in response to the Council of Oxford. The 1407 constitutions, while they were a peremptory intervention in the English Bible debate, did not bring it to an end. Indeed, a version of *First seiþ Bois* was published in 1530 (see the introduction to *FSB*, pp. xlix–liv). Having allowed the English Bible debate time to develop, why did Arundel and the English bishops legislate against the Wycliffite Bible when they must have realized that opponents of translation were out-argued by its advocates, not all of them, by any means, Wycliffite sympathizers? Doubtless one of the main reasons for the prohibition was the fear that Wyclif (in the words of Sir Thomas More) had 'purposely corrupted that holy texte, malycyously plantyng therein suche wordys as myght in the reders erys serue to the profe of suche heresyes as he went about to sow'.[4] That fear was unfounded, but the polemic against the dignitaries of the church and the University of Oxford in the Prologue to the Wycliffite Bible could only have increased the suspicion of Arundel and of other prelatical readers that the translation was a tendentious one. Safer (Arundel must have thought) to wait for an English Bible translated by men of impeccable orthodoxy, a Bible which could be approved with confidence. Had he lived longer, perhaps he would have initiated such a project. In any case, the English Bible debate proved conclusively that lay people were not going to tolerate any attempt on the church's part to 'letten cristen peple to knowe, here, rede, write and speke holy writ in Englisch' (GGII 154–5).

The Prologue to the Wycliffite Bible

The writer of the lengthy Prologue to the Wycliffite Bible (nearly 40,000 words) divides his material into fifteen chapters. The first chapter lists the books of the biblical canon and the apocrypha; the second chapter discusses the old law and its supersession at the coming of Christ; chapters three to eleven contain a synopsis of the Old Testament (much fuller for some books than others); chapters twelve to fourteen contain material on the senses of scripture largely drawn from Augustine's *De doctrina christiana* and Nicholas of Lyra's *Postillae*,[5] and chapter fifteen describes the process of production of the Wycliffite Bible and argues that it should be approved by the English church.[6] Only this last chapter is inherently contentious, but the Prologue contains several highly polemical passages. The first is at the end of chapter one, where the writer quotes Augustine's warning that 'pride and coueitise of clerkis is cause of her blyndnesse and eresie, and priueþ hem fro [deprives them of] veri vndurstonding of

---

[4]   *A Dialogue Concerning Heresies*, III, xiiii, ed. Thomas C.M. Lawler, Germain Marc'hadour and Richard C. Marius, *The Complete Works of St. Thomas More*, vol. VI (New Haven: Yale University Press, 1981), p. 314.

[5]   See the note on PWB 2360.

[6]   On PWB see further Dove, *FEB*, 107–13, 120–36, 145–8.

hooli writ, and makiþ hem go quyk [alive] into helle' (91–3).[7] At the end of the second chapter the writer makes a characteristically Wycliffite distinction between God's law (holy scripture) and ceremonies, customs and laws made by sinful men 'in þe tyme of Sathanas and of antecrist' (130).[8]

For each Old Testament book in turn the writer summarizes the content, more and more fully as he progresses through the historical books from Genesis to Chronicles.[9] After two chapters (eight and nine) summarizing Chronicles we expect the writer to move on to the book of Ezra. Instead, the cry 'But alas, alas, alas!' (1583) heralds a 3,000-word coda arguing that Christian lords 'now, in Ynglond' (1789) do the opposite of the exemplary deeds of the good kings Jehoshaphat, Hezekiah and Josiah, preferring to take their (im)moral lesson from the wicked king Manasseh. Rather than following Jehoshaphat's example by ensuring that God's law is taught openly to the people they are complicit in the offering of worthless pardons;[10] rather than following Hezekiah's example by purifying God's house, they 'bryngen in symonyent [simoniac] clerkis … to stoppe Goddis lawe, þat it be not knowun and kept and freli prechid' (1598–1600), and employ priests in worldly, temporal offices;[11] rather than following Josiah's example by preaching God's law they praise and glorify not the Lord but the letters of friars, 'ful of disseit and leesyngis' (1606). They cruelly persecute those 'þat wolden teche treuli and freli þe lawe of God' (1608–9), and maintain those who preach 'fablis' (1609) and 'synful mennus tradiciouns or statutes' (1610), while inhibiting scripture from being preached, known and observed.[12] The writer then contrasts the hundreds of false prophets who counselled king Ahab with the prophets Elijah and Micaiah who were in sole possession of the truth.[13] He likens the translators' predicament to theirs: 'So now a fewe pore men and idiotis [illiterates] in comparisoun of [contrast with] clerkis of scole moun haue þe treuþe of hooli scripture aȝenus many þousynde prelatis and religious … moost siþ þese pore men desiren oneli þe treuþe and fredom of þe hooli gospel and of hooli scripture' (1616–21).

There follows a diatribe against the followers of Manasseh, unworthy priests and those who promote them, in the course of which the writer cites the *Rosarium super Decreto* of the canon lawyer Guido de Baysio,[14] Gregory the Great's *Regula Pastoralis*, Gratian's *Decretum* and two favourite Lollard authorities, Robert Grosseteste and 'Parisience', Gulielmus Peraldus.[15] Lords and prelates swear by the limbs of God and

---

7   See the note on PWB 91–4 Further details of all quotations from and references to sources in this introduction can be found in the notes to the relevant lines.

8   See the note on PWB 125–30.

9   With the exception of 1 Kings and 1 Chronicles.

10   PWB 1583–92 (and notes); 2 Chron. 17:7–9.

11   PWB 1592–602 (and notes); 2 Chron. 30:13–20.

12   PWB 1603–11 (and notes); 2 Chron. 34:3–5.

13   PWB 1612–16; 3 Kings 18, 22.

14   See the note on PWB 1644.

15   See the notes on PWB 1704–6, 1708–35, 1743–5 and 1767–9.

The Earliest Advocates of the English Bible

Christ and by the saints whom they make into idols, slander good men and 'clepen hem lollardis, eretikis and reisers of debate and of tresoun aʒenus þe kyng' (1796–7), over-tax, extort, and shed blood both in war and by refusing alms to the poor.[16] The coda to Chronicles ends with a plea that God may stir lords and prelates who sin openly, as Manasseh did, to repent, as he did (1833–7).[17]

The Old Testament from Ezra to the Maccabees is summarized in a single chapter (in the course of which the writer points out that the Prophets 'han a general prologe for alle', that is, the Prologue to Isaiah and the Prophets, 2079). When the writer at last turns to address exegetical issues, at the beginning of chapter twelve, he moves swiftly into an abridgment of Augustine's rules, in *De doctrina christiana*, for recognizing spiritual senses.[18] Chapter thirteen begins with Augustine's seven steps to true knowledge and love of God. The Middle English word for steps, 'degres', puts the writer in mind of academic degrees, and of those schoolmen who profess to study and teach the Bible but actually, through their pride and greed, pay homage to Satan (2469–70). In turn, this makes him think of a proposed statute preventing students from studying divinity until they have completed the Arts curriculum and been Master of Arts for two years (2483–6). There follows a commination on the University of Oxford, structured around Jerome's exposition of Amos 1:3.[19] Like Damascus, Oxford commits four great sins: worldliness; sodomy (2520, associated particularly with scholars of divinity); simony and, the greatest sin, the proposed statute. Nevertheless, 'God boþe can and mai, if it likiþ him, spede symple men out of þe vnyuersite as myche to kunne holy writte as maistres in þe vniuersite' (2533–5). The traditional justification of the curriculum was that the liberal arts enabled the Bible to be better understood: the writer of the Prologue, in contrast, associates worldly knowledge with worldliness, a cast of mind that makes it impossible to interpret scripture accurately. Then, a copy of Lyra having just arrived, he proceeds to translate the prologues to the *Postillae* (2555–740).

The final chapter opens with a global perspective: Christ, in the Gospels, and David, in the Psalms (as interpreted by Jerome), proclaim that the word of the Lord shall be preached throughout the world.[20] Specifically, the desire of the English people for holy writ is written into Luke's Gospel, where Jesus says that the stones of the temple would cry out 'hosanna' if the Jews failed so to do (19:40). 'We English men', says the writer, should identify with the stones of the temple, stones being 'heþene men þat worschipiden stoonys for her goddis' (2790), and the ancestors of the English being heathens.[21] Englishmen should, that is, 'crie hooli writ' (2792), since Jews, whose name

---

[16] PWB 1789–833 (and notes).
[17] Manasseh repented according to 2 Chronicles 33:12–16, but not in the account of his reign in 4 Kings 21.
[18] See further the introduction to GGII, pp. lxii–lxiv.
[19] See the note on PWB 2492–5.
[20] See the notes on PWB 2781–7.
[21] See the note on PWB 2789–90.

means 'confession' and signifies 'clerkis', fail to acknowledge their sins and 'dispisen and stoppen hooli writ as miche as þei moun' (2797). Therefore 'wiþ comyn charite to saue alle men in oure rewme which God wole haue saued, a symple creature haþ translatid þe Bible out of Latyn into Englisch' (2800–2).[22] After discussing the process of production of the English Bible and arguing that the translation is comprehensible and accurate, the writer refutes two arguments against a Bible in English, the first being that only men as holy as Jerome was should undertake to translate the Bible. The translators may not be as holy as Jerome was, the writer retorts, but Jerome was not as holy as the apostles and evangelists, and the translators of the Septuagint were far less holy than the writers of the Hebrew sciptures (2875–90). Asked by worldly clerics 'what spirit makiþ idiotis hardi to translate þe Bible now into Englisch' (2906–7) when the four doctors never did, the writer replies that both Augustine and Jerome expounded scripture in the language of the people (2906–31). There is, he claims, a history of translation of scripture into English,[23] and other nations have the Bible in their own language.[24] The English Bible should be understood not as the gift of the translators but as the gift of God to the people, withheld longer from the English than from the French and Bohemians because of the 'falsnesse and necligence of clerkis, or for our puple is not worþi to haue so greet grace and ʒifte of God in peyne of her elde synnes' (2943–4).

We do not know who wrote the Prologue to the Wycliffite Bible. From internal evidence he was closely involved with the production of the Later Version.[25] Early in the eighteenth century the Cambridge theologian Daniel Waterland, looking for a Wycliffite closely associated with Wyclif, guessed (his own word) that John Purvey was the author.[26] In the introduction to their 1850 edition of the Wycliffite Bible, Josiah Forshall and Frederic Madden followed Waterland in attributing the Prologue and the Later Version to Purvey.[27] This turned Waterland's guess into accepted fact, and the Prologue to the Wycliffite Bible and the Later Version of the Wycliffite Bible have been attributed to Purvey ever since.[28] There is some evidence linking Purvey with biblical translation, but none linking him with the Prologue.[29]

The three pieces of evidence for the dating of the Prologue are all found in the commination on the University of Oxford. The 'sleyng of quyke men' (2497) may possibly refer to a riot that took place in Oxford in April 1388, but the reference is

---

[22] See the notes on PWB 2792–801.

[23] See the notes on PWB 2935–9.

[24] See the notes on PWB 2940.

[25] See especially PWB 60 and 2844.

[26] *The Works of Daniel Waterland*, vol. X (Oxford, 1823), pp. 360–61.

[27] In spite of finding Waterland's evidence unsatisfactory, *WB*, I, xxiv–xxv; see Hudson, 'John Purvey: A Reconsideration of the Evidence for his Life and Writings', *LB*, 103.

[28] Hudson, 'John Purvey', *LB*, 103–8, and cf. the list of works ascribed to Purvey in *Manual*, 2, III, 49–56.

[29] Dove, *FEB*, 76–8.

The Earliest Advocates of the English Bible

very imprecise.[30] The proposal to enforce the statute (which had been on the books since 1253) requiring students to become regents in Arts before beginning the study of Divinity (2483–6) must be dated 1387, since on 17 March and 1 August of that year Richard II instructed the university authorities not to proceed with their intention.[31] With regard to 'sodomye and strong meyntenance þerof, as it is knowen to many persoones of þe rewme and at þe laste parlement' (2516–18), Deanesly claimed the writer must be referring to *The Twelve Conclusions of the Lollards* affixed to the doors of Westminster Hall during the parliament of 1395.[32] She therefore dated the Prologue after the parliament of January–February 1395 and before the parliament of January–February 1397.[33] In the *Twelve Conclusions*, however, there is no reference to Oxford, and the test by which one may know sodomitical clergy, 'lik[ing] non wymmen', implies that the framers of *The Twelve Conclusions* are thinking of a non-university context.[34] It is more probable that the Prologue is referring to the parliament in which John Bloxham, Warden of Merton College, was accused of sodomy, according to the *Historia Vitae et Regni Ricardi Secundi*.[35] Bloxham died in 1387, so this may have been the 'Wonderful Parliament' of October–November 1386,[36] in which case the Prologue was written after November 1386 and before the parliament of February 1388. The Prologue may therefore be dated 1387/beginning of 1388.

Most of the Prologue is thoroughly orthodox and conventional, but it is almost certainly because of its unrestrainedly polemical passages, not just because of its length, that it failed to become the standard preface to the Wycliffite Bible. It was the source of thirteen articles brought against Richard Hunne at St Paul's Cross in 1514.[37] The reformist John Gough, printing the Prologue in 1540, felt it necessary to apologize to the reader: 'I humbly requyre you in case ye fynde ony thyng in this boke that shall offend you in the .x. chapiter or in the .xiii. I praye you blame not me

---

[30] Anthony à Wood, *The History and Antiquities of the University of Oxford*, trans. John Gutch, vol. (Oxford: Clarendon Press, 1792), p. 518; the date is accepted in *WB*, I, xxiv, but, as Deanesly says, it 'might refer to any brawl', *LB*, 257.

[31] À Wood, *The History and Antiquities of the University of Oxford*, p. 517, and see *WB*, I, xxiv. Deanesly refers to the statute as an 'anti-Lollard measure', *LB*, 257, but it was primarily anti-mendicant.

[32] Deanesly, *LB*, 257.

[33] This date is also accepted by Hudson, *PR*, 247.

[34] Hudson, *SEWW*, 25/5–7, 30–1. The English text of The Twelve Conclusions derives from Roger Dymmock's *Liber Contra Duodecim Errores et Hereses Lollardorum*, ed. H.S. Cronin (London: Wyclif Society, 1922).

[35] George B. Stow, ed., *Historia Vitae et Regni Ricardi Secundi* (Philadelphia: University of Pennsylvania Press, 1977), p. 135/3011–19.

[36] The *Historia Vitae et Regni Ricardi Secundi*, however, says it was the parliament of 1395; see further Dove, *FEB*, 110–13.

[37] S.R. Cattley and J. Pratt, eds, *The Acts and Monuments of John Foxe*, vol. IV (London: Religious Tract Society, 1877), p. 186.

though I haue folowed myne orygynall and olde copy in worde and sentence'.[38] Only five manuscripts, β P Q S and T, contain complete texts of the Prologue (eleven others contain partial texts or fragments).[39] In only two of the five, P and S, is it placed at the beginning of the Bible as the writer, according to the Prologue to Isaiah and the Prophets, intended: 'of þese foure vndurstondingis [senses] shal be seid pleynliere, if God wole, on þe bigynnyng of Genesis' (PIP 55–6). In that position the Prologue was all too likely to attract the attention of a hostile reader, and no doubt for this reason it is placed between the Old and New Testaments in Q and divided into separate prologues for individual Old Testament books in G. The fact that the first chapter only is included in A and I implies that the editors of those manuscripts chose not to include the rest.

Editions

WB, I, 1–60
Ch. 15 only: Hudson, *SEWW*, 67–72, 189–91

Base manuscript

P Princeton University Library William H. Scheide 12

WB, no. 154; *c.*1395–1410. ii + 405 fols + ii; 12s [collation 1(12) 2(6) 3(5) 4–22(12) 23(15, with 3 stubs) 24–33(12) 34(8) 35(11)];[40] 290 × 190 mm; 210 × 130 mm; 2 columns; 60 lines; one very small and upright bookhand (PWB), probably London. 7-line deep-blue and red initial flourished in both colours at opening of PWB, f. 1r. PWB, fols 1ra–17rb; Lectionary in LV (temporal, commemorations, proper of saints, common of saints), fols 17v–22v; OT in LV, with prologues to Isaiah and Baruch, fols 24r–325r;[41] NT in LV, including four prologues to Galatians, fols 325v–403r,[42] scribal note 'here endiþ þe apocalips & blessid be þe hooly trinite amen amen amen', f. 403r. Above the prologue to the Apocalypse is a note by John Bale, 'Hunc prologum Gilberti Porretani in Apocalipsim transtulit Joannes Wiclevus in Anglicum sermonem', f. 397r.[43]

Dialect of PWB Bucks., *LALME*, I, 154. Shares a few readings (in OT) with A alone, and has some unique LV readings in OT.[44]

---

38   *The Dore of Holy Scripture*, sig. A.6r.
39   N almost certainly originally contained PWB, but in all likelihood it was detached during the fifteenth century; see Ralph Hanna, *A Descriptive Catalogue of the Western Medieval Manuscripts of St John's College Oxford* (Oxford: Oxford University Press, 2002), p. 9. Manuscript ι contains the whole of PWB except the coda to Chronicles.
40   I am grateful to Paul S. Needham for supplying details of the collation.
41   On the contents of OT in LV see Dove, *FEB*, 199–204.
42   On the contents of NT in LV see Dove, *FEB*, 204–9. The prologues to Galataians are also in Takamiya 31, *olim* Boies Penrose (Lindberg, no. 219); see Dove, *FEB*, 206.
43   Dove, *FEB*, 42–3.
44   Dove, *FEB*, 155.

Owned by Robert [or Richard] Mery of Hatfield, Herts, fl.1461–83. This and further ownership notes, fols 403v–405r.[45] The manuscript was sold by Alexander Peregrine Fuller-Acland-Hood to Quaritch in 1931, who sold it to John H. Scheide for £2375. Dove, *FEB*, 41–3, 264–6 (and *passim*).

Other manuscripts and early printed versions

There are four other complete texts of the Prologue to the Wycliffite Bible:

S Corpus Christi College Cambridge 147

WB, no. 116; *c*.1410–30. 454 fols (no modern foliation); 12s; 300 × 195 mm; 215 × 130 mm; 2 columns; 59/61 lines; a rather uneven and angular bookhand (PWB). PWB, fols 1r–18r; Lectionary in LV, fols 18v–23v; OT in LV, fols 24–370; NT in LV, fols 371–454v, breaks off at Apoc. 21:18. Chapter numbers and marginal references in PWB are in the hand of a corrector, who erases and writes over errors made by the first hand. Probably owned by Geoffrey Blyth, bishop of Coventry and Lichfield, 1503–33, since a note by archbishop Parker (or one of his household) says the annotations alongside certain passages of the PWB are in his hand, f. 15r. These nine notes, the first at PWB 125–30 and the last at 2509–14, execrate the errors and heresies of Wyclif and his followers. M.R. James, *A descriptive catalogue of the manuscripts in the library of Corpus Christi College, Cambridge*, vol. I (Cambridge, 1912), pp. 335–6; Christopher De Hamel, *The Book: A History of the Bible* (London: Phaidon, 2001), fig. 123, p. 175; Dove, *FEB*, 174–5, 235–7 (and *passim*).

Q Cambridge University Library Mm.2.15

WB, no. 112; *c*.1410–20. 363 fols; 8s; 375 × 260 mm; 285/90 × 190 mm; 2 columns; 67 lines; one clear and regular bookhand in PWB. OT in LV, fols 5r–271v (fols 272–3 blank); ornamented page with text 'Edoverdus Sextus', f. 274r, and in the same hand 'The true copie of a Prologe whiche John Wicklife wrote to this Bible which he translatid into Englishe about two hundrid yere past, that was in the tyme of kynge Edwarde the thryd, as may iustly be gatherid of the mention that is had of him in diues auncient Cronicles. Anno domini 1550'; PWB, fols 275r–290v; NT in LV, fols 291r–362r.

OT, PWB and NT all begin with a new quire, but some aspects of the decoration imply that PWB was always in its current position. The last four lines of f. 287vb and the first 31 lines of f. 288ra, concerning the sins of Oxford (2480–539), are written in another hand, apparently over an erasure. Dove, *FEB*, 127, 241–2 (and *passim*).

T Trinity College Dublin 75

WB, no. 151; *c*.1425. 281 fols + ii; 295 × 220 mm; 235 × 155 mm (in PWB); 2 columns (in PWB); 41–44 lines (in PWB); hand of PWB bastard anglicana, very similar to script of β.

---

[45] Percy A. Bowyer, 'Notes concerning the Bowyer family', *Sussex Archaeological Collections* 64 (1923), 105–8; Dove, *FEB*, 41–3.

Part I: brief harmony of the Gospels, in Latin, fols 1r–2v; 'Sermo Doctor Curteyse', in Latin, fols 2v–3r; lectionary in EV, fols 4r–11r; prologues to Mark, Luke, John and Apocalypse in LV, fols 11v–13v; NT in EV, fols 14r–217v.

Part II: PWB, fols 218r–251r; Jerome's prologue to Psalms, fols 251r–252r; PWB prologue to Psalms, 2007–14, f. 252r; Rolle's prologue to Psalms, fols 252r–253r; PWB 2007–14 (again), f. 253r; PWB 2166–75, fols 253r–253v; copy of letter in Latin to Cardinal Henry Beaufort, bishop of Winchester from John Witton, curate of Chedynfolde, Surrey, rejecting accusations of heresy (after 1427, when Beaufort became cardinal), fols 255r–257r; OT lections in LV, fols 257r–281r.

John Scattergood and G. Latré suggest Witton owned part II of the manuscript, and perhaps also part I, 'Trinity College Dublin MS 75: a Lollard Bible and some Protestant owners', in J. Scattergood and J. Boffey, *Texts and their Contexts: papers for the Early Book Society* (Dublin, 1997), pp. 229–30. Maureen Jurkowski suggests Beaufort owned it, 'Lollard Book Producers in London in 1414', in Helen Barr and Ann M. Hutchison, *Text and Controversy from Wyclif to Bale: Essays in Honour of Anne Hudson* (Turnhout, 2005), pp. 209–10. See Dove, *FEB*, 77–8, 242–3 (and *passim*).

β University College Oxford 96
WB, no. 105; *c*.1425–40. v + 114 fols; 12s; 175 × 142 mm; 120 × 115+ mm; single column; 18/19 lines; a bastard anglicana with some features of secretary script, similar to **T**. PWB, fols 1r–94r; number of books and chapters in WB, fols 94v–95r; gospel lections for Holy Week and Easter in LV, fols 97r–109v (fols 110–114 blank). S.J. Ogilvie-Thomson, *IMEP* handlist VIII, 109; Dove, *FEB*, 120, 243, 303.

There are also partial texts or fragments in:

ι Cambridge University Library Kk.1.8
WB, no. 110; *c*.1400–20. 196 fols; 410 × 270 mm; 300 × 190 mm; 2 columns; 65 lines; probably written by the same scribe as **G**. PWB (omitting 1583–1837), fols 1r–29r; lectionary in LV, fols 31r–37v; NT in LV, fols 38r–178r; part of OT lections in LV (in later hand), fols 182r–186v. Dove, *FEB*, 284.

Trinity College Dublin 72
98 fols Lectionary, fols 2r–7v; Psalms in LV, fols 8r–86v; Cantica, fols 86v–93r; Dirige in English, fols 93r–96r; prologue to Psalms (PWB 2007–23), fols 96r–v. Dove, *FEB*, 286.

British Library Additional 10046
WB, no. 36; *c*.1430. Opening of PWB ch. 12 (2166–75), f. 4v; Psalms and Canticles in LV, fols 5r–124r. Dove, *FEB*, 289.

British Library Additional 31044
Lindberg, no. 184; *c*.1400–10. Prologue to Ps.–Ecclus (PWB 2007–78), fols 7r–9r; Ps.–Ecclus in LV. Owned by John Parker. Dove, *FEB*, 290.

α British Library Harley 1666
  WB, no. 15; *c.*1400–1425. III fols + iii; 125 × 95 mm; 90 × 62 mm; single column;
  18/26 lines; 2 bookhands (1–4, 5–III). PWB (breaks off at 2793, 'synnes and'), fols
  Ir–IIIv. Dove, *FEB*, 291.

A British Library Royal I C.viii, fols Ir–v
  WB, no. 6; *c.*1400–10. WB in LV. Ch. I of PWB is written in a bookhand of
  *c.*1475–1500 on the original wrapper, fols Ir–v. Dove, *FEB*, 248–9.

I Bodleian Library Bodley 277
  WB, no. 60; *c.*1425–35. Ch. I of PWB, f. Ir; OT in revised LV, fols Iv–301v; NT in
  revised LV, fols 301v–376 (f. 377 blank). Ed. Conrad Lindberg, *King Henry's Bible,*
  MS Bodl 277: the Revised Version of the Wyclif Bible, 4 vols (Stockholm: Almqvist
  and Wiksell, 1999–2004). Dove, *FEB,* 253–5.

G Lincoln College Oxford lat. 119
  WB, no. 96; *c.*1410. iii + 351 fols 8s; 410 × 270 mm; 300 × 190 mm; 2 columns;
  65 lines. WB in LV with OT books prefaced by their descriptions in PWB from
  Exodus onwards; PWB 1–150 follows OT, fols 279r–v. Lacks PWB 1583–837, 2166–
  973. Dialect of PWB Hunts, *LALME,* I, 153. Dove, *FEB,* 262–3.

Huntington Library HM 501
  Lindberg, no. 199. Selections from OT in LV. Opening of prologue to Psalms (PWB
  2007–14), fols 22r–v, and again f. 24r; opening of ch. 12 of PWB (2166–75), fols
  24r–v. Ralph Hanna III, *IMEP* handlist I, 25–30; Dove, *FEB,* 304.

Keio University 170X9/6
  Part of the same volume as Huntington Library HM 501.[46] 35 unnumbered fols;
  145 × 85 mm; 100 × 60 mm; single column; 31 lines; a small, neat bookhand.
  Four bifolia of this unbound manuscript contain nearly-illegible material from chs
  13–15 of PWB; beginning at 'aftirward', 2457, and concluding *c.*2828. Probably the
  manuscript once began with a complete text of PWB, followed by Gen. 1–9 and
  Deut. 1–34:3. Takami Matsuda, ed., *Mostly British: Manuscripts and Early Printed*
  Materials from Classical Rome to Renaissance England in the Collection of Keio
  University Library (Tokyo: Keio University, 2001), pp. 46–8.

Worcester Cathedral Library F.172
  s. xv ex (bef. 1468). Miscellany, including LV Acts, fols 48r–72r; prologue to Ps.–
  Ecclus (PWB 2007–78), fols 167v–168r; Rolle's English Psalter, without commentary,
  Psalms 1–72:19, fols 168v–213v. Written by 'the Hammond scribe', John Multon,
  stationer, active in London 1460–83, and made for John Vale, servant of Sir Thomas
  Cook, mayor of London. Valerie Edden, *IMEP* handlist XV, 62–9; R.M. Thomson,

---

[46] Purchased by Keio University in 1984 from Quaritch catalogue no. 1036, *Bookhands of the Middle*
Ages.

A Descriptive Catalogue of the Medieval Manuscripts in Worcester Cathedral Library (Cambridge: Brewer, 2001), pp. 114–16.

John Gough,[47] ed., *The Dore of Holy Scripture* (London, 1540;[48] STC 25587.5)
128 unnumbered leaves, 135 × 87 mm. The colophon claims that the book was 'perused by doctor Taylor and doctor Barons, Master Ceton and Master Corner' (sig. Q.8v). In the preface, Gough asserts that PWB was 'wryten more then two hondred yeares past' (sig. A.3r), and that he has turned it into the English of his own day 'to the entent that we myght know and perceyue what paynes and labores men toke to / preferre and set forth the word of God in olde tymes passed, to the destruction of the enormityes of the Romysh church which was then in his prosperite' (sig. A.3r–v). He contrasts the 'rude and playne sententious wrytyge' with the eloquence of Chaucer and Gower (sig. A.4r). *The Dore of Holy Scripture* omits many lines and passages of PWB, and 2276–348 (Augustine's version of the rules of Tyconius). The degree of re-writing makes it difficult to identify the text of the copy he works from, but his text has none of the distinctive features of **G ι Q**.

Robert Crowley,[49] ed., *The Pathwaye to Perfect Knowledge* (London, 1550; STC 25588)
136 unnumbered leaves (R.8v blank), 140 × 90 mm. 'The true copye of a Prolog wrytten about two C. yeres paste by John Wyckliffe', cf. **Q** (title), attributing this to John Bale's *Summarium*, i.e., *Illustrium Maioris Britanniae Scriptorum … Summarium* (Wesel, 1548), f. 157r. On reverse of title there is an engraving of Wyclif and a sonnet on his life and the burning of his corpse, *inc.* 'Kyng Edward the iij. did Wicklife defend'. Crowley's text is a careful transcription of **Q**. There are two marginal glosses, 'anentis' (8): 'wyth' (sig. B.1r), and 'Seine' (45): 'is a councell' (sig. B.2v). Thomas James copied extracts from Crowley into his manuscript of portions of Wyclif's writings, Bodleian Library James 3, pp. 249–61.

Choice of base manuscript

Of the five complete texts, **Q** (Hudson's choice of base manuscript for her edition of ch. 15, following *WB*) shares many readings with **G ι** against the other manuscripts. Occasionally the **G ι Q** reading is better than the reading of the other manuscripts, e.g., 'of þo [the idolatrous priests] on þe auteris' (1054) against 'of þo' α S, 'of þe' β, 'on þe' P2, 'on þo' T (see note). Often the **G ι Q** reading is as good as that of the other manuscripts, e.g., 'passynge of Iordan' (402) for 'passage of Iordan', and 'lefte' (1210) for 'hadde sett'. But there are also a number of inferior readings, e.g, 'preest eiþir bishop' (1240–1) for 'prest and bischop', and there are frequent omissions, of words, phrases and complete clauses.

---

[47] Hudson, *PR*, 492–3.
[48] A 1536 edition is listed by Forshall and Madden, *WB*, I, xxiii, but neither the 1926 nor the revised 1976 *Short-Title Catalogue* includes it, and no copies are known.
[49] Hudson, *PR*, 398, 492.

S largely agrees with α (Forshall and Madden's choice of base manuscript for their edition of PWB 1–2793), but the corrector's habit of erasing what was written by the first hand and writing over it makes this an unusably mongrel text. β generally agrees with α S, but also shares some readings with P T, e.g, 'errour eþer eresie' (120), where the other manuscripts read 'heresie'. It has the most plausible reading at 2278, 'spouse' (see note). However, it also has many unique and highly idiosyncratic readings; these are recorded in the apparatus in *WB*, but only occasionally in this edition.

P T are the only manuscripts to preserve the clause 'and þanne brou3t his owne puple þorou3 þe Reed See' (154–5). On the other hand, they sometimes share readings which must be corrections of the archetype, e.g., 'þe firste prologe on Iob' (2890) where the other manuscripts read 'oo prolog on Iob', and 'gaten of Iosue and oþere princes pees and liyf' (432), where α S read 'of iosue pees and lijf and oþer princis' and G ι Q read 'of iosue pees and lyf of iosue and oþere pryncis' (see note). T also has many unique readings: for example, where all other manuscripts read 'hou myche of þe book of Hester and of Danyel is of autorite' (27–8) T *sup. ras.* reads '3it netheles þe book [etc.]', and where all other manuscripts read 'largelier' (1112), T reads 'more largely'. P is therefore the only clean text of PWB relatively free from omissions and idiosyncratic readings, although it is certainly at more than one remove from the archetype.

The Prologue to Isaiah and the Prophets[50]

The Prologue to Isaiah and the Prophets is the only prologue the Wycliffite translators wrote for an Old Testament book. The translations of Jerome's Old Testament prologues in the Earlier Version of the Wycliffite Bible were removed by the revisers producing the Later Version,[51] but when the revisers reached the beginning of Isaiah they decided to include a new prologue in English to serve as 'a general prolog for alle þe bokis of profetis suynge'.[52] This prologue is included in all manuscripts containing Isaiah in the Later Version. It stresses the accessibility of scripture to the reader with little or no formal education, borrowing from Jerome's prologue to Isaiah the reassurance that Isaiah is 'ful open' (1) and as much a gospeller as a prophet. A brief guide to the historical sense of Isaiah follows (13–24), but for the Wycliffite writer (following Lyra) the historical sense is only one aspect of the literal sense; the author's intention is far more significant. He has it on Jerome's authority that all Isaiah's 'bisynesse (*cura*), þat is, principal entent, is of þe cleping [summoning] of heþene men and of þe comyng of Crist' (10–11).

The rules offered for understanding the literal sense of the prophetic books are primarily concerned with Jewish misinterpretation of the Hebrew prophets; they are rooted in the assumption that Jews would understand the christological content of

---

[50] Dove, *FEB*, 106–7, 113–19.

[51] Dove, *FEB*, 103–5. Exceptionally, they retained the prologue to Baruch.

[52] This heading, in E C9 Y, derives from PWB 2079.

their own scriptures if only they would read them literally (25–39). There follows an emphatic assertion of the centrality of the literal sense. Any sense other than the literal must be evidently warranted by the text itself or by plain, evident reason (cf. GGI 23, GGII 111–12, GGIII 26, 60–1 and PWB 1622), on the authority of Augustine, Jerome, Lyra and Richard FitzRalph. With characteristically Wycliffite provocativeness the writer warns against the dangers of spiritual interpretation rooted not in scripture or reason but in delusion. He invites his reader to agree that powerful men have been deceived by preferring the delusions of their imagination to the open sense of the Bible (40–51). Returning to the unexceptionable, he proceeds to name the four senses of scripture, promising to give a fuller account prefaced to Genesis, 'if God wole' (55), and ends with a few lines of guidance for understanding the Prophets' use of figurative language (52–68).

Edition

WB, III, 225–6 (from **A**)

Base manuscript

P Princeton, W.H. Scheide 12, f. 263ra–va

Other manuscripts

S Corpus Christi College Cambridge 147, fols 269v–270r

C9 Emmanuel College Cambridge 21, fols 210v–211r
    WB, no. 118. WB in LV, *c.*1420–30. Dove, *FEB*, 237–8.

C6 Cambridge University Library Additional 6680, fols 227v–228r
    Lindberg, no. 191. WB in LV, *c.*1410. Dove, *FEB*, 238.

R Cambridge University Library Dd.1.27, fols 294v–295r
    WB, no. 106. WB in LV, *c.*1420. Dove, *FEB*, 238–9.

Q Cambridge University Library Mm.2.15, f. 188r–v

Y Trinity College Dublin 67, fols 34v–35r
    WB, no. 149. Proverbs to 2 Maccabees in LV, *c.*1425. (?) Dove, *FEB*, 286.

X Hereford Cathedral Library O.vii.I, fols 211v–212r
    WB, no. 137. WB in LV, *c.*1410–20. R.A.B. Mynors and R.M. Thomson, *Catalogue of the Manuscripts of Hereford Cathedral Library* (Cambridge: Brewer, 1993), p. 46; Dove, *FEB*, 243–4.

E British Library Arundel 104, vol. 2, fols 96v–97r
    WB, no. 29. 2-vol. WB in LV, *c.*1430. Dove, *FEB*, 244–5.

L2 British Library Cotton Claudius E.ii, fols 197v–198r
    WB, no. 9. WB in LV, *c.*1410. Dove, *FEB*, 245–6.

A British Library Royal I C.viii, fols 214v–215r

U Lambeth Palace Library 25, fols 223v–224r

   WB, no. 46. Pentateuch in EV, Joshua–Apoc. in LV, *c*.1390–1410. M.R. James, *A Descriptive Catalogue of the Manuscripts of the Library of Lambeth Palace* (Cambridge, 1930), pp. 40–1; O.S. Pickering and V.M. O'Mara, *IMEP* handlist XIII, 1–2; Dove, *FEB*, 251–2.

V Lambeth Palace Library 1033, fols 136v–137v

   WB, no. 50. 2 Chron. 2:7–Baruch in LV, *c*.1410–20. M.R. James, *A Descriptive Catalogue of the Manuscripts of the Library of Lambeth Palace* (Cambridge, 1930), p. 817; O.S. Pickering and V.M. O'Mara, *IMEP* handlist XIII, 60; Dove, *FEB*, 293.

F Sion College Arc.L.40.2 / E.1, fols 227v–228r (conserved in Lambeth Palace Library)

   WB, no. 42. OT in LV, *c*.1420. N.R. Ker, *Medieval Manuscripts in British Libraries*, vol. I (Oxford, 1969), pp. 287–8; O.S. Pickering and V.M. O'Mara, *IMEP* handlist XIII, 79; Dove, *FEB*, 294.

R91 John Rylands Manchester Eng. 91, f. 46r–v

   Lindberg, no. 209. Proverbs–Apoc. in LV, *c*.1410–20. N.R. Ker, *Medieval Manuscripts in British Libraries*, vol. III (Oxford, 1983), p. 414; Dove, *FEB*, 296.

I Bodleian Library Bodley 277, f. 214r–v

K Bodleian Library Fairfax 2, f. 223r

   WB, no. 71. WB in LV, 1408. Dove, *FEB*, 257–9.

H Corpus Christi College Oxford 20, f. 121r–v

   WB, no. 93. 1 Ezra–2 Macc. in LV, *c*.1400–10. Dove, *FEB*, 261–2.

G Lincoln College Oxford lat. 119, fols 194v–195r

M Queen's College Oxford 388, f. 254r–v

   WB, no. 101. WB in LV, *c*.1410–20. Dove, *FEB*, 263–4.

N St John's College Oxford 7, fols 183v–184r

   WB, no. 103. OT in LV (– Ps.), *c*.1420. Ralph Hanna, *A Descriptive Catalogue of the Western Medieval Manuscripts of St John's College Oxford* (Oxford: Oxford University Press, 2002), pp. 8–9; Dove, *FEB*, 302–3.

Choice of base manuscript

The text of PIP is consistent across all manuscripts.[53] **P** has therefore again been chosen as the base manuscript.

---

[53]   E C9 Y add translational glosses at 4 and 42.

The Twelve Cambridge Tracts[54]

The headings to Cambridge Tracts II–XI make it apparent that an editor has assembled these tracts into a collection advocating scripture in English: Tract II, for example, is headed 'Þis preueþ þat þei ben blessed þat louen Goddis lawe in þere owen langage', Tract IV 'And anoþer sentens comendynge þe gospel in our moder-tunge' and Tract VII 'Þis trettys þat folewþ proueþ þat eche nacioun may lefully haue holy writ in her moder-tunge'. These headings are not found in any other copies of the tracts.[55] Whether the twelfth tract, 'A dialoge as hit were of a wyse man and of a fole denyinge þe trweþe wiþ fablis', should be seen as part of the collection is unsure, but its insistence on the absolute truth of scripture allies it with the other tracts, especially Tract III.

All the Cambridge Tracts give scripture a central place and imply that everyone should have access to it, but only Tracts I (which is the longest, *c*.6,800 words), II, VII and VIII explicitly advocate scripture, particularly the gospel, in the English language. Tracts I and VIII occur only in **C**, but Tract II is a slightly revised version of one of the prologues to the translation of Clement of Llanthony's gospel harmony and Tract VII is a reworking of one of the many Middle English tracts on the Lord's Prayer, *Pater Noster II* (also in this edition, pp. 160–71). The other tracts found only in **C** are Tracts III, IV, V, IX and XII. Tract VI (which is the shortest, *c*.330 words) is one of the tracts associated with the devotional work *The Pore Caitif*. Tract X is the conclusion of the Epilogue to Intermediate/Long Glossed Matthew (GGIII in this edition). Tract XI shares some material with the prologue to the Middle English translation of Robert of Greatham's *Miroir*. In sum, seven of the Cambridge Tracts are unique; three are copies of texts found elsewhere and two are reworkings of other texts.[56]

The Cambridge Tracts are all anonymous, but it is possible that Tract I was written by the same friar who wrote *Dives and Pauper* and the sermons in Longleat 4. The tracts share concerns with writings certainly by Wycliffites: the gospel, it is maintained, is traduced by poorly educated, lazy or worldly clerics,[57] and such clerics prevent the people from attaining knowledge of scripture.[58] A distinction is made between false and true clerics;[59] images are disparaged (at CTI 7–9).[60] Tract IX reveals 'þe armes of antecristis disciplis aȝenes trewe men' (1).[61] Tract X may reasonably be identified as Wycliffite because it is part of a Glossed Gospel epilogue and alludes to

---

[54] Hunt, *TFST*, I, 72–129.
[55] CTVI has a different heading in **L5** and **O3** (see apparatus).
[56] See the introductions to the individual tracts for further details.
[57] E.g., CTI 53–66, CTVII 10–12, 23–5, 49–51, 'pepel' and CTIX 22–6 Cf. *IB* 5–8.
[58] E.g., CTI 76–84 and CTVI 18–19 Cf. PWB 1596–600.
[59] E.g., CTII 39–41, CTVII 57, CTIX 1 and CTX 26–7.
[60] CTI 7, 'and not'–9.
[61] See the note on PWB 2919.

the characteristically Wycliffite distinction between God's law and customs and laws made by sinful men,[62] and Tract XII may reasonably be identified as Wycliffite because it puts the abusive term 'loller' in a positive light (39–46). Can the collection as a whole, however, be characterized as Wycliffite? There is nothing remotely Lollard in tracts III, IV and V. Evidently the editor had considerable interest in and knowledge of texts by Wycliffite writers, but the concept of a collection of texts advocating scripture in English was not in itself Wycliffite, and the Cambridge Tracts, though tinged by Wycliffism, are very diverse indeed.

Tract I almost certainly refers to the third canon of archbishop Arundel's constitutions.[63] The collection may well have been put together in response to the prohibition of the English Bible.[64]

Manuscript

C Cambridge University Library Ii.6.26

*c.*1410–25(?) 103 fols; 1–12(8), 13(8, lacks 1–3); 150 × 107 mm; 97 × 62 mm; single column, 25 lines; bounding-lines carefully drawn in black ink throughout; prickings clearly visible, fols 1–79. Medieval quire (lower-case letters) and folio signatures (dots) are often visible, but no catchwords are visible. Early-modern pagination; modern foliation. One very square bookhand with thick strokes, frequent misdivision of words, alarmingly diverse spellings and inexplicable errors.[65] Errors (even errors producing meaningless text) are frequently left uncorrected. 4-line space for initial left blank, f. 1r; 2-line spaces for initials left blank elsewhere; headings and marginal biblical references sometimes rubricated; red paraphs fols 1–79; capitals touched with red; occasional red and blue decorative line-fillers.

Twelve tracts advocating scripture in English, fols 1–79v (detailed below): *Lucistrye*, i.e., Honorius of Autun, *Elucidarium* (*IPMEP* no. 257), fols 79v–101v (some seven quires of the *Elucidarium* are lost between quires 11 and 12) (fols 102 and 103 blank). The scribe's dialect is central East Midland (Cambridgeshire?); see Hunt, *TFST*, I, 85–6. *A Catalogue of the Manuscripts preserved in the Library of the University of Cambridge*, vol. III (Cambridge, 1861), pp. 524–6.

---

[62]   See the note on PWB 125–30.

[63]   CTI 472–4 and note.

[64]   Hunt, *TFST*, I, 76–8, 127–8, and H. Leith Spencer, *English Preaching in the Later Middle Ages* (Oxford: Clarendon Press, 1993), p. 161. The date given in *Manual*, 2, III, 51 can safely be ignored.

[65]   See, e.g., the notes on CTI 90 and 101.

Tract I: 'Alle cristine peple stant in þre maner of folke', fols 1r–22r
          [unique manuscript]

'Alle cristine peple stant in þre maner of folke' provides the widest range of arguments in favour of English scripture in the Cambridge Tracts. The 'three kinds' are clerics, illiterate laypeople and the literate laity. Evidence from scripture that it is lawful for the laity to read scripture is followed by the charge that the people are ignorant because the clergy are ignorant (1–66). The ability and will to teach God's law are rare, laments the writer, yet so lawless is the country that some who wish to preach are prevented from doing so (67–84). An argument against translation is that scripture in English is full of heresy: *contra*, there is even more heresy in Latin books, and errors can and should be corrected (85–97). The writer argues that those who claim that Hebrew, Greek and Latin are the only languages of scripture ignore Christ's commandment that all nations should be taught the gospel, and in England they should be taught in English (98–124). Just as scripture was translated from Hebrew into Greek and then Latin it should now, he says, be translated into English: students learn to do this in grammar school (125–46). Another argument against translation is that because scripture has many senses it is too difficult for uneducated people to understand: *contra*, it is also too difficult for the majority of the clergy, while many laypeople are literate in Latin (147–66). The nobility and women in religious orders have ready access to scripture in Latin, whether they understand it or not (166–74). Devotional texts everyone should know should be translated into English, sense for sense not word for word (175–82).

Returning to the 'three kinds', the writer repeats that there are two kinds of laypeople, illiterate and literate, and clerics, who should know God's will and law. Illiterates need only basic teaching; literate laypeople, on the other hand, have a duty to learn as much as they can, and the clergy have a duty to teach them. Illiterates are the swine before whom the pearls of the gospel should not be thrown; the literate should feel able to converse with the clergy to the limit of their capability (183–228). The story of the meeting of Philip with the Ethiopian teaches that we should read God's law even when we do not understand it, and be ready to ask for help—especially, he says, 'gentlis and men of lawe' (229–48). There follow examples of laypeople who did God's will: the king of Egypt who had the Hebrew scriptures translated into Greek, the children of Israel and the rich young ruler (249–71). Apostles and church fathers wrote letters of instruction to laypeople, but, he claims, clerics in his own day want laypeople as ignorant as possible, in spite of canon law to the contrary, and refuse to elucidate the epistle and gospel in the vernacular (272–319). Anyone who can read scripture should, without pride or presumption. The adult should not be content with the understanding of a child, for scripture tells us to read and understand, and warns against the incursions of the devil; a warning in Latin is no good to someone who only knows English. Priests pray that laypeople may understand God's law, but prevent them from understanding it (320–408). Ignorance of God's law is likely to lead to disaster, because it is the cause of all instability and sedition (409–56).

Another argument against translation is that speaking about the faith with laypeople is forbidden. The writer retorts that preaching and teaching are not forbidden—they are demanded by every legal code. Laypeople may convert others, as Monica did Augustine, but they should not discuss religious belief in public (457–76). In conclusion, the writer assures his 'dear friends' that laypeople may indeed study God's law (477–96). The conclusion confirms that the kind of people the writer has in mind as readers are devout, educated and well-born laypeople, including lawyers. Although harsh things are said about clerics who are unwilling to teach and unwilling to allow laypeople to read God's law for themselves, they are treated considerably more gently than they are in tracts II, VII, IX and X (see particularly CTI 334–9).

'Alle cristine peple stant in þre maner of folke' shares a short passage, 'For þus seiþ oure Lord God … he haþ takun of God' (19–47), with *Dives and Pauper*, a devotional work written by a friar, probably a Franciscan.[66] There are also similarities of ideas with the sermons of Longleat 4, written by the same friar as *Dives and Pauper*.[67] The Longleat sermons stress the obligation to preach in the vernacular, and argue that it is lawful to read the gospel in the vernacular: 'Crist seyde nout to hym, as prelatis and men of holy cherche don þese dayes to men and wommen þat askin hem questyonys of holy writ, of conscience and of Goddis lawe: O þou borel [ignorant] clerk, what entyrmetyst þu þee wiþ holy writ and wiþ Goddis lawe' (cf. CTI 269–70).[68] Like 'Alle cristine peple stant in þre maner of folke', the Longleat sermons address the reader as 'leue frend', or 'leue frendys'.[69] Their audience, like the audience of Cambridge Tract I, seems to be the devout and privileged laity.[70] 'Alle cristine peple stant in þre maner of folke' may have been written by the friar who wrote *Dives and Pauper* and the Longleat sermons.[71] Certainly he was familiar with the writings of the English Bible debate, probably including the university determinations (see the introduction to *First seiþ Bois*, pp. xlix–liv), and he shared Ullerston's belief that an English Bible 'might actually foster cooperation between laity and clergy'.[72]

Edition

Hunt, *TFST*, II, 265–81

---

[66]   See the note on CTI 19–47 John Whethamstede commissioned a copy of *Dives et Pauper* for the Benedictine Abbey at St Albans, but William Alnwick, bishop of Norwich, thought the work heretical; see Anne Hudson and H.L. Spencer, 'Old author, new work: the sermons of MS Longleat 4', *Medium Ævum* 53 (1984), 228.

[67]   Hudson and Spencer, 'Old author, new work', 220–38; H. Leith Spencer, *English Preaching in the Later Middle Ages* (Oxford: Clarendon Press, 1993), pp. 1–3 [and *passim*], and *Manual*, 11, XXVI, 30.

[68]   Sermon for Trinity 13, f. 90va–b; Hudson and Spencer, 'Old author, new work', 232.

[69]   Hudson and Spencer, 'Old author, new work', 226–7.

[70]   Hudson and Spencer, 'Old author, new work', 233.

[71]   Spencer, *English Preaching in the Later Middle Ages*, pp. 422–3.

[72]   Nicole R. Rice, *Lay Piety and Religious Discipline in Middle English Literature* (Cambridge: Cambridge University Press, 2008), p. 134.

Tract II: 'Oure Lord Iesu Crist verry God and man', fols 22r–25r

'Oure Lord Iesu Crist verry God and man' begins with a *catena* of scriptural authorities on the necessity to love God and keep his law, concluding that it is even more charitable to preach God's law than to give bodily alms (1–17). Only then is the topic of the text introduced: 'Cristyn men owen to trauel myche neȝt and day about þe tixt of holy writ and nameli þe gospel in here moder-tunge' (21–2). The written gospel is uniquely precious and salvific (22–8). Who, the writer asks, may prevent laypeople from knowing it? Worldly clerics reply that laypeople should not concern themselves with religious questions because they will introduce error: *contra*, only a few will be so greedy, and a worldly priest may as easily err against the Latin Bible. Knowledge of God's law is the only way to heaven, and the laity should learn it from God, by good living and by asking 'trwe clerkis' (40). God requires all Christian men and women to learn his law and teach it, and only an antichrist would prevent them from doing so (29–47). Worldly clerics also argue that an English Bible would lead to sedition, but this slanders God and his law, and allies these clerics with the scribes and pharisees who accused Christ of causing dissension. The tract ends with a prayer that Jesus may silence these blasphemies and make his gospel known to his simple brethren (48–58).

'Oure Lord Iesu Crist verry God and man' is one of three additional prologues to *Oon of Foure*, a translation (*c.*1380–90) of Clement of Llanthony's twelfth-century gospel harmony *Unum ex Quattuor*.[73] Clement's own prologue occurs in all copies of *Oon of Foure*: the other additional prologues are *In þe biginnyng* and *Seynt Austyn saiþ* (GGII in this edition, pp. 174–9).[74] All of them argue for scripture in English and blame the clergy for the laity's ignorance: 'Seynt Austyn saiþ' and 'Oure Lord Iesu Crist verry God and man' are harshly critical of worldly clerics, so much so that in manuscript of the end of 'Oure Lord Iesu Crist' (52–8) has been erased, doubtless an act of censorship. It is surely deliberate that the advocacy of English scripture in Cambridge Tract II is not apparent until line 21—a reader checking the prologue's orthodoxy would find its opening unexceptionable.[75]

Tract II is a slightly revised and shortened text of the *Oon of Foure* prologue. All other manuscripts read 'very God and very man', and Tract II omits what Augustine says about figurative language and a passage on the real priesthood of every Christian believer.[76] The focus of the slightly shorter text never moves away from the people's

---

[73] Hunt, *TFST*, I, 65–71, and *Manual*, 2, IV, 37 (where it is dated 1375–1400, and only two additional prologues are mentioned). *Oon of Foure* is ed. Paul M. Smith, *An Edition of Parts I–V of the Wycliffite Translation of Clement of Llanthony's Gospel Harmony* Unum ex Quattuor *known as* Oon of Foure, PhD dissertation, Southampton, 1984.

[74] All three additional prologues occur in **D76 G1 L I P1**; CTII and GGII occur in **D o R77**; GGII occurs in **O6**.

[75] Dove, *FEB*, 52–3.

[76] See apparatus and notes to CTII 42, 47, etc.

need for the gospel. Additional prologues are found in only a third of the manuscripts of *Oon and Foure*, and since they are evidently interpolated in two manuscripts (**L1** and **P1**)[77] they are likely to be somewhat later than the translation itself (*c.*1390–1400). Prologues advocating scripture in English are clearly relevant to any English biblical translation, and it is not surprising that Tract II is also found prefaced to John's Gospel in revised EV and to Matthew's Gospel in LV.

Editions

Hunt, *TFST*, II, 282–8
WB, I, xiv–xv (from **L1**)

Other manuscripts

Extra prologue to *Oon of Foure*:

G1 Glasgow University Gen. 223
Lindberg, no. 195; *c.*1400; 223 fols + stub; 205 × 145 mm; 145 × 95 mm; single column; 26–30 lines. Gospel lectionary in EV, fols 1r–6v; 'In þe bigynnyng of holi chirche', f. 7r; 'Seynt Austyn seiþ', fols 7r–10v; 'Oure Lord Iesu Crist', fols 10v–13r; *Oon of Foure*, fols 13r–189r; Catholic Epistles in EV, fols 190r–212v; Ten Commandments, fols 213r–217r [and other devotional texts].

L1 British Library Arundel 254
s. xiv. ex; 135 fols; 225 × 150 mm; 160 × 100 mm; single column (fols 2–18); 2 columns (elsewhere); 32 lines; hands: anglicana (fols 9–12 and the same hand fols 86v–103v); bookhand (*Oon of Foure*). Preliminaries to *Oon of Foure*, fols 2r–8v; 'In þe biginnyng of holy chirche', f. 9r; 'Seynt Austyn seiþ', fols 9r–11r; 'Oure Lord Iesu Crist very God', fols 11r–12v (these three prologues form a separate quire) (f. 13 blank); gospel lectionary, fols 14r–18r; *Oon of Foure*, fols 19ra–86ra; Catholic epistles in LV, fols 86va–103vb; OT lections in LV, fols 104ra–135vb. Owned by Thomas Howard Earl of Arundel (d. 1646).

o British Library Harley 6333
WB, no. 25; *c.*1400. 366 fols bound as two volumes (medieval wrapper follows f. 144); 272 × 195 mm; 185 × 127 mm; 2 columns; 30 lines; one slightly tremulous bookhand. Preliminaries to *Oon of Foure*, fols 1r–17r; prologues to Matthew, 1) 'Seynt Austyn seiþ' (headed 'a prolog upon þe gospel of Mathew'), fols 18r–20r, 2) 'Oure Lord Iesu Crist verri God', with 52, 'And'–58 erased, fols 20r–21v, 3) LV prologue to Matthew (headed 'þe þridde prolog of Mathew'), fols 21v–22r; LV prologue to Mark, fols 22r–v; LV prologue to Luke, f. 22v; LV prologue to John, with the second half written in the lower margin, f. 22v; *Oon of Foure*, fols 23r–138v; Lectionary in LV, fols 139r–144v; Romans–Apoc., followed by Laodiceans, fols 145r–297v; gospel lections written in full, fols 27v–364v. Dove, *FEB*, 292.

---

77 Hunt argues that they are also interpolated in **o**; *TFST*, I, 68.

P1 Peterborough Cathedral 8 (conserved in Cambridge University Library)
*c.*1400. iii + 123 fols + iv; written space 130 × 80 mm, but in the three prologues 140 × 90 mm; single column. The second quire, containing the additional prologues, is in an anglicana not later than 1400, while *Oon of Foure* is written in bookhand. Preliminaries to *Oon of Foure*, fols 1r–8r, 'In þe begynning of holi chirche', f. 9r, 'Seynt Austyn seiþ', fols 9r–11r, and 'Oure Lord Iesu Crist very God', fols 11r–12v; *Oon of Foure*, fols 13r–122v; the first section of Richard of St Victor, *Benjamin Minor*, fols 123r–v. Owned by Bridgettine Abbey of Syon(?).

Prefaced to revised EV John:

D76 Trinity College Dublin 76
*c.*1400; iv + 122 fols; 235 × 150 mm; 190/205 × 120/140 mm; 2 columns; 36–7 lines. One bookhand, fols 6–122. Extracts from William of Nassyngton, *Speculum Vitae*, fols iʳ–ivʳ (in poor condition); Lectionary in EV, fols 1r–5v; 'In þe bigynnynge of holy chirche' (first prologue to Matthew), f. 6r; 'Seynt Austyn saiþ' (second prologue to Matthew), fols 6r–8r; EV prologue to Matthew, fols 8r–v; Matthew–Luke in revised EV (including EV prologue to Luke), fols 8v–98v; 'Oure Lord Iesu Crist very God', fols 99r–100r; John in revised EV (breaks off at 19:42), fols 100v–122v.

Prefaced to LV Matthew:

D Sächsische Landesbibliothek Dresden Od. 83
Lindberg, nos 182/227; 414 fols; 170 × 115 mm; 120 × 75 mm; 2 columns, 30 lines; one neat bookhand. NT lectionary in LV, fols 1r–14v; 'Saynt Austyn seiþ', headed 'a prologe vpon þe gospel of Mathew', fols 15r–17v; 'Oure Lord Iesu Crist verri God and verri man', fols 17v–19r; 'Mathew þat was of Iudee', headed 'þe þridde prologe', fols 19r–v; NT in LV, fols 20r–352v; OT lections, fols 352v–410r (f. 411 blank); prologue to Romans 'Romayns ben þei þat of Iewis', fols 412r–413v; another short prologue to Romans (not now legible), fols 413v–414r; prologue and epistle to Laodiceans, f. 414r–v. There are several errors and brief omissions in the text of 'Saynt Austyn seiþ', and the text of 'Oure Lord Iesu Crist verri God and verri man' is very close to that in **R77**, with the same omission at 52–3.

R77 John Rylands Manchester Eng. 77
WB, no. 158; *c.*1400. 268 fols; 8s; 190 × 130 mm; 122 × 80 mm; 2 columns; 36 lines; one small and very regular bookhand. Lectionary, fols 4r–12r; prologues to Matthew, 1) 'Seynt Austyn seiþ', fols 13r–15r, 2) 'Oure Lord Iesu Crist verri God and verri man', fols 15r–16r, 3) 'Mathu þat was of Iudee', fols 16r–v; NT in LV, fols 17r–267r. Contains the only surviving 'licence' in a WB manuscript, f. 267v. An elaborately decorated volume. Ralph Hanna, 'English Biblical Texts before Lollardy', in Fiona Somerset, Jill C. Havens and Derrick G. Pittard, eds, *Lollards and their Influence in Late Medieval England* (Woodbridge, Suffolk: Boydell, 2003), pp. 150–1; N. R. Ker, *Medieval Manuscripts in British Libraries*, vol. III (Oxford, 1983), pp. 404–5; G. A. Lester, *IMEP* handlist II, 4–6; Dove, *FEB*, 47–53, 295.

Tract III: 'Oure Lorde Iesu Crist, lord of trouþe', fols 25r–26v
     [unique manuscript]

'Oure Lorde Iesu Crist, lord of trouþe' again asserts the centrality of the gospel, this time as the only way to learn about the life of Christ as well as to learn his law and follow it (1–6). The gospel is a letter sent to humankind sealed with Christ's blood (here the writer echoes the *Charter of Christ* tradition, 6–15). Unlike chronicles, in which truth is mixed with lies, the gospel is absolutely true and, the writer surprisingly claims, is readily available in parish churches (presumably he means in Latin, not in English) (16–24).[78] Even saints' lives are inferior to the gospel because saints erred and the writers of their lives erred (25–31). The gospel surpasses the writings of philosophers in truth and wisdom by as much as God surpasses human beings, and provides a more authoritative moral guide than they do (32–9). There is a break in the sense in CTIII 35, where the writer is arguing that God's law is the best law.[79]

The editor's heading 'Many croniculis ben fals but al þe gospel is trwe' misses Tract III's point that the gospel is truer than *all* other kinds of writing. Since the writer seems to expect his readers to have access to the gospel in the parish church, Tract III may be a translation or adaptation of a Latin original.

Edition

Hunt, *TFST*, II, 289–91

Tract IV: 'Cristen men vnderstonden þat þe foure gospelleris', fols 26v–28v
     [unique manuscript]

The opening of Tract IV establishes that the garden of the Song of Songs should be understood to be the 'gloriose gardyn of Cristis gospel' (10), which is not to be entered by wild pigs (the proud and impenitent, 1–15).[80] If we enter weeping, Christ will give us water to drink; in return we shall give good works and words performed with love. Those who do not enter by one of the four gates (poverty, penitence, patience and prayer) will be hunted out (16–30). The four kinds of work to be done in this garden are reading the gospel, understanding it, acting according to it and persevering to the end: these works will defeat the world, wicked men, the flesh and the devil. Then we shall eat the fruit of the garden, the Eucharist, and not be hunted out by the devil's flesh-hooks (31–43).

According to the editor's heading Tract IV is 'anoþer sentens comendynge þe gospel in our moder-tunge', but it does not contain any arguments for scripture in English. Reading and understanding the gospel and living according to it are the activities proper to the gospel-garden—the only alternative is being hunted out like an animal.

---

[78] See the note on CTIII 23–4.
[79] See the note on CTIII 35.
[80] Mary Dove, 'Love *ad Litteram*: The Lollard translations of the Song of Songs', *Reformation* 9 (2004), 1–5.

The contrast between desire and fear is unpleasantly stark in this highly conventional sermon.[81]

Edition

Hunt, *TFST*, II, 292–5

Tract V: 'The ȝele or feruour of loue of þi hous haþ eten me', fols 28v–40v
[unique manuscript]

'The ȝele or feruour of loue of þi hous haþ eten me' begins and ends with Christ throwing the traders out of the temple (John 2:14–17). This lengthy tract (*c*.3,600 words) consists of a series of extracts from commentaries, sermons and scripture, including Bede's homily on John 2:14–17 (1–14), Augustine on the same passage (17–41), Gregory the Great on Matt. 11:2–10 (42–86), ps.-Chrysostom's *Opus Imperfectum* (90–2), Chrysostom's sermon on the Cross (117–20) and many others. The subjects addressed may very broadly be defined as love for God's house, God's ministers and one's fellow-Christians, and a concomitant hatred of heresy. The most arresting extract is perhaps Gregory the Great's account of the witness of the elements to Christ's divinity, the translation here retaining the poetic quality of the original (93–102). The latter part of Tract V consists of quotations from and summaries of scripture all concerned with witnesses to the words and acts of God, many of these witnesses heathens, such as Nebuchadnezzar and Darius (178–229). The last few lines are a moral interpretation of the throwing of the traders out of the temple, beginning 'Also, bi þe temple may be vnderstonden þe soule of man' (230), as though following on from a gloss on the same passage.

There are no overt links between the various extracts, but each ends with the author's name and the work from which the extract comes, suggesting the format of the gloss. It is tempting to think that this tract may be related more or less closely to Long Glossed John on John 2:14–17 (although Short Glossed John survives, only parts of Long Glossed John are extant, in York XVI.D.2).[82] If, however, the editor had access to the whole of Long Glossed John why did he select this particular section? In spite of the editorial heading, Tract V only occasionally and implicitly touches on the subject of scripture in the vernacular; when, for example, Josiah reads the words of the law to the people, from the greatest to the least (178–82). It is more probable that the writer of Tract V was imitating the mode of the Long Glossed Gospels,[83] and that the editor was impressed by the writer's enterprise.

Edition

Hunt, *TFST*, II, 296–309

---

[81] Hunt agrees that Tract IV derives from 'a sermon, almost certainly one of complete orthodoxy', *TFST*, I, 98.

[82] See the note on GGV 11–12.

[83] As Hunt says, *TFST*, I, 98.

Tract VI: 'Firste wite ech man þat charite', fols 40v–41v

'Firste wite ech man þat charite' opens with the assertion that 'charite is þe principal part of holy writ'. Therefore, to prohibit people from speaking about scripture prohibits them from speaking about God, love, heaven, hell or any aspect of creation, since scripture contains all that is (1–8). Christ would not even prevent the devil from speaking scripture: without it we should not know the difference between good and evil (8–11). Those who break God's law are cursed. In an exemplum drawing on the *Charter of Christ* tradition,[84] the writer says that just as those who prevent a man's testamentary dispositions from being carried out are cursed on earth so are those cursed by God who prevent Christ's testament, the gospel, from being made known to all (12–19).

'Firste wite ech man þat charite' survives in two other copies,[85] both of which are manuscripts of *Pore Caitif*, an unedited collection of devotional tracts *c.*1395–1402.[86] The variants are without significance.[87] *Pore Caitif* is not a Wycliffite work, but Mary Teresa Brady identifies Wycliffite additions and alterations in some manuscripts of *Pore Caitif*, including **O3**.[88] There is nothing specifically Wycliffite in 'Firste wite ech man þat charite', but its argument that if people cannot speak of scripture they cannot speak of anything suggests that the writer sits lightly to academic logic. His concern is to demonstrate the absurdity as well as wickedness of those who prevent laypeople from reading and discussing the gospel.

Edition

Hunt, *TFST*, II, 310–12

Other manuscripts

L5 British Library Harley 2322

s. xiv. ex; iii + 156 fols; 150 × 100 mm; 95 × 65 mm; single column; 20 lines; bookhand. 4-line gold initial filled in blue on square mauve background at openings of Pater Noster tract, f. 4r, Ave, f. 18r, Creed, f. 23r [etc.]. *Pore Caitif* (with the tracts and interpolations in the same order as **O3**), fols 1r–152r, including 'Firste wite ech man þat charite', fols 87r–88r (fols 153–6 blank).

---

[84]   Cf. CTIII 12–13 and note.

[85]   On the closeness of the contents of these two manuscripts see M. Teresa Brady, 'The Pore Caitif: an introductory study', *Traditio* 10 (1954), 533–4.

[86]   It survives complete in 30 manuscripts and in an incomplete or fragmentary state in 24 others; see Jolliffe, B, 65–7, and *Manual*, 9, XXIII, 87. Mary Teresa Brady dates *The Pore Caitif c.*1395–1402, 'Lollard sources of *The Pore Caitif*', *Traditio* 44 (1988), 389.

[87]   **O3** ends at 'testament is' (CTVI 16).

[88]   'Lollard interpolations and omissions in manuscripts of *The Pore Caitif*', in Michael G. Sargent, ed., *De Cella in Seculum: Religious and Secular Life and Devotion in Late Medieval England* (Woodbridge, 1989), pp. 183–203. See also the introduction to CTVII, pp. xliii–xliv.

O3 Bodleian Library Additional B.66

s. xiv. ex; 91 fols (91 a stub); 150 × 105 mm; 95/100 × 67 mm; single column; 23 lines; bookhand. 'The Fifteen Oes', fols 3r–12r (fols 1 and 2 blank);[89] *Pore Caitif*, lacking prologue, fols 12v–90v;[90] 'Firste wite ech man þat charite' is the final tract (incomplete), f. 90r–v.

Tract VII: 'Siþen þat þe trouþe of God stondiþ not in oo langage', fols 41v–46r

'Siþen þat þe trouþe of God stondiþ not in oo langage' begins by asserting that scripture in English sustains common people as scripture in Latin does clerics, and since Christ commanded the gospel to be preached to all there is no reason why scripture may be preached and not written (1–8). The prohibition against written scripture in English, claims the writer, is a heresy, allying its originators with the pharisees. A teacher should make use of any device which helps his pupils to learn, and since written scripture is a means by which common people may reach heaven anyone who prohibits this opposes Christ (8–18). Afraid that their irreligiousness might become known, friars gloss the gospel, as did Mahomet. They are antichrists, traducing scripture (18–25). God's law is sufficient for every need, and Christ commanded it to be taught to all in their own language, because to know God's law and act in accordance with it is a 'hiȝe sacrifice' (32–3). Clerks should do their best to teach God's law; if they do the opposite they are living devils (26–41). God's law strengthens the soul for endless bliss. If the negligence of clerics results in truth's not being spread abroad the writer advises his readers to pray to Christ to ordain preachers and illumine their hearts (42–55). Those who traduce scripture, fail to preach it and persecute true learners and teachers will die in their sins.

The scribes and pharisees, Tract VII continues, were enemies of Christ and incited the people to call for his crucifixion. The scribes were lawyers and the pharisees a religious order who cared more for their own laws then God's (this information is attributed in the margin to Rabanus):[91] Christ said 'woe' to them eight times, and reproved them for breaking God's law (56–69). The writer asks how clerks, especially those in religious orders, compare with the pharisees, answering that, like the pharisees, they claim to keep both God's law and their own rule. Their works, however, prove the contrary, especially their persecution of simple people trying to follow God's law and their slander of those who love it (70–88). The tract ends with a prayer for deliverance from the sin against the Holy Ghost and grace to know and follow God's law (89–95).

The most striking feature of 'Siþen þat þe trouþe of God stondiþ not in oo langage' is its ferocious anti-mendicancy (a characteristic of Wycliffite writings). In other

---

[89] Carleton Brown and R.H. Robbins, *Index of Middle English Verse* (New York, 1943), no. 1672.

[90] Brady, 'Lollard interpolations and omissions in manuscripts of *The Pore Caitif*', p. 532.

[91] See the note on CTVII 62.

Cambridge Tracts worldly clergy (whether in religious orders or not) are identified as the opponents of translation, but the writer of Tract VII represents the friars, successors of the pharisees, as being entirely responsible for this new heresy.[92] Most of Tract VII is very similar to parts of a tract on the Lord's Prayer known as *Pater Noster II* (included in this edition, pp. 160–71). In turn, *Pater Noster II* shares material with *Pater Noster I*[93] and other Middle English expositions of the Lord's Prayer, although none of these include advocacy of scripture in English.[94] The passages *Pater Noster II* and Tract VII have in common are in the same order, but Tract VII omits all *Pater Noster II*'s material on the Lord's Prayer and its separate petitions. On the other hand, Tract VII contains some material not shared with *Pater Noster II*.[95] The writer of *Pater Noster II* apparently recognizes that the material advocating scripture in English is peripheral, for after the equivalent of Tract VII 1–25 he says 'Leue we now þis mater and speke we of the Pater Noster' (*PNII* 27).

It is possible that the writer of *Pater Noster II* borrowed material from 'Siþen þat þe trouþe of God stondiþ not in oo langage', aware that written scripture in English had become a crucial issue, but on balance it is more likely that the editor of the Cambridge Tracts, or someone with the same interests, extracted the material on scripture in English from *Pater Noster II* and reworked it into a tract proving that 'eche nacioun may lefully haue holy writ in her moder-tunge'.[96]

Editions

Hudson, *SEWW*, pp. 107–9, 189–91
Hunt, *TFST*, II, 313–18

Tract VIII: 'Crist seiþ in þe gospel þat þe word', fols 46r–47r
[unique manuscript]

'Crist seiþ in þe gospel þat þe word' argues that since people will be judged on whether they have acted in accordance with Christ's words they must have the opportunity to read, write and speak them. In the Old Testament the (imperfect) law was known to all, and kings were instructed to own and read God's law, which was not forbidden to anyone. 'Whi þanne schulden lewid cristen men be forboden to rede Cristis lawe eiþer to techen it?' (13–14). Christ was not a cleric, neither were his disciples, yet they preached and ministered to others. No apostle forbade man or woman to learn and share God's words (15–25).

---

[92] See the note on CTVII 20 and Hudson, *SEWW*, 190.
[93] Ed. Arnold, *SEW*, III, 93–7, *IPMEP* no. 810, *inc.* 'We schal bileve þat þis Pater Noster þat Crist himsilf tauȝte' [also in Bodleian Library MS Eng. th.e. 181].
[94] See *Manual*, 2, III, 13–14, 57 and 7, XX, 33; Jolliffe, M.3(b) and O.9(b).
[95] CTVII 42–4, 83–8 and 91–5.
[96] Hunt argues that CTVII is 'an adept reworking' of *PNII*; *TFST*, I, 104–5 (quotation at 105). Hudson does not give an opinion on priority, *SEWW*, 189–90.

'Crist seiþ in þe gospel þat þe word' draws an effective contrast between the writer's present and the biblical past. At the time of the old law and in the New Testament period God's word was freely available to men and women after all, not only people of lowly rank but kings and Christ himself were laypeople. As Tract VIII speaks of laypeople being forbidden to read or teach Christ's law (13–14) it was probably written after Arundel's constitutions.[97]

Edition

Hunt, *TFST*, II, 319–21

Tract IX: 'Þese ben þe armes of antecristis disciplis aȝenes trewe men',
       fols 47r–49v

The first weapon of antichrist's disciples against true men (surely here signifying Wycliffites) is the accusation 'hypocrite' aimed at anyone who shows religious tendencies. In reality, the followers of antichrist are the hypocrites, pretending to serve Christ but serving the devil by way of the idols that are the seven deadly sins (1–19). The second weapon is the accusation 'heretic', aimed at anyone leading a godly life, but the accusers are the heretics, traducing holy writ and justifying their sins (20–6). The third weapon, for use against anyone who confesses his sins by reference to scripture, is 'the letter kills' (2 Cor. 3:6).[98] Scripture must be interpreted spiritually. The writer points out that canon law decrees that scripture must be interpreted as the Holy Ghost wills. It is the old law understood literally that kills, says the writer, not the gospel, which must be interpreted literally (a thoroughly traditional point) (27–38). The followers of antichrist make a fool of Jesus by saying that his words are false and by interpreting the gospel in such a way as to make their sins look good. If 'the letter kills' applies to anyone, it applies to them, because God's authority in scripture is absolute and following his law is the only way to be saved (39–49).

From a literary point of view 'Þese ben þe armes of antecristis disciplis aȝenes trewe men' is the most interesting of the Cambridge Tracts, figuring the insults 'trewe men' receive as the weapons of antichrist. It is particularly interesting that the worst weapon is 'þe letter kills'. In his *determinacio* on biblical translation Thomas Palmer (see the introduction to *First seiþ Bois*, pp. xlix–liv) argues 'it is thought that the Jews killed Christ because he taught them to read holy scripture spiritually, since the letter kills, whereas the spirit gives life'. Therefore, if scriptural illiterates who can only understand the plain grammatical sense have the Bible in English, what is to prevent them, says Palmer, from following the Jews' example and persecuting those who expound scripture spiritually?[99]

There is one other copy of 'Þese ben þe armes of antecristis disciplis aȝenes trewe

---

[97] Cf. Hunt, *TFST*, I, 110.

[98] See the note on CTIX 28–48.

[99] Ed. Deanesly, *LB*, 425.

men'. **O5** supplies the words missing in **C** (45–6) and **O5** omits 'in himsilf and his seruauntis' (46).

Edition

Hunt, *TFST*, II, 322–5

Other manuscript

O5 Bodleian Library Laud misc. 524

> s. xiv. ex; 175 fols (f. 2 numbered twice). 218 × 155 mm; 158 × 110 mm; single column; 41/42 lines; one anglicana hand. Rolle, *Emendatio Vitae* (incomplete at opening), fols 1r–7r; Latin sermon *inc.* 'Grauis est nobis ad videndum sapientie', fols 7r–10v; The Ten Commandments (Jolliffe A.1(b)), fols 11r–18v; The Five Wits, fols 18v–20v; 'Litera ocidit', f. 20v; 'Þese ben armys of antecristes disciplys', fols 20v–21r [etc.]; abridgment of Wyclif, *De Mandatis Divinis*, fols 67v–81v [etc.] R. Pyper, 'An Abridgment of Wyclif's *De Mandatis Divinis*', *Medium Ævum*, 52 (1983), 306–10.

Tract X: 'A dere God lord of trwþe', fols 49v–51v

As the editorial heading says, 'A dere God lord of trwþe' laments that human customs and laws, which have no basis in God's law or in reason or in the life of Christ but rather in prelates' pride and covetousness, are made more of than the gospel, confirmed with Christ's blood (1–11). Clerical statutes are taught and upheld while Christ's laws concerning clerical poverty, humility and the studying and teaching of scripture are regarded as erroneous, and those who wish to re-introduce them are persecuted, imprisoned and killed (11–18). The writer asks Christian people why they allow clerics to deprive them of scripture and of their possessions. The blind are leading the blind, but the people have no excuse for their ignorance of God's law, for they have reason and 'trwe prestis' to guide them. The writer begs them to do their utmost to learn and keep God's law and learn and speak about the gospel (19–31). 'A dere God lord of trwþe' ends with a prayer to Christ to make his people know his gospel and rid themselves of antichrist's false teaching, which leads to despair. Never has the need been so great (32–7).

The protest against laws made by sinful men, with no basis in God's law or in reason, is characteristic of Wycliffite writings.[100] More unusual is the writer's insistence that his readers have no excuse for ignorance of God's law. 'A dere God lord of trwþe' is a slightly revised version of the final part of the epilogue to 'intermediate' Glossed Matthew in **O4** and to Long Glossed Matthew in **L** (GGIII 89–118, and see the introduction to GGIII, p. lxiv). Tract X adds 'and peyned to þe deeþ of bodi' (17–18) to **L** and **O4**'s 'cursid and sore prisoned', suggesting a date post 1401.[101] Where Tract X

---

[100] See the note on PWB 125–30.
[101] The bill *De Heretico Comburendo* became law on 10 March 1401.

has 'O ȝe cristen pepel' (19) **L O4** have 'Alas, alas, alas', but 'A dere God lord of trwþe' adds the desperate cries to Christ at the end (35–7).

Edition

Hunt, *TFST*, II, 326–9

Tract XI: 'Holy writ haþ þe lyknesse of a tree þat beriþ fruyt', fols 51v–58v

'Holy writ haþ þe lyknesse of a tree þat beriþ fruyt' begins with an analogy between reading scripture and shaking a fruit tree: the literal meaning is hard but shaking it (studying it and living in accordance with it) leads to the sweetness of goodness. But it must be shaken into a person's own language (1–10). Other languages and evil living are a dark cloud: 'the letter kills' (2 Cor. 3:6) carnal men who break God's law. Those who are ignorant of God's law are in a dry cloud with no dew of grace (11–24). The three estates in the church militant, representing the Trinity, are workers, defenders (responsible for good moral order) and counsellors (the clergy) (25–41). Each of these estates needs to support the other two, and Christ has left a 'bylle', sealed with water and blood (another echo of the *Charter of Christ*). Priests who will neither learn nor teach the gospel, and prevent those who wish to do so, are promised 'woe' (42–59). Such covetous priests fulfill Jeremiah's prophecy about the lack of bread, in which 'bread' is God's word, strengthening the soul (60–5). Those who refuse spiritual alms—that is, prevent God's word from being given to the people in their own language, written or preached—are traitors, because we are commanded to love Christ and his law (66–80). To love it, one must know it; those who do not will be unknown at the last day (1 Cor. 14:38), while those who do will work miracles. Just as those who prevented a medical doctor from curing the people would be greatly blamed, much more blameworthy are those who prevent Christ's cures from being known (81–104) These salves are to be found in the garden of the gospel, for no man or woman may be healed without repentance and mercy; God's word is of incomparable power. By the power of that word everyone will be judged, and those who lived by Christ's light, loving and teaching his word, will dwell with him in bliss. The tract ends with a conventional prayer (105–41).

Tract XI shares about a sixth of its material with the prologue to the Middle English *Mirror*, a mid-fourteenth-century translation of Robert of Greatham's Anglo-Norman *Miroir*, *c.*1250–60, which is a collection of sermons on the Sunday gospels throughout the year and the gospels for the common of saints.[102] The prologue to the *Mirror*, like Tract XI, deplores the state of the clergy; like Tract XI (and Tract I) it

---

[102] The prologue to the Middle English *Mirror* is ed. from Glasgow University Library Hunter 250 by Hunt, *TFST*, II, 430–62, and from Bodl. Holkham Misc. 40 by Kathleen M. Blumreich, *The Middle English* Mirror (Turnhout: Brepols, 2002), pp. 1–19, where an account of the manuscripts and their readings can be found.

quotes Jeremiah's prophecy,[103] and like Tract I and *In þe biginnyng* it quotes Isaiah's prophecy 'as þe peple so is þe prest'.[104] The voice of the writer is very clearly heard throughout the *Mirror* prologue. In the Cambridge Tract, however, there is an uneasy mix of the conventional (for example, the description of the garden of the gospel, 106–9) and the sharply satirical: 'A, Iesu, prestis taken gredeliche þe peny, þe mylke and þe wolle, but þei wolen not do here office in fedynge of her schepe wiþ þe breed of liyf' (60–1).[105]

Edition

Hunt, *TFST*, II, 330–7

Tract XII: '*Non occides*; þis is þe fifþe heste of almy3ti God', fols 58v–79v
          [unique manuscript]

Tract XII begins with the fifth of the ten commandments, 'thou shalt not kill', the wise man warning the fool that causing spiritual death is worse than causing bodily death. Before the fool has a chance to reply, however, the wise man preempts him: 'perauentur þou seist þat þis is noon yuel speche, for it dryueþ awey heuynesse' (10–11). Thus, the wise man says, the fool will call his vanity wisdom and Christ's words folly, and will be guilty of foul heresy. He cites authorities on the need to speak the truth (1–24). But any simple man who speaks in this way is accused of being a 'lollere' (28), in spite of the fact that it is contradicting the word of God that is heresy. The wise man proceeds to distinguish between blessed and cursed 'lollers' in scripture (25–66). He advises his 'dere cristen frendis' (73) not to be ashamed of speaking the word of God and living according to it (73–83).

Only at this point does Tract XII become a dialogue. At last given a chance to speak, the fool points out that speaking God's word does not pay. This provides the wise man with the opportunity to offer a *catena* of scriptural and patristic authorities on persecution, true wisdom and the life-giving quality of scripture (84–161). The fool asks for a romance, instead, and is accused of loving lies. The fool looks back nostalgically to a past of unabashedly carnal pleasures, invoking the wise man's scriptural authorities on evil fathers (162–229). Must we be always sorrowful, asks the fool; yes, if we wish to enjoy a just death and avoid an evil one, answers the wise man (230–83). This is nothing but 'do well and have well' says the fool, quoting *Piers Plowman*. The wise man warns him that death is not the end (*pace* the saducees) and he rehearses the pains of hell and scriptural instances of sudden death. The fool should regret that

---

[103] Lam. 4:4, quoted in the prologue to the *Mirror*, ed. Blumreich, p. 7/15–18, CTXI 62–3 and CTI 64–6.

[104] Is. 24:2 and Hos. 4:9; quoted in the prologue to the *Mirror*, ed. Blumreich, p. 8/13–14, CTI 53 and *IB* 8.

[105] Replacing ten lines of less focused critique in the prologue to the *Mirror*, ed. Blumreich, p. 7/5–14.

scarcely one in a hundred people speaks the word of God (284–377). Repentant, the fool asks how he may find mercy, and the wise man replies with a moralization of the gospel for Epiphany. Wise man and fool end in accord (378–440).

The fiction that Tract XII is a dialogue is not consistently maintained: the fool is not given anything to say until line 85, and at line 162 his words are introduced with 'But sum man seiþ'. His conversion is implausible. Nevertheless, his speeches as fool are made to sound genuinely worldly, and therefore sympathetic (although doubtless the writer did not intend this). Fond of romances, he quotes from *Piers Plowman* and makes two allusions to Chaucer's *Canterbury Tales*,[106] suggesting that the date of this text is likely to be in the later part of the date range 1410–25. The passage distinguishing between blessed and cursed 'lollers' (25–66) shows that this is a self-consciously Wycliffite text.[107]

Edition

Hunt, *TFST*, II, 338–62

First seiþ Bois

A large part of *First seiþ Bois* [Boethius] is a translation or paraphrase of sections of a university *determinacio* on the translation of the Bible into English by Richard Ullerston (*c.*1360–1423), a fellow of Queen's College Oxford, from 1391.[108] Ullerston defended church endowment against the Lollards, and his sixteen *Petitiones* (1408) against papal over-centralization, written for the representatives of the English church at the reformist Council of Pisa, influenced them at the Council of Council (1414–18) as well.[109] There can be no doubt of Ullerston's orthodoxy; yet his 20,000-word *determinacio* published in Oxford in 1401 is unequivocally in favour of an English Bible.[110] Although it is set up as a debate between two doctors, the first opposed to biblical translation and the second advocating it, Ullerston allows his second doctor six times as much space for the refutation of the first doctor's thirty articles against translation as he allows his first doctor for their presentation. Fiona Somerset argues that Ullerston was following in the footsteps of bishops such as Grosseteste, Pecham, Thoresby and FitzRalph, all of whom 'advocated vernacular translation

---

[106] See the notes on CTXII 88–9, 284–5 and 286.

[107] Wendy Scase, *'Piers Plowman' and the New Anticlericalism* (Cambridge: Cambridge University Press, 1989), p. 126.

[108] Archbishop Parker knew this, but not the name of the doctor; see the heading in *FSB* (apparatus).

[109] Margaret Harvey, *ODNB* 55:657–8. Harvey points out that the *Petitiones* make much use of the writings of Grosseteste (see the note on PWB 1711–21).

[110] The unedited *determinacio* is in Vienna, Österreichische Nationalbibl. 4133, fols 195ra–207vb. Ullerston is named as the author and the place and date of publication are given in a colophon following the text (of which only the final leaf survives) in Gonville and Caius College Cambridge 803/807, frag. 36; see Hudson, 'The debate on Bible translation, Oxford 1401', *LB*, 74–5.

while criticizing clerical corruption'.[111] He was certainly urging the bishops of his own day, especially archbishop Arundel, to follow in their footsteps.

Like Wyclif, Ullerston was a secular. Two other surviving determinations on biblical translation were written by Oxford friars, both opposed to translation: the Dominican Thomas Palmer and the Franciscan William Butler; Butler's *determinacio*, like Ullerston's, is dated 1401.[112] Both are much shorter than Ullerston's, and neither has anything like his range of reference or intellectual ambition. We do not know who initiated this Oxford debate on biblical translation, but evidently advocacy of an English Bible was not at that time presumed to be inherently unorthodox.[113]

Although the writer's access to Ullerston's *determinacio* suggests that he may also have been a schoolman, *First seiþ Bois* is not itself a *determinacio*. It begins in the middle of Ullerston's response to article 24 against translation, in which the first doctor argues that all ranks and orders of the church would be brought into disrespect if translations into the vernacular were approved, and in the middle of material drawn by Ullerston from Roger Bacon's *Opus Maius*, in which Bacon is arguing that simple people would do better to read the books of Solomon than versified versions of biblical history. None of this context, however, is apparent in *First seiþ Bois*, which begins with the heading 'Aȝens hem þat seyn þat hooli wriȝt schulde not or may not be drawen into Engliche we maken þes resouns' and then moves directly into the first reason: 'First seiþ Bois, in his boke *De Disciplina Scolarium*'.[114] After this the reasons are not numbered, and the writer moves seemingly randomly from one argument of Ullerston's *determinacio* to another, although he naturally concentrates on the section in favour of biblical translation in English (fols 197va–199rb) which follows the thirty articles against translation and the digression on the meaning of 'translacio'. Frequently the writer of *First seiþ Bois* abridges his original, but sometimes he adds information not in Ullerston's *determinacio*.[115] He intersperses his own material with Ullerston's, although the last section of *First seiþ Bois* (171–90) has no equivalent in the Latin source.

He is writing after the death of Richard II in February 1400 (171–2) and before 1414, for Arundel is still archbishop (180). James Ussher places this text under the date 1410, presumably because Foxe's 1563 version has a prologue linking the text

---

[111] 'Professionalizing translation at the turn of the fifteenth century: Ullerston's *Determinacio*, Arundel's *Constitutiones*', in Fiona Somerset and Nicholas Watson, eds, *The Vulgar Tongue: Medieval and Postmedieval Vernacularity* (Pennsylvania: Pennsylvania State University, 2003), pp. 145–57 (quotation at 152). On Grosseteste, see the note on PWB 1708; on Pecham and Thoresby, *FSB* 114–18, and on FitzRalph, PWB 2361 and *FSB* 128–33.

[112] Butler's *determinacio* is ed. Deanesly, *LB*, 401–18, and Palmer's on 418–37. Palmer's may have been written after 1401. See Hudson, 'The Debate on Bible Translation, Oxford 1401', *LB*, 67–8, 81–2; Kantik Ghosh, *The Wycliffite Heresy: Authority and the Interpretation of Texts* (Cambridge: Cambridge University Press, 2001), pp. 86–111, and the notes on PWB 2935–6 and CTI 147–50

[113] Hudson, 'The debate on Bible translation, Oxford 1401', *LB*, 83.

[114] Actually not Boethius but a thirteenth-century writer: see the note on *FSB* 1–2.

[115] See, e.g., the notes on *FSB* 78–80, 83–4 and 88–91.

directly with Arundel's constitutions.[116] Thomas Arundel takes centre stage at the end of *First seiþ Bois* (180–90), where the sermon he is reported to have preached at the funeral of Queen Anne in 1394 seems to some to herald his withdrawal from public life, much to their satisfaction.[117] The implication is that it was known well before 1407 that Arundel was minded to prohibit the English Bible. The writer's account of John of Lancaster's speech against a parliamentary bill 'to anulle þe Bible þat tyme translatid into Engliche' (171–9) has no basis in fact, but it indicates what short shrift the writer thinks ought to be given to any attempt to censor the English Bible. That Arundel is said to have approved Anne's Glossed Gospels after she had duly submitted them to him (surely extremely unlikely) suggests that *First seiþ Bois* was written with knowledge of the terms of the constitutions, between 1407 and 1414, and that the writer was probably a Wycliffite (see the introduction to the Glossed Gospel Prologues and Epilogue, pp. lx–lxi).

The lack of an overriding structure makes it unsurprising that copies of *First seiþ Bois* have items in different orders, particularly between lines 69 and 91[118] In most copies *First seiþ Bois* occurs in the context of identifiably Lollard material, but, surprisingly, in **N1** it accompanies Nicholas Love's *Mirror of the Blessed Life of Jesus Christ*, which concludes with Arundel's memorandum licensing that work. The four early modern copies of *First seiþ Bois* are collections of texts supposedly heralding the Reformation. On the verge of the Henrician Reformation, in 1530 (Tyndale's New Testament still being under prohibition) Johannes Hoochstraten of Antwerp published a considerably extended version entitled *A compendious olde treatyse shewynge howe that we ought to haue the scripture in Englysshe*, with an introduction on the unbinding of Satan and the rule of Antichrist (cf. PWB 123–5). It continues after the medieval text ends with the deaths of Arundel and of Richard Flemming, bishop of Lincoln (1431) (sig. D.4v), and with an account of the history of the translation of the Bible, including details of Jerome's translations for Paula and Eustochium (sig. D.7r).[119] Antichrist argues with Paul that 'litera occidit', 2 Cor. 3:6 (sig. D.7r),[120] but Christ says 'my wordes ben spritte and lyffe', John 6:64[121] (sig. D.7v). *A compendious olde treatyse* ends with a prayer for the king to remedy the lack of English scripture (sig. D.7v). Apparently the Reformation editor thought the writings of the English Bible debate were as relevant in 1530 as they had been more than a hundred years earlier.

---

[116] James Ussher, *Historia Dogmatica* (London, 1690), pp. 164–6; John Foxe, *Acts and Monuments*, vol. I (London: John Day, 1563), p. 452, col. ii.

[117] See the note on *FSB* 180–90 There is no record of this sermon, and the description may draw on other sermons or public utterances of Arundel. Jonathan Hughes, however, regards *FSB*'s account as historically accurate, *ODNB* 2:566.

[118] Three of the manuscripts begin at *FSB* 68 (**L3 L4 L8**, and the second section of **C1**): see the description of the manuscripts.

[119] Cf. CTI 277–9.

[120] See the note on CTIX 28–48.

[121] Quoted at *FSB* 105–6, and at CTII 11–12, CTXII 151 and *HPD* 218–19.

Editions

C.F. Bühler, ed., 'A Lollard Tract: On Translating the Bible into English', *Medium Ævum* 7 (1938), 167–83 (from **C5**)
Deanesly, *LB*, 437–45 (from **C5**)

Base manuscript

C5 Trinity College Cambridge B.14.50

70 fols; 145 × 110; 100 × 80 mm; single column; 25 lines; two anglicana hands.[122]

Part I: Latin sermon notes on gospels for Sundays and other feasts, fols 1r–13v;[122] miscellaneous Latin notes, fols 13v–16r; an extract from *Speculum Ecclesie*, fols 16v–17r; Latin notes on the sabbath, on the Pater Noster and on confession, fols 17r–18r; Latin extracts from authorities including Grosseteste, Richard Rolle and Wyclif on the duties of pastoral care, fols 18v–20r; on the burial of the dead, fols 20v–25v; notes on pastoral care, f. 25v.

Part II: *First seiþ Bois*, fols 26r–30v; *Sixteen points on which the bishops accuse Lollards* (*IPMEP* no. 676), fols 30v–34r; 'þe eiȝte condiciouns of mawmentrie þat men vsen abouȝte ymages',[123] fols 34r–35r; *Ion and Richard, Dialogus fratrum*, fols 35r–55v; Wyclif, *de fide sacramenti*,[124] fols 56r–58r; *contra temporalia clericorum*, from the *Rosarium*, fols 58r–60r [and other material from the *Rosarium*, fols 60v–67r]; *nota de distinccione fratrum per prophetiam*, ps.–Hildegard of Bingen,[125] fols 67r–68v; *contra adoracionem ymaginum*, from the *Rosarium*, fols 68v–70r (f. 70v blank). M.R. James, *The Western Manuscripts in the Library of Trinity College Cambridge*, vol. I (Cambridge, 1900), pp. 457–9; Linne R. Mooney, *IMEP* handlist XI, 13–15; Hudson, *LB*, 25–6; Fiona Somerset, *Four Wycliffite Dialogues* (EETS 333, 2009).

Other manuscripts and early printed versions

Corpus Christi College Cambridge 100, pp. 227–33 [a transcript of the following]

C1 Corpus Christi College Cambridge 298

A composite s. xvi manuscript, comprising texts relating to ecclesiastical history. Part IV, paper, is in Parkerian hands. *FSB*, fols 242r–245v (fols 64r–67v of Part IV), 30/32 long lines. Owned by archbishop Parker, who notes at the head of

---

[122] Hudson, *LB*, 25.
[123] Hudson, *LB*, 26.
[124] S. Harrison Thomson, 'John Wyclif's "Lost" *De Fide Sacramentorum*', *The Journal of Theological Studies* 33 (1932), 359–65.
[125] Ed. (but not including this manuscript) Kathryn Kerby-Fulton, Magda Hayton and Kenna Olsen, 'Pseudo-Hildegardian prophecy and antimendicant propaganda in late medieval England: an edition of the most popular insular text of *Insurgent gentes*', in Nigel Morgan, ed., *Prophecy, Apocalypse, and the Day of Doom: Proceedings of the 2000 Harlaxton Symposium* (Donington, Lincs., 2004; Harlaxton Medieval Studies, 12), 160–94.

f. 243v, in the middle of *FSB* 68 (Italie / haþ), '… sunt ex quodam lacero fragmento Bibliothece Wigorn'. From here to the end the text is a transcript of this now lost Worcester manuscript, which begins where **L3 L4** and **L8** also begin, while 1–68 is in a different hand, and presumably from another source. M.R. James, *A descriptive catalogue of the manuscripts in the library of Corpus Christi College, Cambridge*, vol. II (Cambridge, 1912), pp. 80–6.

C2 Trinity College Cambridge B.1.26
Augustine *ad Julianam*, Idisore *De Summo Bono* [etc.], in a s. xi/xii hand. *FSB* 1–16, 'stret', in a hand of s. xv. in, squashed into the narrow second column of f. 143v. Linne R. Mooney, *IMEP* handlist XI, 1.

L3 British Library Cotton Vitellius D.vii
s. xvii copies of medieval texts, with upper, left and lower edges destroyed by fire, with consequent loss of text. *FSB, inc.* 'it in Latyn for that is' (l. 68, cf. **L4 L8**), fols 146r–147v (f. 147v is scarcely legible).

L4 British Library Harley 425
Papers of John Foxe, d. 1587. *FSB, inc.* 'hath in Latin' (68, cf. **L3 L8**), fols 1r–2v, 'ex fragmento quodam Ecclesiae Wigorniensis' (cf. **C1**).

L8 Lambeth Palace Library 594
s. xvii copies of medieval religious texts (a Wharton manuscript), including *Pater Noster II* 1–64 (from an unidentified manuscript belonging to archbishop Tenison), p. 6; 'In the biginnynge of holi chirche' (from **L1**), p. 47; extracts from 'Seynt Austyn saiþ' (from **L1**), p. 47, and from 'Oure Lord Iesu Crist' (from **L1**), pp. 47–8. *FSB* (from a manuscript in the Westminster Chapter Library),[126] *inc.* 'hath in Latyn' (l. 68, cf. **L3 L4**), pp. 57–9. O.S. Pickering and V.M. O'Mara, *IMEP* handlist XIII, 56–8.

N1 Pierpont Morgan New York 648
*c.*1445–55; i + 144 fols + i; 285 × 195 mm (item 1), × 180 mm (*FSB*); 200 × 130 mm; 2 columns; 35 lines (item 1), 53 lines (*FSB*); a very small but neat bookhand (*FSB*). Fols 142–4 were originally bound at the beginning of the volume, before the present f. 1.[127] 16 miniatures of the life of Christ. Nicholas Love, *Mirror of the Blessed Life of Jesus Christ*, concluding with Thomas Arundel's memorandum, fols 1r–141v, *First seiþ Bois*, fols 142r–143v; extract from the *Revelationes* of St Birgitta of Sweden, IV, 7, f. 144r.

---

[126] Several Worcester manuscripts were transferred to Westminster Chapter Library in 1623–24; see C.F. Bühler, ed., 'A Lollard tract: on translating the Bible into English', *Medium Ævum* 7 (1938), 168.
[127] I am grateful to Ryan Perry for providing these details.

Hoochstraten *A proper dyaloge betwene a Gentillman and a husbandman* (Marburg, Hans Luft, 1530; but actually Antwerp, J. Hoochstraten; STC 1462.5).

32 unnumbered leaves, 147 × 94 mm. Item 4, *an olde treatyse made aboute the tyme of kynge Rycharde the seconde*, sigs. B.4r–C.3v, and item 6, sigs. C.3v–C.5v, contain material from the Lollard tract *Fundamentum Aliud Nemo Potest Ponere*, ed. Hudson, *WLP*. Item 8 is *A compendious olde treatyse shewynge howe that we ought to haue the scripture in Englysshe*, sigs. C.8r–D.8r. The treatise is preceded by two 7-line stanzas and includes a third. Ed. Douglas H. Parker, *A proper dyaloge betwene a Gentillman and an Husbandman* (Toronto: University of Toronto Press, 1996), pp. 164–73 have lines 1360–1678 and pp. 14–16, 223–40.[128] The single surviving copy is British Library C.37.a.28(5).[129]

A compendious olde treatyse was also printed separately by the same printer (including the 7-line stanazas) in 1530; 8 unnumbered leaves, 140+ × 95+ mm (STC 3021).[130]

Choice of base text

The only two complete texts in medieval hands are **C5** and **N1**. **N1** is damaged, and, like **C1 L3 L4** and **L8**, it omits *FSB* 141–8, 'writynge' and adds these lines after line 191.[131]

Because of the relatively slight medieval evidence for this text, variants from early modern copies and printed texts are also recorded.

The Holi Prophete Dauid

The Holi Prophete Dauid opens with a *catena* of biblical authorities praising God's law (1–22). Some people, says the writer, live according to this law and teach it by example; others study God's law but fail to keep it. They chatter about scripture to their own damnation, as scripture attests; instead of good works they bring forth pride (23–47). Paul orders such men to study scripture soberly, and Bernard of Clairvaux explains that this means abiding by what is necessary to salvation (48–60). Heed should be paid to the order, content and purpose of study: if it does not result in a virtuous life, a troubled conscience and damnation will result (61–84). Study should result in knowledge of God's law and righteous living (85–94). Simple Christians find it very strange that clerics boast of their learning while living a life of worldly pleasure, since scripture proves that wisdom cannot co-exist with sinfulness. These clerics are the devil's prisoners, going alive to hell; fools, they are damned by their own preaching

---

[128] Parker attributes the editorship of the 1530 version of *A compendious olde treatyse* to William Tyndale, pp. 34–50, cf. *Manual*, 2, III, 55, but Hudson doubts this, *PR*, 493 and *WLP*, lxiii.

[129] Items 1–7 of STC 1462.5 have the same text as STC 1462.3 (Antwerp: Hoochstraten, 1529?); see Hudson, *WLP*, xxiii–xxiv and lxi–lxiii.

[130] 2nd edn London: Richard Bankes, *c*.1538; see Hudson, *PR*, 492.

[131] C.F. Bühler, 'A Lollard tract', p. 168.

(95–126). They are like the saducees, reproved by Christ for their ignorance of the scriptures—the writer translates Chrysostom's gloss on Matt. 22:29, to the effect that although the saducees read the scriptures they did not live according to them (127–51). The greatest folly is to assert that God's law is false, since scripture proves the opposite and canon law decrees that anyone who does not interpret scripture as God wills is a heretic, who should (the writer adds) be sharply reproved (152–84). The writer then enumerates six ways in which simple Christians may come to an understanding of scripture (185–211).

There follow the writer's responses to three objections from 'proude clerkis' against uneducated people reading scripture. The first objection is 'the letter kills':[132] on the contrary, scripture proves that God's word is life (185–226). 'The letter kills' means the old law interpreted literally where it should be interpreted spiritually, and the new law interpreted spiritually where it should be interpreted literally. This text should alarm clerics who understand God's law and habitually break it rather than 'symple men of witt' who live in charity (227–62). The second objection depends on what the writer argues is a misinterpretation of Exodus 19:12, according to which the hill the people are commanded not to climb is holy writ. Elsewhere in the Old Testament, the writer demonstrates, God commands that his words should be made known. Without this spiritual food nobody may come to bliss: Chrysostom speaks of scripture as a feast (263–317). The third objection depends on an interpretation of the death of Oza the deacon in 2 Kings 6 as punishment for touching the ark (understood as holy writ) when he had lain with his wife the previous night. The writer responds that the death of Oza is traditionally interpreted as punishment for having oxen carry the ark rather than carrying it himself; this prefigures the vengeance that will come on men who entrust men's souls to ignorant and worldly clergy. As Christ embraced us on the cross, every Christian should embrace the law of God with his whole being (318–51).

In the reply to the third objection, the words 'as Gregor and Grosted seyn, to make vnable curatis is þe hiȝeste wikkidnesse and tresun aȝens God, and is lik synne as to crucifie Crist' (340–2) summarize part of chapter ten of the Prologue to the Wycliffite Bible (1703–36). *The Holi Prophete Dauid* also shares a short passage on the fate of proud clerics (117–20), translated from Augustine's *Enarrationes in Psalmos*, with the Prologue (92–4).[133] This may simply mean that the writer of *The Holi Prophete Dauid* was familiar with the Prologue to the Wycliffite Bible, but it seems to me likely that they are by the same writer, in which case *The Holi Prophete Dauid* was written after 1387/8. Its strictures on the folly and blasphemy of those who deny the truth of holy writ recall Wyclif's writings[134]—which were not, on this topic, in any way unorthodox, even if immoderate in their language. Cambridge Tract III and the Epilogue to Intermediate/Long Glossed Matthew (GGIII in this

---

[132] See the note on CTIX 28–48.
[133] See n. 7, above.
[134] Deanesly, *LB*, 269–70.

edition) also argue for the absolute truth of holy writ, the latter on the authority of Augustine and Jerome.

The unique copy of *The Holi Prophete Dauid* and (in the same hand) commentary on gospel verses and extracts from Long Glossed Matthew open the second part of the common-profit book funded from the estate of John Colop, who was involved in the administration of the Whittington charity associated with St Michael Paternoster Royal in the City of London. The writer of the 'foure errours whiche letten þe verrey knowyng of holy writt' (Part II, fols 98v–99v), 'wordly maner', 'fleschly lust', 'fals couetise' and 'veynglorie', was evidently of the same mind as the writer of *The Holi Prophete Dauid*. Although many of the items in this miscellany are undoubtedly orthodox (for example, the Carmelite Richard Lavenham's *Little Treatise on the Seven Deadly Sins*), Reginald Pecock argued against the conclusion of 'How thu schuldest not adde ne abrigge ouȝt change not ne countre not þe biddingis of God' (Part I, fols 61r–v), showing that he regarded it as a Lollard text.[135]

Edition

Deanesly, *LB*, 445–56 [136]

Manuscript

C7 Cambridge University Library Ff.6.31

163 fols; 142 × 105 mm; 110 × 70 mm; single column; 21 lines (Part II); bookhand, Part II, fols 1–42, anglicana elsewhere. The hand of Part II fols 43–98 is the hand of Bodleian Library Bodley 938 (**O2**) according to A.I. Doyle.[137] 3/2-line deep-blue initials flourished in red (Part II); biblical texts underlined in red (Part II, fols 1–42). The parchment is of uneven quality, carefully mended.

Part I, fols 1–63. Richard Rolle, *Proper Will* (*IPMEP* no. 551), fols 1v–9v; Richard Lavenham, *Little Treatise on the Seven Deadly Sins* (*IPMEP* no. 789), incomplete at beginning, fols 10r–60v; 'How thu schuldest not adde ne abrigge ouȝt change not ne countre not þe biddingis of God', fols 61r–v; 'Sewe not wittis ne lawis of men', fols 61v–63r (f. 64 blank).

---

[135] *Repressor of Over Much Blaming of the Clergy*, ed. Churchill Babington, vol. I (London, 1860; Rolls Series), p. 55. See further Wendy Scase, 'Reginald Pecock, John Carpenter and John Colop's "Common-Profit" Books: Aspects of Book Ownership and Circulation in Fifteenth-Century London', *Medium Ævum* 61 (1992), 267, and Mishtooni Bose, 'Reginald Pecock's Vernacular Voice', in Fiona Somerset, Jill C. Havens and Derrick G. Pitard, eds, *Lollards and their Influence in Late Medieval England* (Woodbridge: Boydell Press, 2003), pp. 230–1.

[136] Selections ed. Stephen Shepherd, in Jocelyn Wogan-Browne Jocelyn, Nicholas Watson, Andrew Taylor and Ruth Evans, *The Idea of the Vernacular: An Anthology of Middle English Literary Theory, 1280–1520* (Exeter: Exeter University Press, 1999), pp. 149–56.

[137] In Alastair J. Minnis, ed., *Latin and Vernacular: Studies in Late-Medieval Texts and Manuscripts* (Cambridge: Brewer, 1989), p. 133.

Part II, fols 1–100. *The Holi Prophete Dauid*, fols 1r–16r; verses from the gospels on meekness, with commentary from Augustine, Chrysostom, etc., f. 16r, 'Crist seiþ tak ȝe my ȝook & lerneþ of me', Matt. 11:30, fols 16v–18r, Matt. 5:2–4, 9, fols 18r–20r, John 13:13–14, fols 20r–27r; 'þe seiyngis of dyuers doctoris vpe þe xxvj. capetil of Matthu', i.e., extracts from Long Glossed Matthew, on Matt. 26:26–8, fols 27v–35v, on Matt. 21:43–4, fols 36r–39r, on Matt. 23:1–3, fols 39r–41r, and on Matt. 23:16–22, fols 41r–42v; *A Tretis of Discrescyon of Spirites* (*IPMEP* no. 240), fols 43r–53r; *A Pistle of Discrecioun of Stirings* (*IPMEP* no. 252), fols 53r–68r; *A Pistle of Preier* (*IPMEP* no. 250), fols 68r–98r; 'foure errours whiche letten þe verrey knowyng of holy writt', fols 98v–99v. This manuscript was John Colop's common-profit book, according to Part II, f. 100r; see Wendy Scase, 'Reginald Pecock, John Carpenter and John Colop's "Common-Profit" Books: Aspects of Book Ownership and Circulation in Fifteenth-Century London', *Medium Ævum* 61 (1992), 267–9; Dove, *FEB*, pp. 50–1.

Pater Noster II[138]

As well as sharing with Cambridge Tract VII material advocating scripture in English and censuring the friars (see the introduction to that tract), *Pater Noster II* shares material with *Pater Noster I* and with the Pater Noster treatise of *Pore Caitif*.[139] In *Pater Noster II* and in *Pore Caitif* the petitions of the Lord's Prayer are each matched with a remedial virtue and its corresponding vice; in *Pore Caitif* each petition is also matched with one of the seven gifts of the Holy Ghost.[140] Predictably, in the manuscripts *Pater Noster II* is usually accompanied by other devotional texts for the literate laity.

Editions

Arnold, *SEW*, III, 98–110 (from **L6**)
Hunt, *TFST*, II, 398–429 (from **O2**)

Base manuscript

L6 British Library Harley 2398
　　*c.*1400; iv (i a stub) + 193 fols; 193 × 115 mm; 132 × 78 mm; single column; 31
　　lines; one anglicana hand. A collection of devotional tracts in English. *Memoriale
　　Credencium* (Jolliffe, A.4), fols 1r–69r; on Christ's wounds, *inc.* 'Womman recluse

---

[138] Hunt, *TFST*, I, 200–2.
[139] See notes to *PNII*, based on the text of *Pore Caitif* in Cambridge University Library Ff.6.34, and M. Teresa Brady, 'Lollard sources of *The Pore Caitif*', *Traditio* 44 (1988), 399.
[140] A.L. Kellogg and Ernest W. Talbot, 'The Wycliffite *Pater Noster* and *Ten Commandments*, with special reference to English manuscripts 85 and 90 in the John Rylands Library', *Bulletin of the John Rylands Library* 42 (1960), 358–62. On the close connection between the Pater Noster treatise of *Pore Caitif* and Glossed Matthew, see Brady, 'Lollard sources of *The Pore Caitif*', 392–401.

and solitarye', fols 69v–70v; Ten Commandments (Jolliffe, A.1(b)), fols 73r–106r; The Five Wits (Jolliffe, D.2), fols 106v–127r (followed by blank unnumbered leaf); 'It byhoueþ specialy to euery man' followed by 'What is þe kynde of man in bodi and in soule' (Jolliffe D.8 + D.13), fols 128r–140r; Thomas Wimbledon's sermon *Redde racionem*,[141] fols 140r–153r; exposition of the Pater Noster from the *Mirror of St Edmund, inc.* 'Ech cristen man oweþ to knowe whiche beth þe seuen axynges', fols 153r–155v; *Visitacio Infirmorum*, fols 156r–160v; 'Of wedded men and wyues', fols 160v–166v; *Pater Noster II*, with the Latin petition in the margin, fols 166v–174r; The Two Ways, fols 174r–175v; sermon for Easter Day, fols 175v–185r (f. 185v blank); 'Whanne þou schapest þe to praye', fols 186r–190v (fols 191–3 blank).

Other manuscripts

C4 Trinity College Cambridge B.14.38
iv + 180 fols English sermons including Thomas Wimbledon's sermon *Redde racionem*; *Pater Noster II* 1–64, fols 148v–150r; Nicholas Love's translation of Bonaventura's *Meditations*, fols 150v–180r. Linne R. Mooney, *IMEP* handlist XI, 11–12.

C8 Cambridge University Library Nn.4.12
60 fols; 130 × 90 mm; 85 × 60 mm; single column; 25 lines; bookhand. Ten Commandments, fols 3r–12v; *Pater Noster II*, fols 12v–25v; Ave, fols 25v–27r; Creed, fols 27r–29v; Visitation of the Sick, fols 29v–37v; Seven Deeds of Mercy, fols 37v–56v (fols 57–60 blank).

R85 John Rylands Manchester Eng. 85
*c.*1400; v + 80 (foliated 2–81) fols + iv; 142 × 95 mm; 93 × 65 mm; single column; 19/20 lines; one bookhand. 'Here bigynneþ þe abcde and next pater noster aue maria and crede [etc.]', fols 2r–37r[142] [including] Þe twelue lettyngis of preier (Jolliffe, M.4), fols 19v–24v, Of diuerse degrees of loue (Jolliffe, G.3), fols 25v–37r; *Pater Noster II*, fols 37r–54r; The Mirror of Sinners (from *Pore Caitif*, Jolliffe, F.8.4), fols 54v–64r; The Charter of Heaven (from *Pore Caitif*), fols 64r–72v; The Three Arrows, *inc.* 'Who þat wole haue in mynde þe dredful day of dome', fols 72v–81v. N.R. Ker, *Medieval Manuscripts in British Libraries*, vol. III (Oxford, 1983), p. 409; G.A. Lester, *IMEP* handlist II, 14–24.

R90 John Rylands Manchester Eng. 90
*c.*1380–1400; v + 64 fols + v (foliated i–iv, 1–70; 1 and 66 are the original wrappers); 343 × 245 mm; 277 × 200 mm (in *Pater Noster II*); 2 columns; 52/55 lines (in *Pater Noster II*); the two items in different anglicana hands. Rolle, *Prick of Conscience*, in eight parts, with interpolations, fols 2r–62v; *Pater Noster II*, fols 63r–65v.

---

[141] Ed. N.H. Owen, 'Thomas Wimbledon's Sermon: *Redde racionem villicacionis tue*', Mediaeval Studies 28 (1966), 176–97.
[142] Including the ten commandments, fols 2v–9r, ed. Kellogg and Talbert, 'The Wycliffite *Pater Noster and Ten Commandments*', pp. 371–6.

N.R. Ker, *Medieval Manuscripts in British Libraries*, vol. III (Oxford, 1983), pp. 413–14; G.A. Lester, *IMEP* handlist II, 30–1.

O2 Bodleian Library Bodley 938

*c.*1400; iv + 280 fols + iii; 180 × 125 mm; 125 × 75 mm; single column; 26 lines; 2 hands, hand 1 fols 1–23v; hand 2 f. 24r to the end. 'Thees ben þe wordis of god in þe olde lawe … of Crist in þe gospel', f. 1r–v; Creed, fols 1v–2r; Ten Commandments, fols 2r–4r; Seven Deadly Sins and remedial virtues, fols 4r–5v [etc.]; *Pater Noster II*, fols 24r–35v; *Pore Caitif*, fols 39v–209r; Rolle, *Form of Living*, fols 209r–236v.

N2 Norwich Castle Museum 158.926.4g(3)

i + 120 fols + i; 168 × 118 mm; 115 × 90 mm; single column; 26 lines; a poor hybrid hand; 2-line deep-blue Lombardic initials. Devotional treatises including 'Prestis dekenes eiþer curatis shulden not be lordes', fols 1r–64r; *Pater Noster II*, fols 64v–75r; *Aue*, fols 75r–78v; Creed, fols 78v–82v. Once in the library of Robert Cotton. N.R. Ker, *Medieval Manuscripts in British Libraries*, vol. III (Oxford, 1983), pp. 521–2.

P2 Princeton University Robert Taylor 16 [*olim* Wrest Park]

*c.*1400; 230 fols; 297 × 233 mm; 236 × 145 mm; two columns; 50 lines; five/seven hands, bookhand (*PNII*), anglicana (sermons). *Vae Octuplex*, fols 1v–4v; *Pater Noster II*, fols 5r–8v; English Wycliffite sermon cycle, fols 8v–223v; 'Of mynystris in þe chirche', fols 223v–230v. *EWS*, I, 64–5.

S1 Huntington Library HM 502

iii + 90 fols + ii; 145 × 105 mm; 105 × 74 mm; single column; 20–3 lines; one bookhand. Thomas of Wimbledon's sermon *Redde racionem*, fols 1r–26v; Rolle, *Form of Living*, fols 27r–34r; Þe Lyfe of Soule (Jolliffe, H.4(c)), fols 35r–60v; *The Mirror of St Edmund*, fols 60v–74r; *Pater Noster II*, fols 74r–87r; 'Pryde wraþþe & envie' (Jolliffe, F.21), fols 87r–90v.

Choice of base manuscript

All manuscripts have some unique readings and unique additions and omissions. This edition, with **L6** as the base manuscript, corrects and revises Arnold's edition.

Glossed Gospel Prologues and Epilogue[143]

The surviving Glossed Gospel prologues and epilogue all make some attempt to explain and justify the nature of the text they accompany. Readers literate in English but not in Latin were likely to be unfamiliar with the layout of a glossed text and with the tradition of commentary on the gospels, so that the writer of the Prologue to Short Matthew feels it necessary to say 'first a sentence of a doctour declarynge [elucidating] þe text is set aftir þe text, and in þe ende of þat sentence þe name of þe doctour seiynge it is set, þat men wite [may know] certeynli hou fer þat doctour goiþ [where that gloss ends]' (25–7). The writer of the Prologue to Intermediate Matthew feels it necessary to say that Rabanus Maurus was an 'olde monk and doctour' (114),[144] and the writer of the Epilogue to Intermediate/Long Matthew, expecting his readers to find the number of glosses from Rabanus surprising, tells them when that doctor was writing and why his commentary is so valuable (11–16) (see the introduction to GGIII, pp. lxiv–lxv). Three of the prologues point out that glosses are taken from canon law only where that law is 'groundid in Goddis lawe and resoun' (GGI 23, cf. GGII 111–12 and GGV 13–14).[145]

There are no surviving prologues to Long Matthew,[146] Short Mark or Long Luke; the prologues to Short Luke and Short John survive in only one of the two copies of each,[147] and there is only one surviving epilogue (GGIII). This suggests that prologues and epilogue may have been a late addition to the Glossed Gospels. The Prologue to Short Matthew was probably written after the Prologue to Short Luke, since it opens with the prophecy of Zacharias (Luke 1:76–7), the second biblical quotation in the Luke prologue. The larger part of the Prologue to Intermediate Matthew is one of the three additional prologues to *Oon of Foure* (see the introduction to CTII, pp. xxxvii–xxxix); the writer then goes on to discuss the sources of Glossed Matthew and condemns those who 'letten cristen peple to knowe, here, rede, write and speke holy writ in Englisch' (154–5). The Epilogue to Intermediate/Long Matthew (the last part of which = CTX) and the prologues to Intermediate Matthew and Short Luke are severely critical of those in authority in the church who keep scripture from the people, although the Epilogue also blames the laity for their forbearance and indolence (108–12).

The compilation of the Glossed Gospels, undertaken by men sympathetic to Wyclif, undoubtedly required a team of scholars and the resources of an academic centre, in all probability Oxford.[148] Hunt suggests that the director of the project wrote all

---

[143] Hunt, *TFST,* I, 181–99.

[144] See the notes on GGI 43 and GGIII 12.

[145] See also the notes on PWB 125–30 and 1623.

[146] But the rubric in **L**, f. 2ra is in effect a mini-prologue.

[147] Short Luke in **O1** and Short John in **C3** lack prologues.

[148] Hudson, *PR,* 248–59, and Henry Hargreaves, 'Popularising Biblical scholarship: the role of the Wycliffite Glossed Gospels', in Willem Lourdaux and D. Verhelst, eds, *The Bible and Medieval Culture* (Louvain: Louvain University Press, 1979), pp. 171–89.

the prologues and the epilogue.[149] This is possible, but Hudson observes that certain aspects of the production of the Glossed Gospels were 'not entirely standardized',[150] and the prologues and epilogue may equally well have been the work of writers adopting similar epithets for themselves ('symple creature', GGI 19; 'symple creature of God', GGV 7; 'pore scribeler', GGIII 4; and 'pore caityf', GGII 116 and GGIV 18) and addressing very similar subject matter from slightly different perspectives. The item of autobiographical information in the Prologue to Short Luke, that the writer was 'lettid fro prechyng for a tyme for causis knowun of God' (18–19), probably relates to the writer of this prologue only.

According to the account of Arundel's sermon at the funeral of Queen Anne in *First seiþ Bois* (180–90), the Glossed Gospels were complete by 1394. However, the writer of *First seiþ Bois* was more concerned with establishing the status of the Glossed Gospels than with historical accuracy.[151] They were probably completed *c.*1400, and the Prologue to Intermediate Matthew may have been written in or after 1407.[152]

I Prologue to Short Matthew, *inc.* 'Þe Holi Goost seiþ bi þe profete Sacarie'

The Prologue to Short Matthew begins by quoting Zacharias's prophecy (Luke 1:76–7) and interpreting 'prophet' as 'teacher' and the 'knowledge of salvation' as knowledge of the gospel (cf. GGIV 3–7). It is a work of charity, the writer says, to teach the gospel to illiterate people and poorly educated priests (1–18). He introduces the content and format of the glossed gospel and provides a key to the short forms of reference used, distinguishing carefully between sources he himself has read ('Whanne Y telle in what omeli of Gregorie eþer of Bede, þanne Y mysilf se [have seen] þat origynal of Gregorie eþer of Bede', 34–7) and sources cited by others, most often Thomas Aquinas (19–47). He believes he has produced an accurate text, but declares it open to correction by the learned because only knowing and acting in accordance with the truth of scripture leads to heavenly bliss (48–58).

Edition

Hunt, *TFST*, II, 365–9

Base manuscript

L7 British Library Additional 41175
   *c.*1380–1400; 164 fols; 355 × 245 mm; 258 × 170 mm; 2 columns; 61 lines. The biblical text is written in bookhand on every other line, in letters twice as large as the glossed text and underlined in red. Openings of Short Glossed Matthew, f. 2r, and Short Glossed Mark, f. 105r, have decorated borders in gold, mauve and blue (cf.

---

[149] Hunt, *TFST*, I, 186–7.
[150] Hudson, *PR*, 251.
[151] Hudson, *PR*, 258, and see n. 117, above.
[152] See the note on GGI 154–7.

British Library Egerton 617/618), and a portrait of the gospeller in the initial 'T'. An exceptionally fine manuscript. Prologue to Short Glossed Matthew, f. 1va–b; Short Glossed Matthew, fols 2ra–103ra (f. 104 blank); Short Glossed Mark, fols 105ra–164ra. A companion volume to **O1**.

Other manuscript

C3 Trinity College Cambridge B.1.38
　　i + i (stub) + 171 fols + i (stub); 180 × 115 mm; 145+– × 90 mm; single column; 60/61 lines; space left for initials. 'Þe prologe of þe schorte exposicioun on Matheu', f. 7r; Short Glossed Matthew, fols 7v–104v; Short Glossed John, fols 105r–171v. Linne R. Mooney, *IMEP* handlist XI, 1–2.

Choice of base manscript

Since the texts in **L7** and **C3** are almost identical, the de-luxe **L7**, a companion volume to **O1**, has been chosen.

II Prologue to Intermediate Matthew, *inc.* 'Seynt Austyn saiþ'

The first 106 lines of the Prologue to Intermediate Matthew are one of the three additional prologues to *Oon of Foure* (see the introduction to CTII, pp. xxxvii–xxxix). The content of this prologue is an abridgment of the rules for recognizing spiritual senses in book III of Augustine's *De doctrina christiana*. In **O4** the prologue continues with the writer naming his sources for Intermediate Glossed Matthew and explaining how he cites his authorities (107–27). He then proceeds to argue for the necessity of scripture in English, the gospel being traduced by the three enemies of the church: worldly priests, members of religious orders and the ecclesiastical authorities (128–66).

　　The abridgment of material from *De doctrina christiana* is very similar to that in chapter twelve of the Prologue to the Wycliffite Bible, although there are significant differences in wording. Although the abridgment in the Matthew prologue is more abbreviated than that in the Prologue to the Wycliffite Bible, it contains some material not in the latter.[153] The writer of the Prologue continues his abridgment after the point where the Matthew prologue ends, and inserts into the material from *De doctrina christiana* some material from a sermon of Augustine 'of þe preisyng of charite' (2275).[154] The biblical quotations in the extracts from *De doctrina christiana* in the Matthew prologue resemble the Earlier Version; in the Prologue to the Wycliffite Bible, the biblical quotations resemble the Later Version, and sometimes quote it directly. Hunt argues persuasively that both abridgements 'are independently derived from some longer source' with the extracts in the same order.[155] It looks as though

---

[153] See the notes on GGII 1–102 and PWB 2191–2357 The Matthew prologue also includes some glosses on the biblical text not included in PWB.
[154] See the note on PWB 2256–75.
[155] Hunt, *TFST*, I, 192–6 (quotation at 196).

Wycliffites made a digest of the teaching about biblical interpretation in *De doctrina christiana* and both the compilers of the Glossed Gospels and the translators of the Wycliffite Bible made use of it.

O4 has a somewhat inferior text of lines 1–106; **D76 G1 L1 O6** and **P1** preserve a better text (see apparatus). The writer of the Prologue to Intermediate Matthew undoubtedly borrowed the *Oon of Foure* prologue and added material relevant to the Glossed Gospel context.

Editions

Deanesly, *LB*, 457–61
Hunt, *TFST*, II, 370–82
WB, I, 44–9

Base manuscript

O4 Bodleian Library Laud misc. 235
    ii (f. ii medieval fly-leaf) + 301 fols; 280 × 190 mm; 220 × 150 mm; 2 columns; 42/44 lines. The biblical text is written on every other line, in letters twice as large as the glossed text. 4-line blue initial flourished in red and with blue and red saw-tooth decoration surrounding the text, f. 1r; 6/4-line blue initials flourished in red. 'Seynt Austyn saiþ', fols 1ra–2vb; Intermediate Glossed Matthew, fols 2vb–263ra; Epilogue to Intermediate Glossed Matthew, 'Þe writere of þis glose purposede' (GGIII in this edition), fols 263ra–264va; LV prologue to the Apocalypse, f. 265ra–va; Glossed Apocalypse, translated from a French original, fols 265va–300ra.[156] (f. 301 blank). Owned by William Laud, archbishop of Canterbury, 1635 (f. iiv).

Other manuscripts of GGII 1–106

Fitzwilliam Cambridge McLean 133 [s. xvi copy of **O4**]
As additional prologue to *Oon of Foure*:

G1 Glasgow University Gen. 223, fols 7r–10v

L1 British Library Arundel 254, fols 9r–11r

o British Library Harley 6333, fols 18r–20r

O6 Christ Church Oxford Allestree L.4.1
    *c.*1400; iii + 126 fols + ii (f. iii medieval fly-leaf); 180 × 130 mm; 150 × 95 mm in second quire, containing 'Seynt Austyn saiþ' and Clement of Llanthony's preface and preliminaries to *Oon of Foure*; single column; 32/34 lines [125 mm × 80 mm, 28 lines, in *Oon of Foure*]; one neat bookhand. 5-line deep-blue and red initials flourished in both colours; 3/2-line deep-blue initials flourished in red

---

[156] Ed. E. Fridner, *An English Fourteenth Century Apocalypse Version with a Prose Commentary* (Lund, 1961; Lund Studies in English 29).

(including 'Seynt Austyn saiþ'). Gospel lectionary, fols 1r–7v (fols iii, 8 blank); 'Seynt Austyn saiþ', fols 9r–10v; *Oon of Foure*, fols 11r–126r. N.R. Ker, *Medieval Manuscripts in British Libraries*, vol. III (Oxford: Clarendon Press, 1983), pp. 595–6; S.J. Ogilvie-Thomson, *IMEP* handlist VIII, 18.

P1 Peterborough Cathedral 8, fols 9r–11r (conserved in Cambridge University Library)

Prefaced to LV Matthew in:

D Sächsische Landesbibliothek Dresden Od. 83, fols 15r–17v

D76 Trinity College Dublin 76, fols 6r–8r

R77 John Rylands Manchester Eng. 77, fols 13r–15r

III Epilogue to Intermediate/Long Matthew, *inc.* 'Þe writere of þis glos purposide'

The Epilogue to Intermediate/Long Matthew begins with the writer's claim that the glossed gospel it follows accurately represents its exemplars, but that it is nevertheless open to correction (1–10). The reason why Rabanus is cited so often, he says, is that he transmits the comments of the church fathers, who are revered for their holiness, learning and virtuous lives, faithful to scripture and reason, and who wanted their writings judged by that same criterion of faithfulness (11–27). Augustine makes it clear that charity is the criterion by which his writings must be judged: Christ's words are infallible but his are fallible, and he welcomes constructive criticism (11–46). The writer quotes at some length from *Contra Faustum*, in which Augustine draws an absolute distinction between canonical writings and those written later, arguing that the latter are open to question but the former are not (47–74). Augustine's statement that the writers of scripture never erred is enshrined in canon law (75–82), and Jerome also writes of the absolute authority of scripture. (The last part of the epilogue is summarized in the introduction to Cambridge Tract X.)

The emphasis on the absolute truth of canonical scripture links this text with Cambridge Tract III and *The Holi Prophete Dauid*, but the writer of the epilogue makes his case through statements from the two most eminent fathers of the church. The closing lament seems at odds with the earlier part of the epilogue and may have existed separately (its existence among the Cambridge Tracts adds weight to this suggestion). 'Þe writere of þis glos purposide' follows Intermediate Matthew in **O4** and Long Matthew in **L**, suggesting that the differences between the two versions were not seen as resulting in separate works.

Editions

Deanesly, LB, 457–61 (from **O4**)
Hunt, *TFST*, II, 383–90 (from **O4**)

Base manuscript

O4 Bodleian Library Laud misc. 235, fols 263ra–264va

Other manuscripts

Fitzwilliam Museum Cambridge McLean 133 [s. xvi copy of **O4**]

L British Library Additional 28026
> i (modern leaf numbered 1) + 189 fols; 290 × 205 mm; 225 × 147 mm; 2 columns; 46/54 lines (53 in epilogue); a regular anglicana hand. 4/2-line simple red Lombardic capitals. Long Glossed Matthew, fols 2r–186r; epilogue, fols 186r–187r; Pater Noster, Ave, Ten Commandments, Five Wits [etc.], fols 187r–189r. Rubric, f. 2r: '[Þ]is is a schort glose on Matheu for lewid men for to vnderstonde þe text, and onely holi writ, holy doctouris, specially seynt Ierom seynt Ioon Crisostom and Gregory and Austyn and Bernard and Rabanus allegynge holy doctouris, ben set in þis gloose'.

Choice of base manuscript

L has a slightly better text than **O4**,[157] but because **O4** provides the base text of the Prologue to Intermediate Matthew the same manuscript provides the epilogue as well.

IV Prologue to Short Luke, *inc.* 'Dauiþ spekynge in þe persone of Crist'

The Prologue to Short Luke opens with prophecies of David (Ps. 21:23) and Zacharias. As in The Prologue to Short Matthew the 'knowledge of salvation' is interpreted as knowing the gospel (without which salvation is impossible) and teaching it to the meek. Proud men will be damned for rebelling against the gospel (1–17). This glossed gospel is compiled for poor but devout men who know little or no Latin. The writer explains the format and content of the glossed gospel, and gives some insight into the authors of the glosses: Bede, for example, 'writes plainly and devoutly and sometimes cuttingly' (32). He goes into some detail about the sources of Aquinas's commentary, naming a number of obscure writers approved in canon law (18–43). He declares the text open to correction by the learned, but points out that the the glosses translate the meaning and not just the words of the originals, and should be trusted only insofar as they are consonant with scripture and reason. Readers of this glossed gospel, says the writer, will be in a good position to understand Luke and imitate the virtuous lives of Christ and the apostles (44–54). They will also be in a good position to eschew the proud lives of antichrist and his followers. Antichrist will certainly come and deceive many, and the best armour against him is scripture and holy living. The prologue ends with a prayer that the people may know and keep God's law and not be led astray by antichrist and his host (54–66).

The writer of the Prologue to Short Luke reveals that he has been 'lettid fro prechyng for a tyme for causis knowun of God' (18–19). Apparently, however, he was not prevented from taking part in the compiling of the Glossed Gospels, which suggests that he was not in prison (or not for long).

---

[157] See the apparatus and notes on GGIII 44, 67 and 81.

The opening of this prologue is in a confused state (see the description of **O** below), but can be confidently reconstructed.

Edition

Hunt, *TFST*, II, 391–5

Manuscript

O Bodleian Library Bodley 143, fols iii^{ra} and iii^{vb}–iv^{va}

iv + 223 fols (fols ii–iv medieval); 300 × 190 mm; 205 × 124 mm; 2 columns; 40 lines; bookhand. The biblical text is written on every other line and in letters twice as large as the glossed text. Gold initials on quartered mauve and blue background, fols 1r and 1v (and green leaves on f. 1v); all margins decorated in gold, mauve and blue, f. 1r. The prologue, written in red ink, begins on f. iii^{ra}, breaks off at 'to all men and seid' (8), and begins again on f. iii^{vb}. The portion of the prologue on f. iii^{ra} and the second attempt as far as 'remissioun '(5) are partly illegible because a layer of paper has been glued over this leaf, obscuring the upper quarter. Short Glossed Luke, fols 1ra–322ra.

V Prologue to Short John, *inc.* 'Oure Lord Iesu Crist veri God'

This prologue justifies the fact that Short John names the authors of the glosses but does not provide bibliographical information by explaining that this is 'to ese þe symple wit and cost of pore, symple men' (11). Full information, the writer says, is included in 'þe grettir gloos writun on Ioon' (11–12), confirming that Long John did once exist, although only a few extracts survive.[158]

Edition

Hunt, *TFST*, II, 396–7

Manuscript

O1 Bodleian Library Bodley 243

s. xiv. ex; iii (ii and iii medieval fly-leaves) + 175 fols; 360 × 230 mm; 260 × 175 mm; 2 columns; 60 lines; two bookhands. The biblical text is written on every other line in letters twice as large as the glossed text, and underlined in red. Gold initial with portrait of Luke, and decorated border in gold, mauve, blue and green at the opening of Luke, f. 1r; gold initial with portrait of John and decorated borders in gold, mauve, blue and green at the opening of John, f. 116r. Short Glossed Luke, fols 1ra–114vb (f. 115 blank); prologue to Short Glossed John, f. 115vb; Short Glossed John, fols 116ra–174vb (f. 175 blank). A companion volume to **L7**.

---

[158] See the note on GGV 11–12 and the introduction to CTV, p. xli.

In þe biginnyng[159]

This short prologue contrasts the situation in the early church with the situation in the time of the writer. Not only do priests no longer ensure that their listeners understand the scripture read in church but they do not understand it themselves (cf. *FSB* 100–8), fulfilling the prophecy in Is. 24:2 and Hos. 4:9 (cf. CTI 53). *In þe biginnyng* is the first of the additional prologues to *Oon of Foure* in three of the manuscripts that contain these (see the introduction to CTII, pp. xxxvii–xxxix), and is the first prologue to revised EV Matthew in **D76**.

Edition

Hunt, *TFST*, II, 363–4 (from **P1**).

Base manuscript

L1 British Library Arundel 254, f. 9r

Other manuscripts

Additional prologue to *Oon of Foure* in:

G1 Glasgow University Library Gen. 223, f. 7r

P1 Peterborough Cathedral 8, f. 9r (conserved in Cambridge University Library)

Prologue to revised EV Matthew in:

D76 Trinity College Dublin 76, f. 6r

---

[159] Hunt, *TFST*, I, 179–80.

THE TEXTS

Editorial procedures

The following conventions have been used in the text and apparatus:

Abbreviations are silently expanded to the most frequent unabbreviated spelling in the manuscript or the individual text; *an'crist* is transcribed as *antecrist*, *ihu(s)* as *iesu(s)*, *g'g'* as *Gregorie* and *wᵗ* as *wiþ*. Double f is modified to F/f, but manuscript i/j and u/v are retained.

Modern capitalization, word-division, punctuation and paragraphing generally replace that of the manuscript. Latin words and short phrases are italicized, but not longer quotations.

Any significant marginal material is recorded in the notes.

In the text:

  | indicates folio-break
  [ ] square brackets enclose added or emended text (see the apparatus for the manuscript reading)
  < > angle brackets enclose reconstruction of damaged material

The apparatus is divided into two sections on each page. The first block includes glosses and biblical references. Glosses are given in the form 'text word(s)': translation; biblical references similarly mention first the text cue if one occurs, followed by the biblical reference. The second block records the corrections made by the scribe or by the present editor; in a text found in more than a single manuscript the material (but not usually the linguistic) variants of copies other than the base manuscript are also given. No lemma is cited when the point of reference is clear.

In the apparatus:

  The spelling of a variant is that of the first-indicated manuscript
  bis the same word copied twice in error
  ] separates lemma from manuscript reading and variants
  / line-break (where this helps to explain scribal error)
  // folio-break (where this helps to explain scribal error)
  ˣ ˣ letters enclosed between ˣ ˣ have been cancelled by subpunction or some other form of deletion
  \ / primes enclose text inserted between the lines or in the margin
  a¹, a², a³ superscript numbers specify which occurrence of a word within a line is intended
  pr. m.; *sec. m.* the first hand; a second hand
  expl. explicit (i.e. ends)
  inc. incipit (i.e. begins)
  om. omitted

See p. xii for a note about the manuscript descriptions.
Psalm numbers are given according to the numbering of the Latin Vulgate.

The Prologue to the Wycliffite Bible

Here bigynneþ þe prologe for alle þe boo<kis> of þe Bible

Chapter 1

f. 1ra | Fyue and twenti bookis of þe elde testament ben bookis of feiþ and
fulli bookis of hooli writ. Þe firste is Genesis, þe secounde is Exodi, þe
þridde is Leuitici, þe fourþe is Numeri and þe fyueþe is De[u]tronomy, and
þese fyue ben bookis of Moises, which ben clepid propirli þe lawe. Þe
5 sixte book is Iosue, þe seuenþe is Iudicum, þat enclosiþ þe stori of Ruth, þe
viij., ix., x. and x<j., xij., xii>j. ben þe foure bookis of Kingis and þe
tw<ei> bookis of Paralipomenon; þe xiiij. book is Esdre, þat comprehendiþ
Nemye, and al is oo book anentis E<breis>, as Ierom seiþ, but anentis
Grekis and Latyns þese b<en twei> bookis; and xv. is Hester, þe xvj. is
10 Iob, þe xvij. is þe Sauter; þe xviij. book, xix. and xx. ben þe þ<re boo>kis
of Salomon, þe firste is Prouerbis eþer Parablis, þe secounde is
Ecclesiastes and þe þridde is Songis of Songis; þe xxj. book, xxij., xxiij.
and xxiv. ben þe foure Grete Profetis, Isaie is þe firste, Ieremye is þe
secounde, Eзechiel is þe þridde and Daniel is þe fourþe; þe xxv. book is o
15 book of xij. Smale Profetis, Osee is þe firste, Ioel is þe secounde, Amos is
þe þridde, Abdie is þe fourþe, Ionas is þe fyueþe and Michee is þe sixte,
Naum is þe seuenþe, Abacuk is þe eiзtþe, So<foni>e is þe nynþe, Aggei is
þe tenþe, Sacarie is þe eleuenþe and Malachie is þe twelueþe, and alle þese
twelue Smale Profetis ben o book and in þis ordre. And whateuere book in
20 þe eld testament is out of þese fyue and twenti forseid shal be set among
apocrifa, þat is, w<iþoute>n autorite of bileue; þerfor þe book of Wisdom
and Ec<clesiastici> and Iudith and Tobie be not of bileue. Þe firste book of

Glosses and biblical references   **5** 'Iudicum': Judges (*gen. pl.*)   **7** 'Paralipomenon': Chronicles
(note)   • 'Esdre': Ezra (*gen. sg.*)   • 'comprehendiþ': includes   **8** 'anentis': with, according to
11 'eþer': or   **15** 'Osee': Hosea   **16** 'Abdie': Obadiah   • 'Michee': Micah   **17** 'Naum': Nahum
• 'Abacuk': Habakkuk   • 'Sofonie': Zephaniah   • 'Aggei': Haggai   **18** 'Sacarie': Zechariah
20 'out of': not included in   **22** 'Ecclesiastici': Ecclesiasticus (*gen.*)   • 'Tobie': Tobit

Variants   **Heading** Prologe on al þe Bible S, a prolog for alle þe bokis of þe oolde testament T, a reule
þat telliþ of þe bookis of þe oolde testament whiche ben of very feiþ [etc.] [title of ch. 1] G   **1–43** A crease
in f. 1ra has caused rubbing of some letters and made others illegible   **2** secounde is Exodi] ij. exodi G
ι Q (etc.)   **3** detornomy   **4** moise^xi^xs   **5** sixte book is Iosue] vj. iosue G ι Q   **12** Songis¹] song A I T
(note)   **15** Osee is þe firste] osee G ι Q (etc.)   **20** out of] wiþoute G ι Q, oute β

Macabeis was foundun writun in Ebreu and þe \<secound\>e book of
Macabeis was writun first in Greek. Ierom seiþ al þis sentence in þe
25   prologe on þe firste book of Kyngis. Also þe book of Baruch and þe Pistle
of Ieremye ben not of autorite of bileue anentis Ebreis, neþer þe Preier of
Manasses, as Ierom witnessiþ, and hou myche of þe book of Hester and of
Danyel is of autorite anentis Ebreis, and in Ebreu lettre, it is teld in þe
same bookis bi Ierom himsilf.

30   Neþeles Ierom, in suynge Ebreis, comprehendiþ alle þese bookis in
xxij., for Ebreis maken o book of þe firste and secounde book of Kyngis
and clepen it Samuel, and þei maken o book of þe þridde and fourþe book
of Kingis and clepen it Ma\<lach\>ym, and þei comprehenden in o book þe
twei bookis of Paralipomenon. But, certis, litle charche is of þis
35   \<rik\>enyng, wheþer þe bookis of Kingis be noumbrid foure, as Latyns don,
eþer tweyne, as Ebreis don; also litil char\<che\> is wheþer Paralipomenon
be departid in two bookis, as Latyns vsen, eþer be a book aloone, as Ebreis
don. And so of þe firste book of Esdras and of Nemye litil charge is wheþer
þei ben tweyne, as Latyns and Grekis vsen, eþer oon aloone, as Ebreis
40   vsen. Neþeles, it semeþ þat Latyns and Greekis han more resoun in þis
rikenyng þan Ebreis han. But houeuere þese bookis ben noumbrid, alle
þese ben of autorite of bileue eþer of cristen feiþ. Þanne, if þe firste book of
Esdre and þe book of Nemye ben noumbrid | rb | for tweyne, as Grekis and
Latyns vsen, and if men taken Iudith for a book of hooli scripture, as þe
45   general congregacioun of clergie dide at þe seyne of Nycene, as Ierom
witnessiþ in þe prologe of Iudith, þanne in þe elde testament ben xxvij.
bookis of bileue. Also Ecclesiastici was writun in Ebreu, and þe book of
Wisdom is not anentis Ebreus but sowneþ Greek eloquence, and summe
elde writers affermen þat þe Iew Filo made it. Þerfor, as hooli chirche rediþ
50   Iudith and Tobie and þe bookis of Macabeis, but resseyueþ not þo among
hooli scriptures, so þe chirche rediþ þese two bo[o]kis Ecclesiastici and
Sapience to edefiyng of þe puple, not to conferme þe autorite of techyngis
of hooli chirche. Ierom seiþ þis pleynli in þe prologe on Prouerbis.

       Also Ierom translatide þe firste book of Esdre and Nemye, and
55   biddiþ þat no man delite in þe dremes of þe þridde and fourþe book of
Esdre þat ben apocrifa, þat is, not of autorite of bileue, for anentis Ebreis þe
wordis of Esdre and of Nemye ben driuun into o book, and þe bookis of þe
elde testament þat ben not anentis Ebreis and ben not of þe noumbre of
hooli writ owen to be cast fer awei. Ierom seiþ in þe prologe of Esdre. And

---

Glosses and biblical references   25–6 'Pistle of Ieremye': Bar. 6 (note)   26–7 'Preier of
Manasses': 2 Chron. 37 (note)   28 'lettre': language   34 'charche is of': weight attaches to
45 'seyne': synod   • 'Nycene': of Nicea   48 'sowneþ': resounds with   52 'Sapience': Wisdom
57 'driuun': compacted

Variants   27 how myche of] ȝit netheles T *sup. ras.*   50 resseyueþ not] þei resseyuen T   51 rediþ] rede
α Q S   • two\b/okis   52 not] and G, *om.* T

60 þerfor I translatide not þe þridde neþer þe fourþe book of Esdre, þat ben
apocrifa, but oneli þe firste and of Neemye, þat ben rekened for tweyne
bookis anentis Grekis and Latyns, and ben of autorite of bileue. Neþeles,
apocrifa ben seid on twei maneres, as *Catholicon* seiþ on þis word
'apocrifa': a book is seid apocrifum eþer for þe auctour is vnknowen and

65 þe treuþe þerof is open, and hooli chirche resseyueþ sich a book not to
preuyng of feiþ but to lernyng of vertues, and siche ben þe bookis of Iudith
and oþere which Ierom noumbriþ in þe prologe on Regum, eþer a book is
seid apocrifum for me doutiþ of þe treuþe þerof, and hooli chirche
resseyueþ not siche bookis, and sich is þe book of þe ʒong childhed of þe

70 Sauyour and þe book of þe takyng up of þe bodi of seynt Marie to heuene.
Catholicon seiþ þis on þat word 'apocrifa'.

   But soþeli alle þe bookis of þe newe testament, þat is foure
gospelers, Matheu, Mark, Luyk and Ioon, xij. epistlis of Poul, seuene
Smale Pistlis, þe Dedis of Apostlis and þe Apocalips, ben fulli of autorite

75 of bileue. Þerfor cristen men and wymmen, elde and ʒonge, shulden studie
faste in þe newe testament, for it is [of ful] autorite and opene to
vndurstonde of symple men as to þe poyntis þat ben moost nedeful to
saluacioun, and þe same sentence is in þe derkest places of hooli writ
which sentence is in þe open places, and ech place of hooli writt boþe open

80 and derk techiþ mekenesse and charite, and þerfor he þat kepiþ mekenesse
and charite haþ þe t[re]we vndurstonding and perfeccioun of al hooli writ,
as Austin preueþ in his sermoun of þe preisyng of charite.

   Þerfor no symple man of wit be afeerd vnmesurabli to studie in þe
text of hooli writt, for whi þo ben wordis of euerlastynge liyf, as Petre

85 seide to Crist in þe sixte chapitre of Ioon. And þe Hooli Goost stirid hooli
men to speke and write þe wordis of hooli writ for þe coumfort and
saluacioun of meke cristen men, as Petir, in þe secounde epistle in þe ende,
and Poul, in xv. chapitre to Romayns, witnessen. And no clerk be proud of
þe veri vndurstonding of hooli writ, for whi ueri vndurstonding of hooli

90 writ wiþouten charite þat kepe[þ] Goddis heestis makiþ a man depper
dampned, as Iamis and Iesu Crist witnessen. And pride and coueitise of
clerkis | f. 1va | is cause of her blyndnesse and eresie, and priueþ hem fro
veri vndurstonding of hooli writ, and makiþ hem go quyk into helle, as
Austin seiþ on þe Sauter, on þat word *descendant in infernum viuentes*.

Glosses and biblical references   **61** 'þe firste and of Neemye': the first book of Ezra and the
book of Nehemiah   **65** 'open': uncertain   **67** 'prologe on Regum': prologue to Kings   **68** 'me
doutiþ of þe treuþe þerof': its truth is in doubt   **78** 'derkest places': most obscure passages
79 'open': clear, plain   **84–5** John 6:69   **85–7** 2 Pet. 1:21   **88** Rom. 15:4   **89–91** Jas. 4:17;
Matt. 23:13   **90** 'heestis': commandments   **92** 'priueþ hem fro': deprives them of   **94** Ps. 54:16
descendant in infernum viuentes: they go living into hell

Variants   **64** apocrifum] apocrifa S, apocrifim T   **76** of ful] ful of   **77** vnderstonde] vndirstonding α β
G ι Q S   **79** place *bis*   **81** twe   **90** þat kepeþ] and kepynge of T, þat kepiþ not G   • kepen

Chapter 2

95   The elde testament is departid into þre partis, into moral comaundementis,
      iudicials, and cerymonyals. Moral comaundementis techen to holde and
      preise and cherische vertues, and to fle and repreue vices, and þese
      comaundementis bynden euere and han strengþe, for þo ben groundid in
      charite and resoun and in þe lawe of kynde. Iudicials techen domes and
100   peynes for orrible synnes, and þe iudicials of Moises lawe weren ful iust
      and profitable for men, for þo weren ordeyned of God, þat mai not erre in
      his domes and lawis and werkis. Neþeles, siþ Crist was maad man and
      ordeyned lawe of merci and of charite, and wole not þe deþ of a synful man
      but repentaunce and saluacioun, cristen men ben not bondun to kepe þe
105   iudicials of Moises lawe, þat was endid in þe tyme of Cristis passioun. But
      ȝit cristen lordis þat han þe swerd and ben Goddis vikeris, in þe xiiij. cᵒ to
      Romayns, moun punysche men þat trespassen openli, in catel and bodili
      prisoun, and sumtyme bi bodili deþ, whanne þe synne mai not ellis be
      distriyed neþer þe comynte mai not ellis be stablischid in pees, as þe foure
110   doctours and oþere lattere preuen openli bi hooli writ and resoun. Bot loke
      þat þis be doon for charite and comyne profyt, wiþ merci and compassioun
      of briþeren, not for coueitise neþer pride, neþer for veniaunce of a mannus
      owne wrong.
      Cerymonyals techen figures and sacramentis of þe elde lawe, þat
115   figuriden Crist and his deþ and þe mysteries of hooli chirche in þe lawe of
      grace, and þese cerymonyals ceessiden vttirli as to obligacioun in þe tyme
      of Cristis deþ, and ben noieful and dampnable to men þat kepen þo. And
      for þat þe gospel is prechid and knowen generali, for, if þo cerymonyes ben
      kept now, þe kepers of þo knoulechen þat Crist is not ȝit comen, neþer
120   suffrid deþ for mankynde, and þis knoulechyng is open errour eþer eresie,
      for whi þe treuþe and fredom of þe gospel sufficiþ to saluacioun wiþout
      kepyng of cerymonyes maad of God in þe elde lawe, and myche more
      wiþout ceremonyes of synful men and vnkunnynge, þat ben maad in þe
      tyme of antecrist and of vnbynding of Sathanas, in þe twentiþe chapitre of
125   Apocalips. Þerfor, as it is open eresie to seie þat þe gospel wiþ his treuþe
      and fredom sufficiþ not to cristen mennus saluacioun, wiþout kepyng of
      cerymonyes of Goddis lawe ȝouun to Moises, so it semeþ opener eresie to
      seie þat þe gospel wiþ his treuþe and fredom sufficiþ not to saluacioun of

---

Glosses and biblical references   106 'vikeris': representatives   106–7 Rom. 13:4
107–8 'catel and bodili prisoun': possessions and imprisonment   112 'coueitise': greed
115 'figuriden': prefigured   116 'as to obligacioun': as far as obligation is concerned
117 'noieful': harmful   123–5 Apoc. 20:2   127 'ȝouun': given

Variants   103 \a\   105 was] weren G ι Q   109 comynte] comynalte G ι Q Gough   • not *om.* α β G ι
Q S   120 errour eþer eresie] heresie α G ι Q S, errore Gough   128 fredom and truþe G ι Q

cristen men wiþout kepyng of ceremonyes and statutis of synful men and
130   vnkunnynge, þat ben maad in þe tyme of Sathanas and of antecrist.

Chapter 3

Symple men of wit moun be edefied eþer holpen myche to heuenli lyuynge
bi redyng and knowyng of þe elde testament, for in þe bigynnyng of
Genesis þei moun knowe hou God made heuene and erþe and alle creaturis
of nouȝt, and made man to his owne ymage and licnesse, and to haue blisse
135   in bodi and soule wiþouten ende. Also men moun knowe hou sore God
punyschide Adam and Eue for brekyng of his comaundement, and hou
Abel pleside God bi feiþ, | vb | mekenesse and charite, and hou Caym
displeside hym bi synnes, and speciali bi enuye, hatrede and manquelling.
Also hou Noe was loued of God, and al þe world outakun eiȝte persoones
140   was distruyed for synne, and hou for pride and oþere synnes God departide
many langagis, þat no man vndurstood oþere in þe tour of Babel. And hou
feiþful and obedient to God Abraham was, þat he ȝede out of his lond into
a straunge cuntre, and was redi to sle his owne sone Isaac at þe wille of
God, and gat þerfor myche reward of God. And hou God distriede Sodom
145   and Gomore and oþere þre citees for lecherie and oþere synnes, þat þo
weren sunken doun, and þe Dead See is now where þo grete citees weren.
Also hou trewe and obedient to God weren Isaac and Iacob and Ioseph, and
hou God kepte hem in alle perels.
     Al þis proces of Genesis shulde stire cristen men to be feiþful and
150   for to drede and loue God, and in alle þingis do his wille.
     Also, in Exodi men moun knowe hou God kepte his symple puple
in Egipt and encreesside hem gretli in þat lond vndur þe persecucioun and
tirauntrie of Farao, and delyueride hem bi many myraclis, and punyschide
Farao and his puple wiþ ten stronge veniaunces, and þanne brouȝt his owne
155   puple þorouȝ þe Reed See, and fedde hem merueilousli in desert fourti
ȝeeris, where no dwelling of men was bifore, and made hem to ouercome
þe strong puple of Amalech. Aftir þis God tauȝte hem wiys gouernail, and
bitook to hem ten comaundementis and oþere iudicialis to punysche gretli
open grete synnes. And þei weren ful bisi to make a costlew tabernacle to
160   þe onour of God bi his biddyng and techyng, þat figuride hooli chirche and
vertues in mennus soulis. At þe laste God took greet veniuance on hem for

Glosses and biblical references   **138** 'manquelling': homicide   **139** 'Noe': Noah   • 'outakun':
except for   **140** 'departide': separated out   **145** 'þat þo': so that those [cities]   **149** 'proces': series
of events   **159** 'costlew': costly

Variants   **131** þis is þe prolog of Genesis Symple G   • edefied eþer holpen myche] edified mych α β G ι
Q S, edefyed or helped greatly Gough   **145** gomo^xi^xre   **149** stire] stire meche β ι *sec. m.* T   **150** wille here
endiþ þe prolog of Genesis G   **151** moun] may G ι Q, mowe β   **153** farao] of kyng farao G ι Q   **154–5** and
þanne … See *om.* α β G ι Q S Gough (note)   **159** And] also α β S

idolatrie, whanne þei forsoken þe feiþ and worschiping of God and
onoureden ȝoten calues bi þe stiryng of þe deuel, and þanne Moises was a
trewe mediatour bitwixe God and þe synful puple, and seide þus to God,
165 for greet trist of his merci and riȝtfulnesse and for greet charite to þe puple,
'eþer forȝyue þou þis trespas to hem, eþer do me out of þi book in which
þou hast writen me'. And for þis deuout preier and greet charite of Moises
God sparide þe synful puple and distriede not sudenli al þe puple, but took
hem to merci and grace.
170   And þis proces of Exodi shulde make men to triste in Goddis help,
and to be trewe in his loue and to eschewe his offence wiþ alle her myȝtis.
     Þe þridde book, clepid Leuitici, techiþ men sacrifices du to God and
for synnes of þe puple in þe tyme of þe elde testament, and þat no man
vnworþi shulde neiȝe to þe seruyce and sacrifice of God. Þese sacrifices
175 owen not to be kept now, for þo figuriden þe passioun and deþ of Crist, and
remyssioun of synnes bi þe blood and merit of Crist in þe law of grace.
Also þis book techiþ men to absteyne fro wedlok of nyȝ kyn and affynyte
wiþinne þe secounde degree, and ordeyneþ peyne of deþ for idolatrie and
wedding wiþinne þe secounde degree of consangwynyte and affynyte. At
180 þe laste þis book techiþ men to kepe Goddis heestis, and for to loue her
neiȝboris and do equite to hem and werkis of merci to nedi men, and
comaundiþ iust weiȝtis and mesures and domes, and forbediþ strongli
idolatrie and wicchecraftis | f. 2ra | and false cuniouryngis, and telliþ
prosperitees þat shal come to hem þat kepen Goddis heestis, and veniaunce
185 and peyne to hem þat breken Goddis heestis.
     And þis process of Leuytici shulde make cristen men afeerd to
breke Goddis heestis and ioiful to kepe þo to liyf and deþ, for reward of
God in euerlastinge blis.
     Þe fourþe book, clepid Numeri, telliþ þe noumbre of puple led out
190 of Egipt, boþe of lewid men and of prestis and of dekenes, and hou God
kepte hem longe in þe orible desert, and punyschide hem alle bi deeþ,
outake Caleph and Iosue, for grucching and mystrist to Goddis word, and
punyschide Marie, Moises sister, wiþ lepre, for bacbityng of Moises, þe
mylde seruaunt of God. Also, whanne God wolde haue destried þe puple
195 for grucchyng aȝens him Moises preiede wiþ al his herte for þe puple þat
wolde stoone hym to deþ. Also God techiþ þere þat he þat doiþ ony synne
bi pride shal be deed, and þat he þat brak þe sabat, ȝhe bi gadering of
stickis, shulde be stoned of al þe puple. Also God punyschide soore
Chore, Dathan and Abiron, þat weren rebel aȝenus Moises and Aaron and

---

Glosses and biblical references   163 'ȝoten': cast in metal   166–7 Exod. 32:32   174 'neiȝe to':
approach   177–9 Lev. 18   177 'nyȝ kyn': close kindred   191–2 Num. 14   192–4 Num. 12
193 'lepre': leprosy   194–6 Num. 14   196–8 Num. 15   197 'ȝhe': yes, indeed   198–205 Num. 16

Variants   170 to triste] trysty α β G ι Q S, to triste Gough   183 wicchecraft G ι Q

200 maden dissencioun in þe puple, so þat þe erþe openyde and deuouride hem
wiþ his tabernaclis and al her catel, and þei ȝeden doun quyk into helle. Ȝit
whanne þe puple grucchide aȝenus Moises and Aaron and wolden sle hem
vniustli, and God killide many þousyndis of þe puple herfor, Moises bad
Aaron preie and offre encense for þe puple, and so he ceesside þe
205 veniaunce.

Also God techiþ þere þat prestis shulden haue þe firste-fruytis and
þe firste-borun þingis, and part of sacrifices and avowes and offringis, and
dekenes shulden haue tiþis of þe puple and ȝyue her tiþis, þat is, þe tenþe
part of tiþis which þei token of þe puple, to þe hiȝeste prest. And prestis
210 and dekenes shulen holde hem apaied wiþ her spiritual part of tiþis and
offringis, and take no possessioun in þe lond of her briþeren, for God
hymsilf shal be þe part and þe eritage of prestis, in þe myddis of þe sones
of Israel.

Also, for Moises and Aaron bileuyd not fulli to Goddis word but
215 doutiden of his biheest at þe watir of Aȝenseiyng, God suffred not hem for
to entre in to þe lond of biheest, but boþe weren deed in þe desert. Also in
þis book ben teld þe dwellingis of þe children of Israel in desert, and þe
batels which þei hadden aȝenus heþene men, and of Balaam, hou he was
hirid to curse Goddis puple, and hou God compellide him to blesse his
220 puple and to seie profesie of Crist. And, for þe puple of Israel dide
fornycacioun and idolatrie, God bad Moises hange up alle þe princes
aȝenus þe sunne, þat þe stronge veniaunce of God were turned awei fro þe
puple [of Israel]. And for as myche as Fynees þe prest killide a duyk of
Israel þat dide fornycacioun wiþ an heþene womman, and dide þis for
225 feruent loue to God, he gat of God euerlastinge presthod for hym and for
his seed, and turned awei Goddis wraþþe fro þe children of Israel.

Also þere is tauȝte who shal be eir of a man, and of halidaies and
sacrifices and offryngis maad in þo, and which avowis shulen be holden
and which not, and of batels, and hou þe preies shulen be departid among
230 þe puple, and what shulde falle to þe prest. And hou þe lond of biheest
shulde be departid to xij. lyna| rb |gis, and dekenes shulde haue citees to
enhabite in þo, and þe subarbis to her sheep and beestis. And citees of
refuyt shulden be ordeyned for hem þat shedden blood vnwilfuli, not of
purpos neþer of hatrede bifor-goyng, and he þat is gilti of mannus deþ shal
235 be slayn wiþouten ony redempcioun.

Glosses and biblical references   206–13 Num. 18   210 'holde hem apaied': reckon themselves
paid   214–16 Num. 20; Deut. 34   215 ' biheest': promise   • 'Aȝenseiyng': contradiction
216–18 'men' Num. 21   218–20 Num. 22   220–6 Num. 25   223 'Fynees': Phinehas   227 'man'
Num. 27:8–11   227–8 'þo' Num. 28–9   228–9 'not' Num. 30   229–30 'prest' Num. 31   230–5
Num. 34–5   232–3 'of refuyt': for refuge   234 'bifor–goyng': previous

Variants   223 of Israel *om.*   223 as myche as myche as   226 w/wraþþe   229 shulen be departid *bis*

Þis process of Numeri shulde stire cristen men for to loue her
enemyes and do good to hem, as Moises and Aaron diden, and to kepe
Goddis heestis and shede out mannus blood nouȝt vniustli.

Þe fyueþe book, clepid Deutronomy, is a rehersyng and confermyng
240   of al þe lawe bifor-going, and stiriþ men gretli to kepe and teche Goddis
heestis, and adde noþing to þo neþer drawe awei onyþing from þo. And
first it techiþ þat wise men and witti shulen be maad jugis and deme iustli
þe pore and þe riche; aftirward, hou þe Iewis ouercamen Seon, þe kyng of
Esebon, and token his lond and alle þe godis þerinne into her owne
245   possessioun, and diden in liyk maner to Og, þe kyng of Basan, and to his
lond and to his goodis. Ferþermore, God comaundiþ men to kepe hise
heestis, and adde noþing þerto neþer drawe onyþing þerfro, and þat þei
drede and loue God wiþ al her herte and al her soule and al her strengþe,
and eschewe idolatrie, and serue and worschipe him aloone, and þat þei
250   teche Goddis heestis to her sones, and þenke on þo heestis in hows and
weie, slepyng and wakyng. Also God comaundiþ his puple to eschewe
weddingis of heþene men and wymmen to her children, lest þei be drawun
to idolatrie, and bihotiþ many blessyngis to hem and myche encreessyng of
goodis if þei kepen treuli his comaundementis, and þat strong veniaunce
255   and distreiyng shulde come on þe Iewis if þei diden idolatrie and weren
vnobedient to God. Also God bad þem haue mynde þat þei weldiden þe
lond of biheest not for here owne riȝtfulnesse and strengþe but for þe
synnes of men þat dwelliden þerinne, and for þe ooþ of God which he
made to Abraham and to oþere hooli men. And þanne God remembriþ to
260   hem many grete synnes, to make hem war þat þei trespassen no more, but
þat þei drede God and loue him in al her herte and soule, and kepe his
comaundementis and swere bi his name, and loue pilgryms eþer
comelyngis.

Eft God biddiþ hem haue his wordis in her hertis and wittis, and
265   haue þo for a signe in þe hondis and bitwixe her iȝen, and þat þei teche her
sones to biþenke on þe wordis of God euere, and þat þei write þe wordis of
God on þe postis and ȝatis of her hows, and telliþ and ȝyueþ his blessyng
to hem if þei kepen his heestis, and ȝyueþ his curs to hem if þei breken his
heestis and worschipen alien goddis. Also þei shulen distroie þe places
270   wherinne heþene men diden idolatrie, and distroie her auteris, ymagis,
wodis and idols, and þei schulen make her sacrifices and offre her tiþis and

---

Glosses and biblical references   241 Deut. 4:2 (note)   241–3 'riche' Deut. 1:13–17   243–6 Deut.
2–3   243 'Seon': Sihon   246–51 Deut. 4–6   251 'weie': [walking in the] way   251–6 Deut.
7   253 'bihotiþ': promises   256–9 Deut. 9:4–6   256 'haue mynde': remember   259–63 Deut.
9–10:19   263 'comelyngis': immigrants   264–9 Deut. 11   269–73 Deut. 12

Variants   238 \nouȝt/   241 drawe ˣonyˣ   242 witti] myȝty α β G ι Q S T (note)   242 shulen] shulden
G ι Q T • iustli] riȝtly G ι Q   247 onyþing] noþing G ι Q   255 shulde] shal α β G ι Q S • diden]
doen α β G ι Q S • weren] ben α β G ι Q S

þe firste-fruytis and ȝiftis and avowis in þe place which þe Lord haþ chose
to his name, and þis was þe temple of Ierusalem. Also a profete eþer a
feynere of dremes þat wole stire men to do idolatrie shal be slayn, and so
275 shal a frend eþer a citee þat doiþ idolatrie, eþer stiriþ oþere men þerto. Also
þou shalt paie tiþis of al fruytis þat growen in erþe, of whete, of wyn and of
oile, and þe firste-borun þingis of neet and sheep, and in þe þridde ȝeer þou
shalt departe anoþere tiþe of alle þingis þat growen to þe, and kepe it
wiþinne þi ȝatis to susteyne þe dekene, pilgrym eþer comeling, | f. 2va |
280 fadirles child eþer modirles and widewe þat ben wiþinne þi ȝatis. Also, in
þe seuenþe ȝeer shal be remyssioun of dette to citeseyns and kynnesmen,
neþeles not to a pilgrym and comelyng, for he mai be compellid to paie.
Vttirli a nedi man and beggere shal not be among Goddis puple, but pore
men shulen not faile in þe lond, þerfor riche men shulen helpe hem wiþ
285 loone, and helpe hem wilfuli in her nede.
    Þanne God techiþ of þre grete solempnytees, of pask, of þe feeste of
woukis eþer Pentecost, and of þe feeste of tabernaclis, and þat maistris and
iugis shulen be ordeyned in alle ȝatis eþer citees bi ech lynage to deme þe
puple bi iust doom, and take not ȝiftis ne persoones. Ferþermore, God
290 techiþ þat whoeuere is conuyct bi twei eþer þre witnessis þat he haþ do
idolatrie, he shal be stooned, first bi þe witnessis and þanne bi al þe puple.
He þat is proud and wole not obeie to þe comaundement of þe hiȝ prest and
to þe doom of þe iugis, in þat þat þei techen Goddis lawe, shal be deed.
Þanne God techiþ what maner kyng þe puple shal make and what shal be
295 his office. Aftirward God techiþ þat prestis and dekenes and alle þat ben of
þe same lynage shulen not haue part and eritage wiþ þe residue puple of
Israel, for þei shulen ete þe sacrifices of þe Lord and þe offryngis of hym,
and þei shulen take noon oþere þing of þe possessioun of her briþeren, for
whi God himsilf is her eritage. Ferþermore, God forbediþ idolatrie and to
300 enquere cuniourers, and to kepe dremes and chiteryng of briddis, and
comaundiþ þat no wicche neþer enchauntere be, and þat men take no
councel at hem þat han spiritis in cloos, neþer at false dyuynours, neþer axe
of deed men þe treuþe. Also God shal reise a profete of her briþeren, þat is
Crist þe Sauyour, and he þat haþ not his wordis shal be punyschid. A
305 profete þat wole speke bi pride in þe name of God þat þing þat God bad not
him, eþer bi þe name of oþere goddis, shal be slayn.
    Also sixe citees of refuyt or of fraunchise shulen be, þat he þat
sleeþ a man not bi hatrede but aȝenus his wille be saued, and he þat sleeþ a

---

Glosses and biblical references   273–5 Deut. 13   275–80 Deut. 14:22–9   280–5 Deut. 15   **285**
'wilfuli': willingly   286–9 Deut. 16   286 'pask': passover   289–95 Deut. 17   290 'þat he haþ
do': of having done   295–306 Deut. 18   300 'enquere cuniourers': ask questions of augurs
(note) • 'kepe': take heed of • 'chiteryng': chirping (note)   302 'in cloos': enclosed within
them (note)   303 'of her': from their   307–11 Deut. 19

Variants   274 wole stire] steriþ G ι Q   293 in þat þei β G ι Q   304 haþ] heriþ G ι Q man bi hatrede and bifor-castyng shal be slayn wiþout merci or raunsun.

310   He þat is conuyct to haue seid fals witnessyng aȝenus his broþer shal haue
þe same peyne to which his broþer shulde be put if he hadde be gilti. Also
prestis shulden coumforte hem þat goen to iust batel to haue trist in God
and drede not her enemyes, and þat ferdful men, and þei þat han newli
bildid an hows, or newli plauntid a vyne or newli weddid a wiyf and not

315   vsid hir, go not to batel. And first werriours shulen profere pees to a citee,
and if þe citee ȝelde itsilf men þerinne shulen lyue vndur tribute, ellis alle
men þerinne shulen be slayn, and þis is vndurstonden of þo citees þat ben
not ȝouun into possessioun to þe puple of Israel. And þere is teld þe
departing of preies, and what trees shulen be kut doun in þe bise[g]yng.

320   Also God techiþ what shal be doon whanne a man is founden slayn
and þe sleere is vnknowen. A child rebel to fadir and modir, and þat ȝyueþ
himsilf to glotenye, leccherie and drunkenesse, shal be stooned of al þe
citee. A man shal kepe þe oxe and sheep of his broþer þat is straied awei
and brynge it aȝen to his broþer, and so of oþere beestis and of ech þing,

325   and if þou knowist not whose þei ben þou shalt kepe þo stille, til þi broþer
seke and resseyue þo. Whoeuere doiþ auoutrie shal be deed; if a man defou
| vb ǁle a virgyn he shal wedde hir and ȝyue fifti siclis of siluer to her fadir.
Þou shalt not take a seruaunt to his lord, which seruaunt fledde to þee, but
he shal dwelle wiþ þee in a place þat plesiþ hym. Noon hoore shal be of þe

330   douȝtris of Israel, neþer a lecchour of þe sones of Israel. Þou shalt not
leene to þi broþer for vsure. If a man hatiþ his wiyf he shal write and ȝyue
to hir a libel of forsaking, but þis is forbeden of Crist in þe gospel of
Matheu, fyueþe chapitre and xix. chapitre. Whanne a man haþ take late a
wiyf, he shal not go to batel neþer ony comyn office shal be putt on him,

335   but oo ȝeer he shal be glad wiþ his wiyf and take heede to his hows. He þat
proloyneþ his broþer which is a fre man, and selliþ hym, shal be slayn. Þou
shalt ȝelde at nyȝt to a pore men his wedde, and in þe same dai þou shalt
paie to a nedi trauelour his hire. Fadris shulen not be slayn for þe sones,
neþer sones for þe fadris. Whanne þou repist corn in þe feeld and forȝetist

340   an handful þou shalt not turne aȝen to take it, but þou shalt suffre þat a
comelyng, fadirles child and widewe take it awei, and so of gaderyng of
olyues and of gaderyng of grapis. Whanne tweie men ben at þe debatyng,
and þe wiyf of oon wole delyuere her hosebonde fro þe hond of þe
strengere and take hym bi þe pryuy membris, she shal leese hir hond

345   wiþouten ony merci. And þere God forbediþ false weiȝtis and mesures, a
more and a lesse.

Glosses and biblical references   **309** 'bifor–castyng': premeditation   **311–19** Deut. 20   **320–3**
Deut. 21   **323–6** Deut. 22:1–3   **326–7** Deut. 22:22–9   **328–31** Deut. 23:15–19   **331–42** Deut.
24   **332–3** Matt. 5:31–2; 19:8–9   **333** 'late': recently   **336** 'proloyneþ': abducts   **337** 'wedde':
pledge   **342–6** Deut. 25:11–16

Variants   **319** bisechyng P, bysekynge α β S   **325** þei] þo α β G ι Q S   **344** streng ˣþeˣ\ere/

Also dekenes shulen pronounce and seie wiþ hiȝ vois to alle þe men
of Israel 'he is cursid þat doiþ idolatrie or brekiþ ony comaundement of
God, or doiþ aȝenus ony part of þe lawe of God', and al þe puple shal seie
350 'amen'. Also God bihotiþ greet prosperite to his puple, if þei kepen his
heestis, and þei shulen be blessid in citee and in feeld, and þe fruyt of her
wombe and þe fruyt of her lond shal be blessid, and alle þingis þat
perteynen to hem shulen be blessid, and þei shulen haue victorie of her
enemyes, and many prosperitees of soule and of bodi shulen bifalle to hem.
355 And if þei kepen not Goddis heestis þei shulen be cursid in citee and in
feeld; þe fruyt of her wombe and alle þingis þat perteynen to hem shulen be
cursid. God shal sende hem hungur, þirst, pestilence, feuyr and coold,
brennynge and heete and corrupt eir, til þei perischen. Enemyes shulen
haue victorie and conquere hem and take hem prisoneris, and ȝit God shal
360 punysche hem wiþ huge veniaunce, þat alle þat heren be astonyed.
Neþeles, if whanne alle þese veniauncis ben fallen on hem þei repenten
verili in þe herte, and turne aȝen to God and obeien to his heestis in al her
herte and al her soule, þe Lord shal haue merci on hem, and brynge hem
aȝen to her lond fro alle folkis among whiche þei weren scaterid, and God
365 shal blesse hem and make hem to be more noumbre þan her fadris weren,
and shal turne alle þese cursis on her enemyes, and God shal ȝyue to hem
abundaunsis in alle werkis of her hondis, and in alle þingis þat perteynen to
hem.

Moises spak alle þese wordis to al þe puple of Israel, and bad hem
370 drede not her enemyes, for God shal go bifor his puple and ouercome her
enemyes. And Moises ordeynede Iosue to be ledere of þe puple bifor al þe
multitude of þe sones of Israel. Moises wroot þis | f. 3ra | lawe and ȝaf it to
prestis, þe sones of Leuy, and to þe eldere men of Israel, and bad hem rede
þe wordis of þis lawe bifor al Israel in þe heryng of alle men and wymmen,
375 litle children and comelyngis eþer conuersis to þe feiþ of Iewis, þat þei
here and lerne and drede oure Lord God, and kepe and fille alle þe wordis
of þis lawe. Moises, bi Goddis comaundement, wroot a greet song and
tauȝte it þe children of Israel, þat it shulde be into witnessyng aȝenus hem,
and Moises clepide togidere alle þe eldere men and techeris and clepide
380 heuene and erþe into witnessing aȝenus hem, and whanne Moises hadde
fillid alle þe wordis of þis grete song he stiede into an hil and was deed
þere, and God biriede hym and man knew not his sepulcre til into þis dai.

Cristen men shulden myche rede and here and kunne þis book of

Glosses and biblical references   347–50 Deut. 27:14–26   350–60 Deut. 28:1–37   361–8 Deut.
30:1–9   369–77 Deut. 31:1–13   375 'conuersis': converts   377–82 Deut. 31:19–28; 32; 34:1–6
378 'into witnessyng': as a testimony   381 'stiede into': climbed up

Variants   351 and blessid in feeld G ι Q   357–8 coold and brennynge G ι Q   366 þese] þe α G ι Q S
pr. m.   379–80 and Moises … hem *om.* Q

Deutronomy, þat comprehendiþ al þe lawe of Moises and disposiþ men for
385   to bileue in Crist and here and kepe his wordis.

Chapter 4

The sixte book is clepid Iosue, and telliþ in general þat Iosue brouȝte þe
puple into þe lond of biheest, and departide it bi lot to hem, and first hou
God bihiȝte to Iosue þat noon shulde mowe aȝenstonde him and his puple
in alle þe daies of his liyf. And God bihiȝte þat Iosue shulde departe bi lot
390   to his puple þe lond of biheest, and God comaundide him to kepe al þe
lawe and bowe not fro it but þenke þerinne boþe daies and nyȝtis, þat he
kepe it and do þo þingis þat ben writun þerinne. Aftir þis Iosue sente aspies
to biholde þe lond and þe citee of Ierico, and þei entriden in to þe hows of a
comyne womman, Raab, and weren saued þere bi counsel and help of þe
395   womman. Þanne Iosue bad þe prestis take þe arke of þe boond of pees of
þe Lord and go bifor þe puple, and þei diden so, and whanne þe prestis
camen wiþ þe arke to þe brynke of Iordan þe grete watir of Iordan wente
awei to þe Deed See, and þe hiȝere watris stoden stille as a wal, so þat þe
puple passide bi þe drie botme and þe prestis stoden on þe drie erþe in þe
400   myddis of Iordan. And Iosue bad twelue men of twelue lynagis of Israel
take xij. grete stoonys fro þe botme of Iordan and sette þo in Galgalis,
where þe puple sette tentis in þe next nyȝt aftir þe passage of Iordan, and
take xij. stoonys of þe lond and putte in þe myddis of Iordan where þe arke
hadde stonde, and bad þat fadris shulden teche her children hou þei
405   passiden bi þe drie botme of Iordan, for God driede þe watris þerof as he
hadde do bifore in þe Reed See. And þe prestis and þe princes and al þe
puple obeide to Iosue.
   Þanne Iosue circumcidid þe puple þat was vncircumcidid xl. ȝeer in
desert, and þe puple made pask in þe xiiij. dai of þe moneþe at euentid, and
410   Iosue siȝ þe aungel of þe Lord, which aungel was prynce of Goddis oost.
Also þe stronge wallis of Ierico felden doun at Goddis ordenaunce whanne
þe prestis breheden wiþ seuene trumpis, and al þe puple cried an hiȝ in þe
seuenþe dai of cumpassyng of þe citee. And þe puple of Israel distroiede
and brente þe citee [and] alle þingis þerinne, outakin Raab and þo þingis
415   þat weren in her hows, and outaken gold and siluer and uessels of bras and
iron, which þei halewiden into þe treserie of þe Lord. And, for Achar dide

---

Glosses and biblical references   **387** 'and first'–**392** Jos. 1   **388** 'mowe': be able to   **392–5** Jos. 2
395–400 Jos. 3   **395** 'boond of pees': covenant   **400–7** Jos. 4   **408–10** Jos. 5   **411–16** Jos. 6
'breheden': sounded   **416** 'halewiden': consecrated   • 'for': because   • 'Achar': Achan

Variants   **388** \to\   • mowe] moun Q, now α β S T   **391** boþe] bi α β G ι Q S   **397** camen wiþ] camen
and brouȝten G ι Q Crowley   **401** sette] settide α β G ι Q S   **402** þe nyȝt α β   • passage] passynge G ι
Q Crowley   **404** children *sup. ras.*   **408** circumcidid] circumcide S, circumsisede β   **414** and] of   • þo]
þo þingis

aȝenus Goddis biddyng and took to | rb | himsilf a þing reserued to Goddis
vss he was stooned and brend, and alle his goodis weren brent wiþ him,
and til þis punysching was doon on him þe puple of Israel myȝte not stonde
420 but was ouercome of her enemyes. Aftir þis punysching of Achar, Iosue
took þe citei of Hai and killid þe kyng and al þe puple, and distriede and
brente þe cite, and hangide þe kyng þerof in a iebat.

Þanne Iosue bildide an auter to God in þe hil of Hebal, and offrid
þeronne brent sacrifice and pesible sacrifices, and wroot þe Deutronomy of
425 Moises lawe on stoones. And first he blesside þe puple of Israel, and aftir
þese þingis he redde alle þe wordis of blessyng and of cursyng, and alle
þingis þat weren writun in þe book of Goddis lawe; he lefte noþing
vntouchid of þese þingis which Moises hadde comaundide, but he declaride
alle þingis bifor al þe multitude of Israel, to wymmen and litle children and
430 to comelingis þat dwelliden among hem.

Also men of Gabaon feyned hem to be of fer cuntrei, and bi þis
fraude þei gaten of Iosue and oþere princes pees and liyf, and for þis fraude
þei and alle her successours were maad boonde to brynge wode and watir
to þe seruyce of þe auter and of al þe multitude of Israel for euere. Also
435 Iosue bi Goddis help ouercam fyue greet kyngis in o dai, and made his
princes trede on þe neckkis of þese kyngis, and aftirward henge þese
kyngis in fyue gebatis. And he ouercam alle þe kyngis and her puplis þat
dwelliden in þe lond of biheest (þat weren xxxj. kyngis), and departide þe
lond of biheest to xij. lynagis of Israel bi lot, and citees of refuyt and citees
440 to prestis and dekenes to dwellen inne, as God comaundide.

Þis proces of Iosue shulde stire cristen men to haue greet trist in
God and drede no man ne puple, as longe as þei seruen treuli almyȝti God.

Þe seuenþe book, clepid Iudicum, telliþ þat þe puple of Israel was
reulid wiþ iugis eþer domesmen aftir þe deþ of Iosue, and sumtyme bi a
445 womman, Delbora. Whanne þe puple fel to grete synnes, and speciali to
idolatrie, God sente aduersaries on hem, þat turmentide þe Iewis ful soore
and killide many þousyndes of þem, and helde oþere vndur tribut and greet
þraldom. And whanne þe puple repentide verili, and cried to God wiþ al
her herte, he sente helpe to hem, and reisid a iuge þat ouercam her enemyes
450 and reulid hem wel in pees and in Goddis lawe.

Þis proces of Iudicum shulde stire cristen men to fle synne and loue
God þat doiþ so greet merci to hem þat repenten verili.

Þis book comprehendiþ þe stori of Ruth, þat was an heþene
womman and lefte her nacioun and idolatrie, and bileuyde in God and

---

Glosses and biblical references   416–20 Jos. 7   420–30 Jos. 8   422 'iebat': gibbet   431–4
Jos. 9   434–8 'kyngis' Jos. 10–11   438–40 Jos. 13–24   449 'a iuge', Samson (Judg. 13–16)

Variants   419 til] al α ι Q S, *om.* G (note)   • him] him for afore þis G ι Q   426 alle *om.* G ι Q   432
of Iosue … liyf] of iosue pees and lijf and oþer princis α S, of iosue pees and lyf of iosue and oþere pryncis
G ι Q (note)   436 aftirward] and þanne he G ι Q   442 seruen] serueden α β G ι Q S

455 kepte his lawe. Þerfor she was weddid to a noble man of þe Iewis, and is
set in þe genologie or kynrede of oure Sauyour.
   Þis storie shulde stire alle men to forsake her synne and serue God
treuli in al her liyf, for rewarde of heuenli blisse.
   Þe firste book of Kyngis telliþ hou þe prest Heli and his sones
460 weren repreuyd and slayn, for þei gouernyden yuele Goddis puple, and for
her synne and necligence þe puple dide myche synne and was ouercome of
heþene men, and þe arke of God was taken of heþene men, and þei killiden
many þousyndis of þe Iewis. And hou þe trewe child Samuel was a feiþful
profete of þe Lord and gouerned wel þe puple in Goddis seruyce and
465 riȝtfulnesse, and dide noon extorsioun | f. 3va | ne took ȝiftis of ony man,
ne coueitid ony mannus good, but dide alle þingis in his office iustli bifor
God and man. And whanne Samuel was eld he sette hise sones iugis on
Israel, and for þei bowiden aftir auerice, and token ȝiftis and peruertiden
doom, þe puple axiden a kyng on hem, to greet indignacioun of God and
470 harm of hemsilf.
   Þanne Saul, þat was pore and meke and souȝte þe assis of his fadir,
was maad kyng and dide wel a litil while, and aftirward for his pride and
coueitise he was repreued of God and pryued fro þe rewme, boþe he and
his kyn, and pore Dauiþ was chose kyng bi Goddis ordenaunce. For his
475 merci, mekenesse and charite, Dauiþ sparide Saul, his enemye, þat
pursuide him to deþ vniustli and was a traitour and blasfemere to God, and
not oneli spared him twies bitaken into hise hondis, whanne he myȝte haue
slayn him and ȝit ascapid harmles, but also lettide hise men to smyte him
whanne þei myȝten haue slayn him and scapid harmles, and ȝit þe wickid
480 tiraunt Saul pursuyde him for enuye and souȝte his deþ in many maneris,
and euere God kepte Dauiþ in alle perels and ȝeldide peyne to Saul for his
tirauntrie and wickidnesse, and made him to be slayn of heþene men.
   Þis process of þe [first] book of Kyngis shulde stire prestis to be not
necligent in her office neþer to be coueitouse, and stire seculer lordis to be
485 meke and iust to God and men.
   Þe secounde book of Kyngis telliþ first hou Dauiþ biweilide gretli
þe deþ of Saul and of Ionatas and of Goddis puple, and Dauiþ killide þe
man of Amalech þat killide Saul vttirli aftir þe deþ wounde of Saul and
brouȝte to Dauiþ þe coroun and bie of Saul. Aftir þis þe lynage of Iuda
490 corownede hym eþer anoyntide Dauiþ in Ebron, þat he shulde regne on þe
hows of Iuda, and þanne was longe werre bitwixe Hisboseth sone of Saul
and bitwixe þe hows of Dauiþ. Dauiþ encreesside euere and wexe strengere

---

Glosses and biblical references   455–6 Matt. 1:5   459–70 I Kings 1–8   459 'Heli': Eli   460
'repreuyd': reproved   462 'of'²: by   468 'bowiden': turned aside   471–82 I Kings 9–31   473
'pryued fro': deprived of   486–9 2 Kings 1   489 'bie': ring   489–96 2 Kings 2–4

Variants   463 þousyndis] þousend G ι Q   470 of] to G ι Q T   471 þat] whil he G ι Q Crowley   478
ascapid] haue scapid G ι Q   483 first *om.* β P S   • \be/   489 \þis/

and strengere, and þe hows of Saul decreessid ech dai, and Dauiþ regnede
seuene ȝeer in Ebron and gat sixe sones. Also Dauiþ made myche sorewe
495 for þe deþ of Abner, whanne Ioab hadde killid hym bi tresoun. Also Dauiþ
killide Banaa and Rechab, þat killiden bi tresoun Hisboseth, his enemye.
Þanne al Israel cam into Ebron and anoyntide Dauiþ into kyng of Israel,
and Dauiþ regnyde on Iuda in Ebron seuene ȝeer and an half, and regnyde
in Ierusalem xxxiij. ȝeer on al Israel and Iuda, and was xxx. ȝeer eld
500 whanne he bigan to regne, and regnyde xl. ȝeer.
Aftir þis þe noble kyng Dauiþ hadde twies victorie aȝenus Filisteis.
Þanne Dauiþ took þritti þousynde of chosen men of Israel to brynge to his
place þe arke of God. For reuerence and deuocioun Dauiþ made grete
mynstrelsie and mekid himsilf bifor þe arke, and suffrid rebukyng of
505 Mychol, þe douȝter of Saul. Þerfor Dauiþ þouȝte to bilde an hows to þe
arke of God. Þanne God telde to Dauiþ þat his sone shulde bilde þis hows,
and þe troone of þe rewme of Dauiþ shal be stable wiþouten ende, and þis
is fillid in Crist. Þanne Dauiþ hadde victorie of many londis, and made þo
tributarie to Israel, and God kepte Dauiþ in alle þingis to which he ȝede
510 forþ. And Dauiþ dide doom and riȝtfulnesse to al his puple, and he dide
merci and curtesie to Mifiboseth, sone of Ionathas.
Aftir þese þingis, Dauiþ dwellide at home, whanne Io| vb |ab and þe
oost wente to batel, and in þat tyme Dauiþ dide avoutrie wiþ Bersabe, þe
wiyf of Vrie, and procurid þe deeþ of Vrie bi tresoun. Þanne God sente
515 Nathan þe profete to repreue Dauiþ of þis synne, and he took mekeli his
repreuyng, and knoulechide þat he synnede aȝenus God, and God forȝaf þe
synne; but swerd and persecucioun ȝede neuere awei fro his hows, for God
killide þe sone of Bersabee, and o sone of Dauiþ killide anoþere, and
Absolon his sone roos aȝenus him and droof him out of Ierusalem and
520 souȝte wiþ stronge oost to sle him. Þanne Dauiþ ȝede out of Ierusalem on
his feet, and stiede wiþ bare feet into þe hiȝnesse of þe hil of Olyuete, and
wepte, and al his puple wepte bittirli. And Dauiþ mekide him to God and
seide 'if God seiþ to me "þou plesist not me", I am redi; do he þat þat is
good bifor himsilf'. Þanne Semei, þat was of þe kyn of Saul, dispiside
525 Dauiþ and clepide him a manqueller and a man of Belial and a rauenour of
þe rewme, and he cursid Dauiþ and castide stoones and erȝe aȝenus Dauiþ
and aȝenus alle þe seruauntis of kyng Dauiþ. And whanne Abisai wolde sle
þis cursere Dauiþ bad him suffre Semei to curse him, and seide God

.

Glosses and biblical references   497–500 2 Kings 5   501–5 2 Kings 6   505–7 'ende' 2 Kings
7   508 'fillid': fulfilled   508–11 2 Kings 8–9   509 'kepte': preserved   512–14 2 Kings 11   514
'Vrie': Uriah   514–20 2 Kings 12:1–14; 13   520–33 2 Kings 15:30–16:12   524 'bifor himsilf': in
his own eyes   526 'erȝe': earth

Variants   500 and he regnide G ι Q   501 twies victorie] twey victories G ι Q S   507 stable] stablichid
T   513 in þat tyme Dauiþ *om.* G ι Q   517 ȝede] wente G ι Q   523 þat þat is] þat is G ι Q

comaundide him þat he curse Dauiþ. And þe kyng seide to Abisai and to
530　alle his seruauntis: 'lo, my sone þat ʒede out of my wombe sekiþ my liyf,
þat is, to sle me. Hou myche more now þis sone of Gemyny suffre ʒe him
to curse bi comaundement of þe Lord, if in caas þe Lord biholde my
turment, and ʒelde good to me for þis cursyng todai'.

Aftirward Absolon defoulide openli his fadris wyues bifor al Israel.
535　Þanne Achitofel ʒaf a fel councel to pursue Dauiþ in þat nyʒt wiþ xij.
þousynde of men and sle him bifor þat he were war, but þis councel was
distroied by Goddis wille and bi a wiys councel of Chusi, þe frend of
Dauiþ. Þanne Absolon gaderide al þe power of Israel to make open werre
aʒenus his fadir. Neþeles, Dauiþ for pitee and charite comaundide þre
540　prynces of his oost to kepe Absolon alyue, þat he myʒte repente and be
saued. And when Dauiþ knew þat Absolon was slayn he made so greet
sorewe þat almoost he was deed, and al þe puple was in poynt to forsake
Dauiþ. Þanne for þis perel Dauiþ lefte his morenyng and sat openli in þe
ʒate to coumforte al his oost. Aftir þis þe council of al Israel cam to Dauiþ,
545　þat þei wolde brynge hym into his rewme worschipfuli, and Dauiþ forʒaf
þe open tresoun to hem þat þei hadden do bifore, and stirid swetli men of
Iuda þat weren speciali his treitours to come and brynge him into his
rewme, and forʒaf her tresoun, and he forʒaf þe souereyn tresoun to
Amasa, þat was of his owne kyn and was prince of þe oost of Absolon to
550　sle Dauiþ, and Dauiþ swoor to make þis Amasa prince nexte Ioab, and
forʒaf þe synne and cursyng and tresoun to Semey, and swoor þat he
shulde not die.

Ʒit bifor þat Dauiþ cam to Ierusalem a newe debate roos bitwixe
men of Israel and þe men of Iuda, for þis bryngyng aʒen of þe kyng was
555　not told first to men of Israel, and bi stiryng of Siba, a man of Belial þat
was of þe kyn of Saul, al | f. 4ra | Israel was departid fro Dauiþ and suede
þis Siba. And in þis tyme Ioab killide bi tresoun þe noble knyʒt Amasa.
Þanne þis Siba passide bi alle þe lynagis of Israel til into Habela and into
Bethmaka, and alle chosun men weren gaderid to hym. And Ioab and his
560　oost bisegiden þese citees and wolde distrie þe greete citee Habela, and a
wiys womman of þe citee sauyde it bi hir councel, and made Siba to be
slayn and al þe puple to be saued on boþe sidis. Also seuene men of þe kyn
of Saul were slayn of Gabonytis, bi suffryng of Dauiþ and bi counsel of
God, for Saul killide wickidli þe men of Gabaon, and for þis synne of Saul

Glosses and biblical references　　532 'in caas': perchance　533 'for': in exchange for　534–8 2
Kings 16:20–3; 17:1–14　538–41 2 Kings 17:24; 18:5　541–52 2 Kings 19:4–23　542 'in poynt to':
on the point of　545 'þat': [saying] that　547 'his treitours': traitors against him　551 'forʒaf
… to Semey': forgave Semey　553–66 2 Kings 20–1:1　554–5 'was not': had not been　563
'suffryng': suffrance

Variants　　529 þat he curse] to curse G ι Q　541 \when/　545 wolde] shulden G ι Q

565 hungur was maad þre ʒeer in þe daies of Dauiþ, and aftir þis veniaunce don
on þe hows of Saul God dide merci to þe lond.

Þanne is set a greet song of Dauiþ which he spak to God whanne he
hadde delyueride him fro þe hond of alle his enemyes. Þanne sueþ þe
noumbre of stronge men of Dauiþ. At þe laste Dauiþ, for pride and aʒenus
570 þe lawe, noumbride þe puple of Israel, and þerfor lxx. þousynde of men
weren deed bi pestilence. Þanne Dauiþ repentide sore and mekid him to
God, and seide þus: 'I it am þat synnede and I dide wickidli. What han þese
men do þat ben sheep', þat is, symple and innocent, 'in comparisoun of
me? I biseche þat þyn hond be turned aʒenus me and aʒenus þe hows of
575 my fadir'. Þanne God sente his profete Gad to him, and bad him make an
auter and offre brent sacrifices and pesible sacrifices, and God dide merci
to þe lond and þe veniaunce ceesside of Israel.

Þe processe of þis secounde book ouʒte to stire kyngis and lordis to
merci and riʒtfulnesse, and euere to be war of idilnesse, þat brouʒte
580 [Dauiþ] to auoutrie and oþere meschefs, and euere to be meke to God and
his prestis, and soore repente of her mysdedis and make amendis to God
and men, and wilfuli forʒyue wrongis don to hem, and euere be war of
pride and extorciouns, lest God take veniaunce on al þe puple as he dide on
Dauiþ and his puple, and euere to be pacient and merciful, as Dauiþ was, to
585 gete remyssioun of synnes bifor don, and to gete pees and prosperite and
heuenli blis wiþouten ende.

Chapter 5

The þridde book of Kyngis telliþ first hou Adonyas, sone of Dauiþ, wolde
haue regned, and Dauiþ in his liyf ordeynede Salomon to be king, and he
regnyde bifor þe deþ of Dauiþ. Þanne Adonyas fledde for drede to þe
590 tabernacle of God, and heeld þe corner of þe auter til Salamon seide þat if
he were a good man he shulde not die, ellis, if yuele were founden in him,
he shulde die. Þanne Dauiþ, in þe tyme of his diyng, chargide Salomon to
kepe wel Goddis lawe, and to quyte to þe sones of Bersalli þe treuþe and
kyndnesse of her fadir, and to punysche Ioab for his trecherous
595 manquelling of Abner and of Amasa in þe tyme of pees, and to punysche
wiseli Semey for his worste cursyng which he dide to Dauiþ. Aftir þese
þingis Salomon made Adonyas to be slayn, for he purposide gilefuli to be
king, and Salamon castide awei Abiathar, þat he was not þe prest of þe
Lord, and exilid him also, for he assentid to Adonyas and was traitour to þe

Glosses and biblical references   567–8 2 Kings 22   568–9 2 Kings 23   569–77 2 Kings
24   570 'noumbride': counted   572 'I it am': I am he   587–92 3 Kings 1   592–606 3 Kings
2   593 'quyte': requite

Variants   574 biseeche þee þat G ι Q   580 Dauiþ *om.*   581 soore] soone S *sec. m.* T   • repente hire
G ι Q

600 kyng. Also Salamon comaundide Ioab to be slayn in þe taber| rb |[na]cle at
þe auter, for he hadde slayn gilefuli twei princes in pees, wiþout wityng of
Dauiþ. And þe kyng ordeyned Sadoch prest for Abiathar. Þanne þe kyng
comaundid Semei þat he shulde not go out of Ierusalem, and if he passide
þe stronde of Cedron he shulde be deed, and Semei acceptid þis, and for he
605 passid þese boondis þe kyng comaundide him to be slayn, and so he was
slayn bi comaundement of þe kyng.

Aftir þese þingis þe rewme was confermed into þe hondis of
Salomon, and he weddide þe douȝtir of Farao kyng of Egipt. Þanne God
bad Salomon axe of him what hym likide, and he axide þat God shulde
610 ȝyue to hym a wiys herte, þat he myȝte deme his puple and make
discrecioun eþer departing bitiwixe good and yuel. And þis axing pleside
God ful myche; þerfore God ȝaf to hym a wiys herte and vndurstonding, in
so myche þat noon bifor him was liyk him, neþer shal rise aftir him. Also
God ȝaf to him richesse and glorie, þat noon among kingis was liyk him in
615 alle daies bifore. Þanne, for Salomon ȝaf a wiys sentence of doom bitwixe
twei comyn wymmen, þat passid þe wit of comyne men, þei dredden þe
king and siȝen þat Goddis wisdom was in him to make doom. Þanne is told
þe worschipful meynee and houshold of Salomon.

Aftir þese þingis Salomon bildide a noble hows to hymsilf and a
620 famouse temple to God in Ierusalem, and aftir þat þe temple was fulli maad
alle þe eldere men and princes of lynagis and þe duykis of meynees of þe
children of Israel weren gaderid to kyng Salomon in Ierusalem to brynge
þe arke of God fro Sion into his owne place in þe temple. Þanne þe kyng
axid of God many preieris and profites for hem þat preiede deuoutli in þe
625 temple, and God grauntide þo. Aftir þese þingis God halewid þe temple
and certefiede to Salomon þat if he kepte alle his comaundementis he
shulde sette þe troone of Salomons rewme in Israel wiþouten ende, and if
þe puple of Israel and her children keptyn not Goddis heestis but
worshipiden alien goddis he shal do awei Israel fro þe face of lond which
630 he ȝaf to hem, and God shal caste awei fro his siȝt þe temple which he
halewide to his name, and Israel shal be into a prouerbe and fable eþer tale
to alle puplis, and þis hows shal be into ensaumple.

After þis þe queene of Saba cam to Salomon, and hadde greet arai
of men and of iewelis, and ȝaf many iewelis to Salomon and he aȝen to hir.
635 Also Salomon tauȝte hir alle þingis þat she hadde in her herte, and she
blesside God and Salomon and his seruauntis, and ȝede into her lond.

Glosses and biblical references   602 'for': in place of   604 'Cedron': Kidron   607–18 3 Kings
3, 4   609 'what hym likide': whatever pleased him   613 'shal': shall [anyone like him]   617
'siȝen': saw   619–32 3 Kings 5–9   631 'into': as   633–41 3 Kings 10   633 'Saba': Sheba   634 'he
aȝen': he [gave many jewels] in return

Variants   600 Also] and G ι Q   • taber/cle   621 dukis and of meynees α G ι Q S *pr. m.* Crowley
(note)   623 in] in to   631 and fable] eiþir fable G ι Q

Þanne Salomon made many sheeldis and bokelers of gold and made a greet
troone of yuer and cloþid it wiþ fyn gold. Þanne kyng Salomon was
magnefied ouer alle kyngis of erþe in richessis and wisdom, and al erþe
640   desiride to se his face and to here his wisdom, which his God hadde ȝeue in
his herte.

    Aftir alle þese þingis Salomon, whanne he was elde, louede gretli
mani heþene wymmen and hadde a þousende wyues, principals and
secoundaries, and þanne his herte was bishrewid and peruertid bi þo
645   wymmen, þat he suede alien goddis and worshipide hem. Þerfor God
reiside an aduersarie to Salomon in his liyf, and departide his rewme in þe
tyme of Roboam his sone, and ȝaf ten lynagis to Ieroboam his seruaunt,
and kepte o lynage to his sone for þe merit of Dauiþ his fadir. And þis
departing | f. 4va | bifel myche, for Roboam forsook þe councel of elde and
650   wise men and suede þe councel of ȝonge men, and spak harde wordis to þe
puple. Þanne Roboam gaderide proudli al þe hows of Iuda and þe lynage of
Beniamyn, an hundrid þousynde and foure score þousynde of chosun men
and werriours, þat þei shulden fiȝte aȝenus þe hows of Israel and brynge
aȝen þe rewme to Roboam þe sone of Salomon. But God forbad þis werre
655   to Roboam and al his puple, for whi þis word of departing of þe rewme was
doon of God.

    Þanne Ieroboam made twei goldun caluys and bad Israel worschipe
þo and stie no more to Ierusalem, and seide 'Israel, lo, þese ben þi goddis
þat ledden þee out of þe lond of Egipt', and he made vnworþi prestis of þe
660   laste men of þe puple, þat were not of þe sones of Leuy, and he made
templis in hiȝ places. Also, whanne Ieroboam stood on þe auter and castide
encense, a man of God cam fro Iuda bi þe word of God and seide 'a sone,
Iosias bi name, shal be bore to þe hows of Dauiþ, and he shal sle on þis
auter þe prestis of hiȝ places þat brennen now encense in þis auter, and he
665   shal brenne boonys of men on þis auter'. And þe profete ȝaf þis signe, þat
þe auter shulde be cleft and þe aischis þerinne shal be shed out. Þanne
Ieroboam helde forþ his hond and bad take þat profete, and his hond was
drie and he myȝte not drawe it aȝen, and bi preier of þe profete þe hond
was heelid. And þe signe bifel on þe auter as þe profete seide, and for þat
670   þe profete eet breed in þat place aȝenus Goddis bidding, ȝhe bi disseit of a
false profete, þe trewe profete of God was slayn of a lioun in þe weie
homward. Aftir þese wordis Ieroboam turnyde not aȝen fro his worste

Glosses and biblical references   **638** 'yuer': ivory   **640** 'ȝeue': given   **642–8** 3 Kings
11   **648–61** 3 Kings 12   **649** 'bifel myche': had important consequences   **653–4** 'brynge aȝen':
return   **654–5** 'forbad þis werre to Roboam': forbade Roboam to wage this war   **660** 'laste
men': men of least rank   **661–76** 3 Kings 13   **662** 'man of God': prophet   **667** 'bad take þat
profete': ordered that prophet to be seized   **668** 'drawe it aȝen': withdraw it

Variants   **639** richessis] richesse β G ι Q T   **643** principals] principal α β S   **648** his ˣseruauntˣ   **665**
signe] tokene G ι Q   **666** aischis] asche α β S   **669** signe] tokene G ι Q

weie, but aȝenward of þe laste puple he made prestis of þe hiȝ places.
Whoeuere wolde fille his hond was maad prest of hiȝ places, and for þis
675 cause þe hows of Ieroboam synnede, and was distriede and doon awei fro
þe face of erþe.

Aftir þis þe profete A[h]ia, þat was blynd for age, knew þe wiyf of
Ieroboam, þat feynede hir to be anoþere womman, and he biforseid to hir
þat hir siyk sone shuld die in her entryng in to hir hows, and þat þe hows of
680 Ieroboam shulde be distroied vttirli for his synnes, and Israel shal be
dryuun out of his good lond for þe synnes of Ieroboam, þat synnede and
made Israel to do synne. Also þe puple of Iuda dide idolatrie; þerfor þe
king of Egipt took awei þe tresours of Goddis hows and of þe kyngis hows,
and þe goldun sheldis of Salomon, for which Roboam made sheldis of bras.
685 And batel was bitwixe Roboam and Ieroboam in alle daies. Þanne Abia
regnyde þre ȝeer on Iuda and ȝede in alle þe synnes of his fadir. Aftir him
roos kyng Asa in Iuda, and he dide riȝtfulnesse bifor God and dide awei
idolatrie and sodomytes fro þe lond, and his herte was parfit wiþ God in
alle daies. And, shortli, among alle þe kingis of Israel was noon feiþful to
690 God. Summe weren good among þe kyngis of Iuda, and þis figureþ þat
among men of hooli chirche ben summe goode, but among eretikis is noon
good outerli, as Ierom seiþ.

Aftir many yuele kyngis of Israel [roos] Achab, þe worste of alle
bifore him, and he weddid Iesabel, an heþene womman, þe douȝtir of
695 Mechael kyng of Sidonyes. And Achab dide manyfold idolatrie. Þanne
roos | vb | Elie þe profete, and seide to Achab þat in þre ȝeer and an half
neþer reyn ne dew shal be. Aftir þis, þe profete Elie hidde hymsilf in þe
stronde of Carith aȝenus Iordan, and drank watir and was fed of rauenes
þere, whiche brouȝten to him breed and fleish in þe euentid and morewtid.
700 And aftir þat þe stronde was dried up, God bad Elie go into Sarepta of
Sidonyes, and þere he was fed of a widewe, and þe pot of meele and þe pot
of oile failide not to þe widewe til God ȝaf reyn on erþe. Þanne Elie reiside
to liyf þe deed child of a womman at whom he was myche susteyned. And
aftir many daies God bad Elie shewe hym to Achab, þat God shulde ȝyue
705 reyn on þe lond, and Elie dide so, and greet hungur was in Samarie. Þanne
Elie apperide first to Abdie, þat dredde God and fedde an hundrid profetis
of God whanne Iesabel killide þe profetis of God. And Elie swoor to Abdie
bi þe Lord of oostis þat he wolde appere in þat dai to Achab. Þanne Achab

---

Glosses and biblical references   674 'fille' [with bribes] (note)   677–85 'daies' 3 Kings 14   677
'knew': had sexual intercourse with   678 'biforseid': prophesied   681 'his': its   683 'of'[2, 3]:
from   684 'for': in place of   • 'Roboam': Rehoboam   685–9 3 Kings 15:1–14   685 'Abia':
Abijah   693–5 'idolatrie' 3 Kings 16:29–33   695–703 3 Kings 17   696 'Elie': Elijah   696 'in':
for   703 'at whom': at whose house   703–15 3 Kings 18

Variants   674 fille] fillide α β S (note)   • hond and was α β P S *sec. m.* (note)   677 abia   • age] eelde α
β G ι Q S   686 \him/   693 roos] was

axide Elie, 'wher þou art he þat disturblest Israel?' And Elie seide 'not I
710 disturblide Israel but þou and þe hows of þi fadir, þat han forsake Goddis
heestis and han sued baalym, han dist[urbl]ed Israel'. Aftir þis þe profete
Elie conuyctid bi an open myracle eiȝte hundrid and fifti profetis of Baal of
open idolatrie, and killide hem alle, wiþ help of þe puple þat bileuyde to
God for þe greet myracle. And aftir þis God sente greet reyn, and Elie ran
715 bifor Achab to þe citee I[e]srael.

Aftir þese þingis Elie fledde for drede of Iesabel, þat manaasside to
sle hym, and whanne he hadde fledde into desert bi þe iournei of oo dai he
axid of God to die, and whanne he slepte an aungel bad him rise and eet
breed baken vndur aischis and drynke watir, and he ȝede in þe strengþe of
720 þat mete xl. daies and xl. nyȝtis, til to Oreb, þe hil of God. And whanne he
was hid þere in a denne, and seide þat he was left aloone a profete of þe
Lord, and þei souȝten to sle hym, God bad him go to Damask and anoynte
Asael kyng on Sirie, and anoynte Hieu kyng on Israel, and anoynte Elisee a
profete for him, and þese þre shulden do veniaunce on trespassours and sle
725 hem. And God left to himsilf seuene þousynde of men in Israel whos knees
were not bowid bifor Baal. Þanne it sueþ hou Elisee suede Elie.

Aftir þese þingis kyng Achab hadde twei grete and meruelouse
victories aȝenus Benadab kyng of Sirie, for he blasfemyde God of Israel,
and for kyng Achab dide fals merci and killide not þis blasfeme[re]
730 Benadab, whom God bitook into his hondis, God sente a profete to Achab
and telde þus, 'for þou suffridist a man worþi þe deþ to go fro þin hond, þi
liyf shal be for his liyf, and þi puple shal be for his puple'. Aftirward
Iesabel þe queene made Nabath to be stooned to deþ bi fals witnesse and
assent of Achab, for he nolde chaunge ne selle his vyner to þe kyng, and
735 whanne Achab ȝede doun to take possessioun of þis vyner God bad Elie
mete him and seie þus: 'þou hast slayn and hast take possessioun. Þe Lord
seiþ þese þingis: in þis place wherinne doggis lickiden þe blood of Nabath,
þei shulen licke also þi blood'. And Achab seide to Elie 'wher þou hast
founde me, þin enemye?'. And Elie | f. 5ra | seide: 'I haue founde, for þou
740 art seeld to do yuele in Goddis siȝt; þerfor God shal distroie and sle ech
man of þe hows of Achab, and ȝyue his hows as þe hows of Ieroboam and
as þe hows of Baasa, for Achab terride God to wraþþe and made Israel to
do synne. Also doggis shulen ete Iesabel in þe feeld of I[e]srael. If Achab
die in þe citee, doggis shulen ete him, if he die in þe feeld, briddis of þe eir

Glosses and biblical references   709 'wher þou art': art thou   711 'baalym': idols   712
'conuyctid': convinced   716–26 3 Kings 19   724 'for him': in his place   725 'left to': retained for
727–32 3 Kings 20   728 'Benadab': Ben–hadad   732–48 3 Kings 21   734 'chaunge': exchange
• 'vyner': vineyard   738 'wher þou hast': hast thou   740 'seeld': sold   742 'terride': provoked

Variants   709 disturblest] distroublist α S, distorbeleth β   711 distried   715 [to] ˣbiˣ\to / • Iesrael]
israel P S, of israel T   717 oo] a G ι Q   729 blasfeme α β P S   730 \god/   743 israel P S T   744 dieþ
α β S

745   shulen ete him'. Noon oþere was sich as Achab, þat was seld to do yuele
      bifor God, for whi Iesabel his wiyf excitid him, and he dide abhomynable
      idolatrie. Þanne Achab dide ful greet penaunce and was mekid bifor God;
      þerfor God brou3te not in þis yuel in his daies, but in þe daies of his sone.
          In þe þridde 3eer aftir þese þingis, aboute foure hundrid profetis of
750   Baal counselide Achab to make werre a3enus þe kyng of Sirie for a cite
      clepid Ramoth of Galaad, and bihi3ten victorie and prosperite to Achab.
      But Mychee, o profete of God, telde to Achab in Goddis name þat þe spirit
      of leesyng disseyuede [him] bi his fals profetis, and þat Achab shulde be
      slayn in þat batel. And so it bifel in dede, but Myche was dispisid and beten
755   of þe false profetis, and was prisoned and purposed to be slayn of þe king,
      whanne he cam a3en in pees. And kyng Iosaphat, a good man, was in þis
      batel wiþ cursid Achab, but Achab was slayn, and doggis lickiden his
      blood, and Iosaphat was saued bi Goddis help. Þanne roos Ocosias kyng of
      Israel for Achab his fadir, and Ocosias worshipide Baal and terride God to
760   ire bi alle þingis whiche his fadir hadde do.
          Þis process of þe þridde book of Kingis shulde stire kyngis and
      lordis to be merciful and pitouse on her sugetis þat trespassen a3enus hem,
      and in alle þingis eschewe idilnesse, leccherie, tresoun, idolatrie and false
      counselours and vnwise, and euere distroie synne, and take councel at hooli
765   scripture and trewe profetis, and triste not to false profetis, be þei neuere so
      many and crie faste a3enus oon or fewe trewe men.

Chapter 6

      The fourþe book of Kingis telliþ in general hou þe rewme of Israel and þe
      rewme of Iuda weren conquerid of heþene men, for many synnes which þei
      diden a3enus God and men [and] weren obstynat and diden not fruytful
770   penaunce in dew tyme. First it telliþ in special hou þe wickid kyng Ocosias
      sente to take councel at Bel3abub wher he my3te lyue and rekyuere of his
      siyknesse. Þerfor God sente Elie þe profete to telle to him þat he shulde die
      and go not doun of his bed. Þanne þis kyng sente to Elie a prince on fifti
      men and fifti men wiþ hym to clepe Elie to þe kyng, and fier cam doun fro
775   heuene and deuouride þis prince and þe fifti men þat weren wiþ him, for in
      scorn þei clepiden Elie þe man of God, and in liyk maner fier deuouride
      anoþere prince and fifti men wiþ him. Þe þridde prince and his fifti men þat
      mekid hem to God and to þe profete were saued on lyue. And God bad Elie

Glosses and biblical references   746 'excitid': incited   749–60 3 Kings 22   752 'Mychee':
Micaiah   753 'leesyng': lying   756 'Iosaphat': Jehoshaphat   758 'Ocosias': Ahaziah   759 'for': in
place of   762 'sugetis': subjects   770–80 4 Kings 1   771 'wher': whether

Variants   753 him *om.*   760 whiche followed by 2-letter erasure   761–2 kyngis and lordis] lordis and
kyngis G ɪ Q   769 and²] þat

go doun wiþ hem to þe kyng and repreue him of his synne, and telle to þe
780   kyng himsilf þat he shal die and go not doun of his bed.

Aftir þis þe profete Elie shulde be rauyschid awei fro erþe, and
Elise knew þis, and sued him in ech place til to þe rauyschyng. And Elie
smoot wiþ his mantil þe watris of Iordan and þo weren departid þerbi, and
Elie and Elisee ȝeden ouer bi þe drie botme þerof. Þanne Elie was
785   rauyschid in a | rb | chare of fier fro Elisee, and stiede bi a whirlewynd into
heuene. And þe double spirit of Elie restide on Elisee, and wiþ þe mantil of
Elie Elise smoot twies þe watris of Iordan, and in þe secounde tyme þo
weren departid and Elisee passide ouer. Aftirward Elise dwellide in Ierico
and heelid þe watris fro bittirnesse and bareynnesse bi puttyng of salt in þe
790   watir. Þanne Elise stiede into Bethel, and as he stiede bi þe weie litle
children ȝeden out of þe citee and seiden to him in scorn 'þou ballard, stie
up!' And he cursid hem in þe name of God, and twei beeris ȝede out of þe
forest and torente of hem xlij. children.

Aftir þese þingis Ioram, þe kyng of Israel, and Iosephat, þe kyng of
795   Iuda, and also þe þridde kyng þat was kyng of Edom, weren in desert and
hadden no watir and weren in poynt of perischyng. Þese þre kingis camen
to Elisee for helpe, and bi spirit of profesie he bad hem make dichis, and
þei sien neþer wynd neþer reyn, and þe botme of dichis was fillid of watris.
And he biforseid þat God shulde bitake Moab into þe hondis of þese
800   kyngis, and þei shulden distroie citees and feeldis and trees, and þus it was
do in dede. Also Elisee multipliede a litil oile and made a pore widewe fille
many vessels þerof, and bad her paie her dettis bi sum þerof, and þat she
and hir sones shulde lyue bi þe residue þerof. Aftirward Elisee biforseid to
a good womman þat herboride him freli and largeli þat she shulde
805   conseyue a sone, and whanne Elisee knew þat þis sone was deed he sente
his seruaunt Gieȝi wiþ his staf to reise him, and neþer vois ne feelyng was
in þe child. Þanne Elisee entride into a closet where þe child lai deed, and
preiede to God, and lai on þe child, and leide his mouþ to þe mouþ of child
and his hondis on þe childis hondis, and þe child ȝoxide seuene siþis and
810   openyde hise iȝen, and Elisee bitook þe child quyk to his modir. Also
Elisee, whanne hungur was in Galgala, heelid þe pot of noiful mete bi
sending in of meele þat no more bittirnesse was in þe mete. Þanne Elisee
made a litil breed to suffice to an hundrid men, and þei leften relifs.

Whanne þe kyng of Sirie sente lettris to þe kyng of Israel þat he

---

Glosses and biblical references   781–93 4 Kings 2   782 'Elise': Elisha   791–2 'ballard, stie up!':
go up, baldhead   793 'torente … children': tore 42 of those children apart   794–801 3 Kings
3   794 'Ioram': Jehoram   798 'sien': saw   801–13 4 Kings 4   804 'herboride him': lodged him
in her house   804 'freli and largeli': unreservedly and generously   806 'Gieȝi': Gehazi   809
'ȝoxide seuene siþis': yawned seven times   811 'noiful': harmful   812 'of meele þat': some flour
so that   813 'relifs': remains   814–26 4 Kings 5

Variants   787 Elise] he G ι Q   799 bitake] bifor take   801 fille] to multiplie G   810 Also] and G ι Q

815 shulde cure Naaman of his lepre, and þe kyng of Israel torente his cloþis
     for sorewe, Elisee bad þat Naaman shulde be waischun seuene siþis in þe
     watir of Iordan, and so he shulde be curid, and þus it was doon in dede.
     And þanne Naaman knoulechide þat noon oþere god is in al erþe [no] but
     oneli þe God of Israel. And Elisee took no ʒifte, ʒhe freli proferid and
820 preesede of Naaman. Þanne Gieʒi ran aftir Naaman, vnwiting or not
     consenting his maister, and made a leesyng þat Elisee sente to him þat he
     shulde ʒyue a talent of siluer and double chaunging cloþis to two ʒonge
     men of þe sones of profetis. And Naaman constreynede him to take þe
     double þat he axide, and ordeynede twei children to bere bifor him. But
825 herfor Elisee seide þat þe lepre of Naaman shulde cleue to Gieʒi and to his
     seed wiþouten ende, and Gieʒi ʒede out fro Elise and was a mesel as snow.
         Whanne þe sones of profetis ʒeden to þe wode to hewe doun wode
     to bilde places to hem to dwelle inne, þe iren of an axe fel doun into watir,
     and Helisee cast doun þe tree or helue, and þe iren houyde and was takun
830 up þerbi. Whanne þe kyng of Sirie sette buyschementis priueli aʒenus þe
     kyng of Israel, Elisee warnyde þe kyng of Israel þerof, and whanne it
     | f.5va | was certefied to þe kyng of Sirie þat Elisee teld his priuytees to þe
     kyng of Israel þe kyng of Sirie sente a greet multitude of þe oost to take
     Elisee, and whanne þe oost cumpasside þe citee Dotaym, wherinne Elisee
835 was, God made þis oost blynde at þe preiere of Elisee. And so he ledde
     hem into þe myddis of Samarie, and whanne þe king of Israel wolde sle
     hem Elise seide nai, but bad make redi a feeste to hem, and let hem go in
     pees to her lord. And whanne ful stronge hungur was in Samarie, þat
     wymmen eten her owne children, oo womman axide doom of þe kyng
840 aʒenus anoþere womman, þat wolde not bi couenaunt brynge forþ her child
     to be eten, whanne þei hadden ete þe child of þe firste womman. Þanne þe
     king, þat werid þe heire next his bodi, torente hise cloþis for sorewe and
     swoor strongli þat in þat dai he wolde girde of þe heed of Elisee. Elise
     bifor-knew þe comyng of þis messanger to do þis dede, and bad men close
845 þe dore and suffre not hym for to entre, for his lord comeþ anoon aftir hym
     to reuoke his ooþ and sentense. Þanne Elisee seide, in Goddis name, þat
     tomorewe in þis tyme a buschel of wheete flour shal be for o statere, þat is,

Glosses and biblical references   **815** 'lepre': leprosy   **820** 'preesede of': pressed upon him by
820–1 'vnwiting … maister': his master not knowing or not consenting   **821** 'made a leesyng':
told the lie   **822** 'double chaunging cloþis': two changes of clothes   **823–4** 'þe double þat he
axide': twice what he asked   **824** 'bere': carry [them]   **826** 'a mesel as snow': afflicted with
leprosy [looking] like snow   **827–46** 4 Kings 6   **828** 'to hem': for themselves   **829** 'tree or
helue': branch or piece of wood   **829** 'houyde': floated   **830** 'buyschementis': ambushes   **837**
'make redi a feeste to': a feast to be made ready for   **840** 'bi couenaunt': as the agreement
was   **842** 'werid þe heire': wore a hair-shirt   **845** 'his' [the messenger's]   **846–55** 4 Kings 7
847 'statere': shekel

Variants   **818** no *om.* P T

a litil quantite of monei as it were a peny, and twei buschels of barli for o
stater, in þe ȝate of Samarie. And Elisee seide to a greet duyk þat bileuyde
850 not to þis word 'þou shalt se it wiþ þin iȝen, and shalt not ete þerof'. And
þus it was in dede, for whanne þe oost of Sirie fledde bi nyȝte, for drede
þat God made among hem, þei leften alle her goodis and fledden nakid and
coueitiden oneli to saue her lyues, and whanne a buschel of wheete flour
was seeld on þe morewe for o statere þe kyng made þat noble duyk kepere
855 at þe ȝate, and þe cumpenye traden him to deþ, as Elisee biforseide. Also
Elisee spak to þe womman whose sone he made to lyue, and bad hir and hir
hows go a pilgrymage eþer go into a straunge lond, whereeuere she foond
couenable, for God shal brynge stronge hungur on þe lond seuene ȝeer, and
[at] þe seuene ȝeeris ende þe kyng restorid to hir alle her þingis and alle þe
860 reentis of feeldis in þe tyme of hir absence.

Benadab kyng of Sirie sente Asael to Elisee to enquere wher þis
kyng myȝte rekeuere of his sikenesse, and God shewide to Elisee þat
Benadab shulde die, and Elisee wepte ful soore whanne he siȝ Asael, for
God shewide to him þat Asael shulde be kyng of Sirie, and do many yuelis
865 to þe children of Israel: brenne her stronge citees, and sle bi swerd þe
ȝonge men of hem, and hurle doun þe litle children of hem, and kerue
wymmen wiþ childe. Ioram, þe sone of Iosaphat, dide yuel in Goddis siȝt,
as þe hows of Achab dide, for þe douȝtir of Achab was his wiyf. But God
nolde distrie Iuda for Dauiþ his seruaunt, as he bihiȝte to hym to ȝyue a
870 lanterne to him and to his sones in alle daies.

Aftir þese þingis Elisee bad oon of þe sones of profetis anoynte
Hieu into kyng of Israel and seie to him 'þou shalt distrie þe hows of
Achab, and God shal make it as þe hows of Ieroboam, and doggis shulen
ete Iesabel in þe feeld of I[e]srael, and noon shal birie hir'. And Hieu
875 killide Ioram king of Israel and Ocosias kyng of Iuda, and Iesabel þe cursid
queene, and doggis eeten þe fleish [of Iesabel], and hir fleish | vb | was as a
toord on þe face of erþe. Þanne Hieu made lxx. sones of Achab to be slayn
of her keperis and nurschers, and he killide xlij. men, briþeren of Ocosias,
and aftir þis doing Hieu feynede hym to worschipe Baal more þan Achab
880 dide, and bi þis feynyng he gaderide togidere alle þe profetis and prestis
and seruauntis of Baal in þe temple of Baal, and killide hem alle, and cast
out of þe temple of Baal his ymage, and brent it and droof it al to dust, and

---

Glosses and biblical references   855 'traden': trod   855–70 4 Kings 8:1–19   856 'made to
lyue': restored to life   857 'hows go a pilgrymage': household make a journey (note)   858
'couenable': suitable   861 'Asael': Hazael   866 'kerue': slit open   869 'for': for the sake of
871–7 4 Kings 9   872 'Hieu': Jehu   877–87 4 Kings 10   878 'keperis and nurschers': guardians
and nurses

Variants   857 eþer go into a straunge lond] eiþer straunge lond α β G ι Q S (note)   859 at *om.*   865
brenne of α G ι Q S   866 hurle doun] hurle G ι Q, hurliden α   874 israel P S   876 of Iesabel *om.*   • as
om. α G ι Q S

distriede þe hows of Baal and made gongis for it, and so Hieu dide awei
Baal fro Israel. Neþeles, Hieu ȝede not awei fro þe synnes of Ieroboam, ne
885   forsook goldun calues þat weren in Bethel and Dan, but, for Hieu dide þis
vengiaunce aȝenus þe hows of Achab, God seide þat his sones til to þe
fourþe generacioun shulen sitte on þe troone of Israel.

Þanne Athalia, þe modir of Ocosias, whanne hir sone was deed
killide al þe blood of þe kyng, and regnyde sixe ȝeer. But Ioas, þe sone of
890   Ocosias kyng, was kept priueli sixe ȝeer in þe temple of God, and in þe
seuenþe ȝeer he was maad kyng bi help of Ioiada þe grete prest, and
Athalia was slayn. Þerfor Ioiada made a boond of pees bitwixe God and þe
kyng and puple, þat it shulde be þe puple of God, and bitwixe þe kyng and
þe puple, and þe puple distriede þe auters of Baal and al tobraken his
895   ymagis, and killiden Mathan þe prest of Baal bifor þe auter. Þis Ioas bigan
to regne whanne he was seuene ȝeer eeld, and regnyde xl. ȝeer in
Ierusalem and dide riȝtfulnesse bifor God in alle þe daies in which Ioiada
þe prest tauȝte him. And Ioas bad prestis take al þe monei þat was offrid
for prys of soulis and bi fre wille to make reparacioun of þe temple, and
900   for prestis weren necligent in þis reparacioun Ioas þe kyng bad þe prestis
ȝelde þis monei to reparacioun, and take it no more. And þe chaunceler of
þe kyng and þe bischop Ioiada helden out of þe arke þe monei, and ȝauen it
into þe hond of maistris of werkmen, and þei spendiden it wel in þis office
and necessarie reparacioun, and maden no rekenyng to souereyns but
905   tretiden þis monei in feiþ and good conscience. For as myche as Asael
kyng of Sirie cam wiþ his oost to werre aȝenus Ierusalem, Ioas kyng of
Iuda took alle þingis whiche hise fadris hadden halewid and which he
hadde offrid, and al þe siluer þat myȝte be founde in þe tresours of þe
temple of God and in [þe paleis] of þe kyng, and sente al to Asael kyng of
910   Sirie, and he ȝede awei fro Ierusalem. Þe seruauntis of Ioas sworen
togidere and killiden him, and Amasias his sone regnyde for him. Ioachas
þe sone of Hieu regnyde on Israel, and dide yuele as Ieroboam dide; þerfor
God bitook Israel into þe hondis of Asael kyng of Sirie and of Benadab his
sone in alle daies, þat þer weren not left to Ioachas of al þe puple of Israel
915   no but fyue hundrid horsemen and ten chares and ten þousynde of footmen.
Þanne Ioachas | f. 6ra| bisouȝte God, and he ȝaf a sauyour to Israel, and
Israel was delyuerid fro þe hond of þe kyng of Sirie.

Þanne Elise fel into a greet sikenesse bi which he was deed, and
whanne Ioas kyng of Israel cam to him and wepte Elisee bad hym brynge a
920   bowe and arowis, and bad him sette his hond on þe bowe, and Elisee sette

---

Glosses and biblical references   883 'gongis for it': latrines in its place   888–96 'eeld' 4 Kings 11
892 'Ioiada': Jehoiada   894 'al tobraken': thoroughly broke in pieces   896–911 4 Kings 12   911–
29 4 Kings 13   911 'Ioachas': Jehoahaz   918 'bi which he was deed': from which he died

Variants   893–4 and bitwixe … puple *om.* G ι Q Crowley   895 Ioas] Iosias   901 chauncel\er/   902
helden] heeldiden G ι Q   909 þe paleis] repareling   919 Ioachas

his hondis on þe kyngis hondis, and bad him shete out at þe eest wyndow
opened. And Elisee seide 'þis is þe arowe of Goddis heelþe aȝenus Sirie,
and þou shalt smyte Sirie in Affech, til þou waaste it'. Eft Elisee bad Ioas
smyte þe erþe wiþ a dart, and whanne he hadde smyte þries, and styntide,

925 Elisee was wrooþ aȝenus him and seide: 'if þou haddest smyte fyue siþis or
sixe siþis or seuene siþis þou shuldist haue smyte Sirie til to þe ending, but
now þou shalt smyte it þries'. Elisee died and was biried, and whanne a
deed bodi was biried in þe sepulcre of Elisee, and hadde touchid þe boonys
of Elisee, þe man lyued aȝen and stood on his feet.

930 Amasias kyng of Iuda regnyde ix. ȝeer and dide riȝtfulnesse in
partie, but not as Dauiþ. He killide ten þousynde men of Edom, and for
pride þerof he terride þe kyng of Israel to werre, and Amasias was
ouercome in þis batel, and þe kyng of Israel took hym prisoner, and brak þe
wal of Ierusalem bi foure hundrid cubitis. And þe kyng of Israel took awei

935 al þe gold and siluer and alle þe vesselis þat weren foundun in Goddis
hows and in þe tresours of þe kyng, and took pleggis, and turned aȝen into
Samarie. At þe laste, þe men of Amasias conspiride aȝenus him and he
fledde into Lachis, and þei senten þidur and killide hym þere, and birieden
him in Ierusalem wiþ his fadris. And Asarie his sone regnyde for him in

940 Ierusalem fifti ȝeer. He dide riȝtfulnesse in parti, as Amasias his fadir dide,
and God smoot him wiþ lepre til into þe dai of his deeþ. And Ioathas his
sone gouerned þe paleis and demyde þe puple of þe lond. And euere þe
kyngis of Israel diden yuele and ȝeden in þe synnes of Ieroboam. And in þe
daies of Manahen, kyng of Israel, Full þe kyng of Assiriens took greet

945 tribute of him to make Manahen strong in þe rewme. And in þe daies of
Face kyng of Israel, þat dide yuele in Goddis siȝt, cam Teglath Falasar
kyng of Assur, and took many places in þe lond of Israel, and he took
Galaad and Galilee and al þe lond of Neptalym, and translatide hem into
Assiriens. Aftirward Achas regnyde on Iuda xvj. ȝeer in Ierusalem, and

950 ȝede in þe weies of kyngis of Israel and dide foul idolatrie.
And aftir þese þingis Osee þe kyng of Israel regnyde ix. ȝeer and
dide yuel, but not as þe kyngis of Israel þat weren bifore hym. And þis
Osee was maad tributarie to Salmanasar kyng of Assiriens, and whanne þis
Osee wolde be rebel and paie not tribute to Salmanasar he bisegide Osee

955 and prisoned [him], and bisegide Samarie þre ȝeer, and took it in þe nynþe

---

Glosses and biblical references   922 [which had been] 'opened'   • 'heelþe aȝenus': salvation
in the face of   923 'waaste it': lay [Syria] waste   924 'smyte þries, and styntide': smitten three
times and stopped   930–9 4 Kings 14:1–20   930–1 'in partie': to a degree   936 'pleggis':
hostages   939–49 4 Kings 15   941 'Ioathas': Jotham   946 'Face': Pekah   • 'Teglath Falasar':
Tiglath–pileser   948 'Neptalym': Naphtali   • 'translatide hem': carried them away   949–50 4
Kings 16   951–64 4 Kings 17:1–33   951 'Osee': Hoshea

Variants   922 heelþe] help G ı Q Crowley   923 and … Sirie *om.* G ı Q Crowley   928–9 and hadde …
Elisee *om.* G ı Q Crowley   944 þe *bis*   955 him *om.*

ȝeer of Oosee, and translatide Israel into Assiriens. Þanne þe scripture
reher[s]iþ many grete synnes of þe puple of Israel, for which þei weren
conquerid and dryuen out of her lond. Þanne þe kyng of Assiriens brouȝte
puple fro Babiloyne and fro many oþere heþene cun| rb |trees, and sette hem
960   in þe citees of Samarie for þe children of Israel, and for þis puple dredde
not God he sente in to hem liouns, þat killiden hem. Þerfor þe kyng of
Assiriens sente þidur a prest of Israel to teche hem þe lawe of God of
Israel, and so þei worschipiden God of Israel and her heþene goddis
togidere.

Chapter 7

965   Eȝechie kyng of Iuda regnyde xxix. ȝeer, and dide good bifor God bi alle
þingis whiche his fadir [Dauiþ] hadde do. He distriede hiȝe places, and al
tobrak ymagis, and hew doun wodis, and brak þe brasun serpent, for þe
children of Israel brenten encense to it, and he hopide in God. Þerfor of alle
þe kyngis of Iuda was noon liyk him aftir him, but neþer among þese
970   kyngis þat weren bifor him. And in þe xiiij. ȝeer of Eȝechie Sennacherib
kyng of Assiriens stied to alle wallid citees of Iuda, and took þo. Þanne
Eȝechie ȝaf to him alle þe siluer þat was founde in Goddis hows and in þe
tresours of þe kyng, for he shulde go awei and distrie not Ierusalem ne
Iudee. And for Sennacherib kepte not couenaunt Eȝechie rebellide aȝenus
975   him, in trist of Goddis help. Þanne Sennacherib sente Rapsaces wiþ stroong
oost to Ierusalem, to blasfeme God and make þe puple to ȝelde hem to him
for drede. Þanne Eȝechie torente his cloþis for sorewe and was hilid wiþ a
sak, and entrid into Goddis hows and sente þe hiȝe prest and oþere eld men
cloþid wiþ sackis to þe profete Isaie, þat he shulde preie to God aȝenus þe
980   blasfemye of Assiriens. And Isaie seide, in Goddis name, þat þei shulde not
drede of þese wordis of Assiriens, for God shal sende a spirit to
Sennacherib, and he shal here a messanger, and he shal turne aȝen into his
lond, and God shal caste him doun bi swerd in his lond. And whanne
Sennacherib ȝede hoom to defende his lond aȝenus þe kyng of Ethiopie he
985   sente blasfeme lettris to Eȝechie, and seide þat his god myȝte not delyuere
him fro his hondis. Þerfor God coumfortide Eȝechie bi þe profete Isaie þat
he shulde not drede Sennacherib, for Sennacherib shal not entre into
Ierusalem, ne sende arowe into it, neþer occupie it ne bisege it, but God
shal defende and saue Ierusalem, for himsilf and for Dauiþ his seruaunt.
990   And in þat nyȝt þe aungel of God killid in þe tentis of Assiriens an hundrid

---

Glosses and biblical references   **960** 'for'¹: in place of   **965–77** 4 Kings 18   **965** 'Eȝechie':
Hezekiah   **968** 'hopide': trusted   **973** 'for he shulde go awei': in exchange for him going
away   **975** 'Rapsaces': Rab–shakeh   **977–93** 4 Kings 19   **979** 'aȝenus': in the face of   **985**
'blasfeme': blasphemous   **989** 'himsilf and for': his own sake and for the sake of

Variants   **957** reherhiþ   **966** Dauiþ *om.* P S T   **984** ȝede] wente G ι Q   **986** hondis] hond G ι Q S T

þousynd and lxxxv. þousynde, and in þe morewtide Sennacherib ȝede into
his lond, and his owne sones killiden him in þe temple of his god, Nestrach,
while he worschipide Nestrach.

Aftir þis, whanne Eȝechie was siyk to þe deþ, Isaie [seide] to him,
995   in Goddis name, 'dispose þin hows, for þou shalt die and not lyue'. And for
Eȝechie wepte gretli God curide him, and made him go into þe temple on
þe þridde dai, and encresside xv. ȝeer to his liyf, and in signe herof God
made þe sunne go bacward bi ten grees. [Aftir] þis doyng þe kyng of
Babiloyne sente lettris, messangeris and ȝiftis to Eȝechie, and bi pride he
1000   shewide alle hise tresours and iewelis to þe messangeris. Þerfor God seide
bi Isaie to him þat 'daies shulen come and [alle] þingis in þin hows shulen
be take awei into Babiloyne'. And Eȝechie seide 'þe word of God is good,
oneli pees and treuþ be in my daies'.

Aftir Eȝechie, Manasses his sone regnyde lv. ȝeer in Ierusalem, and
1005   dide grete yuele in Goddis siȝte and myche idolatrie. And þe puple of Iuda
was disseyued of Manasses, þat þei diden more yuel þan heþen men, which
God distriede fro þe face of þe | f. 6va | sones of Israel. And for Manasses
dide þese worste abhomynaciouns ouer alle þingis which þe men of
Amorreis diden, and he shedde ful myche innocent blood, til Ierusalem was
1010   fillid til to þe mouþ, God seide þat he wolde bringe in yuelis on Ierusalem
and Iuda, þat whoeuere heriþ boþe his eeris tyngle, and he shal do awei
Ierusalem as tablis on bord ben wont to be doon awei, but God shal leue
remenauntis of his eritage and bitake hem in þe hond of her enemyes.
Manasses diede and was biried in þe orcherd of his hows, and Amon his
1015   sone regnyde for him two ȝeer, and dide yuelis as his fadir dide, and
forsook God and seruede vnclennesse[s] and idols as his fadir dide, and
worschipide þo. And his seruauntis settide tresoun to him and killiden hym
in his hows, and þe puple of þe lond killiden alle men þat hadden conspirid
aȝenus þe kyng, Amon. And for him þei ordeyneden Iosie his sone kyng to
1020   hem.

Iosie bigan to regne whanne he was eiȝte ȝeer eld, and regnyde
xxxj. ȝeer in Ierusalem, and he dide þat þat was plesaunt bifor God, and
ȝede bi alle þe weies of Dauiþ his fadir. And in þe xviij. ȝeer of Iosie he
hadde bisynesse þat þe temple of God were reparelid, and whanne þe book

Glosses and biblical references   992 'Nestrach': Nisroch   994–1003 4 Kings 20   995 'dispose þin hows': put your house in order   998 'grees': degrees   1001 'daies shulen come and': the day will come when   1003 'oneli … be': so long as there may be   1004–20 4 Kings 21   1009 'Amorreis': Amorites   1011 'heriþ': hears [of it]   1012 'bord': trestle (note)   1019 'for him': in his place • 'Iosie': Josiah   1021–35 4 Kings 22   1024 'were reparelid': should be restored

Variants   993 worschipide Nestrach] worshipide his god nestarach G ι Q   994 seide *om.* • to² *bis* 998 grees] degrees G ι Q • Aftir] and   999 lettris, messangeris] lettris and messengeris S, lettris by messangeris G ι Q, lettris wiþ messyngers T   1001 alle *om.*   1006 yuel more yuel   1015 yuelis] yuel α β G ι Q S   1016 vnclennesse β G ι P Q T (note)

1025 of lawe was redde bifor þe kyng he torente his cloþis, and sente solempne
messangeris to take councel at God for himsilf and his rewme, for he seide
þat 'greet veniaunce of God [is] kyndlid aȝenus vs, for oure fadris herden
not þe wordis of þis book to do al þat is writen to vs'. And God seide bi þe
profetesse Olda, þe wiyf of Sellum: 'I shal brynge yuelis on þis place and
1030 on þe dwellers þerof, alle þe wordis of þe lawe which Iosie redde, for þei
forsoken me and made sacrifice to alien goddis. And for þou, Iosie, herdist
þe wordis [of þe book] and þin herte was afeerd and þou were mekid bifor
me, and torentist þi cloþis and weptist bifor me, þerfor þou shalt die in
pees, þat þin iȝen se not alle þese yuelis which I shal brynge in on þis
1035 place'.

Þanne Iosie gaderide to him al þe elde men of Iuda and of
Ierusalem, and þe kyng stiede in þe temple of God, and alle men of Iuda
and alle men þat dwelliden in Ierusalem, profetis and prestis, and al þe
puple stiede wiþ hym, and he redde to alle men heringe alle þe wordis of þe
1040 book of couenaunt of þe Lord, þat was founde in þe hows of þe Lord. And
þe kyng stood on þe grees, and smoot couenaunt bifor þe Lord, þat þei
shulden go aftir þe Lord and kepe alle his heestis and witnessingis and
ceremonyes, in al þe herte and in al þe soule, and þe puple assentide to þe
couenaunt. And þe kyng bad þe bischop and preestis and porteris caste out
1045 of Goddis temple alle vessels þat weren made to Baal and to oþere idols,
and he brennyde þo out of Ierusalem in þe valei of Cedron, and bar þe dust
of þo into Bethel. And he distriede idolatours and þe hows[is] of lecchours
þat weren in þe hows of God, and he distriede auteris and hiȝ places of
idols and ymagis, and took out boonys fro sepulcris, and brente þo on þe
1050 auter in Bethel þat seruyde to idolatrie. Also Iosie dide awei alle templis of
hiȝe places þat weren in þe citee of Samarie, which þe kyngis [of Israel]
hadden maad to terre þe Lord to wraþþe, and he dide to þo as he hadde do
in Bethel, and he killide þe prestis of hiȝ places, which prestis weren þere
ouer þe auteris, and he brente mennus boonys [of þo] on þe auteris. Also
1055 Iosie made þe puple to make a solempne pask, and sich pask was not maad
fro þe daies of iugis and | vb | alle kyngis of Israel and Iuda as was þis pask,
maad in þe xviij. ȝeer of Iosie. And he dide awei spiritis spekynge in
mennus wombis and false dyuynours and figuris of idols, and vnclennessis
and abhomynaciouns þat weren in þe lond of Iuda and of Ierusalem. No
1060 king bifor him ne aftir him was liyk him, þat turnede aȝen to God in al his
herte and in al his soule and in al his vertu, bi al þe lawe of Moises.

Neþeles, for þe orible synnes of Iuda God turnyde not awei fro his

---

Glosses and biblical references   1029 'Olda': Hulda   1036–72 4 Kings 23   1041 'grees':
steps   1054 'of þo': of those [priests] (note)   1061 'vertu': strength

Variants   1026 ˣforˣ for   1027 is] was   1030 ˣwˣ/which   1032 of þe book *om.*   1047 hows P α β S T
(note)   1051 of Israel *om.*   1054 of þo on þe G ι Q] of þo α S, of þe β, on þe P, on þo T (note)   • Also]
and G ι Q

strong veniaunce, but seide þat he wolde take awei Iuda fro his face, as he
dide awei Israel, and þat he wolde caste awei þe citee Ierusalem, which he
1065 chees. Þerfor Farao Necao kyng of Egipt killide Iosie in Magedo, and
Ioachas his sone was maad kyng for his fadir, and he regnyde þre moneþis
in Ierusalem, and dide yuel bifor God bi alle þingis whiche hise fadris
hadden do. And þis Farao prisoned him in Reblatha, and took tribute of þe
lond an hundryd talentis of siluer and o talent of gold, and þis Farao made
1070 kyng Eliachym, þe sone of Iosie, and turnyde his name Ioachym, and þis
Farao ledde Ioachas into Egipt. And Ioachym dide yuele bifor God, bi alle
þingis whiche hise fadris hadde do. And þis Ioachym was maad seruaunt
þre ȝeer to Nabugodonosor kyng of Babiloyne. And eft he rebellide aȝenus
Nabugodonosor, and God sente þeuys of Caldeis and þeuys of Sirie and
1075 þeuys of Moab and þeuys of þe sones of Amon into Iuda, þat he shulde
distrie it as he spak bi hise profetis, and speciali for þe synnes of Manasses.
   Þis Ioachym diede, and his sone Ioakyn regnyde þre moneþis in
Ierusalem, and dide yuele bifor God as his fadris hadden doon. In þat tyme
þe seruauntis of Nabugdonosor stieden to Ierusalem and bisegiden it. Þanne
1080 Nabugodonosor cam to Ierusalem to ouercome it, and Ioakyn and his modir
and his seruauntis and princes and chaumburleyns ȝeden out to
Nabugodonosor, and he translatide Ioakyn and his oost, ten þousynde, and
many crafti men into Babiloyne, and took alle þe tresours of Goddis hows
and of þe kyngis hows, and beet togidere alle þe golden vessels which kyng
1085 Salomon hadde maad in þe temple. And Nabugodonosor ordeynede
Mathanye, þe broþer of Iosie, to be kyng, and clepide him Sedechie, and he
regnyde xl. ȝeer in Ierusalem and dide yuele bifor God, bi alle þingis þat
Ioachym hadde do, for God was wrooþ aȝenus Ierusalem and Iuda til he
castide hem awei fro his face.
1090   And Sedechie ȝede awei fro þe kyng of Babiloyne, and in þe nynþe
ȝeer of Sedechie Nabugodonosor cam wiþ al his oost and bisegide
Ierusalem til to þe xj. ȝeer of Sedechie, and þanne þe citee was brokun, and
Sedechie and his werriours fledden bi nyȝte, and þe oost of Caldeis
pursueden and took him, and brouȝte him to Nabugodonosor in Reblatha.
1095 And Nabugodonosor spak doom wiþ Sedechie, and killid his sones bifor
him, and puttide out hise iȝen and boond him wiþ chaynes and brouȝte him
into Babiloyne. Þanne Nabusardan, þe prynce of þe oost, brente Goddis
hows [and þe kingis hows] and þe housis of Ierusalem, and distriede þe
wallis of Ierusalem in cumpas, and he translatide into Babiloyne þe residue

---

Glosses and biblical references   1065 'Magedo': Megiddo   1066 'Ioachas': Jehoahaz   1070
'Ioachym': Jehoiakim   1072–89 4 Kings 24   1077 'Ioakyn': Jehoiachin   1083 'crafti men':
craftsmen   1086 'Sedechie': Zedekiah   1090–1111 4 Kings 25   1091 'Nabugodonosor':
Nebuchadnezzar   1095 'spak doom wiþ': gave judgment on   1099 'in cumpas': round about

Variants   1085 and kyng nabugodonosor G ι Q   1093 ˣandˣ\of/   1098 and þe kingis hows *om.*

1100 puple of Iuda, | f.7ra | outaken a fewe pore men, vynetiliers and erþetiliers.
And he brak alle þe brasun vessels and of metal in þe temple, and bar þe
metal into Babiloyne. Þanne Nabugodonosor made Godolie to be souereyn
of þe puple left in þe lond of Iuda, and þanne alle þe duykis of knyʒtis
camen to Godolie in Maspha, and he made an ooþ to hem þat it shulde be

1105 wel to hem if þei wolden serue þe kyng of Babiloyne. And Ismael, þat was
of þe kingis blood, killid Godolie, and Iewis and Caldeis þat weren wiþ
him, and al þe puple of Iuda and þe princes of knyʒtis fledden into Egipt
for drede of Caldeis. At þe laste, Euylmeradach kyng of Babiloyne reiside
Ioachy[n] fro prisoun, and settide his troone aboue þe troone of oþere

1110 kingis þat weren wiþ him in Babiloyne, and Ioachy[n] eet euere breed in þe
kyngis siʒt of Babiloyne, in alle þe daies of his liyf. Þis process of Godolie,
and þat þat sueþ, is told largelier in þe ende of Ieremye þan here in þe ende
of Kyngis.

Þis process of þe fourþe book of Kyngis shulde stire alle men, and
1115 nameli kyngis and lordis, for to hate synne, as idolatrie and coueitise and
brekyng of Goddis heestis, for which þe puple of Israel and þe puple of
Iuda was þus punyschid and conquerid of heþene men, and for to loue
vertues and kepyng of Goddis heestis and distriyng of open synnes, for
whiche many good kyngis, as Eʒechie and Iosie and many oþere, hadden

1120 greet þank and socour of God in [many] grete perels, and blisse of heuene
wiþouten ende. God for his merci graunte þis blis to vs. Amen.

Chapter 8

The bookis of Paralipomenon ben ful necessarie to vndurstonde þe stories
of þe elde testament in so myche, as Ierom seiþ, þat if ony man wiþouten
þese bookis wole presume to haue þe kunnyng of hooli scriptures he
1125 scorneþ himsilf, þat is, disseyueþ or makiþ hymsilf worþi to be scorned, for
whi þe stories left out in þe bookis of Kyngis ben touchid in þese bookis,
[and vnnoumbrable questiouns of þe gospel ben declarid bi þese bookis].
Þe firste book of Paralipomenon telliþ in þe bigynnyng þe generaciouns fro
Adam til to Iacob and so forþ til to Dauiþ, and touchiþ shortli many stories
1130 of Saul and of Dauiþ, and of Salamon in þe ende þerof, and hou Dauiþ
ordeyned prestis and dekenes in her office, and hou and bi what seruyce þei
shulden serue God.

Glosses and biblical references   1100 'vynetiliers and erþetiliers': viticulturalists and farmers
1102 'Godolie': Gedaliah   1108 'reiside': liberated   1111 'kyngis siʒt of Babiloyne': sight of the
king of Babylon   1115 'nameli': especially   1126 'touchid': narrated   1127 'declarid': elucidated

Variants   1104 to] into   1107 knyʒtis and fledden G ι Q S *pr. m.* Crowley   1109 troone²] troones P α β
S T   1110 ioachym P β G ι S T   1112 largelier] largiere β, more largely T   1120 many *om.* P T   1123 ony]
a G ι Q   1124–5 he scorneþ *sup. ras.*   1125 scorneþ] scorne α G ι Q S   1125 disseyueþ or makiþ] disseyue
eiþir make α S, disseuye and make G ι Q   1126 book\is/   1127 and … bookis *om.* supplied from S

Þe bigynnyng of þe secounde book of Paralipomenon telliþ hou
Salomon axide of God wisdom to deme his puple, and God ȝaf to him
wisdom and kunnyng and riches and glorie, so þat noon among kingis,
neþer bifore ne aftir him, was liyk him. Þanne is teld hou Salomon bildide
þe temple of Ierusalem and an hows to himsilf. Aftir þis þe queene of Saba
cam to Salomon and brouȝte many preciouse iewelis to him, and preued his
kunnyng and wisdom in many þingis. And alle kingis of erþe desiriden to
se þe face of Salamon, for to here þe wisdom of God, which he hadde
ȝouen in his herte.

Aftir þis it sueþ hou Roboam departide þe ten lynagis fro þe hows
of Dauiþ, bi his pride and harde wordis, and bi suynge of þe councel of
ȝong men. And whan þe rewme of Iuda was confermed to him he forsook
þe lawe of God, and al Israel dide þe same wiþ him. Þerfor God sente þe
kyng of Egipt wiþ vnnoumbrable puple on hem, and took awei þe tresours
of Goddis hows and of þe kyngis hows, and þei serue| rb |den þe kyng of
Egipt, to knowe þe dyuersite of Goddis seruyce and of þe seruyce of þe
rewme of þe londis. Aftir hym regnyde Abia his sone, and he tretide wiseli
wiþ þe puple of Israel þat þei shulde forsake her synne and werre not
aȝenus Goddis puple in þe rewme of Iuda, and for þei wolden proudli
werre aȝenus þe rewme of Iuda, and aȝenus þis good councel of Abia, he
killid of hem bi Goddis help fyue hundrid þousynde of stronge men.

Aftir þis councel Abia diede and Asa his sone regnyde for him. In
þe daies of Asa þe lond was in reste ten ȝeer, and Asa dide þat þat was
good and plesaunt in þe siȝt of God, and he distriede auteris of idolatrie
and hiȝ places, and he brak ymagis and heew doun woodis, and
comaundide þe puple of Iuda to seke þe Lord God of her fadris, and do his
lawe and kepe alle his heestis. He regnyde in pees, and bildid strong citees
wiþ wallis and touris and ȝatis and lockis, and he hadde in his oost þre
hundrid þousynde of Iuda, of men berynge sheeldis and speeris, and of
Beniamyn two hundrid þousynde and seuenti þousynde of men of armes
and of archeris. And he ouercam þe king of Ethiopie, þat cam wiþ ten
hundrid þousynde of men and þre hundrid charis, and Asa hadde þe
victorie, for in trist of Goddis help he cam aȝenus þis greet multitude.
Þanne þe profete of God seide to Asa and to al his puple: 'þe Lord is wiþ
ȝou, for ȝe were wiþ him. If ȝe seken him ȝe shulen fynde, and if ȝe
forsaken him he shal forsake ȝou. Many daies shulen passe in Israel wiþout
verri God and wiþout prest and techere and lawe, and whanne þei turnen
aȝen in her angwisch, and crien to God and seken him, þei shulen fynde
hym. Be ȝe coumfortid and ȝoure hondis be not maad vnstidfast, for whi

---

Glosses and biblical references   1133–6 2 Chron. 1   1136–7 2 Chron. 2–8   1137–41 2 Chron. 9
1142–9 2 Chron. 10–12   1149–53 2 Chron. 13   1154–65 2 Chron. 14   1166–81 2 Chron. 15
1171 'ȝoure hondis be not': let your hands not be

Variants   1144 \whan/   1149 \þe/ londis   1152 good *om.* G ɩ Q   1167 fynde] fynde him G ɩ Q

meede shal be to ȝoure werk'. And whanne Asa hadde herd þese wordis
and profesie he was coumfortid, and dide awei alle idols fro al þe lond of
Iuda and of Beniamyn, and fro þe citees which he hadde take of Effraym,
1175 and he gaderide togidere al þe puple vndur him, and he entride in to
Ierusalem to make strong þe boond of pees, þat þei shulden seke þe Lord
God of her fadris in al her herte and al her soule. And he seide 'if ony man
sekiþ not þe Lord God of Israel, die he, fro þe leeste til to þe moost, fro
man til to womman'. And þei sworen wiþ al her herte and wiþ al her wille,
1180 and þei souȝten God and founden him, and God ȝaf reste to hem bi
cumpas.

And whanne þe kyng of Israel werrid aȝenus Asa, Asa sente myche
gold and siluer to þe kyng of Sirie to helpe [him] and to werre aȝenus þe
kyng of Israel, and he dide so. Þanne God blamede Asa gretli for he tristide
1185 in þe kyng of Sirie and not in God, 'and þerfore þe oost of þe kyng of Sirie
ascapid fro þin hond,' seide God, 'and also batels shulen rise aȝenus þee in
present tyme'. And Asa was wrooþ aȝenus þe profete þat telde þis to hym,
and puttide him in þe stockis, and God hadde ful greet indignacioun on þis
þing, and killid ful many men of þe puple in þat tyme. And in þe ende of
1190 his liyf Asa hadde ful greet sikenesse of his feet, and in his sikenesse he
souȝte not þe Lord, but tristide more in þe craft of lechis.

And Asa diede, and Iosephat his sone regnyde for him, and was
strong aȝenus Israel, and kyng Iosephat ordeyned noumbres of knyȝtis in
alle wallid citees of Iuda, and ordeyned strongholdis in þe lond of Iuda and
1195 in þe citees of Effraym which Asa his fadir hadde take. And the Lord was
wiþ | f. 7va | Iosaphat, and he ȝede in þe firste weies of Dauiþ his fadir, and
he hopide not in baalym but in God almyȝti, and ȝede in his
comaundementis and not bi þe synnes of Israel. And God confermyde þe
rewme in þe hond of Iosaphat, and he hadde ful many richessis and myche
1200 glorie, and whanne his herte hadde take trist for þe weies of þe Lord he
dide awei also hiȝe placis and woodis fro Iuda, where þe puple made
offryng out of Iersualem, aȝenus þe lawe. And Iosephat in þe þridde ȝeer
of his rewme sente fyue of his princes þat þei shulden teche in þe citees of
Iuda, and he sente nyne dekenes wiþ hem and two prestis wiþ hem, and þei
1205 hadden þe book of Goddis lawe and tauȝten þe puple in Iuda, and þei
cumpassiden alle þe citees of Iuda and tauȝten al þe puple. Þerfor þe drede
of þe Lord was maad on alle þe rewmes of londis þe weren bi þe cumpas of
Iuda, and dursten not werre aȝenus Iosephat. And he hadde redi at his hond
xl. hundrid þousynde and lx. hundrid þousynde of knyȝtis and men of

Glosses and biblical references   1172 'meede shal be to ȝoure werk': your work will be rewarded
1182–91 2 Chron. 16   1191 'lechis': physicians   1192–1212 2 Chron. 17   1202 'out of': away from
1207 'bi þe cumpas of': round about

Variants   1176 þe bond of boond of pees   1179–80 and þei … him *om.* T   1183 helpe him and to] help
him to G ι Q   1202 out of Ierusalem *om.* G ι Q   1209 hundrid² *om.* G ι Q

1210 armes and archeris, outaken oþere which he hadde set in wallid citees and
in al Iuda. And Filisteis and Arabeis brouȝten to Iosaphat ȝiftis and tributis,
and many þousyndis of sheep and buckis of geet.

And aftir þis doyng Iosaphat was alied to Achab, and ȝede wiþ him
to batel into Ramoth of Galaad, and foure hundrid profetis þat weren
1215 disseyued bi a spirit of leesyng excitiden Achab to þis werre, and bihiȝte
prosperite and victorie to him. But Mycheas, o trewe profete of God, telde
to Achab þat he shulde die in þis batel, and so it was in dede. And Iosephat,
þat was in moost perel of þis batel, was saued bi Goddis help. Aftir þis
batel, Iosaphat turnede aȝen in [pees] to Ierusalem, and a profete of God
1220 mette him and seide: 'þou helpidist þe wickid man and art ioyned in
frenschipe to hem þat haten God, and þerfor þou disseruydist þe wraþþe of
God. But good werkis ben foundun in þee, for þou didist awei woodis fro
þe lond of Iuda and madist redi þin herte to seke þe Lord God of þi fadris'.
Þerfor Iosephat dwellide in Ierusalem, and eft he ȝede out to þe puple fro
1225 Bersabee til to þe hil of Effraym, and clepide hem aȝen to þe Lord God of
her fadris, and he ordeyned iugis of þe lond in alle stronge citees of Iuda bi
ech place, and he comaundide þus to þe iugis: 'Se ȝe what ȝe owen to do,
for ȝe vsen þe doom not of man but of þe Lord, and whateuere þing þat ȝe
shulen deme shulen turne into ȝou. Þe drede of þe Lord be wiþ ȝou, and do
1230 ȝe alle þingis wiþ diligence, for whi neþer wickidnesse ne takynge of
persoones ne coueitise of ȝiftis is anentis ȝoure Lord God'. And in
Ierusalem Iosaphat ordeyned dekenes and prestis and princes of meynees
of Israel þat þei shulden deme to þe dwellers þerof þe doom and cause of
God, and he comaundide to hem and seide: 'Þus ȝe shulen do in þe drede
1235 of þe Lord, feiþfuli and in a parfit herte, ech cause þat comeþ to ȝou of
[ȝoure] briþeren þat dwellen in her citees, bitwixe kynrede and kynrede:
whereeuere is questioun or doute of þe lawe of comaundement, of
ceremonyes, of iustefiyngis, shewe ȝe to hem, þat þei do not synne aȝenus
þe Lord, and wraþþe or veniaunce come not on ȝou and on ȝoure briþeren.
1240 Þerfor do ȝe þus and ȝe shulen not do synne. And Amarie ȝoure prest and
bischop | vb | shal be souereyn in þese þingis þat perteynen to God'.

Aftir þese þingis þe sones of Amon and þe sones of Moab, and wiþ
men of Idumee, weren gaderid togidere to werre aȝenus Iosaphat. Þanne
Iosaphat ȝaf him al to biseche God, and prechid fasting to al Iuda, and al
1245 Iuda was gaderid to biseche þe Lord, and Iosaphat knoulechide þat he
hadde not power to aȝenstonde so greet a multitude of enemyes. Þanne

Glosses and biblical references   1212 'geet': goats   1213–18 2 Chron. 18   1218–41 2 Chron. 19
1229 'turne into': redound upon (note)   1234–5 'do … ech cause': try each case
1238 'iustefiyngis': judgments • 'shewe ȝe' [the truth]   1242–54 2 Chron. 20   1243 'men of
Idumee': Edomites   1244 'ȝaf him al to biseche': gave himself over completely to beseeching

Variants   1210 hadde set] lefte G ɩ Q   1216 mycheˣeˣas   1219 pees *om.*   1221 disseruydist] deseruest β
G ɩ Q   1229 shulen] shal α β Q S   1232 of *bis*   1236 ȝoure] her   1240 and] eiþir G ɩ Q

God coumfortide hym and his puple bi a profete þat þei shulden not drede
þis greet multitude of enemyes, for God hymsilf shal fiȝte and ouercome
her enemyes, wiþout strok of his puple. And so it was in deede. At þe laste,

1250 Iosephat made frenschip wiþ Ocosie kyng of Israel, whose werkis [weren]
ful yuele, and þei weren felowis to make shippis þat shulden go into
Tharsis. Þerfor God bi his profete seide to Iosaphat: 'for þou haddist boond
of pees wiþ Ocosie, God haþ smyten þi werkis, and þe shippis ben al
tobrokun and myȝten not go into Tharsis'.

1255   Þanne diede Iosaphat, and Ioram his sone regnyde for him. Þis
Ioram weddide þe douȝtir of Achab and killid his owne briþeren and ȝede
in þe weies of þe king[is] of Israel, as þe hows of Achab hadde do. And he
dide idolatrie, and made þe dwellers of Ierusalem and also Iuda to breke
Goddis lawe. Þerfor Edom and Lobna ȝeden awei fro his lordschip, for he

1260 hadde forsake þe Lord God of his fadris, and þerfor God reiside aȝenus
him Filisteis and Arabeis, þat costen wiþ Ethiopiens, and þei distrieden þe
lond of Iuda, and token awei al þe catel þat was founde in þe hows of þe
kyng, and token awei his wiyf and sones, outaken Ioachas, þe ȝongest. And
God smoot Ioram wiþ vncurable sorewe of wombe two ȝeer, so þat he

1265 rotide on erþe and castide out his entrails and diede in worste sikenesse.
And his sone Ocosias regnyde for him, and dide yuel as þe hows of Achab,
for whi his modir excitid hym to do wickidli, and þei of þe hows of Achab
weren his councelours into his deeþ, and he ȝede in þe councel of hem.
And þerfor Hieu, whanne he distriede þe hows of Achab, killide Ocosie

1270 and þe prynce of Iuda and þe sones of þe briþeren of Ocosie.
Aftir þese þingis Ioas was maad kyng bi þe help of Ioiada þe prest,
and þe cursid womman Athalia was slayn. Þe prestis and grete men of þe
puple brouȝten out of Goddis hows þe sone of þe king, and settiden a
coroun on his heed and ȝauen in his hond þe lawe to be kept, and maden

1275 him kyng. And Ioiada made couenaunt bitwixe hym and al þe puple and þe
kyng þat þei shulden be þe puple of God, þat is, to forsake idolatrie and
kepe treuli Goddis lawe. Þerfor al þe puple ȝede into þe hows of Baal and
distriede it. and braken þe auteris and symylacris eþer ymagis of him, and
þei killiden bifor þe auter Mathan þe prest of Baal. Þis Ioas dide wel in þe

1280 tyme of Ioiada, and reparelide þe temple of Ierusalem þat was distried bi
Athalia and hir sones. But aftir þe deþ of Ioiada he was flaterid bi þe
princes of Iuda, and þei fellen to idolatrie and forsoken þe temple of God.
And þe wraþþe of God was | f. 8ra | maad aȝenus Iuda and Ierusalem for
his synne, and he sente profetis to hem þat þei shulden turne aȝen to God,

Glosses and biblical references   **1255–65** 2 Chron. 21   **1261** 'costen wiþ': share a border
with   **1266–70** 2 Chron. 22   **1266** 'Achab': Ahab [had done]   **1271–81** 2 Chron. 23
1281–96 2 Chron. 24

Variants   **1250** weren *om.*   **1257** king   **1261** costen] coosteyen α G ι Q S   **1265** rootide G ι Q   **1271**
was maad kyng] was was maad prest kyng P   **1276** \to/   **1281** athalia þe queen and G ι Q

1285 and þei nolden here þese profetis. And Sacarie, þe prest and sone of Ioiada, repreued hem for þis synne, and þei stoneden him to deþ in þe purseynt of Goddis hows, bi comaundement of þe kyng. And whanne þe ȝeer was endid þe oost of Sirie stiede aȝenus him, and cam into Iuda and into Ierusalem and killid alle þe princes of þe puple and senten al þe prai into
1290 Damask, to þe kyng. And, certis, whanne a ful litle noumbre of men of Sirie was comun, God bitook in her hondis a multitude wiþouten ende, for þei hadden forsake þe Lord God of her fadris, and þei vsiden shameful domis in Ioas, and ȝeden forþ and leften hym in grete sorewis. And his seruauntis risiden aȝenus him for veniaunce of þe blood of þe sone of
1295 Ioiada þe prest, and killiden hym in his bed. And Ioas was deed, and Amasie his sone regnyde for him.

Chapter 9

Amasie dide good in parti, but not in a parfit herte, and he killid hem þat hadde slayn þe king his fadir, but he killide not hir sones, as God bad in þe lawe. Þis Amasie foond in al Iuda and Beniamyn, fro xx. ȝeer and aboue,
1300 þritti þousynde of ȝonge men þat ȝeden out to batel and helden spere and sheeld, and he hiride of Israel an hundrid þousynde of ful stronge men for an hundrid talentis of siluer, to fiȝte agenus þe sones of Edom. And a man of God seide to Amasie: 'A, þou kyng, þe oost of Israel go not out wiþ þee, for þe Lord is not wiþ Israel and wiþ alle þe sones of Effraym, þat if þou
1305 gessist þat batels stonden in þe strengþe of oost þe Lord shal make þee to be ouercome of þin enemyes, for it is propir to God for to helpe and for to turne into fliȝt'. Þerfor Amasie departide awei þe oost of Israel and tristili ledde forþ his puple to batel, [and he hadde þe victorie, and killide xl. þousand of hise enemyes in þis bateil]. And aftir þis victorie Amasie
1310 worschipide þe goddis of Edom and brente encense to hem, wherfor God was wrooþ aȝenus Amasie and sente to him a profete þat shulde seie to him 'whi hast þou worschipid goddis þat delyueriden not her puple fro þin hond?' Whanne þe profete [spak] þese þingis to him he answeride to þe profete 'wher þou art a councelour of þe kyng? Ceesse þou, lest
1315 parauenture I sle þee'. Þerfor þe profete ȝede awei and seide 'I woot þat þe Lord þouȝte to sle þee for þou hast do þis yuel, and ferþermore þou assentidist not to my councel'. And so it bifel in dede, for bi pride he terride þe king of Israel to werre, and nolde ceesse for helful councel of þe

Glosses and biblical references 1286 'purseynt': atrium, forecourt 1292–3 'vsiden shameful domis in': executed humiliating judgments against 1297–1324 2 Chron. 25 1298–9 'as God bad in þe lawe': Deut. 24:16 1303 'A ... go not': O king, may the army of Israel not go 1307 'into fliȝt': to flee 1307 'departide awei': separated out 1314 'wher þou art': are you

Variants 1299 Amasie] amasa ι Q 1308–9 and[1] ... bateil *om.* supplied from S 1313 \spak/ *sec. m.* answerid kyng of Israel. Þerfor þe kyng of Israel ouercam þe puple of Iuda, and took

1320 Amasie, and distriede þe wal of Ierusalem bi foure hundrid cubitis, and took awei al þe tresour and vessels which he foond in Goddis hows and in þe kyngis hows. And aftir þis doyng Amasie fledde out of Ierusalem into Lachis, for tresoun don to hym of his men, and þei senten and killiden him in Lachis.

1325   And Osias his sone regnyde for him lij. ȝeer in Ierusalem, and souȝte God in þe daies of Ȝacarie, vndurstondynge and seynge God, and whanne he souȝte God he louyde hym in alle þingis, and God helpid him aȝenus Filisteis and aȝenus Arabeis and aȝenus Amonytes. And Amonytes paieden ȝiftis to Osias, and his name pupplischid til to þe entryng of

1330 Egipt for ofte | rb | victories. He bildid many touris in Ierusalem and also in wildirnesse, for he hadde many beestis and vynes and vyne-tiliers, for he was a man ȝouun to erþe-tilþe. He hadde in his oost ij. þousynde and sixe hundrid prynces of stronge men, and iij. hundrid þousynde and seuene þousynde and fyue hundrid þat weren able to batel, and fouȝten for þe

1335 kyng aȝenus aduersaries. And his name ȝede out fer, for God helpide him and made him strong. But whanne he was maad strong his herte was reisid into his deþ, and he dispiside his Lord God, for he ȝede into þe temple of God and wolde brenne encense on þe auter [of encense], aȝenus þe lawe. And whanne þe bischop and many noble prestis aȝenstood him and telden

1340 þe lawe þat was aȝenus him he was wrooþ, and heeld þe censer and manaasside hem, and anoon lepre roos in his forhed bifor þe prestis in Goddis hows. Þanne prestis puttide him out, and he hastide to go out for drede and for he feelide anoon þe veniaunce of God. Þerfor kyng Osias was leprouse til to þe dai of his deþ and dwellid in an hows departid, and

1345 Ioathan his sone gouerned þe kyngis hows and demed þe puple of þe lond.
     And Ioathan regnyde xvj. ȝeer in Ierusalem, and dide riȝtfulnesse bifor God bi alle þingis whiche Osias his fadir hadde do, outake þat he entride not into þe temple of God, and ȝit þe puple trespasside. He bildide many þingis, and fauȝt aȝenus þe kyng of þe sones of Amon and ouercam

1350 him, and þe sones of Amon ȝaf to him an hundrid talentis of siluer and x. þousynde chorus of barli and as many of wheete, and chorus conteneyneþ þritti buschels. And Ioathan was maad strong, for he hadde dressid hise weies bifor his Lord God. And he was deed, and Achas his sone regnyde for him xvj. ȝeer in Ierusalem.

Glosses and biblical references   1325–45 2 Chron. 26   1325 'Osias': Uzziah (note)   1329 'pupplischid til to þe entryng': proclaimed as far as the borders   1332 'ȝouun to erþe-tilþe': much given to agriculture   1336–7 'reisid into': lifted up, resulting in his   1339 'aȝenstood': withstood   1344 'departid': apart   1346 'Ioathan': Jotham   1346–54 2 Chron. 27   1352 'dressid': prepared

---

Variants   1322 And *om.* G ι Q S   1326 se\ch/ynge   1329 entryng] entre G ι Q   1333–4 and vij. þousend *om.* β G ι Q   1338 of encense *om.*

1355 Þis Achas dide not ri3tfulnesse in Goddis si3t but [3ede] in þe
weies of þe kyngis of Israel and made ymagis to Baal and dide manyfold
idolatrie, and God bitook him into þe hond of þe kyng of Sirie, which kyng
smoot Achas and took a greet preie of his rewme and brou3te into Damask.
And Achas was bitaken into þe hondis of þe kyng of Israel, and was

1360 smyten wiþ greet wounde. And Facee þe sone of Romelie killide of Iuda vj.
scoore þousynde in oo dai, alle þe werriours, for þei hadden forsake þe
Lord God of her fadris, and þe sones of Israel token of her briþeren of Iuda
ij. hundrid þousynde of wymmen and of children and of damesels, and prei
wiþouten ende, and baren into Samarie. And Obed þe profete of God seide

1365 to þe men of Israel þat þei hadde do greet cruelte and synned a3enus God,
and bad hem lede a3en þe prisoneris of Iuda, 'for whi greet veniaunce of þe
Lord nei3iþ to 3ou'. Þerfor þe prynces of Israel maden þe werriours to
forsake þe prei and alle þingis which þei hadde take, and þe prynces
cloþiden hem þat weren nakid, and refreischid hem wiþ mete and drynke

1370 and anoyntyng of oile for trauel, and senten hem hoom benygneli.
    Þanne kyng Achas sente to þe kyng of Assiriens and axid help, and
Idumeis camen and killiden many men of Iuda and toke greet prai, and
Filisteis token many citees of Iuda and dwellid in þo. And God made low
þe puple of Iuda for Achas þe kyng of Israel, for he hadde maad him nakid

1375 of help and for he hadde dispisid God, and God brou3t a3enus him Teglath
Falasar þe kyng of Assiriens, þat turmentide him and distriede, for noon
| f. 8va | a3enstood. Þerfor Achas spuylide Goddis hows and þe hows of þe
kyngis and of princes, and 3af 3iftis to þe kyng of Assiriens, and neþeles it
profitide noþing to him. And Achas in þe tyme of his angwisch encreesside

1380 dispising a3enus God and offride sacrifices to þe goddis of Damask, and he
seide 'þe goddis of Sirie helpe hem, whiche goddis I shal plese wiþ
sacrifices and þei shulen helpe me', whanne a3enward þei weren fallyng to
him and to al Israel. Þerfor Achas rauyschide and brak alle þe vessels of
Goddis hows, and closid þe 3atis of Goddis temple, and made to him

1385 auteris in al þe corners of Ierusalem and in alle þe citees of Iuda to brenne
encense, and terrid God to wraþþe.
    And he diede, and E3echie his sone regnyde for him xxix. 3eer in
Ierusalem. He dide þat þat was plesaunt to Goddis si3t, bi alle þingis
whiche Dauiþ his fadir hadde do. And he openyde þe 3atis of Goddis hows

1390 in þe firste 3eer of his rewme, and made prestis and dekenes to clense and

---

Glosses and biblical references   1355–86 2 Chron. 28   1358 'brou3te': carried [it]   1364 'Obed':
Oded   1366 'lede a3en': return   1374 'for'¹: for the sake of   1377 'spuylide': despoiled   1379–80
'encreesside dispising a3enus': grew even more contemptuous of   1382 'a3enward þei weren
fallyng to': on the contrary they were the ruin of   1383 'rauyschide': seized   1384 'to him': for
himself   1387–1406 2 Chron. 29

Variants   1355 3ede *om.*   1358 and brou3te *om.* α G ι Q S *pr. m.*   1382 weren into fallyng G ι Q   1390
\in/

halowe þe temple and þe auter of God, wiþ alle þe vessels and
purtenaunces of þe temple. And he gaderide togidere alle þe princes of þe
citee and stiede into Goddis hows, and þei offriden seuene boolis and vij.
rammes, vij. lambren and seuene bu[ck]is of geet, for synne, for þe rewme,
1395   for seyntuarie and for Iuda. And he seide to þe prestis, þe sones of Aaron,
þat þei shulden offre on þe auter of God, and þei diden so, and he ordeyned
dekenes in þe hows of God wiþ symbals and sautrees and harpis, bi þe
ordenaunce of Dauiþ and of Gad þe profete of þe kyng and of Nathan þe
profete, for it was þe comaundement of God bi þe hond of his profetis. And
1400   dekens stoden and helden þe orguns of Dauiþ, and prestis helden trumpis,
and Eȝechie comaundide þat þei shulden offre brent sacrifices on þe auter,
and whanne brent sacrifices weren offrid þei bigunnen to synge heriyng[is]
to God, and to sowne wiþ trumpis and dyuerse orguns which Dauiþ þe
kyng of Israel hadde maad redi for to sowne. And Eȝechie and þe princes
1405   comaundiden to þe dekenes þat þei shulden herie God wiþ þe wordis of
Dauiþ and of Asaph þe profete.

And Eȝechie sente to al Israel and Iuda, and wroot epistlis to
Effraym and Manasses, þat þei shulden come to Goddis hows in Ierusalem
and make pask to þe Lord God of Israel. And it pleside þe kyng and al þe
1410   multitude, and þei demyden to sende messangeris into al Israel, fro Bersabe
til into Dan, þat þei shulden come and make pask to þe Lord God of Israel
in Ierusalem. And currours ȝeden out wiþ epistlis, bi comaundement of þe
kyng and of his princes, into al Israel and Iuda, as þe kyng hadde
comaundide and prechid: 'sones of Israel, turne ȝe aȝen to þe Lord God of
1415   Abraham, of Isaac and of Israel, and he shal turne aȝen to þe remenauntis
þat ascapiden þe hondis of þe kyngis of Assiriens. Serue ȝe þe Lord God of
ȝoure fadris, and þe wraþþe of his stronge veniaunce shal be turned awei
fro ȝou, for if ȝe turnen aȝen to þe Lord ȝoure briþeren and ȝoure sones
shulen haue merci bifor her lordis þat ledden hem prisoneris, and þei
1420   shulen turne aȝen into þis lond'. Þerfor currours ȝeden swiftli fro citee into
citee bi þe lond of Effraym and of Manasses til to Ȝabulon, and þei
scorneden and bymoweden þe messangeris. Neþeles, summe of Aȝer and
Manasses and of Ȝabulon assentide to þe councel and camen in| vb |to
Ierusalem. Goddis hond was maad on Iuda þat he ȝaf to hem oon herte, and
1425   þei diden þe word of God bi comaundement of þe kyng and of princes. And
many puplis weren gaderid in Ierusalem to make þe solempnite of pask in

---

Glosses and biblical references   1392 'purtenaunces': equipment   1395 'seyntuarie': sanctuary
1400 'orguns': instruments   1407–29 2 Chron. 30   1410 'demyden to sende messangeris':
decreed that messengers should be sent   1412 'currours': couriers   1422 'bymoweden':
mocked   1424 'Goddis hond was maad on Iuda þat he ȝaf': i.e. God acted in Judah by giving

---

Variants   1394 buckis] buggis   1402 heriyng P T   1406 \of\ Asaph   1410 \in\to   1411 of Israel *om.* G
ι Q   1414 prechid] precheden α β S   • ȝe *om.* G ι Q   1417 ˣwˣ/wraþþe   1421 til to] and of G ι Q

þe secounde moneþe, and þei distrieden þe auters þat weren in Ierusalem, and þei distrieden alle þingis in which encense was offrid to idols, and castiden forþ into þe stronde of Cedron.

1430 Whanne þese þingis weren halewid riȝtli, al Israel ȝede out þat was founde in þe citees of Iuda, and þei braken symylacris or ymagis, and hew doun wodis and distrieden hiȝ places and auteris, and not oneli of al Iuda and Beniamyn but also of Effraym and Manasses, til þei distrieden þo vttirli. And Eȝechie ordeynede cumpenyes of prestis and of dekenes bi her

1435 departingis, ech man in his owne offis as wel of prestis [as] of dekenes, to brent sacrifices and pesible sacrifices, þat þei shulden mynystre and knouleche and synge in þe ȝaatis [of þe castels] or oostis of þe Lord. And Eȝechie comaundide to þe puple to ȝyue to prestis and dekenes her partis, þat is, þe firste-fruytis and tiþis, þat þei myȝten ȝyue tent to þe lawe of

1440 God. And þere is teld myche of þe paiyng and deelyng of tiþis and oþere hooli þingis. Þanne it sueþ hou Sennacherib blasfemed God of Israel, and hou Eȝechie coumfortide þe puple aȝenus his blasfemye and pride. And Eȝechie and Isaie þe profete preieden aȝenus þis blasfemye and crieden til into heuene, and God sente his aungel, and he killide ech strong man and

1445 werriour and prince of þe oost of þe kyng of Assiriens, and he turnyde aȝen wiþ shenschip into his lond, and his owne sones killide hym bi swerd. And God sauyde Eȝechie and þe dwellers of Ierusalem fro þe hond of Sennacherub kyng of Assiriens, and fro þe hond of alle men, and ȝaf to hem reste bi cumpas.

1450 Aftir þese þingis Eȝechie was siyk to þe deþ, and he preiede to God and God herde him. And þe herte of Eȝechie was reisid to pride, and wraþþe was maad aȝenus him and aȝenus Iuda and aȝenus Ierusalem. And aftir he was mekid for his herte was reisid boþe he and þe dwellers of Ierusalem weren mekid, and þerfor þe veniaunce of God cam not in þe

1455 daies of Eȝechie. And Eȝechie was ful riche and noble, and in alle his werkis he dide welsumli whateuere þing he wolde. Neþeles, in þe message of prynces of Babiloyne þat were sent to him to axe of þe greet wondur þat bifel on erþe, God forsook him, þat he was temptid, and alle þingis were knowun þat weren in his herte.

1460 Þanne diede Eȝechie, and Manasses his sone regnyde in Ierusalem lv. ȝeer, and Manasses dide yuele bifor God, bi abhomynacioun of heþene men whiche God distriede bifor þe sones of Israel, and he bildide hiȝ

Glosses and biblical references   1429 'castiden': threw [them]   1430–41 2 Chron. 31
1430 'halewid riȝtli': correctly observed   1435 'departingis': divisions   1437 'castels': [army]
camps   1438 'partis': portions   1439 'ȝyue tent': pay attention   1441–59 2 Chron. 32
1446 'shenschip': disgrace   1456 'dide welsumli': prospered   • 'message': legation
1460–86 'for him' 2 Chron. 33

Variants   1427 weren maad in P T   1435 as²] and   1437 of þe castels *om.*   1442 And *om.* G ɩ Q S   1453
\was reisid/   1457 him ˣofˣ to

places and made auteris to baalym and dide manyfold idolatrie, and
seruyde to wicchcraftis, and sette idols in þe temple of God. And he
1465 disseyuede þe puple of Iuda and þe dwellers of Ierusalem, þat þei diden
yuele more þan heþene men which þe Lord hadde distried fro þe face of þe
sones of Israel. And God spak to him and to his puple, and þei nolden take
heede; þerfor he brou3te on hem þe prynces of þe oost of þe kyng of
Assiriens, and þei token Manasses and boundun him wiþ cheynes and
1470 | f. 9ra | gyues and ledde hym into Babiloyne. And aftir þat he was angwischid
he preiede his Lord God and dide penaunce gretli bifor þe God of his
fadris, and he preiede hertli and bisou3te God, and God herde his preier
and brou3te hym a3en into Ierusalem, into his rewme. And Manasses knew
þat þe Lord hymsilf is God, and he dide awei alien goddis and symylacris
1475 or idols fro Goddis hows, and distriede auteris which he hadde maad in þe
hil of Goddis hows and in Ierusalem, and castide al out of þe citee. And he
restoride þe auter of God and offrid on it sacrifices and heriyng, and
comaundide þe puple of Iuda to serue þe Lord God of Israel, and neþeles
þe puple offrid 3it in hi3 places to her Lord God.
1480 Manasses diede, and Amon his sone regnyde for him ij. 3eer in
Ierusalem, and he dide yuele in Goddis si3t as Manasses his fadir hadde do,
and offride and seruyde to alle idols whiche Manasses hadde maad, and he
reuerencid not þe face of God as Manasses reuerenside, and he dide many
gretere trespassis. And whanne hise seruauntis hadden conspirid a3enus
1485 him þei killiden him, and þe puple killid hem þat hadden slayn Amon, and
made Iosie his sone kyng for him, and he regnede xxxj. 3eer in Ierusalem.
Iosie dide þat þat was ri3tful in Goddis si3te, and 3ede in þe weies of
Dauiþ his fadir, and bowide neþer to þe ri3t side ne to þe left side. In þe
viij. 3eer of his rewme, whanne he was 3it a child, he bigan to seke þe God
1490 of Dauiþ his fadir, and in þe xij. 3eer aftir þat he bigan he clenside Iuda and
Ierusalem fro hi3e places and ymagis and idols. Þei distrieden bifor him þe
auteris of baalym and þe symylacris þat weren put aboue. He kittide doun
and al tobrak woodis and grauen ymagis, and scaterid þe relifs on þe
beriels of hem þat weren wont to offre. Ferþermore, he brente þe boonys of
1495 prestis in þe auteris of idols, and he clenside Iuda and Ierusalem, and
distriede alle idols in þe citee of Manasses and of Effraym and of Symeon,
til to Neptalym.
In xviij. 3eer of his rewme, whanne þe lond and þe temple of God
was clensid, he sente worþi men to reparele Goddis hows, and so þei diden
1500 in dede. And Helchye þe greet prest 3af to Saphan þe scryuen and
solempne messanger þe book of Goddis lawe, and he bar it to þe king. And

Glosses and biblical references   1486–1530 2 Chron. 34   1493 'relifs': remains on the graves
1494 'beriels': graves   • 'offre': sacrifice [to them]   1500 'Helchye': Hilkiah   • 'scryuen': scribe

Variants   1468 prynces] prynce G ι Q   1476 hows *om.* G ι Q   1479 3it *om.* G ι Q

whanne þe kyng hadde herd þe wordis of þe lawe he torente his cloþis, and
he comaundide Helchie and oþere grete men to go and preie þe Lord for þe
kyng and for þe residues of Israel and of Iuda, on alle þe wordis of þe book
1505 of Goddis lawe, 'for whi greet veniaunce of God haþ droppid on vs, for
oure fadris kepten not þe wordis of God, þat þei diden alle þingis þat ben
writun in þis book'. Þerfor Helchie and þei þat weren sent togidere of þe
kyng ʒeden to Olda a profetesse, þe wiyf of Sellum, and God seide bi her
þat he shal brynge in on þis place and dwellers þerof yuelis and alle
1510 cursyngis þat ben writun in þis book of Goddis lawe, for þei forsaken God
and sacrificieden to alien goddis, to terre him to wraþfulnesse in alle þe
werkis of her hondis, 'but for þou, kyng of Iuda, herdist þe wordis of þe
book and were mekid in Goddis siʒt and weptist and torentist þi cloþis, I
haue herd þee,' seiþ God, 'and þou shalt be | rb | borun into þi sepulcre in
1515 pees, and þin iʒen shulen not se al þe yuel which I shal brynge in on þis
place and on þe dwellers þerof'. And whanne Iosie hadde herd þese wordis
he clepide togidere alle þe eldere men of Iuda and of Ierusalem, and he
stiede into Goddis hows, and alle men of Iuda and þe dwellers of Ierusalem
stiden togidere, prestis and dekenes and al þe puple fro þe leeste til to þe
1520 moost, and in audience of hem þe kyng radde in Goddis hows alle þe
wordis of þe book. And he stood in his troone or seete of doom, and smoot
boond of pees bifor God þat he shulde go aftir God and kepe his heestis
and witnessingis and iustefiyngis, in al his herte and in al his soule, and do
þo þingis þat ben writun in þis book which he hadde red. And he chargide
1525 gretli on þis þing þat alle men þat weren foundun in Ierusalem and
Beniamyn and þe dwellers of Ierusalem diden bi þe couenaunt of þe Lord
God of her fadris. Þerfor Iosie dide awei alle abhomynaciouns fro alle
cuntrees of þe sones of Israel, and made alle men þat weren residue in
Israel to serue her Lord God. In alle þe daies of his liyf þei ʒeden not awei
1530 fro þe Lord God of her fadris.

　Aftirward Iosie made pask in Ierusalem, and ordeyned prestis in her
offices and bad hem mynystre in Goddis hows, and bad dekenes serue God
and his puple of Israel, and make hem redi bi her housis and kynredis in þe
departing of ech, as Dauiþ king of Israel comaundide, and bad hem serue in
1535 þe seyntuarie bi þe meynees and cumpenyes and dekenes, and þat þei be
halewid and offre pask, and make redy here briþeren þerto. And Iosie made
such a pask þat noon was liyk it in Israel fro þe daies of Samuel þe profete,
neþer ony of þe kyngis of Israel made pask as Iosie dide, to prestis and
dekenes and to al Iuda and Israel and to þe dwellers of Ierusalem, for he
1540 ʒaf to al þe puple þat was founde in Ierusalem in þe solempnite of pask
xxx. þousynde lambren and kidis and oþere sheep, and þre þousynde of

---

Glosses and biblical references　　1504 'on': concerning　1531–50 2 Chron. 35

Variants　　1511 sacrificieden] sacrifieden β G ι Q　1513 torentist] rentist G ι Q S　1520 ˣhoˣ/hows　1526
þe³] her G ι Q　1536–7 \and make ... pask/

oxen. Aftir þat Iosie hadde reparelid þe temple, Necao kyng of Egipt stiede
to fiȝte in Carcamys and Iosie ȝede forþ aȝens him, and þe king of Egipt
seide to Iosie 'I come not todai aȝenus þee, but I fiȝte aȝenus anoþere hows
1545   to which God [bad and] made me go in haaste; þerfor ceesse þou, kyng of
Iuda, todai aȝenus God which is wiþ me, lest he sle þee'. Iosie nolde turne
aȝen, but made himsilf redi to batel aȝenus þe kyng of Egipt, and assentide
not to þe wordis of þe kyng of Egipt, spoken bi Goddis mouþ. Þerfor Iosie
was slayn of þe kyng of Egipt, and þe puple of þe lond made Ioachas his
1550   sone king in Ierusalem.

He regnyde þre moneþis in Ierusalem, and þe kyng of Egipt puttide
him doun and condempnyde þe lond of Iuda in an hundrid talentis of siluer
and in a talent of gold, and made Eliachym his broþer kyng for him on Iuda
and Ierusalem, and turnyde his name Ioachym. He regnyde xl. ȝeer in
1555   Ierusalem and dide yuel bifor God; þerfor Nabugodonosor took him and
ledde him boundun wiþ chaynes into Babiloyne, and bar þidur þe uessels of
Goddis temple. And Ioakyn his sone regnyde for him þre moneþis and ten
daies in Ierusalem, and dide yuele in Goddis siȝt. Þanne Nabugodonosor
sente men þat ledden him into Babiloyne, and baren out þe preciousest
1560   uessels of Goddis hows. And Nabugodonosor made Sedechie kyng on Iuda
and Ierusalem. He regnyde xj. ȝeer in Ierusalem and dide yuele in Goddis
siȝt, | f.9va | neþer was ashamed of þe face of Ieremye þe profete, þat spak
to hym of Goddis mouþ. He brak þe ooþ maad to Nabugodonosor; þerfor
Nabugodonosor cam and took him and ledde him and alle þe uessels and
1565   tresours of Goddis hows, and of þe king and princes, into Babiloyne, and
killid þe peple, and distried and brent Ierusalem. And þe peple þat was left
aliyf was lade into Babyloyne, and seruyde þe kyng and his sones til þe
kyng of Perses regnyde and til fifti ȝeeris weren fillid, bi Goddis word seid
bi þe mouþ of Ieremye. And Cirus kyng of Perses comaundid to be prechid,
1570   ȝhe bi writyng in al his rewme, þat Iewis shulden turne aȝen into Iudee.

Chapter 10

This processe of Paralipomenon in þe firste and ij. book shulde stire
cristene kyngis and lordis to distrie synne and loue uertu, and make Goddis
lawe to be know and kept of her puple, for here þei moun se hou sore God
punyschyd yuele kyngis þat lyueden yuele and drowen þe puple to idolatrie
1575   or oþere grete synnes, and hou gretli God preisid, rewardide and
cherischide good kingis þat lyueden wel and gouernyde wel þe puple in

Glosses and biblical references   **1551–70** 2 Chron. 36   **1551–2** 'puttide him doun': removed
him   **1563** 'of': from   **1568–9** Jer. 25:12 (note)

Variants   **1545** God bad and made] god made me P, god bad me S   **1553** a] oo G ɩ Q T   • go\l/d   •
kyng *om.* α S   **1559** \in/to   **1565–7** \and killid … Babiloyne/   **1568** fifti] seuenti T (note)   **1572** cristene
kyngis and lordis] kyngis and cristene lordis G ɩ Q S

Goddis lawe and open resoun and good conscience. And þou3 kingis and
lordis knewen neuere more of hooli scripture þan þre stories of þe ij.
bookis of Paralipomenon and of Regum, þat is, þe stori of kyng Iosaphat,
1580   þe storie of king E3echie and þe storie of kyng Iosie, þei my3ten lerne
sufficientli to lyue wel and gouerne wel her puple bi Goddis lawe, and
eschewe al pride and idolatrie, coueitise and oþere synnes.

But alas, alas, alas! Where kyng Iosaphat sente his princes, dekenes
and prestis to ech citee of his rewme wiþ þe book of Goddis lawe to teche
1585   openli Goddis lawe to þe puple, summe cristen lordis senden general lettris
to alle her mynystris and legemen eþer tenauntis þat þe pardouns of þe
bischops of Rome, þat ben open lesyngis, for þei graunten many hundrid
3eeris of pardoun aftir domesdai, be prechid generali in her rewmes and
lordschipis. And if ony wiys man a3enseiþ þe open errours of antecrist, and
1590   teche[þ] men to do her almes to pore nedi men to ascape þe peynes of helle
and to wynne þe blisse of heuene, he be prisoned as a man out of cristen
bileue and traitour of God and of cristen kyngis and lordis. And where
kyng E3echie made him ful bisi to clense Goddis hows and to do awei al
vnclennesse fro þe seyntuarie, and comaundid prestis to offre brent
1595   sacrifice on Goddis auter, and ordeyned dekenes in Goddis hows to herie
God, as Dauiþ and oþere profetis ordeyneden, summe cristen lordis in
name, and heþene in condiciouns, defoulen þe seyntuarie of God and
bryngen in symonyent clerkis ful of coueitise, eresie and ipocrisie and
malice to stoppe Goddis lawe, þat it be not knowun and kept and freli
1600   prechid. And 3it summe cristen lordis holden many prelatis and curatis in
her courtis and in seculer office a3enus Goddis lawe and mannus openly,
and wiþholden hem fro here gostly office and helpynge of cristen soulis.
And where kyng Iosie prechid openli Goddis lawe in þe temple to al þe
puple, and castide awei idols and brente þe boonys of prestis þat diden
1605   idolatrie, summe cristen lordis, in name not in dede, preisen and magnefien
freris lettris ful of disseit and leesyngis, and make her tenauntis and
meynee to swere bi þe herte, boonys, nailis and sidis, and oþere membris of
Crist, and pursuen ful crueli hem þat wolden teche treuli and freli þe lawe
of God, and preisen, mayntenen and cherischen hem þat prechen fablis, lee
1610 | vb |syngis and synful mennus tradiciouns or statutes, and letten gretli þe
gospel to be prechid and hooli writ to be knowen and kept.

But wite þese vnwise lordis þat Elie þe profete oon aloone hadde þe
treuþe of God, and kyng Achab wiþ viij. hundrid and l. prestis and profetis

---

Glosses and biblical references   1585 'general': generic, inclusive   1597 'condiciouns': character-
istics   1598 'symonyent': simoniac (note)   1605 'magnefien': make much of   1612–14 3 Kings
18   1612 'wite þese vnwise lordis': may these foolish lords know

Variants   1578 scripture] writ G ι Q   1579 bookis] book α β G ι Q S   1583–837 *om.*G ι   1590 teche α
β P Q, to teche T   1591 he \schale/ be P *sec. m.* Q T   1601–2 \a3enus … office/   1607 meynee] meynees
Q, many oþer T   1608 pursuen ˣhemˣ ful

of Baal hadde þe false part. And eft Mychee, as oon aloone profete of God,
1615 hadde þe treuþe aȝenus foure hundrid profetis of Baal þat counceliden
Achab go to werre, to his owne shenschip and deþ. So now a fewe pore
men and idiotis in comparisoun of clerkis of scole moun haue þe treuþe of
hooli scripture aȝenus many þousynde prelatis and religious þat ben ȝouun
to worldli pride and coueitise, symonye, ipocrisie and oþere fleischli
1620 synnes; moost siþ þese pore men desiren oneli þe treuþe and fredom of þe
hooli gospel and of hooli scripture, and accepten mannus lawis and
ordenaunces oonli in as myche as þei ben groundid in hooli scripure or
good resoun, and comyne profit of cristen puple. And worldli prelatis and
feyned religiouse grounden hem on synful mennus statutis, þat sow[n]en
1625 pride and coueitise, and letten þe treuþe and fredom of Goddis lawe to be
knowen and kept, and bryngen cristen puple in ne[d]eles þraldom and greet
coost.

   But it is for to drede ful soore lest kyngis and lordis be now in þe
former synnes of Manasses. God graunte þat þei repenten verili and make
1630 amendis to God and men, as he dide in þe ende, for þei setten idols in
Goddis hows and exciten men to idolatrie and sheden innocent blood in
many maneris, as Manasses dide. First þei setten in her herte, þat shulde be
þe temple and special chaumbre of God, þe idol of coueitise or of glotenye
or of pride or of oþere grete synnes, for seynt Poul seiþ þat oure bodies ben
1635 þe temple of þe Hooli Goost, and eft he seiþ þat auerice is þe seruyce of
idols, and eft he seiþ þat glotouns maken her beli her God. And God seiþ bi
Ioob þat þe deuel is kyng ouer alle þe children of pride, and Iesu Crist seiþ
þat þe deuel is prynce of þis world, þat is, as Austyn seiþ, of false men þat
dwellen in þis world. Þanne þei þat setten pride or coueitise or glotenye or
1640 raueyn in her herte setten idols of Baal or of þe deuel in þe temple of God.
   Speciali lordis setten idols in Goddis hows whanne þei maken
vnworþi prelatis or curatis in þe chirche, for whi sich vnable prelatis or
curatis ben idols, as God seiþ in xj. cº of Ȝacharie to an vnable prelat: 'A,
þou sheppard and idol, forsakynge þe floc'. Wherefor Erchedekene in
1645 *Rosarie*, which is oon of þe famous[es]te doctours of þe popis lawe, writiþ
þus: 'an yuel prelat is seid a roring lioun and a wolf rauysching prai', and
in xxxiiij. chapitre of Eȝechiel he is seid to feede himsilf and not þe sheep.

Glosses and biblical references   1614–16 3 Kings 22   1617 'idiotis': illiterates (note)   1618
'religious': men belonging to religious orders   1620 'moost': most of all   1624 'sownen': are
consonant with   1634–5 1 Cor. 6:19   1635–6 Eph. 5:5   1636 Phil 3:19   1636–7 Job 41:25;
'children of pride': proud men   1637–8 John 12:31   1640 'raueyn': greed   1643–4 Zech.
11:17   1647 Ezech. 34:3

Variants   1616 go to] go S, to go β, to Q   1618 ˣwritˣ scripture   1624 sowen β P   1626 nedeles] neþeles
P, endeles Q S Crowley   1628 \ is/   1630 setten] settiden   1631 exciten] excitiden   1633 \þe/ temple •
special] speciali α β S   1635–6 and eft … idols *om.* Q Crowley   1637 children] sones α β S   1645
famouste

Also he is seid to seke his owne profitis temporal; þerfor he is not of
Goddis children, as Austin seiþ in þe viij. cause, j. questioun, cᵒ *Sunt*
1650   *quidam*. And for þis þing power shal be takun awei fro him, as God seiþ in
xxxiiij. cᵒ of Eʒechiel. Also an yuel prelat is seid a wolf, as þe lawe
witnessiþ in lxxxiij. distinccioun, cᵒ *Nichil*. Also, for defaute of gouernail
he is seid an vnchast dogge, | f. 10ra | as Austin witnessiþ in ij. cause, vij.
questioun, cᵒ *Qui nec*. Also he is seid a crowe or a rauene for þe blacnesse
1655   of synnes, as þe lawe witnessiþ þere, in cᵒ *Non omnis*. Also he is seid
fonned salt, not profitable to ony þing, as þe lawe witnessiþ þere, in cᵒ *Non
omnis*. Also he is seid an hog, as þe lawe witnessiþ in þe lxiij. distinccioun,
in cᵒ [*In*] *mandatis*. Also he is seid a cheerl of cherlisched of yuel liyf, as
þe lawe witnessiþ in xlvij. distinccioun, in þe bigynnyng. Also he is seid a
1660   capoun for he haþ þe maner of an hen, for as a capoun crowiþ not so an
yuel prelat crowiþ not in preching; also an yuel prelat gendriþ not bi
prechyng of Goddis word, neþer he fiʒtiþ for his sugetis. Also, as þe
capoun clepiþ not hennes so an yuel prelat clepiþ not pore men to mete.
Also, as a capoun makiþ fat hymsilf so an yuel prelat makiþ fat hymsilf.
1665   Þerfor, siþ he sekiþ plenteuouse metis and richessis, he shal be put into þe
fier of helle, as Ierom witnessiþ on Mychee, and in þe xxxv. distinccioun,
cᵒ *Ecclesie principes*. Erchedekene writiþ al þis in xliij. distinccioun, in cᵒ
Sit rector, on þis word, *muti*.

    Also a doumb prelat is an idol and not a verri prelat; a doumb prelat
1670   is not a verri prelat siþ he vsiþ not þe office of a prelat but he haþ oneli þe
licnesse of a prelat, as an idol þat vsiþ not þe office of a man is oneli liyk a
man but it is no man, wherfor sich doumb prelatis moun riʒtfuli be clepid
symylacris or idols, of which it is seid, in þe vj. cᵒ of Baruch, 'þe trees of
hem ben maad feir of a carpenter, and þo ben araied wiþ gold and siluer
1675   and moun not speke', and þei þat maken sich prelatis ben liyk hem, whiche
makeris shulen be dampned wiþ sich prelatis, bi þat word of Dauiþ 'þei þat
maken þo ben maad liyk þo'. But marke wel þat heþene men hadden
symylacris of sixe kyndis, þat is, of clei, of tree, of bras, of stoon, of siluer
and of gold. We moun fynde þese sixe kyndis in yuele prelatis, for whi
1680   symylacris of clei ben fleischli prelatis, of which God seiþ, in þe Sauter, 'I
shal do hem awei as þe clei of stretis'. Symylacris of tree ben vnwise
prelatis and boistouse and wiþout wit, of which it is seid in hooli scripture
'a tree is wlappid in siluer', and þese ben seid to be maad of nouʒt into
prelatis; þese ben beestis clepid chymeris, þat han a part of ech beest, and

---

Glosses and biblical references   **1650–1** Ezech. 34:10   **1656** 'fonned': savourless, spoiled   **1661**
'gendriþ not': engenders nothing   **1673–4** Bar. 6:7   **1676–7** Ps. 115:8; 135:18   **1680–1** Ps. 17:42
1682 'boistouse': crude, unmannerly   **1683** Bar. 6:7; 'wlappid': clothed   **1684** 'chymeris':
chimeras

Variants   **1654** seid *om*. α β S   **1658** *In om*.   **1665** plenteuouse] plenteousnesse α Q S   **1672** be clepid]
be seid α β Q S   **1682** boistouse] bystowse β, boostours T

1685   sich ben not, no but oneli in opynyoun eþer speche, and not in dede neþer
        in kynde. Symylacris of bras ben þei þat han oneli worldli eloquence, for
        whi bras ȝyueþ greet sown; in þe j. pistle to Cor[intheis], xiij. cᵒ, 'if I speke
        in þe langagis of men and of aungelis, and I haue not charite, I am maad as
        bras sownyng'. Symylacris of stoon ben þei þat ben broken fro riȝtfulnesse
1690   and vertu for temperal strengþe. Þese prelatis ben not þe stoon which is set
        into þe heed of þe corner, but þese ben þe stoon of hirting and of sclaundre.
        Symylacris of siluer ben þei þat ben maad bi monei or richessis, which
        prelatis seien 'what wolen ȝe ȝyue to vs and we shal bitraie Crist to ȝou?'
        Golden symylacris ben þei | rb | þat ben maad oneli for worldli noblei, for
1695   gold signefieþ noblei, and þerfor þe heed of þe ymage of Nabugodonosor
        was of gold, in þe ij. cᵒ of Daniel. Erchedekene telliþ al þis in xliij.
        distinccioun, cᵒ *Sit rector*, on þe word *mutus*. Þouȝ þis doctour of þe popis
        lawe be pleyn and sharp, he seiþ treuþe sesonable, for þe chirche now
        acordiþ wiþ hooli writ and resoun and comyne doctours of hooli scripture,
1700   for in þe xj. cᵒ of ȝacarie God clepiþ an yuele prelat an idol, and in
        Eȝechiel and oþere profetis he licneþ tirauntis and rauenours to liouns,
        wolues, beris and oþere vnresonable beestis, to dispise her synne.

            Here lordis and oþere prelatis moun se in parti hou perelouse it is to
        ordeyne yuele prelatis or curatis in þe chirche, for as seynt Gregorie seiþ in
1705   þe first part of *Pastorals*, þe ij. cᵒ, no man harmeþ more in þe chirche þan
        he þat doiþ weiwardli and holdiþ þe name of ordre or hoolynesse. And þe
        lawe seiþ, *de electionibus*, cᵒ *Nichil*, þat no þing harmeþ more þe chirche of
        God þan þat vnworþi men be taken to þe gouernail of soulis. And Grosted
        seiþ in his sermoun *Premonitus a venerabili patre* þat to make vnable
1710   prelatis or curatis in þe chirche of God is to haue come to þe hiȝest degree
        of trespas. Also, in his sermoun *Dominus noster Iesus Cristus* he writiþ þus
        to þe pope: he þat bitakiþ þe cure of soulis to a man vnmyȝti, vnkunnyng
        or not wilful to kepe duli þe soulis is gilti of alle þe soulis, þouȝ ony ascape
        and is saued bi Goddis grace, and he þat bitakiþ þe cure of soulis to him þat
1715   is openli vnable þerto techiþ to sette more priys bi vnresonable beestis þan
        bi men, and for to loue more erþeli þingis þat passen shortli þan
        euerlastinge þingis, and more þan þe deþ and blood of Goddis sone, and he
        þat ȝyueþ þus þe cure of soulis to vnable men is worse þan Eroude, þat
        pursuyde Crist, and worse þan Iewis and heþene men þat crucifieden Crist.
1720   Grosted seiþ þis pleynli and preueþ it openli bifor þe pope and al his
        clergie. And þei þat procuren benefices and richess to men haten hem to
        which þei procuren þus, as if þei procurid hem to be set in þe cop of þe

Glosses and biblical references   1685 'sich [prelates]'   1687–9 I Cor. 13:1   1690–1 Matt. 21:42;
Mark 12:10; Luke 20:17; Acts 4:11   1695–6 Dan. 2:32   1700 Zech. 11:17

Variants   1693 shal] shulen α β Q S   1696 gold \as it wrytun/ in \þe/ *sec. m.*   1698 sesonable] resonable
Q S, and resonable β   1698–9 now and acordiþ   1706 or] eiþir of α β Q S   1709 þat is to   1711 trespas]
trespasis α β Q S   1713 kepe] helpe Q S   • ascape] ascapiþ α β Q S   1716 \þan/

chirche, in whirlewyndis and grete tempestis. Grosted seiþ þis in his
sermoun *Scriptum est de Leuitis.* And he þat is necligent to drawe soulis
1725 out of þe pit of synne, as myche as he mai bi þe ordre of lawe, and he þat
lettiþ him of þis werk, sleeþ þe soulis, and he þat settiþ more priys bi a
fleischli sheep þan a goostli sheep, þat is, mannus soule; settiþ more priys
bi a peny þan bi þe liyf of Goddis sone, which is worþ al þis world. A
reccheles curat and þat sleeþ sugetis bi yuele ensaumple and wiþdrawyyg
1730 of Goddis word is worse þan vnresonable beestis, and he is worse þan þe
crucifiers of Iesu Crist, for he crucifieþ him in his membris. Good
councelours ben þei aloone þat ben wise men and dreden God, for whi al
coueitouse men ben foolis and vnwise men, and to be led bi þe councel of
hem is to dispose of henne cootis bi þe councel of foxis, and to dispose of
1735 fooldis of sheep bi þe councel of wolues. Grosted seiþ þis in a sermoun
Premonytus a venerabili patre.

Se, ȝe lordis and prelatis þat maken vnable curatis for fleishli
affeccioun and ȝiftis, | f. 10va | and speciali for pleiyng at þe beere and
oþere vnleueful iapis, what tresoun ȝe doon to God and what harme to
1740 Cristis chirche and ȝoure auaunces. Ȝe maken orible abhomynacioun of
discoumfort stonde in þe hooli place, for ȝe maken antecrist to stonde at þe
hiȝ auter in þe stede of Crist, and trete þe hooli sacrament of Cristis fleisch
and his blood ful vnworþili and, as Parisience seiþ, whanne ȝe maken a
coueitouse prest to stonde at þe auter ȝe maken a moldewarp stonde þere in
1745 þe stide of Crist, and whanne ȝe maken a fonned bischop, þat kan not and
loueþ not Goddis lawe, stonde mytrid at þe auter [ȝe maken an hornid asse
stonde at þe auter] in þe stide of Crist, and so of oþere vnresonable beestis,
as liouns, wolues, beeris, apis, dragouns, hoggis, horsis, doggis and oþere
viciouse prestis, proude, coueitouse, rauenouse, wraþful, ipocritis,
1750 trecherouse, glotenouse, leccherouse, enuyouse and bacbiters. And ȝe
transfigure Sathanas into an aungel of liȝt whanne ȝe maken curatis [or]
prelatis þat ben contrarie to Crist to ocupie þe offis of bischop, abbot or of
prest. Lordis and prelatis þat han set sich idols in Goddis hows, as
Manasses dide, sue ȝe Manasses in verri repentaunce and makyng of
1755 amendis to God and men.

Also lordis and prelatis exciten strongli men to idolatrie for þei
sweren customabli, nedelesli and ofte, vnauisili and fals, bi þe membris of
God, of Crist and bi seyntis, in so myche þat ech greet lord and prelat
comynli makiþ him an idol of sum seynt whom he worschipiþ more þan
1760 God. For comynli þei sweren bi oure Ladi of Walsyngham, seynt Ioon þe
Baptist, seynt Edward, seynt Thomas of Cauntirberi and siche oþere

---

Glosses and biblical references   1740 'auaunces': promotees   1744 'moldewarp': mole   **1761**
'seynt Edward' [the Confessor]   1762 'chargen more': attribute more significance to

Variants   1746–7 ȝe … auter *om.* supplied from S   1749 rauenouse] raueynouris α Q S   1751 or]
and   1758 ech lord and greet α β Q S

seyntis, and chargen more þis ooþ þan þou3 þei sweren bi þe Hooli Trinite,
and in al þis þei onouren more þese seyntis þan þei onouren þe Hooli
Trinite. Þou3 it were leueful to swere bi seyntis, þis is idolatrie, to charge

1765   more an ooþ maad bi sich seyntis þan bi God almy3ti or bi þe Hooli
Trinite. Neþeles, Crisostom witnessiþ on þe v. c⁰ of Matheu þat to swere bi
ony creature is to do idolatrie, for, as Ierom þere and þe *Decrees* in þe xxij.
cause, j. questioun, c⁰ *Si quis per capillum* and c⁰ next bifore, and
Decretals, de iure iurando, c⁰ *Et si Cristus* witnessen pleynli, to swere bi a

1770   creature is a3enus Goddis comaundement, and þerfor Crist, in þe v. c⁰ of
Matheu, comaundiþ to swere not bi heuene ne bi erþe, and vndurstondiþ bi
heuene and erþe creaturis of heuene and creaturis of erþe. And in al þe elde
lawe it is not founde where God grauntide to swere be ony creature, but
oneli bi his owne name or bi himsilf. And þerfor þe Wiys Man seiþ in xxiij.

1775   c⁰ of Ecclesiastici 'a man þat sweriþ myche shal be fillid wiþ wickidnesse
and veniaunce shal not go awei fro his hows', and eft he seiþ 'þi mouþ be
not customable to sweryng, for whi myche falling is in it; þe namyng of
God be not customable in þi mouþ', þat is, to swere bi his name in veyn, or
fals, or for an yuel ende, 'and be þou not medlid wiþ þe names of seyntis',

1780   þat is, to swere bi seyntis, 'for þou shalt not be giltles of hem'. Here lordis
and prelatis moun se hou þei doen open idolatrie whanne þei gessen to
onoure seyntis, and her open dedis of idolatrie and blasfemye ben open
bookis of idolatrie and blasfemye to her sugetis. Þerfor, as Gregorie seiþ in
þe secounde book of *Pastorals*, þe v. c⁰, prelatis ben worþi so many | vb |

1785   deþis hou many saumplis of perdicioun þei senden to sogetis, and in xxv. c⁰
of Numeri God bad Moises hange alle þe prynces in gebatis a3enus þe
sunne for þe puple of Israel dide leccherie and idolatrie bi ensaumple and
suffraunce of hem.

Now, in Ynglond, is it a comun proteccioun a3enus persecucioun of

1790   prelatis and of summe lordis if a man is customable to swere nedeles and
fals and vnavysid, bi þe boonys, nailis and sidis and oþere membris of
Crist, and to be proud and leccherouse and speke not of Goddis lawe and
repreue not synne aboute him. And to absteyne fro nedeles oþis and
vnleueful, and to eschewe pride, and to speke onour of God and of his lawe

1795   and repreue synne bi weie of charite is matere and cause now whi prelatis
and summe lordis sclaundren men and clepen hem lollardis, eretikis and
reisers of debate and of tresoun a3enus þe kyng. Now Manasses settiþ idols
openli in þe temple of God and stiriþ men gretli to do idolatrie, and
cherischen hem þat breken openli Goddis heestis, and punysche hem sore,

---

Glosses and biblical references   **1770–1** Matt. 5:34–5   **1771** 'vndurstondiþ': understands
1774–6 Ecclus 23:12   **1776–80** Ecclus 23:9–10   **1779** 'medlid': mixed   **1781** 'gessen': pretend
1784–5 'worþi … saumplis': worthy of as many deaths as the number of examples   **1785–7**
Num. 25:4

Variants   **1797** reisers] riseris α S

1800 as heþene men or eretikis, þat bisien hem to lerne, kepe and teche Goddis
heestis.

Þe þridde [tyme] lordis and prelatis boþe sheden innocent blood, as
Manasses dide, for þei waasten folili her goodis in wakyngis and pleies bi
ny3t and in rere-soperis and oþere vanytees, and taken grete and
1805 vnmesurable taxis of þe comyns, and lesse lordis and prelatis don grete
extorciouns to pore men, and taken pore mennus goodis and paie litil or
nou3t, and out of tyme, for þo. Þerfor, as Myche þe profete seiþ, in iij. cᵒ,
þei hyilden pore men and eten her fleish, and Grosted declariþ wel þis in
his dicte þat bigynneþ þus *Sint lumbi vestri precincti*, and in þe xiij. dicte.
1810 And God seiþ in þe Sauter of sich tirauntis 'þei deuouren my puple as þe
mete of breed'. Hou mych blood lordis sheden in werris for pride and
coueitise, bi councel of false prelatis, confessours and prechours, it passiþ
mannus wit to telle fulli in þis liyf, but of shedyng of blood and sleynge of
pore men bi wiþdrawyng of almes, and in 3yuyng it to deed stockis or
1815 stoonys or to riche clerkis and feyned religiouse, were to speke now, if a
man hadde þe spirit of gostli strengþe.

Now men knelen and preien and offren faste to deed ymagis þat han
neþer hungur ne coold, and dispisen, beten and sleen cristen men maad to
þe ymage and licnesse of þe Hooli Trinite. What onour of God is þis, to
1820 knele and offre to an ymage maad of synful mennus hondis, and to dispise
and robbe þe quyk ymage maad of Goddis hondis, þat is, a cristen man or a
cristen womman? Whanne men 3yue not almese to pore nedi men but to
deed ymagis or riche clerkis þei robben pore men of her owne porcioun and
nedeful sustenaunce assigned to hem of God himsilf, and whanne sich
1825 offreris to deed ymagis robben pore men þei robben Iesu Crist, as he seiþ in
xxv. cᵒ of Matheu 'þat þat 3e diden to oon of þe leest of myne 3e diden to
me'. And if þei shulen be dampned þat 3yuen not mete and drynke and
oþere necessaries to pore men, as Crist seiþ, where shulen þei bicome þat
robben pore men, and so Iesu Crist himsilf? And if þese twei, þat 3yuen not
1830 | f.111a | lyflode and þat robben pore men, shulen be dampned so deep in
helle, where shulen false techeris, [stir]eris and confessours bicome, þat
stiren lordis and riche men to robbe þus pore men, and to [do] þis undur
colour of excellent almes and hoolynesse? But morne we soore for þis
cursidnesse and preie we to God wiþ al oure herte þat, siþ lordis and prelatis
1835 suen Manasses in þese open synnes, God stire hem to sue Manasses in veri
penaunce and make amendis to God and men, lest oure rewme be
conquerid of aliens or of heþene men, for þese open synnes and many mo.

Glosses and biblical references   1803 'wakyngis': nocturnal activities   1804 'rere-soperis': late
[extra] suppers   1807 'out of tyme': after the due date   1807–8 Micah 3:2–3; 'hyilden', strip the
skin from   1808–9 Luke 12:35 (note)   1810–11 Ps. 14:4   1825–7 Matt. 25:40

Variants   1802 tyme] ˣboþeˣ   1803 pleies] pleiyngis α Q S   1809 xiij.] iij. Q, thryde Crowley   1821
quyk *om.* α β Q S   1823 owne] due α Q S, *om.* β   1831 \fla/tereris P, *om.* T   1832 do *om.*

Chapter 11

The firste book of Esdras telliþ hou Cirus kyng of Perseis ȝaf licence to
Iewis to turne aȝen into Ierusalem and Iudee and bilde þe temple of God in
1840   Ierusalem, and bad þat oþere men in his rewme shulde helpe to þis bilding,
and he ȝaf þe vessels herto whiche Nabugodonosor hadde take awei fro
Ierusalem. Þanne is teld þe noumbre of hem þat turneden aȝen into Iudee
vndur Iosue þe prest, þe sone of Iosedech, and vndur Sorobabel þe duyk,
and hou þei bigunnen to bilde þe auter and temple, and what lettyng þei
1845   hadden of enemyes, and what coumfort of God and of his profetis. Þanne is
teld what sorewe Esdras made, for þe prynces and prestis and comunes
token heþene wymmen to wyues aȝenus þe lawe, and hou þe princes and
þe puple repentiden mekeli and verili, and maden amendis to God and men.
     In þe book of Neemye, which is clepid þe secounde book of Esdras,
1850   is teld hou Neemye gat graunt of þe kyng to bilde þe wallis of Ierusalem
and hou he and oþere men, boþe prestis and oþere, prynces and comunes,
bildiden þe wallis and ȝatis and lockis, and touris aboue for defence aȝenus
enemyes, and hou þe enemyes of Iewis purposiden wiþ strong hond to sle
Iewis priueli and distrie her werk. Þanne half þe part of þe ȝonge men
1855   maden þe werk and half þe part was redi to batel; wiþ oon hond þei maden
þe werk and wiþ þe toþer þei helden þe swerd, and ech of hem þat bildide
was girt wiþ his swerd. Þanne it sueþ hou Neemye, duyk of þe puple, dide
freli his office and took no costis assigned to þe duyk, and he dide þus for
pouert of þe puple. Aftir þis doyng Esdras redde in þe book of Goddis lawe
1860   fro þe morewtid til to noon bifor þe multitude of men and wymmen, and
dekenes maden silence in þe puple to here þe lawe. And Esdras radde in þe
book of Goddis lawe fro þe firste dai til to þe laste. Þanne þe children of
Israel camen togidere in fastynge and in sackis or heiris, and erþe was on
hem, and þe seed of þe sones of Israel was departid fro ech alien sone and
1865   þei stoden bifor þe Lord and knoulechiden her synnes and þe wickidnessis
of her fadris. And þei reise[de]n togidere to stonde, and þei radden in þe
book of þe lawe of her God foure siþis in þe dai, and foure siþis in þe nyȝt
þei knoulechiden and herieden her Lord God, and dekenes crieden wiþ
greet vois to her Lord God and baden þe puple rise and blesse God.
1870   Þanne sueþ þe solempne confessioun of Esdras, hou he knoulechide
first þe gloriouse werkis of God and aftirward þe orible synnes | rb | of al þe
puple and of her fadris, and þanne al þe puple made couenaunt and swoor
to kepe Goddis lawe, and to bie not in þe sabat and halidai of hem þat

Glosses and biblical references   1838–42 Ezra 1   1842–5 Ezra 2–8   1845–8 Ezra 9–10   1849–57
Neh. 1–4   1857–9 Neh. 5   1859–69 Neh. 8–9:5   1863 'sackis': sack–cloths   1870–5 Neh. 9:6–
38; 10

Variants   1852 wallis and ȝatis] ȝatis and wallis G ι Q   1856 toþer] oþer α ι Q S   1866 reisen P, reiseden
β, risiden α Q S, risen T

brou3ten vitals to selle, and þei bihi3ten to paie þe firste-fruytis to prestis
1875 and tiþis to þe dekenes, and to brynge al þis to þe temple of God. At þe
laste Neemye suffride neþer Iewis ne straungeris selle ne bie in þe sabatis,
not oneli in Ierusalem but neþer in places ny3 þe wallis, and he rebuykide
and curside and beet men, and made hem ballid, þat token alien wymmen
to be her wyues, as of A3otus, of Amon and of Moab, and chargide hem
1880 gretli in þe Lord þat þei shulden not 3yue her dou3tris to þe sones of
heþene men, and take not of þe dou3tris of heþene men to her owne sones
and to hemsilf.

Þis process of Esdras and of Neemye shulde stire vs to be bisi to
bilde vertues in oure soule aftir turnynge a3en fro caitifte of oure synne,
1885 and to fi3te a3enus temptaciouns and bilde faste vertues, as þei fou3ten wiþ
oon hond a3enus enemyes and bildiden wiþ þe toþer hond; and we shulden
be ful bisi to kepe þe gostli sabat in good werkis and heriyng of God, siþen
þei weren so bisi to kepe þe figuratif sabat.

Þou3 þe book of Tobie is not of bileue, it is a ful deuout stori and
1890 profitable to þe symple puple to make hem to kepe pacience and Goddis
heestis, to do werkis of merci, and teche wel her children, and to take
wyues in þe drede of God, for loue of children and not for foule lust of bodi
ne for coueitise of goodis of þis world. And also children moun lerne here
bi 3onge Tobie to be meke and obedient and redi to serue fadir and modir
1895 in her nede. Þerfor, among alle þe bookis of þe elde testament symple men
of wit shulde rede and here ofte þis book of Tobie, to be trewe to God in
prosperite and aduersite, and eschewe idolatrie, glotenye and coueitise and
to be pacient in tribulacioun and go neuere awei fro þe drede and loue of
God.

1900   Þou3 þe seyne of clerkis or general gaderyng of clergie haþ take þe
book of Iudith among þe noumbre of hooli scriptures, neþeles it is not of þe
canoun or feiþ of þe Bible anentis Ebreies, for þei resseyuen not þe autorite
of þis book; neþeles it was writen in Caldee langage and is noumbrid
among þe stories, as Ierom witnessiþ on þe prolog. But neþeles þis book
1905 comendiþ chastite and abstynence and penaunce and widewehod of Iudith,
and her loue which she hadde to delyuere Goddis puple fro her enemyes,
and to kepe þe feiþ and worschiping of God among his puple. Also þis
book comendiþ þe feiþ and treuþe of Achior, þat was conuertid to Goddis
lawe bi myracle of sleynge of Holofernes bi þe hondis of þe widewe Iudith.
1910 Þanne Iudith repreuyde prestis for þei temptiden God and consentiden to

---

Glosses and biblical references   1875–82 Neh. 13:15–31   1878 'made hem ballid': shaved their
heads   1879 'of A3otus': [women] from Ashdod   1889 'of bileue': canonical   1903 'Caldee':
Syriac (note)   1907–9 Judith 14:5–10   1910–14 Judith 8–9

Variants   1884 oure *om.* α β G ι Q S   1886 oon] þe toon G ι Q   1889 Þou3 ... ful] þe book of tobie is
ful G ι (note)   • is¹] be ι S   1898 drede and loue] loue and drede G ι Q   1900–5 comendiþ] þe book of
iudith comendiþ G (note)   1909 of sleynge] and sleynge G ι Q S

delyuere þe citee to enemyes if God sente not helpe to hem wiþinne fyue
daies, and good prestis token mekeli þis repreuyng of a womman, and she
tauȝte hem hou þei shulden do penauce for þis trespas, and coumforte þe
puple for to triste in God and abide his merci and help, at his owne wille.

1915   Vs nediþ not excuse Iudith fro leesyngis and tresoun to Holofernes, but we
moun fauorabli excuse hir fro dedli synne in þis doynge, for þe grete loue
þat she hadde to Goddis puple, and to sle Holofernes, a blasfemere of God
and distriere of his lawe and puple. And iustli God took þis veniaunce on
Holofernes | f. 11va | for his synnes and harmes do to Goddis puple, and
1920   which he purposide to do if he myȝte lyue longe.

Of þis process proude werriours shulden drede God, þat made
proude Holofernes to be slayn of a womman and al his greet oost to be
scaterid and distried, and cristen men shulden be coumfortid gretli for to
haue ful trist in God and in his [helpe], þat so myȝtili delyueride his puple
1925   fro so greet an enemye and strong oost wiþout persiching of his puple. And
siþ Iudith hadde so greet preisyng for hir doyng, þat was medlid wiþ many
synnes, myche more preisyng shulen þei haue in heuene wiþouten ende þat
putten forþ hemsilf to be martrid for Goddis cause, wiþ trewe menus of
pacience and of charite.

1930   Þe book of Hester telliþ first hou þe queene Vasty was forsaken for
hir pride and was departid fro mariage of kyng Assuerus, and hou Hester,
for hir mekenesse, beute and Goddis grace, was maad queene in þe stide of
Vasti. And þe trewe Mardochee, þe fadir-in-lawe of adopcioun of þis
womman Hester, tauȝte hir to loue God and kepe his lawe, and she was ful
1935   meke and obedient to Mardochee, ȝhe whanne she was queene, as to hir
fadir-in-lawe. Þanne Aaman, of þe kynrede of Agag, conspiride bi sotil
malice to distrie al þe puple of Iewis in þe lond of Assuerus, and hadde
graunt of þe kyng at his owne wille, and þe dai of distriyng and of sleyng
of Iewis was pupplischid þorouȝ al þe rewme. Þanne Mardoche and þe
1940   Iewis diden grete penaunce and maden greet sorewe, and preieden God to
helpe in þat grete nede. And Mardoche sente to Hester þat she shulde do þe
same, and go to þe kyng, in perele of hir liyf, to axe grace of him and
reuokyng of lettris and power grauntid to Aaman, þe enemye of Iewis. And
aftir myche fasting, penaunce and preiere, Hester bitook hirsilf to Goddis
1945   disposicioun and to perele of her deþ, and entride to þe kyng, ȝhe aȝenus
þe lawe of þe lond, whanne she was not clepid, to axe merci and help of þe
kyng for hirsilf and al hir puple. And God turnyde þe fersnesse and cruelte
of þe kyng to mekenesse, merci and benygnyte aȝenus Hester and þe puple

Glosses and biblical references   **1915** 'Vs nediþ not': it is unnecessary for us   **1925–6** 'And
… doyng' Judith 15:8–13   **1930–6** Esther 1–2   **1931** 'departid fro mariage of': separated from
marriage with   **1933** 'Mardochee': Mordecai   **1935** 'ȝhe': yes, indeed   **1936–9** Esther 3
1939–43 Esther 4   **1943–7** Esther 5   **1945** 'disposicioun': control   **1947–53** Esther 6–10, 16:19

Variants   **1913** coumforte] coumfortide G ι Q S T   **1924** puple \helpe/

of Iewis, and þanne he reuokide þe power grauntid to Aaman, and leet
1950 hange him, as he purposide to haue hanged þe trewe Mardoche, and ʒaf
general power to Iewis to sle alle her enemyes in his empire. Aftir þese
þingis þe kyng enhaunside Mardoche and made him grettist next þe kyng,
and ʒaf greet fraunchise and onour to þe Iewis.

Þis storie of Hester shulde stire men to be trewe to God and his
1955 lawe, and putte awei pride and enuye and euere trist in God in alle perels.
And tirauntis shulden be afeerd to conspire aʒenus Goddis seruauntis, lest
God take veniaunce on hem, as he dide on þis [man] Aaman þat conspirid
þe deþ and general distriyng of Iewis.

Þe book of Ioob is ful sutil in vndurstonding, for Ioob argueþ
1960 aʒenus enemyes þat wolde brynge him out of cristen feiþ, and concludiþ
many errours þat suen o[f] her fals bileue and opynyoun. And Ioob
affermeþ not þat al is sooþ þat he spekiþ aʒenus hise aduersaries but
concludiþ hem in her fals bileue, þat many errours suen þerof. And for I
haue declarid in parti in þe glos hou þe harde sentenses of Ioob shulden be
1965 vndurstonde þerfor I passe ouer liʒtli now. First þis book telliþ of þe kyn of
Ioob | vb | and hise richessis, and hooli liyf of him and his children, [and
aftirward it telliþ what tribulacioun bifelde to Iob in his catel, in hise
children] and in his owne bodi, and hou pacientli he suffride þis and þankid
God in al his disesis. Þanne his wiyf, whom þe deuel reseruyde as a special
1970 instrument to him to disseyue Ioob bi his wiyf, as he disseyuede Adam bi
Eue, councelid him to blasfeme God and þerbi die. And Iob repreuyde hir
foli and seide 'if we han resseyued goodis of Goddis hond, whi suffre we
not yuelis, þat is, peynes'? In alle þese þingis Ioob synnede not in hise
lippis.

1975 Þanne sueþ þe disputyng bitwixe Ioob and his frendis, almoost til to
þe ende of þe book. Ioob heelde strongli þe treuþe of cristen feiþ and
speciali of þe risyng aʒen of bodies at domesdai, and hise frendis seiden
many treuþis and medleden falsnesse, and euere purposide an yuel ende
and falsed, for þei helden þat meede is ʒeuen oneli in þis liyf for good
1980 werkis and þat no man is punyschid here, no but for synnes passid, and as
man is punyschid more þan anoþere in þis liyf so he haþ synned more þan
anoþere man lesse punyschid. But al þis is fals, as Ioob preueþ and God

---

Glosses and biblical references   **1949–50** 'leet hange him': had him hanged   **1953** 'fraunchise':
freedom [to live according to their own law]   **1959** 'sutil in vndurstonding': elusive to interpret
1960 'concludiþ': confutes   **1965** 'passe ouer liʒtli': treat it summarily   **1965–74** Job 1, 2:1–10
1969 'disesis': troubles   • 'reseruyde': retained   **1978** 'medleden falsnesse': mixed falsehood
[with truth]   **1978–9** 'purposide an yuel ende and falsed': put forward a wicked and falsified
conclusion

Variants   **1950** purposide] hadde purposid G ɩ Q   **1953** \to/   **1957** þis man aaman α G ɩ Q S   • \Aa/
man   **1960** aʒens hise enemyes α G ɩ Q S   **1961** of] on   **1963–5** And for … now *om.* Gough   **1966–8**
and⁴ aftirward … children *om.* supplied from S   **1973** peynes and in G ɩ Q

confermeþ in þe ende, for whi reward of good dedis is myche more in þe
liyf to-comyng þan in present liyf, and a vertuouse man is punyschid here
1985   for to haue meede in heuene, and comynli a iust man haþ more tribulacioun
in þis liyf þan a wickid man, as it is open of Crist, þat suffride here myche
disese, and of tirauntis þat han prosperite in þis liyf.

And þerfor Ioob telde openli hise goode dedis to coumforte him
aȝenus dispeir, to whiche hise frendis wolden brynge hym, but Ioob dide
1990   þis ouermyche and wiþ sum pride, and iustefied himsilf ouermyche, þat his
frendis conseyueden þat he blasfemyde God and preued God vnriȝtful, and
of þese twei poyntis Ioob repentide in þe ende. Þanne God forȝaf to him þis
litil synne and appreuyd his trewe sentense, and dampned þe errour[s] of
his aduersaries. Þanne Ioob preiede and made sacrifice for hise aduersaries,
1995   and God herde him and dide merci to hem, and God addide alle þingis
double þat Ioob hadde, and he hadde xiiij. þousynde sheep and sixe
þousynde of camelis and a þousynde ȝockis of oxen and a þousynde femal
assis and vij. sones and iij. douȝtris. And Ioob lyuede vij. scoore ȝeeris
aftir his turment, and siȝ his sones and þe sones of hise sones til to þe iiij.
2000   generacioun.

Þis process of Ioob shulde stere men to be iust of lyuyng and to be
pacient in aduersitees, as Ioob was, and to be stidfast in cristen feiþ and
answere wiseli and mekeli to eretikis and aduersaries of oure feiþ, as Peter
and Poul techen, and euere be meke and ful of charite, and preie for oure
2005   enemyes, and loke aftir meede in heuene and not in erþe for oure good
dedis.

Þe Sauter comprehendiþ al þe elde and newe testament and techiþ
pleynli þe mysteries of þe Trinite and of Cristis incarnacioun, passioun,
risyng aȝen and stiyng into heuene and sendyng doun of þe Hooli Goost
2010   and prechyng of þe gospel, and þe comyng of antecrist, and þe general
doom of Crist, and þe glorie of chosun men to blisse and þe peynes of hem
þat shulen be dampned | f. 12ra | in helle; and ofte rehersiþ þe stories of þe
elde testament, and bryngeþ in þe kepyng of Goddis heestis and loue of
enemyes. No book in þe elde testament is hardere to vndurstondyng to vs
2015   Latyns for oure lettre discordiþ myche fro þe Ebreu, and many doctouris
taken litil heede to þe lettre but al to þe gostli vndurstonding. Wel were
hym þat coude wel vndurstonde þe Sauter and kepe it in his lyuyng and

Glosses and biblical references   **1986** 'open of Crist': manifest in relation to Christ   **1993** 'trewe
sentense': the truth of what he said   **1994–2000** Job 42   **1995–6** 'addide alle þingis double þat
Ioob hadde': doubled everything that Job had previously had   **2005** 'loke aftir': anticipate
2011 'chosun': elect   **2015** 'Latyns': members of the Roman Church   • 'oure lettre discordiþ
myche': our text is very different   **2016** 'lettre but al to þe gostli vndurstondyng': literal meaning
but direct all their attention to the spiritual meaning

Variants   **1987** han myche prosperite G ι Q   **1988** him] himsilf G ι Q   **1993** errour   **2001**
lyuyuyng   **2007–23** *om.* G   **2007** elde and newe testament] olde testament and newe ι Q

seie it deuoutli and conuycte Iewis þerbi, for many men þat seien it
vndeuoutli and lyuen out of charite lien foule on hemsilf to God and
2020 blasfemen him whanne þei crien it ful loude to mennus eeris in þe chirche.
Þerfor God ȝyue grace to vs to lyue wel in charite and seie it deuoutli and
vndurstonde it treuli, and to teche it openli to cristen men and Iewis, and
brynge hem þerbi to oure cristen feiþ and brennynge charite.
    Þe Prouerbis or Parablis of Salomon techiþ men to lyue iustli to
2025 God and man; Ecclesiastes techiþ men to forsake and sette at nouȝt alle
goodis in þe world, and to drede God and kepe his heestis; Þe Songis of
Songis techen men to sette al her herte in þe loue of God and of her
neiȝboris, and to do al her bisynesse to brynge men to charite and
saluacioun bi good ensaumple and trewe prechyng, and wilful suffryng of
2030 peyne and deþ, if nede be.
    Prouerbis speken myche of wisdom and keping of Goddis heestis,
in comending trewe techyng and in repreuyng false techyng. And Prouerbis
treten myche of riȝtfulnesse and iust domes and gouernaunce, and of
punysching of auoutrie and oþere falsnessis, and comenden myche iust
2035 lordis and sugetis and repreuen strongli wrongful lordis and rebel sugetis.
Also Prouerbis techen derkli þe mysteries of Crist and of Hooli Chirche,
and techen myche wisdom and prudence for þe soule and þe bodi.
Þerfor lordis, iugis and comynes also, and nameli prestis, shulden studie
wel þis book and reule hemsilf þerbi, to saluacioun of bodi and of soule.
2040   Ecclesiastes is a ful sutil book for Salomon spekiþ in many
persoones and concludiþ her entent and sentense, not in appreuyng þe
sentense of fleischli men, þat preisen more bodili goodis and lustis of þe
bodi þan heuenli goodis and likyng of vertues, and dampneþ many errours
of worldli men, and shewiþ þat al is vanyte til me come to þe drede of God
2045 and kepyng of his heestis. Þerfor men must be ful wel war hou þei
vndurstonde Salomon in þis book, þat þei appreue noon errour and dampne
no treuþe for mysconseyuyng of Salamonis wordis and þe Hooli Goostis
wordis in þis book.
    Þe Songis of Songis touchen derkli þe state of þe synagoge, fro þe
2050 goyng out of Egipt til to Cristis incarnacioun and passioun, and þanne þo
Songis touchen þe state of Cristis chirche and of þe synagoge in þe ende of
þe world, and treten hiȝli of loue to God and neiȝbore also. And þis book is
so sutil to vndurstonde þat Iewis ordeyneden þat no man shulde studie it no
but he were of xxx. ȝeer and hadde able wit to vndurstonde þe gostli

Glosses and biblical references   2018 'conuycte': persuade   2019 'lien foule on': lie foully
concerning   2020 'mennus eeris': i.e., to those hearing them   2041 'concludiþ her entent and
sentense': refutes their intention and meaning   2050 'goyng out of': exodus from

Variants   2024 techiþ] teche α, techen β ι Q T   2026 Songis] song T   2038 iugis *om.* G ι Q   2045
ful *om.* α β G ι Q S, ful war T   2049 Songis¹] song T   2050 ˣinˣto   2052 of loue to God] of þe loue of
god β T

2055 priuytees of þis book, for summe of þe book semeþ to fleischli men to
sowne vncleene loue of leccherie, where it telliþ hi3 gostli loue and greet
priuytees of Crist and of his chirche. Þerfor men moten | rb | be ful wel war
to conseyue wel þe wordis of þe Hooli Goost in þis book, and knowe
whanne Crist spekiþ to þe chirche or to þe synagoge and whanne þe
2060 synagoge spekiþ to God and whanne þe chirche spekiþ to Crist and whanne
God spekiþ to aungels, patriarkis and profetis, and apostlis, and whanne
þese persoones speken to þe synagoge or to þe chirche, or a3enward.

Þe book of Wisdom, þou3 it be not a book of bileue, it techiþ
myche ri3tfulnesse and preisiþ wisdom and repreueþ fleishli men for her
2065 fals bileue and yuel lyuyng and comendiþ myche iuste men sad in bileue
and vertuouse lyuyng, and touchyþ myche of Cristis incarnacioun, his
manhed and godhed togidere, and dampneþ gretli idolatrie and fals
worschiping of idols and false goddis.

Þou3 Ecclesiastici be no book of bileue, it techiþ myche wisdom
2070 and prudence for soule and bodi, and haþ myche þe sentense of Prouerbis,
and comaundiþ men to þenke and speke of Goddis heestis, and for to drede
God and loue him and euere haue mynde of deþ and of þe greete doom, to
kepe men out of synne and in parfit loue to God and man. Also it preisiþ
myche almesse and good preiere and repreueþ gretli extorsiouns and
2075 wrongis, and false oþis and false mesuris and false wei3tis and al fraude,
pryuy and apert. At þe laste it comendiþ good men and herieþ God, þat
delyueriþ fro alle perels. If þis book be wel vndurstonden it is profitable
boþe to gostli gouernours and bodili lordis and iustices, and comynes also.

Þe Profetis han a general prologe for alle, and for I declaride
2080 sumdel þe Greet Profetis and in parti þe Litle Profetis, and þenke soone to
make an ende, wiþ Goddis helpe, of þe glose of þe Smale Profetis, I þenke
now to passe ouer wiþouten ony tariyng.

Þe firste book of Machabeis telliþ hou greet destruccioun and
cruelte Antioke þe noble dide a3enus þe Iewis, and hou many þousynde he
2085 killid of hem þat wolden holde Goddis lawe, and brente þe bookis of
Goddis lawe and defoulide þe temple of Ierusalem and compellid men, for
drede of deþ, to do idolatrie and forsake God and his lawe. And he took
vessels and tresours in þe temple and bar into his lond, and he brente þe
cite of Ierusalem and distriede þe housis þerof and þe wallis þerof in
2090 cumpas, and he took þe hi3 tour of Dauiþ and set men of armes þerinne, to

Glosses and biblical references   2056 'sowne': signify   • 'where': whereas   2062 'a3enward':
vice versa   2070 'haþ myche þe sentense of': is very similar in meaning to   2076–7 Ecclus
44–50   2083–96 1 Macc. 1   2084 'Antioke': Antiochus

Variants   2056 sowne] schewe S *sec. m.*, shewe β   2063 þou3 … bileue it *om.* G (note)   2069 Þou3 …
techiþ] þe book of ecclesiastici teechiþ G (note)   2070 for soule … sentense *om.* G   2075 wrongis] wrong
α β G ι Q S   2079–82 *om.* G Gough   2080 Litle] smale ι Q

let men come to Ierusalem. And þei diden myche harm to þe puple of
Israel, and whoeuere held þe bookis of Goddis testament and kepte his
lawe was slayn, bi comaundement of Antiok þe kyng. And wymmen þat
circumcididen her children weren slayn bi comaundement of Antiok þe

2095   kyng, and þei hangiden children bi þe neckis bi alle þe housis of þe men of
Israel, and killiden hem þat circumcididen children.

Þanne roos Mathathias þe prest and fledde fro Ierusalem into
Modyn, and biweilide gretli þis distriyng of þe puple, of þe temple and
citee and of al þe lond. And he aȝenstood þe kyng and his mynystris and

2100   killide þe kyngis mynystris þat compellide men to do idolatrie, and he
killide a man þat dide idolatrie and distriede þe auter wheronne þe idolatrie
was doon. Þanne Mathathias and his sones fledden into hillis and leften alle
þingis whiche þei hadden in þe cite, and many men þat souȝten doom and
riȝtfulnesse, and wolden kepe Goddis lawe, camen to hem in desert. And

2105   heþene men maden werre on hem in sabatis, and many dieden | f. 12va | in
her symplenesse, for þei nolden make batel in sabatis. Þanne many Iewis
weren gaderid to hym and maden a greet oost, and weren redi to fiȝte in
sabatis, and þei killiden synners in greet wraþþe. And Matatias and his
frendis cumpassiden and distrieden auteris, and circumcididen alle children

2110   which þei founden in þe coostis of Israel, and þei pursuyden þe children of
pride. And þe werk hadde prosperite in her hondis, and þei gaten þe lawe
fro þe hondis of heþene men and of kyngis, and ȝauen not strengþe to þe
synful man. And whanne Matatias was in poynt of deþ he coumfortide hise
sones to putte her lyues for þe lawe of God, bi ensaumple of Abraham and

2115   oþere hooli men bifor-goyng, and he ordeyned Iudas Machabeus to be
duyk of bataile, and ordeyned Symount his sone to be fadir and prest to
hem, for he was a man of councel.

Þanne ben teld many batels of Iudas Machabeus aȝenus heþene
men, and of grete victories bi Goddis help. Þanne Iudas Machabeus made

2120   frenschipe wiþ Romayns, for her prudence, riȝtfulnesse and power. And
whanne Iudas was deed in batel þe puple ordeynede Ionathas his broþer
prince and duyk for to holde werre aȝenus heþene men. Þanne ben teld
many batels of Ionathas, and victories which he hadde aȝenus heþene men.
Þanne Ionathas, aftir many victories, sente to renule frenschip wiþ

2125   Romayns and wiþ Sparciatis, þat weren of þe kyn of Iewis, and Ionathas
and his sones weren slayn at þe laste bi treson of Trifon, þat was an heþene
man and myȝti duyk. Þanne Symount was maad duyk of þe puple in þe
stide of Iudas Machabeus and of Ionathas, and he dide many batels and

Glosses and biblical references   **2091** 'let men come': prevent men from coming   **2097–117**
1 Macc. 2   **2106** 'sabatis': sabbaths   **2118–27** 1 Macc. 3–12   **2124** 'renule': renew   **2125**
'Sparciatis': men of Sparta   **2127–34** 1 Macc. 13–16

Variants   **2098** \and/   **2101** ydolatrie on þe auteer and G ι Q   **2104** And *om.* ι Q   **2109** alle *om.* G ι Q
2110 þe¹] alle þe G ι Q   **2116** to be *om.* G ι Q

stronge and hadde greet victories aȝenus heþene men, and Iewis hadden
2130 myche reste vndur him. And he made strongeholdis and citees in Iuda, and
he renuylide frenschip wiþ Romayns and Sparciatis, and hadde myche
glorie of his folk and of heþene kyngis. At þe laste Symount and his twei
sones weren slayn bi tresoun, and Ioon his sone was prynce of prestis aftir
his fadir dai, and dide many batels aȝenus heþene men.

2135   Þe secounde book of Machabeis telliþ myche þe same sentence as
þe firste book, and haþ a fewe special poyntis of Eliodorus, of Eleaȝarus
and of þe noble widewe and hir vij. sones. Eliodorus was sent of þe heþene
kyng to take awei þe tresours of þe temple of Ierusalem and bere þo to þe
kyng, and þouȝ þe tresours weren kept for þe liyflode of widewes and
2140 fadirles children, and summe weren anoþere mannus goodis, Eliodorus
wolde algate bere alle to þe kyng. But God made him and hise felowis sore
afeerd, and Eliodorus was beten almoost to þe deþ of a ferdful oon sittynge
on an hors þat hadde twei ȝonge men aboute him, and Eliodorus was cast
doun to þe grounde and was born out on a beere, and lai doumb. And
2145 whanne þe hiȝeste prest offride sacrifice and preiede for þe helþe of
Heliodorus God grauntide liyf to him, and he þankid God and þe hiȝeste
prest, and ȝede to þe kyng and tolde him hou it stood, and he witnesside to
alle men þe grete werkis of God, which he hadde seyn wiþ hise iȝen.
        Þanne is teld þe cursid dedis of Iason þe prest, þat cam in bi
2150 symonye and wolde brynge Iewis to idolatrie and sodomye, and to forsake
God and his lawe. Þanne is teld of þe grete cruelte of Antiok which he dide
aȝenus þe Iewis and þe hooli place of Ierusalem, and God suffride þis for
þe | vb | synnes of þe puple, for whi God chees not þe folk for þe place but
þe place for þe folk. Þanne Eliaȝarus ches to die a sharp deþ raþere þan he
2155 wolde breke Goddis lawe in a litil poynt, to ete pork, ȝhe to feyne to ete
pork. Aftir þis it sueþ hou þe blessid widewe and hir seuene sones weren
marterid for þei nolden breke Goddis lawe, and hou gloriousli þe blessid
modir coumfortide hem to take deþ wiþ ioie for þe lawe of God.
        Þis stori and process of Machabeis shulde stire cristen men to holde
2160 Goddis lawe to liyf and deþ, and if knyȝtis shulden vse þe swerd aȝenus
ony cursid men þei shulden vse it aȝenus lordis and and prestis principali
þat wolen compelle men, for drede of prisoun and deþ, to forsake þe treuþe
and fredom of Cristis gospel. But God for his greet merci ȝyue veri
repentaunce to hem þat pursuen þus trewe men, and graunte pacience,
2165 mekenesse and charite to hem þat ben þus pursued. Amen.

Glosses and biblical references   2135–48 2 Macc. 3   2142 'of a ferdful oon': by a fearsome
man   2144 'beere': litter   2149–51 2 Macc. 4   2149–50 'cam in bi symonye': i.e., bought the
position of high priest   2151–4 2 Macc. 5   2154–6 2 Macc. 6   2156–8 2 Macc. 7

Variants   2132 twei *om.* G ι Q Gough   2156 hir vij. seuene   2161 prestis and principali   2165 to …
Amen *om.* β

Chapter 12

But it is to wite þat hooli scripture haþ foure vndurstondyngis: literal, allegorik, moral and anagogik. Þe literal vndurstonding techiþ þe þing doon in deede, and literal vndurstonding is ground and foundement of þre gostli vndurstondingis, in so myche as Austin in his pistle to Vyncent, and oþere

2170 doctours, seyn oneli bi þe literal vndurstonding a man mai argue aзenus an aduersarie. Allegorik is a gostli vndurstonding þat techiþ what þing men owen for to bileue of Crist or of hooli chirche. Moral is a gostli vndurstonding þat techiþ men what vertues þei owen to sue and what vices þei owen to fle. Anagogik is a gostli vndurstonding þat techiþ men what

2175 blisse þei shulen haue in heuene. And þese foure vndurstondingis moun be takun in þis word 'Ierusalem', for whi to þe literal vndurstonding it signefieþ an erþeli citee, as Londoun or sich anoþere; to allegorie, it signefieþ hooli chirche in erþe þat fiзtiþ aзenus synnes and fendis; to moral vndurstonding, it signefieþ a cristen soule; to anagogik, it signefieþ

2180 hooli chirche regnynge in blisse or heuene, and þo þat ben þerinne. And þese þre gostli vndurstondingis ben not autentik or of bileue [no] but if þei ben groundid openli in þe text of hooli scripture in oo place or oþer, or in open resoun þat mai not be distried, or whanne þe gospelers or oþere apostlis taken allegorie of þe elde testament and confermen it, as Poul, in

2185 þe pistil to Galatas, in þe iiij. cᵒ, preueþ þat Sara, þe fre wiyf and principal of Abraham, wiþ Isaac hir sone, signefieþ bi allegorie þe newe testament and þe sones of biheest, and Agar þe handmaide, wiþ hir sone Ismael, signefieþ bi allegorie þe elde testament and fleischli men þat shulen not be resseyued into þe eritage of God wiþ þe sones of biheest þat holden þe

2190 treuþe and fredom of Cristis gospel wiþ endeles charite.

Also hooli scripture haþ many figuratif spechis, and, as seynt Austyn seiþ in þe þridde book of *Cristen Teching*, þat auctours of hooli scripture vsiden moo figures, þat is mo figuratif spechis, þan gramariens moun gesse þat reden not þo figures in hooli scripture. It is to be war in þe

2195 bigynnyng þat we take not to þe lettre a figuratif speche, for þanne, as Poul seiþ, 'þe lettre | f. 13ra | sleeþ but þe spirit, þat is, gostli vndurstonding, quykeneþ'. For whanne a þing which is seid figuratifli is taken so as if it is seid propirli me vndurstond[iþ] fleischli, and noon is clepid more couenabli

---

Glosses and biblical references   **2166** 'to wite': to be known   • 'vndurstondyngis': senses
2171 'aduersarie': opponent [when determining doctrine]   **2176** 'takun': apprehended   **2181**
'autentik': authoritative   **2183** 'distried': demolished   **2184–90** Gal. 4:22–31   **2191** 'spechis':
expressions   **2194** 'moun gesse': may estimate   **2195** 'to þe lettre': literally   **2195–7** 2 Cor. 3:6
2198 'propirli': literally, not figuratively   • 'me vndurstondiþ': it is understood   • 'fleischli':
carnally   • 'couenabli': appropriately

Variants   **2166–973** (chs 12–15) *om.* G   **2181** no *om.* P T   **2197** is³] be α β ι Q S   **2198** me vndirstondiþ]
men vndurstonden P T

þe deeþ of soule þan whanne vndurstonding, þat passiþ beestis, is maad
2200   suget to þe fleish in suynge þe lettre. Whateuere þing in Goddis word mai
not be referrid propirli to honeste of vertues ne to þe treuþe of feiþ þat is
figuratif speche. Honeste of vertues perteyneþ to loue of God and þe
neiȝbore; treuþe of feiþ perteyneþ to knowe God and þe neiȝbore. Hooli
scripture comaundiþ noþing but charite; it blameþ noþing but coueitise, and
2205   in þat maner it enformeþ þe vertues or good condiciouns of men. Hooli
scripture affermeþ noþing but cristen feiþ bi þingis passid, present and to-
comyng, and alle þese þingis perteynen to nursche charite and make it
strong, and to ouercome and quenche coueitise. Also it is figuratif speche
where þe wordis maken allegorie, or a derk licnesse or a parable, and it is a
2210   figuratif speche in þe j. chapitre of Ieremye: 'todai I haue ordeyned þee on
folkis and rewmes, þat þou drawe up bi þe roote and distrie and bilde and
plaunte', þat is, þat þou drawe out elde synnes and distrie þe
circumstaunces or causis of þo, and bilde vertues and plaunte good werkis
and customs.
2215   Alle þingis in hooli scripture þat semen to vnwise men to be ful of
wickidnesse aȝenus a man himsilf or aȝenus his neiȝbore ben figuratif
spechis, and þe priuytees or gostli vndurstondingis shulden be souȝt out of
vs, to þe fedyng or kepyng of charite. Sich a reule shal be kept in figuratif
spechis þat so longe it be turned in mynde bi diligent consideracioun til þe
2220   expownyng or vndurstonding be brouȝt to þe rewme of charite. If ony
speche of scripture sowneþ propirli charite it owiþ not to be gessid a
figuratif speche, and if it forbediþ wickidnesse or comaundiþ profit or good
doyng it is no figuratif speche. If it semeþ to comaunde cruelte eþer
wickidnesse, eþer to forbede profite eþer good doyng, it is a figuratif
2225   speche. Crist seiþ 'if ȝe eten not þe fleisch of mannus sone and drynken not
his blood, ȝe shulen not haue liyf in ȝou'. Þis speche semeþ to comaunde
wickidnesse or cruelte; þerfor it is a figuratif speche, and comaundiþ men
to comyne wiþ Cristis passioun and to kepe in mynde swetli and profitabli
þat Cristis fleish was woundid and crucified for vs. Also, whanne hooli
2230   scripture seiþ 'if þin enemy hungriþ feede þou him; if he þirstiþ ȝyue þou
drynke to him' it comaundiþ benefice or good doyng. Whanne it [seiþ]
'þou shalt gadere togidere coolis on his heed', it semeþ þat wickidnesse of
yuel wille is comaundid; þis is seid bi figuratif speche, þat þou vndurstonde
þat þe coolis of fier ben brennyng weilyngis or morenyngis of penaunce, bi

Glosses and biblical references   2199 'passiþ': surpasses   2199–200 'maad suget': is
subjected   2206 'bi': in relation to   2209 'derk licnesse': obscure image (note)   2209–12 Jer.
1:10   2217 'of': by   2222 'and if it [any expression]'   2225–6 John 6:54   2228 'comyne wiþ':
share in   2229–36 Rom. 12:20

Variants   2201 þat] it α β ι Q S   2204 but[1,2]] no but α β S   2206 but] no but α β ι Q S   2221 gessid
sup. ras.   2222 if it *om.* α β ι Q S   • \if/   2223–5 \if ... speche/   2231 seiþ] is seid

2235 which þe pride of him is maad hool, which sorewiþ þat he was enemye of a
man þat helpiþ and releueþ his wrecchidnesse.

Also þe same word or þe same þing in scripture is takun sumtyme
in good and sumtyme in yuele, as a lioun signefieþ sumtyme Crist and in
anoþere place it signefieþ þe deuel. Also sourdouȝ is set sumtyme in yuel,
2240 where Crist seiþ 'be ȝe war of þe sourdouȝ of Farisees, which is ipocrisie';
sourdouȝ is set also in good, whanne Crist seiþ 'þe rewme of heuenys is
liyk sourdouȝ', etc. | rb | And whanne not o þing aloone but tweyne or moo
ben feelid or vndurstonden bi þe same wordis of scripture, þouȝ þat is hid
þat he vndurstood þat wroot it, þat is no perele if it mai be preued bi oþere
2245 places of hooli writ þat ech of þo þingis acordiþ wiþ treuþe. And in hap þe
autour of scripture seiþ þilke sentense in þe same wordis whiche we wole
vndurstonde, and certis þe Spirit of God, þat wrouȝte þese þingis bi þe
auctour of scripture, bifor-seȝ wiþout doute þat þilke sentence shulde come
to þe redere or to þe herere, ȝhe þe Hooli Goost purueide þat þilke
2250 sentence, for it is groundid on treuþe, shulde come to þe redere or to þe
herere, for whi what myȝte be purueide of God largeliere and
plenteuousliere in Goddis spechis þan þat þe same wordis be vndurstonden
in many maneris, which maneris or wordis of God þat ben not of lesse
autorite maken to be preued. Austin in þe þridde book of *Cristen Teching*
2255 seiþ al þis and myche more, in þe bigynnyng þerof.

Also he whos herte is ful of charite comprehendiþ wiþouten ony
errour þe manyfold habundaunce and largeste techinge of Goddis
scripturis, for whi Poul seiþ 'þe fulnesse of lawe is charite', and, in anoþere
place, 'þe ende of lawe, þat is, þe perfeccioun or fulfilling of lawe, is
2260 charite of cleene herte and of good concience and of feiþ not feyned'. And
Iesu Crist seiþ 'þou shalt loue þi Lord God of al þin herte and of al þi soule
and of al þi mynde, and þi neiȝbore as þisilf, for in þese twei
comaundementis hangiþ al þe lawe and profetis'. And as þe roote of alle
yuelis is coueitise so þe roote of alle goodis is charite; charite bi which we
2265 louen God and þe neiȝbore holdiþ sikirli al þe greetnesse and largenesse of
Goddis spechis. Þerfor, if it is not leiser to seke alle hooli scriptures, to
expowne alle þe wlapping[is] of wordis, to perse alle þe priuytees of
scriptures, holde þou charite where alle þingis hangen, so þu shalt holde þat
þat þou lernedist þere. Also þou shalt holde þat þat þou lernedist not, for if

---

Glosses and biblical references　　2235 'maad hool': healed　　2240 'sourdouȝ': leaven　　• Matt.
16:6　　2241–2 Matt. 13:33　　2244 'þat he vndurstood þat wroot it': what he who wrote it meant
by it　　2245 'in hap': by chance　　2248 'bifor–seȝ': saw in advance　　2249 'purueide': arranged
in advance　　2258 Rom. 13:10　　2258–60 I Tim. 1:5　　2260–3 Matt. 22:37–40　　2263–4 I Tim.
6:10　　2266 'it is not leiser': there is no opportunity　　2267 'wlappingis': wrappings, layers

Variants　　2235 was maad enemye　　2243 is] be ι Q S　　2244 vndurstood] vndirstonde α β ι S　　2245 writ]
scripture α β ι Q S　　2251 forwhi] whi ι Q　　2258 scripturis] scripture ι Q　　2267 wlapping P T

2270   þou knowist charite þou knowist sumþing whereonne also þat hangiþ þat in
       hap þou knowist not, and in þat þat þou vndurstondist in scripturis charite
       is opyn, and in þat þat þou vndurstondist not charite is hid. Þerfor he þat
       holdiþ charite in vertues or in good condicions holdiþ boþe þat þat is open
       and þat þat is hid in Goddis wordis. Austin seiþ al þis and myche more in a
2275   sermoun of þe preisyng of charite.
           Also seuene reulis of Ticonye and of Austin declaren many derk
       þingis of hooli scriptures. Þe firste reule is of Iesu Crist and of his hooli
       bodi or spousesse. O persoone of þe heed and of þe bodi, þat is, of Crist
       and of hooli chirche, is shewid to vs in þis reule, for it is not seid in veyn to
2280   feiþful men 'ȝe ben þe seed of Abraham', whanne þer is o seed of
       Abraham, which seed is Crist. Doute we not whanne scripture goiþ fro þe
       heed to þe bodi, or fro þe bodi to þe heed, and neþeles it goiþ not awei fro
       oon and þe same persoone, for whi o persoone spekiþ in Isaie 'he settide a
       mytre to me as to a spouse, and he o[urne]de me as a spousesse wiþ an
2285   ournement'. And neþeles it is to vndurstonde what of þese twei acordiþ to
       þe heed, þat is, Crist, and what acordiþ to þe bodi, þat is Hooli Chirche, for
       whi a mytre acordiþ to Crist, which is þe spouse, and an ournement acordiþ
       to Hooli Chirche, which is þe spousesse | f. 13va | of Crist.
           Þe secounde reule, as Ticonye seiþ, is of þe bodi of Crist, which
2290   bodi is departid into twei, but certis þis bodi of Crist ouȝte not to be clepid
       so, for treuli it is not þe bodi of Crist, which shal not be wiþ him wiþouten
       ende, but it shulde be seid of þe veri bodi and of þe medlid bodi of Crist, or
       of þe veri bodi and feyned bodi of Crist, for whi ipocritis shulen be seid to
       be not wiþ Crist not oneli wiþouten ende but also now, þouȝ þei semen to
2295   be in þe chirche of Crist. Wherefor þis reule myȝte be clepid þus, þat it
       were seid of þe medlid chirche, þat is, þat comprehendiþ chosen men to
       blis and also ipocritis þat shulen be dampned. And þis reule axiþ a wakyng
       or diligent redere. Whanne it spekiþ of oþere men it semiþ to speke now as
       to þe same men to which it spak bifore, or it semeþ to speke of þe same
2300   men whanne it spekiþ of oþere men, as if o bodi be of euer-eiþer, for
       temporal medlyng and for comynynge of sacramentis. To þis reule it
       perteyneþ þat þe chirche seiþ in Songis 'I am blac and fair, as þe
       tabernaclis of Cedar, as þe skynnes of Salomon'. Þe chirche seide þat she is
       euer-eiþer for temporal vnyte wiþinne oo net of good fischis and of yuele

Glosses and biblical references   2280 Gal. 3:29   2283–5 Is. 61:10   2297 'axiþ a wakyng':
requires a vigilant   2300 'euer-eiþer': each of the two   2301 'temporal medlyng': mixing on
earth   2302–3 Song of Songs 1:4 (note)

Variants   2271–2 \and ... opyn/   2271 scripturis] scripture ι Q   2276–348 *om.* Gough   2276 derk
om. ι Q   2278 bodi or spousesse P T, spirit α ι Q S Crowley, spouse β (note)   2284 onouride α β ι P Q
S (note)   2285 \to/   2288 spousesse] spouse α β ι Q S   2289 of þe bodi *bis*   2290 ˣnotˣ not   2299 to
which] of whiche Q, whiche ι

2305 fischis, for whi þe tabernaclis of Cedar perteynen to Ismael, þat shal not be
eir wiþ þe sone of þe fre wiyf.

Þe þridde reule is of biheestis and of lawe. Þis reule mai be seid
also of þe spirit and lettre. It mai be seid also of grace and of
comaundement, and Ticonye erride in seiynge þat werkis ben ȝouun of
2310 God to vs for merit of feiþ, but feiþ itsilf is so of vs þat it is not of God to
vs.

Þe fourþe reule is of al and of parti, whanne summe of a þing is set
for al or, aȝenward, al is set for a parti.

Þe fyueþe reule is of tymes, and þis is bi a figure clepid
2315 synodoches, whanne a part is set for al or al is set for o part. Oon euangelist
seiþ þat it was doon aftir eiȝte daies whanne þe face of Crist shynede as þe
sunne, and anoþere gospeler seiþ þat it was doon aftir sixe daies. Euer-
eiþer myȝte not be soþ þat is seid of þe noumbre of daies, no but he þat
seide aftir eiȝte daies be vndurstondun to haue set for þe hool dai þe laste
2320 part of þe dai, siþ Crist biforseid it to come, and to haue set for þe hool dai
þe firste part of þe dai in which he shewiþ þat þe apperyng of Cristis face
was fulli doon, and þat he þat seide aftir sixe daies rekenede al þe hool
daies and þe myddil daies and noon oþere. Bi þis kynde of speche, bi
which kynde al is signefied bi a part, þilke question of Cristis rising aȝen is
2325 asoilid. Þe laste part of þe dai wherinne Crist suffride deþ is taken for al þe
dai wiþ þe niȝt passid bifore, and þe firste part of Sundai in whos morewtid
he roos aȝen is taken for al þe Sundai, and þe nyȝt bifor-goinge and þe
sabat wiþ þe hool nyȝt bifor-goyng is al hool dai and nyȝt. If þese nyȝtis
and þese daies ben not takun þus þer moun not be þre daies and þre nyȝtis
2330 in whiche he biforeseid þat he shulde be in þe herte of erþe. Also þis reule
of tymes is taken for lawful noumbris, as ben vij., x. and xij. and sich mo,
for oft sich noumbris ben set for al tyme, as þis þat Dauiþ seiþ 'seuene siþis
in þe dai I seide preisyng or heriyng to þee' is noon oþere þing þan þis, 'his
heriyng be euere in my mouþ'. Also bi an hundrid and xliiij. in Apocalips
2335 is signefied þe | vb | vniuersite or alle þe multitude of seyntis.

Þe sixte reule is of recapitulacioun or rehersyng a þing doon bifore,
not in ordre as it is set, for whi summe þingis ben seid so as if þei sueden in
þe ordre of tyme, or ben teld bi contynuyng of þingis, þat is, þat ben ioyned
next togidere, whanne þe telling is clepid aȝen priueli to þe formere þingis
2340 þat weren left out. And if men vndurstonden not sich seiyng bi þis reule þei
erren, as in Genesis it is seid 'God plauntide paradiys in Eden at þe eest
and settide þere þe man þat he fourmyde, and God brouȝt forþ ȝit of erþe

Glosses and biblical references **2315** 'synodoches': synecdoche **2315–17** Luke 9:28 **2317**
'and … daies' Matt. 17:1; Mark 9:1 **2325** 'asoilid': resolved **2329–30** Matt. 12:40 **2332–3** Ps.
118:164 **2333–4** Ps. 33:2 **2334–5** Apoc. 7:4, 14:1 **2335** 'vniuersite': entirety **2341–3** Gen. 2:8, 9

Variants **2310** \so/ **2317** seiþ] seide α β S **2325–6** wherinne … dai *om*. ι Q Crowley **2328** al hool]
al an hool ι Q, þe hool T **2337** þei] þo α β ι Q S • sueden] suen α β ι Q S

ech fair tre', etc. Þis is seid bi recapitulacioun. In liyk maner 'þe lond was
of o lippe', þat is, speche, is seid bi recapitulacioun.

2345   Þe seuenþe reule is of þe deuel and of his bodi, for he is heed of alle
wickid men þat ben his bodi in a maner and shulen go wiþ him into þe
turment of euerlastinge fier, as Crist is þe heed of hooli chirche which is his
bodi and shal be wiþ him in rewme and glorie euerlastinge.

Also þei þat han likynge for to studie in hooli writ shulen be
2350   charchid þat þei kunne þe kyndis and maneris of spekyngis in hooli
scripturis, and [þat þei] perseyuen dil<igentli> and holden wel in <mynde>
hou a þing is w<ont> to be seid in ho<oli scrip>turis. Also, þat is souereyn
help and moost nedeful, preie þei þat God ȝyue to hem þe veri
vndurstonding of hooli scripture, for þei reden in þo scripturis aboute
2355   which þei ben studiouse þat 'God ȝyueþ wisdom and kunnyng and
vndurstondingis of his face', þat is, ȝifte and grace. Also, if her studie is
doon wiþ mekenesse and loue of cristen lore, it is of God. Austin writiþ al
þis in þe þridde book of *Cristen Techyng*, aboute þe myddil and in þe ende.
Isidere in þe firste book of *Souereyn Good* touchiþ þese reulis shortliere,
2360   but I haue hym not now, and Lire in þe bigynnyng of þe Bible touchiþ
more openli þese reulis, but I haue him not now, and Ardmacan in þe
bigynnyng of his book *De Questionibus Armenorum* ȝyueþ many good
groundis to vndurstonde hooli scripture to þe lettre, and gostli
vndurstondyng also, but I haue him not now.

2365   Also noþing mai seme to me to be wisere, noþing of more
eloquence þan is hooli scripture and þe auctours þerof, þat weren enspirid
of God, and þei ouȝten not speke in oþere manere þan þei diden, and þe
profetis, and moost Amos, weren ful eloquent, and seynt Poul was ful
eloquent in his epistlis. Also þe autours of hooli scripture spaken derkli, þat
2370   þe priuytees þerof be hid fro vnfeiþful men, and good men ben excercisid
or ocupied and þat in expownyng hooli scripture þei haue a newe grace,
diuerse fro þe firste auctours. Austin, in þe bigynnyng of þe iiij. book of
Cristen Techyng.

Also, as þe litle richessis of Iewis which þei baren awei fro Egipt
2375   weren in comparisoun of richessis which þei hadden aftirward in Ierusalem
in þe tyme of Salomon, so greet is þe profitable kunnyng of filosofores
bookis if it is comparisound to þe kunnyng of hooli scriptures, for whi
whateuere þing a man lerneþ wiþouten hooli writ, if þe þing lerned is veyn
it is dampned in hooli writ, if it is profitable it is foundid þere. And whanne

---

Glosses and biblical references   2343–4 Gen. 11:1   2349 'likynge': desire   2350 'charchid þat
þei kunne': charged with knowing   2355–6 Prov. 2:6   2360 'bigynnyng of': prologues to   2365
'me', i.e., Augustine   2374 'as þe litle': as small as the

Variants   2344 speche ˣþatˣ is   2351–2 \þat … scripturis/   2351 þei þat   2355 ȝyueþ] ȝeue ι Q S   2361
armacan Q T, armacam ι   2365 to me to be] to be α ι Q S *pr. m.*   2372 ˣþriddeˣ\ iiij/   2374 as alle
þe   2377 to] ˣinˣ to

2380 a man fyndiþ þere alle þingis which he lerned profitabli in oþere | f. 14ra |
place, he shal fynde myche more plenteuousli þo þingis in hooli scripture
which he lernyde neuere in oþere place, but ben lerned oneli in þe
wondurful [hiȝ]nesse and in þe wondurful mekenesse of hooli scriptures.
Austin seiþ þis in þe ende of þe secounde book of *Cristen Techynge*.
2385 Also hooli writ conteyneþ al profitable treuþe and alle oþere
sciences priueli in þe vertu of wittis or vndurstondingis, as wynes ben
conteyned in grapis, as ripe corn is conteyned in þe seed, as boowis ben
conteyned in þe rootis and as trees ben conteyned in þe kirnels. Grosted, in
a sermoun *Premonitus a venerabili patre*.
2390 Also hooli writ wlatiþ soffyms and seiþ 'he þat spekiþ sofisticali or
bi soffyms shal be hateful, and he shal be defraudid in ech þing', as þe Wise
Man seiþ in þe xxxvij. cᵒ of Ecclesiastici. If filosoforis, and moost þe
disciplis of Plato, seiden ony treuþis and profitable to oure feiþ, not oneli
þo treuþis owen not to be dred but also þo shulen be calengid to oure vse or
2395 profit fro hem, as fro vniust possessours. And as Iewis token bi autorite of
God þe gold and siluer and cloþis of Egipcians so cristen men owen to take
þe trewe seiyngis of filosoforis for to worschipe o God, and of techyngis of
vertues, which treuþis þe filosoforis founden not but diggiden out of þe
metals of Goddis puruyaunce, which is shed eueruwhere. So dide Ciprian
2400 þe swettest doctour and moost blessid martir, so diden Lactancius,
Victorinus and Illarie, and Grekis wiþouten noumbre. Austin, in þe
secounde book of *Cristen Doctryn*.
Bi þese reulis of Austin and bi foure vndurstondingis of hooli
scripture and bi wiys knowing of figuratif spechis, wiþ good lyuyng and
2405 mekenes and studiyng of þe Bible, symple men moun sumdel vndurstonde
þe text of hooli writ and edefie myche hemsilf and oþere men. But for
Goddis loue, ȝe symple men, beþ war of pride and veyn iangling and
chiding in wordis aȝenus proude clerkis of scole and veyn religiouse. And
answere ȝe mekeli and prudentli to enemyes of Goddis lawe, and preie ȝe
2410 hertli for hem, þat God of his greet merci ȝyue to hem veri knowing of
scripturis and mekenes and charite. And euere be ȝe redi whateuere man
techiþ ony treuþe of God to take þat mekeli and wiþ greete þankingis to
God, and if ony man in erþe, or aungel of heuene, teche ȝou þe contrarie of
hooli writ, or ony þing aȝenus resoun and charite, fleeþ fro him in þat as
2415 fro þe foul deuel of helle, and holde ȝe stidefastli to liyf and deeþ þe treuþe
and fredom of þe hooli gospel of Iesu Crist, and take ȝe mekeli mennus

---

Glosses and biblical references   2387 'boowis': boughs   2390 'wlatiþ': abhors   2390–2 Ecclus
37:23   2394 'calengid to': claimed for   2399 'puruyaunce': providence

Variants   2383 wondurfulnesse   2385 writ] scripture α β ι Q S   2390 writ] scripture α β ι Q S   2394
be ˣdoˣ   2395 And as *sup. ras.*   2396 and siluer *om.* ι Q   2407 beþ] be α β S   2411 whateuere] what ι Q
T   2414 fleeþ] fle α β ι Q S   2415 deuel] fend ι Q

seiyngis and lawis oonli in as myche as þei acorden wiþ hooli writ and good consciense, and no ferþere, for liyf ne for deþ.

Chapter 13

Also hooli scripture is betere knowun bi licnessis and bi derknessis. It doiþ
2420 awei anoies, and we owen to þenke and bileue þat þe þing þat is writun in hooli scripture, 3he þou3 it be hid or not knowen, is betere and trewere þan þat þat we moun vndurstonde bi ouresilf. And worschi[p]fuli and helþefuli þe Hooli Goost mesuride so hooli scriptures þat in open places he settide remedie | rb | to oure hungur and in derk places he wipte awei anoies, for
2425 almoost noþing is seie in þo derknessis which þing is not foundeun [seid] ful pleynli in oþere places. Perfor, bifor alle þingis it is nedeful þat a man be conuertid bi Goddis drede, and be mylde bi pitee or cristen religioun, and þat he a3enseie not hooli scripture, wher it be vndurstondun, þou3 it smyte ony synnes of oure, wheþir it be not vndurstondun, as if we moun
2430 vndurstonde betere, or comaunde or teche betere.

Bi þe 3ifte of drede and of pitee me comeþ to degre of kunnyng, for whi ech fructuouse man of hooli scriptures exercisiþ himsilf in þis þing, and to fynde noon oþere þing in þo þan for to loue God for God himsilf and for to loue his nei3bore for God. Þanne þilke drede bi which he þenkiþ on
2435 Goddis doom and þilke pitee bi which he must nedis bileue and 3yue stide to autorite of hooli bookis compelliþ him to biweile himsilf, for whi þis kunnyng of good hope makiþ a man not to avaunce hymsilf but biweil himsilf, and bi þis affeccioun or good wille he getiþ wiþ bisi preieris þe coumfort of Goddis helpe, þat he be not brokun bi dispeir, and he bigynneþ
2440 to be in þe fourþe degree of goostli strengþe, in which he hungriþ and þirstiþ ri3tfulnesse. Þanne in þe fyueþe degre, þat is, in þe councel of merci, he purgiþ þe soule, þat makiþ noise and vnrestfulnesse of coueitise of erþeli þingis, and þanne he dispisiþ filþis of soule and loueþ God and nei3boris, 3he enemyes. Bi þis he stieþ to þe sixte degree, where he purgiþ
2445 þe i3e of soule, bi which i3e God mai be seyn as myche as he mai be seyn of hem þat dien to þis world, as myche as þei moun, for in so mych þei seen God in her soule, þorou3 feiþ and loue, hou myche þei dien to þis world, and in as myche as þei lyuen to þis world þei seen not God. And in þis degree, wherinne a man dieþ to þe world, he neþer preferriþ ne makiþ
2450 euene himsilf ne his nei3bore wiþ þe treuþe of hooli writ. Perfor þis hooli man shal be so symple and cleene of herte þat neþer for plesaunce of men he be drawe awei fro treuþe ne bi cause to eschewe ony harmes of himsilf þat ben contrarie to þis liyf. Sich a child stieþ to veri wisdom, which is þe

Glosses and biblical references   2432 'fructuouse man of': man fruitful in   2442 Matt. 5:6

Variants   2421 be ˣnotˣ hid   2422 ouresilf] vsself α β ı Q S   • worschifuli   2425 seid *om.* P T   2437–8 \but ... himsilf/   2439 and *om.* ı Q   2449 makiþ ˣhiˣ

laste and þe seuenþe, which he vsiþ in pees and in reste. Seynt Austin seiþ
2455 al þis in þe bigynnyng of þe ij. book of *Cristen Techyng.*

Here is a blessid entryng bi þese seuene vertues to þe kunnyng of
hooli scripture in þis liyf, to haue [here] reste of soule and aftirward ful
reste of bodi and soule in heuene wiþouten ende. Alas, what doon proude
and coueitouse wrecchis at hooli scripture, þat seken þe world and fleischli
2460 eese and wolen not conuerte hem fro þese cursidnessis? Þei disseyuen
hemsilf and þe puple þat gessen him wise men whanne þei ben open foolis
and maken hemsilf deppere dampned, and oþere men also þat suen her
folie and blasfemen God. Þese worldli foolis shulden wite þat hooli liyf is a
lanterne to brynge a man to veri kunnyng, as Crisostom seiþ, and þe drede
2465 and loue of God is þe bigynnyng and perfeccioun of kunnyng and wisdom.
And whanne þese fleischli apis and worldli moldewarpis han neþer þe
bigynnyng of wisdom ne desiren it, what doon þei at hooli scripture to
| f. 14va | shenschip of hemsilf and of oþere men? As longe as pride and
coueitise of worldli goodis and honours is rootid in her herte þei maken
2470 omage to Sathanas and offren to him boþe bodi and soule and al her wit
and fynding. Sich foolis shulden þenke þat wisdom shal not entre into an
yuel-willid soule, neþer shal dwelle in a bodi suget to synnes. And Iesu
Crist seiþ þat þe Fadir of heuene hidiþ þe priuytees of hooli scripture fro
wise men and prudent, þat is wise men and prudent to þe world and in her
2475 owne siȝt, and shewiþ þo to meke men. Þerfor, worldli foolis, do ȝe first
penaunce for ȝoure synnes, and forsake pride and coueitise, and be ȝe
meke and drede ȝe God in alle þingis, and loueþ him ouer alle oþer þingis,
and ȝoure neiȝboris as ȝouresilf, and þanne ȝe shulen profite in studie of
hooli writ.
2480 But alas, alas, alas! Þe moost abhomynacioun þat euere was herd
among cristen clerkis is now purposid in Ynglond bi worldli clerkis and
feyned religiouse, and in þe chef vniuersite of oure rewme, as many trewe
men tellen wiþ greet weilyng. Þis orible and deuelis cursidnesse is purposid
of Cristis enemyes and traitours of alle cristen puple, þat no man shal lerne
2485 dyuy[ni]te ne hooli writ no but he þat haþ don his forme in art, þat is, þat
haþ comensid in art and haþ be regent twei ȝeer aftir: þis wolde be nyne
ȝeer or ten bifor þat he lernyde hooli writ, aftir þat he can comynli wel his
gramer, þouȝ he haue a good wit and trauele ful soore and haue good
fynding ix. ȝeer or x. aftir his gramer. Þis semeþ vttirli þe deuelis purpos,
2490 þat fewe men or noone shulen lerne and kunne Goddis lawe.

Glosses and biblical references 2464–5 Ps. 110:10; Ecclus 1:7, 9:10 2471 'fynding': means of
support 2471–2 Wisd. 1:4 2472–5 Matt. 11:25; Luke 10:21 2485 'forme': prescribed course
of study 2486 'regent': Master of Arts 2487–8 'can comynli wel his gramer': knows Latin
reasonably well

Variants 2457 here *om.* P T 2469 honours] onour ι Q 2474 þat is ... prudent *om.* β ι Q 2477
loueþ] loue α β ι Q S • \oþer/ 2478 ȝouresilf] ȝou silf ι Q 2485 dyuyte

But God seiþ bi Amos 'on þre grete trespassis of Damask and on þe
fourþe I shal not conuerte him', where Ierom seiþ þe firste synne is to
þenke yuelis; þe secounde synne is to consente to weiward þou3tis; þe
þridde synne is to fille in werk; þe fourþe synne is to do not penaunce aftir
2495   þe synne and to plese himsilf in his synne. But Damask is interpretid
'drynkyng blood' or 'birlyng blood'. Lord, wher Oxenford drynkiþ blood
and birliþ blood by sleyng of quyke men and bi doyng of sodomye in
leesyng a part of mannus blood wherebi a child my3te be fourmed, deme
þei þat knowen, and wher Oxenforde drynke blood of synne and stireþ
2500   oþere men of þe lond to do synne bi boldnesse of clerkis, deme þei iustli
þat seen it at i3e and knowen bi experiense. Loke now wher Oxenforde is
in þre orible synnes and in þe fourþe, on which God restiþ not tyll he
punysche it. Sumtyme children and 3onge men arsitris weren deuoute and
cleene as aungels in comparisoun of oþere; now men seien þei ben ful of
2505   pride and leccherie, wiþ dispitouse oþis, ne[d]eles and false, and dispisynge
of Goddis heestis. Sumtyme cyuylians and canonystris weren deuout and
so bisi on her lernyng þat þei token ful litil reste on bedde; now men seyn
þat þei ben ful of pride and nyce arai, enuye and coueitise, wiþ leccherie,
glotenye and idilnesse. Sumtyme dyuyns weren ful hooli and deuout and
2510   dispisiden outirli þe world and lyueden as aungels in mekenesse, clennesse,
souereyn chastitie and charite, and tau3ten treuli Goddis lawe in werk and
word; now men seyn þei ben as delicat of her mouþ and wombe | vb | and as
coueitouse as oþere worldli men, and flateren and maken leesyngis in
prechyng to eschewe bodili persecusioun and to gete benifices.
2515   Þe firste grete synne is generali in þe vnyuersite, as men dreden and
seen at i3e. Þe secounde orible synne is sodomye and strong meyntenance
þerof, as it is knowen to many persoones of þe rewme and at þe laste
parlement. Alas, dyuynes þat shulden passe oþere men in clennesse and
hoolynesse, as aungels of heuene passen freel men in vertues, ben moost
2520   sclaundrid of þis cursid synne a3enus kynde. Þe þridde orible synne is
symonye, and forswering in þe semble-hows, þat shulde be an hows of
ri3tfulnesse and hoolynesse, where yuelis shulden be redressid; þis
symony, wiþ purtenaunces þerof, is myche worse and more abhomynable
þan bodili sodomye. 3it on þese þre abhomynaciouns God wolde graciousli
2525   conuerte clerkis, if þei wolden do veri penaunce and 3yue hem hoolich to
vertues, but on þe fourþe moost abhomynacioun purposid now, to lette

---

Glosses and biblical references   2491–2 Amos 1:3; 'him', i.e., Damascus (note)   2494 'fille
in werk': complete the deed   2496 'birlyng blood': giving someone blood to drink   2498 'a
part … fourmed', i.e., semen   2503 'arsitris': students of Arts (note)   2506 'cyuylians and
canonystris': civil and canon lawyers (note)   2509 'dyuyns': theologians   2519 'freel': frail   2521
'semble–hows': meeting-house of convocation

Variants   2496 blood[1] *om.* ι Q   • drynkiþ] drynke α β ι Q S   2503 arsitris] arsetris S *sec. m.*, arsitris
α ι, artitars Q, *om.* Crowley Gough (note)   2505 nedeles] neþeles   2526 moost *om.* ι Q

cristen men, ʒhe prestis and curatis, to lerne freli Goddis lawe til þei han
spendid ix. or x. ʒeer at art, þat comprehendiþ many stronge errours of
heþene men aʒenus cristen bileue; it semeþ wel þat God wole not ceesse of
2530 veniaunce til it and oþere ben punyschid sore, for it semeþ þat worldli
clerkis and feyned religiouse don þis þat symple men of wit and of fynding
knowe not Goddis lawe to preche it generali aʒenus synnes in þe rewme.
But wite ʒe, worldli clerkis and feyned religiouse, þat God boþe can and
mai, if it likiþ him, spede symple men out of þe vnyuersite as myche to
2535 <kunne> holy writte as maistres in þe vniuersite, and þerefor no greet
charge þouʒ neuere man of good wille be poisened wiþ heþene mennus
errours ix. ʒeer or x., but euere lyue wel and studie hooli writ bi elde
doctours and newe, and preche treuli and freeli aʒenus open synnes, to his
deþ.
2540   Se þerfor what Ierom seiþ on Amos: God biforseiþ yuelis to-
comynge, þat men here and amende hemsilf and be delyuerid fro þe perel
neiʒyng, or if þat þei dipisen þei be punyschid iustlier, and God, þat
biforseiþ peynes, wole not punysche men þat synnen but þat þei be
amendid. Ierom seiþ þis in þe ende of þe firste book of Amos. God for his
2545 grete merci graunte þat clerkis here þe grete veniaunce manasid of God and
amende hemsilf treuli, þat God punysche not hem, for if þei amende not
hemsilf þei ben eretikis maad hard in her synnes. But se what Ierom seiþ
aʒenus eretikis and in comending of hooli scripture. He seiþ þus on Amos:
eretikis þat seruen þe wombe and glotenye ben clepid riʒtfuli fattest kiyn
2550 eþer ful of shenschipe. We owen to take hooli scripture on þre maneris:
first, we owen vndurstonde it bi þe lettre, and do alle þingis þat ben
comaundid to vs þerinne; þe ij. tyme bi allegorie, þat is, gostli
vndurstonding, and þe iij. tyme bi blis of þingis to-comynge. Ierom seiþ þis
in þe ij. book on Amos, and in þe iiij. cº [of Amos].
2555   Neþeles, for Lire cam late to me se what he seiþ of þe
vndurstonding of hooli scripture. He writiþ þus [i]n þe ij. prologe of þe
Bible: Ioon seiþ, in v. cº of Apocalips, 'I siʒ a book writen wiþinne and
wiþoutforþ | f. 15ra | in þe hond of þe sittere on þe troone'. Þis book is
hooli scripture, which is seid writen wiþoutforþ as to þe literal
2560 vndurstonding and wiþinne as to þe priuy and gostli vndurstonding. And in
þe firste prologe he declariþ foure vndurstondingis of hooli writ in þis
maner: hooli writ haþ þis specialte, þat vndur o lettre it conteyneþ many
vndurstondingis, for þe principal auctour of hooli writ is God himsilf, in
whose power it is not oneli to vse wordis to signefie a þing, as men doon,
2565 but also he vsiþ þingis signefied bi wordis to signefie oþere þingis. Þerfor,

---

Glosses and biblical references   2557–8 Apoc. 5:1

Variants   2527 curatis *sup. ras.*   2534–5 \as myche … vniuersite/   2540 biforseiþ] bifore seeþ α ι
Q   2543 biforseiþ] bifore seeþ ι Q   2551 do] to ι Q S Crowley   2554 of Amos *om.*   2556 on α *sec. m.*
P   2558 ˣofˣ\on/

bi þe signefiyng bi wordis is takun þe literal vndurstonding or historial of
hooli scripture, and bi þe signefiyng which is maad bi þingis is taken þe
priuy or gostli vndurstonding, which is on þre maneris: allegorik, moral or
tropologik, and anagogik. If þingis signefied bi wordis ben referrid to
2570   signefie þo þingis þat owen to be bileuyd in þe newe testament, so it is
taken þe sense allegorik; if þingis ben refferrid to signefie þo þingis which
we owen to do, so it [is] moral sense or tropologik; if þingis ben refferrid to
signefie þo þingis þat shulen be hopid in blisse to-comynge, so it is
anagogik sense. Þe lettre techiþ what is doon; allegorie techiþ what þou
2575   owist for to bileue; moral techiþ what þou owist for to do; anagogie techiþ
whidur þou owist to go.

   And of þese foure senses or vndurstondingis mai be set ensaumple
in þis word 'Ierusalem', for bi þe literal vndurstonding Ierusalem signefieþ
a citee þat was sumtyme þe cheef cite in þe rewme of Iude, and Ierusalem
2580   was foundid first of Melchisedech and aftirward it was alargid and maad
strong bi Salamon. Bi moral sense it signefieþ a feiþful soule, bi which
sense it is seid, in þe lij. cᵒ of Isaie, 'rise þou, rise þou, sette þou,
Ierusalem'. Bi sense allegorik it signefieþ þe chirche fiȝtyng aȝenus synnes
and feendis, bi which sense it is seid, in þe xxj. cᵒ of Apocalips, 'I siȝ þe
2585   hooli citee, newe Ierusalem, comynge doun fro heuene as a spouse ourned
to her hosebonde'. Bi sense anagogik it signefieþ þe chirche regnynge in
blis; bi þis sense it is seid, in þe iiij. cᵒ to Galatas, 'þilke Ierusalem which is
aboue, which is oure modir, is fre'. And as ensaumple is set in o word, so it
myȝte be set in o resoun, and as in oon so [and] in anoþere. Lire seiþ al þis
2590   in þe firste prolog on þe Bible.

Chapter 14

Neþeles, alle goostli vndurstondingis setten bifore or requyren þe literal
vndurstonding as þe foundement, wherfor as a bilding bowyng awei fro þe
foundement is disposid to falling so a gostli exposicioun þat discordiþ fro
þe literal sense owiþ to be arettid vnsemeli and vncouenable, or lesse
2595   semeli and lesse couenable. And þerefor it is nedeful to hem þat wolen
profite in þe studie of hooli scripture to bigynne at þe vndurstonding of
literal sense, moost siþ bi þe literal sense aloone, and not bi gostli sensis,
mai be maad an argument or pref to þe preuyng or declaryng of a doute, as
Austin seiþ, in his pistle to Vyncent Donatist.
2600   Seynt Isidere, in þe firste book of *Souereyn Good*, þe xx. cᵒ, settiþ
seuene reulis to expowne hooli scripture, | rb | and sum men clepen þese

---

Glosses and biblical references   2582–3 Is. 52:2   2584–6 Apoc. 21:2   2587–8 Gal. 4:26   2589
'resoun': sentence (note)   2589 'and': also

Variants   2572 is *om.*   2589 and *om.* β P T (note)   2592 wherfor] forwhi ɩ Q   2597 sensis] sense β ɩ Q

reulis 'þe keies of scripture', for bi þese reulis þe vndurstondinge of
scripture is openyd in many þingis. Þe firste reule is of oure Lord Iesu Crist
and of his goostli bodi which is hooli chirche, for whi for þe knytting
2605   togidere of þe heed to þe bodi hooli scripture spekiþ sumtyme of euer-eiþer
vndur o resoun, as vndur o persoone, and passiþ fro oon to anoþere. In
ensaumple, in þe lxj. cᵒ of Isaie it is seid 'he cloþid me wiþ cloþis of helþe
and he cumpassid me wiþ cloþing of riȝtfulnesse, as a spouse maad fair
wiþ a coroun and as a spousesse ourned wiþ hir broochis', for whi þis þat is
2610   seid 'as a spouse', etc., is vndurstonden of Crist, and þis þat sueþ, 'as a
spousesse', etc., is vndurstondun of hooli chirche. Also, in þe firste
chapitre of Songis it is seid 'kisse he me wiþ þe coss of his mouþ, for þi
tetis ben betere þan wyn', for whanne it is seid 'kisse he me', etc., it is þe
word of þe spousesse desirynge to haue þe spouse, and þis þat sueþ, 'for þi
2615   tetis', etc., is þe word of þe spouse preisynge þe spousesse. Wherfor, in
siche þingis knyt so togidere bi resoun biforseid, a prudent redere owiþ to
perseyue what acordiþ to þe heed and what to þe bodi.

    Þe secounde reule is þis of þe veri bodi and of þe feyned bodi of
oure Lord Iesu Crist, for whi hooli chirche, which is þe gostli bodi of Crist,
2620   is a net which is not drawen ȝit to þe brynk, and þerfor it haþ yuele men
medlid wiþ good men til to þe doom, in which þese shulen be departid fro
hem. And þerfor in hooli scripture yuele men ben preisid sumtyme wiþ
good men wiþ which þei ben medlid, as, in þe xj. cᵒ of Osee, God seiþ þus:
'Israel is a child and I louyde him', and aȝenward sumtyme good men ben
2625   blamed wiþ yuele men, as, in þe j. cᵒ of Isaie, 'an ox knew his lord and an
asse knew þe cracche of his lord, but Israel knew not me and my puple
vndurstood not'. And sumtyme in þe same resoun it is expressid what
perteyneþ to good men and what to yuele men, as, in þe j. cᵒ of Songis, it is
seid 'I am blac but fair, ȝe douȝtris of Ierusalem, as þe tabernaclis of
2630   Cedar, as þe skynnes of Salomon'. Þese ben þe wordis of þe spousesse,
which for resoun of yuele men conteyned in þe chirche seiþ 'I am blac', but
for resoun of good men it addiþ 'but fair', and þis þat sueþ, as for
ensaumple 'as þe tabernaclis of Cedar' is referrid to yuele men, for whi
Cedar was þe sone of Ismael, as it is seid in xxv. cᵒ of Genesis, of whom
2635   Saracenys camen forþ, and þis þat is addid, 'as þe skynnes of Salomon', is
referrid to good men. Þerfor, bi Salomon here is vndurstondun God himsilf
bi cristen expositours and Ebreis, and þerfor þe skynnes of Salomon ben

Glosses and biblical references   **2607–9** Is. 61:10; 'broochis': ornaments   **2611–13** Song of Songs
1:1   **2614** 'haue': enjoy   **2621–2** 'þese [evil men] … hem' [good men]   **2623–4** Hos. 11:1   **2625–
7** Is. 1:3; 'cracche': cradle   **2628–30** Song of Songs 1:4 (note)   **2633–4** Gen. 25:13   **2635–6** 'is
referrid': relates

Variants   **2606** fro ˣan oþereˣ\oon/   **2608** cloþing] cloþingis ι Q   **2610** etc. *om.* ι Q Crowley   **2624**
sum tyme ˣbeˣ

seid þo wiþ which þe tabernacle was hilid, in which tabernacle good men
worschipiden God.

2640   Þe þridde reule is of þe spirit and of þe lettre. Þis reule is expowned
þus comynli, þat þe historial or literal sense and þe mystik or gostli sense is
taken vndur þe same lettre, for whi þe treuþe of þe storie shal be holden
and neþeles it shal be refferrid to þe gostli vndurstonding. Þis reule mai be
expowned also in anoþere manere, þat it be referrid oneli to þe literal sense,

2645   as oþere reulis ben, aboute which þing it is to se | f. 15va | þat þe same
lettre haþ sumtyme double literal sense. In ensaumple, in þe firste book of
Paralipomenon, þe xvij. cº, God seiþ of Salamon 'I shal be to hym into a
fadir and he shal be to me into a sone', and þis to þe lettre is vndurstonde
of Salamon, in as myche as he was þe sone of God bi grace in ȝongþe;

2650   wherfor Nathan þe profete clepid him amyable to þe Lord, in þe ij. book of
Kingis, xij. cº. Also þe forseid autorite 'I shal be to hym into a fadir', etc.,
is brouȝt in of Poul, in j. cº to Ebreis, as seid to þe lettre of Crist himsilf,
and þis is open bi þis þat Poul bryngiþ it into preef þat Crist is more þan
aungels, but sich preuyng mai not be maad bi goostli sense, as Austin seiþ

2655   aȝenus Vyncent Donatist. Forsoþe, þe forseid autorite was fillid to þe lettre
in Salamon, neþeles lesse parfitli, for he was þe sone of God oneli bi grace,
but it was fillid parfitler in Crist, þat was þe sone of God bi kynde. But
neþeles euer-eiþer exposisioun is literal vttirli, neþeles þe secounde
exposicioun, which is of Crist, is goostli and pr[iuy] in summe maner, in as

2660   myche as Salamon was þe figure of Crist.

Þe fourþe reule is of al and of part, for whi scripture passiþ fro oon
to þe toþer and aȝenward, as, in xiij. cº of Isaie, þe scripture spekiþ first
aȝenus Babiloyne speciali, whanne it is seid 'þe birþene of Babiloyne', and
þanne þe scripture passiþ to vndurstonde þe word generali of al þe wor[l]d,

2665   bi þis þat sueþ: 'þe Lord comeþ fro þe hiȝnesse of heuene and þe vessels of
his strong veniunce comen, þat he distrie al erþe'. Aftirward, þe scripture
turneþ aȝen to speke aȝenus Babiloyne speciali, whanne it is seid 'lo, I shal
reise on ȝou Medeis, þat shulen not seke siluer', for whi Darius Medei, wiþ
Cirus his cosyn, took Babiloyne and killid Balthaȝar þe kyng of Babiloyne,

2670   as it is seid in þe v. cº of Daniel.

Glosses and biblical references   2638 'hilid': concealed   2642 'taken vndur': subsumed
beneath   2645 'se': be seen   2646–8 1 Chron. 17:13   2650–1 2 Kings 12:25 (note)   2652
'brouȝt in of': adduced by   2652 Heb. 1:5   2653 'open ... preef': manifest by the fact that Paul
adduces it as proof   2653 'more': greater   2655 'fillid to þe lettre': fulfilled literally   2658 'euer-
eiþer exposisioun': each of the two interpretations   2660 'was þe figure of': prefigured   2663
'speciali': in particular   2662–3 Is. 13:1; 'birþene': burden   2665–6 Isa 13:5   2667 'turneþ aȝen':
returns   2667–8 Is. 13:17; ' reise on': raise up against   2668–70 Dan. 5:30–1   2668 'Medei': the
Mede   2669 'Balthaȝar': Belshazzar

Variants   2644 oneli] also ι Q   2650 wherfor] herfore S, þerfore ι Q   2651 a ˣlecheˣ (?)   2659 priuy]
preueþ P S T   2664 world] word α β ι P Q S

Þe fyueþe reule is of tymes, which reule bifalliþ in iiij. maneris. In o maner bi a figure clepid synodoches, whanne a part of tyme is set for al þe tyme, as it is seid in þe gospel þat Crist lai þre daies in þe sepulcre, and neþeles þe firste dai and þe þridde weren not hool daies. In anoþere maner

2675 þis reule bifalliþ for smale partis of tyme þat ben noumbrid sumtyme in scripture and sumtyme ben left out, and bi þis þe scripture þat spekiþ of sum noumbre of ʒeeris in many places settiþ sumtyme moo ʒeeris, rekenyng þe forseid smale partis, in anoþere place it settiþ fewere ʒeeris, in leuyng out þe smale partis. In þe þridde maner þis reule falliþ for þat þe

2680 rekenyng of ʒeeris bigynneþ in o place at þe formere terme and in anoþere place at þe lattere terme, as in þe xv. cº of Genesis it is seid to Abraham þat his seed shal be a pilgrym bi foure hundrid ʒeer and in xij. cº of Exodi it is seid of þis pilgrymage þat þe dwelling of þe sones of Israel in þe lond of Egipt was of foure hundrid ʒeer and þritti, for þe rekenyng of þis more

2685 noumbre bigynneþ at þe tyme in which it was seid to Abraham, in xij. cº of Genesis, 'go out of þi lond', etc, and þe rikenyng of þe lesse noumbre bigynneþ at | vb | þe natyuyte of Isaac, þat was þritti ʒeer aftir þe goynge out of Abraham fro Aran. Þe fourþe tyme þis reule bifalliþ for þat hooli scripture spekiþ of þing to-comynge bi þe maner of þing passid, as in ix. cº

2690 of Isaie 'a litil child was borun to vs', etc., and þis is to signefie þe certeynte of profesie, whos bifallyng of tyme to-comynge is so certeyn as if it were passid now, and þis is for certeynte of Goddis bifor-knowing, bi which þe reuelacioun is maad to þe profete. Neþeles, sich maner of speche haþ no place no but in profesie of predestynacioun or ful determynyng of

2695 God, which profesie is whanne a þing to-comynge in nown-certeyn to mannus knowyng is shewid to þe profete in þat maner bi which it is in þe bifor-knowing of God, which bifor-knowing of God biholdiþ so wiþout failyng þingis to-comynge as þingis present and passid. But in profecie of manaassing sich maner speche haþ no place, which profesie of manaas is

2700 whanne ony peyne worþi to be brouʒt in on a puple or on a persoone is shewid to þe profete not bi þat þat is in þe bifor-knowing of God but bi þe ordre of secounde causis, as bi þe yuele deseruyngis of men, as is þilke profesie of Ionas, iij. cº, 'ʒit xl. daies and Nynyue shal be distried', for whi þe synnes of þat citee hadden disserued þis distriyng. Neþeles, for sich a

2705 cause is chaungeable þerfor sumtyme þe effect, þat is, peyne manaassid, sueþ not—as here, for Nynyuytis diden penaunce and so þe Lord brouʒt not in þe peyne manaassid.

Þe sixte reule is of recapitulacioun, þat is, rehersing of þing don

---

Glosses and biblical references   **2681–2** Gen. 15:13   **2682–4** Exod. 12:41   **2685–6** Gen. 12:1   **2689–90** Is. 9:6   **2695–6** 'nown-certeyn to mannus knowyng': uncertainty as far as man's knowledge is concerned   **2697–8** 'wiþout failyng': unfailingly   **2702–3** Jonah 3:4

Variants   **2700** on ony puple ι Q   **2702** þilke] þat ι Q

bifore and of anticipacioun or bifor-takyng, þat is, settyng in of þing bifor
2710   þat it is doon, for in hooli scripture not euere stories and dedis ben writen
in þe same ordre in which þo ben doon. And, þerfor, whanne lattere þingis
ben set bifore it is seid anticipacioun or bifor-takyng, and whanne þe
formere þingis ben set bihynde it is seid recapitulacioun or rehersing of
þingis don bifore, as in þe x. cᵒ of Genesis it is seid of þe sones of Noe 'þe
2715   ilis of heþene folkis in her cuntrees weren departid of þese sones of Noe,
ech man bi his l[ang]age', and wiþinne þe same x. cᵒ it is seid 'þese ben þe
sones of Cham, in kynredis and langagis', and aftirward it is seid in xj. cᵒ
'þe lond was of o langage and of þe same wordis', wherof it is open þat þis
þat is biforseid of þe departing of langagis is seid bi anticipacioun. In liyk
2720   maner in þe ij. cᵒ of Genesis, aftir þat Moises, in þe j. cᵒ, hadde descryued
þe creacioun or making of nouȝt of heuene and erþe, and þe departinge
and ournyng of þe world, he seide 'þese ben þe generaciouns of heuene and
of erþe in þe dai in which þo weren made', wherof it is open þat þis is seid
bi recapitulacioun or rehersing of þing don bifore.
2725   Þe seuenþe reule is of þe deuel and of his bodi, for, as Gregorie seiþ
in þe tenþe omelie, 'certis, þe deuel is heed of alle wickid men, and alle
wickid men ben membris of þis heed', and þerfor, for þe knytting togidere
of | f. 16ra | þe heed [to] þe membris, þe scripture þat spekiþ of oon passiþ
in þe same knyttyng togidere of resoun to speke of þe toþer, as in xiiij. cᵒ
2730   of Isaie, where þe scripture spekiþ of þe kyng of Babiloyne, þat was a
membre of þe deuel, it passiþ to speke of þe prynce of fendis, whanne it is
seid þere 'Lucifer, þat risidist eerli, hou fellist þou doun fro heuene?', and
in xxviij. cᵒ of Eȝechiel, where þe scripture spekiþ of þe prynce of Tire it
passiþ to speke of þe deuel, whanne it is addid 'þou, a signet or a preente of
2735   þe licnesse of God, were ful of wisdom and parfit in fairnesse in þe delices
of paradiys of God'. Lire seiþ al þis in þe secounde prologe on Genesis.
Here Lire rehersiþ þe sentense of seynt Austin and of Isidere in þese reulis,
and declariþ hem openli bi hooli scripture and resoun, and countreþ not
Austin but declariþ him ful myche to symple mennus wittis, and addiþ
2740   more bi scripture and resoun þat Austin touchiþ not.
       Þouȝ þese reulis or keies of scripture bryngen men to greet
vndurstonding þerof, ȝit men moten take heede what is seid of Crist bi his
godhed and what bi his manhed, for Crist bi his manhed is [seid] lesse þan
þe Fadir and bi þe godhed he is seid euene wiþ þe Fadir, and for as myche as
2745   Crist is boþe God and man we graunten þat God is dedli and diede on þe
cros, not bi his godhed but bi þe manhed of Crist, þat was ioyned in oonhed

---

Glosses and biblical references   2714–16 Gen. 10:5; 'departid of': divided by   2716–17 Gen.
10:31; 'Cham': Shem   2717–18 Gen. 11:1   2719–23 Gen. 2:4   2729–32 Is. 14:12   2732–6 Ezech.
28:12; 'a signet or a preente': a sign or an imprint

Variants   2714 þingis] þing α β ι Q S   2716 lynage ι P   2728 to] in   2741 or] and ι Q   2741 bryngen
in men   2743 seid *om.*

of persoone wiþ þe godhed, and we graunten, as þe gospel doiþ, þat
mannus sone while he was dedli on erþe was in heuene, for his godhed was
þere, and he also bi resoun þerof. Also we moun graunte wel þat a man
2750 made heuene and erþe, for Crist bi his godhed, which Crist is and was man,
dide þus.

Also hooli scripture telliþ ofte þe þou3tis of men, and ofte þe
wordis and dedis, and whanne þe þou3tis and þe dedis of men ben contrarie
o gospeler telliþ þe þou3tis, anoþere telliþ þe wordis, and bi þis
2755 equyuocacioun or dyuerse spekyng þei ben acordid, 3he whanne þei semen
contrarie in wordis. Also, ofte in storial matere scripture rehersiþ þe
comyne opynyoun of men and affermeþ not þat it was so in dede. In þis
maner þe gospel seiþ þat Ioseph was þe fadir of Crist, þou3 he neuere
gendrid Crist, for Marie, Cristis modir, was euere clene virgyn. Þus þe
2760 gospeler seiþ þat at þe [bi]heedyng of Ioon Baptist Eroude was sori, and
3it, as docotours seyn, he was ful glad þerof, but he feynede him sori for þe
puple, and þe puple gessid him sori. Also, þou3 scripture rehersiþ hou hooli
men lyueden, and comendiþ hem gretli, it appreueþ not alle her dedis, for
many grete seyntis erriden foul in many poyntis. And, þou3 scripture telliþ
2765 þe stories of yuele men and dampned, it repreueþ not herfore alle þingis
whiche þei diden, for þou3 þei weren hemsilf ful cursid þei diden many
good dedis of kynde, and sumtyme, parauenture, good dedis of vertu, if þei
weren in grace for a tyme.

At þe laste, take 3e good heede whanne scripture spekiþ bi co| rb |
2770 maundement to alle men and whanne it 3yueþ comaundement to certeyn
persoones of dyuerse statis. In þe firste poynt, alle men moten do as it seiþ;
in þe ij. tyme, þe persoonys of statis specified moten nedis obeie. Whanne
scripture spekiþ oneli bi counsel men moun be saued þou3 þei doon not þe
councel, as ful many men and wymmen moun be saued þou3 þei taken not
2775 virgynyte ne contynence, neþer 3yuen alle her goodis to pore men, and 3it
þese ben hi3 councels of Iesu Crist in þe gospel.

Glosses and biblical references   **2756** 'storial matere': historical subject-matter   **2758** John
1:45   **2759–60** Mark 6:26   **2774–5** Matt. 19:12   **2775** Mark 10:21 (cf. Matt. 19:21; Luke 12:33)

Variants   **2748** mannus sone] man α β ι Q S   **2750–1** man and dide ι Q S *pr. m*   **2760** heedyng   **2767**
parauenture manye goode ι Q   **2776** hi3] heere α ι Q S, hye Gough

Chapter 15

For as myche as Crist seiþ þat þe gospel shal be prechid in al þe world, and
Dauiþ seiþ of þe postlis and her prechyng 'þe sown of hem ȝede out into
ech lond and þe wordis of hem ȝeden out into þe endis of þe world', and eft
2780 Dauiþ seiþ 'þe Lord shal telle in þe scripturis of puplis, and of þese princes
þat weren in it', þat is, in hooli chirche, and as Ierom seiþ on þat vers 'hooli
writ is þe scripture of puplis for it is maad þat alle puplis shulden knowe
it', and þe prynces of þe chirche þat weren þerinne ben þe apostlis þat
hadden autorite to write hooli writ, for bi þat same þat þe apostlis writiden
2785 her scriptures bi autorite and confermyng of þe Hooli Goost it is hooli
scripture and feiþ of cristen men, and þis dignete haþ no man aftir hem, be
he neuere so hooli, neuere so kunnyng, as Ierom witnessiþ on þat vers.
Also Crist seiþ of þe Iewis þat crieden 'Osanna' to him in þe temple þat
þouȝ þei weren stille stoonys shulen crie, and bi stoonys he vndurstondiþ
2790 heþene men þat worschipiden stoonys for her goddis. And we English men
ben comen of heþene men, þerfor we ben vndurstonden bi þese stoonys þat
shulden crie hooli writ, and as Iewis, þat is interpretid knoulechyng,
signefien clerkis þat shulden knoulech to God bi repentaunce of synnes and
bi vois of Goddis heriyng, so oure lewid men, suynge þe cornerstoon Crist,
2795 moun be signefied bi stoonys þat ben harde and abiding in þe foundement.
For þouȝ coueitouse clerkis ben wode bi symonye, eresie and many oþere
synnes, and dispisen and stoppen hooli writ as miche as þei moun, ȝit þe
[lewid] peple crie after holy writte to kunne it and kepe it wiþ greet cost
and perel of her liyf.
2800	For þese resouns and oþere, wiþ comyn charite to saue alle men in
oure rewme which God wole haue saued, a symple creature haþ translatid
þe Bible out of Latyn into Englisch. First, þis symple creature hadde myche
trauel wiþ dyuerse felowis and help[er]is to gedere many elde biblis, and
oþere doctours and comyn glosis, and to make o Latyn Bible sumdeel
2805 trewe, and þanne to studie it of þe newe, þe text wiþ þe glose and oþere
doctours as he myȝte gete, and speciali Lire on þe eld testament, þat
helpide ful myche in þis werk. Þe þridde tyme to councele wiþ elde
gramariens and eld dyuynes of harde wordis and harde sentensis hou þo
myȝten be vndurstonde best and translatid. Þe fourþe tyme to translate as
2810 cleerli as he coude to þe sentense, and to haue many good felowis and
kunnynge at þe correcting of þe translacioun.

Glosses and biblical references	2778–9 Ps. 18:4	2780–1 Ps 86:6 (note)	2788–9 Luke 19:40
(note)	2794 'oure' [English]	2794 Matt. 21:42; Mark 12:10; Luke 20:17; Acts 4:11	2804–5
'sumdeel trewe': very accurate	2805 'of þe newe': newly

Variants	2792 þat is *om.* α β ι Q S	2793 synnes and *expl.* α	2797–8 \as miche … writte/	2798
lewid] seid	2803 helpis P α β S T	2809–10 as cleerli ˣas cleerliˣ

Firste it is to knowe þat þe best translating is, out of Latyn into
Englisch, to translate aftir þe sentense and not oneli aftir þe wordis, so þat
þe sentence be as opene or openere in English as in Latyn, and go not fer
2815 fro þe lettre. And if þe lettre mai | f. 16va | not be sued in þe translatyng let
þe sentence euere be hool and open, for þe wordis owen to serue to þe
entent and sentence, and ellis þe wordis ben superflu or false. In
translatyng into Englisch many resoluciouns moun make þe sentence open,
as ablatif caas absolute mai be resolued into þese þre wordis, wiþ þe
2820 couenable verbe, 'þe while', 'for', 'if', as gramariens seyn; as þus, 'þe
maistir redinge, I stonde' mai be resolued þus: 'while þe maistir rediþ, I
stonde', or 'if þe maistir [rediþ]', etc., or 'for þe maistir rediþ', etc. And
sumtyme it wole acorde wel wiþ þe sentence to be resolued into 'whanne'
or into 'aftirward', þus: 'whanne þe maistir redde, I stood', or 'aftir þe
2825 maistir redde, I stood'. And sumtyme it mai [wel] be resolued into a verbe
of þe same tens as oþere ben in þe same resoun and into þis word *et*, þat is,
'and' in Englisch, as þus: *arescentibus hominibus pre timore*, þat is, 'and
men shulen wexe drie for drede'. Also a participle of present tens or
preter[i]t, of actif vois or passif, mai be resolued into a verbe of þe same
2830 tens and a coniunccioun copulatif; as þus, *dicens*, þat is, 'seiynge', mai be
resolued þus: 'and seiþ', or 'þat seiþ', and þis wole in many places make þe
sentence open, where to Englisch it aftir þe word it wolde be derk and
douteful. Also a relatif, which mai be resolued into his antecedent wiþ a
coniunccioun copulatif, as þus: 'which renneþ', 'and he renneþ'.
2835   Also, whanne oo word is onys set in a resoun it mai be set forþ as
ofte as it is vndurstonden, or as ofte as resoun and nede asken. And þis
word *autem* or *vero* mai stonde for 'forsoþe' or for 'but', and þus I vse
comynli, and sumtyme it mai stonde for 'and', as eld gramariens seyn.
Also, whanne riȝtful construccioun is lettid bi relacioun I resolue it openli;
2840 þus, where þis resoun *dominum formidabunt aduersarii eius* shulde be
Englischid þus bi þe lettre 'þe Lord hise aduersaries shulen drede', I
English it þus bi resolucioun: 'þe aduersaries of þe Lord shulen drede
hym', and so of oþere resouns þat ben liyk.
    At þe bigynnyng I purposide, wiþ Goddis help, to make þe sentence
2845 as trewe and open in Englisch as it is in Latyn, or more trewe and more
open þan it is in Latyn, and I preie for charite and for comyne profit of
cristen soulis þat if ony wiys man fynd[e] ony defaute of þe treuþe of
translacioun let him set in þe trewe sentence and open of hooli writ, but
loke þat he examyne treuli his Latyn Bible, for no doute he shal fynde

Glosses and biblical references   2817 'superflu': superfluous   2818 'resoluciouns': separations
into component parts   2827–8 Luke 21:26   2839 'lettid bi relacioun': prevented by syntactical
relation   2840–3 1 Kings 2:10

Variants   2822 rediþ[1] *m.*   2825 wel *om.*   2827 \and\/   2828 pretert   2847 fyndiþ   2849–50 fynde
ful manye ι Q

2850   many biblis in Latyn [ful] false if he loke many, nameli newe. And þe
comyne Latyn biblis han more nede to be correctid, as many as I haue seyn
in my liyf, þan haþ þe Englisch Bible late translatid.
     And where þe Ebreu, bi witnesse of Ierom and of Lire and oþere
expositours, discordiþ fro oure Latyn bookis, I haue set in þe margyn bi þe
2855   maner of a glose what þe Ebreu haþ, and hou it is vndurstonden in sum
place, and I dide þis moost in þe Sauter, þat of alle <oure> bookis discordiþ
m<oost fro Ebrew, for þe chirche rediþ noȝt þe Sauter bi þe laste
translacioun of Ierom, out of Ebreu into Latyn, but anoþere translacioun of
oþere men þat hadden myche lasse kunnyng and lasse hoolynesse þan
2860   Ierom hadde. And in ful fewe bokis þe chirche rediþ þe translacioun of
Ierom, as it mai be preued bi þe propir origenals of Ierom, which he
gloside. And where I haue | vb | translatide as open[li] or opinliere in
Englisch as it is in Latyn, lat wise men deme þat knowen wel boþe þe
langagis and knowen wel þe sentense of hooli scripture, and wher I haue do
2865   þus or nai, no doute þei þat kunnen wel þe sentense of hooli writ and
English togidere, and wolen trauele wiþ Goddis grace þeraboute, moun
make þe Bible as trewe and as open, ȝhe and openere in English þan it is in
Latyn. And no doute a symple man wiþ Goddis grace and greet trauele
myȝte expowne myche openliere and shortliere þe Bible in English þan þe
2870   elde grete doctours han expowned it in Latyn, and myche sharplier and
groundliere þan many late postilatours or expositours han do. But God of
his grete merci ȝyue to vs grace to lyue wel and to seie þe treuþe in
couenable maner and acceptable to God and his puple, and to spille not
oure tyme, be it short be it long at Goddis ordenaunce.
2875   But summe þat semen wise and hooli seyn þus: 'if men now weren
as hooli as Ierom was, þei myȝten translate out of Latyn into Englisch as he
dide out of Ebreu and out of Greek into Latyn, and ellis þei shulden not
translate now', as hem þ[i]nkiþ, for defaute of hoolynesse and of kunnyng.
Þouȝ þis replicacioun seme colourable it haþ no good ground ne resoun ne
2880   charite, for whi þis replicacioun is more aȝenus seynt Ierom and aȝenus þe
firste lxx. translatours and aȝenus al hooli chirche þan aȝenus symple men
þat translaten now into English, for seynt Ierom was not so hooli as þe
apostlis and euangelistis whose bookis he translatide into Latyn, neþer he
hadde so hiȝ ȝiftis of þe Hooli Goost as þei hadden, and myche more þe
2885   lxx. translatours weren not so hooli as Moises and þe profetis, and speciali
Dauiþ, neþer þei hadden so greet ȝiftis of God as Moises and þe profetis

---

Glosses and biblical references   2850 'nameli newe': particularly recent ones   2852 'late':
recently   2861 'propir origenals of Ierom': Jerome's own originals   2871 'groundliere': more
knowledgably   2879 'replicacioun seme colourable': rejoinder may seem plausible

Variants   2850 ful *om.* P T   2854 bookis] biblis ι Q   2856–7 \þat of ... Sauter/   2862 openli]
open   2865 no] ne β ι Q S   2867 openere] opynliere ι Q S   2868 doute to a α ι Q S *pr. m.*   2869 myȝte]
men myȝte α ι Q S *pr. m.*   2878 þenkiþ   2881 al *om.* ι Q   2882 \not/ *sec. m.*

hadden. Ferþermore, hooli chirche appreueþ not oneli þe trewe translacioun
of meene cristen men stidfast in cristen feiþ but also of open eretikis þat
diden awei many mysteries of Iesu Crist bi gileful translacioun, as Ierom
2890 witnessiþ in þe firste prologe on Iob and in þe prologe on Daniel.
Myche more let þe chirche of Ynglond appreue þe trewe and hool
translacioun of symple men þat wolden for no good in erþe, bi her wityng
and power, putte awei þe leeste treuþe, ȝhe þe leeste lettre or titil of hooli
writ þat beriþ substaunce or charge. And dispute þei not of þe hoolynesse
2895 of men now lyuynge in þis dedli liyf, for þei kunne not þeronne and it is
reserued oneli to Goddis doom. If þei knowen ony notable defaute bi þe
translatours or helperis of hem let hem blame þe defaute bi charite and
merci, and let hem neuere dampne a þing þat mai be doon leuefuli bi
Goddis lawe, as weryng of a good cloþ for a tyme or riding on an hors for a
2900 greet iournei, whanne þei witen not wherfor it is doon. For sich þingis
moun be doon of symple men wiþ as greet charite and vertu as summe þat
holden hem grete and wise kunne ride in a gild sadel or vse cuschens and
beddis and cloþis of selk and of gold, wiþ oþere vanytees of þe world. God
graunte pitee, merci and charite | f. 17ra | and loue of comyn profite, and
2905 putte awei sich folidomes þat ben aȝenus resoun and charite.
    ȝit worldli clerkis asken gretli what spirit makiþ idiotis hardi to
translate þe Bible now into Englisch, siþen þe foure grete doctours durste
neuere do þus. Þis replicacioun is so lewid þat it nediþ noon answere [no]
but a stilnesse or a curteis scorn. For þese grete doctours weren noon
2910 English men ne weren not conuersaunt among Englisch men, ne in caas þei
kouden not þe langage of English, but þei ceessiden neuere til þei hadden
hooli writ in þe modir-tunge of her owne puple, for Ierom, þat was a Latyn
man of birþe, translatide þe Bible boþe out of Ebreu and out of Greek into
Latyn, and expownyde ful myche þerto. And Austin and many mo Latyns
2915 expowneden þe Bible for many partis into Latyn, to Latyn men among
which þei weren, and Latyn was a comyne langage to her puple aboute
Rome and biȝende and on þis half, as Englich is comyn langage to oure
puple, and ȝit þis dai þe comyn puple in Italie spekiþ Latyn corrupt, as
trewe men seyn þat han ben in Italie.
2920   And þe noumbre of translatours out of Greek into Latyn passyþ
mannus knowing, as Austin witnessiþ in þe secounde book of *Cristen
Teching*, and seiþ þus: þe translatours out of Ebreu into Greek moun be
noumbrid, but Laten translatours, or þei þat translatiden into Latyn, moun
not be noumbrid in ony maner. For in þe firste tymes of feiþ ech man, as a

Glosses and biblical references   **2893** 'titil': pen-stroke   **2894** 'þat beriþ substaunce or charge':
bearing any substantive meaning   **2905** 'folidomes': foolishnesses   **2918** 'Latyn corrupt': debased
Latin, Italian (note)

Variants   **2890** þe firste] oo α β ι Q S   **2896** kunne\knowen/   **2902** gild] golden S T   **2908** no
om.   **2911** English] english men ι Q   **2912** þe] here ι Q, þer S   **2916** weren] dwelliden α β ι Q S

2925   Greek book cam to him and he semyde [to] himsilf to haue sum kunnyng
  of Greek and of Latyn, was hardi to translate, and þis þing helpide more
  þan lettide vndurstonding, if reders be not necligent, for whi þe biholding
  of many bookis haþ shewid ofte or declarid summe derkere sentensis. Þis
  seiþ Austin þere. Þerfor Grosted seiþ þat it was Goddis wille þat dyuerse
2930   men translatiden and þat dyuerse translaciouns be in þe chirche, for where
  oon seid derkli oon or mo seiden openli.

    Lord God, siþ at þe bigynnyng of feiþ so many men translatiden
  into Latyn and to greet profit of Latyn men, lat o symple creature of God
  translate into Englich for þe profit of Englisch men, for if worldli clerkis
2935   loken wel her cronyclis and bookis þei shulen fynde þat Bede translatide þe
  Bible and expownyde myche in Saxoyn, þat was Englisch or comune
  langage of þis lond in his tyme, and not oneli Bede but also kyng Alurede,
  þat foundide Oxenforde, translatide in his laste daies þe bigynnyng of þe
  Sauter into Saxoyn, and wolde more if he hadde lyued lengere. Also
2940   Frensche men, Beemers and Bretouns han þe Bible and oþere bookis of
  deuocioun and of exposicioun translatid into her modir-langage. Whi
  shulde not Englisch men haue þe same in her modir langage I can not wite,
  [no] but for falsnesse and necligence of clerkis, or for our puple is not
  worþi to haue so greet grace and ȝifte of God in peyne of her elde synnes.
2945   God for his merci amende þese yuele causis and make oure puple to haue
  and kunne and kepe treuli hooli writ to liyf and deþ.

    But in translating of wordis equyuoke, þat is, þat han many
  signeficaciouns vndur o lettre, | rb | mai liȝtli be perel, for Austin seiþ in þe
  secounde book of *Cristen Techyng* þat if equyuok wordis be not translatid
2950   [in]to þe sense or vndurstondyng of þe autour it is errour, as in þat place of
  þe salm 'þe feet of hem ben swifte to shede out blood' þe Greek word is
  equyuok to 'sharp' and 'swift', and he þat translatide 'sharpe feet' erride,
  and a book þat haþ 'sharpe feet' is false and mut nedis be amendid, as þat
  sentence 'vnkynde ȝonge trees shulen not ȝyue deep rootis' owiþ to be þus:
2955   'plauntingis of avoutrie shulen not ȝyue deepe rootis'. Austin seiþ þis þere.
  Þerfor a translatour haþ greet nede to studie wel þe sentence boþe bifore
  and aftir, and loke þat sich equyuoke wordis acorde wel wiþ þe sentence,
  and he haþ greet nede to lyue a cleene liyf and be ful deuout in preieris and
  haue not his wit ocupied aboute worldli þingis, þat þe Hooli Spirit, auctour
2960   of wisdom and kunnyng and treuþe, dresse hym in his werk and suffre him
  not for to erre.

Glosses and biblical references   2940 'Beemers': Bohemians   2950–1 Rom. 3:15 (echoing Prov.
1:16)   2951–2 'is equyuok to': is ambiguous, meaning both   2955 Wisd. 4:3   2960 'dresse':
direct

Variants   2925 to² *om.*   2932 \men/   2937 \not/   2943 no *om.* β P T   2947 han] haþ ι Q   2950 into]
in *om.*   2953 nedis *om.* α β ι Q S   2957 wel *om.* ι Q   2958 haþ ˣaˣ greet   • greet *om.* ι Q   2959 þingis
ˣandˣ þat

Also þis word *ex* signefieþ sumtyme 'of' and sumtyme it signefieþ
'bi', as Ierom seiþ, and þis word *enim* signefieþ comynli 'forsoþe', and, as
Ierom seiþ, it signefieþ cause, þus 'for whi'. And þis word *secundum* is
2965   takun for 'aftir' as many men seyn and comynli, but it signefieþ wel 'bi' or
'up', þus 'bi ȝoure word' or 'up ȝoure word'. Many siche aduerbis,
coniuncciouns and preposiciouns ben set ofte oon for anoþer and at fre
chois of autours sumtyme, and now þo shulen be takun as it acordiþ best to
þe sentence. Bi þis maner, wiþ good lyuyng and grete trauele men moun
2970   come to trewe and cleer translatyng and trewe vndurstondyng of hooli writ,
seme it neuere so hard at þe bigynnyng. God graunte to vs alle grace to
kunne wel and kepe wel hooli writ, and to suffre ioiefuli summe peyne for
it at þe laste. Amen.

Variants   **2962–73** *om.* Gough **2965** and *om.* S T **2970** trewe] truþe ɩ Q S **2971** grace *om.* ɩ
Q **2973** laste to þe plesaunce and wille of god T

2

Prologue to Isaiah and the Prophets

A prologe on Isaie and oþere profetis

f. 263ra | As seynt Ierom seiþ in þe prologe of Isaie, Isaie is ful witti and ful open in his writyng in Ebreu, þou3 þe translacioun into Latyn my3te not kepe þe fairenesse of speche. Isaie is worþi to be seid not oneli a profete but more a gospeler, for he declariþ so openli þe mysteries of Crist and of hooli chirche þat þou gesse him not to
5 ordeyne a profesie of þing to-comynge but to ordeyne a storie of þingis passid. Ysaie profeside in Ierusalem and in Iudee whanne þe ten lynagis [of Israel] weren not 3it led into caitifte, and he ordeyneþ profesie of euer-eiþir rewme; sumtyme of boþe togidere, sumtyme of ech bi itsilf. And whanne Isaie biholdiþ sumtyme to þe present storie, and signefieþ þe comynge a3en of þe puple into Iudee aftir þe caitifte of
10 Babiloyne, neþeles al his bisynesse, þat is, principal entent, is of þe cleping of heþene men and of þe comyng | rb | of Crist. Al þis is þe sentence of Ierom in þe prologe on Isaie.

Here it is to vndurstonde þat Isaie bigan to profesie bifor þat þe ten lynagis weren led into caitifte of Assiriens, as Ierom seiþ here, but he profesiede aftir þis
15 caitifte, aftir E3echies deþ in þe tyme of Manasses, as it is seid in þe iiij. book of Kingis, xx. chapitre, and in many mo places. Þis seiþ a postille on Ieroms prologe on Isaie. For, as Ebreis seien and Lire witnessiþ on þe firste chapitre of Isaie, Manasses ordeynede and demede Isaie to be sawid wiþinne a cedre-tre þat closide him wiþinne itsilf bi myracle, whanne Manasses hadde demed him vniustli to deþ.
20 Also alle profetis þat ben not teld openli in þe text whanne and in what tyme þei profesieden, profesieden in þe same tyme in whiche þe profetis goynge next bifore profesieden þat ben teld in þe text vndur whiche kingis and tymes þei profesieden, as Ierom seiþ in his prologe on Twelue Profetis, and it is set in þe bigynnyng of Osee.

Glosses and biblical references   1 'open': comprehensible   4 'gesse': suppose   5 'storie': history   7 'euer–eiþir': each of the two   11 'þe sentence of Ierom': what Jerome says   13 'to vndurstonde': to be understood   16 'postille': gloss   24 'Osee': Hosea

Variants   **Heading** a prologe on Ysaie and ooþere prophetis F C6 G I K L2 M P Q S U V X, þe prolog of Ysaie and of oþere profetis A, a prologe on þe book of Ysaie and on þe bookis of oþere profetis R91 a general prolog for alle þe bokis of profetis suynge E C9 Y a prologe on Ysaie H, a prolog vpon þe book of Ysaie R, a prolog on þe book of Isaye þe profete N   4 misteries eþer priuetees E C9 Y   • not] not oneli A C6 C9 E K M N P Q R91 Y, not ˣonelyˣ S   6 of Israel *om.*   16 a postille] apostle F, þe apostil C6 K M   23 set] seid U

25   Comunli, alle þe derk places of þe profetis moun be vndurstondun liȝtli bi
þre reulis. Þe firste is þis, þat þe principal entent of þe profetis is to declare þe
mysterie of Cristis incarnacioun, passioun, resureccioun, assensioun and þe comynge
to þe general doom, and þe pupplisching of þe gospel and þe conuersioun of heþene
men, and þe tribulacioun of hooli chirche in þis liyf and þe blis of heuene þerfor. Þe
30   secounde reule is þis, þat þe profetis warnen þe puple of Iewis of her grete synnes,
and exciten hem to do penaunce, and þanne þei shulen gete remyssioun of her
synnes, and grace in present tyme and glorie wiþouten ende; ellis, þei shulen haue
tribulacioun in þis liyf and peyne wiþouten ende. Þe þridde reule is þis, þat þe
profetis rehersen ofte benefices ȝouun of God bifore to þe Iewis, to coumforte hem
35   to ȝyue credence to goodis bihiȝt in her profesies, and þanne þe stories of Moises
lawe eþer of Iosue, Iudicum, Regum and Paralipomenon and of oþere historials
bookis shulen be wel lokid, and, schortli to seie, þe profetis shulen be expowned bi
þe text of Moises lawe and of oþere historials bookis of þe elde testament, eþer bi þe
text of þe newe testament.
40   Þe literal vndurstonding of hooli scripture is þe ground of al goostli
vndurstonding þerof, þat is, of allegorik, of moral and of an[a]gogik. No gostli
vndurstonding is autentik no but it be groundid in þe text openli eþer in open resoun
suynge [of] principlis eþer reulis of feiþ, as seynt Austin witnessiþ openli in his
pistle to Vyncent Donatist, and in his book of *Soliloquies*, and Ierom on Ionas, and
45   Lire on þe bigynnyng of Genesis and in many places of hooli scripture, and
Ardmakan in his book of *Questiouns of Armenyes*. Þerfor men moten seke þe treuþe
of þe text and be war of gostli vndurstonding eþer moral fantasie, and ȝyue not ful
credence þerto, no but it be groundid openli in þe text of hooli writ in o place eþer
oþer, eþer in open resoun þat mai not be avoidid, for ellis it wole as likyngli be
50   applied to falsnesse as to treuþe. And it haþ disseyued grete men in oure daies, bi
ouer-greet trist to her fantasies.
    Literal eþer historial vndurstonding techiþ what þing is don; allegorik techiþ
what we owen for to bileue; moral eþer tropologik techiþ what we owen to do to fle
vices and kepe vertues; anagogik techiþ what we owen to hope of euerlastinge
55   meede in heuene. Of þese foure vndurstondingis shal be seid pleynliere, if God wole,
on þe bigynnyng of Genesis.
    Also it is to wite þat þe profetis spaken sumtyme bi figuratif speche, and
licnen men to vnresonable beestis and clepen men bi figuratif speche liouns, beeris,
culueris and oþere vn| f. 263va |resonable beestis, for certeyn synnes whiche þei

---

Glosses and biblical references   **28** 'pupplisching': spreading abroad   **31** 'exciten': arouse   **34**
'benefices ȝouun of': benefits given by   **35** 'goodis bihiȝt': good things promised   **36** 'Iosue,
Iudicum, Regum and Paralipomenon': of Joshua, Judges, Kings and Chronicles   **37** 'wel lokid':
carefully considered   **43** 'suynge of': following from   **47** 'fantasie': delusion   **49** 'likyngli':
likely   **59** 'culueris': doves

Variants   **36** historial A C6 C9 E F L2 M N Q R91 U, historial[x]is[x] S (note)   **38** historial A C6 C9 E F
L2 M N Q R91 S U   **41** anogogik C6 C9 E F I F K L2 M N P R S U X Y   **42** autentik eþer preuable E
C9 Y   **43** of] þe   **51** to] in E K Q   **55** shal be] is K S X (note)

60 vsen acordinge wiþ þe kyndis of vnresonable beestis, as men ben clepid liouns for
pride eþer raueyn eþer sum oþer synne, and sumtyme a lioun signefieþ Crist, for his
power, and sumtyme a lioun signefieþ þe deuel, for tirauntrie and raueyn. And men
ben clepis beeris for gredynesse eþer glotenye, and mulis for leccherie, and so of
oþere beestis and oþere synnes. Men ben clepid culueris sumtyme for madnesse and
65 sumtyme for innocence, symplenesse and charite. Bi þese reulis, and bisi studiyng of
þe text, men moun liȝtli vndurstonde þe derk places of profetis, and algatis loke wel
þat þe sentence taken of þe text be trewe and acorde wiþ charite, and þanne it is þe
sentence of þe Hooli Goost, as seynt Austin seiþ.

Glosses and biblical references   **61** 'raueyn': greed   **65** 'symplenesse': simplicity   **66** 'algatis':
always

Variants   **67** acorde] acording S K X

Cambridge Tracts

Cambridge Tract I

f. 1r | [A]ll[e] cristine peple stant in þre maner of folke. Sum kunne rede and vnderstonde, as good clerkis and wel-letterd men, and for hem ben ordeyned bookis of Ebrewe, of Grwe and of Latyn. Summe cunnyn neþer rede ne vnderstonde, as lewid peple þat kunnen no letter, and for hem God haþ

5 ordeinede his creaturis in heuene, in erþe and in þe see to schewe his grace and kuyndnesse to men and wymmen þat han discrescion w[hereb]y þei schulden lerne to loue God and drede hym and kepe his comaundementis, and not by peynture and ymagerye madde by mannus hondis, for þe sperite of God seiþ in Dauiþ þe profete 'confundantur omnes qui adorant sc[ul]ptilia', etc. Summe

10 þer ben þat kunnen rede but litil or noȝt vnderstonde, and for hem ben ordent bookis of her moder-tonge, to Frensche | f. 1v | men bokis of Frensche, to Ytaliens bokis of Latyne corrupte, to Duche men bokis [of] Duche, to Englische men bokis of Englisch, in whiche bokis þei mowen rede to konne God and his lawe, and to fulfille it in worde and dede, and so to slee synne in

15 hemself and ech in oþer bi þer power and kunnynge, wherþorouȝ þei mowe desserue eendeles blisse.

   And þat is leful to cristyn peple rede and connen holy scripture in destruccion of synne and incresynge of uertu it is opyne in many placis of Goddis lawe, boþe olde and newe. For þus seiþ oure Lord God: 'Erunt uerba

20 hec que ego precipio tibi hodie in corde tuo, ac narrabis ea fili[i]s tuis et meditaberis sedens in domo tua et ambulans in it[i]nere, dormiens atque consurgens, et ligabis ea quasi signum in manu tua, erunt et mouebuntur ante oculos tuos, scr[i]besque in limine et hostiis domus | f. 2r | tue', Deutº vj. Þese wordis þat I bidde þee þis day schullen be in þi herte; þou schalt telle hem to þi

25 children; þou schalt þenken þerof sittynge in þi hous amongis þi mayne, whan þou goist be þe weye, whan þou goist to slepe and whan þou r[is]est; þou

---

Glosses and biblical references　**1** 'stant in': consists of　**3** 'Grwe': Greek　**4** 'kunnen no letter': are illiterate　**9** 'confundantur … sculptilia': 'let all those who adore graven images be confounded', Ps. 96:7　**12** 'Latyne corrupte': Italian (note)　• 'Duche': German　**18** 'opyne': manifest　**19–23** Deut. 6:6–9

Variants　**1** [ ]lla　**6** whereby] wearely　**9** scluptilia　**12** of *om.*　**18** [in]cresynge *sup. ras.*　**20** filis　**21** itenere　**23** scribesque] screbes que　**24** hem ˣand hemˣ　**26** risest] restest (note)

schalt bynde hem as a tokene in þin hand, in þi dede and in þi werke; þei
schullen be alwey sterynge aforne þe iȝen of þi herte; þou schalt write hem in
þi þresfol[d] and in þi doris of þin hous, þat is to sei, whan þou comyst yn and

30   whan þou goist out, in þe bigynynge and in þe eendenge of euery dede.
Alweye loke þat þou, ne none of þine, forfet aȝens Goddis lawe by cause of
þee.
          Also 'docebis verba mea filios tuos ac nepotes tuos', Deutᵒ iiijᵒ, þou
schalt teche my wordis to þi children, to þi neveuys and to þi kynnesmen. And

35   þerfore seynt Austyn seiþ þat ech man in his owne | f. 2v | houshold schuld do
þe office of a bisshop in techynge and correctynge of comoun þingis. And
Seneca seiþ 'compo[si]tus princeps, id est ben[e] morigeratus, debet
compo[s]itam habere familiam', a wel-ordeyned prince schulde haue a wel-
ordeyned meyne. And þerfor seiþ þe lawe, xxiij. cᵃ, q. vᵃ, trowe þou not þat þe

40   office of techynge and chastisynge longiþ only to þe bisshop, but to euery
gouernoure after his name and his degre, to þe pore man gouernynge his pore
housholde, to þe ryche man gouernynge his mayne, to þe hosbonde
gouernynge his wijf, to þe fader and þe moder gouernynge her childen, to þe
iustice gouernynge his countre, to þe kynge gouernynge his peple. And oone

45   neiȝbore schulde teche anoþer, for seynt Peter seiþ þus, 'vnusquisque sicut
accepit gratiam in alterutrum illam administrantes', prima Petre 4ᵒ, euery man
mynystre to oþer þe grace þat he haþ takun | f. 3r | of God. And þerfore whoso
kan rede bookis in his langage and so knoweþ þe better Goddis lawe, he is
bounden to spende þat kunnynge and þat grace to þe worschipe of God and to

50   helpe of his euene-cristen, to teche hem and to wissen hem after his staat and
his degree. And better it is to ocupie hem and oþere in redeynge of Goddis
lawe and deuocioun þan in redeynge of lesyngis, rebaudie and vanite.
          Ouermore, þe profete Isaye seiþ 'sicut populus, sicut sacerdos', as þe
peple so is þe prest; l[ew]id peple, lewed prest. And for as moche as þe curatis

55   ben often so lewid þat þei vnderstonden not bookis of Latyn for to teche þe
peple, it is speedful not oonly to þe lewed peple but also to þe lewed curatis to
haue bookis in Englisch of needful loore to þe lewed peple, for many curatis
kunnen not construe ne expowne her Pater Noster ne Aue ne crede, ne þe ten
comaunde| f. 3v |mentis ne þe seuene dedely synnes, ne many oþere þingis þat

60   þei ben bounden to knowe and to teche oþere, as þe lawe schewiþ, De
co[nsecratione], d. iiijᵃ, Symb[o]lum; item viij., q. prima, Oportet, et in
Constitucionibus Lam[b]eth, De infor[m]acione sacerdotis. But now it is
fulfillid þat þe prophete seid, 'paruuli petierunt panem et non erat qui frangeret
eis', Treneis iiijᵒ caᵒ, þe smale peple haue axed breed of Goddis worddis to

Glosses and biblical references   **29** 'þresfold': threshold   **33** Deut. 4:9   **45–6** 1 Pet. 4:10
53 Is. 24:2; Hos. 4:9   **54** 'curatis': clergy   **56** 'speedful': profitable   **58** 'Aue': 'Hail [Mary]'
63–4 Lam. 4:4

Variants   **29** þresfolo   **37** compositus] compourtus   •   bene] ben   **38** componitam   **48** is] his   **54**
lewid] lweid   **61** Symbalum   **62** lameth   •   informacione] in fornicacionem

65   sustinans of her soule, and þer was no man to breken it to hem, ne to
      expownen it ne to techen it.
          And þerfore God seiþ in þe gospel 'messis quidem multa, operarii
      autem pauci', etc., þere is moche korun and fewe werkmen; praieþ þanne
      þerfore to þe lord of þe [heruest] þat he sende werkmen into his corne. Fewe
70   þer ben þat wolden be t[au]ȝt; fewe þat kunnen teche, and wol fewere þat
      wolon teche, and so Goddis worde and Goddis lawe is neȝ forȝeten in þis
      lond. Vertu is | f. 4r | forsaken and vice is taken; truþe is in dispit; falshed is in
      worschip; pees and charite ben exilid; synne and malice, [de]baat and
      dissencioun regnen, for wiþouten kepynge of Goddis lawe is no pees. And as
75   þe prophete seiþ 'pax multa diligentibus legem tuam', moche pees, Lord, is to
      hem þat louen þi lawe. And þerfore þei þat letten lawful prechynge and leful
      techynge of Goddis lawe þei mowen dred of þe curse þat God ȝeueþ in þe
      gospel: 'Ve uobis legisperitis qui tulistis cla[uem] sciencie; vos non introistis,
      et eos qui introibant proibuistis', Lucᵒ x[j]. cᵒ. Wo be to ȝou þat schulden after
80   ȝoure staat and ȝoure office ben wyse in Goddis lawe, ȝe þat beren þe keye of
      kunnynge and of wisdom and haue autorite to preche and to teche; ȝe entrid
      not wiþ ȝoure kunnynge into heuene, and þei þat wolden entren ȝe letted hem
      wiþ wickide ensaumpule and wiþholdynge of god techynge, and letten hem þat
      wolden | f. 4v | haue tauȝt.
85   But many men wollen seie þat þer is moche eresie in Englische bookis,
      and þerfore no man schulde haue Goddis lawe in Englische, and I seie, be þe
      same skile þer schulde no man haue Goddis lawe in bookis of Latyn, for þer is
      moche heresie in bookis of Latyn, more þan in Englische bookis, for nyȝ al þe
      heresie þat is in þe peple it comeþ first fro false clerkis and lewed men of holy
90   ch[ir]che, and bi hem it is mayntened. Bookis of heresi schulden be brent, ben
      þei bookis of Latyn or Englische, and bookis of truþe schulden be kepet to
      helpe of mannes soule, for seynt Poul seiþ 'omnis lingua confit[ea]tur', euery
      tunge, euery langag[e] schulde knowlechen Goddis lawe, worschipon oure
      Lord Iesu Crist as euene in blisse wiþ allemyȝti God, þe fader of heuene. And
95   if ony word be myssett in Latyn or in Englische, ȝif it may be excusid lete it be
      | f. 5r | correctid and amendid, as men diden here aforun, for it is aȝens þe
      gospel to distrie þe whete bicause of a litel darnel.
          But summe seynne þat þe gospel ne Goddis lawe schulde not be tauȝt
      but in þre tungis, Ebrew, Grwe and Latyn, for reuerence of Crist þat first tauȝt
100   þe gospel and made þe gospel, and so for reuerence of Crist, wiþ ypocrisee

---

Glosses and biblical references   67–8 Matt. 9:37; Luke 10:2   74–5 Ps. 118:165   78–9 Luke 11:52
(cf. Matt. 23:13)   87 'skile': reason   92 Phil. 2:11   95 'myssett': misplaced, in error   97 'darnel':
weed among corn   98 'not be tauȝt but': only be taught

Variants   67 messis] Messias   69 heruest *om.*   70 be *sup. ras.* • tuaȝt   71 wolon ˣnotˣ teche •
neȝˣteˣ   73 debaat] baat   78 clauem] clamen   79 xj.] x.   90 chriche (note)   92 confitiantur   93
langagis • goddis] gooddis

a3enes Cristis lore, þei wollen distrie þe gospel. For whanne Crist schulde stye
into heuene he seid to his disciplis '*euntes in mundum uniuersum predicate*
euangelium omni creature', Mar. xvj°, 'goiþ', seiþ he, 'al aboute þe world and
preche þe gospel to euery criature', þat is to seye, to eche man and woman, as

105   seiþ seynt Gregorie, and as we fynden in þe last chaptel of seynt Mathew, he
bad h[e]m go and thech alle naciouns and baptise hem in þe name of þe Fader
and þe Sone and Holy Goost. 'And theche hem', seiþ he, to kepe alle þingis
þat I haue boden 3ou.' | f. 5v | Þanne þus God bad his disceplis preche þe
gospel and his lawe to alle men and women and to alle naciouns, but þe most

110   parte of þe world know[eþ] neyþer Ebrew, Grew ne Latyn, ne kouden þat
tyme. Þanne it was Goddis welle and his beddynge þat þei schulden preche
hem þe gospel and Goddis lawe in here langage, for ellis schuld þe peple
neuere haue cowde it. Þerfore on Witsonday, wanne þe Holy Gost li3tted on
Cristi[s] disciplis, he aperid in tongis wiþouten nomber and tau3te hem not

115   oonly Ebrew, Grew and Latyn but alle maner langages, as holy write schewiþ
wel, Actuum ij°, for God wold þat þei schulden teche þe gospel and his lawe,
needful and spe[d]ful, to euery peple in here langage. 3if þe kynge of Englond
sente to cuntrees and citees his patente on Latyn or Frensche to do crie his
lawis, his statutes and his wille to þe | f. 6r | peple, and it were cried oonly on

120   Latyn or Frensche and not on Englisch, it were no worschip to þe kynge ne
warnynge to þe peple but a greet desseyt. Ry3t so þe kynge of heuene wolde
þat his lawe and his welle were cried and tau3t opu[n]ly to þe pepel, and but it
were tau3t hem opunly on Englische, þat þei mowen knowen it, ellis it is a3ens
þe worschip of God, and gret hendrynge.

125   Sume seyne þat Crist tau3tte þe peple þe gospel and þe Pater Noster
frist in Latyn, and þerfor it schulde not be translated into Englische, but it is
not so—he tau3te þe Pater Noster and þe gospel in Ebrew, swych langage as
þe I[e]wis vseden, to whom he prechid. And as nedeful as it was to translate þe
gospel from Ebrewe into Grwe and into Latyn, for helpe of þe peple þat

130   couden noon Ebrwe, now it is nedful and leful | f. 6v | to translate it into
Englysche for helpe of Englisch peple þat kunnen neiþer Ebrewe, Grew ne
Latyn. For þou3 we preche to þe lewid peple Goddis lawe and þe gospel in
Ebrwe, Grwe or Latyn þei schullen neuere be þe wyser, but þei and þe
prechour boþe leesen her tyme. And þerfor men of holy chyrche þat ben

135   comaundid bi God to teche þe peple þe gospel and his lawe schulden teche þe
lewde peple on Englische, for þei vn[der]stonden no Latyn, and þerfor ben
ordeyned skolis of gramer be statute of holy chirche, *ecclesia* li°, v°, ti. [*De*]

Glosses and biblical references   101 'schulde stye': was about to ascend   102–3 Mark 16:15
105–8 Matt. 28:19–20   111 'welle': will • 'beddynge': command   113–16 Acts 2:1–11; 'Actuum
ij°': in the second chapter of Acts   130 'leful': lawful

Variants   101 Crist] cristi (note)   106 hem[1]] him   109 and[1] *sup. ras.* followed by 2-letter erasure   110
knowch   114 cristi   117 speful   118 to do] and not to do (note)   122 opuly   124 henydrynge   125 þat
crist *sup. ras.* • \þe[2]/   128 Iwis • w[x]ho[x]m • ne\de/ful   136 vnstonden   137 De *om.*

magistris, cᵒ *Nonnullis*, þat children in her ȝongþe þat ben disposid to be men
of holy chirche schulden lerne what Englische answeriþ to what Latyn, and so
140   in tyme comynge kunne translate þe gospel of Goddis lawe from Latyn into
Englische to þe vnderstondynge of þe peple. And þerfore in skolis þei
construen þe Sauter, | f. 7r | gospel and pestil on Englische, and so lernen to
make translacion from Latyn into Englische. And þei writen in Englische wiþ
þe Latyn, to rede it aȝen ȝif it nede to haue it freschly in mynde. And we fynde
145   in þe lijf of s[e]ynt Bartholomew þat he translated þe gospel of Mathew into þe
tunge and into þe langage of Indianys.

     But summe seyen þat þe lewid pepel schulde not rede holy write ne
Goddis lawe, ne haue it on Englische, for hooly write haþ so manye
vnderstondynges litera[l] and spiritual þat þe lewid pepel may not
150   vnderstond[e] it. I seie, bi þe same skyl neiþer þe lewid pepel neiþer þe lewid
men of holy chirche, seculere [ne] regulere, schulden haue it ne rede it in
Latyn, for I dar seie þat þe most part of men of holy chirche vnderstonden not
holy write ne þe gospel neiþer literalliche ne spiritualiche, neiþer on Englyche
ne o[n] Latyn. And bi þis skile schulde folowe þat fewe prestis, seculere ne
155   regulere, | f. 7v | schulden saye matinys or masse, for þei vnderstonden not
what þei reden but wel symply. And I dar seie þat þe wysist clerk lyuynge
vnderstonde[þ] not al þe gospil ne al þe Sauter ne al holy write litterallich and
spiritualiche, and þan nedes he muste rede holy write and þat he can not
transalatte to kunne. Ouermore, many men þat kunnen rede Englische þei
160   kunnen rede Latyn and ben letterid, and vnderstonden pistil, gospel and holy
write boþ in Englische and in Latyn as wel or bettere as þe moost part of men
of holy ch[i]rche, whiche kunnynge and vnderstondynge men of holy chirche
mowen not reue h[e]m ne lette hem to kunne be no lawe, but þei moste be here
prestis and seyen hem masse [and] matyns opunly, as seruantis and mynystris
165   of holy chirche, and þe here[r]se schullen vnderstonde after her kunnynge
wiþoute her leue. Lordis, ladies and oþere gentels haue and mowe haue
lawefully in | f. 8r | here chapellis masse-booke and portos, biblis and bookis
of holynes and of Goddis lawe to ocupien hem inne whanne hem likeþ; þer
may no lawe lette hem, weþer þei vnderstonden þe Latyn or nouȝt vnderstonde
170   it. Wymmen of religioun syngen and seyen here office in Latyn, and so reden

---

Glosses and biblical references   138 'ȝongþe': youth   142 'pestil': epistle   144 'to rede': so
that they may read • 'nede': should be necessary   151 'seculere [ne] regulere': whether in
worldly orders or belonging to a religious order   152 'dar seie': venture to assert • 'most part':
majority   154 'bi þis skile': from this cause   156 'but wel symply': except at a very elementary
level   159 'to kunne': in order to understand [it]   160 'letterid': literate   163 'reue': take away
from   163 'lette hem to kunne be no': prevent them from knowing by any   164 'opunly':
publicly   165–6 'after her kunnynge wiþoute her leue': according to their understanding without
the priests' permission   167 'portos': portable breviary   170 'of religioun': in religious orders

Variants   145 synt   149 litera   150 vnderstonde] vnderstondynge   151 ne¹ *om.*   152 \of²/   154 on]
of   156 symplyer (?)   157 vnderstonden   162 chrrche   163 hem] him   164 and² *om.*   165 heresse

myche partie of holy writte, and þou3t þei vnderstonden it no3t 3it it is seid
leefful and medeful to hem, and so leefulliche men and wymen mowen rede
holy writt alþou3t þei vnderstonden it not, and þe beter þei vnderstonden it þe
better and þe more deuoutely þei schullen rede it and seie it.

175   But 3if þe ten comaundementis, þe crede, Pater Noster and Aue, þat al
cristyn peple owiþ kunne, comenne þingis of holy writte, gospellis and pistilis
rede in holy chirche ben welle translatid and truly, sentence for sentence wiþ
good declaracioun, whoso rede it he schal þe better vndersto| f. 8v |nden it,
boþe in Latyn and in Englische, and þe more liking haue in God and in Goddis
180 lawe. But translacioun maad oonly worde for worde is wel derk and perilos
[in] vnderstondynge in alle langages, for euery langage haþ summ apirtee þat
acordiþ not al wiþ anoþer langage worde for worde but sentence for sentence.
        And take heed þat þer is two manner of lewed peple, oon þat kan no
lettrur, as ydiotis þat neuer wenten to skole. Þer is anoþer manner of lewid
185 pepel þat is lettrid but þei ben not seid mynysteris of holy chirche, ne haue
takun [e]ny religion ne holy order of þe bischop. And þus kyngus, princis,
dukis, erles, barons, kny3tus and squiers, men of lawe and oþer men of value,
and communers alle, alþou3 þei ben wel-letterid and better þan þe prest 3it þei
ben toold for lewid men and ben clepid in þe lawe *laici, id est, populares*. And
190 men of holy | f. 9r | chirche alþou3 þei kunnen lesse þan suche lewid folk 3it
þei ben clipid clerkis, a *cleros*, Gr[e]ce, *quod est sors*, Latyne, for þei schulden
be Goddis lott and his part, more ny3e God þan oþere in lyuynge, and
seruynge in Goddis hous, and in knowynge of Goddis lawe and of Goddis
welle.
195   To þe first manere of lewed pepel þat ben iclepid ydiotis it longiþ to
lere Goddis lawe bi herynge, bi techynge and good ensaumple. To hem
schulde be tau3t comoun þingis nedful and speedful, as þe ten
comaundementis, her crede on Englisch, her Pater Noster and Aue on Latyn or
in Englische, or boþe, which ben þe seuene deedly synnes, whiche ben þe
200 seuene sacramentis, seuene deedis of merci, and oþere comoun þingis. But þe
secunde maner of lewed folk mowen and owen to lerre bi herynge, bi redeynge
if þei mowen, and spenden þe grace þat God haþ sente hem | f. 9v | to [h]is
worchip. And wiþ suche folk men of holy chirche schulden trete and speke of
witte and wisdom, redy to answere to here doutis and to here questions
205 whanne þei seen hem willy and hauen lykynge in Goddis lawe.

Glosses and biblical references   172 'medeful': meritorious   176 'owiþ': ought   177 'sentence for sentence': meaning for meaning   178 'declaracioun': elucidation   180 'derk and perilos': obscure and dangerous   181 'apirtee': idiom (note)   182 'but' [does agree]   183–4 'kan no lettrur': has no knowledge of literacy   184 'ydiotis': illiterates   186 'religion': religious order   189 *'laici, id est, populares'*: laymen, i.e., the common people   191 'a' [Lat.]: from   • 'quod est': which is   192 'part': portion   205 'willy and hauen lykynge': willing and taking pleasure

Variants   171 part\i/e   • holy] holy^xnes^x   181 in] and   186 takun eny] takunrny (?)   191 Grece] grace   • sores   200 þingis comoun þingis   202 his] is

For þe firste manere of lewid folk þat ben rude, þat ben not able to take
ne to vnderstonde hiʒe materis, and for hem þat lyuen in synne an hoggis lijf,
ne han no lykynge in gostly þingis but al in þe lust of þe fleisch, redy to turne
aʒen to synne as houndis to her uomyth, for hem Crist seed to his discipilis

210 'nolite sanctum dare canibus neque mittat[i]s margaritas vostras ante porcos',
ʒeueþ not þe holy gospel to houndis, ne castiþ not ʒoure margaritis aforn þe
swyn, for hiʒe materis and priuy materis of þe gospel schulden be hid from
suche manere folk.

For þe secunde maner of lewed folk | f. 10r | seiþ s[e]ynt Poul, prima
215 Cor. ijᵒ, 'sapientiam loquimur inter perfectos', id est, inter auditores iam
capaces, amongis parfite men and wymen, þat is to seie, amongis hem þat ben
able to take it, we speken bi wisedom. And þerfore seiþ þe profete Malachie,
ij. cᵒ, þat 'þe lippis of prestis kepen wisdom', for of wisdom wiþ wise men
schulde be here daliaunce, 'and of his moþe men schullen seke Goddis lawe,
220 for he is þe aungel of þe Lord of hostis', for whan þe pepel is in doute, eiþer
by hereynge eiþer be redeynge, þei schullden b[e] redy to teche hem and to
wissen hem, and not to rebuke hem of here good wille ne to let hem of her
deuocioun to kunne Goddis lawe. And if þei kunnen not teche hem, besi þei
hem to lerre, and not to lette hem þat wolden lerre ne hem þat wolde teche. It
225 is a gret defaute in men of holy cherche as prestis noʒt to kunnen t[o t]eche,
| f. 10v | but it is a greiter nouʒt to welle to teche, but grettist of alle is neiþer to
kunne ne to wille to teche, and þerto to lette hem þat wolden lerne and hem þat
wolden teche.

We fynden in holy writte, Actus viiijᵒ, þat a gret lord of Ethiope,
230 tresorere of Candas, queen and lady of Ethiope, sat in his chare redynge Isaies
profecie as he rood in veyn pilgrimage. Þan God sent his aungle to seynt
Phelip, and bad hym mette wiþ þe lord and go to his chare. He cam and foond
þe heþen lord redynge, and þanne he seid to him 'ser, vnderstondist þou what
þou redist?' The lord answerid 'how myʒte I', seid he, 'vnderstonde it, but
235 sum man declare it to me and teche it me?', for he was an heþen man. And
seynt Phelip declarid to him þe proficie, and conuertid him to þe feþe and
baptisid him, and he wente home wiþ myche ioye and tauʒt þe feþe in his
contre, and was cause of conuersioun of | f. 11r | many þousandis. Here we
mowen see þat it is leeful and medful and spedeful man and woman to rede
240 Goddis lawe in what tunge he can, alþouʒ he wnderstond it not. God was not
myspayde wiþ þe heþen lord þat he redete his lawe and holy writt wiþ
deuocion but he was welle payed, and because of his redynge God ʒaf him
grace to b[e] turned to þe feþe and truþe. To hou moche more God is welle
paied þat cristyne folke redein holy writ and his lawes after her kunnynge, and

---

Glosses and biblical references   **208–9** Cf. Prov. 26:11   **209** 'for': in relation to   **209–10** Matt.
7:6   **214–15** I Cor. 2:6   **217–20** Mal. 2:7   **226** 'welle': be willing   **229–38** Acts 8:26–38

Variants   **209** cristi   **210** mittates   **214** synt   **221** be redy] bi redy   **222** heˣmˣre   **225** to teche]
teheche   **231** sent] seynt   **243** be] b

245 not myspaied, þou3 þei vnderstonden it not al cleerly. Deuout redeynge in holy
writt is cause of grace and cause of lernynge to cr[i]styn peple, as it was to the
lord of Ethiope. And as he was bese to askyn and to lerne, so schullden cristyn
peple þat kunnen rede, and namylyche gentlis and men of lawe.
As telliþ s[e]ynt Ierom and þe master | f. 11v | of stories boþe,

250 Ptholomeus Philathelphus kynge of Egipt dede transalate holy write into his
langage be seuenti and two wise men of Goddis lawe and of ri3t beleue, and
þou3 þe kynge were an heþen man and of false bileue God was welle paied
þerwiþ, for be transalacioun þe lawe of God was knowe welne3t al abowten þe
worlde, and þe feiþe of holy chirche þerby was knowe ferre and wyde, and

255 welle confermed. Aforn þat tym two heþen men, Theopontus and Theotectus,
men of false beleue, wolden haue translatid holy writt on here maner to seche
here worschipe and not Goddis worschipe, and God was myspaied.
Theopo[nt]us wax wod; Theotectus wep bleude, but aftur þei repentiden hem
of here presumcion, and God made hem holle.

260 We fynde, Deut° xviij°, how God bade þat þe children of Israel
schulden do wrytt his holy lawe wel and t[ru]ly, | f. 12r | and rede it al þe days
of here lif, and so lerne to kepe Goddis lawe and to drede him, þou3 many of
hem were no clerkes. We fynden in Luyk, x. c°, þat a man of lawe axide what
he schulde do to haue þe lijf witoutten eende, and þan Crist answerid 'what,'

265 seide he, 'þat is written in þe lawe. How redist [þou]?' 'I rede,' seide he, 'þus:
Diliges dominum deum tuum, etc., þou schalt loue þi God wiþ al þin hert, wiþ
al þi soule, wiþ al my3t, and þi nei3bor as þisilf'. '*Rect[e] respondisti*, þou hast
answerid wel and ry3tfuly; do þis and þou schalt lyue wiþoutten eend'. He
seide not, as men don þese dayes, 'who made þe b[or]el clerk so hardi to rede

270 Goddis lawe?', but he preisid him for his redeynge. And he answerid and bade
him do as he redet.
Seynt Peter, seynt Poul, seynt Ion, seynt Iames and oþere apostlis
writen pistlis feele to comentes of peples of londis and of citees, techynge
| f. 12v | hem Goddis lawe be writynge whan þei my3ten not come to teche hem bi

275 prechynge, and þei baden þat þo pistilis schulden be red oponly in
conggricacion of þe pepel, þat þei my3tyn al heere it þat kouden not reede, and
so boþe bi writynge and prechynge þei tau3ten þe pepel. Seynt Ierom
transalatid moche of þe Bible, and w[ro]ot it first to wymmen þat weren clepid
Paula and Eustochium and to oþere maidonys, wymmen of crafte religion, þat

280 dwelliden wiþ hem. To hem he wrot þat faire sermon of þe Assumpcion, ful of
witte, and it begyneþ þus, '*Cogitis me, O Paula et Eustochium, immo Christi
caritas compellit*', and to oþere holy wymmen he wroot pistilis and bokis feele.

Glosses and biblical references   249 'master of stories': Peter Comestor (note)   258 'wep bleude':
wept blood • 'aftur': afterwards   260–2 Deut. 17:18–19   263–9 Luke 10:25–8
269 'borel': ignorant   273 'comentes': communities   279 'crafte': powerful

Variants   246 crstyn   249 synt   258 Theopontus] Theopouplius   261 truly] turly   262 him and
þou3   265 ˣþouˣ   267 recti   269 broel   278 worot

Seynt Austyn also wroot many a pistil to lordis and ladis and to holy wymmen,
enformynge hem in Goddis lawe, as he schewiþ wel in his pistil *ad Comitem,*
285   *ad sac[ra]s virgines, ad Longinianum, ad Volucianum, ad Lic[e]nti| f. 13r |um,*
ad Arme[n]tarium, ad Paulinam, ad Florentinam, ad Italicam, ad ciues
Yponences, ad Probam et Iuliana[m], et aliis epistulis quam plurim[i]s. Seynt
Ambrose [and] seynt Gregorie diden on þe same maner.
        Here aforn, cl[e]rkys weren besi to write to kingis and princes, lords
290   and ladis, bokis of Goddis lawe, to stere hem to deuocioun and good lyuynge.
But clirkis þese days ben besy to take þis from hem and make þe pepel
ouerlewid, as þei ben hem self for þe moste part, in so moche þat þei wolden
not suffer þet þe pepel kunne here Pater Noster, Aue, ne cred ne þe
comaundementis in here langage, ne vnderston[d] hem. And ȝif it be not
295   leefful to teche hem þese þingis in here langage we schulden teche hem riȝt
not of Goddis lawe in here langage, and so schulde ceesse al prechinge in
Englisch þat is ordennt for þe comoyn pepel, b[oþ] letterid and lewid. Bu[t] þe
lawe, viij. q., prima, *Oportet,* seiþ þat þe | f. 13v | prech[ou]r and þe techer of
Goddis worde schulde so ordeyne his wordis þat þe pepel myȝte vnderstonde
300   him [and] turne Latyn into Englische, not Englische into Latyn corrup, as men
doin þeise days to blende þe pepel and to magnifien hemself, and not seken
Goddis worschipe ne profiȝt of manes soule, as þe lawe schewiþ wel, d. xliij,
dispencacioun.
        Þe pope and holy chirche han ordennte pistil and gospel and oþer
305   offices to be rad opunly in holy chirche in heringe of al þe pepel, þat þei mow
vnderstonde it if þei kunnen, and for þei schulden þe better vnderstonde it ben
ordeyned prechours to expowne pistil and gospel to þe pepel in here langage
from þe beginn[inge]. So þei prechchen in Rome, in Itali, in France, in
Allmayne and in oþere londis. In Itali and at Rome, þere þe pope dwelliþ, þe
310   lewid pepel may in her langage vnderstonde pistil and gospel nyȝ as wel as þe
prest and better þan many prestis in oþere londes, for her langage is Latyn, and
þe | f. 14r | pope ne holy chirche lettiþ hem not to here ne to kunne holy writ
þat is red in holy cherche, ne may let hem be eny lawe, for what holy chirche
rediþ opunly to þe pepel it may be tauȝt hem opunly, as wel on Englische to
315   Englische folk as to þe Romayns in Latyn corrup, or to Duche men in Deuche,
or to Frensche men in Frensch, or let hem telle cause whi þat Englische folk
schulde nouȝt as wel be tauȝt Goddis lawe and þe gospel and holy writte as
wel as oþere naciouns, and whi Englische nacioun schulde more be excludid
from þe blessynge of Goddis lawe more þan oþere naciouns.
320   'Beatus vir qui non abiit in consilio impiorum, et in via peccatorum

---

Glosses and biblical references   292 'ouerlewid': excessively ignorant   301 'blende': blind
320–2 Ps. 1:1–2

Variants   285 sacars   • licinti//um   286 armetarium   287 Iuliana   • plurims   288 and *om.*   289
clrkys   294 vnderston   296 ceesse] creesse   297 boþ] but   • but] bu   298 prechuor   300 and *om.*   308
beginngen   309 and at] and in at   318 nacioun] naciouns   320 abiit] habiit

non stetit, et in cathedra pestalencie non sedit, set in lege domini voluntas eius,
et in lege eius meditabitur die ac nocte'. Blessid be þat man, seiþ he, þat went
not aweye from þe tr[ew]þ of Goddis lawe þorouȝ þe consel of false profites,
shrewis, | f. 14v | and stood not in þe weye of synne[r]s and wickid-doeres, to
325 mayntene synne[s] shrewidnesse, ne sat not in þe chaiere of deeþ to techyn
synne, vanite, errowres and err[esi]e þat leden to eendeles deeþ, ne be
mystechynge ne wiþdrawynge of techynge hid from þe pepel þe weye of lyf,
but sette hijs welle and hijs likynge in oure Lordis lawe, and schal þenke of his
lawe nyȝt and day. *'Beatus qui legit et qui audit uerba prophesee huius',*
330 *Apoca. primo,* blessid be he þat rediþ and heryt þe wordis of þe prophesie, and
kepiþ in mynde and in deede þingis þat ben writen þeryn, what wordis ben seid
to alle cristyn pepel, as þe boke schewiþ wel. And þerfore whoso can rede
Goddis lawe lette him rede it wiþ good deuocioun and wiþ meke hert, and not
be presum[p]tuous of himself ne of his kunnynge ne redynge, ne dispise he
335 men of holy chirche, in þat þat þei suen Iesu Crist, but | f. 15r | hate he he[r]
prid þat ben presumptuous to clepe h[e]mself men of holy cheriche,
contrariy[n]ge Crist in werke and worde, for þis is abhominable to God and to
his chosyn pepel. Neþeles, loue we in him þat þat God made, þat is, body and
soule, and hate we in him þat þat God hatiþ, þat is, wickedenes and synne. Ne
340 no man for his redynge looþe to here Goddis word truly prechid in
distruccioun of synne and encresynge of vertu, but eche man be bysy to kepe
riȝt and trwþe in here word and dedis, as he heerit and rediþ in þe lawe of God,
for boþe to þe reder and to herrer God ȝeueþ his blissynge, if þei kepen it and
don þeraftir. And þer is no þinge þat abateþ so moche temptacion of flessche
345 a[s] loue and lykynge in holy writt, and þerfor seiþ seynt Ierom, *ad Rusticum*
monachum, et ponitur *de con[secratione],* d. vltima, *Nu[m]*|| f. 15v |*quam:*
'ama scienciam scripturarum et carnis vicia non amabis', loue kunnynge of
ho[l]ly writt and of Goddis lawe and þou schalt not loue vicis of þe flesche.
    But sume seien þat þe moder vnderston[de] þe child þat seiþ 'k[e]sse'
350 as him þat seiþ 'chese', and him þat seiþ 'beed' as him þat seiþ 'breed'; moche
more God vndersto[nde] al hise childeren, whateuer tunge þei speken, be it
Latyn or Englisch. Al þis graunte I wel, but ryȝt as þe moder wel loke þat þe
childe, whanne he comeþ to age, schal lerne to speke better and do better and
kunne more good þan he deed in his ȝouþe, or ellis he schal abien it, riȝt so
355 God wol þat we do oure deuer to speke wel, to do wel and to kunne his lawe,
ech man and woman after his state and his degre. For as þe profete Isaie seiþ

Glosses and biblical references   329–30 Apoc. 1:3   331 'what': which   335 'in þat þat': insofar
as   354 'abien': pay the penalty for   356–7 Is. 65:20; 'surely a child shall not die aged a
hundred?'

Variants   323 trweþ   324 synnes   325 synne   326 erriese   328 hijs welle] hijs lyf welle in   330
heryt þe þe   331 þerynni   334 presumtuouns   335 her] hem   336 himself   337 contrariyge   339 we]
ˣbeˣ \we\   345 as] a   346 Nuncquam   348 hohy   349 vnderstonde] vnderston as • kisse (note)   351
vnderstoˣnˣ   352 \þe/2   353 schal ˣitˣ

'where þe child of an hundrid ȝere schal die?' And þerfor seynt Paul beddiþ
þat | f. 16r | men and wymen schulden not in witt and vndertsondynge of
Goddis lawe be alwey children, prima Cor. xiiij. c°. [O]uermore, take hede þat
360 þouȝ þe child seie 'bed' and 'kese' ȝit he vnderstant what he meneþ and woot
what he axsiþ, but þe lewed pepel for seiynge here Pater Noster and cred in
Latyn þei witton not what þei menen, and so in þat þei ben more lewid þan þe
child.

And þerfor, þou lewed man and woman, alþouȝ þou kunne þi Pater
365 Noster, Aue and crede in Latyn, ȝit trauel to wite what þou menyst, or ellis in
cas þe starlynge and þe iaye may kunne þi Pater Noster and þi crede as wel as
þou. And teche it þi childe as wel as þou. Þat is schame þat man or woman of
sixti ȝere schal no better kunne his beleue, ne no more of Goddis lawe, þanne
he code whan he was but fyue ȝere wol[d] or seuen ȝere wol[d]. But þerfor
370 | f. 16v | seiþ þe prophete '*populus non intel[l]igens vapulabit*', Osee iiij. c°, þe
pepel, seiþ he, þat vnderstondit not Goddis lawe schal be ponischid and abyue
it. And þerfor seiþ seynt Poul, ad Ephe. v°, '*nolite fieri imprudentes set
intelligent[e]s que sit uoluntas dei*', beþ not, seiþ he, vnwyse, but vnderstondiþ
what is þe wel of God. God biddiþ in þe gospel þat men schulden vnderstonde
375 what þei heren and what þei reden: '*audite me, omnes, et intelligite*', Mark
vij°; item xiij. c°, '*qui legit, intelligat*', and seynt Poul, prima ad Cor. xiiij° c°,
seiþ þat eche man and woman schulde do his deuer to vnderstonde what he
preiþ, what he rediþ and what hereþ of Goddis lawe, and schewiþ þer bi many
skylis þat it is but a skornworþi and a foly to teche þe pepel in s[uche] tunge
380 þat þei vnderstonden not. And þe same | f. 17r | seiþ þe lawe, *ecclesia*, in
Clementinis, ti. *De magistris*, c° *Inter solicit[u]dines*.

Whoso tauȝte þe lewid Englische man or woman medicyne for his
seknesse oonly in Latyn, and forbede him oonly to lerne it of ony oþer in
Englische to vndertsonde it, he dide litil helpe to þe seke man. Ȝif þe wayte
385 and þe wache in castel seyn enemyes comynge and maden a token or warnede
hem in suche tunge þat no man in þe castel knewe, he were a traytour, for it
were no warnynge. And, as seynt Poul seiþ, if men schulden goen to a batel
and þe tromper trompid in suche maner þat no man wiste what he mente, þer
schulde no man araye h[i]m to batyl ne to witstonde his enemyes. Riȝt so men
390 of holy sch[ir]che, prelatis and prechouris, b[e] ordeyned to be lechis of cristen
soulis and wacche hem in þe castel of holy ch[ir]che, and to be trompris of
Goddis oost to warne folk of | f. 17v | goostly prechynge and to herte hem to
feȝten aȝens þe fendes ooste. And ȝif þei techen þe lewed pepel here Pater

Glosses and biblical references   357–9 1 Cor. 13:11   365 'trauel': labout   369 'code': could
369–70 Hos. 4:14   372–3 Eph. 5:17   374–6 Mark 7:14   376 Mark 13:14 (cf. Matt. 24:15)
376–8 1 Cor. 14:11   387–9 1 Cor. 14:8

Variants   359 euer more   369 wol *bis* (note)   370 inteligens   373 intelligentis   376 legit et
intelligat   379 suche] schuc   381 solicitudines] solicitadinnes   386 knewe þat he   387 batatel   389 him]
hem   390 schriche   • be¹] bi   391 chriche   392 of / of

Noster, Aue and crede and þe ten comaundementis oonly in Latyn, and oþer
395   þingis þat schulden be here goostly boote and gostly armure and warnynge of
myscheuys and of perilis, þei don but dys[e]ysyn þe pepel.

   Men of holy chirche euery day preien to God not only for hemself but
principaly for þe pepel, seynge on þis manere: ʻ*da michi intel[le]ctum et
scrutabor legem tuam et custodiam illam in toto corde meo. Da michi*
400   *intell[e]ctum ut s[c]iam testimonia tua; da michi intell[e]ctum ut viuam*ʼ. Lord,
seiþ he, ȝeue me vnderstondynge and I schal ransake vp þi lawe and kepe it
wiþ al my hert; ȝy[f] me vnderstondynge and I schal kunne þi witnes and þi
comaundementis, and so leue wiþouten eende. And siþen þei preien so bisili
þat cristyne pepel | f. 18r | schulde vnderstonde Goddis lawe wu[n]der I haue
405   whi þei ben so looþe to teche Englysche pepel Goddis lawe in Englische
tunge. For wiþouten Englische tunge þe lewed Englische pepel mowen not
knowe Goddis lawe. And me merueleþ moche why þei ben so besi to let folke
for to vnderstonde Goddis lawe and holy write.

   Huntyngdon telliþ, *De Geestis of Ynglon[d]*, li°, iij°, þat þanne seynt
410   Austyn cam to conuerte Englische pepel to þe feiþ he sent vp to þe Walys[h] to
þe clergie of Bretoneris, preiynge hem and biddynge þat þei schulden come
and helpe to teche and conuerte Englische nacion. Þei hadden but indignacioun
þerof, and wolden not come to teche hem. And þan seid seynt Austyn ʻsyþen
þei wollen not thechyn hem and conuerte hem and han hem breþeren in þe
415   feiþ, þei schullen fele hem fel enemyesʼ. And so it felle, forsoþe, | f. 18v | after
þe kynge of Englond slowȝ of hem, in oo day in oo place, a þousand and t[w]o
hundrid munkis and oþer men of holy chirche, and after he slowȝ moo. And it
is to dred þat it schal falle on þe same manere to þe clerg[i]e of Englond, for
but þei wole teche þe laysee Goddis lawe and þe feiþ beter þan þei done, and
420   nouȝt lette hem to kunne Goddis lawe and þe feiþ of holy chirche, þe laysee
schal, be þe ritful dom of Goddis [lawe], ponysche hem ful harde, for be
defauȝte of techynge of Goddis lawe þe lewed pepel for þe most part ȝeueþ no
tale of God ne man. ʻ*Set ve homini illi per qu[e]m filius hominis tradetur*ʼ, but
woo be to þat man be whom Goddis sone schal be bitrayed and dispisid in his
425   mynisters and hise prestis; ʻ*bonum erat ei si natus non fuisset*ʼ. Not halfundel
þe pepel kunen here feiþ þat þei bonden hem to at þe | f. 19r | fount-ston, ne
here cred, neiþer in Latyn ne in Englische, ne þe ten comaundementis, ne but

---

Glosses and biblical references   395 ʻbooteʼ: remedy   396 ʻdyseysynʼ: make ill   398–9 Ps.
118:34   399–400 Ps. 118:125   400 Ps. 118:144   401 ʻransake vpʼ: search through   422–3 ʻȝeueþ
no tale ofʼ: care nothing about   423–5 Matt. 26:24 (cf. Mark 14:21); ʻbonum erat ei si natus
non fuissetʼ: it would have better for him if he had not been born   426 ʻfount-stonʼ: baptismal
font

Variants   396 dysyseyn   398 intellectum] intelictum   400 intellictum *bis* • sciam] siam   402 ȝyf]
ȝiu   403 eenden   404 wuder   406–7 \mowen not knowe/   409 ynglon   410 walys   416 two] to   418
clerge   421 lawe [or *sim.*] om.   423 quem] quam   427 ne in þe ten

litil of Goddis lawe, and so þe lond, for defaute of techynge and kunnynge of
Goddis lawe, is in poynt to be vndon.

430   And þerfor seiþ Salomon 'erud[i] *filium tuum et refrigerabit te, et dabit*
delicias anime tue. Cum prophecia defecerit, dissipabitur populus; qui custodit
legem beatus est', Prov. xxix°. Teche þi child Goddis lawe and he schal
refresche þe in þin age [and] ȝyue delicis to þi lijf and to þi soule. Whanne
techynge, seiþ he, and declaracioun of Goddis lawe fayleþ þe pepel schal be

435   distroied; whoso kepeþ Goddis lawe he is blessed, for whanne good techynge
fayliþ in hous, þat þe fader or þe moder kunnen not or wollen not teche here
childeren ne[d]ful þingis of þe feiþ and of Goddis lawe, ne þe lord hise | f. 19v |
seruantis, þa[n] þe pepel schal mysfarre, for suche as folke taken in ȝouþe þei
kepen in age. But þe lewed pepel be tauȝt þe feiþe and þe ground of Goddis

440   lawe, whyche ben þe ten comaundementis and oþere comoun þingis, ellis
clerkis prechynge schal do hem but litel profiȝt, for þei wen[en] not what it
mene[þ].

        And þerfor it may be ueryfide of Englische pepel þat is writen in þe
Sauter: '*nescierunt neque intellexunt, in tenebris ambulant; mouebuntur omnia*

445   *fundamenta terre*', þei knowen not Goddis lawe ne vnderstonden it, and þerfor
alle þe groundis of þe lond schullen be stired. For ignoraunce of Goddis lawe
is cause of alle meuynge and vnstabilte in þe comoun pepel, þat þei dreden
neiþer God ne man as þei schulden do: false and vnstable, redi to rebelle aȝens
here souereyns, redi to | f. 20r | mordre and manslauȝter. And so it is to drede

450   þat for ignoraunce of Goddis lawe and falsnesse and schrewidnesse þe lond
schal be moued and chaungid from oure nacion to anoþer nacion, but we
amende us. '*Vtinam saperen[t] et intellegerent ac nouissima prouider[e]nt*',
Deut° xxxij°, wolde God þat men, þe pepel of Englond, kowden Goddis lawe
and vnderstoden it, and aviseden hem and token heede in here doynge allewey

455   of þe laste eende, and wolden þenke what may falle of here deedis, and, att þe
begynnynge of here dede, þenke of þe ende.

        But sum seien þat it is defendid be þe lawe men for to teche þe feiþ or
speke of þe feiþ to þe lewid pepel, for it passiþ here wijt. And I seie, be þe
same skele men schulden not speke þereof amonge clerkis, for it passiþ here

460   wijt. And, ouermore, I seie þat it is not | f. 20v | defendid bi þe lawe to teche ne
to preche þe feiþ to þe lewed pepel, ne to speke þerof in dwe manere in
heerynge of þe pepel be wey of techynge. It is bo[u]ndon bi þe gospel, bi lawe
of holy chirche, bi lawe ceuyle, bi lawe emperial, bi statutis of holy chyrche in

Glosses and biblical references   429 'in poynt to be vndon': on the verge of being ruined
430–2 Prov. 29:17–18   434 'declaracioun': elucidation   443 'of': concerning   443–4 Ps. 81:5; 'in
tenebris ambulant': they walk in darkness   449 'to drede': to be feared   452–3 Deut. 32:29
455 'falle of': result from   457 'defendid': forbidden   460 'ouermore': moreover

Variants   430 erudi] Erud   433 and[1] *om*   434 ˣþe pepelˣ þe pepel   437 neful   438 þan] þat   441
wenen] wente   442 menen   443 englische of   452 saperen • prouiderunt   454 vnderstonden   460
\is/   462 bondon

Ynglond, þat men of holy chirche schulden be besy to teche þe feiþ to þe lewd
465   pepel, boþe cristen and heþen, ȝif þei mowen and kunnen. And whoso kan his
feiþ he may leeffulliche and medfully teche it oþere þat kunnen it not, Iew,
Sarsyn and paynym, for many heþene men and wymmen han be turned to þe
feiþ bi techynge of lewed men and wymen, as seynt Austyn was conuertid bi
his moder, þere alle þe clirkis of Cristendom myȝten not conclude hym ne
470   conuerte him, and seynt Poul seiþ '*saluabitur vir [in]fidelis per mulierem*
fidelem', a man of false bileue schal be | f. 21r | saued bi a woman of riȝ[t]
bileue. But it is defended bi þe lawe þat eiþer clerke or lewed man or woman
schulde dispute þe feiþ or make argumentis aȝenes þe feiþ in audience of þe
pepel, for [bi] suche argumentis and desputyngis to and fro þei myȝten falle
475   into hard temptacion and into gret doute. And þerfore hiȝe materes schulden
be descuscid and disputid amongis clerkis and men of skoole.

      Now, leue frendis, haue I schewed ȝou þat it is leful and nedful to þe
pepel for to knoue Goddis lawe and þe feiþ of holy chirche in here langage,
and þat it is leefful and spedful to hem þat kunne rede, and nameliche to
480   gentellis, to haue Goddis lawe writen in bookis, þat þei mowon red it and so þe
better kunne, for it is a comoun sawe, and soþ it is, 'worde and wynd and
mannes mynde is ful schort, but letter writen dwelliþ'. And, as seynt Austyn
| f. 21v | seiþ *ad Volucianum*, þat man or woman haþ in writynge or in boke he
may rede it alwey whanne he haþ tyme and tome to reden. He may rede
485   whanne he wole and letten whanne he wole wiþouten dissese, but he may not
alwey haue prechynge ne techynge whanne he wolde, and ofte whanne he may
haue a techer he haþ no tome.

      And þerfor, leue frend, siþþen ȝe kunnen rede, spendit ȝoure kunnynge
to þe worship of God, and whanne ȝe haue tome and tyme of deuocion doþ
490   ȝoure deuer after ȝoure staat to kunne and to vnderstonde Goddis lawe. For
Salamo[n] seiþ '*acceptus est regi minister intelligens*', Prov. xiiijº, þe seruaunt
vnderstondynge Goddis lawe is acceptable and plesant to þe kyng of heuene.
And þe bettere þat ȝe vnderstonden what ȝe reden þe more deuocioun ȝe
schullen | f. 22r | haue and þe more knowe ȝoure God, and þe more ȝe knowen
495   him þe more ȝe schullen loue him, and þe more ȝe louen him þe more he schal
loue ȝou. Amen.

Glosses and biblical references   **469** 'conclude': convince   **470–1** 1 Cor. 7:14 (note)   **479**
'nameliche': particularly   **484** 'tome': leisure   **485** 'dissese': inconvenience   **488** 'spendit': use
(*imp. pl.*)   **490–1** Prov. 14:35

Variants   **470** infidelis] fidelis   **471** riȝ   **474** bi (or *sim.*) *om.*   **479** leefful and ˣsuˣ   **488** spendedit   **489**
deuocion and doþ   **491** salomo

Cambridge Tract II

f. 22r | Þis preueþ þat þei ben blessed þat louen Goddis lawe in þere owen langage

[O]ure Lord Iesu Crist, verry God and man, seþ in þe gospel 'blessed ben þei þat
heren Goddis wor[d]e and kepen it'. And eft Crist seþ 'ȝe ben my frendis ȝif ȝe do
þo þingis þat I comande to ȝou'. And eft 'he þat haþ my comaundementis and kepet
hem, he it is þat loueþ me'. Eft Dauiþ seiþ 'blessed be þei þat serchen Goddis
5   witnessynge[s], and s[e]chen God in alle þe herte'. On þe contrarie s[ide], Dauiþ
seiþ 'þei ben cursid þat bowen awey from Goddis hestes', and Poul seiþ 'he [is]
cursid þat loueþ not oure Lord Iesu Crist'. But Crist seiþ 'he þat | f. 22v | loueþ me
schal kepe my word, and he þat lou[e]t not me kepeþ not my wordis'. God seiþ bi
Salamon 'þe preire of him is cursid þat turniþ awey his ere þa[t] he here not þe lawe
10   of God'. And Poul seiþ 'he þat knowiþ not Goddis lawe schal not be knowen of
Crist at þe day of dome for his trwe seruaunt'. Crist seiþ 'þe wordis whiche I haue
spoken to ȝou ben sperit and lyif'. Þerfor Peter seid to Crist 'Lord, to whom schulde
we go? Þou hast wordis of euerlastynge lijf'. Þe Wyse Man seiþ, in þe persoun of
holy writ, 'þei þat declaren me schullen haue euerlastinge liif'. And Dauiþ seiþ
15   'Lord, þe declarynge of þi wordis liȝtne[þ] and ȝeueþ vnderstondinge to meke men'.
Þe prophete Danyel seiþ 'þei þat techen many men to riȝtwisnesse schulden
schiȝ[n]en as þe firmament'. And seþen men doynge iustly bodily al| f. 23r |messe
schullen be saued, as Crist seiþ in þe gospel, myche more þei schullen be of hiȝe
degre in heuene þat ȝeuen in charite þe gret almes of Godis worde, declaringe it
20   riȝtly to þe pepel.
     Cristyn men owen to trauel myche neȝt and day about þe tixt of holy writ
and nameli þe gospel in here moder-tunge, siþen Iesu Crist, verri God and man,
tauȝte þis gospel wiþ his blessed mouþ, and kepte [it] in [h]is lijf, and for kepynge

Glosses and biblical references   1–2 Luke 11:28   2–3 John 15:14   3–4 John 14:21   4–5 Ps. 118:2
(note)   5–6 Ps. 118:21   6–7 1 Cor. 16:22   7–8 John 14:21, 24   8–10 Prov. 28:9   10–11 1 Cor.
14:38   11–13 John 6:64, 69   13 'persoun': role   13–14 Ecclus 24:31   14–15 Ps. 118:130; 'liȝtneþ':
illumines   16–17 Dan. 12:3

Variants   **Heading** *om.* D D76 G1 L1 o P1 R77   • in ˣoþere wunˣ \þere owen/ langage   1 [ ]ure   •
and very man L1 D D76 G1 o P1 R77   2 wore   3 haþ] louiþ L1 D D76 o R77, *om.* P1   5 witnessynge
C, witnessyngis D D76 G1 o P1 R77, witnessis L1   • sechen] schchen C, sekyn out L1 D D76 G1 o P1
R77   • side] seid   6 is *om.*   7 he þat] if eny man L1 D D76 G1 o P1 R77   • me schal] me he schal L1 D
D76 G1 o P1 R77   8 louet] lout   9 turniþ] bowiþ D   • þat[2]] þa   11 þe day of dome] domes day L1 D
D76 G1 o P1 R77   • wichiche   12 seid] seiþ L1 D D76 G1 o P1 R77   • schulde] schul L1 D D76 G1 o P1
R77   15 liȝ\t/ne   16 riȝtwisnesse] ryȝtfulnes L1 D D76 G1 o P1 R77   • schulden] schullen L1 D D76 G1
o P1 R77   17 schiȝen   • and *om.* D D76 G1 L1 o P1 R77   • iustily   • almesse] almesse to nedy men L1
D D76 G1 o P1 R77   19 in heuene] of blis L1 D D76 G1 o P1 R77   • in charite] charitably L1 D D76 G1
o P1 R77   20 þe] cristene L1 D D76 G1 o P1 R77   21 to trauel myche] moche to traueile L1 D D76 G1
o P1 R77   • þe tixt] tixtis D o R77   22 and very man L1 D D76 G1 o P1 R77   23 his[1]] his owne L1 D
D76 G1 o P1 R77   • it *om.*   • his[2]] is

[and] halowynge þerof he schedde his precius blod, and ȝaf it wryten bi his foure
25 gospelleris, Matheu, Mark, Luyk and Jon, þat eche man schulde reule his lif þerbi.
For but if we kepe þis gospel we mow not be saued, and þouȝ we coude noon oþer
lawe mad of synful men we myȝten wel come to heuene, for God seid to Poul 'my
grace sufficiþ to þee'.

Alas, who may for drede of | f. 23v | God lete lewid men to knowe þe gospel
30 and kepe þe gospel and comounly to speke þerof in mekenesse and charite, to
destroie synne and plante vertues in cristyn soulis? But coueitus clerkis of þis world
replyin and seyen þat þe lewid men mo[w]en soone erre, and þerfor þei schullen not
dispute of cristyn feiþ. Allas, allas, what cruelte is it to take awey bod[i]ly mette
from a rewme for a fewe foolis wilen be gloutons and do harm to hemself for þei
35 taken mete vnresonable? And as lyȝtly may a proude wordly prest erre aȝens þe
gospel writyn in Latyn as a lewid man in Englysh, for symple lewid men owen not
to despu[t]e aboute holy write, seyinge wheþer [it] be sooþ or profitable to menis
soulis, but þei owen to beleue truly þat it is sooþ and profitable to alle cristene men,
for þere is non | f. 24r | oþere wey to heuene. Þerfore, lewid men schullen lerne it of
40 God principaly, and be good lyuynge of hemsilf, and studee and axe trwe clerkis þe
expownynge þerof, wher þat it is derke. What resoun were it ȝif a childe faile in his
lessoun þe first day to suffer noon children to come at scole for þis defaute? Who

Glosses and biblical references   26 'but if': unless   27–8 2 Cor. 12:9   29 'lete lewid men to
knowe': prevent uneducated men from knowing   41 'derke': obscure   42 'defaute': deficiency

Variants   24 and] \in/ • halowynge] halewyng and confermyng Lɪ D D76 Gɪ o Pɪ R77 • he] *om.*
D D76 Gɪ Lɪ o Pɪ R77 • schedde] schedinge D R77 • foure *om.* D D76 Gɪ Lɪ o Pɪ R77   25 Matheu,
Mark, Luyk and Jon] to his chirche in erþe Lɪ D D76 Gɪ o Pɪ R77 • man] cristen man Lɪ D76 Gɪ Pɪ •
schulde *om.* D D76 Gɪ Lɪ o Pɪ R77   26 but *om.* D D76 Gɪ Lɪ o Pɪ R77 • we[1, 2]] he D D76 Gɪ Lɪ o Pɪ
R77 • we mow not] he schal Lɪ D D76 Gɪ o Pɪ R77 • saued] saued and ellis in no manere Lɪ D D76
Gɪ o Pɪ R77 • noon] neuere Lɪ D D76 Gɪ o Pɪ R77   27 lawe] lawes Lɪ D76 Gɪ Pɪ • we … heuene] he
may come sufficiently and esely to heuene Lɪ D D76 Gɪ o Pɪ R77   27–8 for god … to þee] *om.* D D76
Gɪ Lɪ o Pɪ R77   29 þe gospel *om.* D D76 Gɪ Lɪ o Pɪ R77   31 synne] synnes Lɪ D76 Gɪ o Pɪ R77   32
þe *om.* D D76 Gɪ Lɪ o Pɪ R77 • moen   33 it to take awey] þis to reeve al Lɪ D D76 Gɪ o Pɪ R77   34 a
rewme] al a rewme Lɪ D76 Gɪ Pɪ • wilen] mowen Lɪ D D76 Gɪ o Pɪ R77   34–5 for þei … vnresonable]
and oþere men be þis mete take mesurably Lɪ D Gɪ Pɪ R77, and … vnmesurably D76 o   35 and *om.* D
D76 Gɪ Lɪ o Pɪ R77 • may sum simple lettride prest o   36 a symple lewid Lɪ D D76 Gɪ o Pɪ R77 • in]
erre aȝeyns þe gospel writyn in Lɪ D D76 Gɪ o Pɪ R77 • for *om.* D D76 Gɪ Lɪ o Pɪ R77   37 despue •
seyinge *om.* D D76 Gɪ Lɪ o Pɪ R77 • it *om.*   37–8 to menis soulis] for mannes soule Lɪ D76 Gɪ Pɪ, to
mannes soule D o R77   38 owen] owen stedfastly Lɪ D D76 Gɪ o Pɪ R77 • truly *om.* D D76 Gɪ Lɪ o Pɪ
R77 • is verrely soþ Lɪ D76 Gɪ Pɪ, is verri sooþ D o R77   39 for þere is … heuene] for wiþoute kunnyng
and kepyng þerof no man may be delyuered fro peynes of helle Lɪ D D76 Gɪ o Pɪ R77   40 and studee
and axe] and bisy traueil of studie and in axyng Lɪ Gɪ Pɪ, and bisi traueile and in axinge D o R77   40–1
clerkis … þerof] clerkis boþe of [in D R77] lyuyng and [in D R77] kunnyng þe verrei exposicioun þerof
Lɪ D D76 Gɪ o Pɪ R77   41 þat *om.* Lɪ D D76 Gɪ o Pɪ R77 • derke] derk for as seynt austyn seiþ þe
same truþe is seid openly in holy writ which truþe is sette in derk figuris profesies and parablis Lɪ D D76
Gɪ o Pɪ R77 • were it] is þis Lɪ D D76 Gɪ o Pɪ R77   42 noon] neuere Lɪ D D76 Gɪ o Pɪ R77 • scole]
lettrure Lɪ D D76 Gɪ o Pɪ R77

schulde be a clerk bi þis proce[sse]? Euery cristen man or woman haþ taken staate,
autorite and bonde of God in his cristondom to be a disciple of holy write, to lerne it
45 and teche it and lyue þerafter al his lif, vpon peyne of dampnacioun or wynnynge þe
blisse of heuene. What ante[cri]st dar for schame of cristen men lette lewide men to
lerne her lesson so hard comaundid of God?

   But wordely clirkis crien and seyn holy writt in Englische wolde make men
at debate, and sougitis to be rebel aȝens | f. 24v | here souereyns, and herfore it schal
50 not be sufferd amonge lewid men. Alas, hou mowe þei more opynly sclaundre God,
auctor of pees, and his holy lawe, þat euere techiþ meken[e]sse, pacience and
charite? And herfor þei moten seie þat þe comountee of cristyn peple is so rebelle in
here synnes as deueles ben, or ellis þei moten sey þat worldly clerkis ben in dispeir
for her synnes. For þus þe false Iiwes, scribis and ph[a]risees criden on Criste þat he
55 madde descencioun in þe pepel. Iesu, þat didest to conferme þi lawe and for raunson
of cristyn soulis, stoppe soone þe blasfemys of antecrist, ȝif it be þi welle, and make
þin holy gospel knowen amonge þi sympel breþeren, and ȝeue vus | f. 25r | grace to
make a good eende. Amen.

Glosses and biblical references   47 'hard': insistently   49 'debate': strife   • 'sougitis':
subjects   52 'rebelle': rebellious   55 'descencioun': dissension

Variants   43 proceses   • or woman *om* D D76 G1 L1 o P1 R77   • haþ taken] takiþ L1 D D76 G1 o P1
R77   44 God in] god ȝhe in D R77   44–5 write … vpon] writ and a real techere þerof in al his lyf vp L1
D76 G1 o P1, writt and a rial techer þerof vp D R77   45 or] and vp L1 D D76 G1 o P1 R77   46 antecrist]
antest   • \for/   47 lesson] holy lessoun L1 D D76 G1 o P1 R77   • God] god eche man is bounden to do so
þat he be saued but eche man þat schal be saued is a real prest maad of god as holy writ and holy doctours
witnessyn pleynly þanne eche lewed man þat schal be saued is a real prest [maad L1 D G1 o P1 R77] of god
and eche man is bounden to be suche a [*om.* D o R77] verri prest L1 D D76 G1 o P1 R77   48 and seyn *om.*
G1 L1 P1 R77   • Englische] englisch tunge D R77   • wolde] wole L1 D D76 G1 o P1 R77   • men] cristen
men L1 D D76 o P1 R77   49 herfore] þerfor L1 D D76 G1 o P1 R77   50 more opynly *om.* D R77   51 þat
euere techiþ] fully techyng L1 D D76 G1 o P1 R77   • mekensse   52 charite] the rest is erased in o   • and
herfor] or ellis L1 D D76 G1 P1 R77   52–3 þe comountee … sey þat *om.* D R77   52 so rebelle] obstinat
L1 D76 G1 P1   53 deueles] fendis L1 D D76 G1 P1   • clerkis] prestis representyng þe state of cristis vikeris
L1 D D76 G1 P1 R77   54 synnes] symony and oþere robberis of cristen men boþe in temporal goodis and
spiritual L1 D D76 G1 P1 R77   • For *om.* D D76 G1 L1 P1 R77   • Iiwes] iewis namely hyȝe prestis L1
D D76 G1 P1 R77   • phrisees   56 soone *om.* D D76 G1 L1 P1 R77   • þe] þese D D76 G1 L1 P1 R77   •
antecrist] antecrist and worldly clerkis L1 D D76 G1 P1 R77   • ȝif it be þi welle *om.* D D76 G1 L1 P1
R77   57 knowen amonge] knowen and kept of L1 D76 G1 P1, knowen and kept in D R77   57–8 and ȝeue
… Amen] and encrese hem in feiþ hope and charite and meknesse and pacience to suffre deþ ioyfully for
þee and þy lawe amen iesu for þy mercy L1 D D76 G1 P1 R77

Cambridge Tract III

fol. 25r | Many croniculis ben fals but al þe gospel is trwe

[O]ure Lorde Iesu Crist, lord of trouþe, of wysdom and of charite, made þe gospel, prechid it, and to conferme it bad his disciplis to preche þe gospel to al manere of men. Also cristen men moten sue Crist in manere of lyue[yn]ge, as Iesu seiþ in Ion gospel, 'he þat seru[i]þ to me, sue he me'. But cristen men knowen not Cristis lijf

5   but be [þe] gospel; þanne owiþ þe gospel to be preched þat men mowe knowe Cr[i]stis [wordis] and sue hem þerafter. Also charite nediþ men to knowe þe gospel, for if þou haue a gret frend in a fer contree and he sende þe a letter wel seelid, in wiche þou my3te knowe his wille, þou woldist se þis letter and knowe þe sentens. Oure Lord Iesu is moste frend þat we mown haue, seþen for oure loue he suffrid gret

10   peyne and deeþ. He | f. 25v | is in heuene and his manhede glorified, and 3it w[e] mo[w]n not see hym bod[i]ly. He sendiþ his gospel to us, in which his wylle is schewid to us, not for his profi3t but for oure auauntage. It is not seelid wiþ wax and dede led as oþere lettris ben, but wiþ þe precious blood of Cristis bodi and hert, for þat we schulde holde it more parfittly in oure soulis and rule oure lyf þerafter. Þen it

15   semet wel þat we schulde lok and kepe þe gospel.

   Also þe gospel is most trwe, most esy and most siker to rule oure lijf by, for Iesu Crist, God and man, spake it, þerfor no falsnes ne defaute may be þerinne, and whoeuere beleu[e]þ þe gospel wiþ lastinge charite and is cristyned schal be saaf, as Crist in þe gospel of Ma[r]ke techiþ. But oþere cronyculis comuly ben mengid wiþ

20   lesyngis, and whedir þei ben soþe or false we witen not, and þou3 we knowe hem not we schul not be dampned. And | f. 26r | oure Iesu seiþ þat his 3ok is softe and his charge is li3t or esy. Also þe gospel is medicen to bringe men out of al sekenes of soule, and to kepe hem holy þat þei falle no more in [su]che siknesse, and it is comuly in eche parische ch[ir]che, redi to iche man wiþout gret coste.

25   Also no seyntis lijf is so p[ar]fi3t and so siker to go spedely to heuene as is [C]ristis lijf tau3t in þe gospel. Þen, si[þ]en men ben so glad to here and to knowe hou holy seyntis haue lyued, to haue ensanple þerbi, moche more schulden cristyne men here and knowe Cristis lyf in þe gospel, se[þe]n alle þis s[e]yntis erreden many tymes in her lijf, and also men erreden in writeynge of her lif. But Iesu Crist my3te

30   not erre in lif, neiþer in þou3t ne word ne dede, ne his appostlis and euangelistis in writynge of þe gospel.

Glosses and biblical references   2–3 Mark 16:15   3–4 John 12:26   15 'lok': pay careful attention to • 'kepe': live in accordance with   18–19 Mark 16:16; 'saaf': saved   19–20 'mengid wiþ lesyngis': mingled with lies   21–2 Matt. 11:30; 'charge': burden

Variants   1[]ure   2 it and bad   3 cristi • lyuenyge   4 he / he þat • seruþ   5 þe¹ *om.*   6 crstis • wordis [or *sim.*] *om.*   10–11 we mown] wmon   11 boodly   13 \but/   16 sikrer   18 beeleuþ   19 make   23 suche] che   24 chriche   25 parfi3t] profi3t • g^{x}o^{x}o   26 ristis • sien   28 seþen] seyn • syntis   30 þou3t/ 3t • ne in his

Also þe gospel passiþ in dignete, wis| f. 26v |dom and truþe al þe techynge of
þe phil[o]sofris and clerkis, as myche as God passiþ synful criaturis, and þat
passynge is wiþouten no[m]ber, for ȝif Crist tauȝte not beste lawe for menns soulis,
35   or hym wanted good welle or wijt or pouere [...] ben eendeles myche. Þanne, siþen
Cristis gospel is of more autorite, more witte and more truþe þan any philosofres
bokis bi a þousand-foold, men owen to preche þe gospel and not philosofres bookis,
but ȝif þei acorden to þe gospel, for synne is more dispisid and vertuis betere preisid
in þe gospel þanne in any philoso[f]ris techynge.

Glosses and biblical references   **32** 'passiþ': surpasses   **35** 'hym wanted': were lacking to
him   **38** 'acorden to': agree with

Variants   **33** philsofris   **34** nober   **35** or hym] our hym   **39** philosoris

Cambridge Tract IV

f. 26v | And anoþer sentens come[n]dynge þe gospel in our moder-tunge

[C]risten men vnderstonden þat þe foure gospelleris ben as foure we[e]lis in þe
foure-horsid carte of þe Lord, þat beriþ him aboute bi prechynge of þe gospel, and
þei may be vnderstonde also þe fo| f. 27r |ure wallis of Cristis blissed g[ar]dyn,
whiche is writen in þe Book of Songis 'my derlinge come doun into his gardyn to ete
5   þe fruyt of his applis', and clepide his spouse to him, which gardyn may vnderstonde
þe letter of loue of Cristis gospel, and þe derlinge of Goddis sone, and þe spouse of
holy chirche, whiche gardyn is ful of heuenly frutis, of pumg[ra]natis and punyk and
hony and mylke and mirre [and] lilies, and alle þinge þat þe Fader of heuene haþ not
plauntid in þis gardyn schal be drawen vp bi þe rote and cast into þe fire. Þerfore,
10 crist[e]n men be ware þat þei enter not in to þe gloriose gardyn of C[ri]stis gospel as
[w]ylde swen deuourynge þis gentel fruyt in her moþe and wiþ hir fete wiþ curius
spekynge and lusty lyuynge, for if proud men, vnpur[u]eied of penaunce and pitee,
as wilde swyn enteren in to his grene gardyn ful of | f. 27v | u[e]rtu þei schullen be
huntid out wiþ hundis of helle, but ȝif þei be made tame wiþ fruytful penance and
15 pete in herte.
        Þerfore Crist, entrenge in þis world to make þis holy gardyn, ȝaf to vs
ensanpule of paciance in his owne persone for perel of þiese houndis, and þerfore
sue we hym and his holy clerkis, and enter we in to þe gardyn wepynge wiþ Marie
Maudeleyn. Appere to vs in fu[l] coumfortable ma[ner]e, and ȝeue us drynke of a
20 welle encelid or closid fro coueitouse men, a pitte of wellynge water of lijf, þat is
writyn in þe Boke of Songis. And þanne we schullen ȝeue to him of a rostid fische
and a parte of an hony-combe, as werkis of liȝt rostid in fire of loue, and wordis of
lif spoken wiþ deuocion vnder dred of hise domes, whiche ben swettere þan honyn-
combe, as þe salme seiþ. And þan schal Crist blowe on us þe holy gost of counforte
25 and of strengþe, and lede us aboute in his gardyn | f. 28r | amonge his precius frutus,
so þat helle houndis honte us not, for many ben honted out of Cristis gardyn, þat is,
þe gospel, for þei entren not be þese foure ȝatus wiþ Crist, þat is pouer[t]e and
penaunce, pacience and pre[i]ere, in mornynge of soule for synne, for bi þese foure
ȝatis entren Cristis derlyngis to here spouse, to pleye wiþ him in his gloriouse
30 gardyn.
        And foure manere werkis ben in þis gardyn, for men þat wollen entre to it. Þe

---

Glosses and biblical references   4 'whiche': as it   • 'book of Songis': Song of Songs   4–5 Song
of Songs 6:1   5 'vnderstonde': be interpreted as   6 'derlinge of': darling as   • 'spouse of': spouse
as   7 'punyk': pomegranate   11 'curius': fastidious   18–19 See John 20:11   19 'Appere': may he
appear   19–21 See Song of Songs 4:12, 15   20 'þat is': as it is   22–4 Ps. 18:10–11

Variants   **Heading** comedynge   1 [ ]risten   • wellis   2 of / of   3 gradyn   7 pumgarnatis   8 and³
om.   10 cristn   • cirstis   11 mylde   12 vnpurieied   13 urtu   15 pete ˣofˣ in   19 ful] fu   • manere] marie
(note)   27 pouerer   28 preere

firste werke is to lerne þe letter bisili; þe secunde to vnderstonde it wis[e]li; þe
þridde to werke þerafter feruentli; þe fourþe to laste into þe ende continuele. And
foure enemys þer ben whiche letten men þat ben cowardis to entere bi þese foure
35 ȝatis and to werke þese foure werkis, þat is, þe world, and wicked men dwellynge
þerin, and þe freel flesche, and þe false fende. But and we entren wysely, as it is seid
before, and werken | f. 28v | strongly, we schullen þanne trede þese iiij. enemyes
vnder oure fete and werke in þis gardyn wit ioye, puttynge aweye al drede and
dispere, and ete þe fruyt þat nowe growiþ in þis gardyn, whiche frwyt is angelis
40 mete hid fro þe world, þat is mynystred of þe Holy [Gost] to þe louers and sueris of
Iesu, þat walken wiþ him in þis gardyn in þe paþis of penaunce and restyn in þe
erber of scilence. And þan schal [þe fende] not honte us out, al ȝif he to-drawe oure
bodi wiþ his fleische hookis.

Glosses and biblical references   **32** 'letter': words of the gospel   **36** 'and'³: if   **39–40** 'angelis
mete': the bread of the eucharist   **40** 'sueris': followers   **42** 'al ȝif he to-drawe': although he may
pull apart

Variants   **32** wisili   **40** gost *om.*   **42** þe fende (or *sim.*) *om.*

Cambridge Tract V

f. 29v | Anoþer sentens schewynge þat þe peple may haue holy writ in her moder-tunge lefully

'[T]he ȝe[e]le, or feruour of loue, of þin hous haþ eten me.' Bi feruent loue of þe fadris hous þe Sauioure cast out of þe temple vnpitous men. Dereworþest breþeren, loue we feruently þe hous of God, and be we besy as moche as we moun þat no schrewid þinge be don | f. 29r | þerinne. Ȝif we schulden see a broþer þat parteyneþ
5   to Goddis hous bolned be pride, or wont to detraccions, or serueynge to drunken[e]s, or made feble to lechere, or trobilid by wraþfulnesse, or borun doun vnder ony oþer vice, stod[i]e we, as moche as pouere sufficiþ, to chaste defoulid þingis and to amende weyward þingis, and, ȝif we mowe, [we] owen to suffer it not wiþoute scharpist sorowe of soule, and moste in þelke house of preier where þe Lordis bodi
10 is sacrid, where presence of aungelis is euere wiþout doute. Do we wiþ alle oure myȝtis, lest ony vnc[o]uenable þing be don, lest eny þinge be which lette oure preiere or briþeren preiere. Bede, in xlv. omelye. Þe Lord cast out of þe temple þese men for þe feruent loue of Goddis hous. Breþeren, eche cristen man in menbris of Crist be et[u]n bi feruent loue of Goddis house.
15   He is etun bi feruent loue of Goddis | f. 29v | hous whiche is bise þat alle we[i]warde þingis whiche he seeþe þere be redressed, and coueitiþ þat þei be amendid. Ȝif he may amende he restiþ not. Þe feruent loue of Goddis house ete eche cristyn man, in wh[i]che hous he is a member; truly þin house, cristen man, is not more þan Goddis hous, where þou hast euerelastynge helþe. Þou entriste in to þin
20 house for temperal reste; þou entr[i]st in to Goddis house for euerlastynge reste. Truly, if þou besiest þe þat no weiward þinge be in þyn hous, w[her]e þou owist to suffer, ȝif þou schalt se ony weiwar[d] þinge in Goddis hous, where helþe and rest wiþoute ende is sett forþ, in ensaunple, þou seist a broþer renne to ve[yn] spectacle, forbed him, moneste, make sorowful, ȝif þe [f]eru[e]nt loue of Goddis hous haþ etun
25 þee. Þou seist oþer men rennen and wilne to be drun| f. 30r |ken, and to wilne þis in holy place which is not semely in ony place. Forbede him þat þou maist, holde him þat þou mayst, ferre him þat þou mayst, speke faer to him þat þou maist; neþeles, nel þou seesse. Ȝif he is a frend, be he monestid liȝtly; ȝif it is þi wijf, be sche refreyned

Glosses and biblical references   1 John 2:17, quoting Ps. 68:10; 'ȝele': zeal   5 'wont to detraccions': accustomed to slanders • 'serueynge to': a slave to   10 'sacrid': consecrated   11 'vncouenable': unseemly • 'eny þinge be which lette': there be anything which may prevent   17 'not' [until he has amended it]   24 'moneste': admonish [him]   27 'ferre': make afraid • 'þat þou mayst': as much as you can   27–8 'nel þou seesse': do not cease

Variants   1 [ ]he • sȝle ('ȝ' *sup. ras.*)   5 detrauccions • drunkens   7 stodie] stonde   8 we² *om.*   11 vncuenable   14 etn   16 wenwarde   18 whche   20 entrst   21 þyn *sup. ras.* • where] werre   22 weiwar   23 veny   24 seruant   25 rennen to be and   28 secesse

most feersly; ȝif it is þin hand-maid, be sche ceessid or made stille. Also be betynge
30 do whateuere þou mayst; for þe persone which þou be[t]ist þou performest þat Crist
seiþ, 'feruent loue of þin hous haþ etun me'. But ȝif þou schalt be coold and
wellowed, lokynge to þe aloone and as [if] sufficient to þisilf, and seiynge in þin
herte 'what is it me to curre oþer menns synnes? My soule sufficiþ to me; I schal
kepe it hool to God', see where þilke seruant whiche hidde þe talent in erþe and
35 wolde not ȝyue comiþ to þe | f. 30v | into mynde, for where he was accusid for he
loste, and not for he kepte wiþout wynnynge. Þerfore, breþeren, here ȝe, so þat ȝe
reste not. I am to-ȝeuynge counsel to ȝou. Ȝyue he þat þat is wiþinne, þat is, Crist in
þe soule, for þouȝ he schal ȝeue bi me, he ȝeueþ. Ȝe witen what ȝe schullen do, ech
man in hous wiþ frende, wiþ tenaunt and wiþ his seruaunt, wiþ more and lasse, as
40 God ȝeuiþ entree, as God openyþ ȝate to his word, nel ȝe ceesse for to wynne to
Crist, for ȝe ben wonen of Crist. Austyn here.

An aungel in Grek and Latyn is a messegere in Englische, þerfore he þat is
sent to schewe þe hiȝe Iuge is riȝtly clepid an aungel, þat he kepe þe dignite and
name whiche he filliþ in worchynge. Truly þe name is hiȝe, but þe lif is not louer
45 þan þe name. Dereworþist breþeren, wolde God þat | f. 31r | we seie not to oure
dampnacioun, for alle prestis ben clepid aungelis, witnesseynge þe prophete þat seiþ
'þe lippis of þe prest kepen kunnynge, and of his mouþ men schulden seke þe lawe,
for he is angel of þe lord of oostis'. But ȝe moun, ȝif ȝe wolyn, disserue also þe
hiȝnesse of þis name, for whiche of vs, in as myche as he sufficiþ, as myche as he
50 haþ take þe gras of heuenly inspirynge, ȝif he aȝenclepiþ his neȝtbor fro
sch[re]widnesse, ȝif he chargiþ to moneste to lyue wel, ȝif he telliþ euerlastynge
rewme or turment to him þat erriþ, whanne he ȝeuiþ wordis of holy monestynge or
tellynge, truly he is aungel. And þerfore no man saie 'I suffice not to teche; I am not
able to monest'. As myche as þou maist ȝeue þou, lest þou be constrained to paie in
55 turmentis þat | f. 31v | þinge yuele kept which þou hast taken, for þe ilke seruant
tooke no but o talent, þat is, vnderstondeynge, whiche studide more to hide it þan to
ȝiue.

By comandement of þe Lord, grete cuppis and litil weren in þe tabernacle.
Be gret cuppis is signified plente[uous] doctryne, and bi litil cuppes is signified litil
60 and streyte kunnynge. Sum man ful of doctrynge of truþe filliþ þe hereris soulis.
Truli, bi þis þat he seiþ he dressiþ a gret cuppe. Anoþer man may not declare clerly
þat truþe þat he feeliþ, but for he telliþ in ony manere þis same truþe, as he may, he
ȝeueþ a taste be a litil cuppe. And þerfore ȝe þat ben sette in holy cherche, þouȝ ȝe
moun not mynyster gret cuppis be wysdom of doctringe, neþ[e]les as myche as [ȝ]e
65 suffisyn for Goddis largenes ȝiue ȝe to ȝoure neiȝboris litil cuppis of [gode] word.

Glosses and biblical references   32 'wellowed': withered   34 'where': whether   34–6 See Matt.
25:24–8   35 'ȝyue': surrender [it]   • 'where': surely   36 'wynnynge': gaining interest   46–8 Mal.
2:7   50 'aȝenclepiþ': recalls   60 'doctrynge': teaching

Variants   30 betist] berist   32 if] a   44 worch×ich×ynge   51 scherwidnesse   56 hidie   59
plenteuotus   63 cheriche (?)   64 neþles   • ȝe] þe   65 goddis (note)

As myche as ȝe beþenkyn þat | f. 32r | ȝe han profitid, enforse ȝe also for to
drawe oþere men wiþ ȝou; desire ȝe to haue felowis wiþ ȝou in þe wey of God.
Breþeren, ȝif ony of ȝou goiþ to chepynge or in hap baþinge, he clepiþ him whom
he seeþ idil for to come wiþ him. Þerfore, þilke ȝoure worldly doynge ar[ous]e or
70 excite ȝou, and ȝif ȝe gone to God be ȝe besy þat ȝe aloone come not to him, for
he[r]fore it is writun 'he þat heriþ, seie: come', þat he which haþ take now in his
herte þe vois of heuenely loue ȝiue also wiþouteforþ þe vois of monestynge or
techynge to neiȝtboris. And in hap he haþ not breed for to dresse almesse to þe nedi,
but it is more which he þat haþ a tunge may ȝyue, for it is more to fede be Goddis
75 word þe soule þat schal lyue wiþoute eende þan to fille by erþely breed þe wombe
| f. 32v | of fleische þat schal die. And þerfore, briþerin, nel ȝe wiþdrawe f[ro] ȝoure
neiȝbowris þe almesse of Goddis word. I moneste ȝou wiþ me, spare we f[ro] ydel
word, flee we to speke vnproftable þinges. As mych as we moun, refrene we þe
tunge; lat no wordis flowe not in veyn, seþen þe Iuge seiþ 'eche idel word þat men
80 han spoken þei schulen ȝelde reson þerof in þe day of dome'. Truly þat word is ydul
which wantiþ þe profiȝt of riȝtfulnes eiþer reson of iust nede. Þerfore, turne ȝe ydil
speches to studie of edificacioun, þat is, to reise soulis to heuene. Biholde ȝe hou
most swiftly þe tymes of þis lijf fleen; perseyue ȝe hou streyt þe domysman schal
come. Sette ȝe him bifore yȝen of ȝoure herte; shewe ȝe him to þe soulis of ȝoure
85 neiȝboris, þat ȝif ȝe ben not necligent to telle | f. 33r | hym as myche as ȝoure myȝtis
suffisen, of him ȝe moun be clepid aungelus. Gregorie, vj. omelie.

Ion euangelist seiþ 'he þat schal se his b[ro]þer haue nede and schal close his
entrailis, þat is, merci, fro hym, how dwelliþ þe charite of God in him?' And Iesu
Crist seiþ, [in] Matheu, xxv. cᵒ, men þat ȝeuen not mete and drynke and cloth and
90 herborow to nedy men schullen be dampned. And seynt Jon Crisostom, alleggynge
Peter and Ion euangelist in þe Pocalip[s]is and þe olde testament, seiþ, fourtiþe
omelie on Matheu, þat ech holy man is a prest.

Doumbe elementis prechidin Crist borun of a virgyn; alle ellementis
witnessiden þat here makere cam. Heuenes knewen Crist to be God, for anoon þei
95 senten a ster; þe see knew, for it ȝaf it silf able to be troden vnder his feet; erþe
knew, for whanne he diede it | f. 33v | tremblede; þe sunne knew, for it hidde þe
beemes of his liȝt; stonys and wallis knew, for in tyme of his deeþ þei weren cleft;
helle knew, for it ȝelde hem whiche it helde deed. And, neþeles, ȝit þe hertis of
vnfeiþful Iewis knewen not hym to be God whom alle vnsenseble elementis feeliden
100 God, and þei, harder þan stonys, nylen be cleft to penaunce, and þei denyue to

Glosses and biblical references   68 'chepynge': market   71 Apoc. 22:17   77 'spare we': let us
refrain   79 'Iuge': Christ   79–80 Matt. 12:36   83 'streyt': unswervingly   87–8 1 John 3:17
88–90 Matt. 25:41–6   90 'herborow': lodging   95 'þe see knew', see Matt. 14:25   95–6 'erþe
knew', see Matt. 27:51   96 'þe sunne knew', see Matt. 27:45   97 'stonys and wallis knew', see
Matt. 27:51–2

Variants   69 arouse] aresone   71 hefore   76 of] by of • for   77 for   78 we³] we þe we   87
borþer   89 in] to • xxv*j*   91 pocalipis   94 markerer   96 dieede

knowleche him whom elementis, eiþer bi tokenes eþer be cleeuyngis, crien God. Grigorie, x. omelie.

Briþeren, whanne ȝe he[e]ren þe Lord seiynge 'where I am, þere also my mynyster schal be', nyle ȝe þenke only good bischopis and clerkis; also ȝe, for ȝoure
105   maner serui[n] to Crist in lyuynge wel and doynge almes deedes, in prechynge his name and doctrine, to whiche men ȝe schullyn mowe, þat eche | f. 34r | man, ȝhe housbounde man, knowe bi þis name þat he owiþ fadris loue to his meynee. Moneste he and teche alle hise for Crist and for euerlastynge lijf; excite he, vnderneme he, ȝyue he good welle, haunte he disciplyne or chastisynge, so in his hous he, seruynge
110   Crist, schal fille þe office of holy chirche, and in sum maner a bischopis office, þat he be wiþ Crist wiþouten ende. For many of ȝoure noumber mynystirden to Crist, ȝe, þe ilke grettis[t] mynystracion or seruice of passion, many not bischopis neþer clerkis, ȝonge men and virgines, elder and ȝounger, many weddid men and widdid wymmen, many housboundmen and ho[u]sewyues mynystrynge to Crist han put ȝhe
115   here lyues in his marturdom. And þe Fader onour[i]nge hem þei han resseyued most glorious crownes. A| f. 34v |ustyn on Ion, in li. omelie.

Whanne þou schalt here 'Crist', vnderstonde þou God and man. Ofte I seie þese same þingis, and I [schal not ceese to seie 'for it is not s]louȝ to me for to seie truly it is sikur to ȝou', for I wol ȝou alle to be made techeris. Crisostom spekynge
120   general[ly] to lewid men in a sermoun of þe cros, þat begynneþ 'What schal I seie?'

Summe false breþeren prechiden þe word of God for enuye, and neþeles Poul seiþ of hem 'and in þis I [i]oye, but also I schal haue ioye', for þei tellden or prechiden Crist by enuye, but neþeles Crist. Se þou not be what seruaunte Crist is prechid to þe; dr[i]nke þou Crist, eschewe enuye; nyle þou sue a[n yue]l prechour
125   but sue þou good Crist whiche is prechid to þee. Austyn on Ion, in v. omelie.

Breþeren, only so be ȝe symple þat ȝe be feruent, | f. 35r | þat is, brennynge in loue. Nele ȝe be stille, ȝe spekynge wiþ brennynge tungis; kyndle colde men. My breþeren, ȝee seen for alle þingis crien aȝenes eritikis, alle þe bokis of God, al proficee, alle þe gospel, alle lettris of postlis, alle mornynge of þe culuer, þat is, holy
130   chi[r]che, and ȝit þei waken not, ȝit þei ben not reisid fro slepe. But ȝif we ben þe culuer, þat is, holy chirch, welle we, suffre we and preie we þe mercy of God schal come, þat þe fire of þe Holy Gost [be] fully borne in ȝoure symplenesse. And þei schullen come. It is not [to] dispeire: preie ȝe, preche ȝee, loue ȝe forsoþe God [al]myȝti. Now þei haue bigunne to knowe her forhed, many han knowe, many
135   weren aschamed. Crist schal com þat also oþere knowe. Austyn on Ion, in vj. omelie, speke| f. 35v |ynge þus generaly to lewide men aȝens eritikis.

Dereworþest breþeren, reule ȝe ȝour sonys, reule ȝoure meynees. As it

Glosses and biblical references   103–4 John 12:26   106 'whiche': whichever   108 'vnderneme': rebuke   112 'passion': suffering   118–19 Phil. 3:1 (note)   121–3 Phil. 1:15–18   129 'culuer': dove

Variants   103 herren   104 clerkis followed by 2-letter erasure   105 seruis   107 owiþ] howiþ   110 officice   112 grettis   114 hosewyues   115 onournge   118 and I ... flouȝ (note)   120 general   120–1 seie put on ȝou Summe (note)   122 I oye   124 drnke   • an yuel] a uenyl   127 loue *sup. ras.*   130 chiche   • waken] walken   132 be *om.*   133 to *om.*   134 almyȝti] is myȝti   135 aschamend

parteyneþ to vs to speke to ȝou in þe cherche, so it parteyneþ to ȝou for to do in
ȝoure housis, þa[t] ȝe ȝelde good resone of þese men þat ben sugettis to ȝou. God
140 loueþ discipline or lore and chast[i]synge; weiward and false innocence is t[o] slake
bridels to synnes, þa[t] is, to ȝiue licence or sufferaunce to synnes. Ful perelosly þe
sone feeliþ þe liȝtnesse of his fader, þat afturward he feele þe fersnesse of God. Þe
synne whiche in þe sone displesiþ not þee, deliteþ þee, but age haþ forsake þee, not
coueitise. Austyn on þe Sauter, in þe l. salm, in þe eende. Þe woman of Samarie
145 l[e]fte here water-pott and prechid þe gospel and þe comynge | f. 36r | of þe Lord.
Austyn in þe book *Of Fourscore Questions and Þre*, in lxiiij. question, in þe eende.
Alle þingis eþer whanne þei offenden eþer ben offendid, eþer whanne þei deliten
eiþer ben delitid, shewyn and prechyn þe vnyte of þe creatoure, þat is, God, þat
makiþ of noȝt. Austyn, in þe secund book *Of Frewille*, xiiij. ca°, in þe ee[n]de. Þis is
150 þe lawe of God[es] puruiaunce, þat no man be holpun of hiȝer þingis for to knowe
and perseyue þe grace of God whiche schal not help lower men to þe same grace for
clene loue. Austyn in þe book *Of Very Religioun*, v. c°, in þe eende.
   God seiþ generally to eche fadre 'þou schalt telle to þi sone in þe day,
seiynge, þis þinge is whiche þe Lord haþ don to me whanne I ȝede | f. 36v | out of
155 Egipt, and it schal be as a tokene in þin honde and as a memorial bifore þin iȝen, þat
þe lawe of þe Lord be euere in þi mowþe'. Þis God seid in Ex[o]dus, xiij. c°. God in
Deutronymye, vj. ca°, 'here þou, Israel, þe Lord ȝoure God is o God. Þou schalt loue
þe Lord þi God of al þi hert and of al þin soule and of al þi strengþe. And þese
wordis whiche I comande to þe today schullen be in þin hert, and þou schalt telle
160 hem to þi sones, and þou schalt þenke on hem sittynge in þin hous and goynge in þe
weie, slepynge and risynge'. Þe Wese Man seiþ, in iij. ca° of Ecclesiasticus, 'þenke
þou euere þo þingis which God comandid to þee'. Eft, in vj. ca°, 'haue þou mynde in
Goddis hestis, and be þou moost besy in þ[e] comaundementis of hym'. | f. 37r | Eft,
in ix. ca°, 'iust men be mete felowis to þe, and gloriynge be to þe [in] þe drede of
165 God, and þe þenkeinge of God be to þe in þ[i] witt, and alle þi tellynge be in þe
heestis of þe Hieste'.
   A man owiþ for to loue his neiȝtbore as hymself, þat he lede for to worschipe
God what man he may, eþer be comfort of go[o]d doynge eiþer be enformynge of
doctringe, eiþer be constre[yn]ynge of disciplyn or chastisynge. Austyn *to*
170 *Macedonye*, xxxiij. pistil, bifore þe ende. Worschipful seruantes of God and
preiseful in Crist, I approue and preise myche þi mornynge of siche eretikis, and þi
wakynge and prudence aȝenes siche eritikis, and I excite and moneste þat þou goo
lastyngly or contynuely in þis weye, and þat þou, symple as a culuuer, | f. 37v | haue
mercy on hem, but yn þat wise as a serpent eschewe h[e]m, and ȝiue þou besynesse

Glosses and biblical references   153–6 Exod. 13:8–9   156–61 Deut. 6:4–7   161–2 Ecclus
3:22   162–3 Ecclus 6:37   163–6 Ecclus 9:22–3   168 'what': whatever   172 'wakynge': vigilance

Variants   139 þat] þa   140 chastsynge • to] t   141 þa   145 lfte   146 and þe þre   149 eede   150
Godes] good (note)   155 iȝen and þat   156 exadius   163 þe] þi   164 in² om.   165 þi¹] þe   166 h\i/este
168 godd   169 constreynge   171 haue approue • and þi] and þei   174 wise] wisse • hem²] hym wise

175 as myche as þou maist þat þei þat cleuen to þe dwelle wiþ þee in riȝt feiþ, eiþer, if
ony ben depraued or peruertid in ony þinge, þat þei be amendid to riȝt feiþ. Austyn
to Maxima, greet lady, lxvij. pistil, aftir þe myddis.

Also kynge Iosie, alle grettur men of Iuda and of Ierusalem clepid togedere,
ascendid into þe hous of þe Lord, and alle men of Iuda and dwelleris of Ierusalem
180 togidere, prestis and clerkis and dekenys and þe pepul, fro þe leste til to þe moste, to
whiche herynge, in þe hous of þe Lord þe kynge redde alle wordis of þe book of
Goddis lawe. And he, stondynge in his trone, made couenaunt bifore þe Lord þat he
schulde go after hym | f. 38r | and kepe his witenessynge and heestis and iustifiynge
in alle his herte and in al his soule, and do þo þingis þat ben writen in þat book
185 whiche he redde, and coniuride or made to swere on þis þinge alle men þat weren
founden in Ierusalem. And Beniamyn and dwelleris of Ierusalem diden vp þe
couenaunde of þe Lord God of here faderis. In iiij. book of Kyngis, xxij. and xxiij.
caᵒ, and in ij. book of Paralipomynon, xxxiiij. caᵒ, in þe ende.

Also kynge Nabugodnosor, ȝit heþen, wroot þus to alle puplis and folkis and
190 langagis in alle erþe: 'Hiȝ God haþ don signis and meraculis anentu[s] me; þerfore it
pleside to me for to preche his signys or mirraclis, for þei b[en] grette, and his
mereuilis, for þei ben gret [and] stronge, and his rewme euerlastynge rewme, and
| f. 38v |his pouere is in generacioun and into generacion. Þerfore þis decre or ful dom
is set of me, þat whoeuere schal speke blasfemye aȝenes God, he perische, and his
195 hous be distryed, for non oþer god is which may saue.'.In ij. and iiij. caᵒ of Danyel.
Also kynge Darius, ȝit heþen, wroot to alle puplis, lynagis and langagis dwellynge in
al erþe: 'Pees be multiplied to ȝou. A dom is ordeyned of me þat in alle þe empere
of my rewme men drede god of Daniel, for he is God lyuynge and wiþout
bigynnynge and endynge, and his rewme schal not be distried, and his pouere schal
200 be til into wiþouten ende. For he is deliuerer and sauyoure, doynge signys and
myrraclys in heuene and in erþe, whiche delyuered Daniel f[ro] þe lake of lyouns. In
| f. 39r | vj. cᵒ of Daniel, in þe ende. Also kynge Cyrus, ȝit heþen man, seide 'men
dwellynge in alle erþe, dred god of Daniel, for he is God lyuynge into worldis, and
delyuerere and sauyoure doynge sygnes and merueilis in heuene and in erþe, whiche
205 delyuered Daniel fro þe lake of lyouns'. In þe ende of Daniel.

Þus heþen men of Nynyue prechiden fastynge and penaunce, and þe heþen
kynge and his princes criden þat men and beestis schulden faste, and þat men be
conuertid fro here yuel weie and fro wickidnesse whiche is in hondis of hem, in iij.
cᵒ of Ionas. Þus þe noble kyngis Esechie, Iosofath and Asa clepiden þe peple fro
210 ydolat[r]ie and of oþere synnes, and tauȝten þe lawe of God in here rewme, as þe
bookis of Kyngis and Paralipomynon witnessen.

Glosses and biblical references   178–88 2 Chron. 34:29–32 (cf. 4 Kings 22–3)   178 'Iosie':
Josiah   189–93 Dan. 3:98–9 [4:1–3]   189 'Nabugodnosor': Nebuchadnezzar   190 'anentus':
towards   193–5 Dan. 3:96 [29]   196–202 Dan. 6:25–7   203 'lake': den   202–5 Dan. 14:42
(note)   203 'into worldis': for ever and ever   206–9 Jonah 3:5–8

Variants   181 þee boke   190 anentur   191 bne   192 and¹ *om.*   194 \h/is *sec. m.*   196 lˣaˣ\yn/ngagis
sec. m.   201 for   210 ydolatie

Also Ion | f. 39v | seid to Crist 'comaunder, we haue seyn sum man castynge out fendes in þ[i] name, and we han forboden hym, for he sueþ not þe wiþ us'. And Iesus seiþ to hym 'nyle ʒe forbede, for he þat is not aʒenes ʒou is for ʒou'. In Luyk,
215   ix. cᵒ, and Marke, ix. cᵒ.

Whanne God bad Moises gader seuenty men of þe elders of Israel and seid 'I schal take aweye of þi spiryte and I schal ʒeue to h[e]m', Eldath and Medath dweltyn in þe tentis, on whiche men þe spirite restide. And þei profecieden in þe tentis. And Iosue, seruaunt of Moises and chosun of manye, seiþ 'my lord Moises,
220   forbed þou h[e]m', and he seiþ 'what, hast þou enuye for m[e]? Who schal lette þat al þe peple profesye, and þat þe Lord ʒiue his spirit to h[e]m?' In xj. cᵒ of Numeri.

'ʒif ony man spekiþe, | f. 40r | speke he as þe worde of God; ʒif ony man mynystre, mynystre he as of þe vertu whom God mynystreiþ, þat in alle þingis God be onourid bi Iesu Crist.' Peter, in his f[ir]st pistle, iiij. cᵒ. And in iij. cᵒ Peter
225   biddiþ generaly to cristyn men 'halowe ʒe þe Lord Crist in [ʒ]oure hertis, euere redy to sati[s]faccioun, þat is, to answer redily to eche man axynge ʒou resoun of þat feiþ and hope þat is in ʒou, but wiþ myldenes and drede, hauynge good conscience þat in þat þinge þat þei mysspeken of ʒou as of yuel-doeris þei be confoundid whiche falsly calengen ʒoure good lyuynge in Crist'.

230   Also, bi þe temple may be vnderstonden þe soule of man, for þe word of God enhabitynge þerinne, in which, bifore þe doctrynge of Iesu, erþely and bestly stiry | f. 40v |ngis weryn. An oxe is tokyn of erþely stiryngis, for he is a tilerre of þe felde. Soþely a schepe, þat is more vnresonable þan oþere beestis, is signe of vnwitty stiryngis, but a culuer is signe of liʒt and vnstable soulis. Soþely, þe tokenes of hem
235   þat semen good ben money, whiche Iesu Crist castiþ out bi worde of techynge þat [in] þe hous of his Fader be no chepinge, whos techynge he graunte us to loue and kepe in worde and werke, þat lyueþ and regneþ wiþouten eende, merciful God. Amen.

Glosses and biblical references   212–15 Mark 9:37, 40; Luke 9:49–50   212 'comaunder': master [*magister*]   214 'nyle ʒe forbede': do not forbid them   216–21 Num. 11:26–9   222–4 I Pet. 4:11   223 'vertu whom God mynystreiþ': power which God administers   224–9 I Pet. 3:15–16   229 'calengen': accuse   233 'vnwitty': ignorant, lewd   234 'liʒt': lacking weight   235–6 John 2:16

Variants   213 þi] þe   217 hym   218 in \þe/ *sec. m.*   220 hem] hym   • me] m   221 hym   224 frist   225 ʒoure] oure   226 satifacioun   235 techichynge   236 in *om.*

Cambridge Tract VI

f. 40v | Þis þat sueþ scheweþ þat al þoo be in gret perel þat letten þe testament of
Crist to be knowen and kept of þe peple

[F]irste wite ech man þat charite is þe principal part of holy writ, and ȝif ony part of
holy writ be taken | f. 41r | from us þanne a part of charite is taken from us. For
Poule seiþ 'if we kepen charite we fulfille al þe lawe'. 'God is charite', and ȝif we
schullen not speke of holy writ we moun not speke of God neiþer of charite. Also
5 Poul seiþ 'ȝif ony man knowiþ not holy writ he schal be vnknowen', and ȝif we
moun not speke of holy writ we moun not blesse God neiþer men, neiþer we moun
speke of heuene neiþer of erþe ne of helle, ne of no criature þat euere God made, for
holy writ spekiþ of alle þe werkis of God. And whanne Iesu Crist was here in erþe
he wolde not lette þe deuel to speke of holy writ, as þe gospel telliþ in þe firste
10 Sonday of Lenten, ne noon oþer synneris, but he tauȝt it himsilf to alle men, good
and yuel, for we knowen not good from yuel but bi wisdom of holy writ.
     And þerfor God cursiþ in his lawe alle men | f. 41v | þat bowen awey here
erres from it, and blessiþ alle men þat heren it and kepen it iustly. And so, as erþely
men deeme hem to be acursid þat letten þe testament of a deede man, so alle heuenly
15 men deemen hem to be acursid þat letten þe testament of Iesu Crist, and his
testament is þe holy gospel þat is comaundide to be prechide to alle criaturis. And he
ordeyned foure holy men to writ[e] þis testament, þat is, Matheu, Mark, Luk and
Jon. And he þat letteþ þis testament to be knowen to þe peple holdiþ wiþ þe fende
aȝens Iesu Crist, and is cursid of God.

Glosses and biblical references   1 'wite ech man': each man should know   2–3 Gal. 5:14   3 1
John 4:8, 16   5 1 Cor. 14:38   8–10 Matt. 4:1–11 (note)   9 'lette þe deuel to speke': prevent the
devil from speaking   12–13 Ps. 118:21

Variants   **Heading** Answeris to hem þat seien þat we schulde not speke of holy writt L5 O3   1 [ ]irste •
wite] know O3   3 seynt poul L5 O3 • lawe of god for god O3   6–7 moun] moun not L5 O3   9 deuel]
fend L5   13 iustyly   16 testament is *expl.* O3 • þat is] *sup. ras.* C, þat he L5   17 writ

Cambridge Tract VII

f. 41v | Þis trett[ys] þat folewþ proueþ þat eche nacioun may lefully haue holy writ in her moder-tunge

Siþen þat þe trouþe of God stondiþ not in oo langage more þan in anoþer, but whoso lyueþ best and techiþ best plesiþ moost God, of what lan| f. 41v |gage þat euere it be, þerfore þe lawe of God writen and tauȝt in Englisch may edifie þe commen pepel as it doiþ clerkis in Latyn, siþen it is þe sustynance to soulis þat schulden be saued.
5   And Crist comaundid þe gospel to be prechid for þe pepel schulde lerne it, kunne it, and worche þerafter. Whi may we not þanne writ[e] in Englische þe gospel and al holy scripture to edificacioun of cristen soulis, as þe prechoure schewiþ it truly to þe pepel? For if it schulde not be writen it schulde not be prechid. Þis eresye and blasfemye schulden cristen men putt fro þeire hert, for it is sprongon [vp] bi þe fend,
10 fader of lesyngis. Ion, in þe viij. caº. And so þe kynrede of pharesces is cursed of God, 'for þei louen not Iesu Crist', as seynte Poul seiþ, but letten þe gospel to be lernyd of þe pepel. For if a master of skole knoweþ a sotilte to make his children clerkis and to spe| f. 42v |de hem in here lernynge, he hidynge þis lore from hem þat ben able þerto is cause of here vnkunnynge. So, if writynge of þe gospel in
15 Englische and of good doctringe þerto be a sotiltee and a mene to þe comoun pepel to knowe þe riȝt and redi weye to þe blisse of heuene, who loueþ lasse Crist, who is more cursed of God þan he þat lettiþ þis [o]on knowynge? For he is a Satana[s], contrarius to Crist. But þe kynrede of Caym, of Daton and Abiron wolden þat þe gospel slepe safe, for þei ben clepid cristyne of manye. Þei prechen sumwhat of þe
20 gospel and gloson it as hem likeþ. And þus diden Makamete and Surge[u]s þe monk: þei maden a lawe after þer owne malice, and token sumwhat of þe gospel to a fleshly vnderstondynge, so þat þorow þe lore of hem heþen pepel vnto þis day ben out of | f. 43r | here bileeue. And þus oure antecristis now, suynge þe farisees, tellen not verilich þe truþe of þe gospel, for þei lyuen contrariously þerto. And Crist biddiþ his
25 children deeme after þe wirkis.
    O, siþ a craft of gret sotilte is myche preised of worldely men, myche more schulde þe glorius lawe of God be loued and preisid of Cristis children! For alle þing þat man nediþ, boþe bodily and gostly, is conteyned in þis blissed lawe, and specialy in þe gospel, and herfore Crist in þe houre of his assencioun comaundid to hise
30 disciplis to preche it to alle pepelis. But, [be we] siker, neiþer only in Frensch ne in

Glosses and biblical references   5 Matt. 28:19   9–10 John 8:44   10–11 1 Cor. 16:22   12 'sotilte': device   15 'doctringe': teaching   19 'slepe safe': may sleep safely   20 'gloson it as hem likeþ': gloss it as it pleases them (note)   21–2 'fleshly vnderstondynge': carnal interpretation   22–3 'out of here bileeue': deprived of their faith   24–5 Matt. 7:16, 12:33; Luke 6:43–4   29–30 Matt. 28:19–20

Variants   **Heading** trettþ   1 [ ]iþen   6 writ ˣitˣ   9 vp *om.* (cf. *PNII* 12)   10 lesyngis *sup. ras.*   17 conknowynge • satana   20 surgens   24 bididiþ   26 siþ] seiþ   30 we be

Latyn but in þat langage þat þe pepel vsed to speke, for þus he tauȝt hymself. And
here is a rule to cristyne folke of what langage so euere þei be: it is an hiȝe
sacrifi[c]e to God to knowe holy writ and to do þeraftur, wher it | f. 43v | be tauȝt or
writen to hem, in Latyn or in Englisch, in Frensche or in Duche, or in ony oþer
35 langage after [þat] þe pepel haþ vnderstondynge. And þus clerkis schulden be glad
þat þe pepel knewen Goddis lawe, and þei hemself bisily, bi alle þe good meenys þat
þei myȝte, schulden ocupie hem to make þe pepel knowe þe truþe of Goddis lawe.
For þis was þe cause þat Iesus bicam man and suffrid deed on þe tree, so þat bi
kepynge of his lor þe pepel myȝte rise fro goostli deed and come to þe blisse þat
40 neuere schal haue eende. And ȝif ony clerke contrarieþ þis, and so endiþ, who schal
be dampned but suche a quyk fende?

    And herfore seid Crist to þe fader of suche clerkis 'not only in bodili breed
lyueþ man, but in eche word þat comeþ out of Goddis mouþ', þe whiche word is
sustynaunce of cristyn menis soulis. For riȝt as bred strengþiþ mannys bodi to
45 traueile, so þe word of God makiþ sad mannis soule in þe Holy Gost, and stronge to
worche þerafter. And þis bred is more needful þan is þe firste breed, as þe soule of
man | f. 44r | is worþier þan his body, for whanne þe body schal lye stynkynge in þe
graue þan þe soule þat louede þis brede and lyued þerafter schal be in eendeles
blysse wiþ Iesu here spouse. And þus ȝif, þorouȝ necligence of oure bischopis and
50 prelatis and oþer fals techer[i]s þat ben in þe chirch, þe truþe of Goddis word be not
sowen to þe pepel, praie we Iesu Crist, bischop of oure soules, þat he ordeyn[e]
prechouris to warne us to leue oure synnes, bi prechynge of his lawe, and þat as he
ensperrede þe prophites wiþ wysdom and kunnynge, and tauȝt þe appostlis þe weie
of al truþe, so lyȝtne he oure hertis wiþ vnderstondynge of his lore, and graunte vs
55 gras to lyue þerafter, boþe in word and werk.

    For þoo þat contrarion þe gospel and þe pistil, and wolden lette it to be
prechid, and pursuen þe trewe techeris and lerneris þerof, louen not Crist; wherfore,
but if þei amende hem whilis þei haue tyme, þei schullen dye in here synnes. Wel we
| f. 44v | witen þat scribis and farisees and princis of prestis in Crist[is] tyme weren
60 more contrarius to his techynge þan þe comoun pepel, for þorouȝ entysynge of hem
þe pepel criden 'do him on þe cros!' Þe scribis weren wyse men of þe lawe, and so
þei weren þe cl[e]rgie of þe I[e]wis; þe farisees weren men of religion þat maden to
hem custoumys and kepten hem as for lawe, and þus þei setten more bi þe laweis þat
þei hadden made þan þei diden bi þe lawe þat God ȝaf to hem and þe pepel, þe
65 whiche was sufficiant to bi ruled bi. Þese ypocritis weren eueremore contrarie to
Crist, and þe comoun pepel wrouȝte myche after þer counseil. And so Crist eiȝte
tymes, as þe gospel telliþ, seid 'sorowe' to h[e]m. And onys þei repreueden Crist for

---

Glosses and biblical references   33 'wher': whether   34 'Duche': German   41 'quyk
fende': living devil   42 'þe fader', i.e., Satan   42–3 Matt. 4:4   45 'sad': steadfast   57
'pursuen': persecute   61 Matt. 27:23; 'do him on þe cros': crucify him   62–3 'to hem': for
themselves   66–7 Matt. 23:13–39 (note)   67 'sorowe': woe   67–9 Matt. 15:2–3

Variants   33 sacrifie   35 þat *om.* (cf. *PNII* 58)   40 \n/euere   45 sad in mannis   50 techerrs   51
ordeynt   59 \in Crist tyme/ (cf. *PNII* 302)   62 clrgie   • iwis   67 hem] him

his disciplis wische[de]n not here hondis whanne þei schulden ete, as here custum
was, and Crist axide of hem whi þei braken Goddis heestis for here feyned lawes.
70   Beholde now wel þese condiciouns, and loke wheþer oure clerkis | f. 45r |
don now as yuel, or worse, and namely oure religio[u]s, þat ben fayners of holines,
þe whiche pursuen Crist in hise membris as þe farisees diden his owne person. And
ȝut þese feyners seyne þat God is her fader, and his lawe þei kepen and here owne
reule boþe, and þis is open falsehed, as here werkis shewen. We knowen þat farisees
75   braken þe lawe þat God ȝaf to hem and to þe pepel for here fayned reule þat þei
hemself maden aȝens þe ordeinaunce of God, and þus, ȝif oure ypocritis seyne now
þat þei kepen here owne reule and Goddis lawe boþe, biholde to here werkis and ȝe
schal fynde þe contrarie. For þe I[e]wis seiden to Crist þat God was here fader, but
Crist seid to hem aȝene ȝif God hadde be here fader þei schulden haue loued h[i]m.
80   So now, in þese daies, þei shewen hem faynet loueres and vntrwe children of Crist
| f. 45v | þat pursuen symple pepel for þei wolde[n] lerne, rede and teche þe lawe of
God in here moder-tonge. And þerfore beddiþ Crist to trowe to þe werkis boþe of
men and wymmen, whatsoeuere here toungis blaberyne. Moreouer, þer ben many,
boþe of men and wymmen, þat ben open enemyes to trouþe and fiȝteris aȝens þe
85   Holy Gost, for þei slaundren þe louers of God and of his word, seiynge þat þei haue
eten fleiȝes þat ȝiueþ hem wysdom and vnderstondynge of al Goddis lawe. Þis is a
cursid speche and a gret blasfemye stiȝynge vp bifore þe Trinyte to be greuously
vengid, but ȝif it be hastily amendid.
        Preie we þerfore hertily to þe Fader of wisdom þat he delyuere us from þis
90   yuel, þat is, synne aȝenes þe Holy Goost, and ȝeue us grace to loue his lawe hertily
and to lyue þerafter to oure departynge of body and soule. For Crist seiþ in þe gospel
'he | f. 46r | þat contynueþ to þe eende' in loue of him and his lawe, wiþ goode and
fruytful werkis, schal haue þe blisse he us graunte, þat suffrid skornys, betyngis,
spettyngis and at þe laste most schameful deeþ, for techynge of þe gospel and
95   lyuynge þeraftur, merciful God. Amen.

Glosses and biblical references   68 'wischen': washed   • 'here'[2], the pharisees'   70
'condiciouns': properties   71 'namely': particularly   74 'open': manifest   78–9 John 8:41–
2   79 'seid ... aȝene': replied   82–3 John 14:11–12   83 'blaberyne': blabber   87 'stiȝynge':
ascending   91–2 Matt. 10:22

Variants   71 religions   78 iwis   79 \be/   • hem   81 woldem   83 \men and/   84 \þe/

Cambridge Tract VIII

f. 46r | Anoþer chapiter strengþinge þe sententis þat goon bifore

[C]rist seiþ in þe gospel þat þe word þat he haþ spok schal deme us in þe laste day, and ȝif we schullen be demed bi Cristis word it is nedeful to lerne his word and to knowe it. Whi þanne schulden not lewid men redyn his word and writen it and speken it?

5   In þe olde testament, þe puple was chargid to knowe Goddis lawe and to wryten it in here housis and to techen it to hire children, and ȝit þat lawe brouȝte no man to parfeccioun, and siþen bi Cristis lawe | f. 46v | we schullen be demed to eendeles blisse eiþer to eendeles peyne it is myche more nedful þat we knowe þat lawe. Also, þouȝ þere weren yn þe oolde lawe prestis ordeyned to teche þe pepel,

10   ȝitt kyngis, þat ben lewide men, weren bedun to haue þe book of Goddis lawe in here warde [and] to rede þerynne ofte syþis, þat þei offende not þe lawe; neiþer þer was no lewid man forboden to haue bookis of þe lawe, ne to rede in hem whanne hem lyked. Whi þanne schulden lewid cristen men be forboden to rede Cristis lawe eiþer to techen it?

15   Crist in his comynge was not of þe order of prestis þat werun ordenet to teche þe lawe, and ȝit he prechide to þe pepel. And his disciplis þat he sent to teche and preche þe gospel to þe pepel weren lewid men, and he ne forbaad any man to speke hese wordis, but he seide generally þat whoso were ashamed to knoweleche | f. 47r | hise wordis tofore men, he wolde be ashamed to knoweleche him tofore his

20   Fader in heuene. Peter biddiþ þat euery man, after þe grace þat he haþ resseuyed of God, he schulde mynystre to oþere, þat in alle þingis God be worschipid. Poul biddiþ men teche here wyues at hoome, and noon apostil forbaad any man ne womman to lerne, rede ne teche Goddis wordis to þe pepel. Whi þan schulden not cristen pepel now lerne, write and rede Godis word, ech to oþere, to plante vertues

25   and distri vices?

Glosses and biblical references   **1** John 12:48   **5–6** Deut. 6:7–9   **10–11** See Deut. 17:18–19   **11** 'warde': keeping   **18–20** Matt. 10:33; Mark 8:38; Luke 9:26   **20–1** 1 Pet. 4:11   **21–2** 1 Cor. 14:35

Variants   **1** [ ]rist   **11** and *om.*   • ˣofteˣ ofte

Cambridge Tract IX

f. 47r | Wordis disp[is]ynge þe loueres of Goddis lawe

Þese ben þe armes of antecristis disciplis aȝenes trewe men þat repreuen here foule
synnes: 'ypocri[t]e', 'heretik', and 'þe letter sleeþ'. First, whan a man begynneþ for
to forsak vanite and fals | f. 47v | liyf of þis world, and to haue mynde of his deeþ-
day and turne hym to Godward, þen antecristis disciplis wol clepe hym an ypocrite
5   to lette hym of his porpos, as ȝif þei weren herde of þe fend to peruerte men and
kepe and cherische h[e]m in synne. But þese antecristis disciplis ben foule ypocritis,
for þei clepen hemself cristen men and ben not but seruauntis of synne and þe fend,
and traitour[s] to Crist and aduersaries to his pepel, as proud, yrous men and enuyus
forsaken Iesu Crist, kynge of mekenesse and of charite, patience and pees, and
10 maken þe fend of helle here fals kynge, as God seiþ in þe booke of Iob. Couetous
men of worldly goodis, þat breken þe heestis of God and don aȝens good conscience
bi fals swerynges, fals mesures, fals weiȝtis and oþer disceitis to wynne a litil muk
or drit of þis world, forsaken in dede God of truþe and | f. 48r | riȝtwisnesse, and
worschipen fals mawmentis, as seynt Poul seiþ in many epistles. Slouþeful men in
15 Goddis seruyse, glotouns, dronken men and lecherous forsaken God, þat techiþ
bysynes in good dedis, mesure in mete and drynke, chastite (at þe lest in verray
matrimonye), and maken here stynkynge baly here fals god, as seynt Poul techiþ
opunly. And þese ben þe ypocritis þat seyn in word þat þei louen and bileuen in
Crist but in here dedis þei forsaken hym, as Poul techiþ in holy writt.
20   Afturward, whan a man telliþ not bi þi[s] word 'ypocrit[e]' but lasteþ in good
lyf and repreueþ hem of here grete synnes, þen þei clepen hym an heretik, to make
hym seesse for more schame, but þei beþ heretikis departid fro God, for þei don
cursed synnes and mentene hem aȝenes holy writ, and excusen and iustifien hem.
For siþen | f. 48v | he is an heritik [þat] maynteneþ bi word an errour aȝenes holy
25 writt, myche more he is an heretik þat maynteneþ suche synnes in doynge, and
iustifieþ hem aȝenes holy writt.
But, at þe laste, ȝif a man stond sadli and alegge holy writt aȝenes h[is]
mysdedis, and to conferme oþere men in vertuous lijf, þei seyn anon þat 'þe letter
sleeþ' but þe goostly understondynge schal be taken, and not as þe letter sowneþ.

Glosses and biblical references   **Heading** 'dispisynge': scorning, insulting   **2** 2 Cor. 3:6; 'þe
letter sleeþ': the literal meaning kills   **5** 'lette hym of': prevent him from   • 'herde of': hired
by   **10** Job 42:25   **14** 'mawmentis': idols   **17–18** Phil. 3:19   **18–19** Titus 1:16   **20** 'telliþ':
reckons   **22** 'departid': separated   **27** 'sadli': steadfastly   **28–9** 2 Cor. 3:6 (note)   **29** 'goostly
understondynge': spiritual interpretation   • 'þe letter sowneþ': the words signify

Variants   **Heading** om. O5   • dispynge   **1** [ ]ese   **2** ypocrice C, ypocrite O5   **5** porpos ȝyf þei may
as O5   • herde] seruantes O5   **6** hym   **8** traitoura   • yrous] angry O5   **11** aȝens here gode O5   **17**
stynkynge] stynken O5   **20** telliþ not bi] cessyth not for O5   • þis] þi   • ypocritis   **24** þat om.   **27** his]
here C, hys O5

30   But here seiþ I[erom] and þe chirches lawe þat he is an heritik þat vnderstondiþ holy
writt oþere weies þan þe Holy Goost wol, and þe Holy Gost vnderstondiþ þus, þat þe
letter of Moyses lawe, vnderstondyn fleischly and not gostly kept, now sleeþ men,
and not so þe lettre of Cristis gospel. And þei þat turnen þis falsly to Cristis gospel
ben perlous heritikes, for if men | f. 49r | kepen now þe lawes of sacrifice in Moises
35   lawe, þat weren figure of Cristis passion and deeþ, þei abiden ȝet þat Crist schal
come and deye. And þis letter, þus vnderstondun, brengeþ men into heresie, and so
sleeþ men, and of þis letter mente Poule and þe Holy Goost þat 'þe letter sleeþ', and
not þe letter of þe gospel.

    For þese disciplis of antecrist seyn preuely in þese wordis þat þe wordis of
40   Iesu Crist ben fals and of non autorite, but þe vnderstondynge þat þei han, to
plesynge of þe fleisch and colourynge of synne, is trewe, and so þei maken Crist a
fool and fals, and hemsilf wiser and trwer þan Crist, siþen þei seien þat here wordis
ben trewe but Cristis ben fals. And be suche fals wordis þe[i] wolden distroie
autorite of holy writt. But ȝif þe letter of holy writ sleeþ ony man it is for here yuel
45   vnderstondynge | f. 49v | and schrewid lyuynge aȝenes it, and not for [falshede of
Godis wordys, seþen] God, auctor of trouþe, spak hem in himsilf and his seruauntis,
and ordeyned hem to be wryten to saluacioun of here soulis, þat lyuen bi his
conceilis in his holy gospel. Now God purge his chirche fro al ypocritis, heresie and
blasfemye. Amen.

Glosses and biblical references   **34** 'perlous': dangerous   **35** 'abiden ȝet þat Crist schal': still
wait for Christ to   **36** 'letter': text   **41** 'colourynge of': giving a speciously fair appearance to

Variants   **30** Ierom O5] Ion C   **31** wol] wold O5   **32** now *om.* O5   **34** o\f/   **35** ˣþei abidenˣ þei
abiden   **43** þe   **45** schrewid] cursede O5   • aȝenes it] þeraȝens O5   **45–6** falshede … seþen *om.* C,
supplied from O5   **46** in himsilf and his seruauntis *om.* O5   **47–8** bi his … gospel] trewli after holi wryt
O5   **48** now *om.* O5   **48–9** ypocritis … blasfemye] feyned ypocrites fals heretikes and cursede blasphemys
O5

Cambridge Tract X

f. 49v | A lamentacion þat þe lawes, statu[t]is and custummes of synful men ben gretly magnified and enhaunsed, but Cristis lawe is leid aslepe and lytel set by of antecrist and of his fals clerkis

[A] dere God, lord of trwþe, my litel witt suffiseþ not to wondre of þe blyndenesse and prid of summe prelatis and prestis whiche con[straine]n cristyn men to beleue to here lawes, statutes and cu[n]stitucions and custummes be peynes of dampnacion, as þei feynen, and bi bodili peynes, þorouȝ blyndenesse | f. 50r | of cristen kyngis and
5   lordis. For cristen pepel kunne not fynde þe ground of manye of þese lawes neiþer in holi writt ne resone, for þei semen aȝenes Cristis lyuynge and techynge and of his apostlis, and brouȝt inne bi prid and couetise of worldly prelatis and prestis to charge more þe pepel in cost þan Crist and his apostlis ordeyneden.
      Alas, good Iesu, louer and sauyour of feiþful soulis, whi ben þese newe
10 statutes of worldly prelatis and prestis magnyfyde aboue þin holy gospel, confermed wiþ þin precius blood and trouþe of þi godheed? A, Iesu, þe trwe spouse of saued soulis, synne haþ gret maistry amonge many þat ben seid cristen, seiþen synful menes ordinaunces ben openly tauȝte and ma[yn]tened bi worldly riche prelatis and prestis | f. 50v | and her maynteneris. But þin holy ordinaunce of wilful pouerte and
15 grettist mekenes of clerkis, and fruytful ocupacioun of hem in studiynge and techynge holy writ, is dispised and holden errour. And þei þat wolden brynge yn aȝen þis, Lord, þi best ordinaunce ben slaundred, pursued, cursed and presond, and peyned to þe deeþ of bodi.
      O ȝe cristen pepel, whi suffren ȝe worldly prelatis and prestis to bereeue ȝou
20 Go[d]dis word, þe sustinaunce of ȝoure soulis? And, ou[e]re þis, þei spoilen ȝou of ȝoure worldly goodis bi vertu of deed leed or roten wax, goten wiþ symonye and coloured wiþ fals ypocrice. I rede ȝou be war, for Crist seiþ 'ȝif þe blynde ledeþ þe

Glosses and biblical references   **Heading** 'set by of': regarded by   **7** 'brouȝt inne': introduced
12 'maistry': mastery   **17** 'pursued': persecuted   **20** 'spoilen': despoil   **22–3** Matt. 15:14; Luke
6:39

Variants   = GGIII 89–118   **Heading** *om.* L O4   • staturis   **1** [ ] dere ('A' supplied from L O4)   • of²]
on L O4   **2** of summe] of owre L   • prelatis and *om.* L O4   • constrainen] contrarion C, constreynen
L O4   **3** custitucions and *om.* L O4   **5** for … manye of] whanne cristen men knowe not þe ground of L
O4   **6** ne resone for] neþer in resoun but L O4   • techynge and lyuynge L O4   **7** bi] for L O4   • prelatis
and *om.* L O4   **9** feiþful] mannis L, mennes O4   • þese *om.* L O4   **10** of þee worldly L   • prelatis and
om. L O4   **11** þin *om.* O4   • a … trwe] alaas goode L O4   • saued] cristen L O4   **12** synne … seiþen]
crist iesu [iesu crist O4] why forsakest þu so myche þy puple þat L O4   **13** manytened   • riche prelatis
and *om.* L O4   • maynteneris] fautoris L O4   • but] and L O4   • holy *om.* L O4   **15** grettist] grettisti C,
greet L O4   • fruytful] contynuel L O4   **16** þei þat] þei holdun cursid and sore prisoned þat L O4   • yn
om. L O4   **17** þis Lord *om.* L O4   **17–18** ben slaundred … of bodi *om.* L O4 (note)   **19** O] alas alas alas
L O4   • prelatis and *om.* L O4   • bereeue ȝou] robbe ȝou of L O4   **20** goodis   • and … of²] and of L
O4   • oure   **21** wiþ] þoruȝ L O4   **21–2** and coloured … ȝou] *om.* L O4

blynde þei fallen boþe into þe diche'. And certis ȝe schal not be excused be
vnkunnynge of Goddis lawe, for ȝe myȝten kno| f. 51r |we it ȝif ȝe wolden axe it of
25 God bi tru deuocioun and good lyuynge, bi þe kyndely resoun þat God haþ writen in
ȝoure soulis. Also, ȝif ȝe wolden seke to be tauȝte of trwe prestis dredynge God as
bisily as ȝe seken worldely goodis of worldly pepel. Wherfore eche cristen man and
womman besi hem wiþ alle her myȝtis to lerne and kepe Goddis comandementis,
and ocupie þei her wittes boþe bodily and gostly in þinkyng[e], lernynge and
30 spekynge Cristis gloriose gospel, for þerynne is al counfort and sekernesse to come
to þe blysse of heuene.
    Nowe, Crist Iesu, wel of mercy and wisdom, rote of loue, frute of charite,
make þi peple to knowe verily and to kepe feiþfulli þin holy gospel, þat þei may
hereþorouȝ caste awey antecristis errours, þat drawen manye men fro veri feiþ and
35 charite, and, | f. 51v | att þe laste, encumbren hem wiþ endeles dispeir. Iesu, mercy!
Iesu, helpe! For now is tyme of nede as gret as euer was fro þe bigynnynge of þe
world vnto þis tyme. Amen.

Variants   23 þe diche] lake L O4   24 vnkunnynge] ygnoraunce L O4   • knowe] cunne L O4   • axe]
seke L O4   25 tru deuocioun] desyre L O4   • bi þe] aftir L O4   • þat … writen] writun of god L O4   26
also … tauȝte] and as bysily seke it L O4   26–7 dredynge … bisily] *om.* L O4   27 pepel] men L O4   •
wherfore] þerfore L O4   28 wiþ alle her] in alle his L O4   • comandementis] hestis L O4   29 to ocupie
his wittis L O4   • boþe … lernynge and] in L O4   • gostyly   • þinkyngis   30 gloriose *om.* L O4   •
sekernesse to] sikirnesse of cristen soulis for to L O4   32 nowe *om.* L O4   • wel] kyng L O4   • mercy …
charite] mercy wisdom and charite L O4   33–4 þat … hereþorouȝ] and to L O4   34 þat drawen] and veyn
bondis þat tarien L O4   • veri *om.* L O4   35 att þe laste *om.* L O4   • hem] many men L O4   • wiþ] in
L O4   35–7 Iesu … amen] *om.* L O4

Cambridge Tract XI

f. 51v | A comendacioun of holy writ in oure owne langage

[H]oly writ haþ þe lyknesse of a tree þat beriþ fruyt—note, peer or appel. Whanne it
is þikke l[e]ued litil or nouȝt is seen of his fruȝt, but whanne men schaken þe tree þe
fruyt falliþ doun faste and þike, and þan swetenesse is knowe þat was hidde aforn,
and whanne men eten it it plesiþ hem wel. So it fareþ bi holy writ. Þe letter semeþ
5   derk and harde, but ȝif a man sette his herte to see þe gostly witt þat is þereynne, and
ȝif he schake it wel, þat is to seie, þorouȝ studyynge þerof and by good lyuynge, by
þe grasce þat God wole | f. 52r | þanne do to hym myche good fruyt he schal fynde
þerynne, þat ben sentenssis of manye good maneris, and þe swetnesse þerof schal
turne him to gret goodnesse, whiche þat a man vnderstondeþ not tyl it be drawen and
10 schaken into his owne langage.
     For holy scripture in Latyn, Grew or Frensche to an Englische man is as a
derk cloude til he haue lerned and vnderstondun þese spechis, but whanne by þe
voys of his owne langage hit entreþ into his soule, it moyste[þ] alle hise wittis, boþe
bodily and gostly, and make[þ] hem to bere fruyt be þe goodnesse of Goddis spirit.
15 Also, be þis derk cloude is vnderstonden wicked lyuynge, þe whiche blyndeþ so his
louers þat þei wanten þe liȝt of gras truly to vnderstonde holy scripture. For Poul
seiþ 'þe letter sleiþ', þat is, fleischly lyuers brekynge þe comaundementis | f. 52v | of
God, 'but þe spirit quikeneþ' alle þoo þat lyuen feiþfully after þe gostly
vnderstondynge of holy writte. Wherfor Poul seiþ 'be ȝee ledde, oþer walke ȝee, wiþ
20 þe Holy Goost and ȝe schullen not fulfile þe synful desires of ȝoure fleische'. Þei
ben alle as [in] a dreye cloude þat vnderstonden not what þei don ne what þei ben
comaunded to do ne what is forboden hem to do, neiþer be holy writyngis ne in her
owne wittis. Þanne þei haue no reyn ne dewe of grace whanne no man techeþ hem
ne writeþ to hem holy scripture.
25   Vnderstondeþ þat þe Holy Trynetee ordent þre ordris in here cherche, þat ben
vynners, defenders and councelours. Vynners ben þe comoun pepel, þat trauellen
sore to susteyn knyȝtis and prestis and hemself boþe. Defendours ben knyȝtis, þat
schulden | f. 53r | kepe Goddis lawe and defende þe louers of it bi her pouer from
alle þe enemyes of trouþe. Also þoo þat leuen contrarie to Cristis lawe, boþe worde
30 and werke, to þe knowynge of trwe peple, ȝif þei wolen not leue her defauȝtis bi
prechynge of trewe prestis ne bi repreuynge of knyȝtis, þane þese defendours ben
boundon bi þe charge þat þei han of God to compelle hem wiþ charitabl
punyschynge to leue her wicked lyuynge, and to turne aȝene to Cristis lawe, be þei

---

Glosses and biblical references   1 'note': nut   2 'his': its   4 'letter': text   16–18 2 Cor. 3:6
19–20 Gal. 5:16   21 'dreye': dry   26 'vynners': winners, workers

Variants   1 [ ]oly   2 lˣoˣued   13 voys *sup. ras.* • moysten   14 make   21 in *om.* • dreye *sup. ras.*

seculeris or prestis. For seynt Poul seiþ not wiþouten cause þei beren þe swerd but to
35 defende hem þat lyuen wel and to chastise hem þat wilfulli and opunly doon amys.
Counceilouris ben prestis þat ben charged of God to teche boþe kny3tis and
comouns hou eche schulde leue in here | f. 53v | degre to þe worschipe of God and
profi3te of here owne soulis. Þese ben þe þre statis þat Crist haþ ordente to be in his
fi3tynge ch[ir]che here in erþe, representynge þe Holy Trinytee. Kny3thod bitokeneþ
40 þe my3t and pouere of þe Fader; presthod þe wisdom and mercy of þe Sone; laborers
þe charite or good welle of þe Holy Goste.
    And euerich of þese þre statis schulde helpe and socoure oþere, as eche
membre of a man serueþ and susteyneþ oþere. Þe feet beren alle þe oþere membris
of a man, so trewe comouns traueielen for þe sustinaunce of kny3tis, prestis and of
45 hemsilf. A mannes armes defenden ofte alle hise oþere membris from bodily harmes,
so kny3tus schulden defende bi h[er]e pouere boþe prestis, laborers and hemself fro
alle harme [and] perellis þat wolden hynder here soulis. | f. 54r | Þe [y]3en in a
mannes heed sch[e]wen to alle his membris breris, buschis, dalis and dichis, to kepe
hem fro stumblynge and fallynge in h[e]m, and to holde hym in þe pl[e]ynne weye
50 and smoþe, and so to kepe hem from hurtynge; so prestis cleuynge to here heed,
Crist, bi cleer lyuynge and feiþful techynge, þei schulden schewe þus to alle pepel þe
pleyn hi3e-weie þat lediþ to blysse, and to flee þo weies þat maken many falle into
þe diche, þe whiche diche is vnderstonden þe perpetual pitte of peyne. And to kepe
us out of þis myre, and to holde us in þe sad weie of grace, oure Sauyoure haþ left us
55 a blessed bylle, þe whiche is his holy gospel, and þis he selid wiþ watur and blod
rennynge fro his blissed herte. O, it schal be ful hard to prestis and oþere þat wollen
not lerne | f. 54v | ne teche þis gospel, ne suffren hem þat fayne wolden, to alle þo
þat han þis condicioun and eenden so. Oure A3enbiere in þe same writynge bi
Matheu bihoteþ hem euerlastynge woo.
60   A, Iesu, prestis taken gredeliche þe peny, þe mylke and þe wolle, but þei
wolen not do here office in fedynge of her schepe wiþ þe breed of liyf. Of suche men
spekiþ Ieremye þe profete, and seiþ þus: 'þe litel children askeden brede, but þer was
non þat wolden brek [it to hem]'; vndirstonde prechynge of Goddis word, for as bred
susteyneþ and strengþiþ mannes body so holy writ makeþ stronge þe soulis of alle
65 þat louen it; to wit, stonde feiþfulli [a3enes] alle goostly temptacioun.
    Now, dere frendis, I preie 3ou were not gretly to blame þat wold lette men
and wymen to 3eue bodily almesse to hem | f. 55r | þat ben in poynt to perische for
nede. 3his, he were greetly to dispise and opunly a3enes charite þat seiþ þese wordis
suynge: 'date et dabitur vobis', þat is, 3eue 3e bodily almes and goostly to hem þat

---

Glosses and biblical references   34 'seculeris': people living in the world   34–5 Rom. 13:4   39
'fi3tynge chirche': church militant (note)   48 'breris': briars   54 'sad': steadfast   55 'bylle':
charter   58 'A3enbiere': Redeemer   58–9 Matt. 23:13   62–3 Lam. 4:4   63 'vndirstonde [by
bread] prechynge'   65 'to wit': that is to say   67 'in poynt to': on the point of   68 'to dispise':
to be scorned   69 Luke 6:38

Variants   39 chriche   41 or ˣandˣ good   46 here] hrer   47 and *om.* • 33en   48 schwen   49 hym •
plynne   63 brekˣyngeˣ   65 a3enes *om.*   66 not he gretly

70   han nede, and þe blisse of heuene schal be ȝeue to ȝou for þis dede. Þanne it sueþ
      opunly þat þei þat leten þe blessid bred of Goddis lawe to be decl[ar]id to þe pepel
      þei ben cursed of God and traitours to his chirche. And for þis traitourie, seiþ Poul,
      'awaite ȝe hem þat letten þe lawe of God, and dele ȝee not wiþ hem'. For God seiþ
      bi Salamon 'þe preier of hym is cursed þat turneþ aweie his eris and wole not here
75   þe lawe of God'. Þanne muste þei nedis be blamed of God þat letten his lawe to be
      written, comyned and preched to þe pepel in here moder-tunge, wherfore Crist seiþ
      'whoso loueþ me he | f. 55v | schal loue and kepe my word, and he þat loueþ not me
      kepeþ not my wordis ne loueþ to here hem'. And Poul seiþ 'he is cursid þat loueþ
      not oure Lord Iesu Crist'. And Crist seiþ it is alle oon, to loue hym and to loue his
80   lawe.
          But hou schulden men loue it but ȝif þei knowen it on sum manere?
      Wherfore seynt Poul reherseþ a dreedful sentence to faynt louers of Cristis lawe,
      seiynge on þis wise 'he þat knoweþ not Goddis lawe boþe in werkis and wordis
      schal be vnknowen and forsaken of God as an vntrwe seruaunt at þe day of dome'.
85   Moreouere, Crist seiþ 'þei þat bileuen in me and louen my word schull[en] caste out
      fendis and voide aweie serpentis; þei schullen speke wiþ newe tunges scharp wordis
      | f. 56r | of trouþe, contrarie to þe werkis and wordis þat þei vsiden bifore. Also þei
      schullen handeel seke men and þei schullen be delyuerd from here disese. And ȝif
      þei drynke deedly venym it schal not harme ne noie hem'. Loo, what vertuys suen
90   hem þat hertily louen God and his lawe!
          Frendis, me semeþ ȝif þe peple weren byten, stongge and enuenemed wiþ
      skorpions, toodis and serpentis, he þat wold lette a man to whom God hadde ȝoue
      kunnynge wiþ salues and oynementis to heele þese woundis and to voide þe venym
      of þese venemous wormes, and þis man wold teche þe peple þis kunnynge, þei þat
95   wolden hate him herfore and lette him of his porpos þei weren in gret perel, and
      namely ȝif þei hemself weren hurte and | f. 56v | defouled wiþ þes deedly venemys,
      for ȝif þei perischiden þorouȝ þes wormes, þei þat weren hemself in cause and worþi
      greet mawgrie of God, myche more perel and wiþouten comparisoun stonden þei yn
      þat letten þe trwe medicynes and holsum salues of oure leche and sauyoure Iesu
100   Crist to be lerned and knowen of þe peple, þorouȝ þe whiche science and kunnynge
      þei schulden voide and distroie al here goostli seknesse and soris wiþ þe whiche þei
      ben defouled or enuenemed be þe bitynge, styngynge oþer sore woundynge of
      summe of here goostli [e]nemyes, þe whiche ben þe freiele fleisch, þis disseyuable
      world [and] þe sotel, slyȝe and fals oolde serpent þe feend, þat is fader of lesyngis.
105   Ȝee, but where schullen we fynde vertu[u]s erbis to make of þis moost
      holsum and heelful oynement? Certis, in þe feire medewe and glorious gardyn of

Glosses and biblical references   72–3 Gal. 6:13–14(?)   73–5 Prov. 28:9   76 'comyned':
communicated   76–8 John 14:21, 24   78–9 I Cor. 16:22   79–80 John 14:21; 'alle oon': one and
the same thing   83–4 I Cor. 14:38   85–9 Mark 16:17–18   98 'mawgrie': displeasure   104 John
8:44   105 'to make of': from which to make

Variants   71 \þei þat/ • declid   74 heris   85 schullne   100 cristi   102 enuenemed woundynge
be   103 nemyes   104 and¹ *om.*   105 vertues

Cristis | f. 57r | gracious gospel, þe whiche is hegged and paleised aboute wiþ þe
writynge of his holy profetis, apostlis and oþere trewe and feiþful disciplis of his
gracious chesynge. O whi is þis gospel so holsum and profitable? Certeyn, for þer
110 was neuer man ne womman heelid fro þe bitynge of þese forseid enemyes wiþouten
þe oynement of repentaunce and mercy writen in Cristis testament. Wherfore seynt
Gregori seiþ '*neque erba neque malagina sanauit eos sed omnipotens sermo tuus,*
domine, qui sanat uniuersa', þat is to seie, Lord God, neiþer erbe neiþer enplaster
[haþ heelid hem] but þi word, þat is almyʒti to heele alle goostly diseses. Loo what
115 vertu is in þe word of God, for bi þis word heuene and erþe weren fourmed and alle
creaturis þat ben in hem, boþe resonable and vnresonable, þe vnresonable to þe vse,
seruyce and profiʒt of þe resonable, | f. 57v | and he wrouʒte þe resonable to ʒeue
seruyce, dreed, loue and worschepe to þe maker of alle þingis. Also, bi þe myʒt
and þe pouer of Goddis word þis world schal be eende[d].
120 Neþeles, as Crist himself seiþ, his wordes schullen dwel wiþouten eende. At
þe last bi strengþe and vertu of [Godd]is word alle men and wymen schullen arise in
body and soule and apere bifore þe euerlastynge word, þat seynt Ion clepeþ þe Sone
of God, and þanne þei þat hatiden þis, þus apperynge bifore þe hiʒe Iustice, þe Sone
of God, bi vertu of þe same word þei schullen be departed wiþouten eende fro þe
125 glorious liʒt of blisse into þe orrible derknesse of peyne. And þe cause whi Crist
reherseþ in þe gospel and seid 'liʒt cam into þis world, and þe cursed peple loueden
more derknes þan þis liʒt for here werkis weren yuel', after þis þei þat loueden
| f. 58r | þe liʒt of Goddis word and ruleden here lyuynge þerafter schulle entre wiþ
Crist in to þat liʒt where is euer day and neuer nyʒt, to þe whiche blisse he brynge us
130 bi þe louynge of his lawe and lyuynge þeraftir, þat schal seie at þe laste to þe techers
and trwe louers of his word þese wordis þat folowen: 'Com, ʒee þe blessed children
of my Fader, and resc[eu]iþ to ʒou euerlastynge kyngdom maad redi to ʒou of my
Fader fro þe bigynnynge of þe world'.
Nowe, Crist Iesu kynge of blisse, þorouʒ þe bisechynge of þi blissed meke
135 maide þi moder, and be þe deuoute preiers of þin holy p[a]triarkis, feiþful prophetis,
trewe apostlis, stedfast martirs, wiþ confessouris and clene vergines, enspire oure
hertis wiþ þe gracius beemys and brennynge sparkis of þe Holy Gost, wherþorouʒ
| f. 58v | we moun loue þee and drede þe in kepynge þin comaundementis and
charitabli to stonde in mekenes and pacience [of] þi gracius gospel to oure lyues
140 eende, boþ in werke and word, what þat euere we suffre þerfore in þis valeye of
teris, gracius God. Amen.

Glosses and biblical references   107 'paleised': fenced   113 'enplaster': salve   120 Mark 13:31;
Luke 21:33   122–3 John 1:14   124 'departed': separated   125–7 'the cause whi ...' [was that]
'after þis'.   126–7 John 3:19   130 'þat': he who   131–3 Matt. 25:34

Variants   114 haþ heelid hem (or *sim.*) *om.* (note)   119 eende   120–1 god at þe last ... of is word   132
resciueþ   135 ptriarkis   139 of *om.*

Cambridge Tract XII

f. 58v | A dialogue as hit were of a wyse man and of a fole denyi[n]ge þe trweþe wiþ fablis

[*Wyse Man:*]
[N]*on occides*; þis is þe fifþe heste of almy3ti God comaundynge ech resonable criature þat noon schulde slee oþer, neiþer bodili ne goostly, but boþe þese slau3tris ben ful comoun and ryue amonge hem þat ben clepid cristyne, and speciali goostly slau3tur, þat leest heede is takun of and moost were to be sorowed for. For late a
5 man come nowadays amonge þe peple, be þei olde or 3onge, he schal ri3t soone heere talis of pride, glotony and lecherie and of alle manere synnes, and he þat can most merely sche| f. 59r |we þese wordis to þe vnwese peple is gretly comendid of hem for þis foli dede, and þei sweren armes, bones, hert and sidis þat he is a good felawe, and þat ech companye is þe betere þat he is amonge. But an holy man seiþ in
10 his writynge 'cursed be þat merþe wherwiþ God is displesed'. But perauentur þou sei[st] þat þis is noon yuel speche, for it dryueþ awey heuynesse and makeþ men li3t and glad. A, þus þou woldist preue þese veyn spechis wisdom and Cristis wordis foli, and þis were f[o]ul erise, for Crist seiþ in þe gospel of euery idel word þat m[e]n speken here, but 3if þei repente it or þei dei 'þei schullen 3eue acountis þerof
15 at þe day of dome'. Seynt Ier[o]m seiþ þat alle wordis þat alle men speken ben veyn and ydel but 3if þei turnen to þe goostli profi3t of þe speker or of þe he| f. 59v |erer. Þanne musten nedis liynge, flatreynge, bacbitynge, slaundrynge, swerynge, cursynge and wordis of rebawdie be preued idil, for þei ben a3ens þe biddynge of Crist and [h]is apostlis. For seynt Peter seiþ 'whan 3e wolen speke, speke 3e as þe wordis of
20 God', þat is euermore trouþe and goodnesse, and neuermore falshede ne wickednesse, for þese hateþ þe Trinyte and loueþ wel þe oþere tweyne. And to þis sentence acorden Poul, Ion, Iames and Iude, þat weren feiþful seruantis of oure leche Iesu Crist. And seynt Gregori seiþ 'he sleeþ hymself þat wol not kepe þe biddyngis of oure heuenli leche, Crist'.
25 But alas, 3if a symple man nowadays louynge þis leche Crist and his lawe wolde schewe to synners þe medicinable wordis of God, to void þese ydel spechis, anoon þei dispisen hym and haten hym and seyn he is an heritik and | f. 60r | a lollere, but [I] rede men be war of þis speche for it is foul eresie opunli a3ens þe Holy Goost to dispise men and wymen spekynge þe word of God to rende vp vices
30 fro mennes soulis and to plante in h[e]m vertues. And Crist seiþ to þe trwe louers

Glosses and biblical references   1–2 Exod. 20:13; Deut. 5:17; '*Non occides*': thou shalt not kill   3 'ryue': prevalent   7 'merely': merrily   8 'foli': foolish   • [by] 'armes'   10 Cf. Eccl. 7:4; Jer. 7:34 13–15 Matt. 12:36; 'or': bifore   18 'rebawdie': lasciviousness   19–20 1 Peter 4:11   21 'hateþ þe Trinyte': the Trinity hates   26 'medicinable': medicinal   28 'opunli': manifestly   30–2 Matt. 10:20

Variants   **Heading** denyige   1 [ ]on   2 goostuly   4 for^xst^x   7 is] þis is   11 seiþ   13 ful   14 man   15 Ierem   19 his] is   22 oure] ouere   28 I *om.*   30 hym

and feiþful speke[r]is of his word 'it ben not ʒe þat speken but þe sperit of my Fader
almyʒti þat spekiþ in ʒou'. Also he seiþ 'whoso synneþ aʒens þe Holy Gost, it schal
not be forʒouen to him in þis wor[l]d ne in þe world to-comynge'. Wherfore, beþ
war þat ʒee replien not aʒens þe word of God, for bi witnesse of seynt Austyn it is a
35 greuous erise.
    And þer þei clepen men lolleris for spekynge of Goddis word, I rede of
tweye manere lollers in þe lawe of grace: summe lolleden to God-ward and summe
to þe fend-ward, and of boþe þese maner loller[i]s I purpose to | f. 60v | reherse
summe. Þe most blessed loller þat euer was or euer schal be was oure Lord Iesu
40 Crist, for oure synnes lollynge on þe rode-tree, and of his leuerey and suyte weren
Peter and Andrew and oþere moo. Þese weren blessed lollers, lollynge on þe riʒt
hond of Iesu wiþ þe repentant þeef, trustynge in Goddis mercy, to whom oure Lord
bihiʒte þe blisse of paradise þe same day. But, goode frendis, what was þe cause þat
Crist and hise suers weren lolled þus? Certis, for her feiþful spekynge aʒens þe
45 synnes of þe peple, and specialli for þei spoken aʒens þe coueitese and synnes of
vntrewe bischopis and of þe fals, feined religious.
    Nowe it were to speke of cursed lollers and vntruwe, denyinge God and his
lawe, eendynge in þis wickedn[e]sse. I rede in a booke of Goddis lawe þat is cleped
Hester how þer | f. 61r | was a wicked loller, whos name was Aman Amalechitees,
50 hatynge and dispisynge þe word of God and þe peple of Israel þat weren þe techeris
of þis word. And for malice and enuye þat was roted in his hert he gat graunt of
kynge Assuere to distroie þis peple þat God hadde chosen, and to parforme þis
malice he made a peire galows fifty cubiti of heiʒte, to haue hanged on blessed
Mardoche, þe conseilour of Goddis peple. Þanne þe kynge of heuen and erþe,
55 þorouʒ his myʒt and mercy, turned þe malice of Aman into his owen heed, for he
was lolled to þe deeþ vpon þe same galowis þat he pur[pos]ed Mardoche schulde
haue hangged vpon. Þis was a wicked lollere, and diede in [h]is synne. Off anoþer
schrewid loller we reden in þe gospel and in þe | f. 61v | Dedes of Apostlis, whos
name was Iudas Scarioth, þat bitraied Crist. And after þis resoun he felle into
60 dispe[ir]e, and ʒede and lollide himself to þe deeþ, and þus he was idampned, and so
he lolled on þe left side wiþ þe þeef þat blasfemed aʒens Crist.
    Now God graunt vs gras to sue þe blessed loll[er]s Crist and hese sueris, and
to flee þe condiciouns of þese cursed lolleris as Aman, Iudas and þe þeef þat lolled
on þe left side of Crist. Whi so? For her lollyngge brouʒte hem to endeles woo. I
65 cannot see but þis: ech man and womman here lolleþ in þe weye to endeles blis-

---

Glosses and biblical references   **32–3** Mark 3:29 (cf. Matt. 12:31; Luke 12:10)   **34** 'replien':
argue   **37** 'lawe of grace': New Testament   • 'lolleden to God-ward': lolled in God's direction
38 'purpose to reherse': intend to give an account of   **40** 'leuerey and suyte': livery and uniform
42–3 Luke 23:40–3   **44** 'suers': followers   **54** 'Mardoche': Mordecai   **55** 'into his owen heed':
upon himself   **57–61** Luke 22:3–6, 47–8 (cf. Matt. 26:47–50, Mark 14:43–5) and Acts 1:16–19
61 Luke 23:39

Variants   **31** spekeis   **33** word   **38** lolliers   **39** oure] ouere   **46** religiouns   **48** wickidnsse   **55** Aman]
a aman   **56** vnpon   • purposed] pursued   **57** is   **60** disperie   **62** lollres   **63** \A/man

ward eiþer in þe weye þat lediþ to lastynge peyne. Neþelese, oure Sauyour seiþ
'large and brood is þe weye þat lediþ to perdicioun, and ful many entren bi þis ȝate
to helle, but ful streyȝt and narowȝ is þe weye þat lediþ to heuene, and ful fewe þer
ben þat entren to | f. 62r | blis bi it'. And þerefore seiþ Crist to þis litil floc 'stryue
70   ȝee to entre bi þe streiȝt ȝat' of tribulacioun and anguische, and þus bi ȝoure
mekenesse and pacient suffrynge ȝe schullen brynge ȝoure soule to blisse and pees
þat neuer schullen ende.
    Dere cristen frendis, beþ not aschamed to speke Goddis word and to lyue
þeraftir, for Crist seiþ 'he þat schameþ me and my wordis bifore men, I schal
75   schame hym before my Fader and hise aungelis'. Wonder ȝee not þouȝ synneris
dispis ȝou and clepe ȝou lolleris for louynge of Cristis gospel, for Salamon seiþ þei
þat walken in þe riȝt weye to heuene in louynge God and his lawe ben dispised of
wicked liuers wandringe in weies contrarie to God and his lawe. And oure samplere
Crist seiþ 'ȝif þ[ei] han cleped þe housbondeman of feiþful soulis Belȝabubbe, how
80   myche raþer þanne schullen þ[ei] dispise his housholde | f. 62v | meyne'? And þis
trwe housbonde Crist seiþ to hise feiþful seruantis 'lerne ȝe of me'; take ȝe
ensaunple of me; sue ȝe me in meke suffrynge; 'preie ȝe for men pursuynge and
hatynge ȝou, þat ȝe mowe be þe trewe children of ȝoure Fader þat is in heuenes'.
But parauenture þou seist:

85   [*Fole*]: I wolde gladli s[pe]ke Goddis word and lyue þerafter, leuynge þis and wordis
of rebawdie, but I am riȝt looth to lese my good þat I haue longe labored fore. And it
is wel knowen þat þouȝ a man speke wordis of harlot[r]ye, swerynge gret ooþes,
vsynge leccherie and oþer gret synnes, herfore he schal not be punysched but bi þe
purse, and ȝif he paye wel þe somnour and þe bischopis offeceris he schal be clepid
90   a manful man and profitable to holy chirche, but ȝif a man speke Goddis word and
leue þerafter, and seseþ not for noo persecucioun ne losse of worldly goodis, anoon
| f. 63r | he schal be cursed and put out of þe cherche, and ȝif he may be cauȝt he
schal [be] brent as an eretyk.

    [*Wyse Man:*] I praie þe, frende, abide and here an answere to þi wordis. Crist seiþ to
95   louers of his lawe 'wondre ȝe not þouȝ þe world hate ȝou, for it hadde me in hate
bifore ȝou'. And God seiþ bi his prophete to alle þat comenden vicis and haten and
dispisen vertues 'woo come to hem þat seien good is yuel and yuel is good, clepynge
liȝt derknesse and derknesse liȝt, swetnesse bitternesse and bitternes swetnesse'.

Glosses and biblical references   66–9 Matt. 7:13–14   69–70 Luke 13:24   73–4 Luke 9:26;
Mark 8:38; 'schameþ': is ashamed of   75–7 Prov. 11:20   78 'samplere': exemplar, model
78–80 Matt. 10:25   80–1 Matt. 11:29   82–3 Matt. 5:44–5; Luke 6:27–8; 'pursuynge':
persecuting   88–9 'but bi þe purse': except financially   90 'manful': brave, manly   92 'put out
of þe cherche': excommunicated   94–6 John 15:18   96–8 Is. 5:20; 'woo come': may woe come

Variants   73 \word/   73–4 \men I schal schame hym before/   78 liuers *sup. ras.*   79 þie   80 þie   81
housbounde   85 sepke   87 harlotye   93 be *om.*   96 to alle þat *sup. ras.*

Gode [frend], mark Cristis wordis þat suen 'who þat forsakeþ not hous, lond, fader,
100   moder, wiyf and child, takynge his cros and suynge me, he may not be my disciple'.
Also he seiþ 'he þat forsakeþ alle þese and leesiþ here his liyf for me and for my
gospel, he schal resseyue an hundrid-fold meede, and haue lor[d]schipe and
euerlasty| f. 63v |nge liyf'. Also he seiþ to þe pacient suffera[ri]s for his lawe
'blessed schullen ȝee be whanne men schullen pursue ȝou and seie alle manere of
105   yuel aȝens ȝou, lyue[n]ge for me and my word. Ioye ȝee þanne and beeþ glad, for
ȝoure mede is plent[eu]us in heuene. Þus also þei slowȝen and pursuden holy
profetis þat weren before ȝou'. Bere we gladly þis cros of tribulacioun, be ensanple
of Crist and his holy apostlis, þat [ȝ]eden ioyynge fro þe biholdynge of wicked
princes, and þe cause whi was þis, þat þe kynge of mercy made hem able and worþi
110   to suffre peyne and dispite for shewynge of his name to þe peple. Þerfore, drynke we
gladly of þe cuppe of Cristis passioun, trustynge stidfastly in Poulis wordis, seiynge
on þis | f. 64r | wise 'ȝif ȝe ben parteners wiþ Crist in tribulaciouns and peynes, þan
dar ȝee not doute ȝe schal be parteners of his eendeles blessis'. Also þe apostle seiþ
'bi manye tribulaciouns it bihoueþ us to entre in to þe kyngdom of heuenes', for 'alle
115   þoo þat wollen lyue mekely in Crist Iesu schullen suffren persecucioun for
riȝtwisnesse'. And Crist seiþ 'ȝee þat suffren tribulacioun for riȝtwis[ness]e schullen
eendelesly be blessid'. And þe profete seiþ 'many ben þe tribulaciouns of iust peple,
and oure Lord schal graciously delyuere hem from alle þoo'. And oure Sauyour seiþ
'nyle ȝee drede hem þat may slee þe bodi, but drede ȝe him þat may slee boþe bodi
120   and soule', and sende hem to peyne or blisse, wher hym likeþ.

    For þese counfortable wordis of oure Aȝenbiere and of hise holy folowers,
eche trewe soule take þe | f. 64v | vois of holy Dauiþ seiynge þus: 'I schal take
gladly þe holsum cupe of tribulacioun, and in drynkeynge of Cristis cuppe I schal
ynwardly clepe his name to helpe'. But men and wymen louynge þe world and þe
125   lusty lyuynge in it sauer[en] litel þis sentence, and no gret wonder, for blissed Ioob
axside a question of God and s[ei]þ 'where schullen we fynde heuenly wysdom?'
And þe Holy Gost ȝeueþ him an answere and seiþ 'þis clere wisdom may not be
founden in þe londe of lusti and fleischly lyuers'. Wherfore Salamon seiþ 'þe
wisdom of God schal not eenter in to a yuel-willed soule, neiþer it schal dwelle in þe
130   bodi þat is suget to synnes'. And Poul, spekynge of fleischli and worldly wisdom,
seiþ þat 'þe wisdom of þis world is folie att God almyȝ[ti]'. And Crist, þe Wisdom
of þe | f. 65r | Fader, spekenge of worldly wise men seiþ on þis wise: 'þe children of
þis world ben more wise and prudent in here fleischely genneracioun' to sauer

Glosses and biblical references   **99–100** Luke 14:26–7 (cf. Mark 8:34, 10:29–30)   **101–3** Matt.
19:29   **103–7** Matt. 5:11–12; 'slowȝen': killed   **111–13** Rom. 8:17   **113–14** Acts 14:21   **114–16**
2 Tim. 3:12   **116–17** Matt. 5:10   **117** 'profete', i.e., David   **117–18** Ps. 33:19   **118–20** Matt.
10:28   **120** 'wher hym likeþ': wherever it pleases him   **122–4** Ps. 115:13 (note)   **125–8** Job 28:12–
13   **128–30** Wisd. 1:4; 'yuel-willed': wishing ill, malevolent   **130–1** 1 Cor. 3:19; 'att': with
131–4 Luke 16:8

Variants   **99** frend *om.*   **102** lorschipe   **103** sufferans   **105** lyuege   **106** \ȝ/oure. • plentus   **107**
gladily   **108** eden   **116** riȝtuwisse   **119** \þe bodi ... slee/   **125** sauerne   **126** sieþ   **131** almyȝit

erþely and fleischly þingis 'þan ben þe children of liȝt', led bi Faderis spirite. And
135 for þis he seiþ to hise foloweris 'I haue chose ȝou fro þis worldli wisdom, and
þerfore þe wor[l]de haþ ȝou in hate'. And Poul seiþ 'be ȝee not confurmed to þis
world', in suche wisdom of þe fleische. And for þis cause he seiþ 'ȝif I wolde plese
to men in such fleischly and erþely wisdom I were not þanne Cristis trwe seruaunte'.
And Crist preied to his Fader to kepe his seruauntis fro þat yuel þat worldly wisdom
140 bryngeþ to men. And seynt Gregori seiþ þat antecrist schal chese men for to preche
his falsnesses þat ben ful of worldly wisdom; fro þis wis| f. 65v |dom God kepe us,
and fastnen his drede in oure soulis. For Salamon seiþ 'þe bigynnynge of heuenli
wisdom is þe drede of oure Lord God'. And herefore seiþ Dauiþ to God 'Lord,
fasten and naile my fleische to þi drede', þat bryngeþ in þis heuenly wisedom, for
145 þei þat han þis drede in here hertis ben clensid from worldly wisdom. And herfore
seiþ Crist 'blessid be men of clene herte, for þei schullen see God', in eendeles
glo[r]ie.
    O, ful blissed is þis worde of God, for it quykeneþ and ȝeueþ liȝt to hise
louers, þat bifore weren drenchid and goostli slayn wiþ synne. And herfore seide
150 Peter to Crist 'Lord, to who[m] schullen we goo but to þee, for þou hast wordis of
euerlastynge liyf'. And Crist seiþ 'þe wordis þat I speke to ȝou ben sprit and liyf'.
Wherfore he seid to Martha, Marie Mawdeleyns suster, 'he þat bileeueþ in me',
turnynge from | f. 66r | synne to good werkis, 'þouȝ þat he were deed', bi synne, 'he
schal lyue', bi vertu of my word wiþouten eende. Dauiþ, seynge þis vertu in sprite,
155 seid to God þese wordis þat folowen: 'Lord, I haue closed þi wordis in myn herte,
þat I offende þe not bi synne'. Ouer þis he seiþ 'Lord, þe declarynge of þi wordis
liȝtneþ and ȝeueþ vnderstondynge to meke men'. Wherfore he seiþ 'blessed be þe
clene peple þat walken in þe lawe', for þi lawe is wiþouten wem, turnynge soulis fro
deeþ to liyf. 'And þe testament of oure Lord is trewe, ȝeuynge wisdom to men l[i]til
160 in malice'. And herfore seiþ Ion in þe Ap[o]calips 'he is blissed þat rediþ and herith'
wiþ good liyf þe blissed and fruytful lawe of oure Lord God.
    But sum man seiþ [*Fole*]: I preie þee, leeue þees spechis, and telle me a mery tale of
Giy of Wariwyk, Beufiȝ of Hamton, eiþer of Sire Lebewȝ, Robyn Hod, | f. 66v |
eiþer of summe welfarynge man of here condiciouns and maners.

165 [*Wyse Man*:] O vn[w]ise man, þou schewist þi self in þis disire to be of þat noumber
þat Isaye repreued and seiþ 'children of frowardnesse, not wellynge to here þe lawe
of God, seien: speke to us plesant þingis, þouȝ þei ben erroris', for be it knowen to

---

Glosses and biblical references   134–6 John 15:19   136–7 Rom. 12:2   137–8 Gal. 1:10   139–40
See John 17:15   142–3 Prov. 1:7   143–4 Ps. 118:120; 'to þi drede': to fear of you (note)   145–6
Matt. 5:8   149 'drenchid': immersed [in]   150–1 John 6:69   151 John 6:64   152–4 John
11:25   154 'in sprite': spiritually   154–6 Ps. 118:11   156–7 Ps. 118:130; 'liȝtneþ': illuminates   157–
8 Ps. 118:1   158 'wem': blemish   159–60 Ps. 18:8   160 Apoc. 1:3   163 'Beufiȝ of Hamtoun':
Bevis of Hampton (note)   • 'Sire Lebewȝ': Lybeaus Desconus (note)   166–7 Is. 30:9–10;
'frowardnesse': perversity; 'þouȝ þei ben': even if they are

Variants   136 worde   147 gloie   150 whon   159 ltil   160 a pacalips   165 vn vise   167 eeroris

alle men þes geestis and rymes of fiȝters, lechours and þeues ben co[ntriui]d of
synneres bi þe idel ymaginacioun of þere hertis. Also þe[i] ben poudred wiþ fals
170 lesyngis, as fore þe most part, and of suche writyngis and talkyngis spekeþ þe
prophete and seiþ 'Lord, wicked peple han tolde to me fablis and tryflys, but
noþinge acordynge to þ[i] lawe'. Also he spekeþ to men of þi disire and seiþ 'how
longe wol ȝee be of heuy hert, and wherto loue ȝee vanitee and lesynge?' And Isaie,
spekynge of suche writeris of trifulys and fablis, seiþ on þis wise: 'þe | f. 67r | werkis
175 of hem ben vnprofitable, and de[e]des of wickidnesse ben in here handis'. And no
doute alle þat han more delite in suche gestis and iapes ben gostli lechouris, for in
þis þei forsaken here spouse, Crist, and his laue, þat is bred of liȝf, and weddyn
Sathanas wiþ his lesyngis þat ben l[a]ues of lastynge sorowe. And herefore seiþ
Dauiþ a dreedful sentence of suche liers: 'Lord God,' he seiþ, 'þou schalt leese alle
180 þat speken lesynge', and þe cause is for þei ben preued in Goddis lawe mansleers of
hemself and many oþere. And for þis, seiþ Austyn, mannes soule dieþ for hunger but
ȝif it be fedde wiþ heuenly breed, þat Crist clepeþ þe breed of lijf. And of þis breed
spekeþ þe prophete and seiþ 'þou haste ȝouen to þyne breed fro heuene, hauynge in
hit al þe deliyt of grace and mercy'. And Ecclesiasticus seiþ 'þe Lord haþ ifedde his
185 chosen noumbre wiþ breed of lijf and | f. 67v | of vnderstondynge'. And seynt
Austyn seiþ 'lyue wel and bileue wel in Crist and þou hast eeten þe breed of liyf'.

[*Fole:*] Ȝe, ȝe, þou sei[st]. I hadde as leyf nouȝt as suche talis. Late us lyue as oure
faders deden, and þanne good inouȝ, for þei weren wel iloued of cheters, wrestlers,
bokeler-pleieris, of daunceris and syngeris, and þei weren wel-welled to haue hem to
190 þe ale; ȝhe, and ofte tymes on þe Sundays for good felowschip þei wolden dyne and
drynke be note and go to ch[ir]ch after, and so late us do nowadays and we schullen
haue þe blissynge of s[e]ynt Thomas of Caunturbere. Ȝhe, man, and ȝif þou haue wel
idrunke att ho[me] þi stomak schal waxe warme, þouȝ it be coolde weeder, and þe
soote sauoure of good ale schal stiȝe into þi br[a]yne and brynge þe mery asleepe,
195 ȝhe, and þouȝ þe prest preche þanne neuer so faste it schal no | f. 68r | more g[r]eue
þi wittis þan þe s[o]une of a myre harpe.

[*Wyse Man:*] A, Iesu, þi wordis ben trewe þere þou seist 'as þe abundans of þe hert
þe mo[u]þe spekeþ'; and þus, vnwise man, it semyth þat in þ[i] herte ben roted ydel
þouȝtis, in þi tunge veyn wordis and in alle þi membris vnprofitable werkes. And so
200 þou preuest þiself in þi wordis yuel and wicked and nouȝt good, and Crist seiþ

Glosses and biblical references   168 'contriuid of': devised by   172 'of þi disire': with desires
like yours   172–3 Ps. 4:3   173–5 Is. 59:6   178–80 Ps. 5:7; 'leese': destroy   180–1 See John
8:44   182 'þat Crist clepeþ þe breed of lijf': John 6:35   183–4 Wisd. 16:20; 'to þyne': to thy
[people]   184–5 Ecclus 15:3   187 'Ȝe, ȝe, þou seist': yeah, yeah, so you say • 'I hadde as leyf
nouȝt': I'd as soon hear nothing   191 'be note': to the accompaniment of music   195 'faste':
earnestly   197–8 Matt. 12:34; Luke 6:45   200 'nouȝt good': no good at all   200–1 Luke 19:22

Variants   168 cointud (note)   169 þe   172 þe   175 dedees   178 loues   187 seiþ   191 chrich   192
synt   193 hoem   194 bryne   195 geue   196 sunne   198 moþe • þe   200 and nouȝt *sup. ras.*

'wicked seruaunt, I deme þee be þi mouþe'. Also he seiþ 'a good man of þe good tresoure of his hert bryngeþ forþe good þingis, but an yuel man for þe schrewed tresoure of his herte bryngeþ forþe wicked þingis'. Also he seiþ 'eche good tree makeþ good fruytes, and eche yuel tree makeþ yuel fruyte, and euery tree is knowen

205 bi þe fruytes þat comen of it'. Wherfore þe enemyes of trouþe seiden | f. 68v | to Peter in þe tym of Cristis passioun 'þou art oon of hem, for þi speche', þat is, þe fruyt of þi tunge, 'makeþ þee knowen to vs'. Now, frend, be ware, for Crist seiþ 'eche tree þat makeþ not good fruyt schal be kutt doune and be cast into þe fire'. Þere þou seist 'we schullen lyue as oure fleischly faderis and synful diden' þis is an

210 vnholsum counsel, for God seiþ of suche fadris and suche children þat he wole punysche here wickednesse into þe þredde and þe fourþ generacioun, etc.

But I trowe þou be of þe noumber of hem þat seien on þis wise: 'Oure faderis han ȝeten a sowre grape and þe teeþ of [sones ben an egge …] synne, and on þis Crist seiþ in þe gospel 'ȝoure synful fadris eten mana in deserte, and for þe[r]

215 vnworþi etenge of hit þei ben deede, but he þat etiþ þe breed of lif, þat is, my word, | f. 69r | he schal lyue wiþowten eende'. And in anoþer place Crist seiþ to þe denyars and haters of his word 'ȝe ben children of þe fader þe deuel, for he was a manslere f[ro] þe begynny[n]ge', and his children ben alle þoo þat louen fantasyes, fablis and lesyngis more þan þe gospel, þat is verey trouþe. Neþeles, God seiþ be [h]is

220 prophete 'þe sone schal not bere þe wi[ckedne]sse of his fader' ȝif he sue him not in his synnes, 'neiþer þe fader schal be punysched for his children', ȝif he tauȝte h[e]m biliuynge and th[ech]ynge to kepe þe comandementis of God. Wherfore, folowe we oure fader God almy[ȝ]ti boþe in þuȝte, werk and word, and flee we þe synful weies of oure fleischly fadris, þat leeden nouȝt to lif but to euerlastynge deeþ, for Crist

225 seiþ he is weie, trouþe and liyf to alle þat schullen be saued. Folowe we oure faderis | f. 69v | and alle peple in þat þei folowen Iesu Crist, but no ferþer, for liyf ne deeþ. For Crist seiþ 'he þat he[e]riþ my wordis and doeþ hem, he is my broþer, suster and moder'. Also he seiþ 'whoso doith þe welle of my Fader, he schal enter in to þe kyngdom of heuenes'.

230 [*Fole:*] What? What þanne be þi tale? We schulden neuere be merie but euer sory? For it semeþ þou woldist haue alle men to speken of Goddis lawe, and to þenke on peynes þat ben ordeyned for synners, and also of here eendynge, and þis wolde make hem die for sorowe.

Glosses and biblical references   201–3 Matt. 12:35; Luke 6:45   203–5 Matt. 7:17 with Luke 6:44   205–7 Matt. 26:73   207–8 Matt. 3:10, 7:19; Luke 3:9   210–11 Exod. 20:5, 34:7; Num. 14:18; Deut. 5:9   212–13 Jer. 31:29–30; Ezech. 18:2 (note)   214–16 John 6:58   216–18 John 8:44   219–21 Ezech. 18:20   224–5 John 14:6   226 'in þat': insofar as   227–8 See Matt. 12:50 (note)   228–9 Matt. 7:21.   230 'be þi tale': may thy tale be

Variants   205 eenemyes   214 þei   216 \a/noþer   218 fro] for   • begynnyge   219 is   220 witnesse   221 him   222 theynge   223 almyti   227 herriþ

[*Wyse Man:*] Certis, þe wordis of þe Wise Man ben preued in þe riȝt trewe, for he

235 seiþ 'malice may be ouercome but hit may not be pesid', and þis þou sch[e]wist wel
in þin answeris, þat ben grounded in folie. Good frend, marke þe wordis of Dauiþ,
þat seiþ 'blessed is þe man wh| f. 70r |os wylle is in þe lawe of þe Lord, and he schal
close his mynde in his lawe boþe be day and be nyȝt'. Also he seiþ 'delite ȝou in þe
lawe of oure Lord and he schal ȝeue to þee þe ryȝthful axyngis of þin hert'. And

240 seynt Austyn seiþ 'close þi mynde in þe biddynges of oure Lord and hise
comandeme[n]tis [be] besie to kepe; þan schal be stabl[e] þin heret in goodnesse,
and ȝeue to þee disires of heuenly kunnynge'. Also he seiþ 'þer is noþinge swetter to
him þat schal be saued þanne to beholde into þe comaundementis of God'. Wherfore
he seiþ 'loue þe sciencis of holy scripture and þou schalt not loue neiþer fulfille þe

245 synful desires of þi flisch'.

    And ful good it is to leue þoo þingis þat bryngen men to helle, and to do þoo
þingis þat bryngen men to heuene, for holy Ioob seiþ þat in helle is noon
redempcioun, wherfore it is clepeid of Crist | f. 70v | þe vtmest derknes, where is
euermore wepynge and grentynge of teeþ. And, as holy doctours seien, þoo peynes

250 þat ben þere ben so greu[u]s and grete þat alle þe peynes in þis liyf ben ioies in
comparisoun of þoo in helle. Þe prophete conseyuynge þe peyne of deeþ of helle
seide on þis wise: 'O þou secoun[d]e deeþ, hou bitter is þe mynde of þee', and
D[a]uiþ spekynge herof seiþ 'þe deeþ of synners is worste' of alle peynes. But Poul
seiþ to þe louers and lyuers after Goddis lawe 'ioie ȝe in ȝoure tribulaciouns, for þei

255 ben nouȝt in comparison to ȝou in þe world to-comynge'. Wherfore he seiþ eftsones
'ioie ȝee, and ȝoure esie pacience be knowen to men, for oure Lord is nyȝ to ȝou'.
And Dauiþ seiþ of suche peple 'o[u]re Lord is nyȝe to hem þat ben troblid in herte
for his lawe, | f. 71r | and ȝif þei dwellen in mekenesse of spirit he schal make hem
saaf'. And oure Sauyour seiþ 'a woman whanne sche is wit childe haþ sorowe, but

260 whanne þe childe is born þe mynde of þe sorowe is passed'. B[i] þis child-berynge is
vnderstondon a trew soule suffrynge in þe bodi manye trybulaciouns, þe whiche att
his departynge is born of þe angels of God into þat world where al blis is closed
ynne. And for þis cause seid seynt Austyn whanne his soule schulde departe from þe
bodi 'welcome deeþ, eende of alle sorowe and traueile and þe [b]igynnynge of alle

265 ioie and reste'. Whi seid he þus to deeþ? Sire, f[or] as deeþ is þe eendynge of ioie
and þe bigynnynge of eendeles peyne to hem þat schullen be dampned, so deeþ is þe
ende of al sorowe to hem þat schullen be saued, and bigynnynge of lastynge ioie.
And herfore seiþ þe prophete 'ful precious is þe deeþ of iust | f. 71v | men in þe siȝt
of God, but þe deeþ of synners is most wicked'. And of þes tweye deeþes spekiþ

Glosses and biblical references   234–5 Wisd. 7:30?; 'pesid': reconciled   236–8 See Ps. 1:1–2;
'close': enclose   238–9 Ps. 36:4; 'axyngis': petitions   241 'stable': establish   248–9 Matt. 8:12;
'grentynge': gnashing   251–2 Ecclus 41:1; 'mynde': recollection   252–3 Ps. 33:22   253–5 Rom.
5:3 with Rom. 8:18   255 'eftsones': later   255–6 Phil. 4:4–5   257–9 Ps. 33:19   259–60 John
16:21   262–3 'closed ynne': enclosed   268–9 Prov. 10:28   269–71 Ecclus 28:6

Variants   235 schwist   241 comandemetis • be *om.* • stabli   250 greus   252 secoune   253 duiþ   257
ore   260 But   264 digynnynge   265 for] fro

270   Salamon and seiþ 'haue þou in þe mynde þe laste þingis and þou schalt not synne
wiþouten eende'. Þis same desire hadde Moises whan he seid þus: 'wolde God þat
men sauereden and vnderstooden and purueyeden for þe laste þingis'.
    Also þe day of doom it is wisedom to haue in mynde, and hereþorouȝ to flee
þoo þouȝtis, wordis and workes þat þan schullen departe men fro God to peyne, and
275   to loue God and his lawe and lyuen þerafter, wherfore men schullen be resceuyd of
God to blisse. For Crist seiþ 'þanne, as a good scheepard departeþ geet fro scheep so
he schal departe þe cursed from þe bless[e]d, þe cursed to eendeles turment, þe
blessed to ioie wiþouten ende'. For þanne schal Crist seie to þe waried noumbre
'goo, ȝe cursed, into euerlastynge fire, þat is ordeyned to þe deuel and alle his
280   aungelis'. After | f. 72r | þat sentence he schal seie to his chosen noumber þese
wordis of loue þat folowen: 'Come, ȝee blessed children of my Fader, and take to
ȝou a kyngedom þat was ordeined to ȝou of my Fader at þe b[i]gynnynge of þe
world'.

    [*Fole*:] Ȝe, ȝe, man, whanne þou haste al seid þer is namore but 'do wel and haue
285   wel', and as good a soule haþ an owle as a cockow, and I trowe as longe as þou hast
lyued þou sawist neuer soule goo a-blacberied; þerfore, be my rede lat us be merye
and sele carre, for amonge an hundrid men, be þei seculeris or prestis, þou schalt
scar[s]ly fynde oon þat wole telle suche talis as þou doist, and whoso doiþ after most
men schal be blamed of leste men. Nowe do be my counsel and þou schalt fynde it
290   for þe beste, as me þynkeþ.

    [*Wyse Man*:] Broþer, haue mynde þat Salamoun seiþ 'þere is a weye þat semeþ to
sum man | f. 72v | ful riȝtful, but þe laste þingis of it leeden to deeþ of soule', and þis
is very truþe, as it may be proued in ydolat[er]is and folk of mysbileue. Frend, þou
seidist bifore 'do wel and haue wel', but to þese tweyne longeþ myche þinge, for
295   þere is neiþer man ne woman þat may be preued a wel-doer but he þat lerneþ þe ten
comaundementis of God and to his pouer kepeþ hem, for it is writen 'he þat seiþ he
loueþ God and kepeþ nouȝt hese heestis, he is a liere and trouþe is nouȝt in him'.
And wite þou wel þat þese ten hestis ben closed in tweyne, þat is, in loue to God
aboue al þinge and to þi neiȝbore as to þiself, and Crist seiþ þat in þese tweyne loues
300   ben closed al þe lawe and þe profetis. And, be witnesse of Poul, he þat loueþ
parfiȝtly haþ fulfilled þe lawe, for whoso loueþ God aboue al þingis, he wol not
breke his comaundementis, and he þat loueþ | f. 73r | his neiȝtbore as himself wole
do noþinge to his neiȝtbore but as he wolde his neiȝtbore dede to him. And whoso

---

Glosses and biblical references   271–2 Deut. 32:29; 'sauereden' (note); 'purueyeden':
provided   274 'departe': separate   276–8 Matt. 25:32–3; 'geet': goats   278 'waried':
cursed   278–80 Matt. 25:41   280–3 Matt. 25:34 (note); 'to ȝou of': for you by   284–5 'do
wel and haue wel': do good deeds and you will be rewarded   286 'goo a-blacberied': go to hell
(note)   287 'sele carre': sell care   288–9 'after most men': what most men do   291–2 Prov.
14:12, 16:25   296–7 1 John 2:4   299–300 Matt. 22:40 (note)   300–1 Rom. 13:8

Variants   277 blessd   282 bgynnynge   284 \do/.   288 scarly   293 ydolatreis   297 lierer

eendeþ in þese tweyne loues he may trewely be seid a wel-doere, and for þis wel-
305 doynge he schal haue more welþe þan herte may þenke oþere tunge telle, þe whiche
ioie and welþe God haþ made redy to alle þat louen him wiþouten feynynge.

3it, broþir, be warre of synful myrþe, for whoso ioieþ and is merye in
brekynge of þe heste of God, he sleeþ hymsilf, and 3if he eende þus he wendiþ to
eendeles care and sorowe. Also þou seist 'as good a soule haþ an owle as a kuckow',
310 and it semeþ bi þis speche þat þou arte of þe noumber of saducees þat seien þere is
noo resurreccioun. And þis foul eresie Crist dampneþ in þe gospel, where he seiþe
on þis wise: 'I am God of Abraham, God of Iacob and God of Isaac'. He is | f. 73v |
God of lyuynge men and nou3t of deede. Of o þinge I am sertyne, who þat þese
fonned wordis spekeþ dispisynge God and his lawe, þe whiche wordis þou haste
315 blabred before, 3if he eende yn hem wiþoute repentaunce he goþ to peyne for
euermore, by witnesse of þe profete þat seiþ 'Lord, þou schalt dampne al þoo þat
speken and mayntene s[u]che fals lesynges'; also bi witnesse of seynt Ion in þe
Pocalip[se]: 'such lyeres schullen dwelle in þe stynkynge poole þat neuer schalle be
quenchd'.

320 Þou spekest of blackeberies. I counceyle þe to leue þi scorneful wordis, lest
þi body and sowle be made a blacke brond in þe lastynge peynes of helle. And 3if
þou wylte witte of þoo peynes whiche þ[ei] ben, I haue red of ix. ful grete whiche
ben þere. Þere is fire most hoot, vnquenchable, as Crist telleþ; þere is watur colder
þan tunge here can telle, as holy | f. 74r | Iob telleþ. Þere [is] contynual wepynge and
325 grentynge of te[e]þ bi [...]withe and palpable, þe whiche weren fygured in Moyses
tyme: 'and derkenesse[s] fellen on cursed pharao and on his peple for her
wyckednesse', but to Moyses þe blessed seruant of God and to his peple þese
derkenesse[s] diseseden noþinge. Pharao and his peple, þat weren in þe se[r]c
derkenes iij. dayes and iij. ne3tes, figureden þe fende wit his retenew, þat schullen
330 dwellen in endles derkenesse by þe ry3twisnesse of þe Fader and of þe Sone and of
þe Holy Goost; Moyses and his peple fygureden Iesu Crist and his chosen noumbre,
þat schullen be in endlesse clerenesse witouten eny derkenesse. Also, in helle is
better stenche witouten eny swotenesses, as Ion, in þe Apocalips, seiþ. Also þere is
þe vretynge worme of eche dampned soules consciens, ful sore | f. 74v | bytynge,
335 and þere is an orible place witouten eny clernesse, and þereto a ful wicked
felouchipe of f[o]ul fendes. Moreouere, þere ben mo glowynge teris þan wateris in
þe see. Þe knetynge togeder of alle þese paynes is dispeyr neuer to go þens but þer to
dwelle witouten ende whosoeuere comeþ þider

Þou seist we schulden do after most folke and þan we schullen haue but litil

---

Glosses and biblical references   310–11 See Matt. 22:23   311–12 Matt. 22:32; Mark 12:26
314 'fonned': foolish   316–17 Ps. 5:7   317–19 Apoc. 21:8   323 Mark 9:43, 45, 47.   323–4 Job
24:19.   324–5 Matt. 8:12, 13:42, 13:50, 22:13, 25:30; Luke 13:28.   325 'fygured': prefigured
326–8 See Exod. 10:21–3   328 'diseseden noþinge': caused no inconvenience at all • 'sere':
colourless   332–3 Is. 3:24 (note)   334 'vretynge': consuming

Variants   315 eenden   317 stiche (?)   318 pocalipes • pool/le   322 þei] þie   324 is *om.*   325 teþþ   326
derkenesse   328 derkenesse • see   333 Ion \seiþ/ in þe apoc. seiþ   337 is] þis

340   blame. But be þis fonde conceyle we schullen not folewe þe dedis of holy prophetis
       ne of Ion Baptist, more þan a prophete, neþere þe werkis of Iesu Crist neiþer of his
       holy apostlis, for ȝif þei hadden wrowte after most men þei hadden not suffred suche
       deþes as þei deden for here repreuenge of synners. Better it is to suffer here blames,
       repreues, sclaunders, dispitis, beetyngis and schameful deeþes, þanne at þe day of
345   dome þe schame of God | f. 75r | and his holy seyntes, and peynes wiþouten ende.
       Frende, I concel þe to leue þi lewde replicaciounes, and holy to sue to God and axe
       of him forȝyu[n]esse of þe[s] wordis þat ben worse þan ydel, for þei ben not only
       aȝeynes man but aȝenes þe maker of alle þingis. Be war, for we reden þat Daton and
       Abiron for þis foly sounken doun to helle al quicke; wyf, child and alle þat longed to
350   hem. Antyocke for þis synne had an oryble ende, and Crist cursed for þis synne þe
       cytees of Be[th]sayda and Corosaynis. Also, for þis wicke[d]nesse Crist seid to his
       obstenant pursueres þei schulden dye in here synnes, and now he w[ar]neþ vs alle
       þat at þe day of iugement þere schal be lesse peyne to Sodom and to Gommore,
       whiche sancken doun to helle for synne, þan to þe cyte or persone þat wollen not
355   resey| f. 75v |ue þe word of God.
          Moreouere, þou seyest þat amounge an hundred persones, prestes or seculers,
       [þou] schalt scarsely fynde oon þat wole speke hoolsomly þe word of God. For þis
       cause boþe þou and I ouȝten for to morne and not to be glad, for Crist seiþ 'blessed
       ben þei þat þus mornen, for þei schullen be coumforted in þe blisse of heuene'. Also
360   he seiþ 'wo to ȝou þat lauȝen', in wickednesse, 'for ȝoure lauȝter schal be turned
       into wepynge and ynto bitternese'. And þat þer ben many þat goon in þe wey of
       wickednese, and ful fewe þat goon in þe wey of goodnesse, Crist and Poule beren
       open wittnesse. Poule seiþ 'many walken þat ben enmes to þe passion of Crist, for
       þei maken þer bellis her god, and her ioie is in þoo þingis þat schullen turne into her
365   confusioun'. And Salamon seiþ 'whoso walkeyþ | f. 76r | in þe riȝte weye, he is
       dispised of hem þat goon in þe wronge weye'. And Crist seiþ 'large and brod is þe
       weye þat ledeþ to dampnacioun, and many entren bi it, but ful narow and streite is þe
       weie and þe ȝate þat leden to blisse, and ful fewe entren in bi him'. And Crist
       bihotyþ to þoo prestes þat han taken þe keye of þe ȝate of kunnynge and wollen not
370   entren to blisse bi hit, ne suffre wolden hem þat fayne wolden, to be rewarded wit
       woo þat haþ non ende. Neþeles, þe kynge of alle criatures seiþ þat 'þere is myche
       repe corne, but þere ben ful fewe werkmen. Praie ȝe þerfore þe lord of þis ripe corne
       þat he wole sende good werkmen into his ripe corne'. Bi þe ripe corne, þis
       vnderstonde, þoo peple þat gladly wolden lyue wi[sl]e ȝif þei westen in | f. 76v |
375   what manere; bi þe werkmen ben vnderstonden prestes þat schulden wit good wordis

Glosses and biblical references   346 'replicaciounes': arguments • 'holy': wholly   348–50
Num. 16:31–5   350 1 Macc. 6:1–16; 'Antyocke': Antiochus   350–1 Matt. 11:21; Luke 10:13   351–2
John 8:21, 24   352–5 Matt. 10:14–15; Mark 6:11; Luke 10:12, 14   358–9 Matt. 5:5   359–61 Luke
6:25   362 Matt. 22:14   363–5 Phil. 3:18–19   365–6 Prov. 14:2   366–8 Matt. 7:13–14   368–71
Luke 11:52 (cf. Matt. 23:13)   370 'hem' [to enter it]   371–3 Matt. 9:37–8; Luke 10:2

Variants   347 forȝyuesse • þer   351 behtsayda • wickenesse   352 wraneþ   353 iugement yt þere   356
an^{x}d^x 357 ^{x}þu^x.   374 wiffe

ket away synnes fro mennes soules, and so make hem able to be caried to þe hyȝe
kynges berne, þat is, þe ryche blisse of heuene.

[*Fole*:] O, now [I] se yn my sowle þat Crist is kynge aboue alle kynges and lord
aboue alle lordis. Also [I] se his lawe is sufficient to be saued wit, and þat alle oþere
380   lawes contrarie to hit of trwe men schulden be dispised. But, good frende, howe
schal I do to geete mercy of þis kynge for my fol þouȝtis, myn ydele wordis and for
my wyked werkes?'

[*Wyse Man*:] Broþer, we reden in þe gospel on twelf[þ]e day þat iij. kyngis sowten
oure Lord fro fer cuntre, and whanne þei haden fonden him þei ofr[e]den [him] gold,
385   encence and myrre. And whan þei haden slept þei wenten home by | f. 77r | anoþer
weye. Þou seiste þou hast syȝte now of þe same Lorde and of his lawe; þan Y
counceyle þe at þe bygynynge þat þou ofer wiþ þese iij. kynges: in stede of gold ofer
þou trew byleue, in stedde of encence ofer to þis lord stydfaste hope, and in stede of
myrre ofer to þis kynge lastynge loue and dred, and loke þat þese iij. vertues
390   contynuelly rest in þi soule, and þan wysely turne home aȝenne wiþ þese kynges, not
by þe same weye þat þou ȝedest out by but by anoþer, for drede of Erowde. Oure
kyndly cuntre is þe blisse of heuene, out of þe wyche blisse mankynd was cast by
brekynge of þe comaundement of God, and for þis trespace he was put vnder þe
þraldom and bondage of Erowde þe fende fyue m., ij. c and ode ȝeris, and þan Crist,
395   boþe God and man, þorw his meke obedience | f.77v | to þe deþ of his manhede,
bouȝte mankynde ouȝte of þe þraldom of þe prince of pride, Lucifer. So we now, in
þat we haue gon out of eny countre by brekynge of þe comaundementis of God,
turne we aȝein by lernynge of hem and by trew kepynge of hem to oure lyues ende.
For Crist seiþ 'ȝif þou w[old]ist entre in to þe bl[i]sse, kepe þou þe comaundementis
400   of God', for þer is non oþere weye to heuene. Ȝif þou haue gon fro þi contre be þe
weie of pride, turne aȝeine by þe vertue of mekenesse; ȝif þou haue gon fro Crist by
þe weie of wraþe, turne aȝeyne to þi cuntre by þe weie of pacience; ȝif þou haue gon
fro þi cuntre be þe weie of enuy, turne aȝeyne be þe weie of loue to God and to þin
euen-cristen; ȝif þou haue gon fro Crist by falsse couytyse, turne aȝeyne by þe weie
405   of almesse-dede and petye to þi | f. 78r | nedi neyȝbore. In þat þou hast gon fro þin
heuenly cuntre by þe stynckynge weyes of gloteny, slouþe and lecherye, turne
aȝeyne bi þe welle-sauered weies of [a]bstinance, of good ocupacioun and schastyte,
and ȝif þou haue gon fro Crist by mysspendynge of þi v. wittis, boþe bodily and
gostly, turne aȝeyne by ocupiynge of hem to þe worchipe of God and profieȝt of þin
410   owne soule. And ȝif þou turne þus to þi cuntre aȝeyne by forsakenge of Erowde þe

---

Glosses and biblical references   383 ' twelfþe day': Epiphany   383–6 Matt. 2:1–12 (note)   391
'Erowde': Herod   394 'fyue m., ij. c and ode ȝeris': 5200⁺ (note)   399–400 Matt. 19:17

Variants   378 I *om.*   379 I *om.*   381 folˣoueˣ   383 twelfye   384 \þei ofrden/   • him² *om.*   394 fende
and fyue   395–6 manhede and bouȝte   397 þat] þat / þat   • \þe/   398 turne] and turne   399 woldist]
wist   • blsse   400 ˣþˣis   • ˣforˣ\fro/   401 turne] and turne   403 \of/ loue   406 turne] and turne   407
obstinanece   409 gostyly

deuele, þat is prince of al manere synnes, and by turnynge to Iesu Crist þat is þe
gronde and bygenere of alle vertues and goodenesse, þan schalt þou not fayle of
mercy, þe whiche he purchased wiþ [h]is o[w]e[n]e blod. For he seiþ by his profette
he wold not þe lastynge deþ of synners but he turne fro his wicked weies and leue. In
415   anoþer place he seiþ to eche synful sowle þus: 'þou haste | f. 78v | don lecherye wiþ
many wicked loueres; neþeles, turne aȝeyne to me and þer I reseyue þe to my
mercy'. And efte he seiþ 'wheþer a moder may forȝete here childer, þat sche haue
not rewþe of þe child of her owne body? Þowȝ sche forȝete I schal not fo[rȝete]
þe[e]; I haue writen þe in myn handis'. And in oþere places he seiþ 'whateuere oure
420   þe sennere forsakeþ his synne, he schal leue and not dye'. And, as þe gospel telleþ,
'hit is gret ioie to þe Fader of heuene and to his aungelis of eche synful man
forsakynge his synne'.
     But no man in triste of mercy be bold to do dedly synne, for many þorowȝ
þis foly han had þe peynes of helle. Nowe take hede to Peter, Poul, Mark, to Matheu
425   and to many mo, þat whan þei forsoken here synnes þei turned not to hem aȝeyne
wilfully but contynueden in vertues and endeden in hem. Þus, by ensan| f. 79r |pul of
hem, go we home by anoþer weye þan we wenten out, and þan schullen we be
fulfillid wit þe vij. ȝiftys of [þe] Holy Goste, and so by vertu of hem we schullen be
gouerned boþe ynward and outward by þe iiij. cardynal vertues. Moreouere, ȝif we
430   ben þus led by þe Hooly Gooste, we schullen, after oure power and kunnynge,
fulfillen þe vij. dedes of mercy boþe bodyly and goostly to pore blynd, to pore feble,
and to pore lame, as Criste byddeþ in þe gospel. And þan we schullen be rewarded
wit þe eyȝte blessynges of Criste rehersed in þe gospel of Alhalewen Day.

435   [*Fole*:] Syr, Y þanke oure mercyful Lord now my desyr[e] is to forsake alle synne
[and] to turne me to vertues to my lyues ende, in louynge God aboue alle þinge and
my ne[yȝ]tbore as myselfe.

[*Wyse Man*:] Broþer, kepe wel þis cloþinge of loue and charite to God and to | f. 79v |
þin euen-cristen; þen at þe daye of dome þou schalt enter wit þe kynge and [wiþ his
louers] in to þe cuntre of endlesse blisse, to þe whiche cuntre he ws brynge, þat
440   lyueþ and rengneþ witouten endynge, merciful God. Amen.

Glosses and biblical references   411–12 See Hebr. 12:2   413–14 Ezech. 18:32   414–17 Jer.
3:1   417–19 Is. 49:15–16; 'wheþer a moder may': may a mother   419–20 Ez. 3:18–21, 33:11
[etc.]   420–2 Luke 15:10   431–2 Luke 14:13–14 (note)   433 'Alhalewen': All Saints'

Variants   413 is • onewe   418 foloo   419 þer   428 þe *om.*   431 goostyly   434 desyry   435 and[1]
om. • turne *sup. ras.* • vertues to my and to my   436 neȝytbore   438–9 wiþ his louers] yueþ þis lyueþ
(note)

4

First seiþ Bois

f. 26r | Aȝens hem þat seyn þat hooli wriȝt schulde not or may not be drawn into
Engliche we maken þes resouns:

First seiþ Bois, in his boke *De Disciplina Scolarium*, þat children schulde be tauȝt in
þe bokis of Senek, and Bede expowneþ þis, seying children schulden be tauȝt in
vertues, for þe bokis of Senek ben morals, and for þei ben not tauȝt þus in her ȝogþe
þei conseyuen yuel maners and ben vnabel to conseyue þe sotil sciense of trewþe,
5   seyinge þe Wise Man 'wisdom schal not entre into a wicked soule', and moche þer of
þe sentence of Bede. And Algasel in his *Logik* seiþ þe soule of a man is as clene
myrour newe polichid, in wiche is seen liȝtliche þe ymage of man. But for þe puple
haþ not konynge in ȝoþe þe[i] han derke soulis and blyndid, so þat þei profiten not
but in falsenes, malice and oþer vices, and moche þer of þis mater.
10   O, siþen heþen philosefris wolden þe puple to profeten in natural science
how myche more schulden cristen men willen þe puple to profiten in science of
vertues, for so wolde God. For wane þe lawe was ȝouen to Moises in þe mounte of
Synay God ȝaf it in Ebrew for þat al þe pupel schuld vnderstonde it, and bad Moises
to rede it vnto hem to þe tyme þei vndrstodyn it, and he rede it, as is pleyn in
15   De[u]tronomie, 31º cº. And Esdrias also redde it from morou to mydday, as it is
pleyn in his first boke, 8º cº, apertily in þe stret, and þe eeres of þe puple weren
enten[t]ly ȝouen þerto and þei vnderstoden it, and þis þei miȝt not haue done but if it
hadde ben redde in þer modr-tounge, so þat þe pupel hering felle into grete
wepinge. In Deut., 32º cº, it is writen 'aske þi fadris and þei schullen schewe to þee,
20   and þin elderis and þei schulen sei to þee'. | f. 26v | Also þe profete seiþ 'how many

Glosses and biblical references   **Heading** 'drawn': translated   **1** 'Bois': Boethius (note)   **5**
Wisd. 1:4   **9** 'moche þer of þis mater': there is much more about the same subject in *Logik*   **10**
'natural science': knowledge of the natural world   **14** 'to þe tyme': until   **15–18** See Neh. 8:1–9
(note)   **16** 'apertily': publicly   **17** 'entently ȝouen þerto': attentively given to the law   **19–20**
Deut. 32:7   **20–3** Joel 1:2–3

Variants   **Heading** This is a determinacioun of a doctor of divinitie agaynst hem that say, it is not
lawfull to haue holy wrytte and other bookes in Englishe. Agaynst hem say that holy wrytt shoulde
not be drawen into Englishe we will make these reasons C1 < > holy writt shule < ... > be drawen into
englyshe we make these < ... > N1 A Notable Discourse for having ye Bible in English in ye time of Thomas
Arundell Bp. of Cant. L4 Tractatus Acephalus De S. Scriptura Anglice Legenda L8   **6** as] a C1 C2   **8**
ȝonnþe • þei] þe   **10** science] sciencis C2 N1   **14** to þe ... it *om.* C1 • þei] they playnly N1   **15**
detronomie • f\r/om   **16** his] the C1 C2 N1 • first] iiᵈᵉ N1 (note) • stret *expl.* C2   **17** entently C5,
intentiuelie C1 • m\i/ȝt   **19** wepinge] lovyng N1 • In] Also in C1

þings he haþ seid vnto oure faderis þei schul make hem knowen vnto her sones, and
þe sones þat scholen be borne of hem schulen rise and schullen teche þes þings to
her sonnes'. And þus seiþ Petre in his first pistile: 'be ȝe redi to fulfille to eche man
þat askeþ ȝouȝ in resoun, in feiþ and hope', and also Peter seiþ 'euery man as he haþ
25 taken grace mynyster he forþe to oþer men'. And in þe Apocalips it is writen: 'þe
housebonde and þe wiffe seyn "come!", and he þat hereþ seiþ he comeþ', þat Crist,
þat is heed of holi chirche is þe housbonde, and parfite prechouris and doctouris, þat
is þe wiffe, clepen þe puple to þe weies of heuene, and iche man þat heriþ clepe
oþer. Þus þis is confermede in Actus of Apostilis: þereas þe apostilis weren but rude
30 men and fischeris þei legeden þe prophecies, as Peter in þe first chapiter seid 'þe
Hooli Goost be þe moutþe of Dauid be Iudas, þat was þe duke of hem þat token
Crist', and more processe þere. In þe 2° c°, Peter seiþ 'it is writun be þe prophete
Ioel it schal be in þe laste daies, seiþ þe Lorde, I shal schede ouȝt of my spirite vpon
iche flesche; ȝoure sones and ȝoure douȝtteris schulen prophecie and ȝoure ȝonge
35 men schullen se viciouns', and more þer in processe. Also, in þe 15° c°, James seiþ,
allegginge þe profecie, 'aftr þes þings I schal turne aȝene [and] I schal make vp þe
tabernacle'. And þus þe apostilis, þat ben cleped ydiotes be scripture, allegeden here
and in many oþer placis þe profecies, and of þis it is notabile þat þe lewde puple in
þe olde lawe knewe ȝe lawe, notwithstandi[n]g þat God for synne hadde departed þe
40 tunges of hem, as it is opon in þe 11 chapitr of Genesis.
     If God wole, he loueþ not lesse vs cristen men in þes daies þan he | f. 27r |
dide þe pupel in þe olde testament but better, as he haþ scheued be þe mene of
Cristis passioun and be þe newe perfite lawe ȝouen to vs. And herfore on þe
Witsondaie he ȝaf to many diuerse nacions knowing of his lawe be on tunge, in
45 tokene þat he wolde alle men knewe his lawe, to his worschipe and her profite. For as
it is writun in þe boke of Numeri, þe 11 c°, wane Moises had chosen seuenty elder
men and þe spirite of God rested on hem and þei profecieden, twey men, as Eldad
and Medad, profeciden in castelis, and on seid to Moises 'sir, forbede hem', and he
seide 'wat enviest þou for me? Wo schal lette þat alle þe puple profecie, if God ȝif
50 hem his spirite?' And in Actus of Apostilis, þe 11° c°, seiþ Peter, wane he had
cristened Cornelie and his felowes repreued hym þerof for he was an heþen man, he
seid to hem 'if God haþ ȝouen to hem þe same grace þat he haþ ȝeuen to vs wiche
beleuen in our Lorde Iesu Crist, wo am I þat may forbede God?' And se[i]nt Poule

Glosses and biblical references   23–4 1 Pet. 3:15; 'fulfille': give satisfaction   25–6 Apoc. 22:17
30–2 Acts 1:16   26 'þat²': in other words   30–2 Acts 1:16; 'be Iudas': [spoke] concerning Judas;
'duke': leader   30 'legeden': cited   32 'more processe': further narrative   32–5 Acts 2:16–17   36
'allegginge': citing   35–7 Acts 15:16 (citing Amos 9:11); 'make vp': build again   30–2 Acts 4:13
39 'departed': divided   40 'opon': evident   43–5 Acts 2:1–11   44 'knowing': knowledge   45–50
Num. 11:25–9   48 'castelis': the camp   • 'on': one [Joshua]   49 'wo schal lette þat alle þe puple
profecie': who shall prevent all the people from prophesying   50–3 Acts 11:17   53–5 1 Cor. 14:5

Variants   22 h ˣyˣ\e/m   25–9 And in ... oþer *om.* Hoochstraten   29 conferm\e/de   30 legeden] allege
C1, alleggyd N1   32–3 it is ... Ioel *om.* C1   33 \of/   35–45 Also ... profite *om.* Hoochstraten   35–6 in þe
15° c° ... allegginge] James he allegeth C1   36 and *om.*   53 sennt

seiþ in 1 Cor., 14° c°, 'I wole euery man to speike wiþ tunges; more, forsoþe, to
55 profecie'; also he seiþ 'I schal preye with spirit and I schal preie with mynde', þat is,
wiþ affeccioun and wiþ vndrstandinge, and þis is myche better þan al-onli to haue
deuocioun in wordes and not in vndrstanding, and þis preueþ þe texte aftr, þat seiþ
'how schal he sei "amen" vpon þis blessing þat wot not wat þou seiste?' And on þis
seiþ þe doctor Lire 'if þe puple vnderstood þe preyour of þe prest it schal þe better
60 be lade into God and þe more deuouteli answere "amen"'. Also, in þe same chapeter,
he seiþ 'I wole raþer fyue wordes be spoken to þe vnderstanding of men þan ten
þousand þat þe[i] vnderstonden not'.

Also seuenti docturis withouten mo byfore | f. 27v | þe incarnacioun
translatiden þe Bibile into Greek ouȝt of Ebrew, and aftur þe ascencioun many
65 translatiden al þe Byble, summe into Greek and summe into Latyne, but seint Ierom
translatide it out of Ebrew into Latine, wos translacioun we vsen most. And so it was
translatid into Spaynesche tunge, Frensche tunge and Almayne, and oþer londes also
han þe Bibel in þer modur-tunge, as Italie haþ it in Latyn for þat is þer modur-tonge,
and be many ȝeeris han had. Worschiful Bede, in his first boke *De Gestis*
70 *Angulorum*, [3]° c°, telliþ þat seint Oswold kyng of Northehumberlond axide of þe
Scottys an holi [b]ischop, Aydan, to preche his puple, and þe kynge of hymself
interpreted it on Engliche to þe puple. If þis blessid dede be aloued to þe kynge of al
hooli chirche, how not now as wel auȝte it to be alowed a man to rede þe gospel on
Engliche and do þeraftur? It was herde of a worþi man of Almaine þat summe tyme
75 a Flemynge, his name was James Merland, translatid al þe Bibel into Flemyche, for
wiche dede he was somoned before þe pope of grete enmyte, and þe boke was taken
to examynacioun and trwly apreued [and] it was deliuered to hym aȝene in
conf[u]cioun to his enmyes. Also venerabile Bede, lede be þe spirit of God,
translatid þe Bibel, or a grete parte of þe Bibile, wos originals ben in many abbeis in
80 Englond. And Sistrence, in his fifte booke, þe 24 c°, seiþ þe euaungelie of Ion was
drawen into Engliche be þe forseide Bede, wiche euaungelie of Ion, and oþer
gospellis, ben ȝ[i]t in many placis of so oolde Englische þat vnneþe can any man
rede hem, for þis Bede regnede an hooly doctor after þe incarnacioun seuene

Glosses and biblical references   55 1 Cor. 14:15   57 'aftr': following   57–8 1 Cor. 14:16   60
'lade into': brought before   60 'answere': he may answer   61 'he', i.e., Paul   61–2 1 Cor.
14:19   63 'withouten mo': i.e., not to mention others   66 'it', i.e. the Hebrew scriptures   69
'worschipful': venerable   69 'his first boke': the first (note) book of his   74 'do þeraftur': act
in accordance with it   76–7 'was taken to examynacioun': went through the process of being
examined   77–8 'in confucioun to': to the discomfiture of   80 'Sistrence': Ranulf Higden
(note)   82 'vnneþe': scarcely

Variants   54 wole euery man to speike] woulde that euery man spake C1   60 answere] sayth C1   61
men] the people C1   62 þei] þe   65–6, summe¹ … most. *om.* Hoochstraten   68 haþ it in Latyn *inc.* L3
L4 L8   70 ȝ C1 L3 L4 L8 N1] 2   71 pischop   • of *om.* C1 L3 L4 L8 N1   73 auȝte] might L8   76 dede]
cause L4   77 and² *om.* C1 C5 L3 L4   78 confucioun C1 L4 L8 N1] conficioun C5, confutation L3   79
bibile] bible into englishe C1 L3 L4 L8 N1   80 was ˣand ˣ   82 ȝit] ȝt   • any man] ony englisshe man C1
L3 L4 L8 N1   83 regnede ˣregned ˣ

hundered | f. 28r | ʒeer and xxxij. Also a man of Loundon, his name was Wyring,
85   hadde a Bible in Englische of norþen speche wiche was seen of many men, and it
semed too houndred ʒeer olde. Also seint Poule seiþ 'if oure gospel is hid, it is hid to
hem þat schal be dampned', and eft he seiþ 'he þat knoweþ not schal not be knowen
of God'. Also Cistrence, in his sext bok, þe 1 c°, seiþ þat Alrede þe kynge ord[e]ined
opone scolis of diuerse artes in Oxenforde and he turnede þe best lawes into his
90   modor-tunge, and þe Sawter also, and he regned aftur þe incarnacioun eiʒt hundred
ʒeer and seuenti and þre.
    Also seint Thomas seiþ þat 'barbarus' is he þat vnderstandiþ not þat he redeþ
in his modor-tunge, and þerfore seiþ þe apostile 'if I kn[o]we not þe vertu of þe
voice to wome I speike I schal be to hym barbarus, and he þat speikeþ to me
95   barbarus, þat is to sey, he vnderstandiþ not wat þat I sey, ne I vnderstande not wat he
seiþ'. Sum men þenkyne hem to be barbaros wiche han not propur vnderstan[din]ge
of þat þat þei reden, to answere þerto in her modor-tunge. Also he seiþ þat Bede
drew into Englische þe liberal artis leste Engliche men schuldon be holden barbarus:
þis [seiþ] seint Thomas super primum *Pol[it]icorum, exponens hoc vocabulum*
100   'barbarus'. Also þe grette sutil clerk Lyncolne seiþ, in a sermon þat bigynneþ
'*Scriptum est de Leuitis*', if, he seiþ, any prest seie he can not preche, oo remedie is
resyne he vp his benefice; anoþer remedie is, if he wol not þus, recorde he in þe
woke þe nakid tixt of þe Soundaie Gospel þat he kunne þe groos story and telle it to
his puple, þat is, if he vndrstonde Latyne, and do he þis euery woke of þe ʒeer
105   forsoþe he | f. 28v | schal profite wel, for þus preched þe Lord seyng, Iohn 6°, 'þe
wordes þat I speike to ʒouʒ ben spirit and lijf'. If, forsoþe, he vndersto[n]de no
Latyn go he to oon of his neiʒtboris þat vnderstandiþ, wiche wole charitabily expone
it to hym, and þus edifie he his flock, þat is, his puple. Þus seiþ Lyncolne. And on
þis argueþ a clerk and seiþ 'if it is leuefful to preche þe naked text to þe pupel it is
110   also lefful to write it to hem, and consequentliche, be proces of tyme, so al þe Bibil'.
    Also a nobil hooly man, Richerde E[re]myte, drewe oon Englic[h]e þe
Sauter wiþ a glose of longe proces, and lessouns of *Dirige* and many oþer tretis, by
wiche many Engliche men han ben gretli edified, and he were cursed of God þat

---

Glosses and biblical references   86–7 2 Cor. 4:3.   87–8 1 Cor. 14:38   89 'opone': public   92
'Thomas [Aquinas]' (note)   93–6 1 Cor. 14:11   97 'answere þerto': respond to it   99 '*exponens
hoc vocabulum*': expounding this word   100 'Lyncolne': Robert Grosseteste (note)   102
'resyne he vp': let him resign   103 'groos': plain, literal   105–6 John 6:64   110 'Bibil [will
be written]'   111 'Richerde Eremyte': Richard Rolle (note)   112 'longe proces': considerable
length   • '*Dirige*': the office for the dead

Variants   84 and xxxij.] xxiiij. ca°. C1 L3 L4 L8 (note)   • Wyring] wearinge L3, wering C1 L4 N1, wernis
L8 (note)   85 seen ˣbeˣ   • of²] wiþ C1 L3 L4 L8   88 of *bis*   • ordeined] ordined C5, meynteyned L4   90
modor] moders C1 L3 L8   93 knewe   96 to be] to be seid C1 L8 N1   • barbarˣuˣ\o/s   • vnderstange   97
þat² *om.* C1 L3 L4 L8 N1   • þer\to/   • Bede drew *sup. ras.*   99 seiþ *om.*   • polecicorum   100 Lyncolne]
Lyncolniensis C1 L8   102–3 in þe ˣbokeˣ woke   106 vnderstode   • no] not C1 L3 L4 L8 N1   108 Lyncolne]
Lyncolniensis C1 L8   110 so *om.* C1 L4 L8   111 hooly *om.* C1 L3 L4 L8 N1   • Richerde] Richard Hampole
L3 L4 N1, Richard Hauepole C1 L8   • Eremyte] emyte   • drewe ˣouteˣ   • englice   113 and] and if he

wolde þe puple schulde be lewder eiþer worse þan þei ben. Also sire Wiliam
115 Thorisby, Erchebischop of 3ork, did do to drawe a tretys in Englisce be a
worschipful clerk wos name was Gaytrik, in þe wiche weren conteyned þe articulis
of þe feiþ, seuene dedli synnes, þe werkes of mercy and þe ten comandementis, and
sente hem in smale pagynes to þe comyn puple to lerne þis and to knowe þis, of
wiche ben 3it manye a copye in Englond. But þer ben summe þat seien if þe gospel
120 were on Engliche men my3ten li3tly erre þerinne, but wel [t]ouchiþ þis holi man
Richa[r]d Hampol suche men, expownyng þis tixte, '*ne auferas de ore meo verbum*
veritatis vsquequaque'. Þer he seiþ þus: 'þer ben not fewe but many þat wolen
sustene a worde of falsenes for God, not willing to beleue to konynge and better þan
þei ben. Þei ben liche to þe frendes of Iob, þat wiles þei enforsiden hem to defende
125 God þei offendeden greuosly in hym. And þou3 suche ben slayne and don myracles
| f. 29r | þei neuerþeles ben stynkyng martirs'. And to hem þat seien þat þe gospel on
En[g]liche wolde make men to erre, wyte wel þat we fynden in Latyne mo heretikes
þan of al[l]e oþer langagis, for þe *Decres* rehersiþ sixti Latyn eretikes. Also þe hooli
euaungelistis writen þe gospelle in diuerse langages, as Matheu in Iudee, Marke in
130 Ytalie, Luck in þe partyes of Achaie and Iohn in Asie, aftur he hadde writun þe
Apocalips in þe yle of Pathomos, and al þes writun in þe langage of þe same cuntre,
as seiþ Ardmakan. Also Ardmakan, in þe *Book of Questiouns*, seiþ þat þe sacrament
mai wel be made in iche comoun langage, for so, as he seiþ, diden þe apostilis. But
we coueyten not þat, but prey anticrist þat we moten haue oure bileue in Englische.
135 Also we þat han moche comyned wiþ þe Iewis knowen wel þat al my3ty men of
hem, in wat londe þei ben born, 3it þei han in Ebrew þe Bible, and þei ben more
actif [in] þe olde lawe þane any Latyn man comonli, 3he, as wel þe lewde men of þe
Iewes as prestis. But it is red in comyne of þe prestis to fulfille þer prestes office and
to edificacioun of porayle þat for slouþe stoudieþ no3t. And þe Grekis wiche ben
140 nobel men han al þis in þer owne langage.

Glosses and biblical references   115 'did do to drawe': had translated   118 'pagynes':
pages (note)   120 'li3tly': easily   121–2 Ps. 118:43; 'ne auferas de ore meo verbum veritatis
vsquequaque': do not altogether take the word of truth from my mouth   123 'for': in the sight
of • 'konynge and better': more learned and virtuous men   124 'enforsiden hem': strove   125
'in': against   132 'Ardmakan': Richard FitzRalph (note)   135 'moche comyned': had many
dealings with   137 'actif in þe olde lawe': practised in the Old Testament • 'Latyn man':
member of the Roman Catholic Church • '3he': yes indeed   138 'in comyne of': together
by   139 'porayle': the poor

Variants   114 be ˣlernedˣ   115 did do to drawe] did draw N1, drew C1 L3 L4 L8   117 þe feiþ] byleve
C1 L3 L4 L8 N1 Hoochstraten   119 copye] componye   120–1 wel … tixte] well to which this holy
man Ric. Hauepole expoundith this textt L8   120 touchiþ] couchiþ C5, teecheth L4 N1, tech< > L3,
toucheth(?) C1 (note)   121 richad   125 don] donn   127 enliche • wolde] will C1 L4 L8 N1 • wyte]
wott ye C1 L3 L4 L8   128 ale • sixti] 66 C1 L3 L4 L8 N1, syxty Hoochstraten (note)   131 þes] þo C1 L4
L8   134 coueteyten • prey *om.* C1 L4 L8, *ras.* N1, *des.* L3 (note) • but prey anticrist þat we moten haue]
but that Antechrist geue us leaue to haue Hoochstraten   135 my3ty] þe gret C1 L3 L4 L8   136 \3it/   137
in] of

But ȝit aduersaries of trewiþ seien, wane men rehersen þat Grekis and Latyns
han al in þer owne langage, þe clerkis of hem speiken gramaticalliche and þe pupel
vndersto[n]diþ it not. Witte þei þat þouȝ a clerke or anoþer man þus lerned can sette
his wordis on Engliche better þan a rewde man it foloweþ not herof þat oure langage
145   schuld be destried. It were al on to sei þis and to kitte oute þe tunges of hem þat can
not speke | f. 29v | þus curiosly. But þei schulde vnderstande þat gramaticaliche is
not ellis but abite of riȝt spekyng and riȝt pronounsyng and riȝt writynge. But frere
Tille, þat seide before þ[e] buschop of Londoun, heerynge an hundrid men, þat
Ierom seide he errid in translatyng of þe Bibel, is lijk to Elymas, þe wiche wolde
150   have lettid a bischope or a iuge to heere þe byleue, to wom Poule seid 'O þou, ful of
al trecherie and of al falace, seching to turne þe buschop from þe beleue, þou schalt
be blynde to a tyme'. Þis [is] writun in þe Dedus of þe Apostilis, 13 cᵒ. For Ierom
seiþ in þe prolog of Kyngis 'I am not knowyng to myself in any maner me to haue
changy[d] anyþinge from þe Ebrew trewiþ. Wel I wot,' he seide, '[þat sum tyme]
155   holy writ was false aftur þe letter'. But aftur, wane Austyn hadde writen to him and
he to him aȝen, he grantid wele þat it was trewe, as he rehersiþ in a pistile and in þe
prolog of þe Bible, and was glad and ioyeful of his translacioun. And þerfor, wane
he haþ rehersi[y]d al þe bookis of þe Bibel, þane he seiþ in þe prolog of Penteteuke
'I praie þe, dere broþer, lyue amonge þese, haue þi meditacioun in þese, knowe noon
160   oþer þing [nor seche non oþer þing] but þese'. But Ierom hadde many enemyes for
translating of þe Bibel, as he rehersiþ in þe first prolog to his enemye þus: 'whi art
þou turmented be enueye? What stirist þou þe willes of vnkunnynge men aȝens me?
If it semeþ to þe þat I haue erred in myn translacion aske þe Ebrew[es], councel wiþ
þe maisteris of diuerse citees'. In þe secunde prolog he seiþ 'þis we seeyn (rehersing
165   þe sentence bifore) leest we ben seen to holde oure pes aȝens [de]batourus'. And in
þe same he seiþ: 'we, hasting to oure contre, schullen passe wiþ | f. 30r | a deffe eere
to þe dedely songis of þe mermaidens'. And þus in many prologis he scorneþ his
enemyes and lettiþ not his hooly werk but seiþ: 'I seide, I schal kepe my weies þat I
trespas not in my tounge; I haue put keping to my mouþ wane þe synful man haþ
170   stande aȝens me'. Þese ben þe wordes of Ierom rehersing þe profiȝte.

Also it is knowen to many men þat in þe tyme of kyng Richerd, whos soule
God asoile, into a parliment was put a bille, be assent of two erchebischopis and of

---

Glosses and biblical references   142 'al [the Bible]'   • 'gramaticalliche': in accordance with
[archaic] grammar   145 'al on': one and the same   146 'curiosly': skilfully   149–52 Acts
13:10–11; 'to': for   150 'lettid … to': prevented from   153 'I am not knowyng to myself': to my
knowledge   155 'false aftur þe letter': inaccurate according to the literal sense   164 'seeyn':
say   168–70 Ps. 38:2   170 'profiȝte', i.e., David   172 'asoile': grant pardon to

Variants   141–7 'writynge'] *om.* and added after line 191 C1 L3 L4 L8 N1 (note)   142 of hem *om.* C1
L3 L4 L8 N1   143 vnderstodiþ   • it not] not what þai seyn C1 L3 L4 L8   148 þe] þi   152 is *om.*   154
changyd] changyng   • þat sum tyme] sum tyme þat C5 N1   158 rehersiþd   160 nor seche non oþer
þing C1 L3 L4 L8 N1, *om.* C5   161 enemye] enemyes   163 Ebrewes] ebrew   165 debatourus] þe batourus
(note)   167 songis] soungyis   170 profiȝte] prophecie C1 L4 L8, *des.* L3

þe clergie, to anulle þe Bible þat tyme translatid into Engliche, and also oþer bokis
of þe gospel translatid into Engliche, wiche, wanne it was seyn of lordis and
175 comouns, þe good duke of Lancastre, Ion, wos soule God asoile for his mercy,
answered þerto scharpely, seying þis sentence, 'we wel not be þe refuse of alle men,
for siþen oþer naciouns han Goddis lawe, wiche is lawe of oure byleue, in þer owne
modur-langage, we wolone haue oure in Engliche, wo þat euere it bigrucche'. And
þis he affermede wiþ a grete oþe.
180   Also þe bischope of Caunturbiri, Thomas Arrundel þat nowe is, seide a
sermoun in Westminster þeras weren many hundred puple at þe biriyng of quene
Anne, of wos soule God haue mercy, and in his comendyngis of hir he seide it was
more ioie of hir þan of any whoman þat euere he knewe, for notwiþstanding þat sche
was an alien borne sche hadde on Engliche al þe foure gospeleris wiþ þe docturis
185 vpon hem. And he seide sche hadde sent hem vnto him, and he seide þei weren
goode and trewe, and comended hir in þat sche was so grete a lady and also an alien
and wolde so lowliche studiee in so vertuous bokis. And he blamed in þat sermoun
scharpeli þe necligence of prelatis | f. 30v | and of oþer men, in so miche þat summe
seiden he wolde on þe morowe leue vp his office of chaunceler and forsake þe
190 worlde, and þan it hadde be þe [b]est sermoun þat euere þei herde.

Glosses and biblical references   173 'anulle': declare invalid   176 'refuse': rejected [ones] (*pa.
p. subst. adj.*)   189 'leue vp': resign

Variants   173 þat tyme *om.* C1 L4 L8 N1   178 modur *om.* C1 L3 L4 L8 N1   • we … Engliche *om.* C1 L3
L4 L8 N1   182 comendyngis] commendatioun C1 L3 L4 L8   184 gospeleris] gospellis C1 L3 L4 L8 N1   190
worlde] wordly busynes and gyue hym to fulfylle his pastoralle office for that he hade seyn and redde in tho
bookes Hoochstraten   • and þan … herde *om.* Hoochstraten   • best C1 L3 L4 L8 N1] lest

The Holi Prophete Dauid

f. 1r | The holi prophete Dauid seiþ, in þe persone of a iust man, 'Lord, how swete ben þi spechis to my chekis', þat is, to myn vndirstondyng and loue, and þe prophete answeriþ and seiþ 'þo ben swettere þan hony to my mowþ'. Eft þe same prophete seiþ, in þe persone of a iust man, 'Lord, I was glad of þine spechis as he þat fyndiþ many spoilis eiþir praies'. Eft þe same prophete seiþ 'þe domes of þe Lord ben trewe and iustified in hemsilf; þo ben more desiderable þan gold and precious stones, and swettere þan hony and honycomb; forwhi þi servant kepiþ þo, and moche reward is to kepe hem'. Þerfore, he seiþ, 'moche pees is to hem þat louen þi lawe, and to hem is no sclandre', for þei 3yuen no sclandre to oþere men bi euel dede ne bi yuel word, and þei ben not sclandrid for tribulacioun and persecucioun, but þei suffre gladli and ioie| f. 1v |fulli tribulacioun and persecucioun for þe laue of God. Eft þe same prophete seiþ 'blessid is þe man þat 3ede not in þe counceil of vnfeiþful men and stood not in the wei of synneris and sat not in þe chaier of pestelence', þat ys, pride eiþir wordli glorie, 'but his wille is in þe lawe of þe Lord and he schal hawe mynde bi ny3t and bi day in þe lawe of þe Lord'. For, as þe same prophete seiþ, 'Lord, þi word is a lanterne to my feet', þat ys, to rule myne affecciouns and myne werkis, 'and þi word is li3t to my paþis', þat is, myne þow3ttis and myne counceilis'. And eft he seiþ 'þe comaundement of þe Lord is li3tful, and li3tneþ i3es of þe sowle', þat is, resoun and wille, and eft he seiþ 'þe declaryng of þyne wordis 3yueþ goostli li3t, and 3yueþ vndirstondyng to meke men'.

For þise auttorites and siche oþere, | f. 2r | sum men of good wille redin besili þe text of holi writ for to kunne it and kepe it in here lyuynge, and teche it to oþere men bi hooli ensample, and for þe staat þat þei stondyn ynne and for þis werk þei han þe blissyng of God, as he seiþ in þe gospel, Luc. xiº, 'blessid ben þei þat heryn þe word of God and kepin it', and, in þe first chapetre of Apocalips, seynt Ioon seiþ 'he is blessid þat heeriþ and rediþ þe wordis of þis prophecie, and kepiþ þo þyngis þat ben writen þerynne'. But oþere veyn men

---

Glosses and biblical references   1 'persone': role   1–3 Ps. 118:103   4–5 Ps. 118:162   5–8 Ps. 18:10–12   7 'desiderable': desirable   8 'forwhi': therefore   9–10 Ps. 118:165   13–16 Ps. 1:1   14 'chaier': seat   17–19 Ps. 118:105   18 'affecciouns': desires   19–20 Ps. 18:9; 'li3tful': luminous   21–2 Ps. 118:130; 'declaryng': elucidation   26–7 Luke 11:28   27–8 Apoc. 1:3

Variants   1 a iust *sup. ras.*   10 scland\r/e   15 of \þe/   17 fe\e/t   24 of ˣoˣ   26 as \he/ seiþ

30 besie hem faste to studie to kunne þe lettre of Goddis lawe, and þei bisie hem
nat treuli to kepe þe sentence þerof, and þerfore þei disceyuen hemself, and in
maner sclaundren þe lawe of God. First þei schulde studie to kunne wel þe
trewe sentence of Goddis lawe, aftirward to kepe it in werk, and þanne to
speke þerof | f. 2v | mekeli and charitabli to þe edificacioun of oþere men; for
35 if þei iangelyn oonli of þis blessid lawe, to schewe here cunnynge abowe oþere
men, and kepe not it opynli in here werkis but doon opynli þe contrarie, þei
ben contrarie to hemsilf, and þis cunnynge turnyþ hem to more dampnacioun.
For Crist seiþ in þe gospel, Luc. xijᵒ, 'a seruant þat knowiþ þe wille of his lord
and dooþ it not schal be betyn wiþ many betyngis'. Iames seiþ, in þe iiij. ch., 'it
40 is synne to hym þat can good and dooþ it not'. And Poul seiþ 'kunnynge
makiþ a man proud', þat is, nakid kunnynge wiþoute goode werkis, whanne it
is medlid wiþ pride, veynglorie and boost. Siche men semen to do goostli
auoutrie wiþ þe word of God, for þere þei schulde take of þe Hooli Goost
trewe vndirstandyng of hooli writ, bi gret meknesse and hooli praier to brynge
45 forþ very charite and goode werkis, þei | f. 3r | takyn þe nakid vndirstondynge
bi presumcioun of mannes witt, and bryngen forȝt pride, veynglorie and boost
to coloure here synnis and disceiue sutilli here neȝebours.
    Siche maner of peple schulden takyn hede what Poul comaundiþ, 'to
kunne no more þan nediþ to kunne, but to kunne to sobirnesse', þat is, as
50 moche as perteyneþ to saluacioun of þin owene sowle eiþir to edificacioun to
oþere mennes. And Bernard expounneþ þis auctorite *On Cantica*, xxxvj.
sermoun, and writiþ þus: 'to vndirstonde to sobernesse' is to kepe most
wakyngli what it bihoueþ to kunne more and sunnere. Þe tyme is schort. Ech
trewe science is good in itsilf, but þou þat hastist for þe schortnesse of tyme to
55 'worche þyn owne helþe wiþ drede and tremblyng', do þi besynesse to kunne
sunnere and more þo þyngis þat ben ner to helþe. Alle metis | f. 3v | ben goode
wiche God haþ fourmed; naþeles, ȝif in takynge hem þou kepist not maner and
ordre þou makist hem not goode. Fele ȝe also þis þing of sciencis which I seie
of metis. Poul seiþ 'he þat gessiþ hymsilf to kunne onyþyng woot not ȝit hou it
60 bihoueþ hym to kunne'. Poul appreueþ not a man þat can manie þyngis, if he
cunne not þe maner of kunnynge. Poul haþ set þe fruit and profit of science in
þe maner of kunnynge; þe maner of kunnynge is þat þou wete bi what ordre,
by what studie and for what entent it behoueþ to kunne alle þyngis. Bi what
ordre: þat þou kunne first þat þyng þat lediþ ripliere to helþe. Bi what studie:

Glosses and biblical references   30 'faste': intently   35 'iangelyn': chatter   36 'opynli':
manifestly   38–9 Luke 12:47   39–40 Jas. 4:17   40–1 1 Cor. 8:1   42 'medlid': mixed   42–3
'goostli auoutrie': spiritual adultery   47 'coloure': pretence   48–9 Rom. 12:3   49 'to sobirnesse':
soberly   51 'mennes' [souls]   • 'þis auctorite', i.e., Rom. 12:3   53 'sunnere': more speedily   55
Phil. 2:12; 'worche þyn owne helþe': work out your own salvation   59–60 1 Cor. 8:2   64
'ripliere': more immediately

Variants   37 þis ˣcˣ   38 seru\a/nt   39 schal \be/   42 men \semen/   45 nakid ˣwordˣ   61 kunnynge
followed by 5⁺-letter erasure   62 w\h/at   63 w\h/at   63 for ˣwaˣ

65 þat þou lerne more brennyngli þat þyng þat lediþ greetliere to þe loue of God
and neȝebour. For what ende: þat þou lerne not to veyn glo| f. 4r |rie eiþir to
coriouste eiþir to ony sich þyng, but oneli to edifiyng of þisilf or of þi
neȝebour. Sum men wolen kunne for þat ende oneli þat þei cunne, and it is
foul coriouste; and sum men wolen cunne þat þei be knowen, and it is a foul
70 vanyte; and sum men wolen cunne for to sille here kunnyng for mony eiþir for
honowris, and it is foul wynnynge. Sum men wolen kunne for to edifie here
neȝebours, and þat is charite; sum men wolen kunne þat þei hemsilf be edified,
and þat is prudence. Þise tweyne laste ben preciable; of alle þe oþere heere þei
Iames seiynge 'synne is to hym þat can good and dooþ it nat'. As mete
75 vndefied gendriþ yuele humours and corrumppiþ þe bodi and not norischiþ, so
moche kunnyng had in mynde if it is not defied bi charite. Whanne þe soule is
not maad good bi | f. 4v | witnessynge of þe liyf of vertues, þilke kunnynge
schal be arettid into synne, as mete þat is turnyd into schrewid and noiful
humors. Wher a man þat can good [is] not dooynge good, schal he not haue
80 bolnyngis and turmentis in his conscience? (as who sei 'ȝhis'). Wher he schal
not hawe so ofte in hymsilf answere of deeþ and of dampnacioun, how ofte þe
word of God þat is seid schal come into his mende? (as who sei 'ȝhis'). 'For a
seruant þat knowiþ þe wil of his lord and dooþ it not schal be betyn wit many
woundis.' All þis is þe sentense of Bernard.
85   Þerfore, alle men þat wolen stodie hooli writ scholden studie to þis
entent, to knowe here owene freelte and defautis and eschewe deedli synnes,
and to kepe wilfulli þe comaundementis of God, and to do þe werkis of merci
and ȝewe hooli ensam| f. 5r |ple to here neȝebours. Wherfore þe Wise Man seiþ
'sone, þou þat desirest wisdam, kepe riȝtwisnesse, and God schal ȝyue it to
90 þe'. And eft 'sone, þou þat neiȝist to þe seruice of God, stonde in drede and
riȝtwisnes, and make þi soule redi to temptacioun', bi Godis grace and þyn
owene besynesse, for 'þe drede of þe Lord is bigynnyng of wisdom'. And
seynt Gregor seiþ hooli writ is to vs to se þerynne oure defautis and amende
hem, and to se goode ensamplis of hooli fadris and to kepe þo in oure lyuynge.
95   Cristene men wondren moche on þe weiwarnesse of diuers clerkis þat
bosten þat þei han passynly þe cunnynge of hooli writ, siþþen þei makyn
hemself most vnable þerto, for þei feynen to studie, kunne and preche hooli
writ for pride of þe word, for couetise of erþeli goo| f. 5v |dis and for wombe
ioie, to lewe in delices bodeli, ese and ydilnesse. Aȝenes hem seiþ God, Prov.

Glosses and biblical references   67 'coriouste': fastidiousness   71 'wynnynge': gain   73
'preciable': worthy   74 Jas. 4:17   75 'vndefied': undigested   78 'arettid into': reckoned as   •
'schrewid and noiful': evil and harmful   80 'bolnyngis': swellings, tumours   • 'as who sei
"ȝhis"' (note)   80–1 'wher he schal not hawe': shall he not have   81 'so ofte … hou ofte': as
often … as   82–4 Luke 12:47   86 'defautis': errors   87 'wilfulli': willingly   88–90 Ecclus
1:33   90–1 Ecclus 2:1; to [encounter] temptation   92 Prov. 1:7   96 'passynly': surpassingly

Variants   78 sch\r/ewid   79 is] and   91 riȝtwisne\s/   95 diu\ers/ followed by 2-letter erasure   96
þa\t/

100 xii° ch., 'he þat suyþ ydilnesse is most fool', and the Lord Iesu seiþ, Mt. xj°
ch., 'Fadir, lord of heuene and of herþe, I knoweleche to þe', þat is, I herie þe,
'for þow hast hid þise þyngis', þat is, preuites of hooli writ, 'fro wise men and
prudent' of þe world, 'and þow hast schewid þo to meke men'. And Crisostom
seiþ þat good leuynge is a lanterne to brynge men to veri vndirstondyng of holi
105 writ, and wiþoute good lyuyng and þe drede of God no man is wise. And þe
Wise Man seiþ, Sapience, ij°, 'wisdom schal not entre into an yuel-willid soule,
neþer schal dwelle in a bodi suget to synnes'. Siþen þese grete synnes bifore-
seid makyn þe dewel to dwelle and to regne in þe sowle of siche veyn clerkis,
no wondir | f. 6r | þou3 he brynge hem to gostli blindnesse and fals
110 vndirstondyng of hooli writ.

 Þese men semen grete foolis þat poisone hemself bi þe mystakynge and
[mys]vndirstondynge of þe hoolsum mete of hooli writ, and þei binde hemsilf
bi ropis of deedli sinnes, and betake hem prisoneris to þe deuyl, and bryngen
þe chayne of deedli synne abowte here nekk, wherbi þei schollen ben hangid
115 in helle. And þerfore hooli writ seiþ, Prov., v. ch, 'þe wikkidnesses of an yuel
man takyn him, and ech is strei3tli bounden wiþ þe ropis of hise sinnes'. Þise
men ben grete foolis in alle maner, for if þei han verili þe vndirstondyng of
holi writ, and doon wetyngli and custumabli þera3enes, þei goon lyuynge doun
to helle, as seynt Austin seiþ on þis word on þe salm *descendant in infernum*
120 *viuentes*. And if þei han not þe trewe vn| f. 6v |dirstondyng of hooli writ, and
bosten þat þei han it passande alle oþere men, þanne be þei opyn foolis, fouli
disseyued of þe deuel, þe world and of þere fleisch. Pryncipali, þise clerkis ben
grete folis þat wiþ sich lyuynge prechen opynli þe lawe of God, for as
Crisostom seiþ on Mt. v. ch., on þat word *vos estis sal terre, vos estis lux*
125 *mundi*, he þat lyueþ yuele opynli in knowyng of þe peple, and prechiþ treuli þe
laue of God, dampnyþ hymself, sclandriþ oþere men and blasfemeþ God.

 Siche proude clerkis and blyndid in peyne of here synnes schulden
taken hede what Crist seiþ, in Mt. xxiij° ch., to þe blynde saduceis, where
Matheu writiþ þus: '3e erren, 3e kunne not þe scripturis neiþir þe vertu of
130 God', wheron Crisostom writiþ þus, in þe xxxviij. omelie: wisli Crist repreueþ
first þe necligence of hem, for þei redden not. | f. 7r | The secunde tyme he
repreueþ here ignorance, for þei knewyn not God, for þe science of God
comeþ of diligence of redynge. Truli, ignoraunce of God is dou3ter of
necligence; treuli, if not alle men redynge knowyn God, hou schal he knowe
135 þat rediþ not? Þanne men redynge knowe no treuþe whanne þei redyn not
wyllynge to fynde treuþe. He þat rediþ scripturis of God and wole fynde God,

Glosses and biblical references   **99–100** Prov. 12:11   **100–3** Matt. 11:25   **101** 'herie':
praise   **105–7** Wisd. 1:4   **106** 'yuel-willid': malevolent   **115–16** Prov. 5:22   **118** 'wetyngli':
knowingly   **118–20** Ps. 54:16 (note)   **123** 'opynli': publicly   **124** Matt. 5:13; '*vos … mundi*': you
are the salt of the earth; you are the light of the world   **128–30** Matt. 22:29

Variants   **112** vndirstondynge   • of¹ followed by an 8/9-letter erasure   • þei followed by a 3-letter
ersasure   **115–16** \of an yuel … strei3tli/   **117** fo\o/lis   **123** wiˣtˣ\þ/   **132** repreueþ ˣfistˣ   **133** of² ˣofˣ

haste he to lyue worþili to God and his good lyuynge is maad as þe leȝt of
lampe bifore hise iȝen of his herte, and openeþ þe wai of treuþe. Treuli, he þat
hàstiþ not to lewe worþili to God and rediþ of God sekiþ not God to his helþe
140   but onli þe kunnynge of God, to ve[y]nglorie. Þerfore, þouȝ he rede euere, he
schal neuere fynde, as neiþir philosophris founden wiche souȝten for þe sa
| f. 7v |me cause. Gessist þou þat prestis of saduceis redden not scripturis? But þei
myȝte not fynde God in hem, for þei wolde not lyue worþili to God. For goode
wordis myȝte not teche hem þe whiche here yuele werkis tauȝten þat is
145   blyndid in errour, forwhi sich is scripture to a man not willynge to lyue aftir
God as if ony man expounne lernynge of bataile to an erþeteliere not hauynge
wille for to fiȝte. And so aȝenward of a knyȝt, [if ony man expounne erþe-
telþe to a knyȝt not hauynge wille to telie þe erþe], þouȝ he here aldai wordis
of his declaryng he mai noþyng vndirstonde or take, for he haþ no desire to his
150   lore; for where is mannes desire þere his witt is dressid. Þis is þe sentense of
Crisistom.
       But of alle foolis blyndid of þe deuel þise ben most folis, þat seyn and
mayntenen opynli þat holi writ is fals. For Dauid seiþ 'alle þe | f. 8r |
comoundementis of þe Lord ben feiþful; þo ben maad in treuþe and equite'.
155   And eft Dauid seiþ to God 'þe begynnynge of þyne wordis is treuþe', and eft
he seiþ to God 'þi laue is treuþe', and eft 'alle þyne comaundementis ben
treuþe'. *Item* God seiþ, þe viij. ch. of Prouerbis, 'alle myne wordis ben riȝtful,
and no schrewid þyng and no weiward þyng is in hem; þo ben riȝtful to hem
þat vndirstonden, and þei ben euene to hem þat fyndyn kunnynge'. Also, in þe
160   xxx. ch. of Prouerbis holi writ seiþ 'euery word of God is a scheld of feir', þat
is, purid in treuþe and charite, 'to hem þat hopyn in hym', and Ion seiþ in þe
ende of Apocalips 'þise wordis of þe Lord ben most feiþful', and oure Lord
Iesu seiþ 'þe Lord is feiþful in alle hise wordis, and he is hooli in alle hese
werkis'. But þise heretikis seyn cur| f. 8v |sidli þat God is fals and his lawe ys
165   fals, for if þe lawe of God is fals, as þei seyn opynly, þanne God is fals, siþen
he is auctour of þis lawe. And ȝit þese folis seyn aȝens hemself whanne þei
seyn þat hooli writ is fals, for yf it is holy it is not fals in ony maner, and,
aȝenward, if it is fals it is not hooli. Þise heretikis mysundirstonden hooli writ,
and þei clepin her ownene errour hooli writ, and þus þe deuyl blyndiþ hem and
170   disseywyþ hem and beiapiþ hem. As a drunke man demeþ of a candele to be
tweyne or þre, so þese foolis demen þat hooly writ haþ many false

---

Glosses and biblical references   146 'erþeteliere': farmer   147 'aȝenward': conversely   149 'his
declaryng': the farmer's teaching   150 'dressid': directed   152 'most': the greatest   153–4 Ps.
110:8   155 Ps. 118:160   156 Ps. 118:142   156–7 Ps. 118:138   157 'item': likewise   157–9 Prov.
8:8–9; 'euene': plain   159–61 Prov. 30:5   161 'hopyn': believe   161–2 Apoc. 19:9   162–4 Ps.
144:17   170 'beiapiþ': tricks

Variants   140 venglorie   147–8 if ony man … þe erþe *om.* (note)   158 sch/r/ewid   • þyng¹] þyngis   160
word of ˣgoddisˣ   162 ende ˣofˣ of   164 godˣdisˣ   168 hooli *sup. ras.*   169 \and þei … writ, and/   170
beiapiþ \hem/   171 foolis *sup. ras.*

vndirstondyngis, where it haþ on oonli trewe vndirstondyng, aftir þe entent of
þe Hooli Gost. Þerfore seynt Ierom and Ysedere seyn, 24 cause, q. 3ª, cº,
Heresis and cº, *Quidam*, whoeuere vndirstondiþ hooli writ oþirwise þan þe
175 Hooli Goost askiþ, of whom is wreten, he may be clepid an heretik. And seynt
Austyn seiþ, in his | f. 9r | epistil to Ierom, if ony part of holy writ were fals al
were suspect. Þise heretikis wolden menyn þus, þat þe text of hooli writ is fals
but here fleischli vndirstondyng is trewe and of auctorite, and þus þei
magnefien hemself and her errour more þan God and hooly writ. And þus þei
180 ben opyn anticristis and moost perilous heretikis þat euere risen up aȝens hooli
chirche, but, as blasfemers of God were stoned of al þe peple bi Goddis doom
in Moises lawe, Leu[i]tici xxiiij., so alle cristene men schulde stone þise
heretikis and blasfemers bi stonis of þe gospel, þat is, scharp and opyn
repreuynge and castynge out of cristene lond.
185   But leue we alle þise cursidnessis bifore-seid and comforte we cristene
peple to take trustili and deyutously þe tixt of hooly writ and þe trewe
vndirstondyng þerof. Cristene men schulden preye deuoutli to God, auctor of
al wisdom and kunnynge, þat he ȝiue to | f. 9v | hem trewe vndirstondyng of
hooli writ. Þus seiþ þe Wyse Man: 'Lord, ȝiwe þou to me wysdom þat stondiþ
190 aboute þi setis', þat I wete what failiþ to me and what is plesaunt befor þee in
al tyme. The secunde tyme, þei schulde meke hemsilf to God in doynge
penaunce, þat God opene to hem þe trewe vndirstondyng of his lawe, as he
openede witt to hise apostlis to vndirstonde hooli scripture. The þridde [tyme],
þei schulden sugette hemself to þe wille of God and bileue stidfastly þat his
195 laue is trewe, and truste feiþfuli in Goddis help, and for þis þei schullen haue
þe blissyng of God and þe blesse of hewene, and schullen graciousli be herd in
here preier, for God despiciþ not þe praier of meke men, and he heriþ þe desire
of pore men þat knowen verili þat þei haue no good but of God. The fourþe
tyme, þei schulden meke hemself to here breþeren and enquere mekeli of
200 euery lerned man, and spe| f. 10r |ciali of wel-wellid men and weel-lyuynge, þe
trewe vndirstondyng of hooli writ, and be þei not obstinat in þer owne wit, but
ȝyue stede and credence to wisere men, þat han þe sperit of wisdom and of
grace. The fifþe tyme, rede þei besili þe text of þe newe testament, and take
þei ensample of þe hooly liyf of Crist and of hise apostlis, and truste þei fulli
205 to þe goodnesse of þe Hooli Goost, wich is spesial techere of wel-willid men.
For Crist seiþ in þe gospel to hise disciplis 'þe Hooli Goost schal teche ȝou al
treuþe þat is necessarie to helþe of soulis', and Ioon seiþ in his epistil 'þat
anoyntyng,' þat is, grace of þe Hooli Goost, 'techiþ ȝow of alle þingis þat
perteyneneþ to helþe of sowle'. The sixte tyme, þei schulden see and studie þe

Glosses and biblical references   173 'Ysedere': Isidore (note)   175 'of whom is': by whom it
is   179 'magnefien': exalt   181–2 Lev. 24:16   183 'scharp and opyn': harsh and public   189–90
Wisd. 9:4   197 Ps. 68:34   200 'wel-wellid': benevolent   206–7 John 16:13   207–9 1 John 2:27

Variants   172 aftir ˣaˣ   182 leuetici   189 wyse \man/   • ȝiwe \þou/   193 ho\o/li   • tyme *om.*   200
we\e/l

210   trewe and opyn expo| f. 10v |sicioun of hooli doctours and oþere wise men, as
       þei may eseli and goodli come þerto.
            Lat cristene men trauaile feiþfulli in þise vj. weies, and be not to moche
       aferid of obiecciouns of enemyes seyynge þat 'þe lettere sleeþ'. Þise enemyes
       menyn þus, þat þe letere of hooli writ is harmful to men and fals and
215   repreuable, siþen þat it sleeþ men bi deeþ of synne. But sekirli þei mystaken þe
       wordis of hooly writ, and here mystakyng and weiward menynge and here
       wickide lyuynge bryngen in deeþ of soule, þat is, synne. But aȝens here fals
       menynge Crist seiþ in þe gospel of Ioon, vj. cap., 'þe wordis wiche I haue
       spoken to ȝou ben sperit and liyf', and in þe same chapetre seynt Peter seiþ to
220   Crist 'Lord, þou hast wordis of euerlastyng liyf'. Poul seiþ, ijᵃ Tess. ij., þat 'þe
       Lord Iesu, bi þe spirit of his mouþ', þat is, his hooli and trewe wordis, 'sch
       | f. 11r |al sle anticrist', and þe prophete Isaie seiþ, xj. ch., þat 'God, bi þe spirit of
       hise lippis schal sle þe wickid man', þat is, anticrist. Þanne, siþen þe wordis of
       Crist ben wordis of euerlastyng liyf, þat is, brynge trewe men to euerlastyng
225   blisse, and siþen þise wordis schulyn sle anticrist, þe wordis of Crist been ful
       hooly and ful miȝty and ful profitable to trewe men.
            But Poul menyþ þus, bi auctorite of þe Hooly Goost, whanne he seyþ
       'þe lettere sleeþ', þat cerymonyes eiþir sacrifices of þe elde lawe wiþoutyn
       goostli vndirstondyng of þe newe lawe, sleeþ men bi errour of mysbileue, for
230   if men holden þat bodeli circumcisioun is nedful now, as it was in þe elde
       testament, it is errour and mysbileue aȝens þe treuþe of þe gospel. Also, if men
       holden þat þe sacrifice of bestes is nedful now, as it was bifore Cristis
       passioun, it is errour and mysbeleue aȝens Crist and his gospel. Þerfore þis
       lettere, vndirstonden þus fleischli, sleeþ | f. 11v | þe mysundirstonders. Þerfore
235   Poul seiþ 'þe sperit quekeneþ', þat is, goostli vndirstondyng of ceremonyes
       and sacrifices of Moises lawe quekeneþ men of riȝt bileue þat now in stede of
       bodeli circumsisioun takyn baptym, tauȝt and comaundid of Crist, and in stede
       of sacrifices of bestis in þe elde lawe takyn now Crist and his passioun, and
       hopyn to be sawid þerbi wiþ his merci and here owene good lyuynge. Also, þe
240   lettere of þe newe testament sleeþ rebel men þat lyuen þeraȝens custumabli
       wiþouttyn amendyng in þis lif, for Crist in þe gospel seiþ to sich a rebel man
       'þe word wich I haue spoke schal deme hym', þat is, dampne hym, 'in þe laste
       day'. Also God seiþ 'I schal sle' false men and rebel aȝens my lawe, 'and I
       schal make to lywe' feiþful men þat kepyn my lawe.
245   Þanne, þouȝ þe letere sleeþ in maner befor-seid, it sueþ not þerfore þat
       þe lettere is fal and harmful to men, as it suiþ not þat God | f. 12r | is fals and
       harmful in his kynde, þouȝ he sleeþ iustli bi deeþ of bodi and of soule hem þat

---

Glosses and biblical references   211 'goodli': conveniently   213 2 Cor. 3:6   215 'repreuable':
open to reproof   218–19 John 6:64   219–20 John 6:69   220–2 2 Thess. 2:8   222–3 Isa. 11:4
234–5 2 Cor. 3:6   241–3 John 12:48   243–4 Deut. 32:39

Variants   225 \schulyn/   229 go\o/stli   229 for ˣcristˣ

rebellen fynaly a3ens his lawe. Also þis sentence 'þe lettere sleeþ' schulde
more make aferid proude clerkis, þat vndirstonden þe treweþe of Goddis lawe
250 and lyuen custumabli þera3ens, þan symple men of witt þat litil vndirstonden
þe lawe of Crist and bisie hem to lywe weel in charite to God and man. For
þise proude clerkis, þe more þei cunne Cristis lawe þe more þei make hemself
dampnable for here hi3 cunnyng and here wickid lyuynge, and þe symple men
for here lytyl cunnyng groundyn hemsilf þe more in meknesse and bisie hem
255 to lerne þe wei of saluacioun. Þus, þou3 þei hawe not tyme and leiser to turne
and turne a3en þe bokis of Goddis lawe to cunne þe lettere þerof, þei han and
kepyn þe fruit and þe veri sentence of al þe lawe of God, þour3 kepyng of
duble charite, as seynt Austyn | f. 12v | seiþ, in a sermoun of þe preisyng of
charite. And of ech sich symple man þe hooli prophete Dauid seiþ þus:
260 'blessid is þe man whom, Lord, þou hast tau3t, and hast enformyd hym of þi
lawe', þat is, charite. And in Deutronomye it is seid þat 'a lawe of fier', þat is,
charite, 'is in þe ri3t ho[n]d of God'.

 The secunde obieccioun is þis: proude clerkis seyn þat lewid men
schulden not entirmete of hooli writ, for in þe xix. chapetre of Exodi God
265 comaundiþ vndir peyne of deeþ þat neiþir beeste neiþir man, outtakyn Moyses
and Aaron, stie into þe hille where God apperid, and bi þis hille þei
vndirstonden hooli writ, which no men schulde touche but onli clerkis, þat ben
vndirstonden bi Moises and Aaron. But þis lewid obieccioun lettiþ as wel
prestis as lewed men to entirmete of hooli writ, which þei vndirstonden to
270 entre into þe hille, for in þe same chapetre aftirward God | f. 13r | comondiþ
þat prestis schulde not stie into þe same hille. Þerfore, þei take fleischli and
weiwardli þis hille to vndirstonde þerbi hooli writ. For God comandiþ Iosue,
primo ch., þat was duk of þe peple and of þe lenage of Effraem, [þat þe peple]
schulde studie boþe ny3t and dai þe lawe of God, and þe same charge God
275 3yueþ to þe kyng in þe xvij. ch. of De[u]tronomye. Also God seiþ generali to
þe peple of Israel, Exodi xij., þat þe laue of God be euere in here mouþ, and þe
Wise Man seiþ, Ecclesiastici vj., to ech man, 'al þi tellyng be in þe
comaundementis of God', and oure Lord Iesu seiþ to hise apostlis, Marc.
vltimo, 'preche 3e þe gospel to euery creature', þat is, to euery staat of men,
280 and God comaundiþ in Moises lawe þat þo bestis þat chewe not code be demid
vnclene, þat is, þat alle þei þat tretyn not and þinke not and speke not of þe
lawe of God aftir þat þei han herd it ben vnclene bi Goddis doom, and vnable
to blisse. Þerfore | f. 13v | Dauid seiþ 'I schal blesse þe Lord in al time; his
heriynge schal be euere in my mouþ'. It is of fendes weiwardnesse to forbede

Glosses and biblical references   258 'duble': two-fold (note)   259–61 Ps. 93:12   261–2 Deut.
33:2   264 'entirmete of': meddle with   264–6 Exod. 19:12   265 'outtakyn': with the exception
of   266 'stie': should climb   270–1 Exod. 19:24   272–4 Jos. 1:8   274–5 Deut. 17:18–19   275–6
Exod. 13:9   276–8 Ecclus 6:37   278–9 Mark 16:15   280–1 Deut.14:7; Lev. 11:4   283–4 Ps. 33:2

Variants   254 hemsilf] hem ˣþeˣ silf   256 \lawe/   260 \hym/   262 hond] hod   265 neiþirˡ ˣmanˣ   271
þei *sup. ras.*   272 þis ˣhisˣ   273 þat þe peple *om.*   275 detronomomye

285 cristene men to fede here soulis on Goddis word, for God seiþ, Deut° viij., 'a
     man liwiþ not in bred alone but in ech word þat comeþ forþ of Goddis
     mou[þ]', and þe same sentense is co[n]fermid bi Crist Iesu in þe gospel, Mᵗ
     iiij°.
         Þanne, siþen Iesu Crist ordayneþ his word to be sustynaunce of mennys
290 sowlis, it is a fendis condicioun to refreine cristene men fro þis goostli mete,
     siþen wiþoutyn it þei mowe not liuen in grace neiþir comen to blisse. Also
     God seiþ, Amos viij°, 'I schal sende hungyr on þe herþe, not hungir of breed
     neiþir þourst of watir but to heere þe word of God'. As it were a gret cruelte to
     wiþholde bodeli mete and drynk fro hungri men and þoursti, and þo
295 wiþholderis schulde ben gelti of bodeli | f. 14r | deeþ of þe same men, so it is a
     moche grettere cruelte to wiþholde goostli mete, þat is, Goddis word, fro
     cristene men þat hungryn and þoursten þerafter, þat is, desiren it gretli to
     kunne and to kepe it and to teche it oþere men for þe staat þat þei stonden inne.
     And þise wiþholders ben cursid of God and ben sleeris of mennys soulis, for
300 God seiþ, Prov. xj°, 'he þat hideþ whete schal be cursid among þe peple'. But
     skilefulli cristene men reden and stodien hooli writ to cunne it and kepe it, for
     Crist seiþ in þe gospel, Mᵗ xxij°, 'I haue maad redi my mete; my bolis and my
     volatilis ben slayn and alle þyngis ben redi; come ȝe to þe weddyngis', wheron
     Crisostom writeþ þus: whateuere þyng is souȝt to helþe of soule, now al is
305 fillid in scripturis. He þat is vnkunnynge schal fynde þere þat þat he owiþ to
     lerne; he þat is rebellour and synnere schal fynde þere þe scourgis of doom to-
     comynge, whiche he owiþ to drede; he þat trawailiþ schal fynde þere | f. 14v |
     þe glorie of biheste of euerlastynge liyf. And while he etiþ þis scripture, þat is,
     bileueþ, kepiþ and holdiþ in mynde, he schal be more sterid to good werk. He
310 þat is of litil corage and sike in his soule schal fynde þere mene metis of
     riȝtwisnesse, and þouȝ þise mene metis makyn not þe soule fat, þat is, parfit in
     goostli lyuynge, naþeles þo suffre not þe soule to die. He þat is of greet corage
     and feiþful schal fynde þere goostli metis of more continent liyf, þat is, more
     parfit liyf, and þise metis bryngyn him niȝ to þe kynde of angels. He þat [is]
315 smetyn of þe deuil and woundid wiþ synnes schal fynde þere medicinable
     metis þat schullen reparaile hym to goostli helþe bi penaunce. Noþyng fayliþ
     in þis feste þat is nedful to helþe of mankynde; þat is, hooli scripture.
         The þridde lewde obieccioun is þis: Goddis lawe telliþ, ij° Reg. vj°, þat
     Oȝa þe dekene was sodeynli slayn bi Goddis veniaunce for he heeld forþ his
320 hond and tou| f. 15r |chide þe arke of God whanne it was in perel to falle, and
     bi þis arke wordli clerkis vndirstonden hooli writ. Þanne siþen þis dekene Oȝa

Glosses and biblical references   285–7 Deut. 8:3   287–8 Matt. 4:4   292–3 Amos 8:11   300
Prov. 11:26   302–3 Matt. 22:4; 'volatilis': fowls (note)   308 'biheste': promise   318–20 See 2
Kings 6:6–7   319 'Oȝa': Uzzah   320 'in perel to falle': in danger of falling

Variants   285 seiþ ˣdetroˣ   286 liwiþ *sup. ras.*   287 mouþ] mouȝ   • corfermid   290 go\o/stli   300
ˣbutˣ But   302 \my/   304 þyng] of þyng   310 \metis/   313–14 \þat is, more parfit liyf/   314 him ˣneˣ   •
is *om.*   318 lawe ˣlaˣ

was slayn of God for he touchide þe arke whanne he hadde leyn wiþ his howne
wif in þe ny3t before, as diuerse doctoris seyn, moche more lewid men
schulden han more weniaunce of God if þei touchyn þar arke, þat is, hooli
writ, whanne þei ben in grettere synnes þanne þis dekene was inne. Þis
obieccioun of wordli clerkis is so lewid and so opynli groundid on falshede þat
it nedeþ noon answere, no but for men of litil vndirstandyng. It is knowe bi þe
text of Moises lawe þat þe dekenes schulde bere þe arke of God on here
schuldres, as it is writen, Num. vij°. Þis dekne hadde þis veniaunce for he putte
þe arke on vnresonable bestis to bere it, whanne he | f. 15v | schulde haue bore
it on his owene schuldres, and not for he lai bi his owene wif in þe ny3t bifore,
for no text of Goddis lawe neþir ony doctur of auctorite telliþ þis cause of
liynge bi his wif, as seynt Ierom and Lire seyn on þe same lettere. But þis
storie þat þe arke was put on vnresonable bestis, and þat þe veniaunce of God
cam sodeynli on him þat putte it on þe bestis, figuriþ þis treuþe, þat þe hi3e
veniaunce of God schal come on hem þat putten þe cure of mennys soulis on
flesc[h]li foolis and vnkunnynge of Goddis lawe, and not wilful to trauaile
aboute helþe of mennys sowlis, wich cure schulde be put oneli on hooli men
and kunnynge of Goddis lawe and wilful to performe þe goostli cure at
ensample of Crist and hise apostlis. For, as Gregor and Grosted seyn, to make
vnable curatis is þe hi3este wikkidnesse and tresun a3ens | f. 16r | God, and is
lik synne as to crucifie Crist.

   Þerfore, notwiþstondynge þise lewide obiecciouns, as Crist strecchid
forþ hise armes and hise hondes to be nailid on þe cros, and hise leggis and
hise feet also, and bowide doun þe heed to schewe what lowe he hadde to
mankynde, so alle cristene peple schulden strecchyn forþ here armes and
hondis and alle here menbris to enbrace to hemsilf þe lawe of God, þour3 veri
bileue and trewe obedience þerto and trewe mayntenaunce þerof, to here lyues
ende, for Crist seiþ in þe gospel 'if a man knowlechiþ me befor men, þanne I
schal knowleche him bifor my Fader and hise angelis'. And eft, 'if a man
schame me and myne wordis I schal schame him bifore þe angelis of God'.

Glosses and biblical references   327–9 See Num. 7:9   329 'Þis dekne', O3a   333 'lettere':
text   335 'figuriþ': prefigures   337 'wilful': willing   340 'Gregor': Gregory the Great (note)   340
'Grosted': Grosseteste (note)   340–1 'make vnable curatis': create incompetent priests   342 'lik
synne as': a sin comparable to   349–51 Luke 12:8–9

Variants   328 schulde followed by 2-letter erasure   331 owene *sup. ras.*   336 soulis ˣofˣ \on/   337 flescli
fo\o/lis   339 go\o/stli   346 strecchyn *sup. ras.*   350 my ˣmaˣ

6

Pater Noster II

f. 166v | Syþþe þe Pater Noster is þe beste prayer þat is, for in it mot alle oþer
prayers be closed yf þey schulle graciouslyche be hurde of God, þerfore scholde men
kunne þis prayour and studie þe wyt þerof. And syþþe þe treuþe of God stondeþ
nouȝt in one langage more þan in anoþer, bot whoeuere lyueþ best [and] techeþ best
5 pleseþ most God of what langage euere he be, þerfore þis prayere declared in
Englysche may edifye þe lewede peple as it doþ clerkes in Latyn. And syþþe it is þe
gospel of Crist, and Crist bad it be preched to þe peple for þe peple scholde lerne and
kunne it and worche þerafter, why may we nouȝt wryte in Englyssche the gospel and
oþere þynges declaryng þe gospel to edificacioun of cristen mennus soules, as þe
10 prechour telleþ it trewelyche [i]n Englyssche to þe peple? For by þe same resoun þat
it scholde nouȝt be wryte it scholde nouȝt be preched. | f. 167r | Þis heresye and
blaspheme scholde men putte out fro here hertes, for it spryngeþ vp by þe fende,
þeras Crist seyþ 'þe fende is fader of lesynges', and so þe kynrede of pharyseys 'is
cursed of God þat loueþ nouȝt Iesu', as seynt Poul seyþ, bot letteþ þe gospel to be
15 lerned of þe peple. For yf þer be any sotilte lyȝtere þan oþer for to kunne a crafte þat
is nedeful, he þat [can] þis sotilte and wol nouȝt teche þe lerner able þerto he is cause
of his vnkunnyng, and so wrytyng of þe gospel in Englyssche of goede lore
acordyng þerto is a sotilte and a mene to þe commune peple to kunne it þe betere.
Who loueþ lasse Crist, who is acursed of God bot he þat letteþ þis mene? For he is
20 Sathanas, contrarie to Crist. Bot þ[i]s wyckede kynrede wolde þat þe gospel slepte,

Glosses and biblical references   2 'closed': enclosed   3 'wyt': wisdom   5 'declared':
elucidated   7 'for': so that   13 John 8:44 • 'kynrede': race   13–14 1 Cor. 16:22   14 'letteþ …
to be': prevents from being   15 'sotilte lyȝtere': device easier   19–20 cf. Matt. 16:23

Variants   **Heading** In þe pater noster beeþ seuene preieres þat God himself ordeyned nedfulliche for
life and soule, þat euery cristen man and womman is iholde to knowe and oft to bidde to God i[n] pater
noster. In þis preiere we beeþ iholde to loue eche man oþer as broþer and sister þat han alle o fader. We
bidden þat his name be halowed in vs þat beeþ icleped cristen men after Crist, and euer in hym to lyue
holiliche. C7 • in] is • declaracioun of þe pater noster R85   3 studie] studie hit and R90   4 whoeuere]
who þat N2 • and² *om.* C7 L6 P2 R85 R90   5 pleseþ] he plesiþ N2   7 to þe peple *om.* C7 N2 O2 P2 R90
S1 • lerne and] lerne it C4 C7 N2 O2 P2 R85 S1, *om.* R90   8 worche] lyue N2 • we] men O2 • nouȝt]
not þanne R85   8–9 and oþere … þe gospel *om.* S1   9 mennus soules] mannes soule O2 R85 R90   10
in englyssche *om.* C4 C7 N2 O2 P2 R85 R90 S1   10 in] an   12 putte] cast O2 • out *om.* C4 N2 P2 R85
R90 S1 • hertes] hert N2 O2 P2   13 þeras] for as C7 • þe fende] he N2 O2, *om.* P2 • kynreden •
lesynges] lesingis Ion þe eiȝte capitle cum loquitur mendacium ex propri[o] se loquitur quia mendax est et
pater eius N2   15 lerned of] loued of O2, prechid to R85   16 nedeful] medeful O2 • can *om.*   17 so]
so
ȝif C4 N2 O2 R90   18 is] be C4 N2 O2 P2 R90 S1, bi R85   20 þis] þes

bot for þey bere þe name of Crist þey preche somwhat þerof, and þus dude þe
Machamete and Surgeus þe monk whanne þey made a lawe after þer owene malys
and toke somwhat of þe gospel to a fleschlyche vnderstondyng, so þat þurghe þe lore
of hem heþene folk to þis day beþ oute of here byleue. And þus þis euele kynrede
25 telleþ nouȝt hollyche þe truþe of þe gospel, for þey leueþ contrariouslyche þerto, and
Crist byddeþ his children deme after þe werkes.

　　Leue we now þis mater and speke we of the Pater Noster þat Iesu Crist made.
Þis holy prayer is ful of wyt and conteyneþ vij. axynges. Þre þe fyrste axynges
answereþ and parteyneþ to þe worschep of þe godhed: þe firste parteyneþ to þe
30 Fader, to whom power is appropried, of whom, as seyþ holy writ, is alle power in
heuene and in erþe. Þe secunde answereþ to þe Sone, to [whom] wysdom is
apropried, for, as seynt Poul seyþ, 'in him beþ alle tresoures of kunnyng and of
wysdom hud'. | f. 167v | Þe þrydde answereþ to þe Holy Gost, to wham is
appropryed loue, and þerfore seyþ seynt Ion 'God is charite, and he þat dwelleþ in
35 charite dwelleþ in God and God in him'. And þe oþer foure axynges parteyneþ to
profyȝt and helpe of mankynde, boþe gostlyche and bodylyche, and so þis blessede
prayer passeþ alle oþere in þre speciale poyntes: in auctorite, in sotylte and profyȝt
to Cristes churche. In auctorite it passeþ, for Crist, boþe God and man, made it and
tauȝte it his disciples, and syþ he is þe wysdom of þe Fader men scholde hertelyche
40 loue þis prayer by cause of þe makere and wyt þat conteyneþ þerynne; in sotylte it
passeþ, for in so schort a prayer is conteyned so muche wyt þat no tonge of man may
telle it al here in erþe, and syþþe a craft of gret sotilte is muche ypreysed of
wordlyche men muche more scholde þis sotylle gospel, þis worþy prayer, be loued
and preysed of Cristis dere chyldren. It passeþ oþer prayers in prophyt to holy
45 churche, for al þyng þat nedeþ to a man gostlyche and bodylyche is conteyned in þis
prayer, and syþþe it is so schort, and so muche mede lyþ þerynne to hem þat beþ of
goed wylle, none excusacioun is to man rekened [negligent] in þis prayer.

　　Wherfore whenne þe disciples axede Crist how þey scholde praye Crist
seyde to hem þey scholde nouȝt wylne to speke muche, as heþene men doþe, [þe
50 whiche] weneþ to be yherde in here muche speche. 'Wille ȝe nouȝt þerfore', seyþ

Glosses and biblical references　　23 'fleschlyche vnderstondyng': carnal interpretation　24 'oute
of here byleue': deprived of their faith　26 Matt. 7:16, 20　28 'axynges. Þre þe fyrste': petitions.
The first three　30–1 Matt. 28:18　32–3 Col. 2:3　34–5 1 John 4:16　48–52 Matt. 6:5–9 and
Luke 11:1–2

Variants　　23–4 þurghe þe lore of hem heþene] þus þe lore of heþene C7　24 kynrede] kynrede　25
þerto] þerto as her dedis schewen O2　27 *capitulum primum* C7, *c.* 2 R85　28 axynges[2] *om.* O2 P2 S1　30
seyþ holy writ] seynt poule seiþ S1　31 Þe] and þe　•　whom] þe whiche　31–2 wysdom is apropried] is
proprid wisdom O2　33 hud] hidde to þe Colosensis ij. capi. in quo sunt omnes thesauri sapiencie et sciencie
absconditi N2　34 Ion in þe firste pistle þe foure capitle deus caritas est N2　38 man followed by 4-letter
erasure　39 disciples for cristen men to vse it and he is most of autorite as oure bileue techiþ vs and N2　40
þat conteyneþ] conteyned N2 O2 P2 R85 R90 S1　41 is sotiliche conteyned N2　•　of man *om.* C7　44
prayers *om.* N2 O2 P2 R85 R90　47 rekened *om.* N2　47 negligent *om.* C4 C7 L6 O2 P2 R85 R90 S1　49
seide in þe gospel orantes autem nolite multum loqui sicut etnici crist seide N2　49–50 þe whiche] þey

Crist, 'be lyche to suche men, bot whanne ȝe schulle praye seyeþ þus: 'Fader oure
þat art in heuenys yhalwed be þy name'. And so he tauȝte hem oute þis prayer, bot,
be þou syker, noþer in Latyn noþer in Frensche bot in þe langage þat þey vsede to
speke, for þat þey knewe best. And here is a reule to cristen men of what langage
55   euere þey be: þat it is an heye sacrifice to God to kunne here Pater Noster, þe gospel
| f. 168r | and oþer poyntes of holy wryt nedeful to here soules, and þey to do
þerafter, wheþer it be ytolde to him or wryten in Latyn or in Englyssche or in
Frensche or in Duchyssche oþer in eny oþer langage after þat þe peple haþ
vnderstondyng. And þus clerkes scholde ioye þat þe peple knewe Goddes lawe and
60   trauayle hemself busylyche by alle þe goede menes þat þey myȝte to make þe peple
knowe þe treuþe. For þis was þe cause þat Iesu Crist bycam man and suffryde deþ
on þe croys, so þat by kepyng of his lore þe peple myȝte ryse fro deþ and come to þe
lyf þat haþ none ende, and yf any clerke wole contrarye þis who schal be dampned
bot suche a quyke fende?

65   Þerfore þe seuene askynges of þis prophetable prayer scholde men lerne and
reule hemself þerafter. Þe firste askyng, þat is answeryng to þe Fader, is seyde on þis
maner: 'Fader oure þat art in heuenes yhalwed be þy name'. Of þis wytty lore of
Crist may be meued þre questiouns: þe firste, why we seye 'oure Fader' and nouȝt
'my Fader'; þe secunde, why we seye 'þat art in heuenes' raþer þan 'in heuene'; þe
70   þrydde, why we seye 'halwed be þy name', seþþe þe name of God in himself may
nouȝt be appaired noþer amended. As to þe firste, we schulle ywwyte þat Crist
whanne he tauȝte ous to seye 'oure Fader' he betoke ous mekenesse and bad ous fle
pryde, and þat we, so lowe and so synful wrecches, whanne we hadde mynde of
heynesse and þe power of oure God, and þerto of grete grace of þis ryche lord, we
75   scholde loue him þe more and myldelyche aske of him, as þe childe of þe fader,
þyng þat ous nedeþ. For þe grettere þat a lord is, þe more gracious þat he is to pore
men, þe more he is to be loued, and þerfore seyth Crist 'lerneþ of me, for I am meke
and mylde of herte, and ȝe | f. 168v | schulleþ fynde reste in ȝoure soules'. Wherfore
we alle scholde be meke, and specialyche prestes, and nouȝt boste of here holynesse
80   and goede dedys þat þey supposeþ þat þey haue ydo, bot wylne for to haue [part] of
gode dedys of here broþeryne, as here broþeryne desyreþ to haue part of herys, and

---

Glosses and biblical references   52 'oute': fully   58 'Duchyssche': German   64 'quyke fende':
living devil   67 'of þis wytty': concerning this wise   71 'appaired': impaired   77–8 Matt. 11:29

Variants   51 suche men] hem N2 O2 R85 R90 S1, men P2 • fader oure] oure fader C7 N2 O2 P2 R85
R90 S1 52 heuenys] heuene C7 • hem al out N2, oute *om.* O2 53 noþer²] ne C4 C7 N2 O2 P2 R85 R90
S1 • langage of þat 55 to god *om.* R90 56 soules] soule O2 P2 S1, soule in her moder tonge N2 57
ytolde to him or *om.* S1 • or wryten *om.* R85 58 or in Duchyssche *om.* O2 • duchyssche] duche C4 C7
N2 P2 R85 R90 S1 • oþer¹] or C4 C7 N2 O2 P2 R85 R90 S1 60 make] teche N2 63 wole] wolde 64
fende *expl.* C4 65 þe] þees O2 R85 R90 66 hemself] hem C7 N2 O2 P2 R85 R90 S1 67 maner pater
noster qui es in celis sanctificetur nomen tuum C7 N2 70 himself] it silf O2 71 noþer] ne N2 O2 P2
R85 R90 S1 76 is¹] is and C7 N2 O2 P2 R85 S1 76–7 pore men] þe pore C7 O2 P2 S1 78 in] to N2 O2
P2 R85 R90 S1 80 þey haue ydo] þei haue C7 N2 P2 R90, to haue O2 R85 • part *om.*

so sulle þey nouȝt to oþere part of here meritys namore þan þey wille bye part of
oþer mennes, for boþe it is symonye and also it longeþ to God to partye suche
meritys, and it is nouȝt in erþelyche mannes powere. Late God þerfore dele as him
85 lykeþ: þus techeþ God in þe gospel and seyþ þus: 'whanne ȝe haue do alle þyng wel
seyeþ "we be vnprofetable seruantȝ"'. And þus knowynge oure owen wyckednesses
mekelyche in þis prayer we schulde clepe God 'oure Fader' and nouȝt 'my Fader',
by stynkynge pryde holdyng ousself worþyer to God þan oþer trewe men.

As to þe secunde poynt, why we seye 'þat art in heuenes' raþer þan 'in
90 heuene', we schulle vnderstonde þat 'heuenes' in þis place beþ vnderstonde cristen
mennes soules þe whiche, as holy wryt seyþ, beþ þe seetes of God. And so alle þylke
þat schulleþ be in blysse after þe dome ryȝtlyche may be cleped holy churche. Bot
now holy churche is seyd to be disposed on [þre] diuers maners: first, it fyȝt here in
erþe and resteþ nouȝt clerlyche fro synne bot ȝit by trauaile and sorwe of hert
95 desyreþ to come to blysse, wherefore it is ryȝtfullyche yclepyd 'þe fyȝtyng churche'.
To þis churche spekeþ Crist and seyþ 'beþ stronge in bataille and fyȝteþ wiþ þe olde
serpent þe deuel, and ȝe schulle take euerlastyng kyngdom'. On þe secunde manere
is þe churche yseyd to be disposed for þulke þat beþ passed out of þis worlde and ȝit
beþ nouȝt come to reste of lyf in blysse, bot resteþ | f. 169r | in purgatorie and
100 suffreþ peyne for synne [and] abydeþ þe mercy of God to delyuere hem oute of
peyne, and whanne þe churche is þus disposed it is ycleped 'þe restyng churche',
and herof spekeþ seynt Poul whanne he seyþ þat fuyr schal preue þe work of
eueryche. On þe þrydde manere is holy churche yseyd to be disposed for þulke þat
beþ ypassed fro sorwe and payne to ioie euerlastyng, haue ouercome þe synne and
105 sorwe of þis worlde and beþ passed payne þat comeþ bot for synne, and haue wonne
þe reste of euerlastyng blysse, and herfore it is ycleped 'the churche ouercomyng'.
Of þis churche spekeþ þe prophete and seyþ 'seyntes schulle ioye in glorie', and so
al holy churche schal be ouercomyng after þe day of dome, and be oute of myschef
of þe worlde and alle oþere paynes, and be in ioye wiþ here spouse Crist Iesu þat
110 techeþ man to be meek and to suppose oþere as goed or betere þan he, by þe dedys

---

Glosses and biblical references   82 'sulle': sell   85–6 cf. Matt. 25:30; Luke 17:10   90 'beþ
vnderstonde': are to be understood as   91 Wisd. 9:4?   95 'þe fyȝtyng churche': the church
militant   96–7 cf. Jas. 4:7; Apoc. 20:2   102–3 I Cor. 3:13   107 Ps. 149:5

Variants   82 sulle þey nouȝt] shulde they not sille R85 R90 • to oþere *om.* S1   85 God] crist N2 O2 P2
R85 R90 S1 • in followed by 8-letter erasure • gospel] gospelle of luke þe seueynteþ chapitur C7 • seyþ
þus] seiþ sic et vos cum feceritis omnia que precepta sunt vobis dicite serui inutiles sumus N2   86 wycked-
nesses] wikkednesse C7 N2 P2 R90 S1, wrecchidnesse O2 R85   91 seetes] sete C7 O2 P2 S1, cite N2   92
ryȝtlyche] ryȝtwyslyche L6 C7   93 þre *om.* C7 L6 O2   96 seyþ] seiþ estote fortes in bello et pugnate cum
antiquo serpente et accipietis regnum eternum N2   98 þulke] þo N2 R85   99 of lyf *om.* N2 S1, lyf in *om.*
O2 • in purgatorie] for a tyme O2, for to synne P2, fro synne N2 R85 R90 (note) • purgatorie til synne
be purged and S1   100 and *om.* C7 L6 O2 P2 R90 • abydeþ] abydynge C7 R90   102 Poul] poule in þe
firste epistel þe thridde chapitur C7   103 eueryche] eueriche vniuscuiusque opus quale sit ignis probabit
N2 • þulke] þo N2 R85   104 and payne *om.* N2 O2 P2 R90, and payne to ioie *om.* S1   106 churche]
churche of   107 seyþ] seiþ exultabunt sancti in gloria N2   109 of þe] of þis C7 N2 O2 P2 R85 R90 S1 •
be in ioye] ioie N2 O2 P2 R90 S1, schal ioie R85

þat he seeþ reuled by Cristes lawe, and so to seye mekelyche in prayer 'oure Fader
þat art in heuenes' and nouȝt 'in heuene', as yf he supposeþ nouȝt his broþer as goed
as himself.

As to þe þrydde questioun, how þe name of God [may be halwid, we schal
115 vndurstonde þat þe name of God] in himself may nouȝt be holyer þan it is, and ȝit it
is seyd to be maad holy whenne cristen m[a]nnes soule, lyche þe Holy Trinite, is
reuled by brennyng loue after Cristes lawe. For take a berille-ston and holde it in a
cleer sonne and so þat ston wol take hete of the sonne and þanne maist þou wiþ
tendre gete fuyre of þat ston to do þerwiþ what þe nedeþ; ryȝt so, put al þy mynde, al
120 þy soule to þe verray sone, Crist Iesu, and þou schalt cacche hete and brennyng loue
to þy God, and þou schalt haue lyȝt of vnderstondyng by þe techyng of his lawe as
muche as is nedeful to þe, and ensample | f. 169v | of goede lyuyng to þy neyȝebores
bysyde. And ryȝt as the berille-ston take nouȝt hete for to ȝeue lyȝt bot by the
sonne, and þe sonne schyne nouȝt in þe berille-ston for to make himself bryȝtere or
125 hattere bot þat þe berille may take hete and ȝeue lyȝt by þe sonne, ryȝt so Crist
techethe ous nouȝt to praye þat his name be halewed for þat we scholde make him
more holy in himself bot þat we, þurghe preysyng of him and trewe reulyng after his
lawe, mowe be maad holy and brennyng in charite to God and to oure euen-cristen,
as þe tendere wex makeþ no preynt in þe seel bot þe seel makeþ a preynt in tendere
130 wex. And so þes proude clerkes, symoniours, silleres of pardoun and indulgences, of
confessiouns and oþer holy dedys, false lawyours, wyckede iurours and cursede
aduocatȝ, disseyuable notaries and alle fals aquestis, grete swerers, vengeable
fendes, proude men and coueytous, glotouns and lecheours, bacbiters and pursuers
of Godes trewe seruantȝ, and oþer suche lymes of þe fende, may nouȝt
135 medefullyche seye 'Fader oure þat art in heuenes, yhalwed be þy name' tylle þey
amende hem of here euel lyuyng. And þerfor seyþ Crist in his gospel 'nouȝt euery
man þat seyþ to me "lord, lord" schal entre into þe kyngdom of heuenes, bot he þat
doþ þe wil of my Fader schal entre into þe kyngdom of heuenes'.

Þe secunde part of þis worþy prayer, þat in a maner is apropried to þe Sone,
140 is seid in þes wordes, 'come to þe þy kyngdom'. Þe kyngdom of God in holy wryt is

---

Glosses and biblical references 119 'tendre': tinder 130 'symoniours': simoniacs 132 'aquestis':
trial-lawyers 136–8 Matt. 7:21 140 Matt. 6:10

Variants 112 supposeþ] supposed C7 N2 O2 P2 S1 114–15 may be … of god *om.* C7 L6 N2 P2 R85 S2,
may be … himself *om.* S1, text supplied from O2 115 nouȝt be] be none C7 P2 R85, be no O2 R90 116
mannes soule] mennes soules C7 L6 S1 • soule \þat/ is lyche O2, soules ben licned to þe S1 118–19 wiþ
tendre gete] gete tynder of C7 120 sone] sone of 129–30 bot … wex *om.* C7 • tendere] vntendere L6,
softe O2, *om.* N2 P2 R85 S1 130 symoniours] symonyans P2 R90, symonyentis N2 O2 R85 S1 131 iurours]
iuriours L6, ioriours C7 132 disseyuable … aquestis *om.* S1 • aquestis] qwestiers R85, questes C7 O2 P2
R90, questmongers N2 133 glotonus P2 • lecheours] leccherouse C7 P2 R90 S1 133 pursuers of gode
trewe cristen men goddis R85 136 euel] wickide N2 O2 P2 R85 R90 S1 • gospel] gospelle of matheu þe
seue[n]þ chapitur C7, gospel non omnis qui dicit michy domine domine intrabit in regnum celorum set qui
facit voluntatem patris mee qui in celis est ipse intrabit in regnum celorum N2 139 part] askynge O2 R85
R90 • \prayer/ 140 wordes] wordis adueniat regnum tuum C7 N2 • come to þe þy kyngdom] come þi
kingdom N2, thi kyngdom come to þe R85

vnderstonde on dyuers maners, and so here it may ry3tlyche be take for þe fy3tyng
churche, þe whiche wolde desyre to regne in blysse wiþ Iesu Crist her spouse as
sone as it is his wille, for vpon þis condicioun we scholde desyre, as seynt Poul
techeþe ous, to passe out | f. 170r | of þis wrecchede lyf and come to þe blysse
145 euerlastyng, for þat is muche bettre. And syþþe Crist is þat noble man þat cam fro
heuene into þe lowe erþe to take ous [for his] kyndom þat byfore were ylost þurghe
Adamis synnes, and þat suffrede deþ on þe rode-tree and bou3te ous alle a3en [fro
deeþ wiþ his precious blood and after turned a3en] to ioye of þe Fader, for
sauacioun of mankynde, wel may þe trewe cristen peple be clepyd Godys kyngdom.
150 And ry3t as we beþ tau3t in þe fyrst axynge to destroye pryde by verraye mekenesse,
whanne we seyeþ 'Fader oure þat art in heuenys, halewede be þy name', ry3t so we
beþ ytau3t in þys secunde axynge to destroye enuye a3ens oure euene-cristen wiþ
parfite charite whanne we seyeþ 'come to þe þy kyngdom'. And as it is nedeful in þe
firste axynge specialyche to haue parfyt feyþ þat God oure Fader is in heuenys, so it
155 nedeþ specialyche in þis secunde axynge þat we haue hope þat alle þylke þat we
supposeþ be his kyngdom schulde regne wiþ him in blysse of heuene.
   Þe þrydde axynge of þys holy prayer, þat is answeryng to þe Holy Goost, is
yseyde in þese wordes: 'be þy wylle ydo in erþe as it is in heuene'. By þese witty
wordes we beþ ytau3t to haue goede wille to oure euen-cristen, and to reule oure
160 soules after þe Holy Gost and nou3t after þe luste of þe flesche, for þe spiryt
coueyteþ contrarious to þe flesche and þe flesche to þe spiryt, as seynt Poul telleþ.
And ry3t as in þe firste axyng we beþ ytau3t to haue parfy3t feyþ, and in þe secunde
goede hope, so in þe þrydde we beþ ytau3t to haue parfy3t charite to God and oure
euen-cristen, for þe most of þese þre vertues, as seynt Poul techeþ, is charite. For
165 fcyþ and hope schulle cesse in man whanne he comeþ | f. 170v | to blysse, for in
stede of feyþ he schal haue clere sy3t in soule of þe godhede of Crist and clere
bodyliche sy3t of þe manhede of Crist, and in stede of hope he schal be syker and
haue parfyt ioye, and so feyþ and hope schulleþ be ychanged and charite schal waxe
more and more, and laste wiþoute end. And þus seyþ seynt Poul, þat 'now we seeþ
170 God by mirrour' and in fer sy3t, by scripture and feyþ, 'bot þanne we schulle see
him as he is', whanne we comeþ to blysse wyþ eye of body and eye of soule. Þerfore
praye we God þat his wylle be don here in erþe among synful men þurghe
amendement of here lyf, as it is ydo yn heuene among his glorious seynt3 wiþoute
medlyng of synne. Nou3t þat he ne may make his wylle to be do in erþe wiþoute

---

Glosses and biblical references   143–5 Phil. 1:23   158 Matt. 6:10   160–1 Gal. 5:17   164 1 Cor.
13:13; 'most': greatest   169–71 1 Cor. 13:12   174 'medlyng': admixture

Variants   144 blysse] lijf N2 O2   146 lowe *om.* N2 P2 R85 R90   • for his] fro þis C7 L6, fro his N2
P2, to his S1   147 rode-tree] tree C7 O2 P2 R90, crosse S1   147–8 fro deeþ … a3en *om.* C7 L6 P2 S1   153
\come/   • come to þe þy kyngdom] come þi kingdom N2, thi kyngdom come to þe R85   154 parfyt *om.*
O2 P2 R85 R90 S1, *des.* N2   155 alle *om.* N2 O2 P2 R85 R90 S1   • þylke] þo N2 R85   157–8 is yseyde] sueþ
C7 O2 P2 R85 R90 S1   158 wordes] wordes fiat voluntas tua sicut in celo et in terra C7 N2   164 charite]
charite fides spes caritas tria hec melior autem horum est caritas N2   173 amendement] amendynge N2
O2 P2 R85 R90 S1

175 oure prayere, bot þat we in charite þus prayenge mowe be corouned in heuene
     blysse. But for þat [þe body] is corrupt it greueþ þe soule, as seynt Poul telleþ, and
     'yf we seye þat we haue no synne we deceyueþ ousself and treuþe is nouȝt in ous',
     as seint Ioon telleþ. Þerfore, whyle we beþ in þis world we may not so parfytlyche
     do þe wille of God as seintȝ in heuene, for corrupcioun of body [and] vnstabelnesse
180 of lyf, and þerfore Crist techeþ ous uittilyche to praye 'be þy wille ydo in erþe as it
     is ydo in heuene', bot nouȝt so parfyȝtlyche in erþe as it is in heuene. And þus as we
     beþ ytauȝte in þe firste and in þe secunde axynge to destroye pryde and enuye wiþ
     mekenesse and charite so we bethe ytauȝt in þis þridde axynge to destroye wraþþe
     wiþ verray loue of herte, and þerfore seyþ Crist 'I ȝeue ȝow a newe maundement,
185 þat ȝe loue togedere as I haue loued ȝow'.
         Þe secunde partie of þis Pater Noster is yordeyned of God for þe infirmite of
     | f. 171r | man, as þe firste parteyneþ to þe worschepe of þe godhed. And it conteyneþ
     [foure] peticiouns, and þese, wiþ oþer [þre], makeþ seuene axynges in þis holy
     prayer. Þe firste of þes foure is seyd on þes wordes: 'oure eche-day[es] bred ȝef ous
190 today'. This peticioun, as seynt Austyn telleþ, ryȝtfulliche is vnderstonde in þre
     maners: ferst, þat þis breed betokeneþ oure sustinaunce and alle oþer necessaryes
     nedeful to oure body, and for [God] made alle þynges to help of mankynde þerfore
     we scholde axe þ[e]s þynges of God as wilfullyche for oþer as for ousself, and þus
     wiþ goede wille and largenesse of herte we scholde desyre oure neyȝebores profyȝt
195 as we wolde þat hy desired oure, and þis is þe remedye aȝens þe cursed couetyse.
     And for man nedeþ eueryche day bodilyche sustinaunce þerfore þese necessaries
     may wel be cleped eche-dayes breede. Also, by þis breede, in þe secunde manere, ys
     vnderstonde þe lore of Godes worde, for ryȝt as breede sa[d]eþ a mannes herte and
     makeþ him stronge to bodylyche trauayle so þe worde of God makeþ saad a mannes
200 soule in þe Holy Gost, and stronge to worche after þe lore þerof, and þis breed is
     more nedeful þan þat firste breed as þe soule of man is worþyere þan his body, for
     whanne þe body lyþ stynkyng in þe graue þanne þe soule is parfyȝtlyche yclensed
     fro synne and ioyeþ in blisse of Iesu Crist, here spouse. And þus, yf þurghe
     necgligence of oure byschepes and prelatȝ and oþer false techers þat ben in holy
205 churche þe truþe of Godes word be nouȝt ysowe in þe peple, praye we Iesu Crist,

---

Glosses and biblical references   176 Wisd. 9:15 (note)   177–8 1 John 1:8   180 'uittilyche':
wisely 184–5 John 13:34 189–90 Matt. 6:11 193 'wilfullyche': willingly 195 'hy': they 198
'sadeþ': satisfies 199 'saad': steadfast

Variants   176 þe body] it L6, þe fleishe N2 R85, *om.* C7 O2 P2, bodi *corr.* S1 • seynt Poul] Sapiens *sup.*
ras. O2 (note)   178 beþ] lyuen R85   179 body and] bodiliche   182–3 pryde … destroye *om.* S1   183 to
destroye wraþþe *om.* C7   187 godhed so þis part parteyneþ to profit and helpe of mankynde boþe bodily
and goostly N2, so þis secound part parteyneþ to worschip of þe manhed of crist O2   188 foure] þre •
þre] foure 189 þes wordes] þis maner N2 O2 P2 R85 R90 S1 + panem nostrum cotidianum da nobis hodie
C7 N2 • dayes] day L6 C7 P2   191 oþer] oþer substaunces and N2, oþer sustynances and P2 S1   192
God *om.*   193 þes] þis   195 hy] he C7 O2 P2 R90 S1   198 sadeþ] saueþ   201 þat] þat of L6, is þe C7
O2 P2 R85 R90   202 soule] soule þat is saued N2   203 synne] synne and regneþ in ioie and blis wiþ Iesu
N2 • of] wiþ O2 P2 R85 R90 S1   204 oþer *om.* N2 S1   205–6 praye … peple *om.* C7

byschepe of oure soule, þat he ordeyne prechours in þe peple to warne hem of synne
and telle hem þe truþe of God. And he þat enspiryde þe prophetes wiþ kunnyng
| f. 171v | and wysdome, and tauȝte þe apostles þe weye of al truþe, lyȝte oure hertes
wiþ vnderstondyng of his lore and graunte ous grace to worche þerafter, and
210 specialiche for ous nedeþ eche day þis breede þerfore pray we mekelyche 'oure
eche-dayes breed ȝyue ous today'. On þe þrydde manere, by þis eche-dayes breed is
vnderstonde þe sacrament, verray Godes body in forme of breed, þe whiche was
ybore of þe mayde Marye and suffrede harde payne and deþ vpon þe croys to
delyuere man fro payne and deþ wiþouten ende. And þerfore seynt Austyn seyþ þat
215 yf we haue resceyued oure creatoure dayes of oure lyf ous nedeþ to haue þis byleue
and so euery day resceyue God and þus euery day to praye 'oure eche-dayes breed
ȝeue ous today'.

Þe secunde peticioun of þis secunde part of þ[e] Pater Noster is seyd on þes
wordes: 'forȝeue ous oure dettes as we forȝeueþ oure dettoures'. By þese wytty
220 wordes of oure Lord Iesu Crist mowe malicious men and vengeable wrecches knowe
þat þey beþ in þe weye to helleward as longe as þey dwelleþ in here cursede malice.
For by þes dettes beþ vnderstonde the synnes aȝens God, and so eueryche day ous
nedeþ to praye God forȝeuenesse of oure synnes, and Crist techeþ ous þat we schulle
praye God forȝeuenesse on þis condicioun, þat we forȝeue oþere, and so yf we praye
225 God to forȝeue ous oure synnes as we forȝeue hem þat trespasseþ aȝens ous, and
þerto holde malice in oure herte, we beþ oute of charite and makeþ oure synnes more
greuous byfore God and axeþ verray vengeaunce to ousself of God, þe hye iustice.
And þerfore techeþ Crist and seyþ 'bot yf ȝe wolle forȝeue oþer men þe trespasse[s]
þat þey haue trespassed to ȝow, ne my Fader of heuene schal nouȝt forȝeue | f. 172r |
230 to ȝow ȝoure synnes'. Þerfore God byddeþ ous to putte awey al malice of oure
hertes þat we may be ysaued. Lo þe goednesse of God how it ous to penaunce
draweþ and techeþ ous to flee slouþe for to turne to him! And þerfore techeþ þe
bouke of wysdom þat we scholde nouȝt tarye to be yturned to God, for yf we do we
synneþ in slouþe of Godes seruice.
235 Lyft vp, wrecches, the eyȝe of ȝoure soules and byholdeþ him þat no spot of
synne was ynne, what payne he suffrede for synne of man. He swatte water and

---

Glosses and biblical references   219 Matt. 6:12   228–30 Matt. 6:14   230–1 cf. Col. 3:7   233–5
Ecclus 5:7   236 'swatte': sweated

Variants   206 prechours] trewe prechours O2 R90 (note)   207 god] god and his lawe N2   209 þerafter]
þerafter to oure lyues ende N2   212 sacrament] sacrament of þe auter S1   214 And þerfore] for O2   215 we]
we beleue þat we haue N2   • haue¹] haue verry Goddis body we haue O2   • dayes] and eche day N2   216
God] god by riȝt byleue crede et manducasti N2   • day²] day us nediþ N2   218 of þe] of þis   219 wordes]
wordes et dimitte nobis debita nostra sicut et nos dimittimus debitoribus nostris [+ þat is N2] C7 N2   219–20
þese wytty wordes L6, þis witti word of lore S1   220 oure Lord Iesu Crist] crist S1, god C7, *om.* N2 O2 P2
R85 R90   • men and wymmen O2 S1   224–5 we praye … synnes *as om.* S1   227 axeþ] askinge O2 P2 R85
R90   • hye] hiȝest O2   228 seyþ] seiþ si non dimiseritis hominibus peccata eorum nec pater meus celestis
dimittet vobis peccata vestra N2   • forȝeue followed by 4-letter erasure   • trespasse   230 al] þe C7 N2 O2 P2
R85 R90 S1   231–2 it drawiþ vs to penaunce O2 P2 R85 R90, he draweþ us to penaunce N2 S1   235 wrecch
þe [þin R85 R90] iȝe of þi soule N2 O2 P2 R85 R90 S1

blood to wassche þe of synne; he was ybounde and ybete wiþ scourges, þe blod
rennyng adoun by his sydes, þat þou scholdest kepe þy body clene in his seruice. He
was corouned wiþ scharpe þornes þat þou scholdest þenke on him and flee alle
240 cursede malice. He was [picch]ed to þe croys wiþ scharpe nayles þurghe honden and
feet, and ystonge to þe herte withe a scharpe spere, þat alle þyne fyue wyttes scholde
be yreuled after him, hauynge mynde on þe fyue precious woundes þat he suffrede
for man. And ry3t in al þis grete payne þis innocent prayde for his enemys to his
Fader and seyde 'Fader, for3eue hem þis gylt, for þey wyteþ nou3t what þey dooþ'.
245 Lat þis sterye 3owre hertes to putte awey slouþe and to serue God wiþ verrey
busynesse to worche after his lawe, and so mekelyche praye oure Fader to for3eue
ous oure trespasses as we for3eueþ oure trespassours.
       Þe þrydde peticioun of þe secunde part of [þ]is holy praier folweþ in þese
wordes: 'and lede ous nou3t into temptacioun'. By þese wytty wordes may we lerne
250 þat þe deuel tempteþ men euere to an yuel ende and God temptede neuere man bot to
a goed en| f. 172v |de, for þus we redeþ þat he temptede Abraham and it was
ar[e]tted to him into ry3twysnesse, bot þe deuel temptede Crist to make him to synne
in glotenye and veynglorie and couetyse, and so Crist techeþ ous nou3t to praye þat
we be nou3t ytempted of þe fende, syþþe þat temptacioun of þe fende profyteþ
255 muche yf it be wiþstonde. For, as seynt Iame seyþ, þat man is blessed þat suffreþ
temptacioun, for whanne he schal be preuyd, or whanne þat he is preuyd, he schal
take þe coroune of lyf þat God haþ behey3t to hem þat loueþ him. And þus seynt
Poul was tempted of þe synne of lecherye, wherefore þryes he prayde God þat he
my3te be delyuered of þis temptacioun, and God answerede him a3en 'my grace
260 sufficeþ to þe'. And he himself knowelecheþ þat þis temptacioun was nedeful leste
he scholde haue had vaynglorie of þe pryue sy3tes þat he sawe whanne he was
rauysched into þe þrydde heuene. Þerfore praye we nou3t God þat we be nou3t
ytempted, syþþe it is so profytable, bot praye we God þat we be nou3t ouercome,
and þat he lede ous nou3t into temptacioun. Þat man is yseyde to be lad into
265 temptacioun þat þurghe his wyckede and vnrepentant herte cont[inu]eþ euere in his
wyckede lyuyng and so is ouercome in temptacioun, and þus it is to be vnderstonde
þat God hardede pharaois herte for þe mysbyleue þat he hadde to God and þe malice

Glosses and biblical references   240 'picched to': impaled upon   243–4 Luke 23:34   249 Matt.
6:13   251–2 Rom. 4:9; 'arettid': reckoned   252–3 Matt. 4:1–11   255–7 Jas. 1:12   257 'behey3t':
promised   257–60 2 Cor. 12:7–9   266–8 Exod. 7:13

Variants   237 þe of synne] awey oure synnes S1   237–8 þe blod rennyng] þat þe blod ran S1   240
picched] nayled L6 O2   243 ry3t] 3it N2 R85 R90, *om.* S1   245 hertis to þenke on hym and putte S1   248
þis] his   249 wordes] wordes et ne nos inducas in tempt[ac]ionem C7 N2   250 euere] neuer but R85, *om.*
S1   250–1 and god … ende *om.* R90   250 neuere man bot] euer men S1   251 redeþ] reden in genesis
N2   • abraham whenne he hadde hym sle isaac his sone and abraham trowide to hym and it was R85   252
aritted   255 seyþ] seiþ in þe firste chapitur C7, seiþ beatus vir qui suffert temptacionem quia cum probatus
fuerit suscipiet coronam vite quam repromisit deus diligentibus se þat is to seie N2   258 of¹] to C7, wiþ
N2 O2 P2 R85 R90 S1   260 leste] leste þe gretnesse of reuelaciouns schulde make hym haue veynglorie
S1   264–6 yseyde … temptacioun *om.* S1   265 continueþ] conteyneþ L6 O2

þat he wroughte to Godes peple. And so, as we beþ ytauȝt in this oþer prayere and
axyng to destroye sleuþe in þe seruice of God in verray busynesse of herte to knowe
270 his lore and worche þerafter, so we beþ ytauȝt in þis peticioun to destroye glotenye
and lecherye wiþ discrete ab| f. 173r |stinence and chastite of herte, and for þes two
beþ synnus of þe flesche, and þat on noryscheþ þat oþer, is þe more perilous yf a
man in him falle. Þefore praye we oure Fader þat he lede ous nouȝt into temptacioun
ne suffre ous nouȝt to be ouercome in þes synnes, ne in none oþer, for, yf we beþ,
275 oure wyckede lyuyng and oure wyckede þouȝtes beþ cause þerof, as God seyþ by
Ieremye þe prophete.

   Þe fourþe peticioun and þe laste of þe secunde part of þe Pater Noster is
yseyd in þis manere: 'bot delyuere ous from yuel'. We schulde vnderstonde þat
euery synne is yuel, and so of alle synnes þat beþ yrekened in þis praier we schul[d]e
280 praye God þat he delyuere ous boþe of yuel þat we doþ in þis wor[ld]e and of yuel of
payne þat wyckede men schulle haue onelyche for synne. For payne comeþ neuere
to man bot be cause of synne, and so on fyue maneres comeþ payne for synne: payne
come to Crist to bigge mannes synne, and payne comeþ to dampny[d] men for to
venge synne in þis worlde, and payne comeþ to Cristes children to purge hem fro
285 synne, and payne comeþ to oþer men to schewe þat God hateþ synne and to kepe
hem þerfrom, and payne comeþ to wyckede men to punysche hem euere for synne.
And so, as God is þe beste þyng in þe worlde so synne is worse þan any oþer þyng,
and þus men scholde flee synne as al maner of yuel. [Bot siþ] synne aȝens þe Holy
Gost is worst of alle oþer, for, as Crist seyþ, þat schal nouȝt be forȝeue in þis worlde
290 ne in þat oþer worlde, þerfore specialiche praye we God to delyuere ous from þis
yuel. Þat man synneþ aȝens þe Holy Gost þat to his lyues ende is rebelle aȝens God,
[and so dieþ in dispeir and goiþ to peyne wiþouten ende, and he is rebel aȝene god]
þat is rebelle aȝens his lore, | f. 173v | and [þerfore seiþ Crist] 'whoso loueþ nouȝt
me he kepeþ nouȝt my word'. And þus eueryche man þat loueþ nouȝt Cristes lore he
295 loueþ nouȝt Iesu Crist, and þus, as seynt Poul seyþ, he is acursed of God. And
þerfore seyde Crist to þe Iewes þat were contrarie to his lore and pursuede him for

---

Glosses and biblical references   275–6 Jer. 11:8; 32:23   278 Matt. 6:13   283 'bigge': redeem
288–90 Matt. 12:33; Luke 6:43–4   293–4 John 14:24   294–5 1 Cor. 16:22   295–7 John 8:21,
24   296 'pursuede': persecuted

Variants   268 peple] puple induratum est cor faraonis et non audiuit eos sicut preceperat dominus
N2   268–9 this oþer prayere and axyng] þe toþer axinge N2 O2 P2 R85 R90 S1   275 and oure wyckede
þouȝtes *om.* S1   276 Ieremye] ysaie *sup. ras. sec. m.* O2   278 manere] manere set libera nos a malo C7
N2   279 schulde] schulle L6 C7   280 þat we han [token O2 R90] of oure first fader and of yuel þat we
don here in N2 O2 R90   • worlde] wordle   283 mannes] man fro N2 O2 P2 R85 R90 S1   • dampnyd]
dampny L6, oþer P2 S1 *sup. ras.* O2   283–5 dampnyd men … payne comeþ to *om.* N2 R85 R90   284 and
payne … fro synne *om.* S1   • purge] clense N2 O2 P2 R85 R90   285 synne] synne in þis world S1   285–6
and to kepe hem þerfrom *om.* N2 O2 R85 R90 S1   286 wyckede] dampnid R85   288 men scholde flee
synne] synne schulde be fledde C7 N2 O2 P2 R85 R90 S1   • bot siþ] by   290 oþer worlde] oþer qui autem
dixerit contra spiritum sanctum non remittetur ei neque in hoc seculo neque in futuro N2   292 and so
… aȝene God *om.* C7 L6   293 þerfore seiþe Crist *om.*   • Crist] crist qui non diliget me sermones meos
non seruat N2

truȝþe þat þey scholde deye in here synnes. And so þes men þat contrarieþ to þe
gospel and to þe epistele, and wolde lette it to be ypreched and pursuwe þe trewe
telleres þerof loueþ nouȝt Crist, and þus þey schulle deye in here synne bot yf þey
300   amende hem whyle þey haueþ tyme.

Wel we wyteþ þat þe scribes and þe pharyseus and þe princes of þe prestes
in Iesu Cristes tyme were more contrarious to his lore þan were oþere commune
peple, for [þurghe] entyssyng of hem þe peple cryde 'do him on þe croos'. Þe scribes
were wyse men of þe lawe and also þey were þe clergie of þe Iewes; þe phariseus
305   were men of religioun þat made customs and kepte hem for lawe, and þus þey sette
more by here lawes þat þey hadde maade þan þey dude by þe lawe þat God ȝaf to
hem and to þe peple, þat was sufficient to be reuled by. Bot þus vnder colour of
parfeccioun þey were departed in customs, in cloþyngis and in many oþer doyngis
fro þe commune peple, as þe maner of religious is nowe, and 'pharise' is as muche
310   for to seye as 'departed in doynge'; þey bereþ here names. Þes ypocrites were most
contrarie to Crist and þe peple wrouȝte muche after here lore, and þerfore Crist, as
þe gospel wytnesseþ, eyȝte tymes seyde 'wo' to hem. And ones þey repreuede Crist
for his disciples wesche nouȝt here hondes whanne þey scholde eete, as here
custome was, and Crist axede hem why þey breke Godes hestes for here feynede
315   lawes. Byholde now wel þese condiciouns and loke | f. 174r | where men doþ after
hem oþer worse, and so þou schalt yknowe þe kynrede of þe phariseus. And þes
fayners of holynesse pursue Crist in hise membres as þe phariseus pursuede Crist
bodilyche, and yf þey seye þat God is here fader, and his lawe þey kepe and here
reule boþe, vnderstonde þat phariseus breke þe lawe þat God ȝaf to hem and to þe
320   peple for here feynede reule þat hy hemself ordeynede. And þus yf þes ypocrites
seyeþ þat hy kepeþ here reule and Godes lawe boþe bot byholde here dedis. For þe
Iewes seyde to Iesu Crist þat God was here fader, bot Crist answerede hem aȝen þat
yf God hadde be here fader þey scholde haue yloued him. And yf þes were trewe
cristene men þey scholde nouȝt pursue Cristes membres for prechynge of þe gospel,
325   and so by here dedys þou schalt knowe hem. And þerfore Crist byddeþ to trowe to

Glosses and biblical references   303 Mark 15:13; Luke 23:21; John 19:6   307 'colour':
pretence   308 'departed': separated   309 'religious': those in religious orders   311–12 Matt.
23:13–39   312–15 Mark 7:1–13 and Matt. 15:2–3   321–3 John 8:41–2   325–6 Matt. 7:16

Variants   297 synnes] synne ego vado et queretis me et in peccato vestro moriemini N2   297–9 And
so … bot *om.* S1   303 þurghe *om.* C7 L6   • croos] cros crucifige eum N2   306–7 þat God … to²] of
god ȝouen to hem þe whiche were sufficient alle men to N2   307 by] by him L6, and to saue her soulis
if þei wolden do þerafter N2   308 departid and as þe dedis schewen oure religious today worþili beren
her name R85   310 doynge] doynge and so C7, doynge þerfore S1, in doynge or deuydide fro þe comune
puple in maner of cloþing and duellynge and synguler customs vsinge N2   312 gospel] gospelle of matheu
witnessiþ in þe þre and twenteþ chapitur C7   • wo] sorowe P2 R85 R90   • hem] hem ve vobis scribe et
farisei ypocrite qui clauditis regnum celorum ante homines N2   316 kynreden   318 fader] fadir as pharisees
þer eldres diden R90   321 bot byholde] biholde to O2 N2 P2 R85 R90 S1   322 fader] fader vnum patrem
habemus deum N2   • aȝen] aȝen si deus pater vester esset diligeretis vtique me N2   323 and yf þes] and
so if oure religious R85   324 prechynge] prechynge and techynge S1

þe workes, and þerfore techeþ seynt Iohn þat whoso bryngeþ nou3t þe lore of Crist
þou schalt nou3t to him seye 'hayl' in confortyng of his synne, ne resceyue him into
þyn hous, for yf þou do þou art partyner of his synne. Praye we þerfore herteliche
oure Fader þat he delyuere ous from yuel of phariseis, þat is, synne a3ens þe Holy
330   Gost, and 3yf ous grace to loue his lore in herte and to werche þerafter in dede, þat
we may come to him in blysse and wonye wiþ him in ioye wiþoute eny ende. Amen.

Glosses and biblical references	**326–8** 2 John 10–11

Variants	**326** Iohn] Iohan in þe secounde epistel þe first chapitur C7	• whoso] whoso comeþ to 3ou
and C7	**327** nou3t] not resceyue hem in to þin hous ne sey S1	• his] here S1	**328** for yf þou do þou art]
for he þat seiþ to him heil is C7	• his] here S1	• synne] synne siquis venit ad vos et hanc doctrinam non
affert nolite recipere eum in domum vestram nec aue ei dixeritis qui ei dicit aue comunicat operibus eius
malignis N2	**331** wonye wiþ him in ioye] ioy O2, ioye with him P2 R90 R85, ioie wiþ hym to reste N2

Glossed Gospel Prologues and Epilogue

I Prologue to Short Matthew

Þe prologe of þe schorte exposicioun on Matheu

f. 1va | Þe Holi Goost seiþ bi þe profete Sacarie of Ioon Baptist 'and þou, child,
schal be clepid þe profete of þe hiȝeste, for þou schalt go bifor þe face of þe Lord
to make redi hise weies, to ȝyue þe science of helþe to hise puple into
remyssioun of her synnes', as Luk witnessiþ in his firste chapitre. Techeris eþer
5   declareris of holi writ ben clepid profetis bi þe speche of holy writ, as Gregorie
witnessiþ ofte in hise bookis. Þis 'science of helþe' is þe holi gospel which oure
Lord Iesu Crist, veri god and veri man, tauȝte in his owne persoone, and
comaundide hise apostlis and disciplis to preche it to alle maner men. And
whoeuer bileueþ þe gospel and kepiþ it in his liyf schal gete remyssioun of alle
10   hise synnes, and he schal haue blis wiþouten ende in bodi and soule, and
whoeuer bileueþ not þe gospel wiþ keping of Goddis heestis and ending in parfit
charite schal be dampned, as Mark witnessiþ in his laste chapitre, wiþ acordyng
of oþere partis of holi scripture. As it is demed a greet werk of mersi and of
charite to teche a vnkunnyng man þe riȝt and sykur weie, whanne many perels
15   ben in wrong weies, and nameli if þe man mut go þat vnknowun weie and ellis
perische in greet meschef, so it is a fer gretter werk of mersi and charite to telle
opynli þe treuþe of þe holi gospel to lewid men and sympli-lettrid prestis, siþen
þe gospel is þe riȝt weie to heuene, wiþout which noon may come to heuene.
    Herfor a symple creature expowneþ schortli þe gospel of Matheu to lewid
20   men in Englische tunge, þat þei mow þe betere knowe it and kepe it, and so be
sauyd wiþouten ende in þe blisse of heuene. In þis schort exposicioun is set oneli
þe text of holy writ wiþ opyn sentensis of elde holi doctours and appreuyd of holi
chirche, and summe lawis of þe chirche groundid in Goddis lawe and resoun. Þe
text of þe gospel is set first bi itsilf, an hool sentence togidere, and þanne sueþ þe

Glosses and biblical references   **1** 'Sacarie': Zacharias   **1–4** Luke 1:76–7; 'science of
helþe': knowledge of salvation   **4** 'declareris': elucidators   **8–12** Mark 16:16   **12** 'acordyng':
agreement   **15** 'nameli': particularly   **16** 'meschef': misfortune   **17** 'sympli-lettrid': literate to an
elementary level   **22** 'sentensis': statements   • 'appreuyd of': approved by

Variants   **10** \hise/   **13** it ˣitˣ

25 exposicioun in þis maner: first a sentence of a doctour declarynge þe text is set
aftir þe text, and in þe ende of þat sentence þe name of þe doctour seiynge it is
set, þat men wite certeynli hou fer þat doctour goiþ, and so of alle doctours and
lawes allegid in þis exposicioun.
    Whanne Y seie 'Ierom here', Ierom seiþ þat sentence on Matheu on þe
30 same text. Whanne Y seie 'Crisostom here', Crisostom in hise omelies on
Matheu þat ben clepid *Werk Vnparfit*, þat is, not fulli endid bi al Matheu, seiþ þat
sentence on þe same text on Matheu. Whanne Y seie 'Austin here', he is aleggid
in hise twey bokis of þe Lordis Sermoun in þe Hil, which sermoun conteyneþ þe
v. and vj and vij. chapitres of Matheu. Whanne Y seie 'Bede in his omeli' eþer
35 'Gregorie in his omeli', and telle not in what omeli, Y | vb | take þat sentence of
Alquyn on Matheu. Whanne Y telle in what omeli of Gregorie eþer of Bede,
þanne Y mysilf se þat orignal of Gregorie eþer of Bede, and, schortli, whateuer
doctour Y alegge and telle not speciali where, Y take þat aleggaunce of Alquyn
on Matheu, for he hadde many mo originals boþe of Grekis and of Latyns þan I
40 haue now, and I haue manye scharpe doctours whiche he hadde not. Whanne I
seie 'Crisostom' and telle not where Y take him of Alquyns rehersyng, and þat
sentence is in Crisostom, in his parfit werk on Matheu. Whanne Y seie 'Origen',
'Illarie', 'Remygie' eþer 'Raban', and telle not where, þo doctours ben on
Matheu as Alquyn rehersiþ hem on þe text expowned, as he witnessiþ in his
45 prologe on Matheu. Whanne Y seie 'a glos' Y take þat glos of Alquyn, and he
aleggiþ so whateuer sentence is takun of lesse doctours þan weren þe elde grete
doctours whose names ben expressid at þe bigynnyng.
    Y purposide wiþ Goddis grace to sette pleynli þe text of holi writ and þe
trewe sentensis of þes doctours in maner biforseid, and, blessid be almy3ti God of
50 his graciouse help, Y am not gilti in mysilf þat Y erride fro þis purpos. If ony
lerud man in holi writ and holi doctours be displesid in ony sentence set here, for
Goddis loue loke he wel trewe originals and Y hope he schal not fynde greet
defaute. Neþeles, if he fynde ony defaute for Goddis loue sette he in þe trewe
sentence and noþing ellis, þat cristen puple may haue sikirli þe trewe
55 vndurstondyng of holi writ, for Y desire noon oþer þing in þis werk no but þat
cristen puple knowe and kepe treuli holi writ, and come bi Goddis mersi þerbi to
þe endles blis of heuene. Iesu, kyng of mersi, of pees and charite, þat scheddist þi
preciouse blood for þe loue of mennus soulis, graunte þis ende! Amen.

Glosses and biblical references   25 'declarynge': elucidating   27 'hou fer þat doctour goiþ':
i. e., where the gloss from that doctor ends   28 'allegid': cited   30 'text' [beneath which
the gloss is written]   31 'fulli endid bi': completely finished on   33 'in þe Hil': on the
Mount   35–6 'of Alquyn': from Thomas Aquinas (note)   37 'se': have seen   38 'aleggaunce':
citation   40 'scharpe': acute   42 'parfit': complete   43 'Illarie': Hilary of Poitiers (note) •
'Remygie': Remigius of Auxerre (note) • 'Raban': Rabanus Maurus (note)   50 'in mysilf':
to my knowledge   51 'lerud': educated   52 'loke he wel': may he look carefully at • 'hope':
believe   53 'defaute':defect, flaw   54 'haue sikirli': securely possess   55 'no but': except

Variants   31 ˣalˣ al   52–3 trewe ... defaute¹ *sup. ras.*

II Prologue to Intermediate Matthew

f. 1ra | Seynt Austyn saiþ, in þe secounde book of *Cristen Docctryne* in þe ende, whateuere þinge a man fyndiþ in any science out of holy writ, if þe þinge founden is veyn it is dampned in holy writ, if þe þinge founden is profitable it is founden in holy writ, and whanne ony man schal fynde in holy writ alle þingis whiche he
5   lernyde profitably in oþer sciens meche plenteuouslyer he schal fynde þer þo profitable þingis þat ben not lerned in ony maner in oþer sciences, no but onely in þe wonderful heiȝnesse and wonderful mekenes of holy scripturis.

Also, in þe iij. bok of [*Cristen*] *Doctryn* Austyn seiþ þus: be þou war þat þou take not figuratyf speche to þe letter, for hereto pert[e]yneþ þe apostlis wordes
10 seyinge 'þe letter sleþ; treuly þe spirit,' þat is, gostly vnderstondyng, 'makiþ lyue'. For whanne þing seid by figure is taken as seid propirly to þe letter it is vnderstonden fleschely. No deþ of soule is seid more couenably þanne whanne vnderstondyng þat is excellentere in þe soule þan beestis is suget to þe fleische in suynge þe letter, þat is, turnynge it to fleischly lustis.
15 Also, a propur speche in holy writ schal not be taken as figuratyf. Whateuer þinge in Goddis word, þat is, holy writ, may not be referrid propirly to oneste of þewes or uertues, neiþer to þe treuþe of feiþ, know þou þat it is figuratif speche. Oneste of þewes pert[e]ineþ for to loue God and þi neiȝbore; treuþe of feiþ pert[e]ineþ for to knowe God and neiȝbore. Treuly to eche man is his hope [and] his
20 owne consciens, as he feliþ himself to profite to þe knowyng and louyng of God and of neiȝbore. Holy writ comaundiþ noþing no but charite neiþer blamiþ anyþing no but couetise, and by þis maner holy writ enformeþ þe condiciouns of men. Holy writ affermeþ not no but general feiþ, bi | rb | þingis passid, present and to-comynge. Tellynge is of þingis passid, bifore-tellynge of þingis to-comynge; shewynge is of
25 þingis present, but alle þes þingis perteynen for to nurche þe same charite and to strengþe it and to ouercome and quenche coueitise.

Also figuratyf speche is whereeuer þe wordis maken allegorye, þat is, gostly vndirstondyng perteynyng to feyþ, or whanne wordes maken derk licenesse or

Glosses and biblical references   2 'out of': outside   10 2 Cor. 3:6; 'gostly vnderstondyng': spiritual interpretation   11 'by figure': figuratively   • 'propirly to þe letter': literally   12 'couenably': appropriately   13 'suget': subjected   15 'propur speche': literal expression   16 'referrid': related   21 'blamiþ': condemns   22 'enformeþ þe condiciouns': fashions the qualities   25 'nurche': nourish   28 'derk licenesse': obscure metaphor

Variants   2 a] ony D o R77   3 if] and whanne D o R77   4 in holy writ alle þingis] alle þingis in holi writt D   5 in ony oþer D o R77   • sciens] sciencis D D76 Gı Lı O6 o Pı R77   6 no] not D D76 Gı Lı O6 o Pı R77   8 *Cristen om.*   9 pertyneþ   • wordes] word D D76 Gı Lı O6 o Pı R77   10 lyue] to liue D D76 Gı Lı O6 o Pı R77   12 No] noon   • is ˣsoˣ seid   14 \it/ *om.* D R77   16–17 oneste of þewes] honest þingis D o R77   18 pertineþ   19 pertineþ   • and²] and D D76 Gı Lı O6 o Pı R77] in   21 of] of þy neyȝbore D D76 Gı Lı O6 o Pı R77   • no¹'²] not D, ˣnotˣ Gı, *om.* D R77   24 tellynge ... passid *om.* D O6 R77   28 derk licenesse] derknesse D D76 Gı Lı O6 o Pı R77 (note)

parable. In alle figuratif speches suche a reule schal be kept þat so longe þat þat is
30   red be ofte turned bi diligent consideracioun or studye til interpretyng or expownyng
be brouȝt to þe rewme of charite. Treuly, if now it sowneþ propu[r]ly charite it is no
figuratyf speche. If þe speche is of comaundyng, forbedyng eiþer corrupcioun of
soule or resoun, eiþer forbedyng trespas aȝeynes neiȝbore or comaundynge profit or
good-doyng, it is no figuratyf speche bote propir to þe letter. Forsoþe, if þe speche of
35   holy writ semeþ to comaunde per[uers]ioun of soule or trespas aȝeines nei[ȝ]bore,
eiþer [to for]bede profite or good-d[o]ynge, it is figuratyf speche. Crist seiþ 'no bot
ȝee schulen ete þe fleich of mannes sone and schulen drynke his blod, ȝe schulen
[n]ot haue lif in ȝou'. It semeþ to comaunde trespas or noyinges of neiȝbore oþer
peruertyng of soule; þerfore it is figuratif speche, comaundynge vs for to comeyne
40   wiþ Cristis passioun and sweteli and profi[t]ably holde in mynde þat his fleich was
woundid and crucified for vs.

Whanne many s[entenc]es ben vnderstonden of þe same wordes of holy writ,
þouȝ þe ilke sentence be hid whiche he þat wroot vnderstood, no perel is if eche of
sentences may be preuyd by oþer partyes of holy scriptures | f. 1va | for to acorde to
45   treuþe, for wiþouten doute þe spirit of God þat spak by þe writer of þis scripture
bifore-say and purueyede þat þis trewe sentence schul[de] come to mynde of þe
reder or herer. For what myȝt be purueied of God large[lyer] and plenteuouslier in
Goddis speches þan þat þe same wordis be vnderstonden in many maners, whiche
oþer scri[p]tures of God of as gret autor[ite] preuen? Austyne þere, in þe iij. book .
50   Autours of holy writ vsen mo figuris þanne gramariens mowen gesse whiche
reden not þe figuris in holy writ: vij. reulis ben sette to vnderstonde holy writ aȝenes
aduersaries. Þe first is of oure Lord Iesu Crist and of his body, þat is, very cristen
men. By þis reule o persoone of þe hed and body, þat is of Crist and of holy chirche,
is schewed to vs, for it is not seid veynly to feiþful men 'ȝe ben þe seed of
55   Abraham', seþen oon holy seed of Abraham is, þat is Crist. [Doute] we not whanne
speche of scripture passiþ fro þe heed to þ[e] body or fro þe body to þe hed, and
neþeles it passiþ not fro oon and þe same persoone, for o persoone spekiþ seyinge

Glosses and biblical references   29 'þat': that which   31 'sowneþ': signifies   36–8 John
6:54   38 'noyinges of': injuries to   39–40 'comeyne wiþ': participate in   42 'sentences':
meanings   44 'acorde to': agree with   46 'bifore-say and purueyede': saw in advance and
provided   51 'vnderstonde' [and defend]   54–5 Gal. 3:29

Variants   29 speches] speche D o R77   33 profit] profity   34 no] not D D76 Gɪ Lɪ O6 o Pɪ R77   35
semeþ] seme D D76 Gɪ Lɪ O6 o Pɪ R77   • peruersioun D D76 Gɪ Lɪ O6 o Pɪ R77] perdicioun   •
neibore   36 for to bede   • dynge   37 b\l/od   37–8 schulen\ot/   38 noyinges] noyinge D D76 Gɪ Lɪ O6 o
Pɪ R77   • oþer] eiþer D D76 Lɪ O6 o Pɪ R77, or Gɪ   39 comeyne] comwne Lɪ O6 R77, comyne D Gɪ   40
wiþ] to D D76 Gɪ Lɪ O6 o Pɪ R77   • holde] to haue D Lɪ O6 o Pɪ R77   42 Whanne] for whanne D o
R77   • sentencis D D76 Gɪ Lɪ O6 o Pɪ R77] swetnesis   44 partyes] placis D D76 Gɪ Lɪ O6 o Pɪ R77   •
scriptures] ˣwriteˣ scriptures   45 þe writer] writ D D76 Gɪ Lɪ O6 o Pɪ R77   46 schul O4 D76, schulde
D Lɪ O6 o   47 purueied] proued O6 o R77   • largelyer] largerly   49 scritures   • autorite] autours O4
D76 o   51 þe] þo D76 Gɪ Lɪ O6 Pɪ   55 Doute] space left for *c.* 5 letters   56 to þ body   57 persoone¹]
persones D D76 Gɪ Lɪ O6 o Pɪ R77

'God settid on me as on spouse a myter, and ourned me as a spousesse wiþ
ournement', and neþeles it is to vnderstonde whiche of þese tw[e]yne acordiþ to þe
60   heed, þat is, Crist, and whiche to þe body, þat is, holy chirche.

[Þe] secounde reule is of Cristis body partid in twey partis, as Tyconye seiþ,
whiche truly ou3te not to be clepid so, for treuly þe ilke is not þe bodi of þe Lord
wheche schal not be wiþ hym into wiþouten ende in blesse but it is to [be] seid of þe
very body of þe Lord and of þe m[e]ddeled body, or very bodi and feyned, for not
65   oonly into wyþouten ende but also now ipocritis schulen not be seid to be wiþ þe
Lord, þou3 þei semen to be in his | vb | chirche. Þerfore þis reule my3te be seid of
meddlyd chirche. Þis reule axiþ a wakynge reder whanne holy writ spekiþ to oþer
men as to þe same [to] whiche it spak bifore, or whanne it semeþ to speke of þe
same men and neþeles spekeþ of oþer, as o body be of hem boþe, for temperal
70   medlyng and comynynge of sacramentis.

Þe þridde reule is of biheestis and lawe, whiche may be seid of spirit and
of letter, or of grace and of maundementis.

Þe iiij. reule is of spice [and] of kynde, þat is, of part and of al þe hool þinge
of whiche þe part is.

75   Þe fi[f]þe reule is of tymes, þat is bi figure synedoche, whanne al is
vnderstonden bi part or part vndirstonden bi al. In þis maner Crist is seid to haue ley
ded in þe sepulcre þre dayes and þre ny3tis: þe laste part of Goode Friday is sette for
al þat day, and þe firste parte of Sunday for al Sunday, and þe Satirday al ful. Or þis
reule of tymes is vndirstonden of noumbris, as seuene, ten and twelue and suche
80   oþer, whiche noumbris ben sette sumtyme for al tyme, as 'seuen siþe[s] in þe day,
Lord, I said preysyng to þe' is noþing elles þanne þis: 'God[dis preysyng] is euer in
my mouþ'. Also in Apocalips bi an hundrid fourety and foure is signyfyed al þe
vniuersite of seyntes.

Þe vj. reule is of [re]capitulacioun. Summe þingis don byfore ben seid as if
85   þei suen in ordre of tyme, or ben teld in next suwynge of þingis whan þe tellynge is
priuely cleped a3eyn to formere þingis þat weren lefte. If scri[p]ture be not
vndirstonden bi þis reule errour is gendrid, as in Genesis, 'God plauntide paradise in
Eden at þe eest, and sette þer man whom he fourmede, and 3et God brou3te forþ of
þe erþe eche feyr tre': þis is seid bi recapitulacioun or rehersyng of þing | f. 2ra | don
90   bifore. Also þere 'and þe lond was of o langage' is recapitulacioun.

Glosses and biblical references   58–9 Is. 61:10   61 'Tyconye': Tyconius   64 'meddeled':
mixed   67 'axiþ a wakynge': requires a vigilant   71 'biheestis': promises   71–2 'spirit
and of letter': spiritual meaning and literal meaning   73 'spice': species   75 'synedoche':
synecdoche   80–1 Ps. 118:164   81–2 Ps. 33:2   82–3 Apoc. 7:4, 14:1   83 'vniuersite':
multitude   86 'cleped a3eyn': recalled   87–9 Gen. 2:8, 9   90 Gen. 11:1

Variants   58 and] and he D D76 G1 L1 O6 o P1 R77   59 tweyne] twyne, *om.* D R77   61 Þe *om.*   •
twey] tweyne   63 wiþ hym *om.* D L1 o R77   • be *om.*   64 myddeled   68 to] þe   72 maundementis]
maundement D76 G1 L1 O6 P1 R77   73 and *om.*   75 fiyþe   78 for al Sunday *om.* D O6 R77   80
siþe   81 god^xdis^x   • preysyng *om.*   • euer] euermore O6 R77   84 recapitulacioun] þe capitulacioun   86
scriture   88 fo\u/rmede   90 and … langage] in þe lond was o langage D o R77

Þe seuenþe reule is of þe deuel and his body, for he is hed of alle vnpitouse
þat ben his bodi in sum maner, þat schulen go wiþ hym into þe turment of
euerelastynge fyre, as Crist is heed of holy chirche þat is his bodi, þat schal be wiþ
him in rewme and glorie euerlastyng.

95   Also, in þe ende of þat bok Austyn seiþ studieris of holy writ schulden kunne
þe kyndes of spechis in holy scripturis and take heed and holde in minde in what
maner a þing is wont to be seid in hem, and also, þat is souereyn and moost nedeful,
preye þei þat þei vnderstonde, for 'þe Lord ȝeueþ wysdom and kunnynge, and
vndirstondynge is of hym'. Al þis seiþ Austyn in þe iij. bok of *Cristen Doctryne*.

100   Autours of holy writ speken derkely þat prudently misteris be hid fro
vnpitouse men, and goode men be excercisid and, in expownynge it, haue grace
vnlik fro þe first autours of holy writ. Austyn in þe iiij. bok of *Cristen Techyng*.
Þerfore seynt Gregorie seiþ in þe xxix. book of *Moralys*, vij. cᵒ, þat Goddis wordis
ben as pyment or preciouse spyceries; hou myche spicerie is more powne[d] bi so

105   myche vertu is encressid in pyment, so hou myche we pownen more Goddis spechis
in expownynge, by þat we, herynge as drynkynge, ben more hol[pen].

For þis cause, a synful caytif, hauynge compassioun on lewed men, declariþ
þe gospel of Mathew to lewid men in Englische, wiþ exposicioun of s[e]yntis and
holy writ, and alleggiþ onely holy writ and olde doctours in his exposicioun, as seynt

110   Austyn, seynt Ierom, seynt Gregorie, seynt Ambrose, seynt Crisostom, seynt
Bernard, Grosted and olde lawes of seyntis and of holy chirche, | rb | wel groundid in
holy writ and resoun, and alleggiþ also þe Maister of Sentence rehersynge olde
seyntis and doctoures, and also Rabanes on Mathew, an olde monk and doctour,
rehersynge copiously olde holy doctouris for hym, as Austyn, Gregorie, Ambrose,

115   Bede, Illarie, Crisostom, Ierom, and many mo.

Þis coward synful caitif alleggiþ Ierom on Mathew on þe same tyxt whiche
he declariþ, and þerfore he alleggiþ þus, 'Ierom here', þat is, on þe same text. First
in glose a word of text is vndirdr[a]wen, þanne comeþ glos and þe doctour seyinge
þat is alleggid inn þe ende of þo glos, and after þat doctour al þe glos suynge is of þe

120   next doctour alleggi[d], so þat þe glos i[s] set bifore and þe doctour all[e]ggid after,
who it is and where. And þe same weye of Crisostom in his werk vncomplete on
Mathew euene on þe text expowned, and þe same maner of Rabanes, for he goþ
þourout on Mathew. Also, in þe sarmoun of þe Lord in þe Hil, þat is on v., vi. and

---

Glosses and biblical references   98–9 Prov. 2:6   102 'vnlik fro': different from that   104
'pyment': spiced wine • 'spyceries': spices • 'powned': pounded • 'hou myche … powned':
the more the spice is pounded   106 'holpen': helped   107 'caitif': wretch • 'declariþ':
elucidates   109 'alleggiþ': cites   112 'maister of sentence' (note)   113 'Rabanes': Rabanus
(note)   113 'for': before   115 'Illarie': Hilary of Poitiers (note)   122–3 'goþ þourout on':
expounds the whole of

Variants   95 writ] scripture D D76 G1 O6 o P1 R77, scripturis L1   96 spechis] spekyngis D D76 G1 L1
O6 o P1 R77   100 speken] spaken D D76 G1 L1 O6 o P1 R77   104 powne   106 holpen D D76 G1 L1 O6
o P1 R77] holsum, *expl.* D D76 G1 L1 O6 o P1 R77   118 vndirdrwen • \þe/   119 \þo/   120 alleggig •
is] it • allggid

vij. chapitris of Mathew, he alleggiþ Austyn on þis maner, 'Austyn here', þat is, on

125　þe same text expowned. Whanne he alleggiþ Gregorie, Bernard or Austyn or Ierom
in oþer bokis, or oþer doctours or lawis, he telleþ in what bok and what chapitre, for
men schulden not be in doute of treuþe.

　　And þis synful caitif, 'seeld vndur synne' as þe postle seiþ, takiþ pleinly and
schortly þe sentence of þ[e]s doctours, wiþ groundis of holy scripturs wiþouten any

130　settyng-to of oþer men, for þe sekenesse of oure peple is so gret þat þei nylen suffre
pore men lyuynge now to reproue her synnes and open heresies, þou3 þei tellen
neuere so pleynly holy writ [and] ensaumple of Cristis lif and his postlis wiþ pleyn
resoun. Þerfore men l[eyi]n | f. 2va | to oure seke peple þe plastre of holy writ wiþ
þes doctours biforseid wiþoute more addynge, if God wol in any maner of his grete

135　mercy make hem to knowe and amende her yuel lyuynge and acorde wiþ holy writ,
byfore þat þei of þis lyf gon.

　　Þre famouse enemyes of holy chirche, cristen pepul, semen to regne now on
þe puple, cristen in name and many of hem semen heþen in condiciouns. Þe firste
ben worldly prestis takynge cure [of] mennes soules by symonye and oþere cursid

140　menes for temperal lucre, worldly onours and bodily ese, whiche prechen Cristys
gospel by word or dede bot ben doumbe in hemselfe fro prechynge of þe gospel, and
letten oþer men þat kunne do þis office of prechyng and wolden do it treuly and
openly reproue synne, as God biddeþ. And 3et, þat is worst, þese strong enemys and
traitouris to Crist and his peple 3yuen ensample of alle curside synnes to her

145　suggitis, and poysenen hem wiþ fendes blasfemyng of pardouns wiþouten noumbre,
for to sle cristen men and sillen openly Cristis fleiche and his blood and alle
sacrementis of holy chirche. Þe secounde slie and fel traitours ben feyned religiouse
in name and colour of seyntis in willeful pouert, chastite and obedience, whiche
magnyfyen more þe trad[ic]ouns of synful men þan þe gospel of Crist wyþ his

150　fredome and ensample of Cristis lyf and his apostlis, in so myche þat if ony of siche
religiouse bounden to siche priuat tradiciouns wolde lyue as Crist and his postlis
diden, and edifie treuly cristen soulis bi þe gospel as þei diden, þe potestatis of
synguler nouelries crien hym a cursed apostata and eretik, distrier of cristen| vb |
dome. Þe þridde sotil enmyes and weiward eretikis letten cristen peple to knowe,

155　here, rede, write and speke holy writ in Englisch, bi feyned colours, seyynge þat þei
shul not preche neþer gedre cumpanyes to here Goddis word spoken and red of
lewed cristen peuple, þou3 charite stire hem neuer so myche þerto.

　　Al [þ]is feynynge is for drede of lesynge of muk of pride and worldly lustis,
lest cristen puple knowe þe treuþe [and] fredom of holy writ and disseitis of mennes

160　tradiciouns, caste aw[ey] þe deuels bondes of ypocris[ie], coueitise and symonye,
and turne to fre and trewe and esi ordinaunce of Crist Iesu and brynge worldly

Glosses and biblical references　　**128** Rom. 7:14; 'seeld': sold　　**130** 'settyng-to': addition　　**152**
'potestatis': powers　　**155** 'feyned colours': specious reasons

Variants　　**129** þes] þis　　**131** heresies] here sices　　**132** and[1] *om.*　　**133** lieyn　　**139** of *om.*　　**149** traciouns　　**158**
þis] is　　**159** and[1] *om.*　　**160** awye　　• ypocrist

clerkis þerto. Þese prestis and phariseys letten Crist to teche fr[e]ly holy writ, lest þe Romayns come and toke her place and folk, and lest þe peple lefte sacrifises and wynnyngys of prestis, as Crisostom seiþ in xl. omele. But, gode Iesu, for þi mechel
165 myȝt, mercy and charite, encresse þe knowynge and kepynge of þi lawe, and bate soone antecristis malice, ipocrisie and tirauntrie. Amen.

III Epilogue to Intermediate / Long Matthew

f. 263ra | Þe writer of þis glos purposide to Goddis onour and helpe of cristen soulis
for to telle treuly holy writ and schortly and pleynly þe moste profitable sentence of
þese byfore-seid doctours and hidurto. Blessid be God of his grete ȝyfte and
graciouse, þis pore scribeler is not gilti in his concience þat he erride fro treuþe of
5 holy writ and very sentence of þese doctouris. If ony lerned man in holy writ se þis
glos, dispise he not it wiþout good examinacioun of olde origynalis of doctouris, for
þis scribeler hadde trauelid wiþ fals bookis to see many and chese þe beste and
clereste sentence acordynge wiþ holy writ and resoun. If ony lerned man in holy writ
fynde ony defaute in þis glos, sette he in þe trewe and cler sentence of holy
10 doctouris, for þis is þe grete desire of þis pore scribeler.
    Wondre not, lewide men, þouȝ Rabanes be myche alleggid in þis glos, for he
was an old doctur almest of sixe hundrid ȝeeris agon | rb | and hadde plente of olde
do[c]turis whiche he rehersiþ in his book þorouout and litil seiþ of himsilf, and ȝit he
touchiþ no but pleyn mater whiche may lyȝtly be prouyd by holy writ and resoun.
15 Þerfore men holden þe sentence profitable and trewe þouȝ he hadde spokun no word
þerof, but we knowen it þe betere for his writynge and declarynge. We ȝeuen greet
credence to þese holy doctouris, namely Austyn, Crisostom, Ierom, Gregorie,
Ambrose and such olde seyntis, namely marterid for holy writ, and þat for þre
causes: oo cause [is] for her oldenesse and holynesse; þe secunde cause is for her
20 grete kunynge and trauel in holy writ and so longe approuynge of holy chirche,
approuynge her bookis for goode and trewe; þe þridde cause and moste of alle is þis,
for þei acordiden so myche wiþ holy writ and resoun in spekynge and lyuynge, and
weren euere meke and redy to be amendid if ony man coude fynde defaute by holy
writ or resoun in her writynge, and þei chargiden neuere neiþer constreynede ony
25 man to take her bookis, but comaundiden men to byleue not to her bokis no but in as
myche as þei weren groundid in holy writ expresly or in pleyn and sufficient resoun.
    Wherfore seynt Austyn, souereyneste of oure Latyn docturis, seiþ on þe lxvj.
salm in þe firste vers 'if Y seye, no man byleue it; if Crist seiþ, wo to him þat
byleueþ not'. Eft Austyn, on þe firste pistil of Ioon in þe ende, seiþ þus to his
30 aduersarie: 'if Y seie, dispise it; if gospel spekiþ, be þou war'. Eft Austyn, in þe
firste book *Of þe Trynyte*, seyþ þus: 'whoeuere rediþ | f. 263va | þese writyngis, where
he is certeyn wiþ me go he wiþ me; where he doutiþ wiþ me seke he wiþ me; where
he knowiþ his errour come he aȝen to me; where he knowiþ myn errour he
aȝenclepe me; so entre we togidere into þe weye of charite, goynge to him of whom
35 it is seid "seke ȝe euere þe face of hym". Y haue maad þis couenaunt pitouse and

Glosses and biblical references   9 'defaute': defect, flaw   11 'alleggid':cited   13 'of himsilf': on
his own account   18 'namely': particularly [those]   20 'approuynge of': having been approved
byȝ   26 'expresly': explicitly   33–4 'he aȝenclepe me': may he call me back   35 Ps. 26:8

Variants   1 helpe] helþ L   2 sentence] sentences L   5 þese] þe L   7 trauelid] trauel L   9 trewe] treuþe
L (cf. PWB 2970)   13 docturis] douturis   15 no word] no þyng L   19 is[1] *om.*   25 beleue and not L

sikere byfore ȝoure Lord God wiþ alle hem þat reden þo þingis þat Y write, and in
alle my writyngis, and moste in þese in whiche þe vnyte of Trynete is souȝt. Also, if
he þat rediþ my writyngis vndirstondiþ oþere men in þat word in whiche [he]
vndirstondiþ not me, leye he my book asidis or cast awey if it semeþ good to him,

40 and ȝeue he trauel and tyme to hem þat he vndirstondiþ. Also he þat rediþ my
writynges and seiþ "Y vndirstonde what is seid, but it is not seid treuly", afferme he
or proue his sentence as it plesiþ, and reproue he my sentence if he may. If he schal
do þis with charite and treuþe, and schal make þis knowen to me, if Y dwelle in lyif
Y schal take þe moste p[lenteu]ous fruyt of þis my trauel'. Also, in þe viij. book *Of*

45 *þe Trynyte* Austyn seiþ 'alle þe bildyngis or makyngis of Goddis bookis risen for
feiþ, hoope and charite to be bildid in mannes soule'.

Eft Austyn seiþ in þe firste bok *aȝenes Faustus*, in xj. cᵒ, 'þe excellence of
autorite of þe olde testament and newe is departid fro bokis of lattere men whiche,
confermed in tyme of þe postlis by successiouns or aftir-comyngis of bischopis and

50 bryngynge forþ of cristen chirches, is set hyȝely, as in sete to whiche alle feiþful and
pitouse vndirston| vb |dyng serueþ, þere if onyþyng myssownynge styre it is not leuful
to seie "þe autour of þis book held not treuþe," but he may seie þe bok is fals, or
interpretour or translatour erride, or þou vndirstondist not. Forsoþe, in litle werkis of
lattere men þat ben conteyned in bokis wiþout noumbre, but in no maner euened to

55 þe alle-holyeste excellence of canoun scripturis or reulis of holy writ, ȝhe in
whicheeuer of hem þe same treuþe is foundun, neþeles þe autorite is fer vneuene
treuly in þese lattere mennes bokis. If ony þyngis in hap ben gessid to discorde fro
treuþe, for þei ben [not] vndirstondun as [þei] ben seid, neþelis þe reder or herer haþ
þere fre demynge bi whiche eþer he approue þat þat plesiþ or reproue þat þat

60 offendeþ. And þerfore alle siche þingis, no but þey be defendid or mayntened by
serteyn resoun or by þe ilke autorite of holy wr[i]t, þat it be schewid eiþer on alle
maner to be so or þat it myȝte be don so þat þing þat is disputid or teld þere, if it
displesiþ to ony man, or he wole not bileue, he is not reproued. But in þe ilke
hiȝnesse of holy scripturis, ȝhe of o profete or postle or gospeler, is declarid by þe

65 ilke confirmacioun of reule to haue set onyþing in his lettris it is not leueful to doute
þat it is soþ, elles no book schal be by whiche þe sekenesse of mannes ignoraunce
schal be gouerned, if þe moste [hel]ful autorite of þese bookis eiþer dispisid be, al
don aweye eiþer forbodun [to] be confoundid'. A litil byfore in | f. 264ra | þe same
chapitre Austyn seiþ 'we ben amonge hem of whiche þe postle seiþ "and if ȝe

70 vndirstonden in oþer maner onyþing also God schal schewe it to ȝou", whiche kynde
of lettris, þat is of latere seyntis, is to be red not wiþ nede of byleuynge but wiþ
fredom of demynge'. And in þe secunde book, xij. cᵒ, 'many men han writun manye
þingis of þe lettris of holye chirche, þat is holy writ, not by autorite of reule but by
sum studie of helpyng or lernynge'.

Glosses and biblical references   48 'departid': distinct   51 'myssownynge styre': sounding amiss
should arise   54 'euened': equal   69–70 Phil. 3:15   73 'autorite of reule': canonical authority

Variants   38 he² *om.*   44 plenteuous L] pituouse (note)   55 þe *bis*   58 not *om.*   • þei² *om.*   60
offenedeþ   61 wrt   67 helful L] leueful (note)   68 to *om.*   73 but by] by by L

75   Also Austyn seiþ þus, and þe comyn lawe rehersiþ him in þis maner, 'Y ȝeue
þis onour to holy writ þat Y dar not seie þat ony of þo autours erride in writynge. If
Y fynde in þo bokis onyþing contrarie to treuþe, Y dar seie noon oþer þing þan þat
þe bok is fals, eiþer þe translatour erride, or Y vndirstonde not it. I rede so oþer
writeris or expositouris þat hou greet euere holynesse or doctryn þey han, not þerfore
80 Y gesse it to be soþe for þey feeliden or vndirstonden so, but for þei myȝten proue
to me by oþer autours þat is of holy wryt, eiþer by resoun of reule eþer probable þat
is soþ þat þei seyen'. Al þis seiþ Austyn.

     Also seynt Ierom, on þe secunde c[hapitre] of Ionas þe profete, seiþ þus: 'Y
vndirstonde þus, þat Crist schal be þre dayes and þre nyȝtis in þe herte of erþe, þat a
85 part of þe firste day be takun for al þe day, and þe Saterday hole, and þe first part of
þe Sunday for al þe Sunday. If ony may betere interprete þe mystries of þis letter,
sue þou his sentence'. Eft Ierom, on xxiij. cᵒ of Matheu, 'for þis seiynge haþ not | rb |
autorite of holy scripturs it is dispisid'.

     A dere God, lord of treuþe, my litle wit suffisiþ not for to wondre on þe
90 blyndenesse and pride of sum prestis, whiche constreynen cristen men for to byleue
to her lawes, statutis and customes, by peynes of dampnacioun as þey feynen, and by
bodily peynes þorou blyndenesse of cristen kyngis and lordis, whanne cristen men
knowen not þe ground of þese lawis neþer in holy writ neþer in resoun, but þei
semen aȝenes Cristis techyng and lyuyng and his postlis, and brouȝt in for pride and
95 coueitise of worldly prestis for to charge more þe puple in cost þan Crist and his
apostlis ordeyneden.

     Alas, gode Iesu, louer and sauyour of mennes soules, whi ben newe statutis
of worldly prestis magnefied aboue þyn holy gospel, confermed wiþ prescious blood
and treuþe of þi godhed? Alas, gode spouse of cristen soulis, Iesu Crist, whi
100 forsakest þou so myche þi puple þat synful mennes ordenaunce[s] ben openly tauȝt
and mayntened by worldly prestis and her fautouris, and þyn ordenaunce of wilful
pouert and greet mekenesse of clerkis, and contynuel ocupacioun of hem in
studiynge and techyng holy wryt, is dispisid and holdun errour, and þey holdun
cursid and sore prisoned þat wolden brynge aȝen þi beste ordenaunce?
105   Alas, alas, alas, ȝe cristen puple, whi suffre ȝe worldly prestis to robbe ȝou
of Goddis word, sustenaunce for ȝoure soules, and of ȝoure worldly goodis by vertu
of deed leed or rotun wex getun þorou symonye? Be ȝe war, for Crist seiþ 'if þe
blynde lediþ þe blynde, þey boþe fallen into lake'. And, certis, ȝe schulen not be
excusid by ignoraunce of Goddis | f. 264va | lawe, for ȝe myȝten kunne it if ȝe
110 wolden seke it of God by disyre and good lyuynge aftir kyndely resoun writun of
God in ȝoure soulis, and as bisily seke it of trewe prestis as ȝe seken worldly goodis
of worldly men. Þerfore eche cristen man and womman bisie hym in alle his myȝtis

---

Glosses and biblical references   80 'gesse': suppose • 'proue' [it]   94 'and his': and the
teaching and life of his   101 'fautouris': supporters   107–8 Matt. 15:14; Luke 6:39   108 'lake':
pit

Variants   81 of] oþer L • probable] profitable L (note)   86 may] man L   90 sum] owre L   98 wiþ]
wiþ þy L   100 ordenaunce   104 beste] beeste

to lerne and kepe Goddis heestis, to ocupye his wittis in spekynge of Cristis gospel, for þereynne is alle counfort and sikirnesse of cristene soulis for to come to þe blisse
115 of heuen. Crist Iesu, kyng of mercy, wysdom and charite, make þi puple to knowe ver[il]y and kepe feiþfuly þyn holy gospel, and to caste awey antecristis errours and veyn bondis þat tarieþ many men fro feiþ and charite, and cumbren many men in endeles dispeyr.

Variants   **116** verily L] very   • feiþfuly] feiþful L

IV Prologue to Short Luke

f. iii^vb |<D>auiþ, spekynge in þe perso<ne o>f Crist, seiþ to God þe <Fadir> 'I shal
telle þi name <to my briþeren; I> shal preise þee in <þe myddis of þe> chirche'.
Also <Sacarie seiþ to Ion Ba>ptist 'and <þou, child, shalt be cle>pid þe prophete of
<þe hiȝest, for þou sh>alt go bifore <þe face of þe Lord to> make <redy hise weies,
5   to ȝiue þe kunn>yng of h<elþe to his puple into re>missioun of her synnes', Luk, i.
c°. <Þe> kunnyng of helþe is þe veri techyng of Cristis gospel, which he tauȝte bi
werk and word, and he diede to conferme it, and he sente his disciplis to preche þis
holy gospel to alle men and seide 'he þat shal bileue and shal be baptisid shal be
saaf; soþely, he þat shal not bileue shal be dampned', Mark, xvi. c°. Also Crist seiþ
10 'it bihoueþ me to preche þe rewme of God for þerfor Y am sent', and eft Crist seiþ
'þe Holy Goost sente me to preche þe gospel to pore men', Luk, iiij. c°. Crist, God
and man, seiþ mekely 'þe Holy Goost sente me' for bi h[i]s manhed he is lesse þan
þe Holy Goost, þouȝ bi his godhed he is euene in maieste wiþ þe Fadir and þe Holy
Goost. And wel Crist seiþ to pore men, þat is, to meke men, for Crist prechide þe
15 gospel to saluacioun of meke men þat wolen gladly obeie to his gospel, but proude
men contynuynge in her pride and cursidnesse sh[u]len be dampned for her rebelte
aȝens Cristis gospel.
      Herfore | f. iv^ra | [a pore] caityf, lettid fro prechyng for a tyme for causis
knowun of God, writiþ þe gospel of Luk in Englysh wiþ a short exposicioun of olde
20 and holy doctouris to þe pore men of his nacioun whiche kunnen litil Latyn eþer
noon, and ben pore of wit and of worldli catel and neþeles riche of good wille to
plese God. Firste þis pore caitif settiþ a ful sentence of þe text togidre þat it may wel
be knowun fro þe exposicioun; aftirward he settiþ a sentence of a doctour declarynge
þe text, and in þe ende of þe sentence he settiþ þe doctouris name, þat men mown
25 knowe verili hou fer his sentence goiþ. Oneli þe text of holy writ and sentence of
olde doctouris and appreuyd ben set in þis exposicioun. Whanne Y alegge 'Ambrose
here' eþer 'Bede here', vndurstonde on þe same text expowned. Whanne Y alegge
eny doctour and telle not in what place, vndirstonde þat Y alegge hym as Alquyn on
Luk rehersiþ him. Ambrose, Ierom, Austyn and Gregorie ben wel knowun for
30 gloriouse lyueris and trewe doctouris of holy chirch; Bede is an olde expositour of
holy writ and telliþ noþing almest no but þe sentence of olde holy doctouris bifore
hym, and he writiþ opynly and deuoutly and sumtyme sharply.
      Whanne Alquyn aleggiþ ony doctour and telliþ not where he takiþ hym on
Luk, as he witnessiþ in his prologe he aleggiþ seint Denyss þe martir, seint | rb |

Glosses and biblical references   1–2 Ps. 21:23 (note)   3 'Sacarie': Zacarias   3–5 Luke 1:76–7
(note)   5 'kunnyng of helþe': knowledge of salvation   8–9 Mark 16:16   9–10 Luke 4:43   10–
11 Luke 4:18, quoting Is. 61:1   16 'rebelte': rebellion   18 'caityf': wretch   23 'declarynge':
elucidating   25 'hou fer his sentence goiþ': i. e., where his gloss ends   26 'alegge': cite   32
'opynly': plainly   • 'sharply': acutely

Variants   12 his] hs   16 There is a small hole in the manuscript between 'sh' and 'len'.   18 a pore *om.*

35 Gregorie Nasansene martir, seint Cipryan martir; he aleggiþ myche Teofile,
Crisostom, Basile, Cirille, Attanasie, Damassene and Gregorie Nycene, and alle þese
ben of a þousand ȝere eþer more, and her bookis ben appreuyd, as þe lawe witnessiþ,
xv. d. in finem, and xvi., de *confirmamus*. Also Alquin aleggiþ myche þe grete
Origen, Epiphanye, Eusebie and Maximus, famouse in omelies; þese ben of a

40 þousend ȝere and more, and famouse doctouris and noble lyueris. Also he aleggiþ
Ysidre, Tite and Greek doctour; þes weren olde men and textual, declarynge wel þe
text. Whanne a sentence is set in þis exposcioun and is aleggid for 'a glos' þanne it
is takun of Alquyn aleggynge oþer doctours, lesse þan þese biforeseid.

If eny lernyd man se þis exposicioun and suppose eny errour þerynne, for

45 Goddis loue loke he wel his originals and sette ynne þe trewe sentence of þese
doctouris, for men desiren noþing in þis exposicioun no but profitable treuþe for
cristen soulis. Y sette shortly and pleynly as Y may and kan þe sentence of þese
doctouris, and not barely her wordis, in as myche as þei declaren þe text and seyen
treuþe groundid in holi scripture eþer quyk resoun, and accordynge wiþ þe blessid

50 lyf of Crist and his apostlis, desirynge þat no man triste more þan þus to her sentence
neþer to eny mannys seying, | f. iv^va | in whateuer staat he be in erþe. Þus, wiþ
Goddis grace, pore cristen men mown sumdel knowe þe text of þe gospel wiþ þe
comyn sentence of olde holy doctouris, and þerynne knowe þe meke and pore and
charitable lyuyng of Crist and his apostlis, to sue hem in vertues and blys, and also

55 knowe þe proude and coueitouse and veniable lyuyng of antecrist and his fautoris, to
fle hem and her cursid dedis and peynes of helle. For no doute, as oure Lord Iesu
Crist and his apostlis profesien pleynli, antecrist and his cursid disciplis shulen come
and disseyue many men by ypocrisie and tyrauntrie, and þe beste armeer of cristen
men aȝens þis cursid cheuenteyn wiþ his oost is þe text of holy writ, and namely þe

60 gospel and veri and opyn ensaumple of Cristis lijf and his apostlis, and good lyuyng
of men, for þanne þei shulen knowe wel antecrist and his meynee bi her opyn dedis
contrarie to Cristis techynge and lyuyng.

Crist Iesu, for þyn endeles power, mercy and charite make þi blessid lawe
knowun and kept of þi puple, and make knowun þe ypocrisie and tirauntrie and

65 cursidnesse of antecrist and his meynee, þat þi puple be not disseyued bi hem. Amen
gode Lord Iesu.

Glosses and biblical references   37 'ben of a þousand ȝere': lived a 1000 years ago   41 'textual':
knowledgable about the text   42 'aleggid for': cited as   48 'barely': merely   55 'veniable':
vengeful • 'fautoris': adherents   59 'cheuenteyn': chieftain

Variants   48 ˣdeˣdeclaren

V Prologue to Short John

f.115vb | Oure Lord Iesu Crist veri God and very man cam to serue pore, meke men
and to teche hem þe gospel, and for þis cause seynt Poul seiþ þat he and oþere
apostlis of Crist ben seruauntis of cristen men bi oure Lore Iesu Crist, and eft he seiþ
'Y am dettour to wise men and vnwise', and eft 'bere 3e þe chargis anoþer of
5 anoþer, and so 3e schulen fille þe lawe of Crist', þat is, of charite, as seynt Austyn
expowneþ.
    Herfor a symple creature of God, willinge to bere in party þe chargis of
symple pore men well-willinge to Goddis cause, writiþ a schort glos in Englisch on
þe gospel of Ioon, and settiþ onely þe text of holy writ and þe opyn and schorte
10 sentencis of holy doctours, boþe Grekis and Latyns, and alleggiþ hem in general for
to ese þe symple wit and cost of pore, symple men, remyttinge to þe grettir gloos
writun on Ioon where and in what bokis þes doctours seyen þes sentences. And
sumtyme he takiþ þe cleer sentence of lawis of þe chirche, maad of seyntis, wel
groundid in holy writ and pleyn resoun, to dispise synnes and comende vertues. First
15 þe text is set and þanne þe sentence of a doctour is set aftir, and þe doctour is aleggid
in þe ende of þe same sentence.

Glosses and biblical references   **2–3** 2 Cor. 4:5   **3–4** Rom. 1:14   **4–5** Gal. 6:2; 'chargis':
burdens **11** 'remyttinge to': postponing until

In þe biginnyng

f. 9r | In þe biginnyng of holy chirche it was forbodyn þat eny man schulde speke in
straunge langage but it were maad op[en] in comwne langage of hem þat herden it,
and þerof waxe a good manere in holy chirche in summe contrees þat whan þe
gospel was pronouncid and rad in chirche aftir þe lettre anoon it schulde be
5   pronouncid to hem þat hadde [herd] it in her comwn langage, and expowned also.
What schulle we do þerfore in oure dayes now, þere fewe or non is founden þat takiþ
hede to þat he rediþ, or þat vndirstondiþ þat he heriþ rad? Wherfore it semiþ now
fulfild þat was seid of old tyme, 'þe prest schal be as oon of þe puple'.

Glosses and biblical references   2 'straunge': foreign   • 'comwne': common, vernacular   3
'manere': practice   4 'aftir þe lettre': according to the [Latin] text   8 Is. 24:2; Hos. 4:9

Variants   2 but] but ʒif G1   • open] opne   5 herd *om.* L1 P1   7 þat¹] þat þat G1   • or] oþer D76 P1

Notes to the texts

1.   The Prologue to the Wycliffite Bible

1–62 PWB begins with a list of the books included in the Hebrew scriptures and of other books included in the Latin Bible. Only the former are included in the canon as 'bookis of feiþ and fulli bookis of hooli writ' (1–2). See Dove, *FEB*, 92–101.

1–24 See Jerome's prologue to Kings, 'Prologus Galeatus' ('helmeted prologue'); PL 28:547–58. Jerome, however, gives the books in the Hebrew order, whereas the Prologue-writer gives them in the order in which they appear in the Greek translation of the Hebrew scriptures known as the Septuagint (LXX; 'the 70'), third to first century BC. On the legendary origin of the Septuagint see CTI 249–59 (and note). Both Hebrew and Septuagint orders are found in early medieval Latin Bibles, but the Septuagint order supersedes the Hebrew from c.1200 onwards, and is the order in which the books appear in WB. See Dove, *FEB*, 85–6.

2–3 'Exodi', 'Leuitici' and 'Numeri' are all genitives.

4 'þe lawe', i.e., the Jewish law, the Torah.

7 'Paralipomenon' (things passed over) is the Septuagint title; the Hebrew title means 'annals'.

11 'Parabolae Salomonis' is an alternative name for this book in the Latin Bible.

12 'Songis of Songis' translates 'Cantica Canticorum', the usual name of this book in the later Middle Ages. 'Song of Songis', translating the Hebrew Shir Ha-Shirim, is more accurate.

19–22 A biblical book 'wiþouten autorite of bileue' cannot be used to determine doctrine; a book 'of bileue', that is, a canonical book, can be used to determine doctrine. The books the writer names are included in the Septuagint but not in the Hebrew scriptures; they are therefore extra-canonical.

25–6 Baruch, written in Greek, is an appendix to Jeremiah; the Epistle of Jeremiah is the sixth chapter of Baruch. Often lacking in Latin Bibles before 1200, Baruch is included in all versions of WB.

26–7 The Prayer of Manasses (Manasseh), 2 Cor. 37, is a Greek addition to the Hebrew text, frequently but not invariably included in medieval Latin Bibles. It is included in all versions of WB, although a gloss in some manuscripts points out that it is not part of the Hebrew text; see Dove, *FEB*, 227–8.

27 'and hou'–**29** Jerome's rubrics indicating the passages of Esther and Daniel that are not in Hebrew are included in all versions of WB.

35 'Latyns': members of the Catholic church of the Roman rite whose Bible is the Latin Bible.

44–6 See Jerome's prologue to Judith; PL 29:39.

47–53 See Jerome's prologue to the Books of Solomon (prefixed to Proverbs); PL 28:1242–3.

54–9 See Jerome's prologue to Ezra; PL 28:1403. In spite of Jerome's contempt, the third book of Ezra (2 Esdras) is included in many medieval Latin Bibles and in the Earlier Version of WB (also in a revised version in Bodleian Library Bodley 277).

60 The writer must be speaking for the translators producing the Later Version as a whole when he says 'I translatide not'; see Dove, *FEB*, 79–80.

62–70 The writer is translating the entry for 'apocrifus' in the *Catholicon*, a dictionary compiled by Johannes Balbus of Genoa, d. 1298, and revised several times. In the edition printed in Venice in 1495 the entry is sig. I.4r.

69–70 On the gospel of the Infancy of the Saviour (the Infancy Gospel of Thomas), see J.K. Elliott, in John Barton and John Muddiman, eds, *The Oxford Bible Commentary* (Oxford: Oxford University Press, 2001), pp. 1319–20. On the *Transitus Mariae*, see Michael O'Carroll, 'Assumption Apocrypha', in *Theokotos* (Dublin: Dominican Publications, 1982), pp. 58–61.

73 The number of Pauline Epistles is usually given as either fourteen or eleven, if 1–2 Corinthians, 1–2 Thessalonians and 1–2 Timothy are counted as one each. The error 'xij.' occurs in all manuscripts and in both Gough and Crowley.

73–4 The 'small epistles' are the seven Catholic (Canonical) Epistles: James, 1–2 Peter, 1–3 John and Jude.

80–2 Augustine, Sermo CCCL; PL 39:1534.

91–4 *Enarrationes in Psalmos* (Ps. 54:16), ed. E. Dekkers and J. Fraipont (Turnhout: Brepols, 1956; CCSL 39), pp. 668–9. Cf. *HPD* 116–20.

109–10 'þe foure doctours': the four pre-eminent doctors of the church in the West are Ambrose of Milan, Augustine of Hippo, Jerome of Stridon and Gregory the Great; see GGIV 29–30.

115–16 'lawe of grace', as opposed to Moses' law.

125–30 For this characteristically Wycliffite distinction between God's law (holy scripture) and customs and laws made by sinful men, including the customs and laws of the church, cf. 1608–11 and 1620–7 below, and CTX 1–8, GGIII 89–96 Beside these lines in S is the first of a series of polemical notes on the Prologue in the hand of Geoffrey Blythe, bishop of Coventry and Lichfield 1503–33.

154–5 'and þanne … See': these words are omitted in all manuscripts except **P** and **T**.

198–201 For other references to this narrative see CTVII 18 and CTXII 347–9.

239 The writer summarizes Deuteronomy considerably more fully than he has the preceding four books.

241 'adde noþing … from þo': this text is the topic of a short treatise in Cambridge University Library (CUL) Ff.6.31, part I, fols 61r–v: see p. lvi (**C7**).

242 P's reading 'wise and witti' translates 'sapientes et gnaros', Deut. 1:13 (all other manuscripts read 'my3ty').

300 'cuniourers', translated 'dyuynouris' in WB in LV (Deut. 18:10); *WB*, I, 510.

300 'chiteryng of briddis' (as in LV; *WB*, I, 510) translates *auguria* (Latin Bible). Nicholas of Lyra (see the note on 2360) says 'diuinationes faciunt per garritum seu volatum auium' (they arrive at divinations through the chirping or the flight of birds).

301 'enchaunter, þat is þat disseyueþ mennus i3en þat a þing seme þat is not' (LV, Deut. 18:11); *WB*, I, 511.

302 'hem þat han spiritis in cloos' (*pythones*, Latin Bible): 'hem þat han a feend spekynge in þe wombe' (LV, Deut. 18:11); *WB*, I, 511, following Nicholas of Lyra (see the note on

2360, below), 'ventriloqui qui habent in ventre daemonem verba exterius preferentem' (ventriloquists who have a demon in their belly proffering words to the outside world). See also 1057–8.

377 The 'greet song' is 'Audite caeli quae loquor', Deut. 32:1.

419 The misreading of 'til' as 'al' spoils the sense of this line in α S, and leads G ι Q to add 'for afore þis þe puple'.

432 'of Iosue and oþere princes pees and liyf': α S read 'of Iosue pees and lijf and oþer princis' and G ι Q 'of Iosue pees and lyf of Iosue and oþere pryncis'. Evidently there was some confusion in the archetype at this point, which has been resolved in β P T.

437–40 Jos. 11–24 receive very short shrift here, and the following book, Judges, is summarized very compendiously.

455–6 Ruth married Boaz, and is named in the genealogy of Christ at Matt. 1:5, 'Booz autem genuit Obed ex Ruth'.

621 α G ι Q S *pr. m.* and Crowley have the erroroneous reading 'dukis and of meynees'.

661 'templis in hiȝ places' were characteristic of the worship of pagan gods in the Canaanite world.

674 'wolde fille his hond was': the reading of α β S *sec. m.* 'fillide his hond and was' is equally good, but P confuses the two: 'wolde fille his hond and was'.

690–2 This quotation, attributed to Jerome, has not been identified.

828 The writer misses the point that axe was borrowed and the borrower was highly distressed when it fell into the water.

857 α β G ι Q S read 'pilgrimage eiþer straunge lond'; the reading of P T is evidently a clarification.

899 'for prys of soulis' translates 'per pretio animae', 4 Kings 12:4. The context suggests that this money was paid as part of the funeral rite.

1012 'as tablis on bord ben wont to be doon awei' translates 'sicut deleri solent tabulae', 4 Kings 21:13.

1016 'vnclennesses' (the reading of α S) accords with 'servivitque immunditiis quibus servierat pater suus et adoravit eas', 4 Kings 21:21.

1024–5 'whanne þe book of lawe was redde': it is surprising that there is no mention of the finding of the book, 2 Kings 22:8. Probably a line or two of the writer's text has been lost.

1047 G ι Q read 'housis', in accordance with 'aediculas effeminatorum', 4 Kings 23:7, and their reading is adopted here.

1054 'of þo on þe': the reading of G ι Q is adopted here, although 4 Kings 23:20 does not specify that the 'ossa humana' are those of the priests, since the range of readings in the other manuscripts—'of þo' in α S, 'of þe' in β, 'on þe' in P and 'on þo' in T—suggests that both prepositional phrases were present in the archetype. Cf. 1604.

1111–13 See Jer. 40–52.

1122–7 Jerome, *Ep.* LIII, *ad Paulinum*; PL 22:548. This is the second prologue to Paralipomenon in WB in EV; *WB*, II, 316.

1229 'turne into ȝou' repeats the translation of 2 Chron. 19:6 in LV, but EV has 'in to ȝou it schal redoundyn'; *WB*, II, 426.

1238 'shewe ȝe to hem': S explains 'shewe ȝe to hem *þe trewþe*' (2 Chron. 19:10); *WB*, II, 426.

1325 Osias (Uzziah) is called Asarie (Azariah) at 4 Kings 14:21, PWB 937

1339–40 'telden þe lawe þat was aȝenus him': see Num. 16:40 and 18:7.

1351–2 'chorus conteneyneþ þritti buschels': this gloss, derived from Nicholas of Lyra (see the note on 2360) is found in ten manuscripts of LV at Ezech. 45:11, though not at 2 Chron. 27:5; *WB*, III, 610.

1471 'he preiede his Lord God': the prayer is recorded in 2 Chron. 37 (see the note on 26–7, above), but is not included in the OT summary in PWB.

1568–9 'fifti ȝeeris' is the number given in all manuscripts except **T**, which correctly reads 'seuenti' in accordance with 2 Chron. 36:21 and Jer. 25:12. Both EV and LV are correct here; *WB*, II, 475.

1579–80 'þe stori of kyng Iosaphat, þe storie of king Eȝechie and þe storie of kyng Iosie': on the history of Josaphat in Kings see 756–8, and in Chronicles 1092–255; on the history of Ezechiah in Kings see 965–1003, and in Chronicles 1387–460; and on the history of Josiah in Kings see 1021–68, and in Chronicles 1486–550.

1585 'summe'–**1589** On arguments against pardons in Wycliffite writings, see A. Hudson, 'Dangerous fictions: indulgences in the thought of Wyclif and his followers', in R.N. Swanson, ed., *Promissory Notes on the Treasury of Merits: Indulgences in Late Medieval Europe* (Leiden: Brill, 2006), 197–214, and R.N. Swanson, *Indulgences in Late Medieval England: Passports to Paradise?* (Cambridge: Cambridge University Press, 2007), pp. 294–309.

1598 'symonyent': simoniac. This term, deriving from Simon Magus, who attempted to buy spiritual power (Acts 8:18–19), denotes a person who buys or sells benefices, ecclesiastical preferments or other spiritual things. Cf. the note on 2149–51.

1600–2 Cf. the sixth of the *Twelve Conclusions of the Lollards*, which draws a similarly sharp distinction between the secular and temporal realms: 'temperalte and spirituelte ben to partys [two parts] of holi chirch, and þerfore he þat hath takin him to þe ton schulde nout medlin him with þe toþir'; ed. Hudson, *SEWW*, 26/62–72, and see pp. 150, 152.

1606 'freris lettris': letters of fraternity, i.e., open letters from one of the orders of friars offering benefactors spiritual benefits in exchange for economic support; see W.G. Clark-Maxwell, 'Some letters of confraternity', *Archaeologia* 75 (1926), 19–60 and 79 (1929), 179–216, and Swanson, *Indulgences in Late Medieval England: Passports to Paradise?*, pp. 142–8, 1300. The Lollard sermon *Omnis plantacio* also accuses the friars of lying 'wiþ her lettre and her general seel', ed. Hudson, *WLP*, 12/246, and see p. 261.

1610 'synful mennus tradiciouns or statutes': customs or laws invented by human beings, as opposed to God's law, revealed in the Bible. See the note on 125–30, above.

1612–14 See 711–14.

1614–16 See 752–4 and 1216–17.

1617 'idiotis in comparisoun of clerkis of scole': illiterates when compared with university scholars. Peter and John are called *idiotae* at Acts 4:13; see *FSB* 37.

1623 'good resoun': i.e., reason evidently following from the rules of faith, as Augustine says, *Epistola* XCIII, *ad Vincentum Donatistum*; ed. K.D. Daur, *Sancti Aurelii Augustini Epistulae*, vol. II (Turnhout: Brepols, 2004; CCSL 31A), pp. 167–206. Cf. 2169–71 and PIP 42–4.

1624 'feyned religiouse': members of religious orders pretending to lead a religious life. This is a favourite Lollard phrase; cf. 1815, 2482, 2531 and 2533, CTXII 46 and GGII 147.

1636 'glotouns maken her beli her god': Paul speaks of the enemies of the cross of Christ whose God is their stomach, Phil. 3:18–19.

1638–9 Augustine, *In Iohannis Euangelium*, LII, 7, ed. D.R. Willems (Turnhout: Brepols, 1954; CCSL 36), p. 449/19–23.

1644 'Erchedekene': a common appellation for Guido de Baysio, archdeacon of Bologna and later of Avignon, author of the commentary on Gratian's *Decretum* known as *Rosarium super Decreto*, c.1296–1300.

1648–50 'Sunt in ecclesia', De Baysio, *Archidiaconus* (*Rosarium super Decreto*) (Venice, 1495), sig. T.9ra.

1651–2 'Nihil ouibus', De Baysio, *Rosarium*, sig. K.6rb.

1652–4 'Qui nec regiminis', De Baysio, *Rosarium*, sig. P.9va.

1654–7 'Non omnes' (not 'omnis'), De Baysio, *Rosarium*, sig. P.9ra.

1657–8 'In mandatis', De Baysio, *Rosarium*, sig. F.4vb. De Baysio cites Matt. 7:6.

1658–9 'Quoniam regula ecclesiastica', De Baysio, *Rosarium*, sig. F.9rb.

1659–68 From 'Sit rector', De Baysio, *Rosarium*, sig. F.4rb.

1665–6 See Jerome, *In Michaeam*, II, vii, ed. M. Adriaen, *S. Hieronymi Presbyteri Opera: Commentarii in Prophetas Minores*, vol. I (Turnhout: Brepols, 1969; CCSL 76), pp. 508–9/163–8.

1667 'Ecclesie epulas' (not 'principes'), De Baysio, *Rosarium*, sig. E.6ra.

1669–97 From 'Sit rector', De Baysio, *Rosarium*, sig. F.4va.

1683 'of nou3t', *ex nihilo*, like the Creation (a scholastic jest).

1704–6 Gregory the Great, *Regula Pastoralis*, I, ii; ed. and trans. H.R. Bramley (Oxford: Parker, 1874), p. 12.

1706–8 'Nihil ouibus', De Baysio, *Rosarium*, sig. K.6rb.

1708 'Grosted': Robert Grosseteste (c.1170–1253), scientist, theologian and Greek scholar, was an administrator in the diocese of Hereford, taught in the university of Oxford and was lector to the Oxford Franciscans before becoming bishop of Lincoln from 1235 to 1253. On his career, see James MacEvoy, *Robert Grosseteste* (Oxford: Oxford University Press, 2000), and R.W. Southern, *ODNB* 24:79–86.

1709–11 There is no modern edition of the sermon *Premonitus a venerabili patre*, the subject of which is the pastoral responsibility of the clergy. For details of manuscripts containing it, see S. Harrison Thomson, *The Writings of Robert Grosseteste Bishop of Lincoln 1235–53* (Cambridge, 1941), pp. 164 (no. 19), 173–4. In BL Royal 6 E.v this sermon is fols 86ra–90vb.

1711–21 Grosseteste's sermon *Dominus noster* is ed. Servus Gieben, 'Robert Grosseteste at the Papal Curia, Lyons 1250: Edition of the Documents', *Collectanea Franciscana* 41 (1971), p. 357. See also Thomson, *The Writings of Robert Grosseteste*, pp. 164 (no. 14), 171. The writer of PWB is paraphrasing Grosseteste. *Dominus noster*, roundly attacking the abuses of the curia, was read aloud to the papal council at Lyons in 1250: Southern points out that Grosseteste's attack on the curia and his reforming zeal endeared him to Wyclif, *ODNB* 24:83.

1721–4 There is no modern edition of the sermon *Scriptum est de Leuitis*. For details of manuscripts containing it, see Thomson, *The Writings of Robert Grosseteste*, pp. 165 (no. 31), 176. In BL Royal 6 E.v this sermon is fols 109ra–112va. For another passage from this sermon see *FSB* 100–10.

1724–35 In BL Royal 6 E.v the quoted passage of *Premonitus a venerabili patre* is on f. 87ra.

1738 'pleiyng at þe beere': performing interludes or playing games beside the coffin?

1743–5 'Parisience', the French Dominican Gulielmus Peraldus, b. c.1200, whose *Summa de Vitiis* was written c.1236. Cf. 'De Avaritia', ch. 7 (Basle, c.1474), sig. G.8v.

1760 'oure Ladi of Walsyngham': the Blessed Virgin Mary, so named for her supposed appearance to Richeldis de Faverches in this Norfolk village in 1061. In the later Middle Ages the Holy House at Walsingham was one of the most popular destinations for pilgrims.

1766–7 The writer of *Opus Imperfectum in Matthæum*, XII, discussing Matt. 5:33–4, argues that oaths are pointless, since the man who fears God will tell the truth whether he has sworn to do so or not, and the man who does not fear God cannot tell the truth, under oath or not; PG 56:697–8. *Opus Imperfectum in Matthæum*, long believed to be by Chrysostom and extremely popular in the later Middle Ages, was probably written by a fifth-century Arian cleric; see J. van Banning, *Opus Imperfectum in Matthaeum: Praefatio* (Turnhout: Brepols, 1988; CCSL 87B), p. v.

1767 Jerome, *Commentariorum in Matheum Libri IV*, ed. D. Hurst and M. Adriaen (Turnhout: Brepols, 1969; CCSL 77), pp. 32–3/644–59.

1767–8 Gratian, *Decretum*, ca. 22, qu. 1, c. 10, *Si quis*, and c. 9, *Clericum*; Richter and Friedberg, I, 863.

1769 Gregory IX, *Decretals*, lib. 2, tit. 24, c. 26, *Etsi Christus*; Richter and Friedberg II, 369–71.

1774 'þe wiys man', *sapiens*, is the epithet commonly given to the writer of Wisdom and Ecclesiasticus.

1783–5 Gregory the Great, *Regula Pastoralis*, III, iv; ed. and trans. Bramley, p. 142.

1785–6 Cf. 220–3, above.

1796 'clepen hem lollardis': the first recorded use of this abusive term, by Henry Crumpe in Oxford, is dated 1382; it is recorded that he called the English heretics 'lollardi'; W.W. Shirley, ed., *Fasciculi Zizaniorum Magistri Johannis Wyclif cum Tritico* (London: Longman, 1858; Rolls Series 5), pp. 289, 311–12. Crumpe was thus linking English heretics with heretical mendicants ('gyrovagi') in continental Europe; see the discussion of the origins of 'lollard' and 'loller' in Wendy Scase, *'Piers Plowman' and the New Anticlericalism* (Cambridge: Cambridge University Press, 1989), pp. 125–60 (on Crumpe, p. 154), and Hudson, *WLP*, 273–4.

1808–9 Grosseteste, Dictum 138, on the text 'sint lumbi vestri precinti' (Luke 12:35), inc. 'Officium enim nostrum qui ad sacros ordines promovemur bipartitum est', in Bodleian Library Bodley 798, fols 113rb–115ra; Dictum 13, on the text 'manus vestre pollute sanguine' (Is. 59:3), inc. 'Alieni sanguinis iniuriosus effusor dicitur sanguinolentas habere manus', in Bodleian Library Bodley 798, fol. 10r.

1889 'Þou3 þe book of Tobie is not of bileue, it is a ful deuout stori': G and ɩ remove the reference to Tobit's extra-canonical status, reading 'þe book of tobie is ful deuout storie'.

1900–4 Jerome's prologue to Judith; PL 29:39. See also 44–6.

1900–5, comendiþ: G replaces this discussion of Judith's canonicity, or lack of, with 'þe book of iudith comendiþ'.

1903 'Caldee', i.e., Syriac; the ancient Semitic language of Syria.

1915–18 A gloss on Judith 10:12 in two manuscripts of WB in LV translates Nicholas of Lyra's gloss (see the note on 2360), which the Prologue-writer evidently has in mind here: 'þese wordis of Judiþ and many mo wordis suynge ben leesinge feyned for delyueraunce of þe puple worschipinge God and for þe castinge doun of proude Holofernes purposinge to distrie Goddis onour, and siche leesing is venyal synne fro which it nediþ not to excuse Judiþ siþen þe postlis hadden venyal synne aftir þe resseyuyng of þe Holy Goost, Lire'; *WB*, II, 622.

1963–5 The writer may be referring to the occasional explanatory glosses within the text of Job in WB in LV, to the marginal glosses—most of which, however, survive in only two LV manuscripts—or to a lost Glossed Job, equivalent to the Glossed Gospels.

2015 'Latyns': see the note on 35, above.

2015 Jerome revised the Old Latin Psalms, which had been translated from the Septuagint, twice: his first translation was the 'Roman Psalter', preserved in liturgical use throughout the Middle Ages; his second revision was the 'Gallican Psalter', popularized by Alcuin: this is the Psalter most commonly found in late medieval Latin Bibles. He also translated Psalms from the Hebrew: the 'Hebrew Psalter'. As the Prologue-writer says, there are many discrepancies between the Gallican and the Hebrew Psalters. In some late medieval Bibles there are parallel Gallican and Hebrew Psalters; WB has the Gallican Psalter only. See also PWB 2857–60 and note.

2049–82 On the interpretation of the Song of Songs in the Middle Ages, understood as concerning 'hi3 gostli loue and greet priuytees of Crist and of his chirche', see E. Ann Matter, *The Voice of my Beloved: The Song of Songs in Western Medieval Christianity* (Philadelphia: University of Pennsylvania Press, 1990).

2049–52 The historical time-frame outlined here, beginning with the exodus from Egypt, derives from Nicholas of Lyra's commentary on the Song of Songs (on Lyra, see the note on 2360); see Mary Dove, 'Nicholas of Lyra and the literal senses of the Song of Songs', in Philip Krey and Lesley Smith, eds, *Nicholas of Lyra: The Senses of Scripture* (Leiden, Brill, 2000), pp. 129–46, and 'Love *ad litteram*: The Lollard translations of the Song of Songs', *Reformation* 9 (2004), 17–20.

2053–4 Other parts of the Bible which Jews regarded as being too subtle for readers under the age of thirty were the beginning of Genesis and the beginning and end of Ezechiel; see Jerome, *Tractatus in Marci Euangelium* (14:5), ed. D. Germanus Morin (Turnhout: Brepols, 1958; CCSL 78), p. 500.

2063 'þou3 it be not a book of bileue': G omits this reference to Wisdom's lack of canonicity (cf. 1889 and 1900–5 and notes).

2069 'Þou3 … techiþ': G replaces this reference to Ecclesiasticus' lack of canonicity with 'þe book of ecclesiastici teechiþ' (cf. the previous note).

2079 'general prologe', i.e., the prologue to Isaiah and the Prophets in WB in LV (no. 2 in this edition).

2079–82 The writer may be referring to glosses within the text in the Wycliffite Major and Minor Prophets in EV and LV, or to marginal glosses surviving in a few LV manuscripts, or possibly to a lost Glossed Prophets. Cf. the note on 1963–5, and see Dove, *FEB*, 124.

2083 'Þe firste book of Machabeis telliþ': in this case, the writer fails to remind the reader of the book's extra-canonical status.

2149–51 Jason's promise of money to Antiochus in return for the position of high priest is a particularly blatant examples of simony, 2 Macc. 4:7–9.

2169 'in so myche'–**2171** *Epistola* XCIII, *ad Vincentum Donatistum*; ed. Daur, *Sancti Aurelii Augustini Epistulae*, vol. II (CCSL 31A), pp. 167–206.

2183 'or whanne'–**2184** 'confermen it': in other words, the spiritual sense of an OT text is authoritative when that text is explicated spiritually by a NT writer.

2191–4 Augustine, *De docrina christiana*, III, xxix; ed. Joseph Martin (Turnhout: Brepols, 1962; CCSL 32), pp. 100–1/1–5.

2194–200 *De doctrina christiana*, III, v; ed. Martin, pp. 82–3/3–9. Cf. GGII 8–14.

2199 'þat passiþ beestis'; Augustine says 'quod … bestiis antecellit' (8).

2200–3 *De doctrina christiana*, III, x; ed. Martin, p. 86/5–9. Cf. GGII 15–21.

2203–8 *De doctrina christiana*, III, x; ed. Martin, p. 87/22–31. Cf. GGII 21–6.

2208–12 *De doctrina christiana*, III, xi; ed. Martin, p. 88/18–22. Cf. GGII 27–9.

2209 'derk licnesse or a parable' translates Augustine's *aenigma* (19).

2215–18 *De doctrina christiana*, III, xii; ed. Martin, pp. 88–9/1–5.

2218–36 *De doctrina christiana*, III, xv, xvi; ed. Martin, pp. 91–2/3–5, 1–18.

2218–20 Cf. GGII 29–31.

2220–9 Cf. GGII 31–41.

2237–9 *De doctrina christiana*, III, xxv; ed. Martin, p. 98/14–16.

2239–42 *De doctrina christiana*, III, xxv; ed. Martin, p. 98/7–11.

2242–54 *De doctrina christiana*, III, xxvii; ed. Martin, pp. 99–100/1–5, 10–18. Cf. GGII 42–9.

2253 'which maneris'–**2254** The translation in GGII is clearer here: 'whiche oþer scri[p]tures of God of as gret autor[ite] preuen', GGII 48–9.

2256–75 Augustine, Sermo CCCL; PL 39:1533–5. Cf. *HPD* 258–62.

2276–348 Augustine summarizes the seven rules for understanding scriptural metaphors written by Tyconius Afer, a Donatist, fl. 1370–90, *Liber de Septem Regulis*; PL 18:15–66.

2276–7 *De doctrina christiana*, III, xxx; ed. Martin, p. 102/1–6. Cf. GGII 51–2.

2277–88 *De doctrina christiana*, III, xxxi; ed. Martin, p. 104/1–11. Cf. GGII 52–60.

2278 'bodi or spousesse': according to *De doctrina christiana*, the first rule is 'capitis et corporis, id est Christi et ecclesiae'; 'bodi or spousesse' is the reading of **P** and **T**; **β** reads 'spouse'; **α ɪ Q S** and Crowley read 'spirit'; GII 52 reads 'body'. Here **β P T** are probably correcting an early *lectio facilior*, 'hooli spirit' for 'hooli spouse'.

2284 'onouride', the reading of all manuscripts except **T**, is a surprising error. GGII 58 correctly reads 'ourned'.

2289–306 *De doctrina christiana*, III, xxxii; ed. Martin, pp. 104–5/1–20. Cf. GGII 61–70.

2302 'blac and fair': the Latin Bible reads 'nigra sum sed formonsa' (I am black but beautiful); 'fusca sum *et* speciosa', 'blac *and* fair', is the Old Latin (pre-Jerome) reading.

2305 Cedar is named as a son of Ishmael at Gen. 25:13; see 2633–5.

2307–11 *De doctrina christiana*, III, xxxiii; ed. Martin, pp. 105–6/1–10. Cf. GGII 71–2.

2312–13 *De doctrina christiana*, III, xxxiv; ed. Martin, p. 106/1–3. Cf. GGII 73–4.

2314–35 *De doctrina christiana*, III, xxxv; ed. Martin, pp. 110–11/1–35. Cf. GGII 75–83.

2336–44 *De doctrina christiana*, III, xxxvi; ed. Martin, pp. 111–13/1–13, 44–5. Cf. GGII 84–90.

2345–8 *De doctrina christiana*, III, xxxvii; ed. Martin, p. 114/1–5. Cf. GGII 91–4.

2349–57 *De doctrina christiana*, III, xxxvii; ed. Martin, pp. 115–16/37–45. Cf. GGII 95–9.

2356 'of his face' translates Augustine's Old Latin 'facie eius' (43) rather than the Latin Bible's 'ore eius' (from his mouth).

2359 Isidore of Seville's summary of Augustine's account of the Tyconian rules is sometimes obscure; *De Summo Bono* I, ch. 25 (Paris, 1538), fols 21r–22v.

2360 'Lire': the Franciscan Nicholas of Lyra, 1270–1349, was 'the greatest biblical exegete of the fourteenth century and perhaps the greatest in the West since Jerome', Philip Krey and Lesley Smith, eds, *Nicholas of Lyra: The Senses of Scripture* (Leiden: Brill, 2000), p. 1. Lyra's hugely influential commentary on the Bible, the *Postillae super totam Bibliam*, 1322–31, concentrates on the literal sense of scripture, and in the Old Testament it is everywhere evident how much he has learned from Jewish exegetes of the Hebrew scriptures, especially Rashi (Solomon ben Isaac of Troyes, 1045–1105) and his school; see, e.g., the notes on 300, 302, 1351–2 and 2806 Wyclif's *Postilla in totam Bibliam*, which survives in an incomplete state, is heavily dependent on Lyra, whom he regarded highly; see Dove, *FEB*, 24–5.

 Lyra's prologues to the Bible in his *Postillae* are translated and summarized 2555–740.

2360–1 'touchiþ more openli þese reulis': see 2600–740.

2361 'Ardmacan': or 'Ardmachanus', Richard FitzRalph, b. bef. 1300–60, was Chancellor of the University of Oxford 1332–34, Dean of Lichfield Cathedral from 1335, and, from 1346, archbishop of Armagh. As archbishop he was a noted opponent of the friars, against whom he wrote *De pauperie Salvatoris*, and the legal proceedings between FitzRalph and the friars remained undecided at his death. See Katherine Walsh, *A Fourteenth-Century Scholar and Primate: Richard FitzRalph in Oxford, Avignon and Armagh* (Oxford: Oxford University Press, 1981), and Walsh, *ODNB* 19:917–22.

2362 FitzRalph's *Summa in Questionibus Armenorum*, written in Avignon between 1337 and 1344, argues against errors attributed to the Armenian church by way of literal interpretation of the Bible. It was a favourite text of the Lollards, and its discussion of *dominium* (lordship) influenced Wyclif. On FitzRalph and the literal sense of scripture see Alastair J. Minnis, '"Authorial intention" and "literal sense" in the exegetical theories of Richard FitzRalph and John Wyclif: an essay in the medieval history of Biblical hermeneutics', *Proceedings of the Royal Irish Academy* 75, Section C, no. 1 (Dublin, 1975), pp. 5–10, and Christopher Ocker, *Biblical Poetics before Humanism and Reformation* (Cambridge: Cambridge University Press, 2002) p. 118. See also *FSB* 128–33 and *PIP* 47.

2365–9 *De doctrina christiana*, IV, vi, xi–xxi (summarized); ed. Martin, pp. 122/6–7, pp. 134–57.

2369–72 *De doctrina christiana*, IV, viii; ed. Martin, p. 131/1–11. Cf. GGII 100–2.

2374–83 *De doctrina christiana*, II, xlii; ed. Martin, p. 76/1–12.

2385–9 Grosseteste, *Premonitus a venerabili patre*; see the note on 1709–11 In BL Royal 6 E.v the quoted passage is on fols 89vb–90ra.

2390–2 *De doctrina christiana*, II, xxxi; ed. Martin, p. 66/15–17.

2391–2 'þe Wise Man': see the note on 1774.

2392–401 *De doctrina christiana*, II, xl; ed. Martin, pp. 73–4/1–33.

2399–400 'Ciprian': Cyprian, bishop of Carthage, martyred 258. See GGIV 35–6.

2400 'Lactancius': 240–*c*.320, Christian apologist, author of *Divinae Institutiones*.

2401 'Victorinus and Illarie': Victorinus, bishop of Pettau/Ptuj, was martyred in the Diocletian persecutions at the beginning of the fourth century. Nearly all his writings have been lost, but he was highly regarded by Jerome as well as Augustine. On Hilary, *c*.300–*c*.368, bishop of Poitiers and writer against heretics, see also GGI 43.

2419–26 *De doctrina christiana*, II, vi; ed. Martin, p. 36/32–42.

2426–30 *De doctrina christiana*, II, vii; ed. Martin, pp. 36–7/1–2, 7–10.

2431–41 'riȝtfulnesse', *De doctrina christiana*, II, vii: ed. Martin, p. 37/13–17, 25–32.

2431 'to degre of kunnyng' ('scientiae gradum'). In *De doctrina christiana* this is the third step of knowledge, but the Prologue-writer omits the first two steps.

2441–54 *De doctrina christiana*, II, vii; ed. Martin, p. 38/38–48, 53–61.

2463–4 This quotation, attributed to Chrysostom here and at *HPD* 103–5, has not been identified.

2464–5 Also *De doctrina christiana*, II, vii; ed. Martin, p. 38/61–2.

2474–5 'þat is wise … siȝt': this gloss on 'wise men and prudent' derives from Lyra (see the note on 2360).

2475 'meke men': in the Latin Bible *parvulis* (children) echoes the *Glossa Ordinaria*'s 'humilibus spiritu' (to those humble in spirit).

2491–2 The Hebrew means 'for three transgressions and for four I shall not reverse the punishment due'.

2492–5 Jerome commenting on Amos 1:3; ed. Adriaen, *S. Hieronymi Presbyteri Opera: Commentarii in Prophetas Minores*, vol. I (CCSL 76), p. 219/231–8.

2495–6 Jerome, *Liber Interpretationis Hebraicorum Nominum*, ed. P. Antin (Turnhout: Brepols, 1959; CCSL 72), p. 64 (Damascus). In *The Dore of Holy Scripture* John Gough paraphrases PWB: 'but here Damasco is vnderstand blood sopers'.

2501–32 In Q these lines are written in another hand over an erasure which was presumably an act of censorship.

2503 'arsitris': this term for students of Arts, the root 'ars' being the plural of 'art', occurs as 'arsetris' in S *sec. m.* and T, as 'arsistris' in α and ι, and as 'artitars' in Q. Both Crowley and Gough omit it, presumably not recognizing the word. It is not recorded in MED.

2506 'cyuylians and canonystris': civil lawyers, specializing in Roman civil law as distinct from English common law, and canon lawyers, specializing in the law of the church. Most students took degrees in both laws.

2516–18 'sodomye … parlement': see the introduction to PWB, p. xxiv, and Dove, *FEB*, 110–13.

2522–4 'þis symony … sodomye': on simony as a graver sin than sodomy, see Wyclif, *De Simonia*, ed. Sigmund Herzburg-Fränkel and M.H. Dziewicki (London: Wyclif Society, 1898), p. 8, and Guillelmus Peraldus (see the note on 1743–5), *Summae Virtutum ac Vitiorum*, 'De Avaritia', VII; vol. II (Antwerp, 1571), p. 51. These passages are discussed by Carolyn Dinshaw, *Getting Medieval: Sexualities and Communities, Pre-Modern and Postmodern* (Durham, N.C.: Duke University Press, 1999), pp. 62, 241–2. Wyclif, following Peraldus, says that sodomy is an act against the law of nature, simony against the law of grace.

2540–4 Jerome, *In Amos*, II, iv; pp. 257–8/59–61.

2547–53 Jerome, *In Amos*, II, iv; pp. 261–2/196–9.

2547–50 Here Jerome is commenting on Amos 4:1.

2551–2 Jerome subsumes the moral under the literal sense, so that four senses are reduced to three.

2555–740 There is no modern edition of Nicholas of Lyra's *Postillae* on the Bible (see the note on 2360). Extracts from Lyra's first and second prologues are translated in Alastair J. Minnis and A.B. Scott with David Wallace, eds, *Medieval Literary Theory and Criticism c. 1100–c. 1375: The Commentary-Tradition*, rev. ed. (Oxford: Clarendon Press, 1991), pp. 266–70.

2556–60 The opening of Lyra's second prologue.

2560–90 From Lyra's first prologue.

2589 'resoun' translates Lyra's *oratio*.

2589 'so [and] in anoþere': translates Lyra's 'ita et in aliis'. β P and T omit 'and', presumably taking it to be an error.

2591–736 From Lyra's second prologue to the Bible, the writer continuing from where he left off at 2560.

2591 'setten bifore eiþir requyren' translates Lyra's *praesupponunt* (presuppose).

2598–9 See the note on 2169–71.

2600 See the note on 2359.

2607–9 Cf. 2283–5.

2614 'to haue'; Lyra's verb is *frui* (enjoy).

2628–30 Cf. 2302–3.

2629 'blac but fair' is the normal Latin Bible reading; see the note on 2302.

2646 'double literal sense' translates Lyra's *duplex sensus litteralis*, i.e., two literal meanings rather than a literal and a spiritual meaning. See Dove, *FEB*, 134–5.

2650 'amyable to þe Lord': 'amabilis domino' translates the Hebrew 'beloved of the Lord'.

2654–5 See the note on 2169–71.

2673–4 Cf. 2323–30.

2725–7 Gregory the Great, *Homiliae in Evangelia*, XVI, on Matt. 4:1–11; ed. Raymond Étaix (Turnhout: Brepols, 1999; CCSL 141), p. 110/10–12.

2737–40 The Prologue-writer asserts that there is no contradiction between Lyra's account of the seven rules and Isidore and Augustine's.

2741–76 No source has been found for this passage.

2759–62 Lyra's gloss on Mark 6:26 reads 'dicit Beda quod licet tristaretur in facie, laetabatur tamen in corde' (Bede says that he chose to look sad, but he rejoiced in his heart).

2780–1 The reading of the Hebrew Psalter (see the note on 2015) is quite different: 'Dominus numerabit scribens populos ipse natus est in ea'; 'the Lord shall count when he writeth up the people that this man was born there' (AV).

2781–7 Jerome, *Tractatus in Psalmos*, 86:6, ed. Morin (CCSL 78), p. 116/198–9, 204–10. In his *determinacio* on translation of the Bible into English, in his response to article 30 against translation, Richard Ullerston (see the introduction to *First seiþ Bois*, pp. xlix–liv) refers to Jerome's commentary on the same verse (f. 206ra–b).

2788–9 In his commentary on this verse, Bede says that stones should be interpreted as 'gentium nationes incredulas aliquando ac duricordes' (the unbelieving and even hard-hearted Gentile nations), PL 92:570.

2792 'By "Jews" is understood confessing or acknowledging', Jerome, *Liber Interpretationis Hebraicorum Nominum*, ed. Antin (CCSL 72), p. 154.

2800–1 'to saue … wole haue saued': as Christina von Nolcken points out, the comma after 'rewme' in Forshall and Madden's edition of PWB (*WB*, I, 57/6) implies that God wishes to save everyone in England, whereas the writer means all whom God wishes to save: 'Lay literacy, the democratization of God's Law and the Lollards', in John L. Sharpe III and Kimberly Van Kampen, eds, *The Bible As Book: The Manuscript Tradition* (London: British Library, 1998), p. 181.

2801 'a symple creature': the writer's description of himself. Cf. GGI 19, 'a symple creature of God', GGV 7; 'pore scribeler', GGIII 4, 10, and 'pore caityf', GGIV 18, 22 (and the *Pore Caitif* tracts, see the introduction to CTVI, pp. xlii–xliii).

2806 'speciali Lire on þe eld testament': see the note on 2360, and, on the influence of Nicholas of Lyra on the WB OT, see Dove, *FEB*, 163–71.

2812–43 For a discussion of this passage about translation strategies, with examples from the various versions of WB, see Dove, *FEB*, 145–8.

2812–15 Jerome argues the case for translating meaning for meaning and not word for word in *Epistola* LVII, *ad Pammachium*, V, ed. G.J.M. Bartelink, *Liber de Optimo Genere Interpretandi* (Leiden: Brill, 1980; *Mnemosyne*, supplement 61), pp. 43–63.

2817–20 'seyn': the writer's point is that absolute participial constructions in Latin (constructions where there is no temporal verb) may be made clear in English by turning the participle into a temporal verb and adding an appropriate conjunction (which may be a copulative conjunction). This involves the translator in interpreting the relationship between two temporal verbs; see Hudson, *SEWW*, 175.

2828–33 The second strategy the writer recommends is that all kinds of Latin verbal participles may be translated by a copulative conjunction and a temporal verb.

2833–4 The third strategy the writer recommends is that the Latin relative, when used as a resumptive subject, should be translated by repeating the antecedent and adding 'and'.

2835–6 The fourth strategy the writer recommends is that a word which appears only once in Latin may be repeated as often as necessary in English.

2836–8 The fifth strategy the writer recommends is that common Latin words such as *autem* should be translated according to the context and not by fixed equivalents.

2839–43 The sixth strategy the writer recommends is that where word for word translation does not make sense because English has a less flexible word-order than Latin natural English word-order should be substituted. (Sense for sense translation obviously demands this.)

2849–50 'no doute … nameli newe': there was no one 'Paris Bible' text; see Guy Lobrichon, *Les Éditions de la Bible Latine dans les Universités du XIIIe Siècle*, in Giuseppe Cremascoli and Francesco Santi, eds, *La Bibbia del XIII Secolo: Storia del Testo, Storia dell'Esegesi* (Florence: SISMEL, 2004), pp. 15–34. Nevertheless, the writer is correct in saying that Latin bibles written in the thirteenth and fourteenth centuries typically contain more errors than earlier Latin bibles. Knowing this, when the translators wanted to establish an accurate text from which to translate they set out to 'gadere many elde biblis' (2803). It was, however, largely through their study of Nicholas of Lyra's *Postillae* that they were alerted to common errors in the Latin text and in WB in EV, many of which are emended in LV. See Dove, *FEB*, 172–88, 222–34.

2852 'late translatid': in context the writer is clearly referring to what we call the Later Version of WB.

2853–7 'Ebrew'. In the Pentateuch and in 1–2 Chronicles there are many marginal glosses matching this description in several manuscripts of LV, but they are very infrequent or absent elsewhere in the Old Testament. There is only a smattering of such glosses in Psalms, except in the Glossed Psalter Bodleian Library Bodley 554. See Dove, *FEB*, 160–1.

2857–60 See the note on 2015, but the writer's low regard for the Gallican Psalter becomes clear only here. Given his preference for the Hebrew Psalter, it is surprising that WB Psalms are translated from the Gallican Psalter.

2860–2 The writer correctly observes that the corrupt state of the text in most books of the Latin Bible could be estimated by the differences between their text and the biblical text preserved in the verse-by-verse analysis in Jerome's commentaries, although this text was not, of course, identifiable with Jerome's 'propir origenal'; see Hudson, *SEWW*, 176.

On the use of Jerome's commentary on Isaiah in the biblical *correctoria* of the first half of the thirteenth century, see *Biblia Sacra*, xl–xli.

2880–1 'þe firste lxx. translatours': the translators of the Septuagint. See the note on CTI 249–59.

2889–90 Jerome accuses the Jews of deliberately mistranslating their own scriptures to erase references to the mysteries of Christ in his prologues on Job and Daniel, PL 28:1082 and 1293–4.

2907 'þe foure grete doctours': see the note on 109–10.

2918 'Latyn corrupt': debased or contaminated Latin: evidently here meaning Italian, as at CTI 12, although this usage is not recorded in MED.

2919 'trewe men': this is a distinctively but not exclusively Lollard usage; see Matti Peikola, *Congregation of the Elect: Patterns of Self-Fashioning in English Lollard Writings* (Turku: University of Turku Press, 2000; Anglicana Turkuensia 21), pp. 81–229.

2920–8 Augustine, *De doctrina christiana*, II, xi, xii; ed. Martin, p. 42/21–6, 1–4.

2929–31 Cf. Grosseteste, Dictum 19, inc. 'Liber iste sacra scriptura est'; ed. James R. Ginther, 'Natural philosophy and theology at Oxford: an edition and study of Robert Grosseteste's Inception Sermon', *Medieval Sermon Studies* 44 (2000), 108–34.

2935–6 'Bede translatide þe Bible': according to *First seiþ Bois* Bede 'translatid þe Bibel, or a grete parte of þe Bibile' (79), following Richard Ullerston's *determinacio* on biblical translation, f. 198rb–va; see the note on *FSB* 78–80 Also following Ullerston, f. 198va, *First seiþ Bois* reports that Ranulf Higden says Bede translated the gospel of John; see further the note on *FSB* 80–3 In his *determinacio* on biblical translation, c.1400–07, the Oxford Dominican Thomas Palmer (see the introduction to *First seiþ Bois*, pp. xlix–liv) reports that Bede is said to have translated the Bible, but he asserts that Bede only translated those parts necessary for salvation; ed. Deanesly, *LB*, 419/17–18 and 435/31–5.

2937 'but also'–**2939** According to Higden's *Polychronicon*, VI, i, Alfred translated the first part of the Psalter (psalms 1–50); ed. Joseph Rawson Lumby, vol. VI (London, 1876; Rolls Series 41), pp. 354–6. Higden's comments on Alfred are repeated in Richard Ullerston's *determinacio* on biblical translation, f. 198va; see *FSB* 88–91 and note.

2940 'Frensche men': on the various versions of the Old French Bible, see C.A. Robson, 'Vernacular scriptures in France', in G.W.H. Lampe, ed., *The Cambridge History of the Bible*, Volume 2: *The West From The Fathers To The Reformation* (Cambridge: Cambridge University Press, 1969), pp. 436–52, and Clive R. Sneddon, 'On the creation of the Old French Bible', *Nottingham Medieval Studies* 46 (2002), 25–44. According to the interpolated chapter on biblical translation in the English translation of *De Officio Pastorali*, 'As lordis of Englond han þe Bible in Freynsch so it were not aȝenes resoun þat þey hadden þe same sentense in Engliȝsch', John Rylands Manchester Eng. 86, f. 10r.

2940 'Beemers': in *De Triplico Vinculo Amoris*, c.1383, Wyclif states that Anne of Bohemia, first queen of Richard II, owned the Gospels in Czech as well as German and Latin; ed. Rudolf Buddensieg, *John Wyclif's Polemical Works in Latin*, vol. II (London: Wyclif Society, 1883), p. 168/9–11; see also *FSB* 184–5.

2940 'Bretouns': as far as is known, there was no medieval Breton Bible. Andrew Breeze argues that 'Britons' means Welsh; there are devotional books but no scriptures in medieval Welsh: 'The Wycliffite Bible Prologue on the scriptures in Welsh', *Notes and Queries* n.s. 46 (1999), 16–17.

2947–61 Augustine, *De doctrina christiana*, II, xii; ed. Martin, p. 44/33–52.

2962–3 The souce of these linguistic comments, attributed to Jerome, has not been identified.

2. The Prologue to Isaiah and the Prophets

1–3 'In sermone suo disertus sit, quippe ut vir nobilis et urbanae elegantiae nec habens quicquam in eloquio rusticitatis admixtum, unde accidit ut prae ceteris florem sermonis eius translatio non potuerit conseruare', Jerome, prologue to Isaiah, *ad Paulam et Eustochium*; PL 28:771.

3–6 'Ita enim uniuersa Christi ecclesiaequae mysteria ad liquidum persecutus est ut non eum putes de futuro vaticinari sed de praeteritis historiam texere', Jerome, *Epistola* LIII *ad Paulinum*; PL 22:547.

17–19 This information is provided in what the *Glossa Ordinaria* calls the 'Argumentum' on Isaiah, a gloss on Jerome's prologue.

20–4 The Prologue-writer takes from Jerome's prologue to the Minor Prophets (prefixed to Hosea) the reassuring point, as far as the historical sense is concerned, that where the context in which a prophet prophesied is not apparent in the biblical text it can be assumed to be the same as that of the previous prophet, or the most recent prophet in the Hebrew order for whom the title does provide historical information (the Hebrew order is different from the Septuagint order); PL 28:1072.

25–39 No source for these rules for understanding the prophets has been identified.

36 'historials', the reading of **I K P S** *pr. m.* **V** and **X**, has the form of a French plural adjective.

37–9 From the time of Abelard it had been accepted that in Jewish–Christian debate evidence should as far as possible be drawn from the OT and not the NT; see Theresa Gross-Diaz, 'What's a good soldier to do? Scholarship and revelation in the Postills on the Psalms', in Philip D.W. Krey and Lesley Smith, eds, *Nicholas of Lyra: The Senses of Scripture* (Leiden: Brill, 2000), pp. 110–28.

38 'historials': see note on PIP 36.

40–6 From the second prologue to Lyra's *Postillae*, trans. Alastair J. Minnis and A.B. Scott with David Wallace, eds, *Medieval Literary Theory and Criticism c. 1100–c. 1375: The Commentary-Tradition*, rev. ed. (Oxford: Clarendon Press, 1991), p. 268. Lyra is drawing on *Epistola* XCIII, *ad Vincentum Donatistum*; ed. K.D. Daur, *Sancti Aurelii Augustini Epistulae*, vol. II (Turnhout: Brepols, 2004; CCSL 31A), pp. 167–206.

45 The writer is doubtless thinking of the role of Reason in leading Augustine to right understanding and truth in the *Soliloquies* (written 386–7).

45–6 In his preface to Jonah, Jerome argues that the Christian meaning is the literal meaning, not the Jews' historical interpretation; ed. M. Adriaen, *S. Hieronymi Presbyteri Opera: Commentarii in Prophetas Minores*, vol. I (Turnhout: Brepols, 1969; CCSL 76), pp. 377–9.

46 'Lyre on þe bygynnynge of Genesis', i.e., the second prologue to Lyra's *Postilla*, see note on 40–6, above.

46 On 'Ardmakan', Richard FitzRalph, archbishop of Armagh, see the note on PWB 2361, and on his *Questiouns of Armenyes* (*Summa in Questionibus Armenorum*) see the note on PWB 2362.

55–6 The writer is referring to PWB chapters 12–14.

55 K S X alter 'shal be' to 'is', PWB having already been written.

60–6 Augustine, *De doctrina christiana*, III, xxv; ed. Martin, p. 98/14–20.

67–9 Augustine, *De doctrina christiana*, I, xxxvi; ed. Martin, p. 29/1–7.

3.   The Twelve Cambridge Tracts

Tract I

12 'Latyne corrupte': i.e., Italian; see the note on PWB 2918.

19–47 This passage also occurs in *Dives and Pauper*, IV, xi; ed. P.H. Barnum, vol. I (Oxford; Oxford University Press, 1976; EETS OS 275), pp. 327–8/10–33. See the introduction to the Cambridge Tracts, pp. xxxiii–xxxiv.

26 'risest' ('restest'); *Dives and Pauper*, 'arysist', p. 327/14), translating 'consurgens' (as at CTV 161).

34 'neveuys' is an over-literal translation of *nepotes*; in context it means 'mene', as at *Dives and Pauper*, p. 328/22.

34–6 Augustine, *Sermo* XCIV; PL 38:580–1. Moreover, says Augustine, the householder is responsible for preventing wife, son, daughter and servant from falling into heresy.

37–8 This maxim, lacking in *Dives and Pauper*, has not been located in Seneca, but recalls what Seneca says about the man who leads a happy life, that he is 'compositum ordinatumque' and 'magnificum' (magnanimous) in his dealings with his household; see *De Vita Beata*, 8, 3, ed. Pierre Grimal (Paris: Presses Universitaires, 1969), p. 50/5–6. 'Morigerari' properly means 'to be compliant'.

39 'þe lawe', i.e., canon law.

39–44 Richter and Friedberg, I, 915–16, in fact a quotation from qu. 4, c. 35, *Duo*. *Dives and Pauper* also cites qu. 5, c. 36, *Non putes* (*Corpus Iuris Canonici*, I, 940), p. 328/31.

51–2 Cf. CTXII 162–86, *The Mirror of St Edmund*, ed. C. Horstman, *Early Yorkshire Writers*, vol. I (London: Sonnenschein, 1895), p. 232/15–16 ('I say þe sikerly þat it es a foule lechery for to delyte in rymmes and slyke gulyardy'), and the prologue to the Middle English translation of Robert of Greatham's *Mirror*, ed. Kathleen Blumreich, *The Middle English Mirror* (Turnhout: Brepols, 2002), pp. 1–2.

60–1 Gratian, *Decretum*, dist. 4, c. 56; Richter and Friedberg, I, 1382; causa 8, qu. 1, c. 12, *Pro ingenio*; 'Oportet eum qui docet et instruit animas rudes esse talem ut pro ingenio discentium semet ipsum possit aptare et uerbi ordinem pro audientis capacitate dirigere', Richter and Friedberg, I, 594.

62 *De informatione simplicium sacerdotum*, canon 9 of the Council of Lambeth, 7–10 October, 1281; ed. F.M. Powicke and C.R. Cheney, *Councils and Synods II, A.D. 1205–1313*, vol. II (Oxford: Clarendon Press, 1964), pp. 900–5. This canon requires that even simple priests should teach the people in the mother tongue, 'absque cuiuslibet subtilitatis textura fantastica', i.e., literally and simply (p. 901), the fourteen articles of the Creed, the ten commandments, the two dominical commandments, the six works of mercy, the seven deadly sins, the seven theological virtues and the seven sacraments.

63–4 Lam. 4:4 is also quoted at the beginning of *De informatione simplicium sacerdotum* (see previous note), p. 900.

72–4 These lines belong to a 'complaint' topos based on Is. 59:14 ('judgment is turned away backward and justice standeth afar off, for truth is fallen in the street and equity cannot enter', AV); see Siegfried Wenzel, *Preachers, Poets, and the Early English Lyric* (Princeton: Princeton University Press, 1986), pp. 174–208. These lines belong to Wenzel's 'Type B', syntactically 'a complete predication with verb' expressing 'the idea of degeneracy through time', p. 182.

78–84 Cf. the exposition of the first 'woe' to the Pharisees (Matt. 23:13) in *Vae Octuplex*, ed. Arnold, *SEW*, II, 379/16–20; cf. CTVII 66–7, CTXI 56–9, CTXII 369–72 and *PNII* 311–12.

85–8 Richard Ullerston makes a similar point in his *determinacio* on translation of the Bible into English (see the introduction to *First seiþ Bois*, pp. xlix–liv): 'Nam si propterea non permitteretur ewangelium scribi in anglico quia sunt multi tractatus anglicani continentes hereses et errores, iam pari siue a fortiori prohiberent scripturam in latino, que per totam christianitatem posset disseminari' (for if the gospel were not allowed to be written in English because there are many English treatises containing heresies and errors, likewise, or even more so, they should prohibit it from being written in Latin, which could be disseminated throughout christendom), f. 199ra; cf. *FSB* 126–7 and note.

90 'chirche': the scribe writes 'chriche', as at CTI 391, CTIII 24 and CTXI 39.

98–9 Hebrew, the language of most of the OT, Greek, the language of the NT, and Latin, the language into which Jerome translated large parts of the Bible, were regarded as 'the chief languages'. As Ullerston says at the beginning of his *determinacio* (see note on 85–8, above), the question had only recently arisen whether scripture could be translated into 'alias lingwas minus principales et famosas' (other languages less important and less well known), f. 195ra.

101 'Crist': the scribe writes 'cristi', as he frequently does for both 'Crist' and 'Cristis'.

104–5 Gregory the Great, *Moralia in Iob*, VI, xvi; ed. M. Adriaen, vol. I (Turnhout: Brepols, 1979; CCSL 143), p. 298/27–8.

107 'theche': 'th' is often substituted for 't' in C.

118 Manuscript 'and not to do': possibly the scribe was expecting the text to continue 'and not on englisch' as at 120.

137–8 Gregory IX, *Decretals*, 5, titulus 5, *De Magistris*, etc., c. 4, *Quia nonnullis*; Richter and Friedberg, II, 770.

144–6 See Jacobus de Voragine, *Legenda Aurea*, rev. ed. G.P. Maggioni, vol. II (Florence: Galluzzo, 1998), p. 834. De Voragine attributes this information to the second- or third-century St Dorotheus of Tyre, ibid.

147–50 One who argued in this way was Thomas Palmer (see the introduction to *First seiþ Bois*, pp. xlix–liv), ed. Deanesly, *LB*, pp. 422–4. See Dove, *FEB*, 10–11, and Kantik Ghosh, *The Wycliffite Heresy: Authority and the Interpretation of Texts* (Cambridge: Cambridge University Press, 2001), pp. 100–2.

166–70 A well-educated and well-to-do layman of the early fifteenth century (perhaps a member of the Throckmorton family), who carried in his purse instructions in Latin for devout living, was recommended to 'look at the books of the church' during Mass, and on feast days to look at the gospel and epistle lections, commentary on the gospel, and the *Legenda Sanctorum*; see W.A. Pantin, 'Instructions for a devout and literate layman', in J.J.G. Alexander and M. Gibson, eds, *Medieval Learning and Literature: Essays presented to R.W. Hunt* (Oxford, 1976), pp. 399, 404–5, 421.

180–2 Cf. PWB 2812–15, 2839–43 and notes.

181 'apirtee' literally means 'openness', but here evidently means 'idiom'.

183 'þer is two manner of lewed peple': the writer's distinction between two classes of laypeople, 'ydiotis' (illiterates) and the literate, is an unusual one.

184–6 The writer evidently regards lay literacy as a recent phenomenon, needing explanation.

191 Greek *kleros* (sg.) means allotment, portion, as does Latin *sors* (sg.).

209 'for hem'–**213** On the identification of the laity as the swine of Matt. 7:6 see Dove, *FEB*,

6–9. Identifying the 'swine' as the illiterate rather than the laity as a whole enables the writer to argue for the education of the literate laity.

229–38 The meeting of Philip with the eunuch is also narrated in *Lanterne of Liȝt*, ed. Lilian M. Swinburn (London, 1917; EETS OS 151), p. 102/12–20.

231 'veyn pilgrimage': this allusion to the uselessness of pilgrimages is the only Wycliffite moment in CTI.

249–59 'þe master of stories', Peter Comestor (d. *c.*1178), in *Historia Scolastica* (Lyons: 1534), f. 170r; Jerome, 'Desiderii mei desideratus accepi epistolas', *Praefatio in Pentateucum*; PL 28:150–1, and *Commentariorum in Danielem*, III, xi, 5; ed. F. Glorie (Turnhout: Brepols, 1964; CCSL 75A), p. 901/906–12. This legend of the inspired origin of the Septuagint derives ultimately from the *Letter of Aristeas* to Philocrates, claiming to be written in the reign of Ptolemy Philadelphus but probably no earlier than first-century BC, trans. R.H. Charles, *The Apocrypha and Pseudopigrapha of the Old Testament*, vol. II (Oxford: Clarendon Press, 1963), pp. 83–122. Flavius Josephus paraphrases the letter in his *Antiquitates Judaicae*, XII; trans. H.St.J. Thackeray, *Josephus*, vol. VII (London: Heinemann, 1967; Loeb Classical Library), pp. 2–59. The number 'seuenti and two' (251) derives from the supposition that there were six translators from each of the twelve tribes. According to Josephus, Theopompos (a Greek historian) was driven mad because he planned to include earlier material, rejected in the Torah, in his writings, and Theodectes (a tragedian) suffered from cataracts because he planned to dramatize parts of the Torah (pp. 53–7). Jerome does not mention Theopompos and Theodectes.

268–70 Cf. the sermon for Trinity xiiii in MS Longleat 4, f. 90va–b: 'Crist seyde nout to hym, as prelatis and men of holy cherche don þese dayes to men and wommen þat askin hem questyonys of holy writ, of conscience and of Goddis lawe: O þou borel clerk, what entyrmetyst þu þee wiþ holy writ and wiþ Goddis lawe?'; Anne Hudson and H.L. Spencer, 'Old author, new work: the sermons of MS Longleat 4', *Medium Ævum* 53 (1984), 232.

278–9 Jerome names Paula and her daughter Eustochium as the recipients of his translation in the prologues to Esther (PL 28:1434), Isaiah (PL 28:774), Jeremiah (PL 28:849), Daniel (PL 28:1294) and the Minor Prophets (PL 28:1015–16), and he names Eustochium, after Paula's death, as the recipient of Joshua and Judges (PL 28:464) and the Catholic Epistles (PL 29:831).

280–2 Jerome, *Ep.* IX *ad Paulam et Eustochium*; PL 30:122–42.

282 A frequently cited letter is *Ep.* CXXX, *ad Demetriadem*, on preserving virginity; PL 22:1107–24. In his *determinacio* on biblical translation, in his response to article 16 against translation, Ullerston (see the note on 85–8) uses what Jerome says about the benefits of reading widely in scripture as an argument in favour of an English Bible (f. 203rb).

282–7 Augustine, *Ep.* CLXXXIX, *ad [Bonifacium] Comitem*, PL 33:854–7; *ad sacras virgines* (unidentified); CCXXXIII, *ad Longinianum*, col. 1030, and CCXXXV, cols 1032–3; CXXXII, *ad Volucianum*, cols 508–9, and CXXXVII, cols 515–25; XXVI (1), *ad Lic[e]ntium*, ed. K.D. Daur, *Sancti Aurelii Augustini Epistulae*, vol. I (Turnhout: Brepols, 2004; CCSL 31), pp. 76–7; CXXVII, *ad Arme[n]tarium*, PL 33:483–7; CXLVII, *ad Paulinam*, cols 596–622; CCLXVI, *ad Florentinam*, cols 1089–91; XCII, *ad Italicam*, ed. K.D. Daur, *Sancti Aurelii Augustini Epistulae*, vol. II (Turnhout: Brepols, 2004; CCSL 31A), pp. 160–5, and XCIX, vol. II, pp. 235–6; LXXVIII, *ad ciues Yponenses [Hipponenses]*, ed. Daur, *Sancti Aurelii Augustini Epistulae*, vol. II (CCSL 31A), pp. 83–91, and CXXII, PL 33:470–2; CL, *ad Probam et Iulianam*, col. 645.

287 'et aliis epistulis quam plurim[i]s', and in very many other letters.

287–8 For the letters of Ambrose, see PL 16:875–1286; his letters to his sister and to laymen are trans. M.M. Beyenka, *Saint Ambrose: Letters* (New York: Fathers of the Church, 1954), pp. 365–495. Gregory's letters are ed. D. Norberg, *S. Gregorii Magni Registrum Epistularum*, 2 vols (Turnhout: Brepols, 1982; CCSL 140, 140A): only a few, such as those to Adeodata, VIII, 34 and XI, 5 (vol. 2, pp. 559–60, 866), are addressed to laypeople.

294 'vnderston[d]': Final 'd' is also omitted at 369 and 409.

297–300 See the note on CTI 62.

302–3 Gratian, *Decretum*, dist. 43, c. 5 ('the preacher who does not scatter the seed of the divine word incurs the punishment of eternal damnation'); Richter and Friedberg, I, 156.

328 The scribe's 'but sette hijs lijf welle in & hijs likynge' is an extreme example of his disregard for sense.

345–8 Jerome, *Ep.* CXXV, *ad Rusticum monachum*, PL 22:1078; Gratian, *Decretum*, dist. 5, c. 33; Richter and Friedberg I, 1420–21 (quotation 1421).

349 Manuscript 'kisse' is emended to East Midland 'kesse' to make the mother's understanding plausible (cf. 360).

357–9 'When I was a child I spake as a child, I understood as a child, I thought as a child; but when I became a man I put away childish things', 1 Cor. 13:11 (AV).

369 'wol[d]': MED gives 'wold' as a variant of 'old'. Final 'd' is also omitted at 294 and 409.

378–80 In his *determinacio*, Ullerston makes similar points about 1 Cor. 11:14–15, f. 198ra, and see also *FSB* 53–62.

380–1 Clementine V, titulus I *De magistris*, c. 1 *Inter sollicitudines nostris*; Richter and Friedberg, II, 1179. This chapter concerns the provision of university posts for the teaching of the languages of scripture.

409–18 Henry of Huntingdon, *Historia Anglorum*; ed. T. Arnold (London, 1879; Rolls Series 74), pp. 77–9.

409 'Ynglon[d]': see the note on 369

437 'ne[d]ful': here medial 'd' is omitted.

446–9 Cf. Wyclif, *De Veritate Sacre Scripturae*, ed. Rudolf Buddensieg, vol. III (London: Wyclif Society, 1907), p. 99/13–16; and see Margaret Aston, 'Lollardy and Sedition, 1381–1431', *Past and Present* 17 (1960), 1–44, and Dove, *FEB*, pp. 19–20.

463 'lawe ceuyle' and 'lawe emperial' both mean Roman civil law, as distinct from English common law, but here 'lawe emperial' seems to mean specifically the law of the Holy Roman Empire.

468–9 'seynt Austyn was conuertid bi his moder': Augustine's mother, Monica, is an important presence throughout his *Confessiones*, but the writer is no doubt thinking particularly of the end of book VIII, where Monica is overjoyed at her son's conversion, and where Augustine recalls the vision she had in Carthage of his future conversion, at a time when she was full of sorrow for his sinful life; *Confessions* VIII, xii, trans. William Watts, vol. I (Cambridge: Mass., Harvard University Press, 1968), p. 466, and III, xi, pp. 136–8.

470 'saluabitur': the best manuscripts of the Latin Bible read 'sanctificatus est'.

472–4 The writer is almost certainly referring to the third canon of archbishop Arundel's *Constitutions*; ed. David Wilkins, *Concilia Magnae Britanniae et Hiberniae*, vol. III (London, 1737), p. 316, although H. Leith Spencer points out that the canon reaffirms earlier principles, *English Preaching in the Later Middle Ages* (Oxford: Clarendon Press, 1993), pp. 174–5.

481–2 B.J. Whiting cites this proverb from this manuscript, *Proverbs, Sentences and Proverbial Phrases*, W632 (Cambridge, Mass: Harvard University Press, 1968), p. 668.

482–7 Augustine, *Ep.* CXXXII, *ad Volusianum*; PL 33:508–9.

494–5 Cf. 'Hou þe office of curatis is ordeyned of God', ch. 27, where the writer argues that priests should not prevent men from knowing scripture because 'þe more goodnesse þat þei knowen of God þe more þei schullen loue God'; ed. F.D. Matthew, *The English Works of Wyclif Hitherto Unprinted* (London: EETS, 1880), p. 159/18–19.

Tract II

5 Ps. 118:2 reads 'beati qui scrutantur testimonia [testimonies] eius', and all manuscripts except C reproduce the plural noun. C is therefore emended here.

8 'louet': 't' for 'þ' is also found at CTIII 15 ('semet').

13 'Þe wyse man': see the note on PWB 1774

17–18 Probably referring to the account of the last judgment in Matt. 25:31–46, where those who have performed works of mercy are promised life eternal.

26–8 See the note on PWB 125–30

43 'man or woman': all other manuscripts read simply 'man', so this reading shows deliberate inclusiveness on the editor's part.

47 Following 'God', this tract omits the passage about the priesthood of true believers in all other manuscripts: 'eche man is bounden to do so þat he be saued, but eche man þat schal be saued is a real prest maad of God, as holy writ and holy doctours witnessyn pleynly. Þanne eche lewed man þat schal be saued is a real prest of God, and eche man is bounden to be such a verri prest' (BL Arundel 254; see apparatus).

Tract III

12–13 Cf. CTX 10–11, CTXI 54–6 and the long version of the Middle English *Charter of Christ*, in which the legal deed granting mankind title to the kingdom of heaven is identified with the crucified body of Christ, the sealing-wax with his blood: 'And selyng wex was dere ibought / At myn hert rote it was sought / Alle itemperyd wythe fyn vermylone / Of my red blode that ran adovne' (CUL Ee.2.15, fols 108v–109r); see M.C. Spalding, *The Middle English Charters of Christ* (Bryn Mawr, 1914; Bryn Mawr College Monographs), pp. xlii–xliii, 65, and Mary Teresa Brady, 'The *Pore Caitif*: An Introductory Study', *Traditio* 10 (1954), 539–40.

23–4 The writer cannot mean that the gospels (or gospel lections) are commonly found in each parish church in English, since before 1409 it would have been unusual for a church to possess gospels (or gospel lections) in English, and after 1409 it was illegal. Presumably, therefore, the writer expects his readers to be literate in Latin (or more likely is translating or adapting a Latin text): that the Latin gospels were available in churches is suggested by the 'Instructions for a devout and literate layman' discovered by W.A. Pantin; see note on CTI 166–70.

35 There is evidently some text missing here; the writer must be making the point that Christ's is the best law, and that he did not lack good will, or wit, or power.

Tract IV

1 'Cristen men': the direct address suggests an oral presentation.

4–5 'dilectus meus descendit in hortum suum' (my beloved has come down into his garden) Song of Songs 6:1, conflated with 'veniat dilectus meus in hortum suum ut comedat fructum pomorum suorum. Veni in hortum meum soror mea, sponsa' (let my beloved come into his garden so that he may eat the fruit of his apples. Come into my garden, my sister, my spouse) Song of Songs 5:1. See Mary Dove, 'Love *ad litteram*: the Lollard translations of the Song of Songs', *Reformation* 9 (2004), 1–5.

19 'manere': the scribe repeats 'marie' from the previous line.

21–2 'a rostid fische and a parte of an hony-combe': the food the disciples gave the risen Christ during the last of his resurrection appearances, Luke 24:42.

35–6 'þe world … and þe freel flesche, and þe false fende': this trio of enemies of humankind became a devotional commonplace from the twelfth century. According to Hugh of St Victor (1096–1141), 'Tres sunt qui bellum suscitant contra nos: videlicet diabolus et mundus et caro nostra', *In Salomonis Ecclesiasten*, homily XVI; PL 175:235.

Tract V

1–14 Bede, Homily CVIII; PL 94:513.

7 'stonde' must be an error for 'stodie', translating Bede's *studeamus*.

15–17 'not': Augustine, *In Iohannis Evangelium*, X, 9; ed. D.R. Willems (Turnhout: Brepols, 1954; CCSL 36), p. 105/4–6.

17–41 Augustine, *In Iohannis Evangelium*, X, 9; ed. Willems, p. 106/13–40.

23 've[yn] spectacle' translates Augustine's *theatrum* (21).

32 'wellowed' translates Augustines' *marcidus* (29).

37–8 'þat is, Crist in þe soule' is the translator's gloss.

42–86 Gregory the Great, *Homiliae in Evangelia*, VI (on Matt. 11:2–10), ed. Raymond Étaix (Turnhout: Brepols, 1999; CCSL 141), pp. 42–4/95–153.

41/2 The writer makes no attempt to provide a link between these lines. At 55–6 it becomes clear that the link is the parable of the talents.

42 Immediately before this passage Gregory has quoted Matt. 11:10: 'This is he of whom it is written: I send my angel before your face, who has prepared your way before you'.

51–2 'ʒif he telliþ euerlastynge rewme or turment to him þat erriþ' translates 'si aeternum regnum uel supplicium erranti denuntiat', p. 43/107–8.

54–5 'lest þou be constrained to paie in turmentis þat þinge yuele kept' translates 'ne male seruatum quod acceperas in tormentis exigaris', p. 43/111–12.

56 'þat is, vnderstondeynge' is the translator's gloss.

58 'grete cuppis and litil' translates Gregory's *phialae* and *cyathi*, p. 43/114, 115; Exod. 25:29.

59 'plenteuous doctryne' translates 'doctrina exuberans', p. 43/116.

60 'doctrynge' translates *doctrina*, p. 43/117. Apparently a gerund, this form is not recorded in *MED*, but occurs also at CTV 64, 169, 231 and CTVII 15.

60 'soulis' translates *mentes*, p. 43/118.

65 'gode word'; Gregory has 'boni uerbi', p. 43/123, and the English text's 'Goddis word' has been emended accordingly.

66 'enforse ʒe'; the translator's text evidently included the words 'uobiscum satagite' in the apparatus in Étaix's edition, p. 43/125.

69–70 'ar[ous]e or excite'; Étaix's text has *conueniat* (may come together), p. 43/128–9. Either the translator's original was at fault here, or this is a mistranslation.

77–80 The translator's text of these lines is Étaix's type β.

82 'þat is, to reise soulis to heuene' is the translator's gloss.

90–2 Ps.–Chrysostom, 'Non omnis sacerdos sanctus est, sed omnis sanctus sacerdos',

Opus Imperfectum in Matthæum, XLIII; PG 56:876. On this work, see the note on PWB 1766–7.

93–102 Gregory the Great, *Homiliae in Evangelia*, X (on Matt. 2:1–12), ed. Étaix, pp. 66–7/19, 23–35.

93 'borun of a virgyn' is the translator's addition.

103–16 Augustine, *In Iohannis Evangelium*, LI, 13; ed. Willems, p. 445/1–17.

117–20 Chrysostom, *In venerabilem atque vivificam crucem ... homilia*; PG 50:819. Chrysostom's text reads 'Saepe enim dixi et dicere non cessabo "mihi enim non pigrum est dicere vobis autem tutum"' (quoting Phil. 3:1). The words in brackets **118** are speculative.

120 The words 'put on ʒou', which follow 'seie' in the manuscript, are inexplicable.

121–5 *In Iohannis Evangelium*, V, 19; ed. Willems (see note on 15–17), p. 52/6–12.

123–4 'Se þou not be what seruaunte Crist is prechid to þe': Augustine has 'Non per quid sed quem uide. Per inuidiam tibi praedicatur Christus?' (See not by what but whom. Was Christ preached to you by envy?), p. 52/10–11. The translator's 'seruaunte' shows that he does not appreciate that 'quid' refers back to 'inuidiam'; nevertheless, the text makes sense as it stands, although it is an inaccurate translation.

124 'drinke' is an inexplicable error; Augustine has *vide* (see), p. 52/11.

126–7 'men' Augustine, *In Iohannis Evangelium*, VI, 4; ed. Willems, p. 55/20–2.

127–36 Augustine, *In Iohannis Evangelium*, VI, 24; ed. Willems, pp. 65–6/1–10.

129–30 'þat is, holy chirche' is the translator's gloss.

131 'þat is, holy chirch' is the translator's gloss.

137–44 Augustine, *Enarrationes in Psalmos* (Ps. 50), 24; ed. E. Dekkers and J. Fraipont (Turnhout: Brepols, 1956; CCSL 38), vol. I, pp. 615–16/7–16, 20–1.

140 'or lore and chast[i]synge' is the translator's addition.

141 'þat is, to ʒiue licence or sufferaunce to synnes' is the translator's addition.

144–6 A summary of Augustine, *De Diversis Quaestionibus Octoginta Tribus*, qu. 64; ed. Almut Mutzenbecher (Turnhout: Brepols, 1975; CCSL 44A), p. 146/210–13.

147–9 Augustine, *De Libero Arbitrio*, III, xxiii, 70; ed. W.M. Green (Turnhout: Brepols, 1970; CCSL 29), p. 316/97–9.

148–9 'þat is, God, þat makiþ of noʒt' is the translator's addition.

149–52 Augustine, *De Vera Religione*, XXVIII (51); ed. Martin, pp. 220–1/19–22.

150 Since Augustine has 'lex est diuinae prouidentiae', line 19, 'good' is emended to 'Godes'.

167–70 Augustine, *Ep. CLV, ad Macedonium*; PL 33:673.

170–7 Augustine, *Ep. CCLXIV, ad Maximam*; PL 33:1085.

172 'wakynge' translates Augustine's *vigilantiam*.

201 'lake' (translating *lacu*, den) is an inferior reading; good manuscripts of the Latin Bible have *manu* (power) at Dan. 6:27.

202–5 This final verse of Daniel is relegated to the textual apparatus (as having dubious authority) in Weber, *Biblia Sacra*.

209–11 The deeds of Hezechiah are detailed in 4 Kings 18–20 and 2 Chron. 29–32, of Jehoshaphat in 3 Kings 22 and 2 Chron. 17–20, and of Asa in 3 Kings 15:9–23 and 2 Chron. 14–16.

223 'whom' should properly be 'which', since the antecedent is an abstract noun.

230 The writer returns to John 2:17.

230–5 'money': no source has been identified for these lines.

Tract VI

3–4 '3if we schullen not speke of holy writ': cf. CTI 457–8 and CTII 29–31.

8–10 Matt. 4:1–11 was the prescribed gospel for the first Sunday in Lent according to the Sarum rite.

13–16 On the gospel as the testament of Christ see Mary Teresa Brady, '*The Pore Caitif*: an introductory study', *Traditio* 10 (1954), 539–40, and M.C. Spalding, *The Middle English Charters of Christ* (Bryn Mawr, 1914; Bryn Mawr College Monographs).

Tract VII

1–25 Cf. *PNII* 3–26.

6–8 On the importance of scripture in English being written cf. CTI 477–87.

10–12 Cf. CTII 54–5.

18 'Caym': the name of Cain (Gen. 4:8) is commonly altered in anti-mendicant writings to make the word an acronym of the four orders of friars, Carmelites, Augustinians, Jacobins (Dominicans) and Minorites (Franciscans).

18 In Numbers 16:31–5, Dathan and Abiram, with others, rebel against Moses in the wilderness, and the earth opens and swallows them up, cf. CTXII 347–9.

20 'gloson it as hem likeþ': the charge here is that the friars ignore the literal meaning of the gospel and substitute their own self-serving interpretation. If this were true, it would falsify scripture. Cf. the interpolated chapter on biblical translation in the English translation of *De Officio Pastorali*: 'freris wolden lede þe puple in techinge hem Goddis lawe, and þus þei wolden teche sum and sum hide and docke [cut] sum, for þanne defautis in þer lif shulden be lesse knowun to þe puple, and Goddis lawe shulde be vntreweliere knowun, boþe bi clerkis and bi comyns', Matthew p. 430/17–21. Cf. CTIX 39–43 and (in a different context) CTXII 12–13, and see Hudson, *WLP*, 260.

20–3 Wyclif mentions Mahomet and Sergius together in *Tractatus de Apostasia*, saying that they were not 'copiously and regularly heretics, as the irreligious despots of the church are today'; ed. M.H. Dziewicki (London: Wyclif Society, 1889), p. 67/23–5.

26–8 'lawe': cf. *PNII* 42–6.

30 'But'–**41** Cf. *PNII* 53–64.

44 'For ri3t'–**55**, 'þerafter': cf. *PNII* 197–211.

56–82 'werkis': cf. *PNII* 297–326.

62 'Rabanus' is written in the margin beside this line, cf. *PNII* 301, 305; see Hrabanus Maurus' commentary on Matt. 3:7, ed. B. Löfstedt, *Expositio in Matthaeum*, vol. I (Turnhout: Brepols, 2000; CCCM 174), p. 77/20–9.

66–7 Christ's eightfold invocation of 'woe' on the pharisees, Matt. 23:13–39, is the subject of Wyclif's *Vae Octuplex* and the English translation of that work, ed. Arnold, *SEW*, II, 379–89. Cf. also CTI 78–84, CTXI 56–9, CTXII 368–71 and *PNII* 311–12.

85–6 Cf. *Lanterne of Li3t*, where it is 'prelatis and freris' who slander the simple people in this way; ed. Lilian M. Swinburn (London, 1917; EETS OS 151), p. 11/4–9.

Tract VIII

6 'þat lawe', the law of Moses.

21–2 In Ullerston's *determinacio*, in article 13 against translation, 1 Cor. 14:35 is used as an argument against scripture in the vernacular since this might lead to women preaching in church, f. 195va. Ullerston's counter-argument is that scripture in the vernacular, a desirable thing, should not be forbidden because it may lead to undesirable ends any more than one should refrain from making a window for fear someone might hang himself from it, f. 202va.

Tract IX

Heading For 'dispisynge' in a similar context see CTXII 314.

2 'þe letter sleeþ', 2 Cor. 3:6; see the note on 28–48, below.

14 E.g. 1 Cor. 10:7; 2 Cor. 6:16; Col. 3:5; Eph. 5:5 and Gal. 5:20.

16–17 'chastite (at þe lest in verray matrimonye)': chastity, if not complete continence then at least chaste sexuality in legal marriage.

24–5 Gratian, *Decretum*, causa 24, q. 3, c. *Heresis*; ed. Richter and Friedberg, I, 998.

28–48 Cf. the discussion of the same text in CTXI 16–19, *EWS*, I, 652–3/44–70, *HPD* 215–65, and in Palmer's *determinacio* on biblical translation, ed. Deanesly, *LB*, 424; see also Rita Copeland, *Pedagogy, Intellectuals, and Dissent in the Later Middle Ages: Lollardy and Ideas of Learning* (Cambridge: Cambridge University Press, 2001), pp. 103–4, and Dove, *FEB*, 11–13. Immediately preceding CTIX in Bodleian Library Laud misc. 254, fol. 20v, is a short Latin exposition of 'Littera occidit spiritus autem viuificat', ascribed in the margin to 'Haymo'.

30–1 Jerome, *In Hieremiam*, V, lxiv; ed. S. Reiter (Turnhout: Brepols, 1960; CCSL 74), p. 278/17–19; 'and þe chirches lawe', see note on 24–5.

45–6 The text missing in C is supplied from O5.

Tract X

= GGIII 89–118.

Heading 'leid aslepe', cf. CTVII 18–19.

1–8 For this characteristically Wycliffite protest against laws made by sinful men, with no basis in the Bible (God's law) or in reason, see the note on PWB 125–30.

10–11 See the note on CTIII 12–13

21 'deed leed or roten wax': the seals of papal bulls and other official documents, which take the means of life from the people.

22–3 Cf. CTXI 52–3; *EWS*, I, 339/89–90; *Lanterne of Liȝt*, 69/5–15. In Wyclif's sermon on Matt. 6:16 it is the friars who are the blind leading the blind; ed. J. Loserth, *Sermones*, vol. IV (London: Wyclif Society, 1890), p. 56/3–8.

Tract XI

1–9 Cf. *The Middle English* Mirror, ed. Kathleen Blumreich (Turnhout: Brepols, 2002), p. 5/6–14.

6 'þat is … good lyuynge': there is no equivalent in the *Mirror*.

10 'into his owne langage': there is no reference to the languages of scripture at this point in the *Mirror*.

11–12 'cloude': 'Ffor þe letter of holy wryt is as it were a derk clowde', Blumreich, *The Middle English* Mirror, p. 5/15.

16–19 See the note on CTIX 28–48 Here the writer makes the entirely traditional point that scripture should be understood spiritually and not literally.

20 'Þei'–28, 'lawe': cf. Blumreich, *The Middle English* Mirror, p. 6/7–14.

21 'dreye': there is no equivalent in the *Mirror*.

23 'ne dewe of grace': there is no equivalent in the *Mirror*.

26 In the *Mirror* the third order are 'assailyours', p. 6/11.

39 On the 'fiʒtynge chirche' see *PNII* 93–7.

54–6 See the note on CTIII 12–13.

56–9 See the note on CTI 78–84.

61 'Of'–**64** Cf. Blumreich, *The Middle English* Mirror, p. 7/15–19.

63 The quotation from Lam. 4:4 is completed from CTI 65 See also the note on CTI 63–4.

63, 'for as'–**65** Cf. CTVII 44–6.

103–4 See the note on CTIV 35–6.

111–13 The words 'omnipotens sermo tuus, Domine [thy all-powerful word, O God]' occur many times in Gregory's *Liber Antiphonarius*, which perhaps is why the writer attributes Wisd. 16:12 to Gregory.

114 'haþ heelid hem': 'sanauit eos' is missing in the translation.

Tract XII

9–10 Cf. Luke 6:25 (CTXII 360–2), and Chrysostom, *Homiliae XC in Matthæum*, VI; 'de luctu saepe Christus nos admonet et eos qui lugent beatos praedicat, illos vero qui rident miseros declarat … Non enim Deus id dat ut ludamus, sed diabolus'; PG 57:70.

15–16 Jerome, *Commentariorum in Matheum*, II, ed. D. Hurst and M. Adriaen (Turnhout: Brepols, 1969; CCSL 77), p. 96/530–43, commenting on Matt. 12:36.

22 Paul, John, James and Jude are, with Peter, the writers of the Catholic (canonical) epistles. See PWB 73–4.

23–4 This quotation, said to be from Gregory, has not been identified.

25–71 See the discussion of 'loller' and 'lollard' in Wendy Scase, *'Piers Plowman' and the New Anticlericalism* (Cambridge: Cambridge University Press, 1989), pp. 125–60, and the note on PWB 1796.

33–5 See the note on CTIX 24–5.

39–40 Scase (see the note on 25–71) mentions these lines as an example of 'lollen', meaning 'to hang', *'Piers Plowman' and the New Anticlericalism*, p. 154.

40–1 The crucifixion of Peter is described by Jacobus de Voragine in the *Legenda Aurea*, rev. ed. G.P. Maggioni, vol. I (Florence: Galluzzo, 1998; SISMEL), pp. 567–8, and that of Andrew in vol. I, pp. 31–2.

84 From the heading of this text until this point there has been no indication that this is a dialogue.

88–9 'he schal … þe purse': the writer seems to be recalling the portrait of the Summoner in the General Prologue to the *Canterbury Tales*, I, 653–6: 'if he foond owher a good felawe, / He wolden techen him to have noon awe / In swhich caas of the ercedekenes curs, / But if a mannes soule were in his purs'; ed. Larry D. Benson, *The Riverside Chaucer* (Oxford: Oxford University Press, 1988), p. 34. Cf. CTXII 286.

123 'in drynkeynge of Cristis cuppe' is the writer's gloss.

124–47 This part of the text contrasts heavenly with worldly wisdom.

135 'fro þis worldli wisdom' glosses 'de mundo' (from the world).

140–1 Gregory the Great, *Moralia in Iob*, XIII, x; ed. M. Adriaen, vol. I (Turnhout: Brepols, 1979; CCSL 143), p. 676/31–6.

144 'fasten and naile my fleische to þi drede' mistranslates 'confige timore tuo carnes meas' (transfix my flesh with fear of you). The Hebrew Psalter reads 'horripilavit a timore tuo caro mea' (my flesh has bristled for fear of you).

152 'Marie Mawdeleyns suster': Mary of Bethany, sister of Martha and Lazarus, was traditionally identified with Mary Magdalen.

157–8 'þe clene peple' translates *immaculati* (Ps. 118:1).

159–60 'men litil in malice' glosses *parvulis* (Ps. 18:8).

162–4 See note on CTI 51–2.

163 The romance of *Guy of Warwick* is ed. J. Zupitza, 3 vols (London: Paul, Trench and Trübner, 1883–91; EETS ES 25–7); Guy is mentioned in the prologue to *The Middle English* Mirror, ed. Blumreich, p. 1/15–16. The romance of *Bevis of Hampton* is ed. Ronald B. Herzman, Graham Drake and Eve Salisbury, *Four Romances of England: King Horn, Havelok the Dane, Bevis of Hampton and Athelston* (Kalamazoo, Michigan: Medieval Institute Publications, Western Michigan University, 1999). The romance of *Lybeaus Desconus* is ed. M. Mills (London: Oxford University Press, 1969; EETS OS 261). There are many references to Robin Hood in the thirteenth, fourteenth and early fifteenth centuries, but no surviving Robin Hood texts in English can be dated before about 1450; see Stephen Knight, *Robin Hood: A Complete Study of the English Outlaw* (Oxford: Blackwell, 1994), pp. 46–8, 262–5.

168 'co[ntriui]d' (devised): 'countid' (recounted) would be closer to the scribe's 'cointud', but the context suggests the word means 'composed'.

171–2 This quotation, said to be from Psalms, has not been identified.

181–2 This quotation, said to be from Augustine, has not been identified.

184 'ifedde': this is one of several distinctively Southern past participles in CTXII; cf. 'iloued' (188) and 'idrunke' (193).

185–6 This quotation, said to be from Augustine, has not been identified.

212–13 'sones ben on egge' is taken from WB in LV; further text is evidently missing at this point.

220 'wickednesse' (witnesse manuscript) translates *iniquitatem* (Ezech. 18:20).

221–2 'tauȝte h[e]m biliuynge and th[ech]ynge to kepe þe comandementis': even emended, the text reads very awkwardly here.

227–8 Christ's brother, etc., is 'whoever will do the will of the Father' (Matt. 12:50).

234 'þe Wise Man': see the note on PWB 1774.

239–42 This quotation, said to be from Augustine, has not been identified.

242–3 This quotation, said to be from Augustine, has not been identified.

243–5 This quotation, said to be from Augustine, has not been identified, but closely resembles the quotation from Jerome's *Ep.* CXXV, *ad Rusticum monachum* at CTI 345–8 (see note).

247–8 These words are not found in the Book of Job, but occur in the responsary of the seventh lection (Job 17) of the Office of the Dead, in the third nocturn: 'Quia in inferno nulla est redemptio miserere mei Deus et salva me' (have mercy on me, God, and save me because in hell there is no redemption). See Francis Procter and C. Wordsworth, *Breviarum ad usum insignis ecclesiae Sarum*, vol. II (Cambridge: Cambridge University Press, 1879), p. 278.

263–5 Perhaps a paraphrase of Augustine, *De Moribus Ecclesiae Catholicae*, XXII, 40; PL 32:1328.

272 'sauereden' (savoured, delighted in) is a mistranslation of *saperent* (knew) (Deut. 32:29).

280 'After þat sentence': in Matt. 25 Christ addresses his chosen ones before the damned.

284–5 'do wel and haue wel' is a quotation from *Piers Plowman*, VII, 116, where the priest tells Piers that the 'pardon' sent by Truth amounts to nothing but 'do wel and haue wel'; ed. George Kane and E. Talbot Donaldson, *Piers Plowman: The B Version* (London: Athlone Press, 1975), p. 376.

286 'þou sawist neuer soule goo a-blacberied': in his prologue, the Pardoner of the *Canterbury Tales* says that he cares nothing for the fate of the souls to whom he preaches: 'I rekke neuere whan that they been beryed / Though that hir soules goon a-blakeberyed', i.e. go to hell (see MED and CTXII 321–2); *Canterbury Tales*, VI, 405–6; ed. Benson, *The Riverside Chaucer*, p. 195.

299 'loues': Christ says 'in these two commandments (*mandatis*)', Matt. 22:40, but it seems from line 305 below that the writer understands Christ as saying 'loues', not 'laues'. The text is therefore not emended.

321–38 Cf. the ten pains of hell in 'Sermon of Dead Men', in *Lollard Sermons*, ed. G. Cigman (Oxford, 1989; EETS 294), pp. 230–4/839–957; also Lilian M. Swinburn, ed., *Lanterne of Liȝt* (London, 1917; EETS OS 151), p. 136/6–12.

325 The end of the third and the beginning of the fourth pain of Hell are missing in the manuscript.

332–3 In the Apocalypse there are many references to brimstone and pitch, but not to sweetness. The mistake probably arises from the fact that the writer is summarizing a text resembling 'Sermon of Dead Men', p. 232/897–906, which adduces first John in the Apocalypse and then Is. 3:24.

333–4 The worm of conscience is the fourth pain of Hell in 'Sermon of Dead Men', between weeping and darkness, p. 232/879–85.

368–71 See the note on CTI 78–84.

383–6 For other Epiphany sermons see Pamela Gradon, ed., *English Wycliffite Sermons*, vol. II (Oxford: Clarendon Press, 1988), pp. 236–9, and Gloria Cigman, *Lollard Sermons* (Oxford, 1989; EETS 294), pp. 74–9.

394 'fyue m., ij. c and ode ȝeris': the supposed number of years from the Fall to the birth of Christ.

400–10 Cf. Cigman, ed., *Lollard Sermons*, p. 78/192–200.

428 'þe vij. ȝiftys of [þe] Holy Goste'; these are detailed in e.g., Trinity College Dublin 70, fols 185r–186r, and Glasgow University Gen. 223, f. 222v.

429 'þe iiij. cardynal vertues': temperance, prudence, justice and fortitude; see Jolliffe, G.22.

431 'þe vij. dedes of mercy boþe bodyly and goostly'; see *Manual*, 7, XX, 50 and 51.

431–2 'to pore blynd, to pore feble, and to pore lame': this translation of Luke 14:13 understands 'pauperes' as an adjective qualifying 'debiles', 'claudos' and 'caecos', rather than as a plural noun. This interpretation, implying that the idle poor should not receive alms, was ammunition in the anti-mendicant debate of the fourteenth century; see Scase, *'Piers Plowman' and the New Anticlericalism*, pp. 63–4, 152.

433 Matt. 5:1–12 was the gospel for All Saints Day, 1 November, according to the Sarum rite.

438–9 'wiþ his louers' (yueþ þis lyueþ C): this is a speculative emendation.

4.   *First seiþ Bois*

1–2 'Senek': cf. Ullerston's *determinacio*: 'Boecius, inquit, in libro *de disciplina scolarium*, docet quod pueri primo instruendi sunt in libris Senece' (response to article 24 against translation, f. 205rb). *De disciplina scolarium* was in fact written between 1230 and 1240; see Olga Weijers, ed., *Pseudo-Boèce: De Disciplina Scolarium* (Leiden: Brill, 1976).

2–3 'and ... morals': cf. Ullerston's *determinacio*: 'et Beda exponit quod hoc dicit quia primo sunt docendi in moralibus, quia libri Senece sunt morales', f. 205rb. Ullerston probably attributes the commentary to Bede because in seven manuscripts of *De Disciplina Scolarium* there is an introduction claiming that Bede found the text among Boethius' books in Rome; see Weijers, pp. 170–2. The commentator is expounding the first of *De Disciplina Scolarium*'s list of recommended authors, Seneca, p. 95/21. Weijers lists the many commentaries on this text, pp. 18–30, including that by William Wheatley written at Stamford in 1309, pp. 23–4, but this gloss is not in Wheatley's commentary (and has not been located).

3 'morals' is here a plural adjective, but *Moralia* was also the title given to the moral works of Seneca.

3–5 'and ... soule': cf. Ullerston's *determinacio*: 'Et ideo iuuenes concipiunt malos mores a iuuentute et quando temptauerunt semper crescunt in eis, et inde accidit quod sunt inhabiles ad ueritatem sciencie magnificam, quia scriptura dicit quod *in maliuolam anima non intrabit sapiencia nec in corpore subdito peccatis* [Wisd. 1:4]' (response to article 24 against translation, f. 205rb). Quoting Roger Bacon, *Opus Majus*, ed. John H. Bridges, vol. II (Oxford: Clarendon Press, 1897), p. 170.

5–6 'moche þer of þe sentence of Bede': much [more] of what Bede says there [in the gloss on *De Disciplina Scolarium*].

6–9 Cf. Ullerston's *determinacio*: 'Et anima deturpata peccatis est sicut speculum rubiginosum et uetus in quo non possunt species rerum apparere, ut pulchre dicit Algazel, in *Logica*, et anima ornata uirtute est sicut speculum nouum et pollitum, in quo apparent clare rerum ymagines. Et ideo, inquit, quia uulgus nescit hanc scienciam a iuuentute homines habent animas obscuras et excecatas, quod numquam possunt proficere nisi in vanis et falsis et malis cauilloribus et magnis infeccionibus sapere' (response to article 24 against translation, f. 205rb). Quoting Roger Bacon, *Opus Majus*, ed. Bridges, vol. II, p. 170, and see Al Ghazzâli, *Logica et philosophia Algazelis Arabis* (Venice, 1506), sig. A.2v.

12–19 The writer is paraphrasing Ullerston's *determinacio*, f. 197vb.

16 'first' (in all copies of *FSB* except N1) is an error for 'second', Nehemiah being the second book of Ezra (see PWB 7–8, 38–40 and 54).

19–20 Cf. Ullerston's *determinacio*: 'Si enim laici humiliter petant questiones ad eorum salutem pertinentes ordinat eis remedium diuina scriptura, Deut 32ᵐ, dicens: *Interroga patres tuos et anunciabunt tibi, maiores tuos et dicent tibi* [Deut. 32:7]' (response to article 24 against translation, f. 205va).

23–4 'hope'. This quotation immediately follows Deut. 32:7 in Ullerston's *determinacio* (response to article 24 against translation, f. 205va).

25–6 'comeþ': Apoc. 22:17, with 'spiritus' translated as 'housebonde', and 'venit' (comeþ) in place of 'veni' (come); cf. CTV 71.

37 'þat ben clepid ydiotes be scripture': cf. Ullerston's *determinacio* (response to article 20 against translation, f. 204ra); Peter and John are called 'idiotae' at Acts 4:13.

45–50 Cf. Ullerston's *determinacio* (response to article 15 against translation, f. 203ra).

53–60 Cf. Ullerston's *determinacio*: 'et ideo dicit apostolus, 1 Cor. 14°, *orabo spiritu orabo et mente*, id est, affectu et intellectu, et probat consequenter quod hoc est multo melius quam solum habere deuocionem in uerbis, ipsa non intelligendo, quam ostendit consequenter, ita dicens: *ceterum si benediccionis quis supplet locum ydiote. Quomodo dicit amen super tuam benediccionem quoniam quid dicas nescit.* Quam literam exponens doctor Delira [Lyra] ita scribit: si populus, inquit, intelligat oracionem sacerdotis melius reducitur in deum et deuocius respondet amen' (f. 198ra). 'Id est affectu et intellectu' is Nicholas of Lyra's gloss on 1 Cor. 14:15. (On Lyra, see the note on PWB 2360).

63 'seuenti docturis': the legendary translators of the Hebrew scriptures into Greek. See further CTI 249–59 and note.

66–72 Cf. Ullerston's *determinacio*, f. 198rb.

67 'Spaynesche tunge, Frensche tunge and Almayne': in Spanish, the earliest Bible was in thirteenth-century Castilian; see Margherita Morreale, 'Vernacular scriptures in Spain', in G.W.H. Lampe, ed., *The History of the Bible*, Volume 2: *The West From The Fathers To The Reformation* (Cambridge: Cambridge University Press, 1969), p. 470 (and 465–91). On the Bible in Old French, see the note on PWB 2940 In German, the earliest complete Bible is the Mentel Bible, 1466, but its language is early fourteenth century; see W.B. Lockwood, 'Vernacular scriptures in Germany and the Low Countries before 1500', in Lampe, ed., *The History of the Bible*, Volume 2, p. 433 (and 415–36). See also the note on PWB 2940.

69–72 Bede, *Ecclesiastical History of the English People*, III, iii (not I), ed. B. Colgrave and R.A.B. Mynors (Oxford: Clarendon Press, 1969), pp. 218–21. Bede explains that Oswald 'had gained a perfect knowledge of Irish [the language of the Scots] during his exile', while Aidan 'was not completely at home in the English language', p. 221.

74–83 'rede hem': cf. Ullerston's *determinacio*, f. 198rb–va.

74–5 Jacob van Maerlant (*c*.1235–*c*.1300) translated Peter Comestor's *Historia Scolastica* (see note on CTI 249–59), into rhyming couplets; ed. J. David, *Rymbybel*; 3 vols (Brussels, 1858).

74 'It was herde' replaces Ullerston's *audiui* (I have heard).

78–80 Cf. Ullerston's *determinacio*: 'Nonne credis quod anglicus noster Beda uenerabilis spiritu dei ductus / transtulit bibliam in uulgare anglicum sui temporis' (f. 198rb–va); 'or a grete parte of þe Bibile' is added by the writer of *FSB*. See the note on PWB 2935–6.

80–3, 'rede hem': cf. Ullerston's *determinacio*, f. 198va, citing 'Cestrensis' ('Sistrence', the Chester scholar), *Polychronicon*, V, xxiv; ed. Joseph Rawson Lumby, *Polychronicon Ranulphi Higden*, vol. VI (London, 1876; Rolls Series 41), p. 224. Cuthbert's Letter on the Death of Bede says Bede translated John 1:1–6:9; Colgrave and Mynors, *Bede's Ecclesiastical History of the English People*, p. 583.

83–4 Bede's death, not mentioned by Ullerston, is included under the year 734: Higden, *Polychronicon*, V, xxiv; ed. Lumby, vol. VI, p. 218. **C1 L3 L4** and **L8** read 'xxiiij. ca°', but this reference has already been given at 80.

84–6 No Wyring or We[a]ring has been identified. Paul's letters exist in a Northern English translation of the fourteenth century: see M.J. Powell, ed., *The Northern Pauline Epistles* (London, 1916; EETS e.s. 116). Possibly the reference is to *Cursor Mundi*, *c*.1300.

88–91 Cf. Ullerston's *determinacio*: 'scribit enim Cestrensis, libro 6°, in principio, de rege Aluredo, fundatore vniuersitatis Oxoniensis … optimas leges in lingwam anglicam conuertit; tandem psalterium transferre aggressus, uix parte prima explicata' (f. 198va). Higden, *Polychronicon*, VI, i; ed. Lumby, vol. VI, pp. 354–6. The writer of *FSB* omits the fact that Alfred completed only the first part of the Psalter (psalms 1–50), but supplies his regnal year (actually 871).

92–100 Cf. Ullerston's *determinacio*: 'Dicit enim sanctus Thomas, super primum *Politicorum*, exponens hoc uocabulum *barbarus* per hunc modum: quidam dicunt omnes hominem barbarum esse qui lingwam eius non intelligit, bene, inquit, apostolus dicit que *si nesciero uirtutem uocis ero ei cui loquor* barbarus *et qui loquitur michi* barbarus [1 Cor. 14:11], quibusdam autem illos uidetur barbaros dici qui non habent literalem locucionem in suo uulgari ydiomate rudentem. Bene, inquit, Beda dicitur in lingwam anglicam liberales artes transtulisse ne anglici barbari reputarentur' (response to article 9 against translation, f. 201vb). Ullerston is quoting Thomas Aquinas's commentary on Aristotle's *Politics* (trans. William of Moerbeke, *c.*1260), Book I (Rome, 1492), f. 2v.

100–10 Cf. Ullerston's *determinacio*, f. 198va–b, quoting Robert Grosseteste, 'Scriptum est de Leuitis', BL Royal 6 E.v, f. 109va. See the notes on PWB 1708 and 1721–4.

108 'þat is, his puple' is the translator's addition.

109 'argueþ a clerk': i.e., Ullerston.

111 'þe Sauter': cf. Ullerston's *determinacio*, f. 198va, but Ullerston does not mention Richard Rolle's gloss, the Dirige or other treatises. Rolle's Psalter (*c.*1340) is ed. H.R. Bramley, *The Psalter or Psalms of David … by Richard Rolle* (Oxford: Clarendon Press, 1884). A new edition is being prepared by Jill C. Havens and Karl Gustaffson.

114–19 Cf. Ullerston's *determinacio*, f. 198vb. John (not William, *pace* Ullerston and *FSB*) Thoresby, archbishop of York 1352–73, wishing to improve the religious knowledge of the laity issued an injunction in 1357 outlining a programme of education modelled on that promulgated in 1281 by John Pecham, archbishop of Canterbury (see the note on CTI 62). An expanded English version, now known as *The Lay Folk's Catechism*, was made for Thoresby by John Gaytryge, a Benedictine monk of St Mary's Abbey, York.

118 'in smale pagynes': cheap booklets in small format. This detail has no basis in fact.

119–26 Cf. Ullerston's *determinacio*, f. 199ra, quoting Rolle's gloss on Ps. 118:43.

120–1 'but wel [t]ouchiþ þis holi man Richard Hampol suche men' is the equivalent of Ullerston's '… sed eo deterius eis continget [but it impacts even less favourably upon them, i.e. those who argue against vernacular scripture] quod bene notat Ricardus Hampole'. **C5**'s 'couchiþ' (puts down, quells) is possible, but 'touchiþ' (cf. **C1** and 'to which' **L8**) probably translates *continget*.

122 'not fewe but many' translates *nonnulli*.

123 'better' translates Ullerston's *melioribus*, but other manuscripts of Rolle's Psalter-commentary read *sapientioribus* (wiser).

126–8 'langagis': cf. Ullerston's *determinacio*: 'Nam, si propterea non permitteretur ewangelium scribi in anglico quia sunt multi tractatus anglicani continentes hereses et errores, iam pari siue a fortiori prohiberent scripturam in latino, que per totam christianitatem posset disseminari' (f. 199ra). Cf. also CTI 85–8 and note.

128 'for … eretikes': according to Gratian's *Decretum*, causa 24, qu. 3, c. 39, *Quidam*, there were sixty-eight Latin heresies, as well as 'others without a founder or a name'; Richter and Friedberg, I, 1001–6.

128–33 Cf. Ullerston's *determinacio*: 'et dominus Ardmacanus, nono libro *de questionibus armenorum*, ca° 1°, ubi querit an consecracio in uulgari lingua possit fieri, sic respondet: nemo enim christianus dubitat quin ita vere consecratur in vna lingua sicut in alia, quam sic fecerunt apostoli et sic facere tradiderunt. Matheus enim ewangelium scripsit in hebraico et Iohannes in greco et Marcus in ytalico et Paulus epistulam ad Romanos, in qua de ista consecracione fit mencio eciam scripsit in greco, singuli in illis linguis in quibus scripserunt non dubium docuerunt, vnde, inquit, constat in singulis linguis consecracionem posse fieri, quo uidetur quod lingue omnes ob hoc erant dite apostolica, sicut legitur Actuum, 2° ca°, ut modum consecracionis huius sacramenti et alia salutis documenta singulis nacionibus singularum linguarum crederent exercenda' (response to article 18 against translation, f. 204vb). Ullerston is quoting Richard FitzRalph, archbishop of Armagh, *Summa Domini Armacani in Questionibus Armenorum*, IX, i (Paris, 1512), sig. L.6r. (On FitzRalph, see the note on PWB 2361, and on his *Summa in Questionibus Armenorum* see the note on PWB 2362) *FSB* omits the logical connection FitzRalph makes between the languages in which the apostles wrote and the language in which the sacrament is celebrated.

134 'prey anticrist þat we moten haue oure bileue in Englische': the notion of praying to Antichrist evidently daunted scribes; 'prey' is erased in **N1** and omitted in **C1 L4** and **L8**. By 'anticrist' the writer surely means the church authorities who are denying the people the Bible in English.

135–9 The writer's claim to have had many dealings with Jews is surprising in England at the beginning of the fifteenth century.

139–40 The writer is presumably referring to the Septuagint and the Greek New Testament.

141–7 Cf. Ullerston's *determinacio* (response to article 20 against translation, f. 204ra–b). To clinch his argument, Ullerston quotes Augustine, 'quid est igitur integritas locucionis nisi consuetudinis conseruacio loquencium veterum auctoritate firmata?', *De doctrina christiana*, II, xiii; ed. Martin, p. 45/26–8. These lines are misplaced at the end of *FSB* in **C1 L3 L4 L8** and **N1**.

148–9 'Bibel': One John Dille was provincial of the Dominican friars in England from *c*.1404 until 1410; see A.G. Little, 'Priors and vicars of the English Dominicans', *The English Historical Review* 33 (1918), 497. The sermon Tille/Dille is said to have preached recalls the preamble to the seventh article of Arundel's *Constitutions*, in which Jerome's comments on the danger of translation and his confession that he had often erred preface the prohibition of translation in any form. See David Wilkins, ed., *Concilia Magnae Britanniae et Hiberniae*, vol. III (London, 1737), p. 17.

152–5 Cf. Ullerston's *determinacio* (response to article 9 against translation, f. 202ra), quoting Jerome's prologue to Kings, 'Prologus Galeatus' ('helmeted prologue'); PL 28:557–8.

155–6 'trewe': Jerome's replies to Augustine's arguments on holy scripture are included among Augustine's correspondence: Jerome's letters LXVIII, ed. K.D. Daur, *Sancti Aurelii Augustini Epistulae*, vol. II (Turnhout: Brepols, 2004; CCSL 31A), pp. 29–31, and LXXII, vol. II, pp. 40–3, reply to Augustine's letter LXVII, ed. Daur, vol. II, pp. 27–8; Jerome's letter LXXV, ed. Daur, vol. II, 54–76, replies to Augustine's letters XXVIII, ed. K.D. Daur, *Sancti Aurelii Augustini Epistulae*, vol. I (Turnhout: Brepols, 2004; CCSL 31), pp. 92–7, XL, ed. Daur, vol. I, pp. 159–65, and LXXI, ed. Daur, vol. II (CCSL 31A), pp. 36–9; Augustine's letter LXXXII, vol. II, pp. 97–122, replies to Jerome's letters LXXII, LXXV and LXXXI, vol. II, p. 96. On Augustine's reply to Jerome's charge that scripture is sometimes false, cf. *HPD* 174–6, and the note on those lines.

156 'as'–**160** Jerome, 'Frater Ambrosius tua mihi munuscula perferens', *Ep.* LIII, *ad Paulinum*; PL 22:540–9 (quotation at 549).

160–4 'Desiderii mei desideratus accepi epistolas', *Praefatio in Pentateucum*; PL 28:152.

164–7 Jerome's prologue to Joshua; PL 28:464.

165 '[de]batourus' translates *calumniantibus*.

168 'I'–**170** The end of Jerome's prologue to Kings (see note on 152–5); PL 28:558.

170 'rehersing þe profi3te': Jerome is quoting Ps. 38:1–2.

171–9 This account has no basis in fact, and it was not for parliament to legislate on such matters.

171–2 'whos soule God asoile': Richard died in February 1400.

175 John of Lancaster died in 1399.

180–90 These details of Thomas Arundel's sermon at the funeral of Anne of Bohemia, first queen of Richard II, d. 1394, are not recorded elsewhere. This account is perhaps a composite of several sermons of his, although the sermon is accepted as historical by Jonathan Hughes, *ODNB* 2:566. The implication is that it was known well before 1407 (though hardly as early as 1394?) that Arundel was minded to prohibit the English Bible.

180 'bischope … nowe is': Arundel was archbishop of York in 1394; he was translated to Canterbury in 1396. 'þat nowe is' dates *FSB* before Arundel's death in 1414.

184–5 'on Engliche … vpon hem': surely a reference to the Glossed Gospels (see the introduction to the Glossed Gospel Prologues and Epilogue, pp. lx–lxi). In *De Triplico Vinculo Amoris*, *c*.1383, Wyclif states that Anne of Bohemia owned the Gospels in Czech, German and Latin; ed. Rudolf Buddensieg, *John Wyclif's Polemical Works in Latin*, vol. II (London: Wyclif Society, 1883), p. 168/9–11. It is extremely unlikely that Anne possessed all the Glossed Gospels, or that Arundel approved them.

190 'and þan … herde': it is difficult to gauge the tone of these words, but presumably those who thought Arundel would 'forsake þe worlde' judged it 'þe best sermoun þat euere þei herde' because he would no longer be in a position to prohibit the English Bible.

5. *The Holi Prophete Dauid*

2 The Latin Bible's 'faucibus' properly means 'throat', not 'cheeks'.

51–84 This passage is an abbreviated version of part of Bernard of Clairvaux, *Sermones in Cantica Canticorum* 36, ed. H. Hurter (Innsbruck, 1888; Sanctorum Patrum Opuscula Selecta 5), pp. 318–20.

56–7 Cf. Peter's vision in Acts 10:10–16.

65–6 'of God and ne3ebour' is the translator's addition.

73 The word 'preciable' replaces Bernard's 'non inveniuntur in abusione scientiae' (are not found in the wrongful use of knowledge).

80 'as who sei 3his' alerts the reader to the fact that this is a rhetorical question expecting the answer 'yes'.

88 'þe Wise Man': see the note on PWB 1774.

92–4 Gregory the Great, *Moralia in Job*, II, i; ed. M. Adriaen, vol. I (Turnhout: Brepols, 1979; CCSL 143), p. 59/1–5.

103–5 This quotation, attributed to Chrysostom here and at PWB 2463–4, has not been identified.

118–20 Augustine, *Enarrationes in Psalmos* [Ps. 54:16], ed. E. Dekkers and J. Fraipont (Turnhout: Brepols, 1956; CCSL 39), pp. 668–9. Cf. PWB 91–4.

122 'þe deuel, þe world and of þere fleisch': see the note on CTIV 35–6.

124–6 Ps.-Chrysostom on Matt. 5:16, *Opus Imperfectum in Matthæum*, X; PG 56:687. (See the note on PWB 1766–7).

126 'sclandriþ' (is a cause of moral harm to) is stronger than ps.-Chrysostom's 'scandalizat' (is a cause of moral outrage to).

130–50 Ps.-Chrysostom on Matt. 22:29, *Opus Imperfectum in Matthæum*, XLII; PG 56:870–1.

144–5 'þat is blyndid in errour' has no equivalent in *Opus Imperfectum*, 871.

146 'lernynge of bataile' translates 'bellicam disciplinam', 871.

147–8 The translation of 'nolenti colere terram agriculturam exponat', necessary to the sense, is lacking. The words in brackets are a speculative translation.

173–5 Gratian, *Decretum*, ca. 24, c. 3, *Heresis* (quoting Jerome); Richter and Friedberg I, 997; c. 39, *Quidam*, para. 70 (quoting Isidore of Seville); I, 1006.

175–7 Augustine, *Ep.* XXVIII, *ad Ieronimum*; ed. K.D. Daur, *Sancti Aurelii Augustini Epistulae*, vol. I (Turnhout: Brepols, 2004; CCSL 31), p. 95/84–96.

212–62 See the note on CTIX 28–48.

255–9 Augustine, *Sermo* CCCL; PL 39:1534. Cf. PWB 80–2, 2256–75.

258 'duble charite': love of God and neighbour.

263 The first objection is 'þe letter sleeþ'.

263–72 Cf. also Heb. 12:20, cited by Ullerston in his *determinacio* on biblical translation (see the introduction to *First seiþ Bois*, pp. xlix–liv), in article 22 against translation: 'bestia, per quam intelligitur populus rudus et carnalis, si tetigerit montem lapidabitur' (an animal, by which is understoood crude and fleshly people, will be stoned if it touches the mountain) (f. 196ra), and by Palmer (see the introduction to *First seiþ Bois*, pp. xlix–liv), ed. Deanesly, *LB*, 430. Ullerston's counter-argument is that although simple people may not understand the subtler points of scripture they can understand its essential truths, which the clergy have a duty to explain to them (f. 204vb).

279 See the note on CTI 104–5.

302–3 The Latin Bible reads 'tauri mei et altilia' (my bulls and my fatlings), not 'fowls'. Most manuscripts of the Wycliffite Bible in EV and LV have the same error; see Dove, *FEB*, 180, 233.

303 'wheron'–**317** Ps.-Chrysostom on Matt. 22:4, 'et omnia iam parata', *Opus Imperfectum in Matthæum*, XLI; PG 56:862.

306 'rebellour' translates *contumax*.

308 'þe glorie of biheste of euerlastynge liyf': *Opus Imperfectum* has 'glorias et promissiones vitae perpetuae' (the glories and promises of eternal life).

308–9 'þat is, bileueþ, kepiþ and holdiþ in mynde' is the translator's gloss.

310 'in his soule' is the translator's gloss.

310 'mene' translates *mediocres*.

311–12 'þat is, parfit in goostli lyuynge' is the translator's gloss.

313–14 'þat is, more parfit liyf' is the translator's gloss.

316 'schullen reparaile' translates *revocent*.

316 'penaunce': Ps.-Chrysostom provides several examples, including the Israelites' stoning of Achar, which averted God's wrath (Jos. 7:24–6); see PWB 416–20.

317 'þat is, hooli scripture' is the translator's gloss on 'feste'.

318–20 'falle' Cf. 1 Chron. 13:7–10.

329–33 Lyra's gloss on 2 Kings 6:6–7 says that according to the Jews Oza was killed because he sinned in failing to carry the ark on his shoulders. In *Quaestiones Hebraicae in Librum I Paralipomenon*, Jerome (or ps.-Jerome), commenting on 1 Chron. 13:7, says that Oza and his brother (better manuscripts have 'brothers'; *Biblia Sacra*) should have carried the ark on their shoulders, but in his *Ep.* XXII, *ad Eustochium*, Jerome implies that Oza's failure to maintain virginity was the cause of his death; PL 22:409.

340–2 See PWB 1703–36 and the notes on that passage.

6. *Pater Noster II*

28–42 'erþe': cf. the Pater Noster tract in *Pore Caitif*, except for the references to authority, subtlety and profit; in CUL Ff.6.34, fols 52v–53r.

36–7 On the excellence of the Pater Noster, see Wyclif: 'ista oracio excedit omnes alias in hiis quinque. In dignitate, in compendiositate, in utilitate, in subtilitate et omnimoda bonitate', *De Mandatis Divinis*, ed. J. Loserth and F.D. Matthew (London: Wyclif Society, 1922), p. 259–60/15–20 (quotation p. 259/15–17), and *De Oracione Dominica*, ed. J. Loserth, *Opera Minora* (London: Wyclif Society, 1913), pp. 383–4. See also *Pater Noster I*, ed. Arnold, *Select English Works*, III, 93/1–3, and *The Mirror of St Edmund*, ed. C. Horstman, *Early English Writers*, vol. I (London: Sonnenschein, 1895), p. 232/3–4. Many other parallels could be cited.

71–3 On the structuring of vices and their remedial virtues in this text, see A.L. Kellogg and Ernest W. Talbot, 'The Wycliffite *Pater Noster* and *Ten Commandments*, with special reference to English manuscripts 85 and 90 in the John Rylands Library', *Bulletin of the John Rylands Library* 42 (1960), 360–2.

90–1 Cf. *Pore Caitif*: 'þe soule of a iust man and wel liuinge is þe sete of wisdome, þat is, of Crist', CUL Ff.6.34, f. 59r.

99 Only three manuscripts, **C7 L6** and **S1**, mention purgatory.

145–9 'syþþe' ... kyngdom': cf. the Pater Noster tract in *Pore Caitif*; CUL Ff.6.34, f. 57v.

151–3 'kyngdom': cf. the Pater Noster tract in *Pore Caitif*; CUL Ff.6.34, f. 58v.

151 *Pore Caitif*'s reading is better here: 'whanne we seyn *oure* fadir and not *myn*', CUL Ff.6.34, f. 58v.

157–8 Cf. the Pater Noster tract in *Pore Caitif*; CUL Ff.6.34, ff. 58v–59r.

160 'for'–1 Cf. the Pater Noster tract in *Pore Caitif*; CUL Ff.6.34, f. 59r.

176 All manuscripts read 'seynt Poul' except **O2**, where 'Sapiens' is written over an erasure.

181 'And'–5 Cf. the Pater Noster tract in *Pore Caitif*; CUL Ff.6.34, ff. 59v–60r.

190–217 Cf. Augustine, *De Sermone Dei in Monte*, II, 7, 25; ed. Almut Mutzenbecher (Turnhout: Brepols, 1967; CCSL 35), pp. 113–16/515–83. Augustine, unlike the writer of *PNII*, is concerned with the question of whether the sacrament should be received daily.

198–200 'for ... þerof': cf. (but not word for word) *Pore Caitif*; CUL Ff.6.34, f. 60v.

205–11 'praye' ... 'today': cf. the Pater Noster tract in *Pore Caitif*; CUL Ff.6.34, f. 61r–v.

206 *Pore Caitif* reads 'trewe techeris', CUL Ff.6.34, f. 61r.

218–26 'ous': cf. the Pater Noster tract in *Pore Caitif*; CUL Ff.6.34, f. 61v.

236 'He'–244 Cf. the Pater Noster tract in *Pore Caitif*; CUL Ff.6.34, f. 63r.

262–4 'praye ... temptacioun': cf. the Pater Noster tract in *Pore Caitif*; CUL Ff.6.34, f. 63r–v.

268–9 'And ... God': cf. the Pater Noster tract in *Pore Caitif*; CUL Ff.6.34, f. 64r.

273–4 'Þefore ... synnes': cf. the Pater Noster tract in *Pore Caitif*; CUL Ff.6.34, f. 65r.

277–95 On the similarity between this passage and the fourth petition of the Pater Noster treatise in *Pore Caitif*, see M. Teresa Brady, 'Lollard sources of *The Pore Caitif*, *Traditio* 44 (1988), 399.

279–81 'and so ... synne': cf. the Pater Noster tract in *Pore Caitif*; CUL Ff.6.34, f. 65r.

291–5 'Þat ... God': cf. the Pater Noster tract in *Pore Caitif*; CUL Ff.6.34, f. 65v.

301 'Rabanus' is written in the margin beside line 301 in manscripts **L6**, **P3** and **R90**, and beside line 305 in **N2**. See the note on CTVII 62.

305 See previous note.

311–12 See the note on CTVII 66–7.

7. Glossed Gospel Prologues and Epilogue

I Prologue to Short Matthew

4–6 'Prophetae quippe in sacra eloquio nonnumquam doctores vocantur' (teachers are sometimes called prophets in holy writ), Gregory the Great, *Regula Pastoralis*, II, iv; ed. and trans. H.R. Bramley (Oxford: Parker, 1874), p. 22.

17 'and sympli-lettrid prestis': cf. *IB* 5–8, CTI 53–66 and CTII 35–6 (variants).

19 'a symple creature': the writer of PWB describes himself in the same way; see the note on PWB 2801.

23 On the role of reason, cf. GGII 111–12, GGIII 26, 60–1 and PIP 42–3.

29–30 Jerome, *Commentariorum in Matheum Libri IV*, ed. D. Hurst and M. Adriaen (Turnhout: Brepols, 1969; CCSL 77).

30–1 Ps.-Chrysostom, *Opus Imperfectum in Matthæum*; PG 56:611–946; see note on PWB 1766–7.

32–4 Augustine, *De Sermone Domini in Monte* (a commentary on Matt. 5–7), ed. Almut Mutzenbecher (Turnhout: Brepols, 1967; CCSL 35).

34 'Bede in his omeli': Bede's commentary on Matthew; PL 92:9–132.

35 'Gregorie in his omeli': Gregory the Great, *Homiliae in Evangelia*, ed. Raymond Étaix (Turnhout: Brepols, 1999; CCSL 141).

36 'Alquyn on Matheu': the commentary of Thomas Aquinas (1225–74) on Matthew is ed. A. Guarienti, *Catena Aurea in Quatuor Evangelia*, vol. I (Turin: Marietti, 1953), pp. 9–425.

42 'his parfit werk on Matheu': Chrysostom, *Homiliae XC in Matthæum*; PG 57–8.

42 'Origen': the (now incomplete) commentary of Origen of Alexandria (b. 185–d. 254) on Matthew is ed. E. Klostermann with E. Benz, *Mattäuserklärung* (Leipzig: Hinrich, 1935; Die griechischen christlicher Schriftsteller 38).

43 'Illarie': the commentary of Hilary of Poitiers (*c.*300–*c.*368) on Matthew is ed. PL 9:915–1078.

43 'Remygie': on the commentary of Remigius of Auxerre (b. bef. 850–908), see F. Stegmüller and N. Reinhardt, *Repertorium Biblicum Medii Aevi* (Madrid: Consejo Superior de Investigaciones Científicas, 1950–80), nos 7226–7.

43 'Raban': the commentary on Matthew of Rabanus (or Hrabanus) Maurus (*c.*780–856), pupil of Alcuin, is ed. B. Löfstedt, *Expositio in Matthaeum* (Turnhout: Brepols, 2000; CCCM 174, 174A).

II Prologue to Intermediate Matthew

1–7 Augustine, *De doctrina christiana*, II, xlii; ed. Martin, p. 76/6–12; cf. PWB 2378–83.

8–14 *De doctrina christiana*, III, v; ed. Martin, pp. 82–3/3–9; cf. PWB 2194–200.

12–14 The translation in PWB 2199–200 is clearer here: 'vndurstonding, þat passiþ beestis, is maad suget to þe fleish in suynge þe lettre', translating 'id etiam quod in ea bestiis antecellit, hoc est intelligentia, carni subicitur sequendo litteram'.

15–21 *De doctrina christiana*, III, x; ed. Martin, p. 86/5–12; cf. PWB 2200–203.

21–6 *De doctrina christiana*, III, x; ed. Martin, p. 87/22–31; cf. PWB 2203–8.

27–9 *De doctrina christiana*, III, xi; ed. Martin, p. 88/18–20; cf. PWB 2208–9, 'parable'.

28–9 'derk licenesse or parable' translates Augustine's *aenigma* (19). Here **O4** and PWB have a better reading than **D D76 G1 L1 O6 o P1 R77**.

29–31 *De doctrina christiana*, III, xv; ed. Martin, p. 91/3–5; cf. PWB 2218–20.

31–41 *De doctrina christiana*, III, xvi; ed. Martin, pp. 91–2/1–9; cf. PWB 2220–9.

42–9 *De doctrina christiana*, III, xxvii; ed. Martin, pp. 99–100/1–5, 10–18; cf. PWB 2242–54.

50–1 *De doctrina christiana*, III, xxix; ed. Martin, p. 101/1–5; cf. PWB 2191–4.

51–2 *De doctrina christiana*, III, xxx; ed. Martin, p. 102/1–6; cf. PWB 2276–7.

51 See notes on PWB 2276–348.

52–60 *De doctrina christiana*, III, xxxi; ed. Martin, p. 104; cf. PWB 2277–88.

52 'and of his body': see the note on PWB 2278.

58 'ourned': see the note on PWB 2284.

61–70 *De doctrina christiana*, III, xxxii; ed. Martin, pp. 104–5/1–13; cf. PWB 2289–306.

71–2 *De doctrina christiana*, III, xxxiii; ed. Martin, pp. 105–6/1–4; cf. PWB 2307–11.

73–4 *De doctrina christiana*, III, xxxiv; ed. Martin, p. 106/1–3; cf. PWB 2312–13.

75–83 *De doctrina christiana*, III, xxxv; ed. Martin, pp. 110–11/1–3, 15–38; cf. PWB 2314–35.

84–90 *De doctrina christiana*, III, xxxvi (1–13, 44–5); ed. Martin, pp. 111–12, 113; cf. PWB 2336–44.

91–4 *De doctrina christiana*, III, xxxvii; ed. Martin, p. 114/1–5; cf. PWB 2345–8.

95–9 *De doctrina christiana*, III, xxxvii; ed. Martin, pp. 115–16/37–45; cf. PWB 2349–57.

100–2 *De doctrina christiana*, IV, viii; ed. Martin, p. 131/1–11; cf. PWB 2369–72.

103–7 Gregory, *Moralia in Iob*, XXIX, viii, ed. M. Adriaen, vol. III (Turnhout: Brepols, 1985; CCSL 143B), p. 1447/43–7.

110 'Austyn': see the note on GGI 32–4; 'Ierom': see the note on GGI 29–30; 'Gregorie': see the note on GGI 35; 'Ambrose': (on Luke), see the note on GGIV 26; 'Crisostom': see the notes on GGI 30–1 and 42.

111 'Bernard': Bernard of Clairvaux (1090–1153), whose sermons on the Song of Songs are quoted at *HPD* 51–84.

111 'Grosted': Robert Grosseteste, see the note on PWB 1708.

112 'þe Maister of Sentence': Peter Lombard (*c*.1100–1160), scholastic theologian and author of the *Quatuor Libri Sententiarum*.

113 'Rabanes on Mathew': see the final note on GGI 43.

115 'Bede': see the note on GGI 34; 'Illarie': Hilary of Poitiers, see the note on GGI 43.

121 'Crisostom in his werk vncomplete': see the note on GGI 30–1.

123 'þe sarmoun of þe Lord in þe Hil': see the note on GGI 32–4.

138 'cristen in name … heþen in condiciouns': cf. PWB 1596–7.

145 'pardouns wiþouten noumbre': see the note on PWB 1585–9.

154–7 These lines seem to refer to the terms of the third of Arundel's constitutions, in which case this prologue was written in or after 1407.

162–4 Similar points are made by ps.-Chrysostom on Matt. 23:2, *Opus Imperfectum in Matthæum*, XLIII; PG 56:876–9.

III Epilogue to Intermediate / Long Matthew

3 'byfore-seid': see GGII 109–15.

12 'almest of six hundrid ȝeeris agon': Rabanus (see the final note on GGI 43) was writing in the first half of the eighth century, suggesting this text was written *c*.1400.

27–9 Augustine, *Enarrationes in Psalmos*, Ps. 66:1, 44–5; ed. E. Dekkers and J. Fraipont (Turnhout: Brepols, 1956; CCSL 39), vol. II, p. 857.

29–30 'Ego dico, contemne; evangelium loquitur, cave', Augustine, *In Epistolam Joannis ad Parthos* (1 John); PL 35:2062.

30–7 Augustine, *De Trinitate*, I, III, 1–8; ed. W.J. Mountain, vol. I (Turnhout: Brepols, 1968; CCSL 50), p. 32.

37–40 *De Trinitate*, I, III, 15–19; ed. Mountain, pp. 32–3.

40–4 *De Trinitate*, I, III, 32–7; ed. Mountain, p. 33.

44 'uberrimum fructum', p. 33/36; **O4**'s 'pitouse' is therefore emended to L's 'plenteuous'.

44–6 *De Trinitate*, VIII, IV, 16–19; ed. Mountain, p. 275.

45 'bildyngis or makyngis' translates Augustine's *machinamenta*.

47–68 Augustine, *Contra Faustum*, XI, 5; ed. J. Zycha (Vienna: Tempsky, 1881; CSEL 25), pp. 320/18–30–321/1–14.

49 'or aftir-comyngis' is the translator's gloss.

55 'canoun' is evidently an adjective here, translating Augustine's *canonicarum*.

55 'or reulis of holy writ' is the translator's gloss.

67 L's 'helful' translates Augustine's *saluberrima*, p. 321/13.

68–72 *Contra Faustum*, XI, 5; ed. Zycha, p. 320/12–15.

71 'þat is of lattere seyntis' is the translator's gloss.

72–4 Augustine, *Contra Faustum*, XXXIII, 6; ed. Zycha, p. 792/8–9.

73 'of reule' translates Augustine's *canonica* (9).

75–82 Gratian, *Decretum*, dist. IX, c. 5, *Ego solis*; ed. Richter and Friedberg, I, 17; Augustine, *Ep.* LXXXII, *ad Hieronymum*, ed. K.D. Daur, *Sancti Aurelii Augustini Epistulae*, vol. II (Turnhout: Brepols, 2004; CCSL 31A), pp. 98–9/50–60.

81 'by resoun of reule eþer probable': by reason grounded in the biblical canon or by probable reason, that is, following from the principles of faith (cf. PIP 42–3).

83–7 Jerome, *In Amos*, 2:1, ed. M. Adriaen, *S. Hieronymi Presbyteri Opera: Commentarii in Prophetas Minores*, vol. I (Turnhout: Brepols, 1969; CCSL 76), pp. 393–4/18–41. Only the last sentence is a direct translation. Cf. Augustine, *De doctrina christiana* III, xxxv; ed. Martin, pp. 110–11, translated PWB 2323–30, and the second prologue to Lyra's *Postillae*, translated PWB 2673–4.

87–8 See Jerome, *Commentariorum in Matheum*, ed. D. Hurst and M. Adriaen (Turnhout: Brepols, 1969; CCSL 77), Lib. II, on Matt. 12:40; p. 97/560–69.

107 'deed leed or rotun wex getun þorou symonye': see the note on CTX 21.

IV Prologue to Short Luke

1–2 Illegible text supplied from Ps. 21:23 in LV; *WB*, II, 758.

3–5 Illegible text supplied from Luke 1:76–7 in LV, *WB*, IV, 147. Both EV and LV, however, read 'science', as does GGI 3.

14 'to pore men, þat is, to meke men': glossing 'pore' as 'meke' suggests an anti-mendicant interpretation; cf. the note on CTXII 431–2.

26 Ambrose's commentary on Luke is ed. M. Adriaen, *Expositio evangelii secundum Lucam* (Turnhout: Brepols, 1957; CCSL 14).

27 Bede's commentary on Luke is ed. D. Hurst (Turnhout: Brepols, 1960; CCSL 120), pp. 5–425.

28–9 'Alquyn on Luk': Thomas Aquinas's commentary on Luke is ed. A. Guarienti, *Catena Aurea in Quatuor Evangelia*, vol. II (Turin: Marietti, 1953), pp. 3–319.

34 'seint Denyss þe martir': pseudo-Dionysius (Dionysius the Areopagite), who wrote *c*.500, was formerly identified with the martyr Dionysius of Paris (d. *c*.250).

34–6 'seint Gregorie Nasansene': Gregory of Nazianzus (329–87); 'seint Cipryan': Cyprian of

Carthage (d. 258); 'Teofile': Theophilus of Alexandria (d. 412); Chrysostom (*c*.347–407); Basil of Caesarea (*c*.329–79); Cyril of Alexandria (*c*.378–444); 'Attanasie': Athanasius of Alexandria (*c*.293–373); 'Damassene': John of Damascus (*c*.676–749); Gregory of Nyssa (d. aft. 394).

37 'as'–**38** Gratian, *Decretum*, d. 15, c. 3, *Sancta Romana*; Richter and Friedberg I, 36–41; d. 16, c. 7, *Quoniam*; I, 44–5.

39 On Origen, see the note on GGI 42; Epiphanius of Salamis (*c*.315–403); Eusebius of Caesarea (*c*.263–33); Maximus of Turin (*c*.380–aft. 465).

41 'Ysidre': Isidore of Seville (*c*.560–636) (?); 'Tite': Titus of Bostra (d. *c*.378). 'Greek doctour' translates Aquinas's anonymous 'Graecus'.

V Prologue to Short John

5–6 See Augustine's discussion of Gal. 6:2, question 71 of his *De Diversis Quaestionibus Octoginta Tribus*, ed. Almut Mutzenbecher (Turnhout: Brepols; CCSL 44A), pp. 200–7.

11–12 'remyttinge to þe grettir gloos writun on Ioon … sentences': this is evidence that Long Glossed John, now lost, did once exist. The only textual evidence for it is in York Minster XVI.D.2 (see Hudson, *PR*, 249) and in Tokyo, Takamiya 31; see Anne Hudson, 'Two notes on the Wycliffite *Glossed Gospels*', *Philologia Anglica: Essays Presented to Professor Yoshio Terasawa on the Occasion of his Sixtieth Birthday* (Tokyo, 1988), pp. 379–84. See also the introduction to CTV, p. xli.

8. *In þe biginnyng*

There are no notes for *In þe biginnyng*.

Glossary

The Glossary is a selective one, and should be used in conjunction with the glosses accompanying the text on each page; in a very few cases further information is offered in the Notes. It is assumed that users of this book will be familiar with the normal language of Chaucerian English, and with the usual grammatical abbreviations found in editions of the medieval vernacular. Citation of the texts here is normally in alphabetical order of the abbreviated text title, and not by the order in which the texts are here printed.

Initial i/y and u/v are included in the same alphabetical sequence. Initial ʒ follows g.

abien, *v.* pay the penalty for CTI 354

affecciouns, *sb. pl* desires *HPD* 18

aʒenclepe, *v.3sg.pres.subj.* recall GGIII 34

aʒenward, *adv.* conversely, vice versa *HPD* 147 PWB 2062

aleggaunce, *sb.* citation GGI 38

alegge, *v.* cite GGIV 26, **alleggiþ**, *3sg.pres.* GGII 109, **allegid**, *pa.p.* cited GGI 28 GGIII 11

anentis, *prep.* according to, with PWB 8 (etc.), towards CTV 192

apert, *adj.* open PWB 2076, **apertily**, *adv.* publicly *FSB* 16

apirtee, *sb.* idiom CTI 181 (note)

aquestis, *sb.pl.* trial-lawyers *PNII* 131 (app.)

arettid, *v.pa.p.* reckoned *HPD* 78 *PNII* 252 (app.) PWB 2594

arsitris, *sb.pl.* students of Arts PWB 2503 (note)

asoilid, *v.pa.p.* resolved PWB 2325

auauunces, *sb.pl.* promotees PWB 1740

Aue, *interj.* Hail [Mary] CTI 58

auoutrie, *sb.* adultery PWB 326 (etc.) *HPD* 43

autentik, *adj.* authoritative PIP 42 PWB 2181

axynge, *sb.* petition *PNII* 150 (etc.)

ballard, *sb.* bald head PWB 791

bate, *v.* abate GGII 165

beere, *sb.* bier PWB 1738, 2144

beheyʒt [see **bihoteþ**]

beiapiþ, *vb.3sg.pres.* tricks *HPD* 170

better, *adj.* bitter CTXII 333

bie, *sb.* ring PWB 489

biforseid, *v.3sg.pa.* prophesied PWB 678, 799

bigge, *v.* redeem *PNII* 283

bihoteþ, *v.3sg.pres.* promises **PWB 253,** **bihotyþ** CTXII 369, **bihiʒte**, 3sg.pa. CTXII 43, **beheyʒt**, *v.pa.p. PNII* 257, **bihiʒt**, *pa.p.adj.* PIP 35

bymoweden, *v.3pl.pa.* mocked PWB 1422

bihe(e)st(e, *sb.* promise *HPD* 308 PWB 215 (etc.)

birlyng, *ger.* giving to drink PWB 2496

blasfeme, *adj.pl.* blasphemous PWB 985

blende, *v.* blind CTI 301

bileue (**book of**), *sb.*, canonical book, book used to determine doctrine PWB 22

boistouse, *adj.* crude, unmannerly PWB 1682 (app.)

bolnyngis, *sb.pl.* swellings, tumours *HPD* 80

borel, *adj.* ignorant CTI 269

bowiden, *v.3pl.pa.* turned aside PWB 468

buyschementis, *sb. pl.* ambushes PWB 830

bylle, *sb.* charter CTXI 55

canoun, *adj pl.* canonical GGIII 55 (note)

canonystris, *sb.pl.* canon lawyers PWB 2506

certis, *adv.* indeed PWB 34

cevyle, *adj.* civil CTI 463

chaier, *sb.* seat *HPD* 14

chare, *sb.* chariot PWB 785

charche, *sb.* significance, weight PWB 34

chargen, *v.3pl.pres.*attribute significance to PWB 1762

cheuenteyn, *sb.* chieftain GGIV 59

chymeris, *sb.pl.* chimeras PWB 1684

cyuylians, *sb pl.* civil lawyers PWB 2506

cleped a3eyn, *prep.v.pa.p.* recalled GGII 86

code, *sb.* cud *HPD* 280

colourable, *adj.* plausible, superficially attractive PWB 2879

colour(e, *sb.* pretence, disguise *HPD* 47 *PNII* 307, **colours,** *sb pl.* specious reasons GGII 155

comentes, *sb.pl.* communities CTI 273

comyned, *v.3sg.p.* communicated CTXI 76, **com(e)yne wiþ,** *v.* participate in GGII 39–40 PWB 2228, **comynynge,** *ger.* GGII 70

comwn(e, *adj.* common, vernacular *IB* 2, 5

comountee, *sb.* community CTII 52

conclude, *v.* convince CTI 469, **concludiþ,** *3sg. pres.*confutes PWB 1960

conuycte, *v.* convince, persuade PWB 2018

coriouste, *sb.* fastidiousness *HPD* 67

costen, *v.3pl.pres,* share a boundary with PWB 1261

costlew, *adj.* costly PWB 159

couenable, *adj.* suitable PWB 858, **couenably,** *adv.* appropriately GGII 12

cracche, *sb.* cradle PWB 2626

crafte, *adj.* strong CTI 279

culver, *sb.* dove CTV 129 (etc.)

curatis, *sb.pl.* clergy CTI 54 *HPD* 341 PWB 1600

currours, *sb.pl.* couriers, runners PWB 1412

cuschens, *sb pl.* cushions PWB 2902

darnel, *sb.* cockle, weed among grain CTI 97

declaracioun, *sb.* elucidation CTI 178, 434

declareris, *sb.pl.* elucidators GGI 5

declaryng, ger. elucidation *HPD* 21, teaching *HPD* 149

declariþ, *v.3sg.pres.* elucidates PWB 1808, **declaren,** *3pl.pres.* PWB 2276, **declaride,** *1sg.pa.* PWB 2079, *3sg.pa* PWB 428, **declared,** *pa.p.adj.* *PNII* 5

defaute, error GGI 53, **defautis** *HPD* 86

derk(e, *adj.* obscure, figurative CTI 180 CTII 41 PWB 80 (etc.)

deyutously, *adv.* dutifully *HPD* 186

departid, *pa p.adj.* apart, standing alone PWB 1344, distinct GGIII 48, **departed,** separated *PNII* 308

departing, *sb.* division PWB 1534, discernment PWB 611 **departingis,** *pl.* divisions PWB 1435

desiderable, *adj.* desirable *HPD* 7

dis(s)ese, *sb.* distress, trouble PWB 1987, inconvenience CTI 485, **disesis,** *pl.* PWB 1969

dyseysyn, *v.* disease CTI 396 (app.), **diseseden,** *v.3pl.pa* inconvenienced CTXII 328

disturblest, *v.2sg.pres.* bring trouble upon PWB 709 (app.)

do [one's] **deuer,** *v* + *sb.* to do [one's] best CTI 355

doctrynge, *sb.* teaching, doctrine CTV 60 (etc.) (note)

dreye, *adj.* dry CTXI 21

dresse, *v.* guide, direct PWB 2960, **dressid,** *pa. p.* *HPD* 150 PWB 1352

drit, *sb.* dirt CTIX 13

duble, *adj.* two-fold *HPD* 258

Duche, *sb.* German CTI 12, **Duchyssche** *PNII* 58 (app.)

Ebrewes, *sb.pl.* Jews *FSB* 163, **Ebreu,** *subst. adj.* Hebrew language PWB 28, **Ebrewe** CTI 3

emperial, *adj.* imperial CTI 463 (note)

enplaster, *sb.* salve, plaster CTXI 113

entent, *sb.* intention, purpose PIP 10 PWB 2041

entirmete of, *prep. v.* meddle with *HPD* 264

euene, *adj.pl.* plain *HPD* 159

euened, *pa.p.adj.* equal GGIII 54

euer-eiþer, *cj.* each of the two PIP 7 PWB 2300

falsed, *v.pa.p.* falsified PWB 1979

fautouris, *sb.pl.* adherents, followers GGIII 101

feele, *adj.following noun*, many CTI 273, 282

feyned, *pa.p.adj.* pretend, invented PWB 1624 (note), **feined** CTXII 46 GGII 147

feynere, *sb.* inventor PWB 274

feir, *sb.* fire HPD 160

ferre, *imp.sg.* make afraid CTV 27

figuriþ, *vb.3sg.pres.* prefigures HPD 335, **figuriden** *3pl.pa.* PWB 115 (etc.)

fi3tynge, *pres.p.adj.* militant CTXI 39, **fy3tyng** PNII 95

fynding, *sb.* means of support PWB 2471

foli, *adj.* foolish CTXII 8

folidomes, *sb.pl.* foolishnesses PWB 2905

fonned, *v.pa p.* savourless PWB 1656, spoiled PWB 1745, foolish CTXII 314

for, *prep.* for the sake of PWB 869, in exchange for PWB 973, in place of PWB 602, in relation to CTI 209

fount-ston, *sb.* baptismal font CTI 426

forme, *sb.* prescribed course of study PWB 2485

geet, *sb.pl.* goats PWB 1212

gessen, *v.* estimate PWB 2194, *3pl.pres.* pretend PWB 1781, **gesse**, *1sg.pres.* suppose GGIII 80, **gesse**, *2sg.pres.sbj.* PIP 4

gongis, *sb.pl.* latrines PWB 883

goodli, *adv.* conveniently HPD 211

grentynge, *ger.* gnashing CTXII 325

Grete, *adj.* Major PWB 13

groos, *adj.* plain, literal FSB 103

Grwe, *subst.adj.* Greek language CTI 3

3ele, *sb.* zeal CTV 1 (app.)

3he, *adv.* yes, indeed PWB 197 (etc.), **3his** HPD 80

3ongþe, *sb.* youth CTI 138 FSB 3 PWB 2649

3oxide, *v.3sg.pa.* yawned PWB 809

3oten, *pa.p.adj.* cast in metal (MED yeten 7b,b) PWB 163

halfundel, *sb.* half-portion CTI 425

heestis, *sb.pl.* commandments PWB 90 (etc.)

helue, *sb.* piece of wood PWB 829

herberow, *sb.* lodging CTV 90

herboride, *v.3sg.pa.* lodged PWB 804

herde, *v.pa.p.* hired CTIX 5

herie, *vb.1sg.pres.* praise HPD 101

hyilden, *v.3pl.pres.* strip the skin from PWB 1808

hi3, *adj.* exalted PWB 2056, **hi3li**, *adv.* in an exalted manner PWB 2052

historial, *adj.* historic-literal [sense] PIP 52 PWB 2566, *historials*, *pl.* historical PIP 36 (note), 38

holy, *adv.* wholly CTXII 346

hopyn, *v.3pl.pres.* believe HPD 161, **hopide**, *3sg.pa.* trusted PWB 968

houyde, *v.3sg.pa.* floated PWB 829

iangelyn, *v.3pl.pres.* chatter HPD 35

ydiotis, *sb.pl.* illiterates CTI 184, **idiotis** PWB 1617 (note)

iebat, *sb.* gibbet PWB 422

item, *adv.* likewise HPD 157

Latyns, *sb.pl.* members of the Roman Church PWB 35 (note), 2015

laysee, *sb.* laity CTI 419, 420

le3t, *sb.* light HPD 137

lepre, *sb.* leprosy, PWB 193 (etc.)

lerud, *adj.* educated GGI 51

letterid, *adj.* literate CTI 160

lett(e)r(e, *sb.* text CTIX 36 CTXI 4 HPD 333 IB 4 PWB 2015 (etc.), literal meaning CTIX 2 PWB 2016, **l. to þe**, *adv.phr.* literally GGII 9 PWB 2195 (etc.)

lettrur(e, *sb.* literacy CTI 184, CTII 42 (app.)

likynge, *ger.* desire PWB 2349

loke aftir, *prep.v.* anticipate PWB 2005

lokid, *pa.p.adj.* considered PIP 37

magnefien, *v.* exalt HPD 179, make much of PWB 1605

manful, *adj.* brave, manly CTXII 89

mawgrie, *sb.* displeasure CTXI 98

mawmentis, *sb.pl.* idols CTIX 14

medlyng, *ger.* admixture PNII 174

mende, *sb.* mind HPD 82

mesel, *sb.* person afflicted wih leprosy PWB
    826
message, *sb.* legation, diplomatic mission
    PWB 1456
myche, *adv.* greatly CTIII 33, 35 PWB 2064
mo(o)st, *adj.superl.* greatest *HPD* 152 *PNII* 164
    PWB 2480

neet, *sb.* cattle PWB 277
no but, *cj.* unless PWB 818 (etc.)
noiful, *adj.* harmful *HPD* 78
note, *sb.* nut CTXI 1
nown-certeyn, *sb.* uncertainty PWB 2695
nurche, *v.* nourish GGII 25

on, *prep.* concerning PWB 1504, 2019
opon(e, *adj.* evident, public *FSB* 40, 89, **open,**
    clear, plain PIP 1, PWB 79, uncertain
    PWB 65, **opyne,** manifest CTI 18
opynli, *adv.* manifestly *HPD* 36, **opunly,**
    publicly CTI 164
outakun, *prep.* except PWB 139 (etc.),
    outtakyn *HPD* 265
overmore, *adv.* moreover CTI 460

paleised, *pa.p.adj.* fenced CTXI 108
parfit, *adj.* complete GGI 42
passande, *v.pres.p.* surpassing *HPD* 121
passynly, *adv,* surpassingly *HPD* 96
pesid, *v pa.p.* appeased, reconciled CTXII
    235
picched to, *prep.v.pa.p.* impaled upon *PNII*
    240 (app.)
pyment, *sb.* spiced wine GGII 104
pistle, *sb.* epistle PWB 25 (etc.)
porayle, *sb.* the poor *FSB* 139
portos, *sb.* portable breviary CTI 167
potestatis, *sb.pl.* lords GGII 152
powned, *v.pa.p.* pounded, pulverized GGII
    104 (app.)
punyk, *sb.* pomegranate CTIV 7
preciable, *adj.* worthy *HPD* 73
preesede, *v.pa p.* pressed PWB 820
proloyneþ, *v.3sg.pres.* abducts PWB 336
propur, *adj.* literal GGII 15, **propirli/y,** *adv.*
    appropriately PWB 4, literally GGII 11
    PWB 2198

purseynt, *sb.* atrium, forecourt PWB 1286
pursuen, *v.* persecute CTVII 57, *3pl.pres.*
    PWB 1608, **pursuede,** *3sg.pa.* *PNII* 296
purtenaunces, *sb.pl.* equipment PWB 1392

ransake vp, *prep.v.* search through CTI 401
raueyn, *sb.* greed PIP 61, 62 PWB 1640
rebel(le), *adj.* rebellious, CTII 49, 52
rebelte, *sb.* rebellion GGIV 16
refuse, *pa.p.subst.adj.* rejected [ones] *FSB* 176
relifs, *sb.pl.* remains PWB 813, 1493
religion, *sb.* religious order CTI 186
religious, *sb.pl.* those in religious orders *PNII*
    309 PWB 1618 (etc.)
renule, *v.* renew PWB 2124
reparaile, *v.* recover *HPD* 316
replicacioun, *sb.* rejoinder PWB 2880
repreuable, *adj.* open to reproof *HPD* 215
rere-soperis, *sb.pl.* late [extra] suppers
    PWB 1804
resoun, *sb.* sentence PWB 2835
ripliere, *comp.adv.* more immediately *HPD* 64

sa(a)d, *adj.* steadfast CTVII 45 *PNII* 199
    PWB 2065
sadeþ, *v.3sg.pres.* satisfies *PNII* 198 (app.)
Sarsyn, *adj.* Saracen CTI 467
seyne, *sb.* synod PWB 45, 1900
semble-hows, *sb.* meeting-house of
    convocation PWB 2521
symylacris, *sb.pl.* images PWB 1278 (etc.)
symonyent, *adj.* simoniac PWB 1598 (note)
symoniours, *sb.pl.* simoniacs *PNII* 130
synodoches, *sb.* synecdoche PWB 2315, 2672,
    synedoche GII 75
Smale, *adj.pl.* Minor PWB 15
soote, *adv.* sweet CTXII 194
sotilte, *sb.* device *PNII* 15 (etc.)
sowne, *v.* signify PWB 2056, be consonant
    with PWB 1624, **sowneþ,** *3sg. pres.*
    signifies GGII 31, resounds with
    PWB 48
spe(e)dful, *adj.* profitable CTI 56, 117 (app.)
spendit, *imp.pl.* use CTI 488
spice, *sb.* species GGII 73
stie, *v.* climb PWB 658, *3sg. pres. sbj.*
    HPD 266

storial, *adj.* historical PWB 2756

straunge, *adj.* foreign *IB* 2

suget, *pa.p.adj.* subjected GGII 13 PWB 2200

sugetis, *sb.pl.* subjects PWB 762

sulle, *v.3pl.pres.sbj.* sell *PNII* 82

sunnere, *comp.adj.* sooner *HPD* 53, 56

swatte, *v.3sg.pa.* sweated *PNII* 236

swen, *sb.pl* swine CTIV 11

tale, *sb.* account CTI 423

tent, *sb.* attention PWB 1439

terride, *v.3sg.pa.* provoked, incited PWB 742 (etc.)

titil, *sb.* pen-stroke PWB 2893

tome, *sb.* leisure CTI 484, 487

touchen, *v.3pl.pres.* concern PWB 2049

traitourie, *sb.* treachery CTXI 72

þresfold, *sb.* threshold CTI 29 (app.)

veniable, *adj.* vengeful GGIV 55

vndefied, *pa.p.adj.* undigested *HPD* 75

vyner, *sb.* vineyard PWB 734

vynner, *sb.* winner CTXI 26

vynetiliers, *sb.pl.* viticulturalists PWB 1100

vniuersite, *sb.* entirety PWB 2335

vnneþe, *adv.* scarcely *FSB* 82

volatilis, *sb.pl.* fowls *HPD* 303 (note)

vretynge, *ger.*, gnawing CTXII 334

wakyng, *sb.* vigilance CTV 172, *adj.* vigilant PWB 2297

warde, *sb.* keeping, custody CTVIII 11

waried, *pa p.adj.* accursed CTXII 278

wel-wellid, *adv.+pa.p.adj.* benevolent *HPD* 200

wellowed, *adj.* withered, shrivelled CTV 32

wetyngli, *adv.* knowingly *HPD* 118

wher, *interrog.* whether PWB 709 (etc.)

where, *cj.* whereas *HPD* 172 PWB 2056

wilful, *adj.* willing *HPD* 337 PWB 1713, **wilfuli**, *adv.* willingly PWB 285, **wilfullyche** *PNII* 193

willy, *adj.* willing CTI 205

wlappingis, *sb.pl.* wrappings, layers PWB 2267 (app.)

wlatiþ, *v.3sg. pres.* abhors PWB 2390

wold, *adj.* old CTI 369 (note)

Index of biblical quotations

The Index lists those references that are given in the 'Glosses and biblical references' section below the text on each page, but omits those references that consist only in a biblical book without chapter (see especially PWB 1–75) and the sequential listing of the contents of those books (as in PWB). Citation of the texts here is normally in alphabetical order of the abbreviated text title, and not by the order in which the texts are here printed.

Mark 14:43–5 CTXII 57–61
Mark 15:13 *PNII* 303
Mark 16:15 CTI 102–3, CTIII 2–3,
    HPD 278–9
Mark 16:16 CTIII 18–19, GGIV 8–9,
    GGI 8–12
Mark 16:17–18 CTXI 85–9

Luke 1:76–7 GGI 1–4, GGIV 3–5
Luke 3:9 CTXII 207–8
Luke 4:18 GGIV 10–11
Luke 4:43 GGIV 9–10
Luke 6:25 CTXII 359–61
Luke 6:27–8 CTXII 81–2
Luke 6:38 CTXI 69
Luke 6:39 CTX 22–3, GGIII 107–8
Luke 6:43–4 CTVII 24–5, *PNII* 288–90
Luke 6:44 CTXII 203–5
Luke 6:45 CTXII 197–8, 201–3
Luke 9:26 CTVIII 18–20, CTXII 73–4
Luke 9:28 PWB 2315–17
Luke 9:49 CTV 212–15
Luke 9:50 CTV 215–17
Luke 10:2 CTI 67–8, CTXII 371–3
Luke 10:12 CTXII 352–5
Luke 10:13 CTXII 350–1
Luke 10:14 CTXII 352–5
Luke 10:21 PWB 2472–5
Luke 10:25–8 CTI 263–9
Luke 10:33 CTXII 347–8
Luke 11:1–2 *PNII* 48–52
Luke 11:28 CTII 1–2, *HPD* 26–7
Luke 11:52 CTI 78–9, CTXII 368–71
Luke 12:8–9 *HPD* 349–51
Luke 12:10 CTXII 32–3
Luke 12:35 PWB 1809
Luke 12:47 *HPD* 38–9, 82–4
Luke 13:24 CTXII 69–70
Luke 13:28 CTXII 324–5
Luke 14:13–14 CTXII 431–2
Luke 14:26–7 CTXII 99–100
Luke 15:10 CTXII 420–2
Luke 16:8 CTXII 131–4
Luke 1710 *PNII* 85–6
Luke 19:22 CTXII 200–1
Luke 19:40 PWB 2788–9
Luke 20:17 PWB 1690–1, 2794

Luke 21:33 CTXI 120
Luke 21:26 PWB 2827–8
Luke 22:3–6 CTXII 57–61
Luke 22:47–8 CTXII 57–61
Luke 23:21 *PNII* 303
Luke 23:34 *PNII* 243–4
Luke 23:39 CTXII 61
Luke 23:40–3 CTXII 42–3

John 1:14 CTXI 122–3
John 1:45 PWB 2758
John 2:16 CTV 235–6
John 2:17 CTV 1
John 3:19 CTXI 126–7
John 6:35 CTXII 182
John 6:54 GGII 36–8, PWB 2225–6
John 6:58 CTXII 214–16
John 6:64 CTII 11–12, CTXII 151,
    FSB 105–6, *HPD* 218–19
John 6:69 CTII 12–13, CTXII 150–1,
    HPD 219–20, PWB 84–5
John 8:21 CTXII 351–2, *PNII* 295–7
John 8:24 CTXII 351–2, *PNII* 295–7
John 8 41–2 CTVII 78–9, *PNII* 321–3
John 8:44 CTVII 9–10, CTXI 104,
    CTXII 180–1, 216–18, *PNII* 13
John 11:25 CTXII 152–4
John 12:26 CTIII 3–4, CV 103–4
John 12:31 PWB 1637–8
John 12:48 CTVIII 1, *HPD* 241–3
John 13:34 *PNII* 184–5
John 14:6 CTXII 224–5
John 14:11–12 CTVII 82–3
John 14:21 CTII 3–4, 7–8, CTXI 76–8,
    79–80
John 14:24 CTII 7–8, CTXI 76–8,
    PNII 293–4
John 15:14 CTII 2–3
John 15:18 CTXII 94–6
John 15:19 CTXII 134–6
John 16:13 *HPD* 206–7
John 16:21 CTXII 259–60
John 17:15 CTXII 139–40
John 19:6 *PNII* 303

Acts 1:16 *FSB* 30–2
Acts 1:16–19 CTXII 57–61

1 Pet. 3:15 *FSB* 23–4
1 Pet. 3:15–16 CTV 224–9
1 Pet. 4:10 CTI 45–6, *FSB* 24–5
1 Pet. 4:11 CTV 222–4, CTVIII 20–1,
    CTXII 19–20

2 Pet. 1:21 PWB 85–7

1 John 1:8 *PNII* 176–7
1 John 2:4 CTXII 296–7
1 John 2:27 *HPD* 207–9
1 John 3:17 CTV 87–8
1 John 4:8 CTVI 3
1 John 4:16 CTVI 3

1 John 4:16 *PNII* 34–5

2 John 10–11 *PNII* 326–8

Apoc. 1:3 CTI 329–30, CTXII 160,
    HPD 27–8
Apoc. 5:1 PWB 2557–8
Apoc. 7:4 GGII 82–3, PWB 2334–5
Apoc. 14:1 GGII 82–3, PWB 2334–5
Apoc. 19:9 *HPD* 161–2
Apoc. 20:2 PWB 123–5, *PNII* 96–7
Apoc. 21:2 PWB 2584–6
Apoc. 21:8 CTXII 317–19
Apoc. 22:17 CTV 71, *FSB* 25–6